1900 Cen

TISHOMINGO COUNTY, MISSISSIPPI

Tishomingo County Historical & Genealogical Society
P.O. Box 273
Iuka, MS 38852

TURNER PUBLISHING COMPANY

ACKNOWLEDGEMENT

This book is a cumulative effort of the some of the members of the Tishomingo County Historical & Genealogical Society. This has been a goal of the Society since 1996. The committee and TCHGS accept no responsibility for misspelled names, misplaced dates, subjects which were left out, or other human errors.

The 1900 Tishomingo County Mississippi Census would not have been possible without the efforts of the following individuals. Special thanks goes to:

June Bullard
Eddie Carson
Carolyn Gaines
C.D. & Sybil Holley
Nelda McRae
Cindy Nelson
Brenda Whitfield

Turner®
PUBLISHING COMPANY

TCHGS
P.O. Box 273
Iuka, MS 38852
Email: tchgslibrary@nadata.net

TABLE OF CONTENTY

LEGEND

Row 1: HH#

Row 2: Name

Row 3: Relationship to Head

Row 4: Color

Row 5: Sex

Row 6: Month & Year of birth

Row 7: Age

Row 8: M/S

Row 9: Number of years married

Row 10: Mother of how many children

Row 11: How many living

Row 12: Person's birth place

Row 13: Father's birth place

Row 14: Mother's birth place

Row 15: Occupation

ABBREVIATIONS

Adp D	Adopted Daughter	**GM**	Grandmother	**S**	Son
Adp S	Adopted Son	**GS**	Grandson	**Ser**	Servant
Aunt	Aunt	**H**	Head of Household	**SiL**	Sister-in-Law
Bdr	Boarder	**HH**	Hired Hand	**Sis**	Sister
BiL	Brother-in-Law	**HK**	Housekeeper	**SD**	Step-Daughter
Bro	Brother	**Husb**	Husband	**SS**	Step-Son
Cou	Cousin	**IND**	Indian Territory	**UN**	Unknown
D	Daughter	**M**	Mother	**Unc**	Uncle
DiL	Daughter-in-Law	**MiL**	Mother-in-Law	**Ward**	Ward
F	Father	**Nce**	Niece	**W**	Wife
FiL	Father-in-Law	**Nep**	Nephew	**Wd**	Widow
GD	Granddaughter	**OT**	No explanation		
GF	Grandfather	**Rel**	Relative		

3

1	2	3	4	5	6	7	8	9	10	11	12	13	14	15
1	Ford, Sam	H	W	M	Aug 1867	32	M	1			MS	SC	SC	Typesetter
	Daisie L.	W	W	F	Mar 1880	20	M	1	0	0	MS	SC	SC	
2	Long, Jacob L.	H	B	M	Mar 1874	26	M	4			MS	MS	MS	Teacher
	Ida S.	W	B	F	Aug 1875	24	M	4	3	3	MS	AL	TN	
	Henry M.	S	B	M	Sep 1896	3	S				MS	MS	MS	
	Hubert E.	S	B	M	Jun 1897	2	S				MS	MS	MS	
	Lancaster	S	B	M	Jan 1899	1	S				MS	MS	MS	
	Tena	F	B	F	Feb 1829	71	Wd	29			MS	VA	VA	
3	Bonds, Demby	H	B	M	Jul 1869	30	M	11			MS	GA	UN	Day Laborer
	Millie W.	W	B	F	Aug 1872	27	M	11			AL	NC	AL	
	Dickson, Henry	Ward	B	M	Feb 1887	18	S				AL	UN	AL	
	Susan	Ward	B	F	May 1890	10	S				AL	UN	AL	
4	Parker, Aaron, Sr	H	B	M	May 1862	38	Wd	16			MS	SC	SC	Hotel Clerk
	Aaron, Jr	S	B	M	Mar 1884	16	S				MS	MS	MS	
	Henry	S	B	M	Jan 1882	14	S				Ms	MS	MS	
	Nora	D	B	F	Nov 1888	11	S				MS	MS	MS	
	Fannie	D	B	F	Nov 1882	8	S				MS	MS	MS	
	Winter	F	B	M	Jan 1822	78	Wd	45			SC	VA	SC	
	Baily, Ada	UN	B	F	Feb 1840	40	M	22	1	1	MS	MS	MS	Housekeeper
5	Fry, Charlie	H	B	M	Jan 1841	58	M	22			SC	UN	UN	Day Laborer
	Sylvia	W	B	F	Apr 1858	41	M	22	2		MS	UN	TN	
6	Vermer, Mary	H	B	F	Aug 1859	40	Wd	5			MS	UN	MS	Cook
	Harris, Mary	Nce	B	F	Feb 1884	16	S		1	1	AL	UN	MS	
	Aosuyale	Nep	B	M	Aug 1888	1	S				MS	AL	AL	
7	Williams, Fannie	H	B	F	Dec 1844	50	Wd		5	4	VA	VA	VA	Wash Woman
	Lucy	D	B	F	Jan 1866	34	M	10	0	0	MS	VA	VA	
	Thomas, Fran	D	B	F	Mar 1873	27	M	3	1	1	MS	AL	VA	
	Harold	GS	B	M	Sep 1899	9/mo	S				MS	MS	MS	
8	Carter, Will	H	B	M	Apr 1878	22	M	2			MS	UN	MS	R.R.Brakeman
	Bama	W	B	F	Apr 1881	19	M	2	1	1	MS	UN	AL	
	Evelyn	D	B	F	Dec 1898	1	S				MS	MS	MS	
9	Cummins, Abe	H	B	M	Jan 1845	55	S				MS	MS	MS	Day Laborer
10	Powell, John	H	B	M	Mar 1842	58	S				VA	VA	VA	Day Laborer
11	Adams, Harriet	H	B	F	Dec 1849	50	S				NC	NC	NC	Cook
	Thompson, Pheba	Nce	B	F	Dec 1861	13	S				MS	NC	MS	
	Jim	Nep	B	M	Apr 1879	21	M	3			MS	MS	NC	
	Mary	Nce	B	F	Feb 1881	19	M	3	2	2	MS	VA	VA	
	Wiliord	Nep	B	M	Dec 1897	2	S				MS	MS	MS	
	Claidy	Nep	B	M	Apr 1900	1/mo	S				MS	MS	MS	
12	Nelson, Ben L.	H	B	M	Sep 1856	43	M	24			MS	AL	AL	Day Laborer
	Chana	W	B	F	Dec 1863	36	M	24	5	2	MS	MS	MS	
	Author	S	B	M	Mar 1881	19	S				MS	MS	MS	
13	Nelson, Wiley	H	B	M	May 1878	22	M	4			MS	MS	MS	Day Laborer
	Lula	W	B	F	Mar 1877	23	M	4	1	1	MS	MS	MS	
	John S.	S	B	M	Nov 1896	3	S				MS	MS	MS	
	Williams, Mattie	Nce	B	F	Sep 1892	8	S				MS	MS	MS	

1	2	3	4	5	6	7	8	9	10	11	12	13	14	15
14	Nelson, Mary	H	B	F	UN UN	UN	Wd	4	3		UN	UN	UN	Day Laborer
	Robert T.	S	B	M	Mar 1874	26	M	3			MS	MS	MS	RR Hand
	Bertha	D	B	F	Aug 1877	22	M	3	0	0	MS	UN	UN	
	Sam	S	B	M	May 1892	8	S				MS	UN	UN	
15	Mason, Millie	H	B	F	UN UN	UN	Wd	11	10	3	AL	UN	AL	Cook
	Francie	D	B	F	Apr 1885	15	S				MS	TN	AL	
	Lula	D	B	F	Jan 1894	5	S				MS	TN	AL	
	Givens, Jim	D	B	F	Aug 1871	28	M	7	3	3	MS	TN	AL	
	Charlie	GS	B	M	Jan 1893	6	S				MS	AL	MS	
	Lucile	GD	B	F	Jul 1895	4	S				MS	AL	MS	
	Henry	GS	B	M	Oct 1898	1	S				MS	AL	MS	
	Nelson, Millie	GD	B	F	Sep 1899	4/mo	S				MS	MS	MS	
	Morris, Fate	SiL	B	M	Oct 1875	24	M	3			MS	UN	UN	RR Brakeman
	Hattie	D	B	F	Jan 1881	19	M	3	1	1	MS	TN	MS	
	Nalon	GS	B	M	Oct 1897	2	S				MS	UN	MS	
16	Coman, Stephen	H	B	M	UN UN	UN	M	2			UN	UN	TN	Farmer
	Mollie	W	B	F	Oct 1867	32	M	2	1	1	AL	MO	MS	
	Sallie	D	B	F	Jun 1872	27	S				MS	UN	TN	Teacher
	Darius	S	B	M	Jul 1899	4/mo	S				MS	MS	MS	
17	Crayton, Tim	H	B	M	Oct 1830	70	M	6			NC	NC	NC	Farmer
	Melia	W	B	F	May 1842	58	M	6	0	0	AL	NC	AL	
18	Jones, Harry C.	H	B	M	Jan 1852	48	M	19			AL	AL	TN	Farmer
	Bettie	W	B	F	May 1864	36	M	19	9	4	AL	AL	VA	
	Homer	S	B	M	Aug 1885	14	S				MS	AL	AL	
	Harry C.	S	B	M	Jun 1888	11	S				MS	AL	AL	
	Kelle F.	S	B	M	Aug 1897	2	S				MS	AL	AL	
	Charolette E.	D	B	F	Apr 1900	2/mo	S				MS	AL	AL	
19	Jones, Homer P.	H	B	M	Aug 1856	48	M	20			AL	AL	TN	Farmer
	Charolette	W	B	F	Sep 1858	41	M	20	0	0	AL	GA	AL	
20	Biggs, Hannah	H	B	F	Aug 1849	50	Wd		12	8	MS	TN	GA	Farmer
	Brown, Lucile	D	B	F	Feb 1881	18	M	0			MS	VA	MS	
	Fannie	D	B	F	Sep 1885	14	S				MS	VA	MS	
	Monroe	SiL	B	M	Dec 1878	21	M	0			MS	UN	MS	Day Laborer
21	Brown, Bob	H	B	M	Nov 1830	70	M	40			MS	MS	MS	Day Laborer
	Laura	W	B	F	UN UN	UN	M	40	10	8	MS	UN	UN	
	Roberts, Joseph	D	B	F	Jun 1874	25	M	1	4	4	MS	UN	UN	
	Brown, Bell	D	B	F	Dec 1881	19	S				MS	UN	UN	
	Roberts, Willie	GS	B	M	Apr 1886	14	S				MS	MS	MS	
	Annie	GD	B	F	Jun 1898	6	S				MS	MS	MS	
	George	GS	B	M	Jan 1896	3	S				MS	MS	MS	
	Maybell	GD	B	F	Jun 1898	1	S				MS	MS	MS	
22	Comans, Sarah	W	B	F	Mar 1870	30	M	8	7	6	MS	UN	UN	Day Laborer
	Jim	H	B	M	Aug 1870	30	M	8			MS	GA	GA	
	Albert	S	B	M	Mar 1886	14	S				MS	MS	MS	
	Mattie	D	B	F	Sep 1887	13	S				MS	MS	MS	
	Bobbie	S	B	M	Feb 1890	10	S				MS	MS	MS	
	Mary	D	B	F	Oct 1893	6	S				MS	MS	MS	
	Paura	D	B	F	Jul 1895	4	S				MS	MS	MS	
	Jesy	D	B	F	Mar 1898	2	S				MS	MS	MS	
23	Pace, James W.	H	W	M	Feb 1861	39	M	10			MS	TN	TN	Farmer
	Matilda	W	W	F	Feb 1869	31	M	10	4	4	GA	GA	GA	
	Ethel	D	W	F	Apr 1893	7	S				MS	MS	GA	
	Edgar	S	W	M	Nov 1894	5	S				MS	MS	GA	
	Earl	S	W	M	Dec 1895	4	S				MS	MS	GA	

1	2	3	4	5	6	7	8	9	10	11	12	13	14	15
	Lelia	D	W	F	Apr 1897	3	S				MS	MS	GA	
24	Webb, George W.	H	W	M	Jul 1818	81	M	33			VA	VA	VA	Farmer
	Elizabeth	W	W	F	Jul 1837	62	M	33	9	7	AL	GA	GA	
	Andy	S	W	M	Nov 1870	29	S				AL	VA	AL	
25	Sherd, Charlie	H	B	M	Aug 1817	82	M	16			AL	UN	UN	Farmer
	Margie	W	B	F	Mar UN	UN	M	16			MS	UN	AL	
26	McRae, Will	H	B	M	Aug 1867	32	M	5			MS	UN	UN	Farmer
	Della	W	B	F	Mar 1870	30	M	5	3	3	AL	UN	UN	
	Lena	D	B	F	Jun 1886	14	S				AL	MS	AL	
	Auther	S	B	M	Dec 1888	11	S				AL	MS	AL	
	Luster	S	B	M	Nov 1890	10	S				AL	MS	AL	
27	Adams, Louis B.	H	W	M	Oct 1837	62	M	41			NC	NC	NC	Farmer
	Mary Ann	W	W	F	Jul 1838	61	M	41	9	4	AL	SC	SC	
	Louisa A.	D	W	F	Nov 1873	26	S				MS	NC	AL	
	Fannie L.	D	W	F	UN 1875	25	S				MS	NC	AL	
28	Harris, Della	H	B	F	UN 1864	36	M	14	5	5	AL	AL	AL	Farmer
	Minnie	D	B	F	UN 1881	12	S				AL	AL	AL	
	Mamie	D	B	F	UN 1889	11	S				AL	AL	AL	
	Oscar	S	B	M	UN 1891	9	S				AL	AL	AL	
	Erve	S	B	M	UN 1894	6	S				AL	AL	AL	
	Tod	S	B	M	UN 1897	3	S				AL	AL	AL	
29	Crenshaw, Columbus	H	B	M	Dec 1852	48	M	20			AL	AL	AL	RR Section Hand
	Martha	W	B	F	Feb 1861	39	M	20	9	6	AL	AL	AL	
	Fallis	D	B	F	Jul 1881	18	S				AL	AL	AL	
	Mary B.	D	B	F	Jun 1884	15	S				MS	AL	AL	
	Clidie	S	B	M	Jan 1889	11	S				MS	AL	AL	
	Clarence	S	B	M	Jan 1891	9	S				MS	AL	AL	
	Eddie	S	B	M	May 1895	5	S				MS	AL	AL	
	Robert	S	B	M	Jun 1889	11/mo	S				MS	AL	AL	
	Ora Lee	DiL	B	F	Jul 1899	10/mo	S				MS	AL	AL	
30	Jackson, Charlie	H	B	M	UN 1868	41	M	14			AL	UN	UN	Farmer
	Pennie	W	B	F	UN 1862	38	M	14	4	4	AL	UN	UN	
	Minnie	D	B	F	May 1883	17	S				MS	AL	GA	
	Charlie	S	B	M	Jan 1887	13	S				MS	AL	GA	
	Lithy	D	B	F	Dec 1888	11	S				MS	AL	AL	
	Mary	D	B	F	Apr 1890	10	S				MS	AL	AL	
	Cooper	S	B	M	Feb 1892	8	S				MS	AL	AL	
	Vasiline	D	B	F	Jan 1896	4	S				MS	AL	AL	
31	Scruggs, Simon	H	B	M	Dec 1851	48	M	21			MS	UN	GA	Farmer
	Queen	W	B	F	Sep 1853	36	M	21	7	4	MS	VA	VA	
	Hattie	D	B	F	Mar 1881	18	S				MS	MS	MS	
	Mattie	D	B	F	Oct 1883	16	S				MS	MS	MS	
	Marshall	S	B	M	Oct 1889	10	S				MS	MS	MS	
	Garrett	S	B	M	Jun 1894	5	S				MS	MS	MS	
32	Coman, Sallie	H	B	F	Dec 1824	76	Wd	20	10	3	VA	UN	UN	Day Laborer
33	Patten, Jacob	H	B	M	Nov 1863	36	M	9			GA	UN	UN	
	Jennie	W	B	F	Feb 1876	24	M	9	5	3	AL	AL	AL	
	Rebecca	D	B	F	Sep 1892	8	S				AL	AL	AL	
	Arrena	D	B	F	Aug 1894	6	S				AL	AL	AL	
	Odie	D	B	F	May 1896	4	S				AL	AL	AL	
34	Rogers, William	H	B	M	Mar 1835	65	M	38			VA	UN	UN	Farmer
	Mary	W	B	F	Jan 1830	70	M	38	6	4	TN	UN	UN	

6

1	2	3	4	5	6	7	8	9	10	11	12	13	14	15
	Creca	D	B	F	Apr 1864	36	S				MS	UN	UN	
	Whitesides, Donna	GD	B	F	Feb 1877	23	M	5	2	2	MS	UN	UN	
35	Crosby, A.	H	W	M	Feb 1833	67	M	40			NC	VA	SC	Day Laborer
	Martha	W	W	F	Jul 1828	71	M	40	5	4	TN	KY	KY	
36	Williams, Joel	H	W	M	Mar 1870	30	M	9			AL	GA	TN	Day Laborer
	Emma	W	W	F	Nov 1870	29	M	9	3	3	TN	NC	TN	
	Delbert	S	W	M	Aug 1892	7	S				AL	GA	TN	
	Fred	S	W	M	Jul 1894	5	S				MS	GA	TN	
	Hyde	S	W	M	Sep 1896	3	S				MS	GA	TN	
	Williams, Joseph	Bro	W	M	Jan 1877	23	S				AL	GA	TN	
37	Coman, Stephen	H	B	M	Jan 1874	26	M	5			MS	MS	MS	Farmer
	Victoria	W	B	F	Oct 1880	19	M	5	1	1	MS	MS	MS	
	Auston	S	B	M	Nov 1893	3	S				MS	MS	MS	
	Campbell, Mattie	SiL	B	F	Mar 1888	12	S				MS	MS	MS	
38	Hubbard, Lem D.	H	W	M	Sep 1845	54	M	35			GA	SC	SC	Farmer
	Nancy	W	W	F	Apr 1848	52	M	35	11	9	AL	AL	GA	
	Amy	D	W	F	Mar 1884	16	S				MS	GA	AL	
	Paul	S	W	M	Jun 1887	12	S				MS	GA	AL	
	Paulus	S	W	M	Jun 1887	12	S				MS	GA	AL	
	Mattie	D	W	F	Feb 1891	9	S				MS	GA	AL	
	Allen	S	W	M	Dec 1893	6	S				MS	GA	AL	
39	Martin, Francis	H	W	M	Dec 1859	40	Wd		2	2	MS	UN	UN	Farmer
	Ather	D	W	F	May 1885	15	S				MS	MS	MS	
	Furley	S	W	M	Oct 1880	19	M	4			MS	MS	MS	Teamster
	Fannie	DiL	W	F	Apr 1880	20	M	4	2	2	MS	GA	AL	
	Frank	GS	W	M	Mar 1898	2	S				MS	MS	MS	
	Fred	GS	W	M	Sep 1899	8/mo	S				MS	MS	MS	
40	Adams, Mac D.	H	W	M	Apr 1845	55	M	24			NC	NC	NC	Farmer
	Addie D.	W	W	F	Feb 1856	44	M	24	3	3	MS	GA	GA	
	Parilie	D	W	F	Dec 1893	16	S				MS	NC	MS	
	Ollie	D	W	F	Aug 1896	13	S				MS	NC	MS	
	Curtell	D	W	F	Mar 1895	5	S				MS	NC	MS	
41	Chenault, John W.	H	W	M	Oct 1860	39	M	15			MS	AL	GA	Farmer
	Ara B.	W	W	F	Oct 1855	44	M	15	6	6	MS	AL	SC	
	Sallie V.	D	W	F	Sep 1887	13	S				MS	MS	MS	
	Ida V.	D	W	F	Apr 1888	12	S				MS	MS	MS	
	Ottie S.	D	W	F	Jan 1890	9	S				MS	MS	MS	
	Bettie A.	D	W	F	Jan 1892	7	S				MS	MS	MS	
	Clara L.	D	W	F	Sep 1896	3	S				MS	MS	MS	
	John B.	S	W	M	May 1896	2	S				MS	MS	MS	
42	Fairless, Meade	H	W	M	Feb 1837	63	M	30			TN	NC	NC	Farmer
	Francis	W	W	F	Aug 1845	54	M	30	4	4	GA	GA	GA	
	Robert M.	S	W	M	Jul 1873	26	S				MS	TN	GA	
	John W.	S	W	M	Dec 1881	18	S				MS	TN	GA	
	Hafford	S	W	M	Jan 1884	15	S				MS	TN	GA	
43	Clark, James	H		M	Jul 1873	26	M	6			AL	TN	GA	Farmer
	Eugenia	W		F	Aug 1872	27	M	6	2	2	AL	GA	AL	
	Horace L.	S		M	Sep 1895	4	S				MS	AL	AL	
	Luther	S		M	Jul 1898	1	S				MS	AL	AL	
44	Prewit, George H.	H	W	M	Jul 1854	45	M	25			GA	GA	SC	Jeweler, Photogr.
	Amelia	W	W	F	May 1858	42	M	25	6	4	MS	SC	SC	
	Lula A.	D	W	F	Mar 1872	28	S				MS	GA	MS	
	Flora Lee	D	W	F	Aug 1882	18	S				MS	GA	MS	

1	2	3	4	5	6	7	8	9	10	11	12	13	14	15
	Willie C.	S	W	M	Dec 1885	14	S				MS	GA	MS	
	Oscar C.	S	W	M	Apr 1887	13	S				MS	GA	MS	
	Randle, Willie T.	HH	W	M	Aug 1877	22	S				TN	GA	MS	Hired Hand
	Taylor, Jim	HH	B	M	Nov 1887	12	S				MS	MS	MS	Hired Hand
45	Wadkins, Dave	H	W	M	Apr 1870	30	M	11			TN	GA	AL	Farmer
	Ella N.	W	W	F	Jun 1870	30	M	11	5	5	TN	GA	AL	
	Paulie	S	W	M	Nov 1889	10	S				MS	GA	AL	
	Blanch	D	W	F	May 1892	8	S				MS	TN	AL	
	Mollie	D	W	F	Aug 1894	5	S				MS	TN	AL	
	Clora	D	W	F	Oct 1897	2	S				MS	TN	AL	
	Flora	D	W	F	Jan 1900	6/mo	S				MS	TN	AL	
46	Wadkins, Henry	H	W	M	Jun 1840	59	M	39			GA	GA	GA	Farmer
	Liza	W	W	F	Jun 1840	59	M	39	8	7	AL	NC	SC	
	Walker, Ellen	D	W	F	May 1877	23	Wd		1	1	MS	GA	AL	
	Henry F.	GS	W	M	Jun 1898	1	S				MS	UN	MS	
47	Wadkins, Author	H	W	M	Jun 1879	20	M	0			MS	GA	AL	Farmer
	Otha	W	W	F	Apr 1887	19	M	0			MS	UN	UN	
48	Thompson, Josie	H	W	F	Dec 1866	33	M	2	5	5	AL	AL	AL	Farmer
	George W.	S	W	M	Sep 1886	13	S				AL	AL	AL	
	Mattie	D	W	F	Dec 1890	9	S				AL	AL	AL	
	Cleveland	S	W	M	Oct 1888	11	S				AL	AL	AL	
	Minnie	D	W	F	Dec 1893	6	S				AL	AL	AL	
	Stephen	S	W	M	Sep 1895	4	S				AL	AL	AL	
49	Hyatte, Joe B.	H	W	M	Feb 1825	75	M	12			AL	NC	NC	Farmer
	Susan	W	W	F	Jun 1850	50	M	12	5	5	MS	SC	SC	
	Leatherwood, Willie	SS	W	M	May 1881	19	S				MS	AL	MS	
	Hyatte, J.B.	S	W	M	Aug 1880	9	S				MS	AL	MS	
50	Sanders, Gustus	H	B	M	Jun 1837	62	M	32			AL	AL	AL	Farmer
	Kate	W	B	F	Jun 1845	54	M	32	8	5	AL	VA	TN	
	Augustus, Jr	S	B	M	May 1876	24	S				AL	AL	AL	
51	Harris, Tom	H	B	M	Dec 1838	61	M	25			AL	VA	SC	Farmer
	Marie	W	B	F	UN UN	UN	M	25	6	6	AL	AL	AL	
	Tomie	S	B	M	Aug 1883	13	S				AL	AL	AL	
	Katie	D	B	F	Jun 1890	10	S				Al	AL	AL	
	Nora	D	B	F	Jun 1893	6	S				AL	AL	AL	
52	Smith, Anderson	H	B	M	Jan 1833	66	Wd				AL	AL	AL	Saw Cutter, Saw Mill
53	Hobbs, Henderson	H	B	M	Mar 1859	41	M	5			AL	AL	AL	Farmer
	Alabama	W	B	F	Feb 1869	31	M	5	1	1	AL	AL	AL	
	Dixon, Jim	SS	B	M	Jun 1880	20	S				AL	AL	AL	
54	Derrick, Clay	H	B	M	May 1871	29	M	6			MS	UN	TN	Day Laborer
	Pracilla	W	B	F	Sep 1872	27	M	6	1	1	GA	GA	GA	
	Essie	D	B	F	Sep 1894	5	S				MS	MS	GA	
55	Jones, Isiah	H	B	M	Feb 1875	25	M	2			MS	MS	MS	Preacher
	Claudie	W	B	F	Oct 1882	17	M	2	1	1	TN	VA	TN	
	I.H.	S	B	M	Feb 1899	1	S				MS	MS	TN	
56	Simson, Henry	H	B	M	UN UN	UN	M	5			AL	UN	UN	Day Laborer
	Sallie	W	B	F	UN UN	UN	M	5	1	1	AL	UN	UN	
	Sam S.	S	B	M	Dec 1894	5	S				MS	AL	AL	
57	Scroggins, Elsby	H	W	M	Mar 1822	78	M	22			GA	GA	GA	Farmer
	Mattie	W	W	F	Aug 1860	39	M	22	7	7	MS	AL	GA	

1	2	3	4	5	6	7	8	9	10	11	12	13	14	15
	Jim	S	W	M	Dec 1882	17	S				MS	GA	MS	
	Sudie	D	W	F	Mar 1885	15	S				MS	GA	MS	
	Liza	D	W	F	Nov 1887	13	S				MS	GA	MS	
	Dave	S	W	M	Jan 1888	12	S				MS	GA	MS	
	John	S	W	M	Sep 1891	8	S				MS	GA	MS	
	Lou	D	W	F	Jul 1881	19	S				MS	GA	MS	
58	Wadkins, Wilson	H	W	M	Mar 1860	40	M	8			MS	TN	TN	Farmer
	Mary A.	W	W	F	May 1868	32	M	8	10	3	TN	Ger	AL	
	Mattie L.	D	W	F	Oct 1871	12	S				MS	MS	TN	
	Minnie M.	D	W	F	Jun 1893	7	S				MS	MS	TN	
	Maggie P.	D	W	F	Aug 1896	3	S				MS	MS	TN	
59	Thomas, Robt. E.L.	H	W	M	Feb 1874	26	M	2			TN	SC	AL	Farmer
	Maude	W	W	F	Sep 1876	23	M	2			MS	MS	MS	
60	Lambert, Robt. E.	H	W	M	Jul 1857	48	M	31			GA	GA	GA	Farmer
	Elizabeth	W	W	F	Jan 1851	49	M	31	2	2	AL	GA	AL	
	Williams, Leslie B.	Ward	W	M	Aug 1884	15	S				MS	AL	AL	
	Baker, Amelia	Ward	W	F	May 1887	13	S				MS	UN	TN	
61	Yow, Jeff D.	H	W	M	Jan 1862	38	M	15			MS	SC	SC	Farmer
	Martha E.	W	W	F	Sep 1867	32	M	15	6	6	MS	MS	MS	
	George A.	S	W	M	Jun 1887	12	S				MS	MS	MS	
	Jimmie	S	W	M	Oct 1889	10	S				MS	MS	MS	
	Stonie E.	S	W	M	Feb 1893	7	S				MS	MS	MS	
	Carrie C.	D	F	M	Dec 1894	5	S				MS	MS	MS	
	John S.	S	W	M	Aug 1897	2	S				MS	MS	MS	
	No Name	S	W	M	Apr 1900	1/mo	S				MS	MS	MS	
62	Comans, Adaline	H	B	M	Dec 1876	23	S				MS	MS	MS	Day Laborer
63	Comans, Sinda	H	B	M	Dec 1835	64	Wd		5	5	MS	MS	MS	Day Laborer
	Willie	D	B	F	Jul 1884	16	S				MS	MS	MS	Day Laborer
	Clay	D	B	F	Dec 1889	13	S				MS	MS	MS	Day Laborer
	Morgan	S	B	M	Nov 1894	11	S				MS	MS	MS	Day Laborer
	George W.	S	B	M	Aug 1890	9	S				MS	MS	MS	Day Laborer
	John	S	B	M	Feb 1880	20	S				MS	MS	MS	
	Marie	GD	B	F	May 1895	5	S				MS	MS	MS	
	Elizabeth	GD	B	F	Jun 1897	2	S				MS	MS	MS	
	Tohow	S	B	M	May 1878	22	S				MS	MS	MS	Farmer
	Nelson	S	B	M	May 1873	21	S				MS	MS	MS	Day Laborer
	Taylor	S	B	M	Jun 1875	25	S				MS	MS	MS	Day Laborer
64	Hubbard Peter W.	H	W	M	Apr 1812	88	Wd				SC	SC	NC	Farmer
	George D.	S	W	M	Dec 1831	68	Wd				GA	SC	NC	Farmer
	Coman, Lucy	UN	B	F	Nov 1860	40	S				MS	MS	MS	Cook
65	Hubbard, George T.	H	W	M	Feb 1867	33	M	8			MS	GA	GA	Farmer
	Hattie	W	W	F	Apr 1873	27	M	8	4	4	MS	MS	MS	
	Clyde	D	W	F	Aug 1894	5	S				MS	MS	MS	
	Olivia	D	W	F	Oct 1895	4	S				MS	MS	MS	
	Lena	D	W	F	Aug 1897	2	S				MS	MS	MS	
	Ray	S	W	M	Jan 1899	1	S				MS	MS	MS	
66	Hubbard, Jim C.	H	W	M	Mar 1862	38	S				MS	GA	GA	Farmer
67	Coman, Dena	H	B	M	Feb 1872	28	Wd		6	6	MS	MS	MS	Farmer
	Della	D	B	F	Mar 1886	14	S				MS	MS	MS	Day Laborer
	Jim	S	B	M	Jul 1889	10	S				MS	MS	MS	
	Leona	D	B	F	May 1892	8	S				MS	MS	MS	
	Paul	S	B	M	May 1894	6	S				MS	MS	MS	
	Jennie	D	B	F	Apr 1895	5	S				MS	MS	MS	

1	2	3	4	5	6	7	8	9	10	11	12	13	14	15
	Calie	S	B	M	Aug 1898	1	S				MS	MS	MS	
	Tom	Bro	B	M	May 1870	30	S				MS	MS	MS	
68	Prewit, Wm. H.	H	W	M	Jul 1832	67	M	21			GA	SC	SC	Farmer
	Sallie C.	W	W	F	Jan 1845	55	M	21	7	6	MS	AL	AL	
	Fannie B.	D	W	F	Sep 1880	19	S				MS	GA	AL	
	William P.	S	W	M	Oct 1884	15	S				MS	GA	AL	
69	Kimbell, Robt. H.	H	W	M	Jan 1870	29	M	7			AL	UN	AL	Farmer
	Rosa L.	W	W	F	Nov 1874	25	M	7	5	4	MS	UN	AL	
	John H.	S	W	M	Jan 1893	7	S				MS	AL	MS	
	Ernest F.	S	W	M	Jan 1895	5	S				MS	AL	MS	
	Isaac L.	S	W	M	Jan 1898	2	S				MS	AL	MS	
	Kenneum, Tildon	HH	W	M	Dec 1877	22	S				MS	UN	MS	
70	Cane, Lidie	H	W	F	Sep 1857	42	Wd		13	5	AL	AL	AL	Farmer
	Isham	S	W	M	Jul 1882	17	S				TN	MS	AL	
	Bama	D	W	F	Sep 1886	13	S				TN	MS	AL	
	Sydnie	S	W	M	Nov 1887	12	S				TN	MS	AL	
	Ceney	D	W	F	Apr 1894	6	S				TN	MS	AL	
71	Hubbard, John D.	H	W	M	Nov 1832	67	M	42			GA	SC	GA	Farmer
	Martha C.	W	W	F	Jul 1839	60	M	42	12	10	GA	UN	GA	
	Alice	D	W	F	Apr 1872	28	S				MS	GA	GA	
	Blanch	D	W	F	May 1887	23	S				MS	GA	GA	
	Pauline	D	W	F	Nov 1880	17	S				MS	GA	GA	
	Edward R.	S	W	M	Oct 1884	15	S				MS	GA	GA	
	McRae, Ben	HH	B	M	UN 1886	14	S				MS	MS	MS	
72	Glenn, Robt. W.	H	W	M	Apr 1851	49	M	25			MS	SC	AL	Farmer
	Martha E.	W	W	F	Nov 1859	40	M	25	6	6	MS	TN	AL	
	Lora	D	W	F	Feb 1885	15	S				MS	MS	MS	
	Rochester	S	W	M	Aug 1886	13	S				MS	MS	MS	
	Estell V.	D	W	F	Sep 1888	11	S				MS	MS	MS	
	Grover C.	S	W	M	Jan 1893	7	S				MS	MS	MS	
	Petty, Scint	HH	W	M	Nov 1860	40	Wd				MS	MS	MS	Hired Hand
73	Glenn, Willie C.	H	W	M	Oct 1869	30	M	11			MS	SC	AL	Farmer
	Febe L.	W	W	F	Jul 1872	27	M	11	6	6	MS	AL	AL	
	Virgie E.	D	W	F	Nov 1889	10	S				MS	MS	MS	
	Wm. N.	S	W	M	Oct 1891	8	S				MS	MS	MS	
	David L.	S	W	M	Aug 1893	6	S				MS	MS	MS	
	Minnie P.	D	W	F	Jun 1895	4	S				MS	MS	MS	
	Jimmie A.	S	W	M	Jul 1897	2	S				MS	MS	MS	
	Maurie L.	D	W	F	Mar 1899	1	S				MS	MS	MS	
74	Bonds, Green B.	H	W	M	Mar 1846	54	M	33			MS	AL	AL	Farmer
	Josephine	W	W	F	Sep 1849	50	M	33	10	7	MS	MS	MS	
	Elmer L.	S	W	M	Feb 1879	21	S				MS	MS	MS	
	Jimmie	S	W	M	Mar 1882	18	S				MS	MS	MS	
	Clarence F.	S	W	M	Jul 1885	14	S				MS	MS	MS	
	Evey E.	D	W	F	Apr 1888	12	S				MS	MS	MS	
	May P.	D	W	F	Mar 1893	7	S				MS	MS	MS	
	Janie	D	W	F	Feb 1898	2	S				MS	MS	MS	
75	Kennedy, Martha	H	W	F	Apr 1839	61	Wd		9	7	TN	UN	UN	Farmer
	Taylor	S	W	M	Mar 1877	23	S				MS	AL	TN	
	Louise	D	W	F	Oct 1878	21	S				MS	AL	TN	
76	Taylor, Leander	H	W	M	Sep 1877	22	M	3			MS	AL	AL	Farmer
	Sallie	W	W	F	Feb 1882	18	M	3	1	1	AL	AL	UN	
	Leona	D	W	F	Sep 1898	1	S				MS	MS	AL	

1	2	3	4	5	6	7	8	9	10	11	12	13	14	15
77	Kennedy, Sam R.	H	W	M	Mar 1870	30	M				MS	UN	TN	Farmer
	Mary J.	W	W	F	Jan 1875	25	M				MS	UN	UN	
	Hattie R.	D	W	F	Nov 1890	9	S				MS	MS	UN	
	Lillie C.	D	W	F	May 1893	7	S				MS	MS	UN	
	Charlie	S	W	M	Sep 1894	5	S				MS	MS	UN	
	Willind	S	W	M	Nov 1898	1	S				MS	MS	UN	
78	Kennedy, Jess	H	W	M	Aug 1872	27	M	3			MS	TN	AL	Farmer
	Sarah J.	W	W	F	Apr 1873	27	M	3	1	1	MS	MS	MS	
	Dora W.	D	W	F	Aug 1898	1	S				Ms	MS	MS	
	Susie	D	W	F	Jan 1900	1/mo	S				MS	MS	MS	
79	Gattis, John	H	W	M	Sep 1863	36	M	13			TN	MS	VA	Farmer
	Bettie	W	W	F	Nov 1865	35	M	13	10	5	TN	UN	UN	
	Mandy	D	W	F	Aug 1890	9	S				MS	TN	TN	
	Walter	S	W	M	Oct 1891	8	S				MS	TN	TN	
	Maggie	D	W	F	Oct 1893	6	S				MS	TN	TN	
	Malcolm	S	W	M	Aug 1897	2	S				MS	TN	TN	
80	Yow, John F.	H	W	M	Nov 1859	40	M	14			MS	UN	UN	Farmer
	Mary J.	W	W	F	Dec 1861	38	M	14	5	5	MS	AL	MS	
	Virgie C.	D	W	F	Dec 1886	13	S				MS	MS	MS	
	Hattie E.	D	W	F	Sep 1888	11	S				MS	MS	MS	
	George T.	S	W	M	Dec 1889	10	S				MS	MS	MS	
	Minnie L.	D	W	F	Aug 1893	6	S				MS	TN	MS	
	Fannie C.	D	W	F	Mar 1896	4	S				MS	MS	MS	
81	Roberson, WM. J.	H	W	M	Feb 1867	33	M	14			MS	MS	MS	Farmer
	Mary	W	W	F	Nov 1870	29	M	14	6	5	MS	MS	SC	
	Larry R.	S	W	M	Jun 1887	12	S				MS	MS	MS	
	Nancy A.	D	W	F	Feb 1890	10	S				MS	MS	MS	
	Thomas A.	S	W	M	Feb 1892	8	S				MS	MS	MS	
	Maschal E.	S	W	M	Dec 1893	6	S				MS	MS	MS	
	Beulah G.	D	W	F	Feb 1895	5	S				MS	MS	MS	
	Maybell	D	W	F	Nov 1897	2	S				MS	MS	MS	
82	McCoy, WM.	H	W	M	Jan 1860	40	Wd				MS	MS	MS	Farmer
	Clarence	S	W	M	Feb 1885	15	S				MS	MS	MS	
	Cloy B.	D	W	F	Apr 1887	13	S				MS	MS	MS	
	Willie B.	D	W	F	Jul 1888	11	S				MS	MS	MS	
	Virdie E.	D	W	F	Dec 1890	9	S				MS	MS	MS	
	James N.	S	W	M	Sep 1894	6	S				MS	MS	MS	
	Fred A.	S	W	M	Mar 1893	5	S				MS	MS	MS	
	Odie L.	D	W	M	Jan 1900	4/mo	S				MS	MS	MS	
83	Bonds, WM.	H	W	M	Sep 1866	33	M	4			MS	SC	MS	Farmer
	Nellie E.	W	W	F	Jan 1874	26	M	4	3	3	MS	MS	MS	
	Willie E.	D	W	F	Aug 1891	8	S				MS	MS	MS	
	Thomas	S	W	M	Feb 1896	4	S				MS	MS	MS	
	Roxie	D	W	F	Jul 1898	1	S				MS	MS	MS	
84	Wadkins, James	H	W	M	May 1827	73	M	42			TN	Ire	TN	Farmer
	Sarah W.	W	W	F	Apr 1842	58	M	42	11	7	TN	NC	NC	
	Margaret E.	D	W	F	Aug 1877	22	S				TN	TN	TN	
	Charlie L.	S	W	M	Aug 1880	19	S				MS	Tn	TN	
	Ida E.	S	W	M	Oct 1882	17	S				MS	TN	TN	
	Alex C.	S	W	M	Aug 1886	13	S				MS	TN	TN	
85	Barrett, Sam	H	W	M	Sep 1857	42	M	22			AR	AL	AL	Farmer
	Sarah E.	W	W	F	Jun 1859	40	M	22			AR	AL	AL	
86	Kirk, James M.	H	W	M	Dec 1823	76	M	13			NC	VA	NC	Farmer
	Ara	W	W	F	Nov 1854	45	M	13			TN	TN	TN	

1	2	3	4	5	6	7	8	9	10	11	12	13	14	15
	Ellington, Martha	Sis	W	F	Mar 1842	58	Wd				TN	VA	VA	
	Shull, Rebecca	Sis	W	F	Feb 1838	62	Wd				TN	VA	VA	
87	Barrett, Wm.	H	W	M	Apr 1871	28	M	10			AL	UN	UN	Farmer
	Eliza P.	W	W	F	Nov 1872	27	M	10	4	4	TN	TN	TN	
	Sarah E.	D	W	F	Dec 1892	7	S				MS	TN	AL	
	James E.	S	W	M	Feb 1895	5	S				MS	TN	AL	
	E.B.	S	W	M	Jul 1897	2	S				MS	TN	AL	
	Ida B.	D	W	F	Apr 1900	2/mo	S				MS	TN	AL	
88	Davis, Thomas	H	W	M	May 1863	37	M	14			MS	AL	UN	Farmer
	Effie L.	W	W	F	Mar 1871	29	M	14	6	5	MS	MS	AL	
	James E.	S	W	M	Nov 1887	12	S				MS	MS	MS	
	Thomas P.	S	W	M	Feb 1890	9	S				MS	MS	MS	
	Wm. D.	S	W	M	Sep 1891	8	S				MS	MS	MS	
	Elmore D.	S	W	M	Aug 1895	4	S				MS	MS	MS	
	Alford E.	S	W	M	May 1898	2	S				MS	MS	MS	
89	Linton, Julius C.	H	W	M	Mar 1854	46	M	19			AL	SC	SC	Farmer
	Bellzory	W	F	M	Jan 1862	38	M	19	8	6	MS	AL	NC	
	Claude K.	S	W	M	Apr 1883	17	S				MS	AL	MS	
	Cody J.	S	W	M	Mar 1885	15	S				MS	AL	MS	
	John W.	S	W	M	Apr 1887	13	S				MS	AL	MS	
	Jeff A.	S	W	M	Nov 1889	10	S				MS	AL	MS	
	Ina M.	D	W	F	Mar 1891	8	S				MS	AL	MS	
	Nellie	D	W	F	Mar 1897	3	S				MS	AL	MS	
90	Morris, John	H	W	M	Mar 1849	51	M	30			AL	UN	AL	Farmer
	Malinda	W	W	F	Feb 1850	50	M	30	10	2	TN	UN	AL	
	Fred W.	S	W	M	Nov 1880	19	S				AL	AL	TN	
	Charlie F.	S	W	M	Sep 1886	13	S				AL	AL	TN	
91	Washington, Mahala	H	B	F	UN UN	UN	Wd		8	4	MS	MS	MS	Farmer
	Andrew	S	B	M	Sep 1880	19	S				MS	MS	MS	
	Rosa B.	D	B	F	Apr 1889	11	S				MS	MS	MS	
92	Gilchrist, John	H	W	M	Apr 1858	41	M	15			TN	TN	TN	Farmer
	Anna	W	W	F	Sep 1865	34	M	15	7	7	MS	AL	AL	
	Frank E.	S	W	M	Aug 1885	14					MS	TN	MS	
	George W.	S	W	M	Aug 1887	12					MS	TN	MS	
	Wm. C.	S	W	M	Jun 1890	9					MS	TN	MS	
	John M.	S	W	M	Jan 1894	6					MS	TN	MS	
	James W.	S	W	M	Jun 1895	4					MS	TN	MS	
	Emma R.	D	W	F	Apr 1897	3					MS	TN	MS	
	Minnie M.	D	W	F	Apr 1898	1					MS	TN	MS	
93	Brewer, A.M.	H	W	M	Jan 1855	45	M	19			AL	AL	AL	Farmer
	Sara	W	W	F	Oct 1857	42	M	19	9	8	GA	GA	GA	
	Albert	S	W	M	Dec 1881	18	S				AL	AL	GA	
	Mary J.	D	W	F	Apr 1883	17	S				AL	AL	GA	
	Joseph M.	S	W	M	Oct 1887	12	S				AL	AL	GA	
	Ruben E.	S	W	M	Jul 1891	8	S				MS	AL	GA	
	Rutha E.	D	W	F	Jul 1891	8	S				MS	AL	GA	
	Grover	S	W	M	Feb 1892	7	S				MS	AL	GA	
	Cleveland	S	W	M	Feb 1892	7	S				MS	AL	GA	
	Laur P.	D	W	F	Feb 1896	4	S				MS	AL	GA	
94	Clifton, Frank C.	H	B	M	Nov 1860	39	M	15			MS	VA	VA	Farmer
	Anna	W	B	F	Apr 1862	38	M	15	8	6	AL	UN	UN	
	Wiley H.	S	B	M	Apr 1887	13	S				MS	MS	AL	
	Jim	S	B	M	Apr 1894	6	S				MS	MS	AL	
	Willie	S	B	M	Apr 1893	7	S				MS	MS	AL	
	Rosa B.	D	B	F	May 1897	3	S				MS	MS	AL	

1	2	3	4	5	6	7	8	9	10	11	12	13	14	15
	Malone, Geo.	BiL	B	M	Jan 1887	13	S				MS	UN	UN	
95	Clifton, Jake	H	B	M	May 1790	110	M	55			VA	UN	UN	Farmer
	Mary	W	B	F	Feb 1815	85	M	55	11	3	VA	UN	UN	
	Flemen	GS	B	M	Jan 1878	22	S				MS	UN	MS	
	Thomas, Douglas	GS	B	M	Nov 1878	21	S				MS	MS	MS	
	Mary	GD	B	F	May 1882	18	S				MS	MS	MS	
96	Hale, John H.	H	W	M	Feb 1861	39	M	15			MS	UN	MS	
	Lorena	W	W	F	Oct 1868	31	M	15	6	6	GA	SC	GA	
	Dovie E.	D	W	F	Jul 1887	12	S				MS	MS	GA	
	Henry D.	S	W	M	Aug 1889	10	S				MS	MS	GA	
	Maundy L.	D	W	F	Oct 1891	8	S				MS	MS	GA	
	Jacob W.	S	W	M	Nov 1893	6	S				MS	MS	GA	
	Nellie D.	D	W	F	Jan 1896	4	S				MS	MS	GA	
	Wm. G.	S	W	M	Nov 1898	1	S				MS	MS	GA	
97	Farris, Margaret	H	W	F	Feb 1862	38	Wd		5	4	MS	VA	TN	Farmer
	Bertha E.	D	W	F	Feb 1887	13	S				MS	MS	MS	
	Collin M.	S	W	M	Mar 1890	10	S				MS	MS	MS	
	Mary A.	D	W	F	Apr 1894	6	S				MS	MS	MS	
	Myrtle M.	D	W	F	Mar 1896	4	S				MS	MS	MS	
98	Davis, Warren W.	H	B	M	Aug 1865	34	M	5			MS	GA	SC	Farmer
	Annie B.	W	B	F	Feb 1875	25	M	5	3	3	MS	MS	MS	
	Warren W. Jr	S	B	M	Feb 1896	4	S				MS	MS	MS	
	Celia A.	D	B	F	Jun 1897	2	S				MS	MS	MS	
	Fred C.	S	B	M	Mar 1900	2/mo	S				MS	MS	MS	
	Manus, Mary	Bdr	B	F	UN UN	UN	M	30			MS	UN	UN	
99	Counts, Richard H.	H	W	M	Oct 1860	39	M	8			MS	VA	MS	Farmer
	Fannie	W	W	F	Aug 1863	36	M	8	2	2	MS	SC	SC	
	Blanch O.	D	W	F	Oct 1891	8	S				MS	MS	MS	
	Howell J.	S	W	M	Jun 1894	6	S				MS	MS	MS	
100	Foote, Thomas J.	H	W	M	Nov 1867	32	M	6			MS	SC	SC	Farmer
	Willie	W	W	F	Dec 1875	24	M	6	2	2	MS	MS	MS	
	Author	S	W	M	Sep 1894	5	S				MS	MS	MS	
	Lillian	D	W	F	Mar 1898	1	S				MS	MS	MS	
	Elizabeth J.	M	W	F	Mar 1832	68	Wd				SC	GA	SC	
	Garrett, Elijah	HH	W	M	Dec 1878	21	S		6	5	TN	VA	NC	Hired Hand
101	Sloan, Willie	H	B	M	Nov 1845	54	M	3			MS	MS	MS	Day Laborer
	Frances	W	B	F	Dec 1862	37	M	3	0	0	MS	MS	MS	Laundress
102	Malone, Ben	H	B	M	Aug 1850	49	M				MS	UN	UN	Carpenter
	Celia	W	B	F	Mar 1860	40	M	3	0	0	MS	UN	UN	
	Colwell, Mary	MiL	B	F	Jun 1835	65	Wd		5	2	NC	UN	UN	
103	Dixon, Willie	H	B	F	Apr 1884	16	S				MS	UN	UN	Cook
	Madie P.	D	B	F	May 1898	2	S				MS	MS	MS	
104	Ducket, Albert	H	B	M	May 1850	50	M	10			AL	AL	UN	Day Laborer
	Jennie	W	B	F	Apr 1857	43	M	10	7	7	TN	MS	SC	
	Sam C.	D	B	F	May1880	20	S				MS	AL	TN	
	Shelton	S	B	M	Jun 1890	9	S				MS	AL	TN	
	Minnie	D	B	F	Feb 1894	6	S				MS	AL	TN	
	Pue	S	B	M	Sep 1896	4	S				MS	AL	TN	
	Ollen	S	B	M	Nov 1898	2	S				MS	AL	TN	
105	Patterson, Charlie A.	H	B	M	Jan 1862	38	M	12			MS	UN	UN	Farmer
	Katie	W	B	F	Dec 1862	37	M	12	7	7	MS	UN	VA	
	Novell	S	B	M	Nov 1888	11	S				MS	MS	MS	

1	2	3	4	5	6	7	8	9	10	11	12	13	14	15
	Wadell F.	S	B	M	Jun 1891	9	S				MS	MS	MS	
	Lottie C.	S	B	F	Oct 1893	6	S				Ms	MS	MS	
	Chester D	S	B	M	Sep 1896	3	S				MS	MS	MS	
	Mattie P.	D	B	F	Sep 1899	9/mo	S				MS	MS	MS	
106	Evans, Rube	H	B	M	Mar 1870	30	M	7			MS	MS	MS	Farmer
	Manerva	W	B	F	Apr 1875	25	M	7	9	7	AL	UN	UN	
	Lizzie B.	D	B	F	Aug 1885	14	S				MS	MS	AL	
	Louis S.	S	B	M	Mar 1898	2	S				MS	MS	AL	
	Worlie M.	S	B	M	Mar 1900	1/mo	S				MS	MS	AL	
	White, Emiley	D	B	F	UN UN	UN	Wd		16	6	TN	TN	TN	
107	McRae, Crede	H	B	M	Aug 1847	52	M	20			AL	VA	AL	Farmer
	Henrietta	W	B	F	UN UN	UN	M	20	9	6	AL	UN	VA	
	Henry S.	S	B	M	Aug 1881	19	S				AL	AL	AL	
	Lizzie	D	B	F	Aug 1887	12	S				MS	AL	AL	
	Oscar	S	B	M	May 1889	10	S				MS	AL	AL	
	Bessie	D	B	F	Dec 1890	8	S				MS	AL	AL	
	Maggie T.	D	B	F	Sep 1896	3	S				MS	AL	AL	
108	Comer, Sallie A.	H	W	F	Jul 1861	38	Wd		1	1	MS	AL	IND	Farmer
	Clyde M.	S	W	M	Jan 1882	18	S				MS	TN	MS	
109	Scott, Malinda	H	B	F	Apr 1854	46	Wd		4	4	AL	UN	GA	
	Ida	D	B	F	Oct 1873	16	S				MS	MS	AL	
	Jeff L.	S	B	M	Oct 1886	13	S				MS	MS	AL	
	Dorch, Matilda	M	B	F	Jul 1804	95	Wd		6	3	GA	GA	GA	
	Scott, Eddie	GS	B	M	Jul 1898	1	S				MS	MS	MS	
	George	GS	B	M	Jun 1898	1	S				MS	MS	MS	
110	Herd, Geo. E.	H	W	M	Sep 1846	53	M	19			IA	NY	NY	Mechanic
	May E.	W	W	F	Sep 1863	37	M	19	3	3	MO	AtSea	NC	
	John E.	S	W	M	Jan 1883	17	S				MS	IA	MO	
	Charlie	S	W	M	Dec 1885	14	S				MO	IA	MO	
	Lucian	S	W	M	Jul 1888	11	S				MO.	IA	MO	
111	Vaughn, James T.	H	W	M	Aug 1857	42	M	19			MS	TN	TN	Farmer
	M.J.	W	W	F	Apr 1860	40	M	19	7	5	MS	NC	MS	
	Roxie	D	W	F	Sep 1882	17	S				MS	MS	MS	
	Mandy J.	D	W	F	Aug 1886	13	S				MS	MS	MS	
	Russ O.	S	W	M	May 1890	10	S				MS	MS	MS	
	Cleopatra	D	W	F	Nov 1891	8	S				MS	MS	MS	
	Nellie M.	D	W	F	Jun 1895	4	S				MS	MS	MS	
112	McKenney, James D.	H	W	M	Jul 1869	30	M	12			MS	UN	UN	Day Laborer
	Mary E.	W	W	F	Jul 1871	28	M	12	3	3	AL	KY	TN	
	Lillie R.	D	W	F	Jul 1889	10	S				MS	MS	AL	
	Wm. D.	S	W	M	Jun 1893	6	S				MS	MS	AL	
	Robert H.	S	W	M	Sep 1895	4	S				TN	NC	VA	
	Moore, Mary E.	MiL	W	F	Jan 1844	54	Wd	2	2		TN	NC	VA	
	Williams, James	Bdr	W	M	Jan UN	UN	S				UN	UN	UN	Day Laborer
113	Brewer, Jesse J.	H	W	M	Jan 1872	28	M	9			AL	UN	UN	Day Laborer
	Georgia	W	W	F	Jun 1868	31	M	9	4	3	AL	MS	AL	
	Sallie P.	D	W	F	Apr 1892	8	S				AL	AL	AL	
	Lurlie J.	D	W	F	Sep 1894	5	S				AL	AL	AL	
	Myrtle L.O.	D	W	F	Aug 1899	11/mo	S				AL	AL	AL	
114	McKenny, Rebecca	H	W	F	Dec 1855	45	S				AL	AL	AL	Day Laborer
115	Curtis, Joe H.	H	W	M	Jul 1849	50	M	26			MS	TN	TN	Day Laborer
	Rebecca A.	W	W	F	Jan 1858	42	M	26	5	4	MS	TN	NC	
	Henry D.	S	W	M	Apr 1882	18	S				MS	MS	MS	

1	2	3	4	5	6	7	8	9	10	11	12	13	14	15
116	Wagner, Clarence F.	H	W	M	Oct 1869	30	M	11			WV	WV	WV	RR Car Insp.
	Jennie M.	W	W	F	Oct 1865	34	M	11	4	1	TN	TN	TN	
	Chester	S	W	M	Mar 1894	6	S				TN	TN	TN	
117	Coffman, Wm. E.	H	W	M	Feb 1878	22	M	0			AL	TN	AR	RR Car Repairman
	Effie D.	W	W	F	May 1883	17	M	0	0	0	MS	UN	MS	.
118	Jamison, Shade D.	H	W	M	Sep 1850	49	M	31			MS	GA	TN	Gris Mill Op.
	Corm R.	S	W	M	Apr 1880	20	S				AL	MS	MS	
119	Kilgore, Dave	H	B	M	Jun 1878	22	S				MS	MS	MS	
120	Curtis, Sam	H	W	M	Sep 1874	25	M	5			MS	MS	MS	Day Laborer
	Emmra	W	W	F	Oct 1880	19	M	5	2	2	MS	MS	MS	
	Lawrence E.	S	W	M	Jan 1887	3	S				MS	MS	MS	
	Clarence J.	S	W	M	Nov 1899	6/mo	S				MS	MS	MS	
121	Curtis, John T.	H	W	M	Nov 1877	22	M	0			MS	MS	MS	Day Laborer
	Lou	W	W	F	Jun 1880	20	M	0	0	0	MS	MS	MS	
	Douthout, Whitten J.	Bdr	W	M	Feb 1873	27	S				AL	MS	AL	Switchman
	Julliam, Jack L.	Bdr	W	M	Sep 1880	15	S				AL	AL	AL	Operator
	Bond, Wm. P.	Bdr	W	M	Mar 1876	22	S				TN	UN	TN	Locom. Fireman
	Whitson, Will	Bdr	B	M	Apr 1884	16	S				MS	MS	MS	Day Laborer
	Stewart, Charlie	Bdr	B	M	Jun 1881	19	S				MS	MS	MS	Day Laborer
	Boyd, Whash	Bdr	B	M	May 1876	23	S				MS	MS	MS	Day Laborer
122	Nix, Ambus	H	W	M	Mar 1853	47	M	20			AL	GA	GA	Day Laborer
	Brittioms	W	W	F	Sep 1861	38	M	20	7	6	TN	UN	UN	
	Felix P.	S	W	M	Oct 1879	20	S				MS	AL	TN	
	James A.	S	W	M	Sep 1882	17	S				MS	AL	TN	
	Agnes	D	W	F	Feb 1888	12	S				MS	AL	TN	
	Robert P.	S	W	M	Sep 1890	9	S				MS	AL	TN	
	Maggie O.	D	W	F	Mar 1895	5	S				MS	AL	TN	
	Mary E.	D	W	F	Jun 1893	7	S				MS	AL	TN	
123	Clark, Wm. H.	H	W	M	Jan 1873	27	M	12			IL	MS	MS	Day Laborer
	Elizabeth	W	W	F	UN UN	UN	M	12	6	5	AL	UN	UN	
	Johnnie	S	W	M	May 1888	12	S				AL	IL	AL	
	George	S	W	M	Apr 1889	11	S				AL	IL	AL	
	Sam	S	W	M	Jun 1895	5	S				AL	IL	AL	
	Wesley	S	W	M	Mar 1897	3	S				AL	IL	AL	
	Charlie	S	W	M	Dec 1899	4/mo	S				AL	IL	AL	
124	Wadkins, Geo. H.	H	W	M	Jul 1864	35	M	17			AL	SC	AL	Farmer
	Lena J.	W	W	F	Jan 1865	35	M	17	9	8	UN	UN	UN	
	Joe F.	S	W	M	Feb 1885	15	S				MS	AL	MS	
	George H.	S	W	M	Mar 1887	13	S				MS	AL	MS	
	Oscar L.	S	W	M	Dec 1888	11	S				MS	AL	MS	
	James J.	S	W	M	Nov 1890	9	S				MS	AL	MS	
	Lish H.	S	W	M	Sep 1892	7	S				MS	AL	MS	
	Peter	S	W	M	Oct 1894	5	S				MS	AL	MS	
	Lidie V.	D	W	F	Sep 1896	3	S				MS	AL	MS	
	Wm. F.	S	W	M	Oct 1898	1	S				MS	AL	MS	
125	Kenum, Frances E.	H	W	F	Nov 1844	55	Wd		7	6	AL	KY	KY	Farmer
	Mary	D	W	F	May 1869	21	S				AL	SC	AL	
	Wm. F.	S	W	M	Jun 1896	. 4	S				MS	GA	SC	
126	Locket, Alford	H	B	M	UN UN	UN	M	6			UN	UN	UN	Farmer
	Manda	W	B	F	UN UN	UN	M	6	6	5	AL	AL	AL	
	Elzada	D	B	F	Jul 1884	15					MS	UN	UN	
127	Baily, Eda	H	B	M	Jun 1880	19	S				MS	UN	UN	

1	2	3	4	5	6	7	8	9	10	11	12	13	14	15
	Hattie	Sis	B	F	Apr 1876	24	Wd		2	2	MS	UN	UN	
	Johnie	Sis	B	F	Jul 1893	6	S				MS	UN	UN	
	Coon	Sis	B	F	Jan 1896	3	S				MS	UN	MS	
128	Locket, Cornelius	H	B	M	Mar 1872	23	M	6			MS	MS	AL	Section Hand RR
	Ida	W	B	F	Sep 1880	19	M	6	4	4	AL	UN	UN	
	Andrew	S	B	M	Aug 1895	4	S				MS	MS	AL	
	Neely	S	B	M	Aug 1897	2	S				MS	MS	AL	
	Ola	D	B	F	Sep 1899	8/mo	S				MS	MS	AL	
	Nola	D	B	F	Sep 1899	8/mo	S				MS	MS	AL	
	Baily, Alice	Ward	B	F	Feb 1882	18	S				MS	UN	UN	
	Anna B.	Ward	B	F	Mar 1900	3/mo	S				MS	UN	MS	
129	Wilson, Columbus	H	B	M	UN UN	UN	M	19			GA	GA	GA	Farmer
	Nancy	W	B	F	Jun 1873	26	M	19	4	3	GA	SC	AL	
	Joe E.	S	B	M	Jan 1885	15	S				AL	GA	GA	Farm Hand
	Maude E.	D	B	F	Sep 1889	10	S				AL	GA	GA	
	Luida	D	B	F	Sep 1892	7	S				AL	GA	GA	
	Tubberville, Joe	UN	B	M	UN UN	UN	UN				MS	MS	UN	Farm Hand
130	Kimberly, George	H	W	M	Jun 1847	52	M	29			MS	MD	AL	Farmer
	M.E.	W	W	F	Mar 1858	52	M	29	0	0	AL	TN	TN	
131	Woods, Iveny V.	H	W	M	Feb 1849	51	Wd		6	6	NC	NC	NC	Farmer
	Petter L.	S	W	M	Apr 1878	22	S				MS	AL	NC	Nightwatch RR
	Ethelbert	S	W	M	Nov 1880	19	S				MS	AL	NC	
	Nignon A.	S	W	M	Dec 1882	17	S				MS	AL	NC	
	Susie E.	D	W	F	Feb 1887	13	S				MS	AL	NC	
	Adams, Susie	M	W	F	Mar 1812	88	Wd				NC	VA	NC	
	Redmon, John J.	Bdr	W	M	Mar 1873	27	S				Ire	Ire	Ire	Craner
	Wyle, Sam	Bdr		M	Dec 1871	28	S				MO	UN	UN	Fireman
132	Blunt, Andrew	H	W	M	Jun 1844	53	Wd				AL	MO	TN	Blacksmith
	Sallie	D	W	F	UN UN	UN	S				MS	AL	MA	
	Katie	D	W	F	UN UN	UN	S				MS	AL	MS	
	Walter	S	W	M	UN UN	UN	S				MS	AL	MS	Day Laborer
133	Mars, John S.	H	W	M	Dec 1858	41	M	18			AL	UN	AL	Farmer
	Lucy	W	W	F	Jul 1859	40	M	18	8	5	Al	UN	AL	
	John	S	W	M	Dec 1883	16	S				MS	AL	AL	Farm Hand
	James H.	S	W	M	Jan 1887	13	S				MS	AL	AL	Farm Hand
	W.F.	S	W	M	Dec 1889	10	S				MS	AL	AL	
	Frank	S	W	M	Mar 1892	8	S				MS	AL	AL	
	Locrecy	D	W	F	Feb 1898	2	S				MS	AL	AL	
134	Archy, Jackson	H	W	M	Apr 1829	71	M	46			TN	VA	TN	Farmer
	Mary	W	W	F	May 1849	51	M	46	11	9	AL	VA	VA	
	Ida	D	W	F	UN UN	UN	S				AL	TN	AL	Teacher
	William	S	W	M	Dec 1878	21	S				AL	TN	AL	Farm Hand
	Erwin, James	HH	W	M	Mar 1879	20	S				AL	AL	AL	Farm Hand
135	Smith, James	H	W	M	Nov 1860	39	M	11			MS	GA	GA	RR Section Hand
	Mollie A.	W	W	F	Sep 1869	34	M	11	6	6	MS	TN	AL	
	Maude L.	D	W	F	Oct 1889	10	S				MS	MS	MS	
	Tom W.	S	W	M	Apr 1891	9	S				MS	MS	MS	
	Owen J.	S	W	M	Feb 1893	7	S				MS	MS	MS	
	Mary L.	D	W	F	Nov 1894	5	S				MS	MS	MS	
	Charlie C.	S	W	M	Sep 1896	3	S				MS	MS	MS	
	Annie L.	D	W	F	Sep 1898	1	S				MS	MS	MS	
136	Fincher, Clark	H	W	M	Mar 1876	24	M	8			GA	GA	GA	RR Section Hand
	Dillie	W	W	F	Jul 1877	22	M	8	3	1	AL	AL	AL	
	Ella M.	D	W	F	Aug 1893	6	S				AL	AL	AL	

1	2	3	4	5	6	7	8	9	10	11	12	13	14	15
137	Murphy, Wm. A.	H	W	M	Oct 1841	58	M	33			MS	UN	UN	Farmer
	Sarah	W	W	F	May 1845	55	M	33	6	6	AL	AL	AL	
	Charlie	D	W	F	Dec 1867	32	S				MS	MS	AL	Farm Hand
	John W.	S	W	M	Feb 1878	21	S				MS	MS	AL	Farm Hand
	Marcus W.	S	W	M	Jul 1881	18	S				MS	MS	AL	Farm Hand
138	Woods, Ky	H	W	M	May 1862	38	M	11			MS	UN	TN	Day Laborer
	Sarah A.	W	W	F	Oct 1869	30	M	11	4	4	MS	MS	MS	
	Dixie I.	D	W	F	Feb 1890	10	S				MS	MS	MS	
	Sarah E.	D	W	F	Jun 1893	6	S				MS	MS	MS	
	Math A.	S	W	M	Jun 1897	2	S				MS	MS	MS	
	Walter S.	S	W	M	Mar 1900	2/mo					MS	MS	MS	
139	Chamberg, John W.	H	W	M	Jul 1874	25	M	11			AL	UN	AL	Farmer
	Spicy	W	W	F	Nov 1864	35	M	11	5	3	IL	VA	AL	
	Mary A.	D	W	F	Nov 1891	9	S				MS	AL	IL	
	Perlie	D	W	F	Jan 1894	6	S				MS	AL	IL	
	Earlie	S	W	M	Aug 1897	2	S				MS	AL	IL	
140	Lindley, John J.	H	W	M	Jan 1866	34	Wd				AL	UN	AL	Farmer
	James	S	W	M	Mar 1890	10	S				AL	AL	AL	
	Mary A.	D	W	F	Oct 1892	7	S				AL	AL	AL	
	Colley A.	D	W	F	Apr 1895	5	S				AL	AL	AL	
141	Lindley, Bill	H	W	M	Oct 1865	34	M	12			AL	AL	AL	Farmer
	Nancy J.	W	W	F	May 1871	29	M	12	5	4	AL	AL	AL	
	Beca J.	D	W	F	Jun 1889	10	S				AL	AL	AL	
	Ella D.	D	W	F	Sep 1890	9	S				AL	AL	AL	
	John W.H.	S	W	M	Mar 1894	6	S				TN	AL	AL	
	Annie B.	D	W	F	Sep 1897	3	S				MS	AL	AL	
142	Thomas, Mary E.	H	W	F	Dec 1842	57	Wd				AL	AL	AL	Farmer
	John J.	S	W	M	Oct 1870	29	M	8			AL	AL	AL	Farm Hand
	Pearlie	D	W	F	Apr 1884	16	S				MS	AL	AL	
	Lou	DiL	W	F	May 1876	24	M	8	3	3	AL	SC	AL	
	Walter	S	W	M	Jun 1893	7	S				MS	MS	AL	
	Modena	GD	W	F	Jun 1894	5	S				MS	MS	AL	
	Etta	GD	W	F	Dec 1897	2	S				MS	MS	AL	
143	Mitchel, John W.	H	W	M	Jun 1874	25	M	2			IN	IN	IN	Day Laborer
	Mary J.	W	W	F	Apr 1872	28	M	2	1	1	MS	VA	AL	
	Joseph A.	S	W	M	Nov 1898	1					MS	IN	MS	
144	Hannon, James W.	H	W	M	Aug 1875	24	M	5			MS	UN	MS	Day Laborer
	Bell	W	W	F	Oct 1874	25	M	5	3	3	MS	UN	AL	
	Robert	S	W	M	Aug 1896	3	S				MS	MS	MS	
	Everett	S	W	M	Oct 1897	2	S				MS	MS	MS	
	Ora	D	W	F	Feb 1900	4/mo	S				MS	MS	MS	
145	Wadkins, Dock	H	W	M	Sep 1875	24	M	3			MS	UN	UN	Day Laborer
	Viora	W	W	F	May 1880	20	M	3	1	1	AL	UN	UN	
	Wm. T.	S	W	M	Mar 1898	2	S				MS	MS	MS	
146	Thomas, Dave A.	H	W	M	Oct 1866	33	M	11			AL	AL	AL	Farmer
	Sallie	W	W	F	Nov 1872	27	M	11	5	4	MS	GA	TN	
	Joe C.	S	W	M	May 1890	10	S				MS	AL	MS	
	Luther V.	S	W	M	Feb 1892	8	S				MS	AL	MS	
	Rosa L.	D	W	F	Jan 1894	6	S				MS	AL	MS	
	John F.	S	W	M	Jan 1898	1	S				MS	AL	MS	
	Manley, Wm. F.	BiL	W	M	May 1886	14	S				AR	GA	TN	Farm Hand
	McKinney, Julia	M	W	F	Jul 1818	81	Wd		10	5	AL	UN	UN	
	Tubberville, Frank	Nep	W	M	Oct 1886	13	S				MS	AL	AL	

1	2	3	4	5	6	7	8	9	10	11	12	13	14	15
147	McKinney, Bob	H	W	M	Feb 1876	24	M	2			MS	UN	AL	Day Laborer
	Lizzie	W	W	F	Mar 1880	20	M	2	1	1	AL	MS	AL	
	Maude	D	W	F	Sep 1899	9/mo	S				MS	MS	MS	
148	Curtis, Jennie	H	W	F	Apr 1855	45	Wd		4	4	AL	UN	UN	Farmer
	Jim	S	W	M	May 1883	17	S				MS	MS	MS	Farmer
149	Yarbrough, L.B.	H	W	M	Mar 1861	39	M	17			MS	SC	SC	Farmer
	Josie	W	W	F	UN UN	UN	M	17	5	5	UN	UN	UN	
	Emma	D	W	F	Oct 1884	15	S				MS	MS	UN	Farm Hand
	Jim	S	W	M	Jul 1886	13	S				MS	MS	UN	Farm Hand
	Tom	S	W	M	Apr 1891	9	S				MS	MS	UN	
	Wm.	S	W	M	Dec 1894	5	S				MS	MS	UN	
	Mollie	D	W	F	Feb 1898	2	S				MS	MS	UN	
150	Yarbrough, Wills	H	W	M	Aug 1864	35	M	8			MS	GA	GA	Farmer
	Edna	W	W	F	Feb 1878	22	M	8	3	3	MS	MS	MS	
	Fly L.	D	W	F	Sep 1893	6	S				MS	MS	MS	
	Celestial	S	W	M	Feb 1896	4	S				MS	MS	MS	
	Ollie	D	W	F	Feb 1898	2	S				MS	MS	MS	
151	Wingo, Dan W.	H	W	M	May 1860	40	M	19			AL	AL	AL	Farmer
	Bettie	W	W	F	Jan 1864	36	M	19	8	7	AL	AL	AL	
	Edia H.	D	W	F	Feb 1882	18	S				AL	AL	AL	
	Jane D.	D	W	F	Sep 1884	12	S				AL	AL	AL	
	John H.	S	W	M	Sep 1886	13	S				AL	AL	AL	
	Lucresia L.	D	W	F	Jan 1889	11	S				MS	AL	AL	
	Dan W.	S	W	M	Jul 1891	7	S				MS	AL	AL	
	Clarence O.	S	W	M	Jul 1894	5	S				MS	AL	AL	
	Myrta L.	D	W	F	Jan 1899	1					MS	AL	AL	
152	Campbell, Mack	H	W	M	Aug 1862	37	M	20			SC	SC	SC	Farmer
	Plannie	W	W	F	Jun 1857	42	M	20	11	8	AL	TN	TN	
	Ben L.	S	W	M	Oct 1882	17	S				AL	SC	AL	Farm Hand
	Annie	D	W	F	Sep 1883	16	S				AL	SC	AL	Farm Hand
	Nancy E.	D	W	F	Dec 1884	15	S				AL	SC	AL	Farm Hand
	India E.	D	W	F	Apr 1887	13	S				AL	SC	AL	Farm Hand
	Mary I.	D	W	F	Apr 1891	9	S				AL	SC	AL	
	Plina B.	D	W	F	Apr 1892	8	S				AL	SC	AL	
	Emma M.	D	W	F	Sep 1896	4	S				AL	SC	AL	
	Mattie A.	D	W	F	Apr 1897	3	S				AL	SC	AL	
153	Edward, Tom	H	W	M	May 1858	42	M	18			MS	AL	MS	Farmer
	Lettice	W	W	F	Apr 1861	39	M	18	4	3	MS	TN	TN	
	Sydnie	S	W	M	Aug 1882	17	S				MS	MS	MS	Farm Hand
	Virgie	D	W	F	Feb 1888	12	S				MS	MS	MS	
	Blanche	D	W	F	Jan 1891	9	S				MS	MS	MS	
154	Dean, Ruben C.	H	W	M	Aug 1867	32	M	4			MS	MS	MS	Farmer
	Lula B.	W	W	F	UN 1871	29	M	4	3	2	MS	MS	SC	
	Carrie	D	W	F	Jan 1896	4	S				MS	MS	MS	
	Elmo F.	S	W	M	Jun 1899	1	S				MS	MS	MS	
155	Wood, Charles	H	W	M	Aug 1848	51	M	20			AL	AL	AL	Farmer
	Ella A.	W	W	F	Sep 1859	40	M	20	6	5	AL	AL	AL	
	Ella	D	W	F	Feb 1861	14	S				AL	AL	AL	
	Ida	D	W	F	Jun 1888	11	S				MS	AL	AL	
	Eddie K.	D	W	F	Feb 1861	10	S				MS	AL	AL	
	Charles F.	S	W	M	Feb 1892	8	S				MS	AL	AL	
	Esten J.	S	W	M	Feb 1894	6	S				MS	AL	AL	
	Carr, Duncan E.	HH	W	M	Nov 1878	21	S				MS	AL	TN	Hired Hand
	Batey, Bob	Bdr	W	M	UN 1864	66	M	22			MS	MS	UN	Teacher

1	2	3	4	5	6	7	8	9	10	11	12	13	14	15
156	Oliver, J.M.	H	W	M	Jan 1863	37	M	5			IL	TN	KY	Day Laborer
	Sarah	W	W	F	Mar 1878	21	M	5	3	2	MS	TN	TN	
	Cala	S	W	M	Nov 1897	2	S				TN	IL	MS	
	Elizabeth	D	W	F	Nov 1898	7/mo	S				TN	IL	MS	
	Bailey, Sarah	Bdr	W	F	Jul 1824	75	M	22			MS	AL	AL	
157	Thomson, Tom	H	W	M	Jan 1863	37	M	13			MS	AL	AL	Farmer
	Lucy	W	W	F	Mar 1863	37	M	6	5		MS	VA	UN	
	James E.	S	W	M	Apr 1888	12	S				MS	MS	MS	Farm Hand
	Lang C.	S	W	M	May 1891	9	S				MS	MS	MS	
	William F.	S	W	M	Nov 1893	6	S				MS	MS	MS	
	Zeke C.	S	W	M	Sep 1895	4	S				MS	MS	MS	
	Julius C.	S	W	M	Oct 1897	2	S				MS	MS	MS	
	Ennus	S	W	M	Feb 1900	3/mo	S				MS	MS	MS	
158	Akers, William T	H	W	M	Oct 1848	51	M	33			MS	VA	GA	Farmer
	H.V.	W	W	F	Jan 1846	51	M	33	7	7	MS	SC	SC	
	Dean J.	S	W	M	May 1880	20	S				MS	MS	MS	Farm Hand
	Zeb	S	W	M	Apr 1884	16	S				MS	MS	MS	Farm Hand
	Hill, Clarence	HH	B	M	UN UN	17	S				MS	MS	AL	Farm Hand
159	Bonds, James C.	H	W	M	Dec 1867	32	M	11			MS	AL	SC	Farmer
	Lillie M.	W	W	F	Apr 1870	30	M	11	5	4	MS	MS	MS	
	Annie B.	D	W	F	Dec 1891	8	S				MS	MS	MS	
	Bessie L.	D	W	F	Jan 1894	6	S				MS	MS	MS	
	Elsie M.	D	W	F	Mar 1896	4	S				MS	MS	MS	
	Florence A.	D	W	F	Feb 1898	2	S				MS	MS	MS	
160	Wisdom, John E.	H	W	M	Mar 1863	37	M	12			MS	UN	UN	Farmer
	Frances	W	W	F	May 1873	27	M	12	6	6	MS	UN	MS	
	Alford	S	W	M	Aug 1889	10	S				MS	MS	MS	
	Jesse	S	W	M	Sep 1892	8	S				MS	MS	MS	
	Homer	S	W	M	Nov 1893	6	S				MS	MS	MS	
	Mary L	D	W	F	Aug 1895	4	S				MS	MS	MS	
	Eula P.	D	W	F	Mar 1897	3	S				MS	MS	MS	
	Minnie S.	D	W	F	Mar 1899	1	S				MS	MS	MS	
161	Wood, Robert W.	H	W	M	Jan 1874	26	M	4			MS	AL	NC	Teacher/Carpenter
	Mattie S.	W	W	F	Jul 1871	28	M	4	1	1	MS	MS	MS	
	Susie A.	D	W	F	Apr 1897	3	S				MS	MS	MS	
162	Blunt, James J.	H	W	M	Mar 1871	29	M	4			MS	AL	MS	Carpenter
	Eva	W	W	F	Sep 1876	23	M	4	2	2	MS	AL	AL	
	Ruth	D	W	F	May 1897	3	S				MS	MS	MS	
	Lenard	S	W	M	Dec 1898	1	S				MS	MS	MS	
163	Alexander, William	H	W	M	Oct 1858	41	M	14			MS	SC	TN	Farmer
	Caroline	W	W	F	Aug 1861	38	M	14	5	5	MS	AL	AL	
	Clide	S	W	M	Feb 1887	13	S				MS	MS	MS	
	Frank	S	W	M	Jan 1890	10	S				MS	MS	MS	
	William	S	W	M	Jun 1892	7	S				MS	MS	MS	
	Ezekiel	S	W	M	Dec 1894	5	S				MS	MS	MS	
	Lenand	D	W	F	Mar 1896	4	S				MS	MS	MS	
164	Yarbrough, Louis F.	H	W	M	Feb 1827	73	M	45			GA	SC	GA	Farmer
	Susie	W	W	F	Jul 1831	61	M	45	7	4	SC	SC	SC	
	Haney, Nancy	D	W	F	Oct 1859	40	Wd		1	1	MS	GA	SC	
	Riley	GS	W	M	Nov 1881	18	S				MS	IL	MS	Farmer
165	Yarbrough, Dan	H	W	M	Feb 1857	43	M	21			GA	GA	GA	
	Melia	W	W	F	Jul 1860	39	M	21	2	2	MS	UN	UN	
	Eula M.	D	W	F	Jul 1897	2	S				MS	GA	MS	

1	2	3	4	5	6	7	8	9	10	11	12	13	14	15
166	Blunt, Wm.	H	W	M	Jul 1865	34	M	3			MS	TX	MS	Farmer
	Louisa C.	W	W	F	Sep 1867	32	M	3	3	2	AL	AL	AL	
	Oscar E.	S	W	M	Jul 1887	13	S				MS	MS	MS	
	Mary M.	D	W	F	Nov 1889	10	S				MS	MS	MS	
167	Webb, Annie	H	W	F	Mar 1868	31	Wd		2	2	MS	MS	MS	Farmer
	Lillie M.	D	W	F	May 1888	11	S				MS	MS	MS	
	Henry B.	S	W	M	Mar 1897	3	S				AL	MS	MS	
	Sallie	D	W	F	May 1900	1/mo	S				MS	MS	MS	
168	Maxwell, J.M.	H	W	M	Jan 1834	66	M	14			GA	GA	GA	Farmer
	Sallie	W	W	F	UN UN	UN	M	14			KY	TN	UN	
	Powell, Annie	Ward	W	F	Dec 1892	7	S				MS	MS	MS	
169	Miller, William	H	W	M	Apr 1850	50	M	20			AL	UN	UN	Farmer
	Elizabeth A.	W	W	F	Sep 1864	35	M	20	4	2	AL	NC	NC	
	Wm. H.	S	W	M	Feb 1880	20	S				AL	AL	AL	Farm Hand
170	Gassaway, John	H	W	M	Mar 1841	59	M	29			GA	SC	SC	Farmer
	Mary C.	W	W	F	Feb 1856	44	M	29	14	12	AL	TN	TN	
	John T.	S	W	M	Mar 1878	22	S				AL	GA	AL	
	Laura B.	D	W	F	Jul 1877	21	S				AL	GA	AL	
	Lonie L.	D	W	F	Apr 1881	19	S				AL	GA	AL	
	Sam F.	S	W	M	Oct 1882	17	S				AL	GA	AL	
	Fannie D.	D	W	M	Feb 1886	14	S				TN	GA	AL	
	Annie C.	D	W	M	Jan 1889	11	S				TN	GA	AL	
	Robert L.	S	W	M	Oct 1890	9	S				AL	GA	AL	
	Minnie P.	D	W	F	Jan 1893	7	S				TN	GA	AL	
	Martha M.	D	W	F	Jun 1893	7	S				TN	GA	AL	
	Bernis	D	W	F	Jul 1897	2	S				AL	GA	AL	
171	Haynes, James L.	H	W	M	May 1866	34	M	3			AL	VA	AL	Farmer
	Ella L.	W	W	F	Apr 1876	24	M	3	2	2	AL	AL	AL	
	Wm. A.	S	W	M	Oct 1897	2	S				MS	AL	AL	
	Crystine	D	W	F	Apr 1899	1	S				MS	AL	AL	
172	Haynes, James A.	H	W	M	Jun 1861	38	M	11			AL	VA	AL	Farmer
	Dinnie	W	W	F	Feb 1869	31	M	11	3	3	MS	TN	MS	
	Walter S.	S	W	M	Jul 1890	9	S				MS	AL	MS	
	Clora E.	D	W	F	Jul 1892	7	S				MS	MS	MS	
	Clarence M.	S	W	M	Aug 1894	5	S				MS	MS	MS	
173	Haynes, Mary E.	H	W	F	Dec 1838	61	Wd		10	9	AL	TN	AL	Farmer
	Wilks C.	S	W	M	Jan 1877	23	S				MS	DC	AL	Day Laborer
	Robert H.	S	W	M	Mar 1878	22	S				MS	DC	AL	Farm Hand
	Tinnie	D	W	F	May 1880	20	S				MS	DC	AL	
	Pearl C.	D	W	F	Dec 1881	18	S				MS	DC	AL	
174	Coman, Hardy	H	B	M	May 1864	35	Wd				MS	MS	MS	Farmer
	Elvie	D	B	F	May 1887	13	S				MS	MS	MS	Farm Hand
	Perdie	S	B	M	Jun 1888	11	S				MS	MS	MS	Farm Hand
	Annie	D	B	F	Jun 1892	7	S				MS	MS	MS	
	Willie	S	B	M	Jun 1893	6	S				MS	MS	MS	
	Annie D.	D	B	F	Jun 1894	5	S				MS	MS	MS	
175	Thompson, James	H	W	M	Feb 1820	80	M	40			AL	UN	UN	Farmer
	Mary J.	W	W	F	Mar 1825	75	M	40	2	2	TN	UN	UN	
	Wm. J.	S	W	M	Dec 1864	35	S				AR	AL	TN	
176	Moore, William	H	W	M	Jul 1867	32	M	1			MS	MS	UN	Farmer
	Virginia	W	W	F	Jan 1874	26	M	1	0	0	AL	UN	GA	
177	Winbush, John W.	H	W	M	Jan 1860	39	M	7			MS	UN	UN	Farmer

1	2	3	4	5	6	7	8	9	10	11	12	13	14	15
	Mary I.	W	W	F	Nov 1872	27	M	7	2	1	MS	MS	UN	
	Mennie E.	D	W	F	Jul 1897	2	S				MS	MS	MS	
178	Moore, James	H	W	M	Jan 1839	61	M	33			MS	UN	TN	Farmer
	Mary	W	W	F	Jan 1845	55	M	33	8	5	MS	VA	VA	
	Martha A.	D	W	F	Jun 1874	25	S				MS	MS	MS	
	John M.	S	W	M	Oct 1876	23	S				MS	MS	MS	
	Letha	D	W	F	Jul 1879	20	S				MS	MS	MS	
179	Brown, Sam	UN	W	M	UN UN	UN	Wd				MS	MS	MS	Farmer
	John A.	S	W	M	Mar 1872	28	S				MS	MS	MS	
	Mary A.	D	W	F	Nov 1881	18	S				MS	MS	MS	
	Wilson, May	HH	W	F	Apr 1850	50	Wd				MS	MS	MS	Farm Hand
	Nell, Roman	HH	W	M	May 1887	13	S				MS	MS	MS	Farm Hand
180	Wood, William A.	H	W	M	Mar 1867	33	M	5			TN	VA	TN	Farmer
	Lula	W	W	F	Nov 1877	22	M	5	3	2	MS	MS	MS	
	Solathie	D	W	F	Jan 1897	3	S				MS	TN	MS	
	Emma	D	W	F	Feb 1900	3/mo	S				MS	TN	MS	
181	Adams, David	H	W	M	Sep 1857	42	M	10			MS	TN	TN	Farmer
	Dollie	W	W	F	UN 1866	34	M	10	5	5	MS	TN	AL	
	Webster L.	S	W	M	Jul 1892	8	S				MS	MS	MS	
	Candia A.	D	W	F	Dec 1893	6	S				MS	MS	MS	
	John S.	S	W	M	Dec 1895	4	S				MS	MS	MS	
	Garfield	S	W	M	Dec 1897	2	S				MS	MS	MS	
	May	D	W	F	May 1900	1/mo	S				MS	MS	MS	
182	Flynt, Mary	H	W	F	May 1837	63	Wd		9	2	TN	NC	NC	Farmer
	Charles	S	W	M	Oct 1875	24	S				MS	AL	TN	Teacher
183	Davis, Alford	H	W	M	Dec 1868	31	M	7			MS	AL	MS	Farmer
	Hattie	W	W	F	Mar 1870	30	M	7	1	1	MS	AL	AL	
	Blanche	D	W	F	Dec 1897	2	S				MS	MS	MS	
184	Moore, John	H	W	M	Feb 1835	65	M	30			AL	NC	AL	Lawyer
	Frances A.	W	W	F	Oct 1839	60	M	30	3	1	MS	AL	TN	
	Moseley, George S.	SS	W	M	Mar 1863	37	M	18			TN	TN	TN	Machine
	Lula B.	SD	W	F	Sep 1863	37	M	18	5	4	MS	MS	MS	
	Willord	GD	W	F	Feb 1888	11	S				MS	TN	MS	
	Adell	GD	W	F	Dec 1892	7	S				MS	TN	MS	
	Reed	GS	W	M	Apr 1896	4	S				MS	TN	MS	
	Georgia	GD	W	F	Jun 1900	6/mo	S				MS	TN	MS	
185	Broughton, Charles	H	W	M	Feb 1869	31	M	11			MS	SC	MS	Farmer
	Liza E.	W	W	F	Jul 1863	36	M	11	5	5	MS	MS	MS	
	Bertha E.	D	W	F	Sep 1891	8	S				MS	MS	MS	
	Ina H.	D	W	F	Feb 1894	6	S				MS	MS	MS	
	Horace T.	S	W	M	Feb 1896	4	S				MS	MS	MS	
	Paul E.	S	W	M	Aug 1897	2	S				MS	MS	MS	
	Ruth	D	W	F	Oct 1899	8/mo	S				MS	MS	MS	
186	Broughton, John	H	W	M	Jan 1839	61	M	30			SC	SC	SC	Farmer
	Elizabeth	W	W	F	May 1850	50	M	30	3	3	MS	TN	MS	
	Maude	D	W	F	Aug 1875	24	S				MS	SC	MS	
	G.G.	D	W	F	Jan 1881	19	S				MS	SC	MS	
	Pearl	D	W	F	Sep 1884	15	S				MS	SC	MS	
187	Akers, Charles	H	W	M	Mar 1874	26	M	6			MS	MS	MS	Farmer
	Maude	W	W	F	Mar 1876	24	M	6	0	0	MS	MS	MS	
188	Jordan, George T.	H	W	M	Feb 1856	42	M	33			TN	KY	AL	Farmer
	Mattie E.	W	W	F	Apr 1872	28	M	33	6	5	AL	AL	AL	

1	2	3	4	5	6	7	8	9	10	11	12	13	14	15
	Cora L.	D	W	F	May 1884	16	S				TN	TN	AL	
	Roxie E.	D	W	F	Mar 1885	15	S				TN	TN	AL	
	Chester C.	S	W	M	Feb 1894	6	S				TN	TN	AL	
	Minnie B.	D	W	F	Dec 1892	7	S				TN	TN	AL	
	Wilmer	S	W	M	Feb 1895	5	S				TN	TN	AL	
	Mamie B.	D	W	F	UN 1898	2	S				TN	TN	AL	
	No Name	D	W	F	May 1900	0	S				MS	TN	AL	
189	Dean, Sam C.	H	W	M	Sep 1867	32	M	8			MS	MS	MS	Farmer
	Bettie	W	W	F	Feb 1872	28	M	8	3	3	MS	MS	MS	
	Paul	S	W	M	Feb 1893	7	S				MS	MS	MS	
	Rubie	D	W	F	Sep 1894	5	S				MS	MS	MS	
	Ora	D	W	F	Mar 1898	2	S				MS	MS	MS	
190	Dean, John F.	H	W	M	Aug 1856	43	M	22			MS	SC	SC	Farmer
	Hettie K.	W	W	F	Sep 1862	37	M	22	8	8	MS	MS	MS	
	Florence	D	W	F	Feb 1880	20	S				MS	MS	MS	
	Cordie	D	W	F	Mar 1881	19	S				MS	MS	MS	
	Lucius	S	W	M	Feb 1883	17	S				MS	MS	MS	
	John A.	S	W	M	Feb 1886	14	S				MS	MS	MS	
	Josie	D	W	F	Mar 1890	10	S				MS	MS	MS	
	Nellie	D	W	F	Jan 1892	8	S				MS	MS	MS	
	Ivy	D	W	F	Feb 1898	7	S				MS	MS	MS	
	Lucille	D	W	F	Jan 1896	4	S				MS	MS	MS	
191	Harwell, Dewitt	H	W	M	Nov 1859	40	M	15			TN	UN	UN	Farmer
	Minnie	W	W	F	Mar 1865	35	M	15	5	5	MS	MS	MS	
	Wilford	S	W	M	Feb 1887	13					MS	TN	MS	Farm Hand
	Nellie	D	W	F	Feb 1891	11					MS	TN	MS	
	Ernest	S	W	M	May 1894	9					MS	TN	MS	
	Ina	D	W	F	Feb 1897	6					MS	TN	MS	
	Mary E.	D	W	F	Feb 1894	3					MS	TN	MS	
192	Boyd, William	H	B	M	Jan 1873	27	M	7			MS	SC	SC	Farmer
	Mary	W	B	F	Aug 1864	35	M	7			TN	MS	MS	
	Harriett	M	B	F	Feb 1830	70	Wd		9	5	SC	VA	VA	
	James, Minnie	Nce	B	F	Mar 1885	15	S				TN	TN	MS	
	Ed	Nep	B	M	Mar 1883	17	S				MS	TN	MS	
	Green, Mamie	Nce	B	F	Feb 1892	8	S				MS	MS	MS	
193	Young, Jennie	H	B	F	Jun 1872	28	M	6	2	2	AL	TN	TN	Laundress
	Dave	H	B	M	UN UN	UN	M	6			AL	UN	AL	Day Laborer
	Kringes, Rosa	Sis	B	F	Sep 1883	16	S				AL	TN	AL	Chamber Maid
	Phyle, Pheby	Ward	B	M	UN 1884	16	S				AL	TN	AL	Cook
	Kringes, Frank	Nep	B	M	Jan 1900	6/mo	S				MS	AL	AL	
194	Smith, Sam	H	B	M	UN UN	UN	M	1			UN	UN	UN	Shoe Maker
	Tabitha	W	B	F	UN UN	UN	M	1			MS	UN	UN	Laundress
195	Wingo, Sallie	H	W	F	Mar 1849	51	S				AL	UN	UN	
	Cath	Bro	W	M	Sep 1858	41	S				AL	UN	UN	Farmer
	Bunt, Shelley	Nce	W	F	May 1870	30	Wd		1	1	MS	AL	MS	
	Jimmie	Nep	W	M	Sep 1890	9	S				MS	AL	MS	
196	Green, Eucima	H	W	F	Jan 1877	23	S				AL	NC	MS	Seamstress
	Kendrick	S	W	M	Apr 1896	4	S				MS	AL	MS	
	Della	Sis	W	F	Jul 1879	20	S				AL	NC	NC	Nursing
197	Brandson, James	H	W	M	Sep 1872	27	M	6			MS	UN	UN	RR Sect. Hand
	Mollie	W	W	F	Apr 1876	24	M	6	2	2	MS	SC	AL	
	Bessie	D	W	F	Mar 1895	5	S				MS	MS	MS	
	Maggie	D	W	F	Jun 1896	3	S				MS	MS	MS	
	Clark, Martha	MiL	W	F	Oct 1839	60	Wd		5	3	AL	NC	NC	

1	2	3	4	5	6	7	8	9	10	11	12	13	14	15
	Alice	Sis	W	F	Mar 1872	28	S				MS	SC	AL	Day Laborer
198	Harris, John	H	B	M	UN UN	UN	S				UN	UN	UN	Day Laborer
	Green, Allie		B	F	Nov 1867	33	M	13	12	6	AL	UN	AL	Laundress
	Oscar	Ward	B	M	Apr 1897	3	S				MS	AL	AL	
	Lizzie	Ward	B	F	Feb 1900	3/mo	S				MS	UN	AL	
	Bankhead, Wiley	Ward	B	M	Dec 1878	21	S				AL	AL	AL	Day Laborer
199	Campbell, William F.	H	W	M	Aug 1860	39	M	12			MS	NC	SC	Farmer
	Beulah	W	W	F	Dec 1860	39	M	12	4	2	MS	TN	AL	
	Mitchell D.	S	W	M	Jun 1890	10	S				MS	MS	MS	
	Merion	D	W	F	Jun 1896	3	S				MS	MS	MS	
	Mitchell, Sarah C.	MiL	W	F	Jul 1825	74	Wd		10	4	AL	GA	MS	
200	Rodgers, Sam	H	B	M	Mar 1841	59	M	33			VA	VA	VA	Farmer
	Nancy	W	B	F	Jul UN	48	M	33	11	10	MS	UN	UN	
	Bell	D	B	F	Jan 1876	24	S				MS	VA	MS	
	Oscar	S	B	M	Sep 1881	18	S				MS	VA	MS	
	Berta	D	B	F	Feb 1884	16	S				MS	VA	MS	
	Robert	S	B	M	Aug 1886	13	S				MS	VA	MS	
	Frank	S	B	M	Jan 1890	10	S				MS	VA	MS	
	Floy	D	B	F	Dec 1892	7	S				MS	VA	MS	
	Viola	D	B	F	Mar 1895	5	S				MS	VA	MS	
	Davis, Henry	GS	B	M	Jun 1890	9	S				MS	MS	MS	
201	Whitesides, Alex	H	B	M	Jan 1830	70	M	28			AL	UN	UN	Farmer
	Mandy	W	B	F	Apr 1858	42	M	28	13	13	MS	UN	UN	
	Velma	D	B	F	Mar 1883	17	S				MS	AL	MS	
	Pennie	D	B	F	Feb 1886	14	S				MS	AL	MS	
	Sylvester	S	B	M	Dec 1888	11	S				MS	AL	MS	
	Robert	S	B	M	May 1890	10	S				MS	AL	MS	
	Willie	S	B	M	Jan 1892	8	S				MS	AL	MS	
	Abraham	S	B	M	Oct 1893	6	S				MS	AL	MS	
	Velma	D	B	F	May 1895	5	S				MS	AL	MS	
	Jones, Sonnie	GS	B	M	Dec 1898	6	S				TN	MS	MS	
	Mattix, Alex	GS	B	M	Oct 1896	3	S				MS	MS	MS	
	Hill, Manda	GD	B	F	Jun 1896	3	S				MS	MS	MS	
202	Rolen, John M.	H	B	M	Dec 1859	40	M	19			AL	AL	AL	Farmer
	Rebecca	W	B	F	May 1858	42	M	19	3	3	TN	TN	MS	
	Sallie C.	D	B	F	Oct 1891	8	S				MS	AL	TN	
203	Reed, Manda	H	B	F	UN UN	UN	S		4	3	VA	UN	UN	Cook
	Harris, Katie	D	B	F	Apr 1874	26	M	3	1	1	MS	UN	VA	Cook
	Margaret	GD	B	F	Jan 1894	6	S				MS	AL	MS	
	Oscar	SIL	B	M	Feb 1866	34	M	3			AL	UN	UN	Day Laborer
204	Carter, John R.	H	W	M	Jan 1858	42	M	21			AL	GA	GA	Farmer
	Georgia A.	H	W	F	Nov 1859	42	M	21	7	7	MS	UN	AL	
	Mollie	W	W	F	Apr 1884	16	S				MS	AL	MS	
	Oscar C.	S	W	M	Feb 1885	15	S				MS	AL	MS	
	Shelley	S	W	M	Jan 1887	13	S				MS	AL	MS	
	Dora	D	W	F	Jan 1889	11	S				MS	AL	MS	
	Myrta A.	D	W	F	Jun 1893	7	S				MS	AL	MS	
205	Carter, Jim H.	H	W	M	Sep 1879	20	M	0			MS	AL	MS	Farmer
	Jennie W.	W	W	F	Mar 1879	20	M	0	0	0	MS	UN	UN	
206	Walker, Levy	H	W	M	Mar 1858	42	M	18			MS	UN	UN	Farmer
	Marguerette	W	W	F	Jan 1863	37	M	18	7	7	TN	AL	UN	
	Fred	S	W	M	May 1883	17	S				AR	MS	TN	
	Myrtle	D	W	F	Jul 1880	14	S				MS	MS	TN	
	Auston	S	W	M	Nov 1887	12	S				MS	MS	TN	

1	2	3	4	5	6	7	8	9	10	11	12	13	14	15
	Bertha	D	W	F	Mar 1890	10	S				MS	MS	TN	
	Lester	S	W	M	Oct 1892	7	S				MS	MS	TN	
	Eugene	S	W	M	Dec 1893	6	S				MS	MS	TN	
	Corrie	D	W	F	Mar 1897	3	S				MS	MS	TN	
207	Walker, John	H	W	M	Jan 1868	37	M	14			MS	UN	UN	Farmer
	Edie K.	W	W	F	Apr 1867	33	M	14	5	5	TN	UN	UN	
	Lillie	D	W	F	Jun 1886	13	S				MS	MS	TN	
	Lawrence B.	S	W	M	Jan 1889	10	S				MS	MS	TN	
	Velma J.	D	W	F	Jun 1892	7	S				MS	MS	TN	
	Ellis W.	S	W	M	Jul 1898	6	S				MS	MS	TN	
	Colton T.	S	W	M	UN 1897	2	S				MS	MS	TN	
208	Kirk, Sidney	H	W	M	Mar 1871	29	M	9			MS	UN	UN	Farmer
	Nicy	W	W	F	UN 1873	26	M	9	3	3	MS	UN	UN	
	Dolphus L.	S	W	M	Sep 1892	7	S				MS	MS	MS	
	Lucille	D	W	F	UN 1894	4	S				MS	MS	MS	
	Lum	S	W	M	Dec 1898	1	S				MS	MS	MS	
	Medley, Till	Bdr		M	UN 1882	18	S				MS	MS	MS	
209	Gant, John J.	H	W	M	Jan 1820	80	Wd				SC	SC	SC	Farmer
	Beasley, Comalia M.	Ward	W	F	Oct 1868	31	S				MS	UN	UN	House Keeper
210	Anderson, David L.	H	W	M	Feb 1861	39	M	5			MS	SC	SC	Farmer
	Martha	W	W	F	Dec 1868	31	M	5			MS	UN	MS	
	Martha A.	M	W	F	Jan 1821	79	Wd		7	6	GA	SC	SC	
	Lewis, Charlie	HH	W	M	UN 1882	18	S				MS	MS	UN	Hired Hand
211	Thorne, John S.	H	W	M	Oct 1873	26	M	3			AL	AL	UN	Farmer
	Leona	W	W	F	UN 1880	20	M	3	2	2	MS	UN	UN	
	Jim K.	S	W	M	Mar 1898	2	S				AL	AL	MS	
	Sidney E.	S	W	M	Nov 1899	6/mo	S				MS	AL	MS	
212	Dexter, M.J.	H	W	M	Apr 1861	39	M	14			MS	Eng	MS	Farmer
	Ida	W	W	F	Jun 1866	34	M	14	8	8	MS	NC	GA	
	Onnie	D	W	F	Mar 1887	13	S				MS	MS	MS	
	Lema	D	W	F	Nov 1888	11	S				MS	MS	MS	
	Jesse	D	W	F	Apr 1891	9	S				MS	MS	MS	
	Roxie	D	W	F	May 1893	7	S				MS	MS	MS	
	Mattie	D	W	F	Apr 1895	5	S				MS	MS	MS	
	Jimmie	S	W	M	Mar 1896	4	S				MS	MS	MS	
	Roy	S	W	M	Jun 1898	2	S				MS	MS	MS	
	No Name	S	W	F	May 1900	1/mo	S				MS	MS	MS	
213	Medley, William J.	H	W	M	Oct 1853	46	M	27			MS	MS	MS	Farmer
	Pricilla	W	W	F	Nov 1851	48	M	27	9	7	MS	VA	TN	
	Charlie	S	W	M	Aug 1874	25	S				MS	MS	MS	Farm Hand
	Bob	S	W	M	May 1879	21	S				MS	MS	MS	Farm Hand
	Burt	S	W	M	Sep 1881	18	S				MS	MS	MS	Farm Hand
	Jim	S	W	M	Jun 1884	16	S				MS	MS	MS	Farm Hand
	Jennie L.	D	W	F	Mar 1887	13	S				MS	MS	MS	Farm Hand
	Ed	S	W	M	Aug 1889	10	S				MS	MS	MS	Farm Hand
	Lou E.	D	W	F	Mar 1893	7	S				MS	MS	MS	
215	Cagle, Charles	H	W	M	Aug 1869	30	M	4			MS	AL	AL	Farmer
	Bell	W	W	F	Dec 1869	30	M	4	0	0	MS	UN	UN	
216	Tigner, Edward	H	W	M	Sep 1870	29	M	2			MS	TN	MS	Farmer
	Ellen	W	W	F	Mar 1866	34	M	2	6	6	MS	Eng	UN	
	Savanah G.	D	W	F	Nov 1897	2	S				MS	MS	MS	
	Allen O.	S	W	M	Nov 1899	6/mo	S				MS	MS	MS	
	Busby, Adie M.	SD	W	F	UN 1889	11	S				MS	MS	MS	
	John M.	SS	W	M	UN 1891	9	S				MS	MS	MS	

1	2	3	4	5	6	7	8	9	10	11	12	13	14	15
	Edgar	SS	W	M	UN 1893	7	S				MS	MS	MS	
	Willie	SS	W	M	UN 1895	5	S				MS	MS	MS	
217	Biggs, Jesse S.	H	W	F	Oct 1867	32	M	14			MS	NC	GA	
	Mary F.	W	W	F	Sep 1864	35	M	14	5	5	MS	Eng	MS	
	Wm. J.	S	W	M	Oct 1887	13	S				MS	MS	MS	
	Nancy H.	D	W	F	Apr 1889	11	S				MS	MS	MS	
	Julia	D	W	F	Sep 1892	7	S				MS	MS	MS	
	Charlie C.	S	W	M	Jul 1894	5	S				MS	MS	MS	
	Albert E.	S	W	M	Jun 1897	2	S				MS	MS	MS	
217	Goode, John	H	W	M	Sep 1831	68	M	33			AL	SC	KY	Farmer
	Sallie	W	W	F	UN UN	UN	M	33	5	4	AL	UN	UN	
	Willie M.	D	W	F	Mar 1870	30	S				MS	AL	AL	
	Lillie L.	D	W	F	Aug 1878	22	S				KY	AL	AL	
218	Crause, Rufus	H	W	M	Aug 1854	45	M	20			MS	UN	UN	Farmer
	Maggie	W	W	F	Oct 1868	31	2M	20	2	2	UN	UN	UN	
	Ethel	D	W	F	Mar 1890	10	S				MS	MS	MS	
	Ora E.	D	W	F	Apr 1894	6	S				MS	MS	MS	
	Maty L.	D	W	F	Jun 1883	17	S				MS	MS	MS	
	Ada E.	D	W	F	Aug 1884	15	S				MS	MS	MS	
	Lila B.	D	W	F	Jul 1889	10	S				TN	MS	MS	
	Clayton A.	S	W	M	Jul 1891	8	S				TN	MS	MS	
219	Clark, Lucrus	H	W	M	Nov 1868	31	M	12			MS	SC	AL	Farmer
	Minnie	W	W	F	Nov 1869	30	M	12	9	6	MS	UN	MS	
	Leland	S	W	M	Dec 1888	11	S				MS	MS	MS	
	Clarence H.	S	W	F	May 1893	7	S				MS	MS	MS	
	Arch	S	W	M	Mar 1895	5	S				MS	MS	MS	
	Mattie E.	D	W	F	May 1896	4	S				MS	MS	MS	
	Homer	S	W	M	Dec 1897	2	S				MS	MS	MS	
	Dexter	S	W	M	Apr 1900	3/mo	S				MS	MS	MS	
220	Kimberly, Sam	H	W	M	Jul 1864	36	M	12			AL	UN	AL	Farmer
	Edna	W	W	F	Feb 1872	28	M	12	4	4	MS	AL	NC	
	Victoria	D	W	F	Oct 1889	11	S				MS	AL	MS	
	Perry	S	W	M	Oct 1881	7	S				MS	AL	MS	
	Elma	S	W	M	Sep 1895	4	S				MS	AL	MS	
	Edward	S	W	M	Dec 1897	2	S				MS	AL	MS	
221	Roler, Geo. M.	H	W	M	Jan 1837	63	M	41			AL	AL	AL	Farmer
	Mary C.	W	W	F	Jan 1836	64	M	41	7	1	AL	TN	TN	
	Webb, Matilda	Nce	W	F	Mar 1846	53	S				AL	UN	AL	
222	Erwin, Felix G.	H	W	M	Jul 1846	53	M	23			TN	SC	SC	Farmer
	Martha	W	W	F	Mar 1846	54	M	23	3	2	TN	PA	SC	
	Julia W.	D	W	F	Nov 1878	20	S				MS	TN	TN	
223	Erwin, Joe D.	H	W	M	Nov 1880	19	M	0			MS	TN	TN	
	Coffey C.	W	W	F	UN 1883	17	M	0			TN	TN	TN	
224	Carter, William J.	H	W	M	Jan 1868	32	M	13			AL	UN	UN	Farmer
	Sarah L.	W	W	F	Mar 1871	29	M	13	4	3	TN	UN	AL	
	Walker C.	S	W	M	Sep 1890	9	S				MS	AL	TN	
	Maggie	D	W	F	Nov 1894	5	S				MS	AL	TN	
	Jim	S	W	M	Mar 1898	2	S				MS	AL	TN	
225	Atkins, George	H	W	M	Aug 1865	34	M	13			AL	SC	SC	Farmer
	Jane	W	W	F	UN UN	UN	M	13	5	4	AL	UN	AL	
	Minnie	D	W	F	Apr 1888	12	S				MS	AL	AL	
	Henry	S	W	M	May 1889	11	S				MS	AL	AL	
	Mattie	D	W	F	Jan 1896	4	S				MS	AL	AL	

1	2	3	4	5	6	7	8	9	10	11	12	13	14	15
226	Sanders, John	H	W	M	Feb 1876	24	M	5			MS	UN	AL	Farmer
	Lou	W	W	F	May 1877	23	M	5	3	2	MS	UN	AL	
	Elmore	S	W	M	Sep 1895	4	S				MS	MS	MS	
	Lish	S	W	M	Dec 1892	2	S				MS	MS	MS	
227	Sanders, Pearly	H	W	M	Jun 1855	44	S				AL	NY	AL	Day Laborer
	Harriett	Sis	W	F	Feb 1868	32	S				AL	NY	AL	Day Laborer
	Tinsey	Nce	W	F	Aug 1888	11	S				MS	AL	MS	Farm Hand
228	Carter, James M.	H	W	M	Sep 1879	20	M	0			MS	AL	MS	Farmer
	Jennie	W	W	F	May 1882	18	M	0	0	0	MS	UN	UN	
229	Joshlin, James	H	W	M	Nov 1828	71	Wd				AL	NC	AL	Farmer
	Sanders, Martin	HH	W	M	Jan 1886	14	S				MS	AL	MS	Farm Hand
	Langster, Callie	HH	W	F	Sep 1860	39	Wd				MS	UN	UN	Farm Hand
	Joslin, Henry	HH	B	M	Oct 1877	22	S				MS	UN	UN	Farm Hand
	Ann	HH	B	F	UN UN	UN	S				MA	UN	UN	Farm Hand
230	Sanders, William	H	W	M	Jun 1870	29	M	0			MS	AL	MS	Farmer
	Sallie	W	W	F	May 1874	26	M	0			MS	MS	MS	
231	Sanders, George	H	W	M	Apr 1879	21	M	0			MS	AL	MS	Farmer
	Maude	W	W	F	Apr 1878	22	M	0			AL	AL	UN	
232	Sanders, James	H	W	M	Jul 1848	51	M	31			AL	NY	AL	Farmer
	Francis	W	W	F	May 1850	50	M	31	9	8	MS	MS	MS	
	James R.	S	W	M	Jun 1882	17					MS	AL	MS	Farm Hand
	Burk	S	W	M	May 1886	14					MS	AL	MS	Farm Hand
	Mamie	D	W	F	Sep 1889	10					MS	AL	MS	
	Myrta	D	W	F	Jul 1892	7					MS	AL	MS	
	Waters, Mack C.	SiL	W	M	UN 1866	33	M	10			AL	UN	UN	Sawmill
	Jennie	D	W	F	Nov 1873	26	M	10	3	3	MS	AL	MS	
	James	GS	W	M	Oct 1890	9	S				MS	AL	MS	
	Bob	GS	W	M	Feb 1893	7	S				MS	AL	MS	
	Addie	GD	W	F	Oct 1895	4	S				MS	AL	MS	
	Sanders, Sam T.	Bdr	W	M	Oct 1876	23	Wd				MS	AL	MS	Farmer
233	Sanders, Otha B.	H	W	F	Jul 1882	17	S				MS	AL	MS	Farmer
	Cook, Tilda C.	HH	W	M	Apr 1861	39	Wd				MS	TN	TN	Farm Hand
	Langster, Milton	Bro	W	M	May 1892	7	S				MS	MS	MS	
	Ella	Sis	W	F	Apr 1881	19	S				MS	MS	MS	Day Laborer
234	Booker, Richard W.	H	W	M	Dec 1859	40	M	22			MS	VA	SC	Farmer
	Texanna	W	W	F	Jul 1862	37	M	22	9	9	MS	MS	MS	
	James F.	S	W	M	Apr 1880	20	S				MS	MS	MS	
	Hattie	D	W	F	Feb 1882	18	S				MS	MS	MS	
	Effie E.	D	W	F	Jan 1884	16	S				MS	MS	MS	
	Dolphus L.	S	W	M	Dec 1885	14	S				MS	MS	MS	
	Jossie B.	D	W	F	Aug 1887	12	S				MS	MS	MS	
	Anna L.	D	W	F	Oct 1890	9	S				MS	MS	MS	
	Carl V.	S	W	M	Feb 1893	7	S				MS	MS	MS	
	Richard	S	W	M	Nov 1896	3	S				MS	MS	MS	
235	Null, Rebecca	H	W	F	Jul 1860	39	Wd		6	6	AL	NC	AL	Farmer
	Tilden	S	W	M	Jan 1882	18	S				MS	MS	AL	Farm Hand
	Athler	D	W	F	Jan 1884	16	S				MS	MS	AL	Farm Hand
	Elzadie	D	W	F	Apr 1886	14	S				MS	MS	AL	Farm Hand
	Rufus	S	W	M	Feb 1882	13	S				MS	MS	AL	Farm Hand
	Ronnie	S	W	M	Oct 1887	12	S				MS	MS	AL	Farm Hand
	Bennie	S	W	M	Sep 1889	10	S				MS	MS	AL	Farm Hand
236	Kirk, Columbus	H	W	M	Dec 1830	69	M	40			NC	SC	NC	Farmer
	Lou E.	W	W	F	Sep 1840	59	M	40	10	9	MS	SC	SC	

1	2	3	4	5	6	7	8	9	10	11	12	13	14	15
	Ida	D	W	F	Apr 1863	37	S				MS	NC	MS	HouseKeeper
	Oscar	S	W	M	Mar 1875	25	S				MS	NC	MS	Farm Hand
	Everett	S	W	M	Jun 1880	19	S				MS	NC	MS	Farm Hand
	Julian, Sallie	SiL	W	F	Oct 1838	61	S				MS	SC	SC	
237	Beard, William C.	H	W	M	Aug 1863	36	Wd				TN	TN	TN	Fisherman
238	Aldridge, George W.	H	W	M	Feb 1867	33	M	11			MS	AL	AL	Farmer
	Emma	W	W	F	Jan 1866	34	M	11	2	2	MS	MS	TN	
	Walter L.	S	W	M	May 1895	5	S				MS	MS	MS	
	James E.	S	W	M	Nov 1899	5/mo	S				MS	MS	MS	
239	Roler, Robert L.	H	W	M	Dec 1881	18	M	0			MS	AL	UN	Farmer
	Josie	W	W	F	Jan 1882	18	M	0	0	0	MS	UN	MS	
240	Hendrix, Noah	H	W	M	UN UN	UN	Wd				UN	UN	UN	Farmer
	Lucy	D	W	F	Jan 1874	26	S				MS	UN	MS	
	Roxie	D	W	F	Apr 1882	18	S				MS	UN	MS	
	Arta B.	D	W	F	Sep 1885	14	S				MS	UN	MS	
241	Booker, James M.	H	W	M	Feb 1858	42	M	2			MS	VA	TN	Farmer
	Mary J.	W	W	F	Mar 1874	26	M	2	1	1	MS	TN	TN	
	Albert B.	S	W	M	Jul 1898	1	S				MS	MS	MS	
242	Long, Samuel G.	H	W	M	Mar 1874	26	M	9			AL	TN	MS	Farmer
	Margarett	W	W	F	Mar 1875	25	M	9	3	1	MS	MS	TN	
	Ada C.	D	W	F	Aug 1891	8	S				MS	AL	TN	
243	Hill, William D.	H	W	M	Dec 1866	33	M	10			MS	AL	AL	Farmer
	Mary E.	W	W	F	Sep 1871	28	M	10	5	5	Ms	MS	MS	
	Clyde	D	W	F	Dec 1890	9	S				MS	MS	MS	
	Carl D.	S	W	M	Jul 1892	7	S				MS	MS	MS	
	Ruth	D	W	F	Apr 1894	6	S				MS	MS	MS	
	Willie M.	D	W	F	Mar 1897	3	S				MS	MS	MS	
	No Name	S	W	M	Dec 1898	1	S				MS	MS	MS	
244	Hill, Columbus A.	H	W	M	Nov 1845	54	M	23			AL	TN	SC	Farmer
	Jennie E.	W	W	F	Sep 1857	48	M	23	5	5	AL	AL	AL	
	Zula E.	D	W	F	Jun 1877	22	S				MS	AL	AL	
	Mattie E.	D	W	F	Dec 1882	17	S				MS	AL	AL	
	Blanch	D	W	F	Dec 1883	14	S				MS	AL	AL	
245	Williams, Nancy	SiL	W	F	Sep 1841	58	Wd				AL	AL	AL	
	Medley, Burt	Bdr	W	M	UN UN	UN	S				MS	MS	MS	Boarder
	Hill	Bdr	W	M	UN UN	UN	S				MS	MS	MS	Boarder
246	Higdon, Martha	H	W	F	Oct 1845	54	Wd		3	2	GA	SC	VA	Farmer
	Ethela A.	D	W	F	Aug 1852	17	S				MS	UN	GA	
	Bryant, Wm. H.	SiL	w	M	Jan 1860	40	M	3			TN	UN	UN	Stone Cutter
	Mattie	D	W	F	May 1870	30	M	3	1	1	AL	GA	GA	
	Joseph W.	GS	W	M	Jul 1888	11	S				AL	AL	AL	
247	Clement, Wheller	H	B	M	UN UN	41	M	10			MS	MS	MS	Farmer
	Liza	W	B	F	UN UN	35	M	10	3	3	MS	UN	UN	
	Hettie	D	B	F	UN UN	6	S				MS	UN	UN	
	Bee	D	B	F	UN UN	4	S				MS	UN	UN	
	Anna L.	D	B	F	UN UN	2	S				UN	UN	UN	
248	Lenard, Teddie	H	B	M	Aug 1845	54	M	30			MS	UN	UN	Farmer
	Lucy	W	B	F	Jun UN	UN	M	30	11	5	KY	KY	KY	
	Henry	S	B	M	Jan 1877	25					MS	MS	MS	
	Willie	S	B	M	Apr 1885	15					MS	MS	KY	
	Bertha	D	B	F	Feb 1887	13					MS	MS	KY	

1	2	3	4	5	6	7	8	9	10	11	12	13	14	15
	Terry, Elizabeth	MiL	B	F	UN UN	UN	Wd				KY	UN	KY	
249	Barton, Nettie	H	B	F	Jun 1862	37	M	6	3	3	UN	UN	UN	Farmer
	Sim	Husb	B	M	UN UN	UN	M	6			AL	UN	UN	
	Johnson, Hattie	D	B	F	May 1884	16					MS	UN	UN	
	Robert	S	B	M	Feb 1886	14					MS	UN	UN	
250	Johnson, Charlotte	H	B	F	UN 1850	50	Wd		4	1	AL	AL	AL	
251	Castleberry, Ike	H	B	M	Jun 1850	50	M	28			MS	MS	MS	Farmer
	Harriett	W	B	F	Mar 1858	42	M	28	8	3	MS	VA	MS	
	Katie	D	B	F	Nov 1880	19	S				MS	MS	MS	Farm Hand
	Frank	S	B	M	May 1881	19	S				MS	MS	MS	Farm Hand
	Coger, Frank	GS	B	M	Dec 1896	3	S				MS	AL	MS	
	Lawrence	GS	B	M	Aug 1898	1	S				MS	AL	MS	
252	Woodruff, Andy	H	B	M	Aug 1836	63	M	30			MS	UN	MS	Farmer
	Mary	W	B	F	May 1850	50	M	30	8	6	TN	TN	TN	
	Zuma	D	B	F	Mar 1883	17	S				MS	MS	TN	Farm Hand
	Jannis	D	B	F	May 1885	15	S				MS	MS	TN	Farm Hand
	Evie	D	B	F	Mar 1889	11	S				MS	MS	TN	Farm Hand
	Berry, Laura	D	B	F	Oct 1871	28	S				MS	MS	TN	
	Gonzo	GS	B	M	Apr 1898	2	S				AL	AL	MS	
	Augusta	GD	B	F	Jun.1900	5/mo	S				MS	AL	MS	
253	Briggs, George	H	B	M	May 1861	39	M	14			MS	UN	UN	Farmer
	Annie	W	B	F	Aug 1867	32	M	14	7	2	MS	UN	UN	
	Clarence	S	B	M	May 1888	12	S				MS	MS	MS	
	Myrta	D	B	F	Mar 1895	5	S				MS	MS	MS	
254	Briggs, Frank	H	B	M	Jan 1872	28	M	10			MS	UN	UN	Farmer
	Ermma	W	B	F	Feb 1870	29	M	10	5	4	AL	UN	UN	
	Royal	S	B	M	Sep 1890	9	S				MS	MS	AL	
	Walter	S	B	M	Feb 1893	7	S				MS	MS	AL	
	Hattie E.	D	B	F	Jul 1896	3	S				MS	MS	AL	
	McKinley	S	B	M	Mar 1898	2	S				MS	MS	AL	
	Mays, Ann	MiL	B	F	UN UN	UN	Wd				UN	UN	UN	
255	Crouch, H.P.	H	W	M	Jun 1855	44	M	20			IL	IL	IL	Farmer
	Mary	W	W	F	Dec 1854	45	M	20	5	5	MS	AL	AL	
	William	S	W	M	Jun 1881	18	S				MS	IL	MS	
	George T.	S	W	M	Apr 1885	15	S				MS	IL	MS	
	John E.	S	W	M	Jan 1887	13	S				MS	IL	MS	
	Paul	S	W	M	Sep 1890	9	S				MS	IL	MS	
	Mary	D	W	F	May 1894	6	S				MS	IL	MS	
256	Walker, Martha	H	W	F	Apr 1879	71	Wd				AL	VA	TN	Farmer
	Owen	S	W	M	Jul 1864	35	S				AL	AL	AL	
	Wallace, Susie	D	W	F	May 1867	33	Wd				AL	AL	AL	
	Mattie	GS	W	F	May 1885	15	S				MS	MS	AL	
	Ed	GS	W	M	Jul 1887	12	S				MS	MS	AL	
	Elmore	GS	W	M	Nov 1887	10	S				MS	MS	AL	
257	Briggs, Ann	H	B	F	UN UN	UN	Wd				AL	AL	AL	Farmer
	Ella	D	B	F	Sep 1882	17	S				MS	VA	AL	
258	Massey, Lafayette	H	W	M	Jan 1860	40	M	19			MS	MS	MS	Farmer
	Julia	W	W	F	Feb 1863	37	M	19	6	4	MS	MS	MS	
	Leona E.	D	W	F	Sep 1881	18	S				MS	MS	MS	
	Charles C.	S	W	M	Jun 1884	15	S				MS	MS	MS	Farm Hand
	Savanah	D	W	F	Feb 1891	3	S				MS	MS	MS	
	Griff E.	D	W	F	Nov 1899	7/mo	S				MS	MS	MS	

1	2	3	4	5	6	7	8	9	10	11	12	13	14	15
259	Long, Arch	H	W	M	Dec 1867	32	M	0			AL	UN	UN	Farmer
	Myrta	W	W	F	Jan 1876	26	M	0	0	0	MS	MS	MS	
	Emma	D	W	F	May 1893	7	S				MS	AL	MS	
	Grace	D	W	F	Oct 1895	4	S				MS	MS	MS	
	Briggs, Barton	GS	W	M	Aug 1895	4	S				AL	MS	MS	
	Letra	GD	W	F	Nov 1896	3	S				AL	MS	MS	
260	Medley, Charlie	H	W	M	Jan 1875	25	M	2			MS	MS	MS	Farmer
	Lettie A.	W	W	F	Aug 1879	20	M	2	1	1	MS	SC	TN	
	Mollie	D	W	F	Nov 1899	8/mo	S				MS	MS	MS	
	Alexander, Sarah E.	MiL	W	F	Feb 1841	59	Wd				TN	NC	NC	
261	Garlon, West	H	B	M	UN UN	28	M	2			AL	TN	AL	Farmer
	Lou	W	B	F	Feb 1872	28	M	2	1	1	MS	TN	AL	
	Letha	D	B	F	Apr 1899	1	S				MS	AL	MS	
262	Payne, W.T.	H	W	F	Dec 1873	53	Wd		3	3	AL	NC	AL	Farmer
	Edgar	S	W	M	Jul 1875	24	M	1			MS	AL	AL	
	Mollie	DiL	W	F	Jun 1889	26	M	1			MS	NC	MS	
263	Clement, Ammie	H	B	F	UN UN	UN	Wd		4	4	MS	UN	UN	Farmer
	Ed	S	B	M	Dec 1883	16	S				MS	UN	MS	Farm Hand
	Lessie	S	B	M	Apr 1886	14	S				MS	UN	MS	Farm Hand
	Ada	D	B	F	Feb 1889	11	S				MS	UN	MS	Farm Hand
264	Payne, Joe C.	H	W	M	Apr 1848	52	M				MS	TN	SC	Farmer
	Mary V.	W	W	F	Apr 1866	34	M		6	6	MS	AL	AL	
	Josie B.	D	W	F	Jun 1879	20	S				MS	TX	MS	
	Arstead F.	S	W	M	Aug 1883	17	S				MS	TX	MS	
	Luther S.	S	W	M	Jun 1885	14	S				MS	TX	MS	
	Willie B.	S	W	M	Aug 1888	12	S				MS	TX	MS	
	Mary E.	D	W	F	Dec 1892	7	S				MS	TX	MS	
	Samuel C.	S	W	M	Jul 1894	5	S				MS	TX	MS	
265	Dean, John	H	B	M	Nov 1874	25	S				MS	MS	MS	Farmer
	Goodlow, Allen	Bdr	B	M	UN 1850	49	S				VA	VA	VA	
	Solomon	Bdr	B	M	UN 1888	12	S				AL	VA	VA	
	Ben	Bdr	B	M	UN 1890	10	S				AL	UN	UN	
266	Dean, William	H	B	M	Mar 1854	66	M	UN			SC	SC	SC	Farmer
	Sarah	W	B	F	UN UN	42	M	UN	1	1	KY	UN	UN	
	Rufus	S	B	M	UN 1890	10	S				MS	SC	KY	
267	Busby, James N.	H	W	M	May 1849	51	M	27			MS	UN	UN	Farmer
	Augusta	W	W	F	Nov 1853	47	M	27	9	9	AL	AL	AL	
	John	S	W	M	Jun 1874	25	S				MS	MS	AL	
	Minnie	D	W	F	UN 1880	20	S				MS	MS	AL	
	James E.	S	W	M	UN UN	UN	S				MS	MS	AL	
	Mary F.	D	W	F	UN UN	UN	S				MS	MS	AL	
	Laura A.	D	W	F	Apr 1889	UN	S				MS	MS	AL	
	Ella	D	W	F	Jul 1891	UN	S				MS	MS	AL	
	Bertha	D	W	F	Oct 1893	UN	S				MS	MS	AL	
268	Busby, R.W.	H	W	M	Jul 1855	44	M	21			MS	MS	MS	
	L.A.	W	W	F	Jul 1862	37	M	21	4	4	Ms	MS	MS	
	Thomas J.	S	W	M	Jul 1883	16	S				MS	MS	MS	
	Ivy P.	D	W	F	Oct 1887	12	S				MS	MS	MS	
	Edward L.	S	W	M	Dec 1893	6	S				MS	MS	MS	
	Ruben W.	S	W	M	Oct 1897	2	S				MS	MS	MS	
	Broadway, W.E.	HH	W	M	Jan 1876	24	S				TN	TN	TN	Hired Hand
	Robinson, Wm.	HH	W	M	Dec 1873	27	S				AL	AL	AL	Hired Hand
269	Jameson, William	H	W	M	Mar 1845	55	M	28			AL	TN	TN	Farmer

1	2	3	4	5	6	7	8	9	10	11	12	13	14	15
	Mary E.	W	W	F	Sep 1842	55	M	28	10	3	AL	AL	AL	
	Mary	D	W	F	Apr 1876	24	S				AL	AL	AL	Farm Hand
	Martha J.	D	W	F	Apr 1883	17	S				AL	AL	AL	Farm Hand
	James T.	S	W	M	Mar 1887	13	S				AL	AL	AL	Farm Hand
	Effie	D	W	F	Mar 1888	12	S				AL	AL	AL	Farm Hand
	John A.	S	W	M	Mar 1890	10	S				AL	AL	AL	Farm Hand
270	Busby, Sarah	H	W	F	Aug 1826	74	Wd		0	0	MS	SC	MS	Farmer
	White, Martha	HH	W	F	Jan 1873	27	S				TN	UN	UN	Hired Hand
271	Province, Rube	H	W	M	Jan 1875	25	M	0			UN	UN	UN	Farmer
	Annie	W	W	F	Oct 1882	17	M	0			MS	UN	UN	
272	Milligan, Thomas	H	W	M	Mar 1868	32	M	13			TN	UN	UN	Farmer
	Nancy A.	W	W	F	Nov 1869	30	M	13			MS	MS	MS	
	Hellen	D	W	F	Aug 1889	10	S				MS	TN	MS	
	Flauda	D	W	F	Jun 1892	8	S				MS	TN	MS	
	Shelby	D	W	F	Dec 1893	6	S				MS	TN	MS	
	Virgie	D	W	F	Dec 1895	4	S				MS	TN	MS	
	Retha	D	W	F	May 1898	2	S				MS	TN	MS	
	Matthew	S	W	M	Jun 1900	2/mo	S				MS	TN	MS	
273	Wood, David	H	W	M	Nov 1871	28	M	4			MS	MS	??	Farmer
	Nettie	W	W	F	Nov 1880	19	M	4	2	1	AL	AL	AL	
	Flora	D	W	F	Jan 1899	1	S				MS	MS	AL	
274	Goodman, Robert	H	W	M	Jul 1845	54	M	8			TN	TN	AL	
	Mary C.	W	W	F	Dec 1854	46	M	8	1	1	MS	SC	UN	
	Ruby G.	D	W	F	Dec 1854	6	S				MS	TN	MS	
	Walter	S	W	M	Feb 1884	16	S				MS	TN	MS	Farm Hand
	Clay H.	S	W	M	Mar 1885	15	S				MS	TN	MS	Farm Hand
	Hilda B.	D	W	F	Dec 1886	14	S				MS	TN	MS	
275	Province, Ed. D.	H	W	M	Mar 1850	50	M	26			UN	UN	UN	Farmer
	Mary	W	W	F	Aug 1844	55	M	26	8	8	MS	UN	UN	
	Lou E.	D	W	F	Oct 1883	16	S				MS	UN	MS	Farm Hand
	Caldonia	D	W	F	Mar 1885	15	S				MS	UN	MS	Farm Hand
	Ben F.	S	W	M	Oct 1886	13	S				MS	UN	MS	Farm Hand
276	Hudson, Elijah A.	H	W	M	Aug 1853	46	M	19			MS	TN	AL	
	Fannie	W	W	F	Sep 1859	40	M	19	1	1	MS	UN	UN	
	Ollie C.	D	W	F	Oct 1896	3	S				MS	MS	MS	
277	Hudson, Z.B.	H	W	M	Jan 1848	52	M	32			MS	TN	AL	
	Mary A.	W	W	F	Feb 1852	48	M	32	3	3	MS	NC	NC	
	Tishomingo	D	W	F	Apr 1877	23	S				MS	MS	MS	
278	Helton, William E.	H	W	M	Feb 1871	29	M	9			AR	GA	GA	
	Nerva D.	W	W	F	Nov 1869	30	M	9	3	3	MS	UN	UN	
	Elmore J.	S	W	M	Aug 1893	6	S				MS	AR	MS	
	Willie	S	W	M	Oct 1894	5	S				MS	AR	MS	
	Floid	S	W	M	Feb 1898	2	S				MS	AR	MS	
	Johnson, Josey	Cou	W	F	Jul 1887	12	S				TN	UN	MS	
279	Jackson, William M.	H	W	M	Apr 1879	21	M	5			AL	AL	AL	
	Jessie L.	W	W	F	Sep 1879	20	M	5	1	1	MS	UN	UN	
	Frank C.	S	W	M	Oct 1899	7/mo	S				MS	AL	MS	
	Kizzie L.	Sis	W	F	Mar 1873	27	S				AL	AL	AL	
280	Miller, Silas B.	H	W	M	Dec 1868	31	M	10			MS	UN	UN	
	Nancy E.	W	W	F	Jun 1872	27	M	10	3	3	MS	MS	MS	
	Charlie C.	S	W	M	Sep 1891	8	S				MS	MS	MS	
	Sydney P.	S	W	M	Jan 1895	5	S				MS	MS	MS	

1	2	3	4	5	6	7	8	9	10	11	12	13	14	15
	Luther B.	S	W	M	Jun 1897	2	S				MS	MS	MS	
281	Clement, Jack	H	B	M	UN UN	UN	M	UN			MS	SC	SC	
	Annia	W	B	F	May UN	UN	M	UN	7	7	SC	SC	SC	
	Emma	D	B	F	Dec 1872	27	S				MS	MS	SC	
	Joe T.	S	B	M	Sep 1874	25	S				MS	MS	SC	
	Fannie H.	D	B	F	Sep 1877	22	S				MS	MS	SC	
	Lee	S	B	M	Dec 1881	18	S				MS	MS	SC	
	Melia	D	B	F	Sep 1883	16	S				MS	MS	SC	
	Mary	D	B	F	Aug 1887	12	S				MS	MS	SC	
	Mattie	D	B	F	Aug 1890	9	S				MS	MS	SC	
282	Dexter, William	H	W	M	Mar 1856	44	Wd				MS	Eng	MS	Farmer
	Florence	D	W	F	Mar 1882	18	S				MS	MS	MS	
	Oscar	S	W	M	Aug 1885	14	S				MS	MS	MS	
	Hellen	D	W	F	Sep 1887	12	S				MS	MS	MS	
	Dan	S	W	M	Jan 1891	9	S				MS	MS	MS	
	Ellen	D	W	F	Mar 1893	7	S				MS	MS	MS	
	Berdie	D	W	F	Mar 1896	4	S				MS	MS	MS	
	Clora	D	W	F	Nov 1898	1	S				MS	MS	MS	
283	Dexter, Edward	H	W	M	Mar 1880	20	M	0			MS	MS	MS	Farmer
	Ada	W	W	F	Dec 1879	21	M	0	0		MS	MS	MS	
284	Bonds, Joe R.	H	W	M	May 1850	50	M	30			MS	UN	UN	Farmer
	N.H.	W	W	F	Jan 1852	48	M	30	7	5	MS	Eng	MS	
	May	D	W	F	Feb 1882	18	S				MS	MS	MS	
	Jack	S	W	M	Aug 1887	12	S				MS	MS	MS	
	Matthew	S	W	M	Oct 1889	10	S				MS	MS	MS	
285	Graham, John L.	H	W	M	Mar 1870	30	M	9			UN	UN	UN	Farmer
	Flora	W	W	F	Jan 1872	28	M	9	4	2	MS	MS	MS	
	Lettie B.	D	W	F	Oct 1893	6	S				MS	AL	MS	
	Maggie	D	W	F	Oct 1893	1	S				MS	AL	MS	
286	Roberson, I.C.	H	W	F	Feb 1874	26	M	7			MS	MS	MS	Farmer
	Blutha	D	W	F	Aug 1893	6		S			TN	MS	AL	
	Elbert	S	W	M	May 1896	4		S			TN	MS	MS	
	Nancy	D	W	F	Dec 1899	7/mo		S			TN	MS	MS	
287	Parker, J.B.	H	W	M	Nov 1860	39	M	16			AL	NC	AL	Farmer
	M.M.	W	W	F	Jul 1845	54	M	16	4	3	GA	GA	GA	
	Skinner, R.C.	Bdr	W	M	Nov 1838	61	S				AL	KY	AL	
288	Tuberville, Marion R.	H	W	M	Jan 1861	39	M	20			AL	AL	UN	Farmer
	Cyrena	W	W	F	Mar 1859	41	M	30	9	7	AL	SC	AL	
	Wm. T.	S	W	M	Sep 1879	20	S				MS	AL	AL	
	Daniel R.	S	W	M	Feb 1883	17	S				MS	AL	AL	
	Susan E.	D	W	F	Apr 1886	14	S				MS	AL	AL	
	Minnie E.	D	W	F	Apr 1888	12	S				MS	AL	AL	
	John R.	S	W	M	Mar 1892	8	S				MS	AL	AL	
	Sam H.	S	W	M	Mar 1894	6	S				MS	AL	AL	
	Other	D	W	F	Sep 1896	3	S				MS	AL	AL	
289	Green, Henry	H	B	M	UN UN	UN	M	UN			GA	UN	UN	Farmer
	Emely	W	B	F	UN UN	UN	UN	UN			UN	UN	UN	
	Lee	D	B	F	Dec 1876	23	UN				MS	GA	MS	Farm Hand
	George	S	B	M	Jan 1868	32	UN				MS	GA	MS	Farm Hand
	Jennie	DiL	B	F	UN UN	UN	UN				KY	KY	KY	Farm Hand
	Lou A.	DiL	B	F	Jun 1874	25	S				MS	GA	MS	Farm Hand
	Allen, Will	SiL	B	M	UN UN	UN	M				UN	UN	UN	
290	Ross, Mary	H	B	F	Aug 1865	84	M		5	5	MS	GA	MS	Farmer

31

1	2	3	4	5	6	7	8	9	10	11	12	13	14	15
	Ed	S	B	M	Jan 1882	18	S				MS	UN	MS	
	Ada	D	B	F	Aug 1885	14	S				MS	UN	MS	
	Willie	S	B	M	Jul 1889	10	S				MS	UN	MS	
	Ellen	D	B	F	Oct 1891	8	S				MS	UN	MS	
	Harrion	S	B	M	Oct 1884	5	S				MS	UN	MS	
	Lena	SD	B	F	Jul 1894	5	S				MS	UN	MS	
291 Hill, Calvin		H	B	M	Nov 1824	75	M	45			AL	VA	VA	
	Collene	W	B	F	UN UN	UN	M	45	6	4	UN	UN	UN	
292 Luster, Celia		H	B	F	Dec 1862	37	Wd	UN	2	2	MS	MS	UN	Farmer
	Clora	D	B	F	UN UN	UN	S				MS	MS	UN	
	Robert	S	B	M	UN UN	UN	S				MS	MS	UN	
293 Willis, Mary		H	B	F	Feb 1874	25	D		3	3	MS	MS	UN	Farmer
	Carl	S	B	M	UN UN	UN	S				MS	UN	MS	
	Virginia	D	B	F	UN UN	UN	S				MS	UN	UN	
294 Boyd, Alf.		H	B	M	UN UN	UN	M	18			MS	UN	UN	Farmer
	Ann	W	B	F	UN UN	UN	M	18	6	6	MS	UN	UN	
	Rosalie	S	B	M	Jan 1883	17	S				MS	MS	MS	
	Cora	D	B	F	May 1885	15	S				MS	MS	MS	
	Marcus	D	B	F	Mar 1888	12	S				MS	MS	MS	
	Sidney	S	B	M	Oct 1892	7	S				MS	MS	MS	
	Hittie	D	B	F	Jan 1895	5	S				MS	MS	MS	
	Hattie	D	B	F	Jan 1895	5	S				MS	MS	MS	
	Julia	D	B	F	Mar 1897	3	S				MS	MS	MS	
	Sam	S	B	M	Dec 1899	7/mo	S				MS	MS	MS	
295 Brewer, Joe B.		H	W	M	Apr 1871	29	M	7			AL	SC	AL	Farmer
	Sallie	W	W	F	Aug 1870	29	M	7	2	2	MS	MS	MS	
	Elmore	S	W	M	Oct 1894	5	S				MS	AL	MS	
	Minnie	D	W	F	Nov 1896	3	S				MS	AL	MS	
296 Dean, Wiley		H	W	M	Nov 1827	72	M	29			SC	SC	SC	Farmer
	Sarah A.	W	W	F	Sep 1845	54	M	29	8	5	AL	GA	SC	
	Joseph L.	S	W	M	Jun 1871	28	S				MS	SC	AL	
	Williams, Jack	HH	B	M	UN 1881	19	S				MS	MS	MS	Hired Hand
297 Dean W.P.		H	W	M	Jun 1838	61	M	34			MS	SC	TN	Farmer
	Mary E.	W	W	F	Jan 1846	54	M	34	11	9	MS	SC	SC	
	G.A.	S	W	M	Mar 1872	28					MS	MS	MS	Farmer
	Robert N.	S	W	M	Jan 1875	25					MS	MS	MS	Farmer
	John D.	S	W	M	Mar 1879	21					MS	MS	MS	Farm Hand
	M.M.	S	W	M	May 1885	15					MS	MS	MS	Farm Hand
298 Miller, Joe E.		H	W	M	May 1845	55	M	12			Ire	Ire	Ire	Farmer
	Laura	W	W	F	Aug 1870	29	M	12	3	2	AL	AL	AL	
	Blount, Nora J.	SS	W	F	Mar 1889	11	S				MS	MS	AL	
	Miller, Jonie	SS	W	M	Jun 1898	1	S				MS	Ire	AL	
299 Wynn, G.P.		H	W	M	Dec 1829	70	m	49			TN	NC	NC	Farmer
	Elizabeth	W	W	F	Apr 1833	67	M	49	11	8	AL	AL	TN	
	Dolly E.	D	W	F	Mar 1873	27	S				MS	TN	AL	
300 Foote, John M.		H	W	M	Nov 1867	32	M	10			MS	UN	SC	Farmer
	Rebbie	W	W	F	UN 1870	30	M	10	4	4	MS	SC	SC	
	Dean	S	W	M	UN 1890	9	S				MS	MS	MS	
	Claude	S	W	M	UN 1893	6	S				MS	MS	MS	
	Bobb	S	W	M	UN 1896	3	S				MS	MS	MS	
	No Name	S	W	M	UN 1899	6/mo	S				MS	MS	MS	
301 Davis, S.M.		H	W	M	Jan 1847	53	M	30			AL	AL	AL	Farmer

1	2	3	4	5	6	7	8	9	10	11	12	13	14	15
	Mary M.	W	W	F	Dec 1847	52	M	30	9	7	AL	UN	AL	
	Auther N.	S	W	M	Jun 1876	23	S				AL	AL	AL	
	Oscar S.	S	W	M	May 1886	14	S				AL	AL	AL	
	May C.	D	W	F	Jul 1881	18	S				AL	AL	AL	
	Bradley W.	S	W	M	Jan 1888	12	S				AL	AL	AL	
302	Hudson, William T.	H	W	M	Jul 1855	44	M	15			MS	MS	MS	Farmer
	May	W	W	F	Mar 1862	38	M	15	9	4	AL	AL	AL	
	Luther	S	W	M	Mar 1886	14	S				MS	MS	AL	Farm Hand
	George W.	S	W	M	Oct 1888	11	S				MS	MS	AL	Farm Hand
	Minnie B.	D	W	F	Feb 1894	6	S				MS	MS	AL	
	Mamie B.	D	W	F	Jul 1899	11/mo	S				MS	MS	AL	
303	Broughton, Joe	H	W	M	May 1868	32	M	8			MS	SC	AL	Farmer
	Katie	W	W	F	Jan 1868	32	M	8	4	4	MS	VA	MS	
	Lenna	D	W	F	Dec 1892	7	S				MS	MS	MS	
	John T.	S	W	M	Mar 1895	5	S				MS	MS	MS	
	Georgia	D	W	F	Apr 1897	3	S				MS	MS	MS	
	No Name	D	W	F	Jul 1899	11/mo	S				MS	MS	MS	
	Kay, Sid	Bdr	W	M	UN 1877	23	S				MS	UN	UN	Farmer
304	McAnnally, W E.	H	W	M	UN UN	UN	M				AL	AL	AL	Farmer
	Jane	W	W	F	UN UN	UN	M				MS	MS	AL	
	John H.	Bro	W	M	Oct 1847	52	M	26			AL	AL	AL	
	H.D.	DiL	W	F	Sep 1856	44	M	26	10	5	MS	MS	AL	
	Lou E.	Nce	W	F	Oct 1878	21	S				MS	AL	MS	
	Maggie	Nce	W	F	Sep 1881	18	S				MS	AL	MS	
	Lizzie J.	Nce	W	F	Feb 1887	13	S				MS	AL	MS	
	Joseph B.	Nep	W	M	Jan 1890	10	S				MS	AL	MS	
305	Broughton, William A.	H	W	M	Feb 1841	59	M	35			SC	UN	SC	Farmer
	Sara J.	W	W	F	Feb 1843	57	M	35	9	9	AL	VA	AL	
	Myrtle	D	W	F	Jan 1882	18	S				MS	SC	AL	
	Edgar H.	S	W	M	Oct 1885	15	S				MS	SC	AL	
306	Wheeler, John W.	H	W	M	UN 1843	57	M	31			AR	UN	AL	Farmer
	Elizabeth	W	W	F	UN 1833	67	M	31	6	3	SC	NC	SC	
	Ella E.	D	W	F	UN 1875	24	S	S			AL	AR	SC	Farm Hand
	John W.	S	M	M	UN 1877	22	S	S			AL	AR	SC	Farm Hand
307	Broughton, James	H	W	M	Sep 1872	27	M	1			MS	SC	AL	Farmer
	F.P.	W	W	F	Nov 1878	21	M	1	2	2	TN	TN	TN	
	Lowery	S	W	M	Sep 1898	1	S				MS	MS	TN	
	No Name	S	W	M	Apr 2000	2/mo	S				MS	MS	TN	
308	Bonds, Lem C.	H	W	M	Oct 1839	59	M	39			MS	TN	SC	Farmer
	Tabitha	W	W	F	Jan 1845	54	M	39	8	7	TN	TN	TN	
	Nella C.	D	W	F	Mar UN	UN	S				MS	MS	TN	
	Ezra D.	S	W	M	Aug 1889	10	S				MS	MS	TN	
309	Grisham, W.F.	H	W	M	Feb 1859	41	M	21			MS	TN	SC	Farmer
	L.C.	W	W	F	Sep 1863	36	M	21	7	7	MS	UN	MS	
	Cora	D	W	F	Dec 1880	19	S				MS	MS	MS	
	Ora	D	W	F	Oct 1883	16	S				MS	MS	MS	
	Charlie	S	W	M	Jul 1886	13	S				MS	MS	MS	
	Marshall	S	W	F	Feb 1890	10	S				MS	MS	MS	
	Letha	D	W	F	Feb 1893	7	S				MS	MS	MS	
	Roy	S	W	M	Oct 1894	5	S				MS	MS	MS	
	Ommie	D	W	F	Jun 1898	1	S				MS	MS	MS	
310	Grisham, M.E.	H	W	M	May 1866	34	M	13			MS	TN	SC	Farmer
	E.M.	W	W	F	Nov 1866	33	M	13	4	3	MS	AL	AL	
	Robert	S	W	M	Oct 1887	12	S				MS	MS	MS	Farm Hand

1	2	3	4	5	6	7	8	9	10	11	12	13	14	15
	Florence	D	W	F	Apr 1893	7	S				MS	MS	MS	
	Gillie	D	W	F	May 1898	2	S				MS	MS	MS	
311	Brown, W.R.	H	W	M	Dec 1869	30	M	10			MS	AL	AL	Farmer
	Nancy	W	W	F	Jan 1874	26	M	10	5	5	TN	TN	TN	
	Mary H.	D	W	F	Aug 1890	9	S				MS	MS	TN	
	Lizzie B.	D	W	F	Mar 1891	8	S				MS	MS	TN	
	Jennie	D	W	F	Jan 1894	6	S				MS	MS	TN	
	John T.	S	W	M	Oct 1896	3	S				MS	MS	TN	
	Wm. R.	S	W	M	Feb 1900	9/mo	S				MS	MS	TN	
312	Hudson, John	H	W	M	Sep 1825	74	M	45			TN	UN	NC	Farmer
	R.J.	W	W	F	Aug 1837	62	M	45	9	7	TN	NC	NC	
	Oscar	S	W	M	Jan 1881	19	S				MS	TN	TN	Farm Hand
	Milton E.	S	W	M	Jan 1878	22	S				MS	TN	TN	Farmer
313	Brown, G.W.	H	W	M	Dec 1873	25	M	3			MS	AL	AL	Farmer
	Lizzie	W	W	F	UN 1879	21	M	3	2	2	MS	MS	MO	
	Altha	D	W	F	Mar 1897	3					MS	MS	MO	
	Almy	D	W	F	Jan 1898	1	MO				MS	MS	MO	
314	Hudson, James	H	W	M	Apr 1871	29	M	7			TN	TN	TN	Farmer
	Lillie	W	W	F	Dec 1874	25	M	7	3	3	MS	UN	MS	
	Hester	D	W	F	Jun 1894	5	S				MS	TN	MS	
	Wm. E.	S	W	M	Mar 1897	3	S				MS	TN	MS	
	Nettie A	D	W	F	Nov 1899	11/mo	S				MS	TN	MS	
315	Johnson, John T.	H	W	M	Mar 1855	45	S				MS	UN	NC	Farmer
	Smith, Mollie	Sis	W	F	UN 1869	31	M	2	3	2	MS	UN	NC	
	Paulie	Nep	W	M	UN 1890	10	S				MS	TN	MS	
	No Name	Nep	W	M	May 1900	1/mo	S				MS	TN	MS	
	Guss	BiL	W	M	UN 1869	31	M	2			GA	GA	GA	
316	Helton, Dan	H	W	M	Feb 1833	67	M				GA	TN	GA	Farmer
	Sarah	W	W	F	UN 1843	57	M		11	6	GA	GA	GA	
317	Whitesides, J.T.	H	W	M	Mar 1834	66	M	23			TN	VA	VA	Farmer
	Annie	W	W	F	Apr 1840	59	M	23	0	0	AL	TN	GA	
	Beasley, Mary C.	Ward	W	F	Apr 1878	23	S				MS	UN	MS	
318	Brown, Rebecca	H	W	F	Aug 1850	49	Wd		10	8	AL	AL	AL	Farmer
	John	S	W	M	Jan 1875	25	S				MS	AL	AL	Farm Hand
	Mary	D	W	F	Apr 1881	19	S				MS	AL	AL	Farm Hand
	Lottie	D	W	F	May 1885	15	S				MS	AL	AL	Farm Hand
	Luther	S	W	M	May 1887	13	S				MS	AL	AL	Farm Hand
319	Hudson, Charles	H	W	M	Dec 1873	26	M	3			MS	TN	TN	Farmer
	Willie	W	W	F	Mar 1881	19	M	3			MS	TN	MS	
320	Brown, Lewis T.	H	W	M	Mar 1875	22	M				MS	AL	AL	Farmer
	Mollie	W	W	F	Jan 1885	15	M				TN	MS	UN	
321	Massey, Henry S.	H	W	M	Dec 1857	42	M	21			MS	SC	SC	Farmer
	Mary E.	W	W	F	Jul 1860	39	M	21	10	9	MS	AL	AL	
	Edward E.	S	W	M	Mar 1880	20	S				MS	MS	MS	Drummer
	Oscar L.	S	W	M	Dec 1882	18	S				MS	MS	MS	Drummer
	Benton C.	S	W	M	Apr 1883	15	S				MS	MS	MS	Farm Hand
	John F.	S	W	M	Jun 1887	12	S				MS	MS	MS	
	Gordon F.	S	W	M	Aug 1889	10	S				MS	MS	MS	
	Minnie	D	W	F	Oct 1891	8	S				MS	MS	MS	
	Whit W.	S	W	M	Dec 1893	6	S				MS	MS	MS	
	Malcolm F.	S	W	M	Mar 1896	4	S				MS	MS	MS	
	Schley Henry	S	W	M	Oct 1898	1	S				MS	MS	MS	

1	2	3	4	5	6	7	8	9	10	11	12	13	14	15
322	Osborn, Sallie	H	W	F	Dec 1822	77	Wd				SC	VA	VA	Farmer
	Sarah	D	W	F	Mar 1861	39	S				AL	SC	SC	Farm Hand
	Francis	D	W	F	Sep 1862	37	S				AL	SC	SC	
	Lizza	D	W	F	Apr 1867	33	S				AL	SC	SC	
	Cagle, James	GS	W	M	Sep 1876	23	S				MS	AL	GA	Farm Hand
323	Bonds, Frank	H	W	M	Mar 1866	33	M	4			MS	UN	UN	Farmer
	Susan	W	W	F	Mar 1865	35	M	4			TN	TN	TN	
	Poole, Wm. E.	SS	W	M	Oct 1886	13	S				TN	TN	TN	Farm Hand
	George E.	SS	W	M	Oct 1888	11	S				TN	TN	TN	Farm Hand
	Ethel R.	SS	W	F	Mar 1892	8	S				TN	TN	TN	
	John W.	SS	W	M	Sep 1893	6	S				TX	TN	TN	
	Bonds, Hattie A.	D	W	F	Apr 1897	3	S				MS	MS	MS	
	Gertrude	D	W	F	Apr 1899	1	S				MS	MS	MS	
324	Bonds, Lem.	H	W	M	Dec 1829	70	Wd				AL	NC	NC	Farmer
	Viola	D	W	F	Apr 1876	23	S				MS	AL	AL	
	Josie	D	W	F	May 1880	20	S				MS	AL	AL	
	Jacob	GS	W	M	Jun 1890	10	S				MS	AL	AL	Farm Hand
325	Belue, Senia A.	H	W	M	Oct 1840	59	Wd		1	1	GA	UN	GA	Farmer
	Roberson, Hutton	SiL	W	M	Oct 1875	25	M	2			MS	MS	AL	Farmer
	Lillie	D	W	F	Jan 1879	21	M	2	1	1	MS	KY	GA	
	Lorenza	GS	W	M	Jan 1900	6/mo					MS	MS	MS	
326	Roberson, Julian	H	W	M	Dec 1860	34	M	13			AL	SC	NC	Farmer
	Mattie	W	W	F	Sep 1867	32	M	13	5	4	AL	UN	UN	
	Adam G.	S	W	M	Sep 1888	11	S				MS	AL	AL	Farm Hand
	Grover C.	S	W	M	Sep 1890	9	S				MS	AL	AL	
	Ruben	S	W	M	Jul 1892	7	S				MS	AL	AL	
	Wm. C.	S	W	M	Aug 1894	5	S				MS	AL	AL	
327	Roberson, M.	H	W	M	Mar 1853	47	M	27			AL	SC	AL	Farmer
	C.L.	W	W	F	Feb 1856	44	M	27	7	6	MS	UN	MS	
	W.G.	S	W	M	Mar 1877	23	S				MS	AL	MS	Farm Hand
	O.I.	S	W	M	Feb 1880	20	S				MS	AL	MS	Farm Hand
	J.L.	S	W	M	Oct 1883	16	S				MS	AL	MS	Farm Hand
	Berdie L.	D	W	F	Apr 1883	14	S				MS	AL	MS	
328	Curtis, Jeff D.	H	W	M	Aug 1862	37	M	18			MS	TN	TN	Farmer
	Mary	W	W	F	Oct 1852	47	M	18	10	8	AL	SC	GA	
	Wm. M.	S	W	M	Feb 1882	18	S				MS	MS	AL	Farm Hand
	John H.	S	W	M	Feb 1883	17	S				MS	MS	AL	Farm Hand
	Albert	S	W	M	Jul 1884	15	S				MS	MS	AL	Farm Hand
	Susan E.	D	W	F	Mar 1888	12	S				MS	MS	AL	
	Joe	S	W	M	Mar 1889	11	S				MS	MS	AL	
	Rosie	D	W	F	Mar 1890	9	S				MS	MS	AL	
	Bell	D	W	F	Jul 1892	7	S				MS	MS	AL	
	Jeffie	D	W	F	Jul 1895	9	S				MS	MS	AL	
	Moses	F	W	M	Jun 1828	72	Wd				TN	SC	SC	
329	Scruggs, Job H.	H	W	M	Nov 1817	82	M	56			TN	VA	TN	Farmer
	Mary	W	W	F	Apr 1825	75	M	56	10	9	AL	NC	NC	
	Joe	S	W	M	Sep 1860	39	Wd				MS	TN	AL	Farm Hand
	Allen	GS	W	M	Sep 1895	4	S				MS	MS	TN	
	Job	GS	W	M	Sep 1897	2	S				MS	MS	TN	
330	Counts, Max H.	H	W	M	UN 1861	39	M	12			MS	VA	UN	Farmer
	Julia	W	W	F	Apr 1866	39	M	12	2	2	MS	MS	TN	
	Ruth	D	W	F	Aug 1890	9	S				MS	MS	MS	
	Fred	S	W	M	Dec 1895	4	S				MS	MS	MS	
331	Patrick, John	H	W	M	Jul 1877	22	M	1			MS	MS	MS	Farmer

35

1	2	3	4	5	6	7	8	9	10	11	12	13	14	15
	Cotie	W	W	F	Aug 1866	23	M	1			MS	MS	MS	
	Roberson, L.M.	H	W	M	Dec 1872	27	M	8			AL	AL	AL	Farmer
	Lou	W	W	F	Nov 1875	24	M	8	2	2	MS	MS	MS	
	Marion	S	W	M	Oct 1893	6	S				MS	AL	MS	
	Lizza	D	W	F	Apr 1896	4	S				MS	AL	MS	
	Dunahoo, Liza	MiL	W	F	May 1847	53	Wd		1	1	MS	UN	UN	
332	Morris, Dan J.	H	W	M	Oct 1864	36	M	8			MS	UN	UN	Farmer
	Marion	W	W	F	Apr 1870	30	M	8	3	3	MS	UN	UN	
	Clora	D	W	F	Jun 1893	6	S				MS	MS	MS	
	Lenna G.	D	W	M	Jul 1897	2	S				UN	UN	UN	
	Wm. C.	S	W	M	Feb 1900	5/mo	S				UN	UN	UN	
	James	Bro	W	M	UN 1880	20	S				MS	MS	UN	Day Laborer
333	Morris, Wm. A.	H	W	M	UN 1838	62	M	42			MS	AL	UN	Farmer
	Caroline	W	W	F	Feb 1849	57	M	42	3	3	MS	TN	AL	
	John W.	S	W	M	Oct 1881	18	S				MS	MS	MS	Farm Hand
	Julia	D	W	F	Feb 1886	16	S				MS	MS	MS	
	Joseph W.	S	W	M	Jul 1881	8	S				MS	MS	MS	
334	Davis, Robert	H	W	M	Jan 1856	44	M	13			MS	MS	MS	Farmer
	Twilley	W	W	F	Jul 1859	40	M	13	6	6	MS	TN	MS	
	Roxie	D	W	F	May 1887	12	S				MS	MS	MS	
	Nettie	D	W	F	Jan 1890	10	S				MS	MS	MS	
	Mimmie	D	W	F	Jun 1892	8	S				MS	MS	MS	
	Dee	S	W	M	Apr 1894	6	S				MS	MS	MS	
	Paul	S	W	M	May 1896	4	S				MS	MS	MS	
	Fred	S	W	M	Feb 1899	1	S				MS	MS	MS	
335	McDougal, William F.	H	W	M	Mar 1832	68	M				AL	UN	UN	Farmer
	Martha F.	W	W	F	UN 1844	56	M		6	6	AL	UN	UN	
	Virgie L.	D	W	F	Aug 1878	21	S				MS	AL	AL	
	James M.	S	W	M	Aug 1883	16	S				MS	AL	AL	Farm Hand
336	Cutshall, George W.	H	W	M	Mar 1880	20	M	1			MS	KY	UN	Farmer
	Ola	W	W	F	May 1881	19	M	1	0	0	TN	UN	UN	
337	Helton, James D.	H	W	M	Apr 1877	23	M	3			MS	GA	AL	Farmer
	Winnie	W	W	F	Oct 1882	17	M	3	1	1	MO	MS	MO	
	George D.	S	W	M	Dec 1898	1	S				MS	MS	MO	
	Shook, Will	HH	W	M	UN UN	UN	S				UN	UN	UN	Farm Hand
338	Pickens, William	H	W	M	Sep 1847	52	S				MS	SC	SC	Farmer
	Elizabeth	M	W	F	Jan 1811	88	Wd		1	1	SC	UN	UN	
	Smith, Sallie A.	Sis	W	F	Sep 1837	62	Wd				GA	SC	SC	
	Pickens, Nancy E.	Sis	W	F	May 1839	61	S				GA	SC	SC	
	Margaret E.	Sis	W	F	Jan 1844	56	S				GA	SC	SC	
339	Cutshall, John W.	H	W	M	Nov 1839	60	M	30			KY	PA	KY	Farmer
	Malvina	W	W	F	Jun 1847	52	M	30	6	6	GA	GA	GA	
	Wm. H.	S	W	M	Aug 1872	27	S				KY	KY	GA	Farm Hand
	D.C.	S	W	M	Jan 1885	15	S				TN	KY	GA	Farm Hand
	Bessie C.	D	W	F	Mar 1891	9	S				MS	KY	GA	
340	Woodin, John	H	W	M	UN 1872	27	M	2			KY	LA	GA	Farmer
	Dora A.	W	W	F	UN 1873	26	M	2	1	1	MS	UN	AL	
	Ednia E.	D	W	F	UN 1899	11/mo	S				MS	KY	MS	
	Joe G.	F	W	M	UN 1834	65	M	32			IN	LA	IN	Farm Hand
	Sarah C.	M	W	F	UN 1843	56	M	32	9	5	GA	SC	GA	
	James M.	Bro	W	M	UN 1879	21	S				MS	IN	GA	Farm Hand
	Julia M.	Sis	W	F	UN 1889	11	S				MS	IN	GA	
341	Cutshall, John J.	H	W	M	UN 1874	25	M	1			KY	KY	GA	Farmer

1	2	3	4	5	6	7	8	9	10	11	12	13	14	15
	Martha	W	W	F	UN 1884	16	M	1	1	1	MS	UN	UN	
	Ommie C.	D	W	F	UN 1900	2/mo	S				MS	KY	MS	
342	Ramsey, Albert	H	W	M	May 1875	25	M	3			AL	AL	AL	Farmer
	Annie C.	W	W	F	Sep 1874	25	M	3	1	1	OH	KY	UN	
	Ollie G.	D	W	F	Sep 1898	1	S				MS	AL	OH	
343	Hendrick, John	H	W	M	Feb 1878	32	M	11			MS	SC	MS	Farmer
	Lizzie B.	W	W	F	Feb 1870	30	M	11	4	4	MS	AL	AL	
	James L.	S	W	M	Apr 1891	9	S				MS	MS	MS	
	Cleveland	S	W	M	Feb 1894	6	S				MS	MS	MS	
	Rubie	D	W	F	Jan 1895	5	S				MS	MS	MS	
	Lunie	S	W	M	Apr 1897	3	S				MS	MS	MS	
344	Ramsey, John	H	W	M	Jan 1839	61	M	28			AL	AL	AL	Farmer
	J.A.	W	W	F	Oct 1861	38	M	28	3	2	MS	UN	MS	
	Willie	S	W	M	Jan 1883	17	S				MS	AL	MS	Farm Hand
	Mintie	D	W	F	May 1886	14	S				MS	AL	AL	
	Rosco	S	W	M	Jan 1887	13	S				MS	AL	AL	Farm Hand
	Edgar	S	W	M	Aug 1890	9	S				MS	AL	MS	
345	Ramsey, S.E.	H	W	M	May 1870	30	M	2			AL	AL	AL	Farmer
	Dasie	W	W	F	Jan 1878	22	M	2	1	1	MS	MS	MS	
	Etta	D	W	F	Jul 1898	1					MS	AL	MS	
346	Garnett, Martha	H	W	F	Feb 1850	50	Wd		5	4	GA	GA	GA	Farmer
	Mary	D	W	W	Nov 1860	39	S				MS	MS	MS	
	George	S	W	M	Jan 1880	20	S				MS	MS	GA	
	Willie	S	W	M	Jul 1882	17	S				MS	MS	GA	
347	Roberson, Calvin	H	W	M	Apr 1873	27	M	8			UN	UN	UN	Day Laborer
	Rachael	W	W	F	Mar 1874	26	M	8	3	3	UN	GA	GA	
	Kendrick	S	W	M	Aug 1893	6	S				MS	UN	UN	
	Robert	S	W	M	Feb 1896	4	S				MS	UN	UN	
	Mattie	D	W	F	Jan 1898	2	S				MS	UN	UN	
348	Reaves, John	H	W	M	Oct UN	27	M	8			TN	TN	SC	Farm Hand
	Lucy E.	W	W	F	Nov UN	25	M	8	4	4	AL	SC	AL	
	Wm. L.	S	W	M	May UN	7	S				TN	TN	AL	
	Gertie V.	D	W	F	Dec UN	5	S				AL	TN	AL	
	Lillie E.	D	W	F	May UN	3	S				MS	TN	AL	
	No Name	S	W	M	May UN	3/mo	S				MS	TN	AL	
349	Walker, J.B.	H	W	M	Nov 1825	74	M	54			AL	AL	TN	Farmer
	Sarah C.	W	W	F	Oct 1825	74	M	54	9	8	AL	KY	NC	
350	Flanagan, Louis	H	W	M	Apr 1866	34	M	11			TN	UN	UN	Farmer
	Mattie B.	W	W	F	Jan 1869	31	M	11	5	5	MS	UN	UN	
	Margurett B.	D	W	F	Aug 1889	10	S				MS	TN	MS	
	Letha J.	D	W	F	May 1893	7	S				MS	TN	MS	
	Willie L.	S	W	M	Jun 1895	4	S				MS	TN	MS	
	Johnie M.	S	W	M	Mar 1888	2	S				MS	TN	MS	
	Hern	HH	W	M	Dec 1885	14	S				MS	TN	MS	Farm Hand
351	Walker, Wm. C.	H	W	M	Sep 1847	52	M	34			TN	TN	TN	Farmer
	Sarah A.	W	W	F	Oct 1847	52	M	34	3	3	MS	UN	UN	
	Wm. H.	S	W	M	Mar 1883	17	S				AR	TN	MS	Farm Hand
	Levi	S	W	M	Apr 1887	13	S				AR	TN	MS	Farm Hand
	Dasie M.	D	W	F	Jun 1890	9	S				MS	TN	MS	
	Choate, George W.	GS	W	M	Apr 1884	16	S				AR	KY	MS	Farm Hand
	Auston	GS	W	M	Aug 1887	12	S				AR	KY	MS	Farm Hand
	Kennedy, W.B.	HH	W	M	Dec 1876	23	S				MS	SC	AL	Farm Hand

1	2	3	4	5	6	7	8	9	10	11	12	13	14	15
352	Johnson, Robert	H	W	M	Feb 1867	33	M	7			MS	AL	AL	Farmer
	Nancy E.	W	W	F	Jan 1874	25	M	7	3	3	MS	GA	GA	
	Hattie M.	D	W	F	May 1894	6	S				MS	MS	MS	
	Wm. Elmore	S	W	M	Aug 1896	4	S				MS	MS	MS	
	Samuel S.	S	W	M	Aug 1899	1/mo	S				MS	MS	MS	
	Thomas M.	Bro	W	M	May 1873	27	Wd				MS	AL	AL	
353	Tolliver, Matilda	H	W	F	Jul 1818	81	Wd		8	2	AL	NC	NC	Farmer
	Phillip	S	W	M	Aug 1849	50	S				AL	AL	AL	Farm Hand
354	Johnson, William	H	W	M	Oct 1824	75	M	12			AL	SC	SC	Farmer
	Elizabeth	W	W	F	Apr 1858	42	M	12	3	3	AL	AL	AL	
	Elijah J.A.	S	W	M	Jan 1889	11	S				MS	AL	AL	Farm Hand
	Edward W.	S	W	M	Dec 1890	9	S				MS	AL	AL	
	James M.	S	W	M	Jul 1893	6	S				MS	AL	AL	
355	Osborn, John	H	W	M	Mar 1869	31	M	9			AL	MS	MS	Farmer
	Elizabeth	W	W	F	Apr 1873	27	M	9	4	3	MS	MS	MS	
	Tishie L.	D	W	F	Jun 1893	6	S	S			MS	AL	MS	
	Virgie A.	D	W	F	Jun 1896	3	S	S			MS	AL	MS	
	Mary H.	D	W	F	Mar 1899	11/mo	S	S			MS	AL	MS	
356	Osborn, Sarah M.	H	W	F	Mar 1834	66	Wd		11	10	GA	SC	SC	Farmer
	E.R.	D	W	F	May 1854	45	S				AL	SC	SC	Farm Hand
	Sam	S	W	M	Jan 1867	33	S				AL	SC	SC	Farm Hand
	Mattie	D	W	F	Nov 1871	29	S				AL	SC	SC	Farm Hand
357	Osborn, W.L.	H	W	M	Nov 1860	39	M	20			AL	SC	SC	Farmer
	Mary A.	W	W	F	Jan 1859	40	M	20	5	5	AL	UN	UN	
	James W.	S	W	M	Dec 1880	19	S				MS	AL	AL	Farm Hand
	Alford	S	W	M	Nov 1883	16	S				MS	AL	AL	Farm Hand
	Marion F.	S	W	M	Dec 1888	11	S				MS	MS	MS	
	Myrtle L.	D	W	F	Mar 1893	7	S				MS	AL	AL	
	Daniel E.	S	W	M	Feb 1895	5	S				MS	AL	AL	
358	Blakney, W.H.	H	W	M	Mar 1832	64	Wd				TN	TN	KY	Merchant
359	Bonds, John	H	W	M	Nov 1854	45	Wd				MS	AL	SC	Farmer
	Pru	Sis	W	F	Feb 1858	42	S				MS	AL	SC	
	Jesse L.	Sis	W	M	Apr 1885	15	S				MS	MS	MS	Farm Hand
	Ella O.	D	W	F	Jun 1895	4	S				MS	MS	MS	
360	Hubbard, Milton	H	W	M	Nov 1855	46	M	15			MS	MS	GA	Farm Hand
	Susan P.	W	W	F	UN UN	UN	M	15	3	3	MS	TN	TN	
	Oscar	S	W	M	Jan 1886	14	S				MS	MS	MS	Farm Hand
	Wheeler	S	W	M	Apr 1888	12	S				TN	MS	MS	Farm Hand
	Minnie	D	W	F	Dec 1893	6	S							
361	Higgins, James	H	W	M	Apr 1881	19	M	2			AL	AL	AL	Farm Hand
	Virginia	W	W	F	Feb 1879	21	M	2			MS	MS	MS	
	Jackson, George	HH	W	M	UN UN	UN	UN				UN	UN	UN	Farm Hand
362	Bugg, Able W.	H	W	M	Nov 1852	44	S				MS	GA	MS	Farmer
	Mary A.	M	W	F	Jan 1831	69	Wd		2	2	MS	TN	GA	
	A. L.	Bro	W	M	Dec 1865	34	S				MS	GA	MS	Farm Hand
	Davis, Anna K.	Nce	W	F	Jan 1882	18	S				MS	TN	MS	
363	Bugg, D.R.	H	W	M	Nov 1867	31	M	3			MS	GA	MS	Farm Hand
	Alma P.	W	W	F	UN 1880	20	M	3	2	2	MS	MS	MS	
	Harriet A.	D	W	F	May 1898	2	S				MS	MS	MS	
	Aba L.	D	W	F	May 1899	1	S				MS	MS	MS	
364	Milligan, William	H	W	M	Jan 1843	57	M	40			TN	TN	TN	Farmer

1	2	3	4	5	6	7	8	9	10	11	12	13	14	15
	Margaret	W	W	F	Nov 1841	59	M	40	4	4	TN	TN	TN	
	John Y.	S	W	M	Mar 1884	16	S				MS	TN	TN	Farm Hand
365	Brown, James	H	W	M	May 1850	50	M	27			AL	UN	AL	Farmer
	Nancy	W	W	F	Jul 1850	50	M	27	12	6	TN	TN	KY	
	Emma E.	W	W	F	Feb 1883	17	S				TN	AL	TN	
	Robert T.	S	W	M	Feb 1883	17	S				TN	AL	TN	Farm Hand
	Annie A.	D	W	F	Feb 1885	15	S				MS	TN	AL	
	Amelia F.	D	W	F	Jan 1887	13	S				MS	TN	AL	
	Charlie	S	W	M	Jul 1891	9	S				MS	TN	AL	
	Joseph	S	W	M	Sep 1893	6	S				MS	TN	AL	
366	Davis, Alexander	H	W	M	May 1854	46	M	20			TN	TN	SC	Farm Hand
	Louise	W	W	F	Feb 1856	44	M	20	4	4	MS	GA	MS	
	Mattie L.	D	W	F	Jan 1880	20	S				TN	TN	MS	
	Anna K.	D	W	F	Jan 1882	18	S				TN	TN	MS	
	Mary C.	D	W	F	Jan 1889	11	S				MS	TN	MS	
	Luther L.	S	W	M	Jul 1891	8	S				MS	TN	MS	
367	Brown, Robert	H	W	M	Sep 1848	51	M	27			AL	GA	AL	Farmer
	Minnie J.	D	W	F	Apr 1882	18	S				MS	GA	MS	
	William T.	S	W	M	Jun 1880	20	S				MS	GA	MS	Farm Hand
	Victoria A.	W	W	F	Nov 1844	55	M	27	3	3	MS	GA	GA	
368	Wisdom, Doctor F.	H	W	M	Apr 1834	66	M	33			TN	UN	UN	Farmer
	Emily	W	W	F	Jan 1828	72	M	33	12	4	AL	UN	UN	
	Tennessee A.	D	W	F	Mar 1860	40	S				AL	GA	AL	
	Dickerson, Maggie	Ward	W	F	May 1878	22	S				MS	UN	UN	
	Rubie	D	W	F	Jul 1898	1	S				MS	UN	MS	
369	Bonds, Sydney F.	H	W	M	Apr 1867	33	M	15			MS	MS	MS	Day Laborer
	Dotie J.	W	W	F	Apr 1862	38	M	15	5	5	AL	SC	GA	
	Minnie L.	D	W	F	Oct 1886	13	S				MS	MS	AL	
	Robert E.	S	W	M	Oct 1888	11	S				MS	MS	AL	
	William T.	S	W	M	Jul 1889	10	S				MS	MS	AL	
	Edie E.	D	W	F	Jul 1892	7	S				MS	MS	AL	
	John A.	S	W	M	Feb 1895	5	S				MS	MS	AL	
370	Holder, William	H	W	M	Jul 1868	31	M	15			MS	MS	MS	Merchant
	Mary	W	W	F	Feb 1869	31	M	15	7	4	MS	AL	MS	
	Ollie E.	D	W	F	Jul 1886	13	S				MS	MS	MS	
	Elmore	S	W	M	Apr 1891	9	S				MS	MS	MS	
	Paulie D.	S	W	M	Mar 1893	7	S				MS	MS	MS	
	David C.	S	W	M	Aug 1896	3	S				MS	MS	MS	
371	Hubbard, E. A.	H	W	M	May 1880	70	Wd		8	8	GA	GA	GA	Farmer
	Watley, Nicy	Ward	W	F	Jan 1857	43					MS	UN	UN	
372	Glover, Dorman	H	W	M	Nov 1868	31	M	7			UN	UN	UN	
	Cora	W	W	F	May 1868	32	M	7			UN	UN	UN	
	Berdie	D	W	F	Sep 1894	5	S				UN	UN	UN	
	Effie	D	W	F	Jan 1897	3	S				UN	UN	UN	
	Mattie E.	D	W	F	Nov 1899	6/mo	S				UN	UN	UN	
373	Hubbard, Sydney	H	W	M	Mar 1857	42	M	1			MS	AL	GA	Farmer
	Della	W	W	F	May 1874	26	M	1	0	0	MS	TN	TN	
374	Hubbard, Jack C.	H	W	M	Nov 1870	29	M	4			MS	AL	GA	Farmer
	Julia C.	W	W	F	Jan 1874	26	M	4	2	2	MS	TN	TN	
	Connie	D	W	F	Feb 1894	4	S				MS	MS	MS	
	Lenna	D	W	F	May 1898	1	S				MS	MS	MS	
375	Hubbard, Robert	H	W	M	Aug 1865	34	M	4			MS	AL	GA	Farmer

1	2	3	4	5	6	7	8	9	10	11	12	13	14	15
	Sudie	W	W	F	UN 1874	26	M	4	2	2	MS	MS	TN	
	Lee	S	W	M	Oct 1895	4	S				MS	MS	MS	
	Lue G.	D	W	F	Oct 1897	2	S				MS	MS	MS	
376	Johnson, Jack	H	W	M	Mar 1851	49	M	18			MS	UN	UN	Farmer
	Julia	W	W	F	Dec 1859	40	M	18	2	2	MS	Eng	MS	
	Bertha	D	W	F	Jul 1883	16	S				MS	MS	MS	
	Dixie	D	W	F	Jul 1885	14	S				MS	MS	MS	
377	Meeks, J.J.	H	W	M	Nov 1845	54	M	29			TN	TN	TN	Farmer
	Margaret	W	W	F	Mar 1846	54	M	29	11	7	TN	TN	TN	
	Jennie O.	D	W	F	Apr 1882	18	S				AL	TN	TN	
	Otis F.	S	W	M	Nov 1884	15	S				TN	TN	TN	Farm Hand
	Arpie	D	W	F	Aug 1886	13	S				MS	TN	TN	
	Almer F.	D	W	F	Feb 1890	10	S				MS	TN	TN	
378	Meeks, E. A.	H	W	M	Sep 1878	20	M	0			AL	TN	TN	Farm Hand
	Frances	W	W	F	UN UN		M	0			MS	MS	AL	
	Dorothy	D	W	F	Oct 1894	5	S				MS	AL	MS	
379	Meeks, James	H	W	M	Apr 1854	26	M	0			MS	TN	TN	Farm Hand
	Mollie	W	W	F	May UN	26	M		3	1	AL	AL	AL	
	Erwin	S	W	M	Apr 1899	1	S				MS	MS	AL	
380	Meeks, John	H	W	M	Sep 1878	22	M	4			TN	TN	TN	Farm Hand
	Almeter	W	W	F	Sep 1871	28	M	4			MS	NC	NC	
	Loula B.	SD	W	F	Jul 1890	9	S				MS	UN	TN	
	Macha A.	D	W	F	May 1898	3	S				MS	TN	MS	
	Almer P.	D	W	F	Feb 1900	5/mo	S				MS	TN	MS	
381	Sowell, W.R.	H	W	M	Feb 1859	41	M	7			TN	TN	TN	Day Laborer
	Sarah	W	W	F	Sep 1870	29	M	7	4	3	TN	TN	AL	
	Samuel	S	W	M	Sep 1882	17	M	0			TN	TN	TN	Farm Hand
	Ednie V.	DiL	W	F	Aug 1885	14	M	0			TN	TN	TN	
	Jennie	DiL	W	F	Jun 1888	11	S				TN	TN	TN	
	Lizzie	DiL	W	F	Jul 1891	8	S				TN	TN	TN	
	Luther	S	W	M	Jul 1894	5	S				TN	TN	TN	
	Gilbert	S	W	M	Feb 1898	2	S				TN	TN	TN	
	Venie	D	W	F	May 1885	15	S				TN	TN	TN	
382	Ridge, Harvey	H	W	M	May 1872	28	M	8			MS	NC	MS	Timberman
	Annie	W	W	F	Jan 1868	32	M	8	6	4	MS	MS	MS	
	Elbert	S	W	M	Dec 1892	7	S				MS	MS	MS	
	Freddie	S	W	M	May 1894	6	S				MS	MS	MS	
	Nora	D	W	F	Dec 1898	2	S				TN	MS	MS	
	Paulie	D	W	F	Jan 1899	1	S				AL	MS	MS	
383	Johnson, Ziphor	H	W	M	May 1835	45	S				MS	NC	NC	Farmer
	S.E.	Sis	W	F	Jan 1833	48	S				MS	NC	NC	
	Bugg, S.L.	Nep	W	M	Jun 1872	28	S				MS	GA	TN	Farm Hand
384	Bullard, George	H	W	M	Mar UN	UN	M	36			MS	AL	AL	Farmer
	Mary	W	W	F	Nov 1833	65	M	36	5	4	TN	SC	TN	
385	Johnson, Morris	H	W	M	UN UN	UN	M	13			MS	MS	MS	Mill Hand
	May A.	W	W	F	Oct 1865	34	M	13	4	4	TN	TN	MS	
	Joe W.	S	W	M	Feb 1888	12	S				MS	MS	TN	Farm Hand
	May A.	D	W	F	Jan 1890	10	S				MS	MS	TN	
	Hattie E.	D	W	F	May 1892	8	S				MS	MS	TN	
	Julia C.	D	W	F	Sep 1899	9/mo	S				MS	MS	TN	
386	House, Jack	H	W	M	Aug 1874	28	M	9			MS	AL	AL	Mill Hand
	E.B.	W	W	F	Aug 1874	28	M	9	9	3	AL	AL	AL	

1	2	3	4	5	6	7	8	9	10	11	12	13	14	15
	Eddie W.	S	W	M	Oct 1892	7	S				MS	MS	AL	
	Allen	S	W	M	Oct 1894	5	S				MS	MS	AL	
387	Bullard, Bill	H	W	M	Apr 1874	24	M	1			MS	MS	TN	Farmer
	Delia	W	W	F	Oct 1878	21	M	1			AL	AL	AL	
	Mary S.	Ward	W	F	Nov 1896	3	S				MS	MS	MS	
388	Willis, Sin	H	W	M	Jan 1881	19	M	2			AL	AL	AL	
	Roxie	W	W	F	Jan 1881	19	M	2	1	1	AL	AL	AL	
	Ada	D	W	F	Dec 1898	1	S				AL	AL	AL	
	Sallie	Sis	W	F	Oct 1886	13	S				AL	AL	AL	
389	Beckman, Len	H	W	M	Oct 1870	28	M	9			TN	TN	TN	Sawyer
	Olla	W	W	F	Mar 1874	26	M	9	2	1	AL	AL	AL	
	Harold	S	W	M	May 1895	5	S				AL	TN	AL	
390	Bullard, C.A.	H	W	M	Aug 1840	59	M	8			MS	TN	AL	Farmer
	R. E.	W	W	F	Dec 1843	56	M	8	8		TN	TN	GA	
	Bonds, Sallie	D	W	F	Apr 1870	30	Wd	3	3		MS	MS	MS	Farm Hand
	Bobine	GD	W	F	Sep 1889	10	S				MS	MS	MS	
	Bertha	GD	W	F	Jun 1892	7	S				MS	MS	MS	
	William	GS	W	M	Oct 1893	6	S				MS	MS	MS	
	Johnson, Della	D	W	F	Sep 1875	24	Wd	1	1		MS	MS	MS	Farm Hand
	Sallie	GD	W	F	Jan 1899	1	S				MS	MS	MS	
	Bullard, Charlie	S	W	M	Dec 1877	22	S				MS	MS	MS	Farm Hand
	Lizzie	D	W	F	Jun 1882	17	S				MS	MS	MS	Farm Hand
	Janie	D	W	F	Jun 1883	16	S				MS	MS	MS	Farm Hand
	Maggie	D	W	F	Jun 1885	14	S				MS	MS	MS	Farm Hand
391	Bullard, Ben	H	W	M	Jan 1838	42	M	20			MS	TN	AL	Tie Inspector
	Mary	W	W	F	UN UN	43	M	20	7	7	MS	TN	MS	
	Jeff	S	W	M	Nov 1881	18	S				MS	MS	MS	Day Laborer
	Artie	D	W	F	Jul 1884	15	S				MS	MS	MS	
	John Allen	S	W	M	Aug 1886	13	S				MS	MS	MS	
	Cora	D	W	F	Aug 1889	10	S				MS	MS	MS	
	Andrew	S	W	M	Oct 1890	9	S				MS	MS	MS	
	Olen	S	W	M	Jan 1894	6	S				MS	MS	MS	
392	Bullard, Dick	H	W	M	Jul 1873	26	M	1			MS	TN	AL	Day Laborer
	Jane	W	W	F	Jul 1882	17	M	1	1	1	MS	MS	MS	
	Polk	S	W	M	Jan 1900	4/mo	S				MS	MS	MS	
393	Massey, Tom	H	W	M	UN UN	UN	M	UN			TN	TN	TN	Day Laborer
	Mary	W	W	F	UN UN	UN	M	UN	7	7	TN	TN	TN	
	M.	S	W	M	UN UN	14	S				TN	TN	TN	
	Rid	S	W	M	UN UN	17	S				TN	TN	TN	
	Dora	D	W	F	UN UN	18	S				TN	TN	TN	
	Cora	D	W	F	UN UN	11	S				TN	TN	TN	
	Lula	D	W	F	UN UN	7	S				TN	TN	TN	
	Etta	D	W	F	UN UN	5	S				MS	TN	TN	
	Ross	S	W	M	UN UN	1	S				MS	TN	TN	
394	Bullard, T.H.	H	W	M	Dec 1863	36	M	11			MS	TN	AL	Farmer
	Susie	W	W	F	Apr 1869	31	M	11	6	5	TN	TN	TN	
	Julia	D	W	F	Jan 1891	9	S				MS	MS	TN	
	Tomie	S	W	M	Aug 1892	7	S				MS	MS	TN	
	Alvy	D	W	F	Feb 1895	5	S				MS	MS	TN	
	Berdie	D	W	F	Sep 1895	5	S				MS	MS	TN	
	Bertha	D	W	F	Jan 1898	2	S				MS	MS	TN	
395	Lutts, William	H	W	M	Jan 1865	35	M	8			TN	NC	NC	Mill Man
	Lula D.	W	W	F	Sep 1864	35	M	8	2	2	NC	NC	NC	
	Flora	D	W	F	Jan 1893	7	S				TN	TN	NC	

1	2	3	4	5	6	7	8	9	10	11	12	13	14	15
	Lucy	D	W	F	Feb 1895	5	S				TN	TN	NC	
396	Tacket, N. J.	H	W	M	Jul 1850	49	Wd	3	3		TN	TN	TN	Farmer
	Bell Z.	D	W	F	Nov 1886	13	S				MS	TN	TN	
	Thomas	S	W	M	Sep 1888	11	S				MS	TN	TN	
397	Bullard, Jeff	H	W	M	Jan 1862	38	M	5			MS	TN	AL	Farmer
	Pennsylvania	W	W	F	Jul 1876	24	M	5			AL	AL	AL	
	Henry	S	W	M	Jan 1887	13	S				MS	MS	AL	
	Lu O.	D	W	F	May 1889	11	S				MS	MS	AL	
	Ivy	D	W	F	May 1886	4	S				MS	MS	AL	
	George	S	W	M	Jan 1896	4	S				MS	MS	AL	
	Allen B.	S	W	M	Apr 1898	2	S				MS	MS	AL	
	Mannie	S	W	M	Oct 1899	7/mo	S				MS	MS	AL	
398	Dillahunt, James	H	W	M	Jun 1867	32	M	12			UN	UN	UN	Day Laborer
	Josie	W	W	F	Aug 1874	25	M	12	4	3	MS	MS	MS	
	Willie	S	W	M	Oct 1889	10	S				MS	UN	MS	Day Laborer
	Lillie	D	W	F	Mar 1892	8	S				MS	UN	MS	
	Arthor	S	W	M	Jun 1895	4	S				MS	UN	MS	
399	Morgan, Mary	H	W	F	Jul 1849	52	Wd		6	6	TN	TN	UN	Farmer
	Olive	S	W	M	Mar 1883	17	S				TN	MS	TN	Farm Hand
	John L.	S	W	M	May 1885	15	S				MS	MS	TN	Farm Hand
	Eula C.	D	W	F	Feb 1888	2	S				MS	MS	TN	Farm Hand
400	Wallace, N.C.	H	W	M	Mar 1859	61	Wd	UN	10	7	MS	AL	AL	Farmer
	Borden, Rebecca	D	W	F	Aug 1874	25	M	0			MS	TN	MS	
	David E.	SiL	W	M	Jun 1875	25	M	0			AL	AL	AL	Farm Hand
	Wallace, James M.	S	W	M	Dec 1878	21	S				MS	TN	MS	Farm Hand
401	Bullard, John	H	W	M	UN UN	UN	M	2			MS	UN	UN	Farm Hand
	Bettie	W	W	F	May 1878	22	M	2	1	1	MS	TN	MS	
	Laura	D	W	F	Jan 1892	8	S				MS	MS	MS	
	Jemie	D	W	F	Mar 1893	7	S				MS	MS	MS	
	Auston	S	W	M	May 1895	5	S				MS	MS	MS	
	Pony	S	W	M	Sep 1899	9/mo	S				MS	MS	MS	
402	Borden, William	H	W	M	Feb 1851	49	M				AL	AL	AL	Day Laborer
	Sarah	W	W	F	Jun 1848	51	M		11	10	AL	AL	AL	
	Jim	S	W	M	Jan 1881	19	S				AL	AL	AL	Farm Hand
	Nancy L.	D	W	F	May 1883	17	S				AL	AL	AL	
	David	S	W	M	Mar 1888	12	S				AL	AL	AL	Farm Hand
	James	S	W	M	Jun 1891	8	S				AL	AL	AL	
	Isac A.	S	W	M	Jan 1892	8	S				AL	AL	AL	
	Hayne, Julia A.	D	W	F	Nov 1876	23	Wd		1	1	AL	AL	AL	
	Hayne, Melson	GS	W	M	Oct 1896	3	S				AL	MS	AL	
403	Tigner, George	H	W	M	UN UN	UN	M	0			AL	MA	MS	Day Laborer
	Fannie	W	W	F	Jan 1879	21	M	0	0	0	MS	MS	MS	
404	Tigner, Joseph M.	H	W	M	Aug 1846	53	M	28			MA	Fra	KY	Farmer
	Elizabeth	W	W	F	Jan 1860	40	M	28	7	7	MS	TN	TN	
	Mary E. J.	D	W	F	May 1880	20	S				MS	MA	MS	
	Charlie	S	W	M	Nov 1882	17	S				MS	MA	MS	
	William M.	S	W	M	Feb 1882	16	S				MS	MA	MS	
	John M.	S	W	M	Jan 1889	12	S				MS	MA	MS	
	Josiah A.	S	W	M	Jan 1896	4	S				MS	MA	MS	
405	Curtis, Tom	H	W	M	UN UN	UN	M	5			MS	MS	MS	Tieman
	Lena	W	W	F	UN UN	UN	M	5			MS	MS	MS	
	Milton D.	S	W	M	Jul 1895	4	S				MS	MS	MS	
	Oscar L.	S	W	M	Feb 1898	2	S				MS	MS	MS	

1	2	3	4	5	6	7	8	9	10	11	12	13	14	15
	Carmack	S	W	M	May 1900	4/mo	S				MS	MS	MS	
406	Curtis, William	H	W	M	Jan 1838	62	M	38			MS	UN	SC	Farmer
	Jemima	W	W	F	Oct 1850	49	M	38	12	10	MS	UN	UN	
	William	S	W	M	Apr 1866	34	S				MS	MS	MS	
	John	S	W	M	May 1868	32	S				MS	MS	MS	
	Tommie	D	W	F	Aug 1870	29	S				MS	MS	MS	
	Georgia A.	D	W	F	Sep 1872	27	S				MS	MS	MS	
	Rebecca	D	W	F	Oct 1874	25	S				MS	MS	MS	
	Fannie	D	W	F	Dec 1876	23	S				MS	MS	MS	
	Marshall	S	W	M	Jun 1878	22	S				MS	MS	MS	
	Andrew	S	W	M	UN 1882	18	S				MS	MS	MS	
	Luther	S	W	M	UN 1885	14	S				MS	MS	MS	
	Joe	S	W	M	Sep 1891	8	S				MS	MS	MS	
407	Bullard, W.M.	H	W	M	Feb 1820	80	M	58			AL	SC	SC	Farmer
	Rebecca	W	W	F	Jan 1824	76	M	58	12	8	AL	GA	AL	
	Harrison, Lottie	Ser	W	F	UN UN	UN	S				TN	UN	UN	Servant
	Bullard, William	GS	W	M	Oct 1882	17	S				MS	MS	MS	Farm Hand
	Black, Jack	HH	B	M	Jan 1882	18	S				AL	UN	UN	Farm Hand
	Morgan, Ida	GD	W	F	Mar 1886	14	S				MS	UN	MS	
	Harrison, Emily	Ser	W	F	Apr 1888	12	S				MS	UN	TN	
	Bullard, Dosky	GS	W	M	Jul 1889	2	S				MS	MS	MS	
408	Jones, Elonza	H	W	M	UN UN	UN	M				IN	UN	UN	Farm Hand
	Nancy	W	W	F	UN UN	UN	M				IN	UN	UN	
	Jennie E.	D	W	F	Apr 1886	14	S				TN	IN	IN	
	Nettie M.	D	W	F	Dec 1888	11	S				KY	IN	IN	
	Henry E.	S	W	M	Oct 1891	8	S				KY	IN	IN	
	Elonza W.	S	W	M	Dec 1895	4	S				KY	IN	IN	
	Ezra W.	S	W	M	Jan 1898	2	S				MS	IN	IN	
409	Ganong, Cornelius	H	W	M	Aug 1844	55	M	35			GA	UN	UN	Carpenter
	Katie	W	W	F	Jul 1849	50	M	35	66		At Sea	Eng	Ire	
	Parker	S	W	M	Feb 1881	18	S				MS	GA	At Sea	
	Cornelius	S	W	M	Jul 1882	17	S				MS	GA	At Sea	
410	Alridge, John	H	W	M	Dec 1869	30	M	5			TN	TN	AL	Blacksmith
	Nelie	W	W	F	Aug 1864	35	M	5	6	6	MS	GA	Eng	
	Johnson	SS	W	M	Dec 1885	14	S				MS	AR	MS	
	Lucille	SS	W	F	Sep 1889	10	S				MS	AR	MS	
	Elwood	SS	W	M	Jul 1891	8	S				MS	AR	MS	
	Ida	SS	W	F	Oct 1899	5/mo	S				MS	MS	MS	
411	Mackey, D.J.	H	W	M	Sep 1829	70	M	7			SC	Ire	SC	Blacksmith
	Dora	W	W	F	Oct 1861	38	M	7	4	4	MS	MS	MS	
	Charles H.	S	W	M	Nov 1895	5	S				MS	SC	MS	
	Walter S.	S	W	M	Oct 1891	8	S				MS	SC	MS	
	Thomas L.	S	W	M	Feb 1898	2	S				MS	SC	MS	
	Zeke C.C.	S	W	M	May 1900	1/mo	S				MS	SC	MS	
412	Castleberry, Frances	H	W	F	UN UN	UN	UN		8	4	TN	UN	UN	
	John P.	S	W	M	UN 1860	39	S				MS	GA	TN	RR Section Hand
	Kate	D	W	F	UN UN	20	S				MS	GA	TN	
413	Davis, Sam	H	W	M	Jan 1848	52	M	22			MS	AL	GA	Farmer
	Sallie	W	W	F	UN UN	UN	M	22	5	5	MS	MS	MS	
	James	S	W	M	May 1881	21	S				MS	MS	MS	
	Mollie	D	W	F	Oct 1887	12	S				MS	MS	MS	
	Ben	S	W	M	Apr 1880	10	S				MS	MS	MS	
	Susie	D	W	F	Jun 1892	7	S				MS	MS	MS	
414	Bonds, Sam	H	W	M	Dec 1876	23	M	4			MS	MS	MA	Day Laborer

1	2		3	4	5	6	7	8	9	10	11	12	13	14	15
	May		W	W	F	Mar 1877	21	M	4	1	1	MS	MS	MS	
	Willie		S	W	M	May 1898	2	S				MS	MS	MS	
415	Daniel, Jim		H	W	M	Jun 1860	40	M	5			MS	GA	MS	Farm Hand
	Annie		W	W	F	Feb 1870	30	M	5			TN	MS	MS	
416	Brown, James		H	W	M	UN UN	UN	M	UN			SC	UN	UN	Carpenter
	Jennie		W	W	F	UN UN	UN	M	UN			UN	UN	UN	

End of numeration for District #1

1	2	3	4	5	6	7	8	9	10	11	12	13	14	15
1	Doan, J.F.	H	W	M	Aug 1837	62	M	15			MS	NC	SC	Farmer
	Hattie W.	W	W	F	Sep 1853	46	M	15	7	3	AL	NC	SC	
	Hattie S.	D	W	F	Oct 1885	14	S				MS	MS	AL	
	Jno. F.	S	W	M	Aug 1891	8	S				MS	MS	AL	
	Mamie W.	D	W	F	Jan 1894	6	S				MS	MS	AL	
	Williams, Sallie B.	SiL	W	F	Feb 1844	56	S				AL	NC	SC	
	Mamie A.	SiL	W	F	Jun 1859	40	M	20	1	1	AL	NC	SC	
2	Marks, Claraney	H	B	F	UN UN	61	Wd		10	5	AL	SC	TN	Laundress
3	Johnson, Lucy	H	B	F	UN UN	70	Wd		2	1	AL	UN	UN	Laundress
	Hodges, Mattie	GD	B	F	Apr 1880	20	S				MS	MS	GA	Laundress
4	Jackson, Richard	H	B	M	UN UN	24	M 5mo				AL	UN	AL	Day Laborer
	Mary	W	B	F	UN UN	30	M 5mo		8	7	MS	UN	TN	
	Armstrong, Alex	SS	B	M	UN UN	24	M	1			MS	UN	MS	Day Laborer
	Terry	SS	B	M	UN UN	16	S				MS	UN	MS	Boot Black
	Anna	SD	B	F	UN UN	15	S				MS	UN	MS	Laundress
	Eva	SD	B	F	UN UN	14	S				MS	UN	MS	Laundress
	Minnie	SD	B	F	UN UN	12	S				MS	UN	MS	Laundress
	Sulivan	SS	B	M	UN UN	7	S				MS	UN	MS	
	Bankhead, Rose	MiL	B	F	UN UN	60	Wd		1	1	TN	UN	UN	Cook
5	Cotton, Albert	H	W	M	Oct 1871	29	M	6			MS	MS	MS	Bookkeeper
	Carrie L.	W	W	F	Feb 1874	26	M	6	3	3	MS	MS	TN	
	Linda C.	D	W	F	Oct 1895	4	S				MS	MS	MS	
	Haley	S	W	M	Jul 1897	2	S				MS	MS	MS	
	Emma	D	W	F	Mar 1900	2/mo	S				MS	MS	MS	
6	Simmons, M.A.	H	W	M	Mar 1820	80	M	13			TN	NC	NC	Farmer
	Nancy E.	W	W	F	Apr 1859	41	M	13	2	2	TN	AL	AL	
	Ennis	S	W	M	Oct 1883	16	S				AL	AR	AL	
	Minnie	Adp D	W	F	Apr 1886	14	S				MS	AL	AL	
7	McKinney, Linda	H	W	F	Oct 1842	57	Wd		9	8	TN	NC	TN	
	Sallie	D	W	F	Aug 1875	24	S				MS	MS	TN	
	Jas. B.	S	W	M	Feb 1878	22	S				MS	MS	TN	Drummer
	Joe T.	S	W	M	Apr 1882	18	S				MS	MS	TN	Bookkeeper
	Charles W	S	W	M	Apr 1885	15	S				MS	MS	TN	Clerk
8	Moody, Mary	H	B	F	UN UN	UN	Wd		3	3	UN	UN	UN	
	Gilbert	S	B	M	UN UN	UN	Wd				UN	UN	UN	Day Laborer
	Nancy	D	B	F	UN UN	UN	S		1	1	MS	UN	UN	Cook
	Sam	S	B	M	UN UN	UN	S				MS	UN	UN	Day Laborer
	Ada	GD	B	F	UN UN	18	S				MS	UN	UN	
	Jim	GS	B	M	Feb 1884	16	S				MS	UN	UN	Day Laborer
9	Ramsey, V.C.	H	W	M	May 1850	50	M	1			AL	Ire	UN	Merchant
	Amana S.	W	W	F	UN 1843	57	M	1	1	1	MS	UN	SC	
10	McRae, Jasper	H	B	M	Aug 1855	44	M	23			MS	GA	NC	Day Laborer
	Edith	W	B	F	May 1860	40	M	23	13	8	MS	MS	MS	
	James	S	B	M	UN UN	17	S				MS	MS	MS	Day Laborer
	Gus	S	B	M	UN UN	13	S				MS	MS	MS	
	Ed	S	B	M	UN UN	11	S				MS	MS	MS	
	Virginia	D	B	F	UN UN	9	S				MS	MS	MS	
	Hosey	S	B	M	UN UN	7	S				MS	MS	MS	
	Channy B.	D	B	F	UN UN	5	S				MS	MS	MS	

1	2	3	4	5	6	7	8	9	10	11	12	13	14	15
	Bob Lee	S	B	M	UN UN	1	S				MS	MS	MS	
11	Kenell, Sylvia	H	B	F	UN UN	29	Wd		5	5	AL	AL	AL	Laundress
	Jno. H.	S	B	M	May 1892	8	S				MS	MS	AL	
	Ford	S	B	M	Oct 1894	6	S				MS	MS	AL	
	Jessie	S	B	M	Apr 1895	5	S				MS	MS	AL	
	Lottie	D	B	F	Feb 1897	3	S				MS	MS	AL	
	Edward	S	B	M	Mar 1899	1	S				MS	MS	AL	
12	Roberts, Ella	H	B	F	UN UN	UN	M		1	1	VA	UN	UN	Laundress
	Davis, Lena	D	B	F	UN UN	24	Wd				MS	TN	MS	Cook
	Roberts, Hattie	Ad-D	B	F	UN UN	14	S				MS	TN	MS	
13	Armstrong, Geo.	H	B	M	Feb 1832	68	M	2			MS	UN	MS	Barber
	Eva	W	B	F	UN UN	31	M	2			AL	UN	TN	
14	Holcom, Alex	H	B	M	Jan 1859	41	M	4			LA	LA	MS	Day Laborer
	Alla Bell	D	B	F	May 1880	20	S				MS	LA	MS	Cook
15	Moody, Louis	H	B	M	UN UN	40	M	18			AL	UN	UN	Day Laborer
	Bell	W	B	F	Apr 1865	35	M	18	6	5	MS	SC	NC	Laundress
	Will	S	B	M	Jul 1872	17	S				MS	AL	MS	Day Laborer
	Branch	D	B	F	Mar 1887	13	S				MS	AL	MS	Laundress
	Harvey	S	B	M	Jan 1890	10	S				MS	AL	MS	
	Richard	S	B	M	Apr 1891	9	S				MS	AL	MS	
	Laura	D	B	F	Jun 1891	4	S				MS	AL	MS	
16	Bonds, Paul	H	B	M	UN UN	81	M	40			GA	UN	GA	
	Harriett	W	B	F	UN UN	80	M	40	11	6	MS	UN	UN	
	Malissie	D	B	F	Sep 1872	27	S				MS	GA	MS	Laundress
	Ada	D	B	F	Apr 1881	19	S				MS	GA	MS	Laundress
17	Cooper, Burt	H	B	M	UN UN	50	M	20			AL	AL	AL	RR Brakeman
	Lena	W	B	F	UN UN	40	M	20			TN	UN	VA	
18	Coman, Garrett	H	B	M	UN UN	21	M	3			MS	UN	MS	Day Laborer
	Pheba	W	B	F	UN UN	30	M	3	2	2	AL	AL	AL	
	Clarence	S	B	M	UN UN	13	S				MS	MS	AL	
	Simpan-yell	D	B	F	UN UN	4	S				MS	MS	AL	
19	McKinney, W.D.	H	W	M	Sep 1856	43	S				MS	UN	NC	
20	O'Malley, Mathew	H	W	M	Dec 1832	67	M	28			Ire	Ire	Ire	Day Laborer, Pedler
	Ruby	W	W	F	Nov 1842	57	M	28	7	3	TN	NC	NC	
	Joseph	S	W	M	May 1883	17	S				MS	Ire	TN	Hdwe Clerk
	Charley	S	W	M	Oct 1885	15	S				MS	Ire	TN	Beef Maker
21	Payne, Matlin	H	W	F	Aug 1854	45	M		1	1	GA	SC	SC	
	Turner, Hattie	D	W	F	Dec 1878	21	S				GA	NC	GA	
22	Morgan, W.N.	H	W	M	Jan 1857	43	M	22			MS	KY	MS	
	Mittie S.	W	W	F	Jan 1861	39	M	22	8	7	TN	VA	TN	
	James A.	S	W	M	May 1881	19	S				TN	MS	TN	Meat Maker
	Clara Bell	D	W	F	Jul 1883	16	S				TN	MS	TN	
	William N.	S	W	M	Jul1886	13	S				TN	MS	TN	
	Mack R.	S	W	M	Sep 1892	7	S				TN	MS	TN	
	Ada Lou	D	W	F	May 1894	6	S				TN	MS	TN	
	Walter C.	S	W	M	Jan.1900	4/mo	S				TN	MS	TN	
23	Allen, Mattie F.	H	W	F	Jun 1841	59	Wd		9	5	MS	NC	MS	
	Maggie L.	D	W	F	May 1874	26	S				MS	VA	MS	Millinery
	Sam	S	W	M	Sep 1878	21	S				MS	VA	MS	Civil Engineer
	Jno. Henry	S	W	M	Aug 1853	16	S				MS	VA	MS	

1	2	3	4	5	6	7	8	9	10	11	12	13	14	15
	Wilson, Virge	D	W	F	Jul 1876	23	M		2	2	MS	VA	MA	Millinery
	Lura	GD	W	F	Nov 1896	3	S				MS	MS	MS	
	Virginia	GD	W	F	Aug 1898	1	S				MS	MS	MS	
24	Jackson, William O.	H	W	M	Jan 1859	41	M	10			AL	SC	AL	Drummer
	May	W	W	F	Jan 1867	33	M	10	4	4	MS	VA	MS	
	Mattie Allen	D	W	F	Jul 1891	8	S				MS	AL	MS	
	Isaac M.	S	W	M	Feb 1894	6	S				MS	AL	MS	
	Nalla	D	W	F	Jun 1895	4	S				MS	AL	MS	
	Robert Harrison	S	W	M	Dec 1897	2	S				MS	AL	MS	
25	Smith, Martha A.	H	W	F	Oct 1821	78	Wd		1	0	TN	UN	UN	
	Minnie May	GD	W	F	Oct 1893	6	S				TN	MS	MS	
	Donald, Ida E.	UN	W	F	Dec 1880	19	S				MS	SC	MS	Housekeeper
26	McKnight, Charles W.	H	W	M	Jan 1850	49	M	8			MS	SC	TN	Merchant
	Lilla	W	W	F	Jan 1870	30	M	8	8	6	MS	MS	MS	
	Anna Ford	D	W	F	Aug 1885	14	S				MS	TN	MS	
	Charley	S	W	M	Aug 1887	13	S				MS	TN	MS	
	Alma	D	W	F	Sep 1891	9	S				MS	TN	MS	
	Elsie	D	W	F	May 1894	6	S				MS	TN	MS	
	William	S	W	M	Jun 1895	4	S				MS	TN	MS	
	Robert	S	W	M	Oct 1899	1	S				MS	TN	MS	
	Schrock, Nancy A.	GM	W	F	Aug 1819	85	Wd		1	1	SC	PA	SC	
	Cotton, Willie B.	SiL	W	F	May 1867	33	S				MS	MS	MS	
	Meek, Julius	Nce	W	F	Jan 1890	10	S				MS	MS	MS	
27	Angley, Pernaley	H	W	F	Dec 1841	59	Wd		8	5	AL	VA	AL	Dress Maker
	Mollie	D	W	F	Jun 1886	33	S				AL	AL	AL	Dress Maker
	Oria	D	W	F	Aug 1870	28	S				AL	AL	AL	Dress Maker
	Anna	D	W	F	Mar 1874	25	S				AL	AL	AL	Dress Maker
	Carrie	D	W	F	Oct 1879	20	S				AL	AL	AL	Telephone Ex
28	Golston, Cherry	H	B	F	UN UN	60	Wd		1	0	AL	UN	UN	Laundress
29	Davis, Nancy	H	W	F	Feb 1822	78	Wd		13	5	AL	NC	VA	
	Maggie E.	D	W	F	Sep 1844	55	S				AL	AL	AL	
	Bessie	GD	W	F	Mar 1883	17	S				UN	UN	UN	
30	Barnett, John W.	H	W	M	May 1853	47	M	18			TX	LA	MS	Merchant
	Linda	W	W	F	Jun 1851	48	M	18	5	0	TN	TN	TN	
	Ernest	S	W	M	Feb 1883	17	S				MS	TN	AL	
	Louise	D	W	F	Mar 1885	15	S				MS	TN	MS	
	Walter	S	W	M	Nov 1888	11	S				MS	TN	MS	
31	Bishop, Ben L.	H	W	M	Nov 1870	29	S				AL	SC	AL	Cattle Dealer
32	Barnett, Shelly	H	W	M	Apr 1868	32	M	5			MS	TN	MS	Postal Clerk
	Lillian W.	W	W	F	Apr 1876	24	M	5	1	1	TN	TN	TN	
	Harrell	S	W	M	Jun 1898	1	S				MS	MS	TN	
33	Doan, Jno. E.	H	W	M	Sep 1863	36	M	17			MS	AL	MS	Drummer
	Virginia	W	W	F	Apr 1868	32	M	17	1	1	MS	SC	SC	
	Arabia	D	W	F	Oct 1884	15	S				MS	MS	MS	
34	Chambers, Andrew	H	W	F	Dec 1865	34	M	14			MS	SC	TN	Farmer
	Nancy A.	W	W	F	Oct 1865	34	M	14	6	6	MS	SC	SC	
	William C.	S	W	M	Oct 1887	12	S				MS	AL	MS	
	Robert C.	S	W	M	Sep 1889	10	S				MS	AL	MS	
	Florence E.	D	W	F	Mar 1891	9	S				MS	AL	MS	
	Harvey L.	S	W	M	Nov 1893	6	S				MS	AL	MS	
	Virginia Ann	D	W	F	Jan 1896	4	S				MS	AL	MS	
	Birdie D.	D	W	F	Jul 1898	1	S				MS	AL	MS	

1	2	3	4	5	6	7	8	9	10	11	12	13	14	15
35	Davis, William	H	W	M	Feb 1819	81	M	45			TN	VA	VA	Day Laborer
	Cathran	W	W	F	Oct 1833	66	M	45	6	6	AL	SC	SC	
	Howell	GS	W	M	Nov 1887	17	S				MS	UN	AL	
36	Holmes, Frances E.	H	W	F	Oct 1822	77	Wd		6	3	TN	PA	TN	
37	Jenkins, George	H	B	M	Sep UN	23	M	4			AL	SC	AL	Day Laborer
	Anna	W	B	F	Apr 1874	26	M	4	3	3	MS	UN	TN	
	Willie W.	D	B	F	May 1890	10	S				MS	AL	MS	
	Lovie	D	B	F	Mar 1897	3	S				MS	UN	MS	
	Alman	S	B	M	Mar 1899	1	S				MS	UN	MS	
	Green, Henry	FiL	B	M	UN UN	70	M				UN	UN	UN	
	Emily	MiL	B	F	UN UN	55	M				TN	UN	UN	
	Derrick, Homer	BiL	B	M	Sep 1884	15	S				MS	UN	UN	Day Laborer
38	Davis, Frank	H	W	M	Feb 1872	28	M	8			MS	AL	AL	Farmer
	Ruben	W	W	F	Nov 1875	24	M	8	1	1	MS	AL	AL	
	Olen	S	W	M	Dec 1897	2	S				MS	MS	MS	
39	Traylor, Loyd S.	H	W	M	Nov 1861	38	M	9			AL	MS	MS	Clerk
	Della	W	W	F	May 1865	35	M	9	4	4	MS	SC	MS	
	Samuel L.	S	W	M	Oct 1892	7	S				MS	AL	MS	
	Sarah L.	D	W	F	Jun 1894	5	S				MS	AL	MS	
	Essa Maud	D	W	F	Jun 1896	3	S				MS	AL	MS	
	Nancy M.	D	W	F	Apr 1900	1/mo	S				MS	AL	MS	
40	Sullivan, Lizzie	H	B	F	Jun 1869	36	Wd				MS	UN	UN	Laundress
41	Robinson, Lou	H	B	F	UN 1866	34	M	UN			AL	UN	AL	Cook
42	Milsaps, John L.	H	W	M	Jan 1851	49	M	15			MS	NC	GA	Carpenter
	Thurseal	W	W	F	UN UN	47	M	15			MS	NC	GA	
43	Alexander, Mary C.	H	W	F	Jul 1849	50	Wd		1	1	MS	NC	VA	
	Ennis	D	W	F	Sep 1867	32	S				MS	NC	VA	
	Coman, Sallie J.	Sis	W	F	Aug 1845	55	S				AL	NC	VA	
	Rebecca	Sis	W	F	Sep 1853	46	S				AL	NC	VA	
44	Dean, H.A.	H	W	M	Mar 1844	56	M	2			TN	TN	TN	Teaching
	S.E.	W	W	F	Sep 1852	48	M	2	2	2	TN	TN	TN	Teaching
	Guy D.	S	W	M	Mar 1877	23	S				TN	TN	TN	Teaching
	Miller, Lillie	Bdr	W	F	Jan 1874	21	S				MS	TN	IN	Stenographer
45	Brown, J.E.	H	W	M	Aug 1867	33	M	3			MS	SC	MS	Teacher
	A.L.	W	W	F	Feb 1875	25	M	3	1	1	MS	NY	MS	
	Anna L.	D	W	F	Jul 1899	10/mo	S				MS	MS	MS	
	Shoemaker, W.	Bdr	W	M	Nov 1875	24	S				MS	AL	MS	Teacher
	Hall, Claud	Bdr	W	M	Nov 1877	22	S				MS	MS	MS	Teacher
	Hill, D.C.	Bdr	W	M	Dec 1881	19	S				MS	MS	MS	
	Wier, V.A.	Bdr	W	M	Dec 1877	22	S				MS	MS	MS	
	Clifton, C.A.	Bdr	W	M	Nov 1885	14	S				MS	MS	MS	
	Barr, B.M.	Bdr	W	M	Dec 1876	23	S				MS	NC	NC	
	Gurney, J.O.	Bdr	W	M	Dec 1881	18	S				MS	TN	MS	
	McMinn, C.H.	Bdr	W	M	Jan 1874	26	S				MS	MS	MS	Teacher
	Houston, L.	Bdr	W	M	Jun 1879	20	S				LA	GA	LA	
	Holmes, P.K.	Bdr	W	M	Mar 1882	18	S				AR	MS	MS	
	Jaynes, D.A.	Bdr	W	M	Mar 1882	17	S				MS	MS	MS	
	Harris, H.L.	Bdr	W	M	Nov 1883	17	S				CA	TN	OH	
	Neal, D.A.	Bdr	W	M	Sep 1861	38	Wd				MS	SC	SC	Teacher
	Church, J.J.	Bdr	W	M	Sep 1878	21	S				MS	MS	MS	
	Hadnett, J.R.	Bdr	W	M	Apr 1878	21	S				MS	MS	NC	
	Kelly, R.P.	Bdr	W	M	May 1875	25	S				MS	SC	MS	Teacher

1	2	3	4	5	6	7	8	9	10	11	12	13	14	15
	Puckett, L.E.	Bdr	W	M	Nov 1882	19	S				MS	SC	SC	
	Fraiser, J.S.	Bdr	W	M	Feb 1879	21	S				MS	TN	MS	
	Sherrill Carrie E.	Bdr	W	F	Dec 1879	19	S				AL	AL	AL	
	O'Dell, Kittie	Bdr	W	F	Feb 1883	17	S				AL	NY	MS	
	Myrtice, Leggett	Bdr	W	F	Feb 1882	18	S				MS	MS	MS	
	Puckett, Ida	Bdr	W	F	Aug 1880	19	S				MS	SC	SC	
46	Harris, L.A.	H	W	M	Jul 1879	20	M				CA	TN	OH	
	J.D.	W	W	F	Feb 1880	20	M				MS	NY	OH	
	Lennard, Mary	Bdr	W	F	Dec 1882	18	S				MS	AL	MS	
	Turnage, Quinona	Bdr	W	F	Jan 1882	18	S				MS	MS	AL	
	Davis, Edna	Bdr	W	F	Jan 1882	18	S				MS	MS	MS	
	Anthony, L.E.	Bdr	W	F	Nov 1879	20	S				TN	TN	TN	Music Teacher
47	McIntire, L.P.N.	H	W	M	Jun 1852	57	Wd		1	1	NC	NC	NC	Physical Cult.
	Z.E.	D	W	F	Feb 1883	17	S				MS	NC	NC	
	Clower, May	Bdr	W	F	Oct 1878	21	S				MS	MS	MS	
	McCauley, Addie	Bdr	W	F	Mar 1880	20	S				MS	MS	MS	
	Williams, Ada	Bdr	W	F	Un 1880	20	S				MS	GA	AL	
	Coman, James G.	Nep	W	M	Apr 1885	15	S				MS	MS	NY	
	Celia R.	Nce	W	F	Dec 1887	13	Wd				MS	MS	NY	
	Jane	UN	B	F	Jun 1832	67	UN				AL	AL	AL	
48	Stone, Mary G.	H	W	F	Aug 1841	59	Wd				AL	NC	VA	
	Jenny	Adp D	W	F	Jul 1879	20	S				TN	TN	TN	
	Maggie	Adp D	W	F	Oct 1882	17	S				TN	TN	TN	
49	Reed, E.N.	H	W	M	Apr 1864	66	M	10			TN	NC	NC	Clerk
	Anna Lou	W	W	F	Aug 1866	33	M	10	3	2	MS	VA	AL	
	Emmett M.	S	W	M	Nov 1891	9	S				MS	TN	MS	
	Mattie Cook	D	W	F	Dec 1897	3	S				MS	TN	MS	
	Scruggs, Mat	Nurse	B	M	UN UN	14	S				MS	MS	MS	Nurse
	Marrett, W.B.	Bdr	W	M	Dec 1864	30	S				MS	AL	MS	Merchant
50	Pyle, J.A.E.	H	W	M	Oct 1858	41	M	10			AL	GA	GA	Attorney
	Alice H.	W	W	F	Oct 1870	29	M	10	4	3	MS	AL	AL	
	Ida Lee	D	W	F	Nov 1893	6	S				MS	AL	MS	
	Evlin	D	W	F	Sep 1895	4	S				MS	AL	MS	
	Calvin H.	S	W	M	Sep 1899	8/mo	S				MS	AL	MS	
	Coman, Etta	Ser	B	F	Jan 1876	24	S				MS	AL	AL	Cooking
51	Nance, E.E.	H	W	F	Nov 1831	68	M		8	5	GA	NC	SC	
	Fannie B.	D	W	F	Aug 1868	31	S				MS	AL	GA	Dress Maker
	Long, Jesse	Ser	B	F	UN UN	11	S				MS	AL	AL	Servant
52	Alexander, J.F.	H	W	M	Sep 1871	28	M	5			AL	AL	AL	Physician
	Mary Lane	W	W	F	Sep 1874	25	M	5	2	2	AL	AL	AL	
	Turner	D	W	F	Oct 1895	4	S				MS	AL	AL	
	Mary A.	D	W	F	May 1900	10/mo	S				MS	AL	AL	
53	Curry, Esten D.	H	W	M	Jun 1865	34	M	4			TN	UN	UN	Drummer
	J.E.	W	W	F	Aug 1873	26	M	4	0	0	AL	AL	AL	
	Castleberry, Rufus	Bdr	W	M	Mar 1832	68	Wd				GA	GA	GA	Town Marshall
54	Williams, J.B.	H	W	M	Aug 1872	28	M	2			MS	NC	MS	Clerk
	M.L.	W	W	F	Feb 1876	24	M	2			MS	MS	MS	
	Laura E.	D	W	F	UN 1899	1	S				MS	MS	MS	
	Dewoody, L.M.	MiL	W	F	Nov 1849	50	Wd		7	2	TX	NC	NC	
	Brown, Willie	Ser	B	M	UN UN	13	S				MS	MS	MS	Servant
55	Lyle, Mattie, Mrs	H	W	F	Jul 1837	62	Wd				MS	NC	NC	Boarding House
	Moore, Della	Sis	W	F	Aug 1848	52	S				TX	NC	NC	

1	2	3	4	5	6	7	8	9	10	11	12	13	14	15
56	Watson, M.C.	H	W	F	Aug 1854	45	Wd		6	4	AL	TN	TN	
	Mattie	D	W	F	Jan 1882	18	S				AL	SC	AL	
	Willie C.	S	W	M	Jun 1885	14	S				MS	SC	AL	
	Marilla H.	D	W	F	Mar 1890	10	S				MS	SC	AL	
	Oscar E.	S	W	M	Nov 1894	6	S				MS	SC	AL	
57	Moon, W.J.	H	W	M	Dec 1831	68	M	35			AL	NC	TN	Boarding House
	T.A.	W	W	F	Apr 1833	65	M	35	1	1	AL	AL	TN	
	J.N.	S	W	M	Jan 1869	31	S				MS	AL	AL	Merchant
58	Hill, O.L.	H	W	M	Mar 1878	22	M	1			TN	TN	TN	Electrician
	Minnie	W	W	F	Aug 1879	20	M	1	0	0	MO	MO	MO	
57	McRae, B.F.	H	W	M	Sep 1851	48	M	25			MS	UN	UN	Drygds Clerk
	E. Jimmie	W	W	F	Jun 1855	44	M	25	9	7	MS	AL	AL	
	Ben F.	S	W	M	Apr 1879	21	S				TN	MS	MS	
	Ottie	D	W	F	May 1885	15	S				MS	MS	MS	
	Tom	S	W	M	Feb 1888	12	S				MS	MS	MS	
	Mable O.	D	W	F	Apr 1892	8	S				MS	MS	MS	
	Kenneth	S	W	M	Apr 1897	3	S				MS	MS	MS	
	McRae, Kenneth F.	Cou	W	M	Mar 1869	31	S				MS	NC	NC	Dentistry
60	Marckle, M.L.	H	W	M	Mar 1850	50	M	19			PA	UN	UN	
	J.E.	W	W	F	Mar 1860	40	M	19	3	3	IN	NJ	NJ	
	B.C.	S	W	M	Oct 1876	23	S				IL	PA	IN	
	Maud R.	D	W	F	Mar 1878	22	S				IL	PA	IN	
	Julia P.	D	W	F	Jan 1885	15	S				IL	PA	IN	
	McRae, Clary	Ser	B	F	UN UN	13	S				MS	MS	MS	Servant
61	Merell, Ed	H	W	F	Dec 1838	61	M	39			AL	KY	TN	Cotton Buyer
	Ada E.	W	W	F	Dec 1841	58	M	39	5	5	TN	Ire	TN	
	Birdie	D	W	F	Jun 1885	14	S				MS	AL	TN	
62	McDonald, T.M.	H	W	M	Oct 1872	28	M	1			TN	TN	TN	Drummer
	L.M.	W	W	F	Apr 1876	24	M	1	1	1	MS	AL	TN	
	Mildred V.	D	W	F	May 1900	0/mo	S				MS	TN	MS	
63	Hodges, W.A.	H	W	M	Sep 1856	44	Wd				MS	TN	AL	Physician
	Southall, M.L.	Cou	W	F	Sep 1850	50	Wd				AL	NC	GA	
64	Hubbard, C.I.	H	W	F	Apr 1838	61	Wd		10	6	GA	NC	SC	
	Sallie A.	D	W	F	Feb 1866	34	S				MS	SC	GA	
	Clara	D	W	F	Dec 1877	22	S				MS	SC	GA	
	Hern D.	S	W	M	Jan 1880	20	S				MS	SC	GA	Meat Mkt.
65	Krouce, A.A.	H	W	F	Dec 1841	58	Wd		2	2	Ger	Ger	Ger	
66	Howard, T. J.	H	W	M	Feb 1863	37	M	7			GA	GA	GA	
	Alice A.	W	W	F	Oct 1873	26	M	7	1	1	MS	Ger	Ger	
	Henry H.	S	W	M	Jan 1897	3	S				MS	GA	MS	
67	James, Sarah C.	H	W	F	Feb 1837	63	Wd				AL	VA	VA	
	Coffee, A.N.	Sis	W	F	May 1826	74	Wd				AL	VA	VA	
68	Hearn, Henry	H	W	M	Jan 1837	63	M	34			AL	GA	TN	Farmer
	Margaret A.	W	W	F	Sep 1844	55	M	34	4	4	SC	SC	SC	
	Ollie Alice	D	W	F	Apr 1877	23	S				MS	SC	AL	
	Henry G.	S	W	M	Nov 1882	17	S				MS	SC	AL	
	Oscar Lee	S	W	M	Jun 1885	14	S				MS	SC	AL	
	Mary R.	D	W	F	UN 1888	12	S				MS	SC	AL	
	Payne, P.P.	Bdr	W	M	Mar 1876	24	S				MS	AL	AL	Merchant
	Reed, George C.	Bdr	W	M	Dec 1878	21	S				MS	MS	MS	Drug Clerk

1	2	3	4	5	6	7	8	9	10	11	12	13	14	15
69	Derrick, Clay	H	B	M	May 1869	29	M	6			MS	TN	TN	Day Laborer
	Percilla	W	B	F	UN UN	27	M	6	1	1	GA	GA	GA	Cook
	Essa	D	B	F	Sep 1894	5	S				MS	MS	GA	
	McGee, W.H.	Bdr	W	M	Dec 1877	22	S				MS	MS	MS	
70	Aldridge, Canvass	H	B	F	UN UN	42	Wd		11	8	MS	UN	UN	Cook
	Mollie	D	B	F	UN UN	30	Wd		4	1	UN	UN	UN	Cook
	Dora	D	B	F	UN UN	13	S				MS	UN	UN	Laundress
	Rosanna	D	B	F	UN UN	15	S				MS	UN	UN	Nurse
	Anna	D	B	F	UN UN	13	S				MS	UN	UN	Nurse
	Willis	S	B	M	UN UN	10	S				MS	UN	UN	Hotel Master
71	Moore, Jno.	H	B	M	Mar 1865	35	M	10			MS	MS	MS	Teamster
	Julia	W	B	F	UN UN	27	M	10	4	3	MS	GA	MS	
	Lylia	D	B	F	UN UN	8	S				MS	MS	MS	
	Jno Archey	S	B	M	UN UN	4	S				MS	MS	MS	
	Lawrence	S	B	F	UN UN	1	S				MS	MS	MS	
72	Harris, Dave	H	B	M	UN UN	UN	S	5			AL	UN	UN	Day Laborer
	Margaret	W	B	F	Un UN	50	M	5	2	2	AL	AL	AL	
	White, Emps	SS	B	M	UN UN	15	S				MS	AL	AL	Day Laborer
	Jake	SS	B	M	UN UN	UN	S				MS	AL	AL	Day Laborer
73	McKnight, R.L.	H	W	M	Apr 1840	60	M	30			TN	NC	TN	Clerk
	Elsie	W	W	F	Dec 1848	51	M	30	2	2	AL	TN	AL	
	Penn, Patty Lou	Bdr	W	F	Mar 1877	23	S				TN	TN	AL	Music Teacher
74	Herrig, Tilman	H	W	M	Mar 1820	80	Wd				GA	UN	NC	Farmer
75	Jourdan, Hattie	H	B	F	UN UN	60	M		12	4	AL	UN	UN	Laundress
	Alice	D	B	F	UN UN	22	S				MS	UN	AL	
76	Patterson, Phil W.	H	W	M	Nov 1845	54	M	UN			AL	OH	AL	Chan.Ct.Clerk
	Mary A.	W	W	F	May 1845	55	M	UN			MS	TN	TN	
	Drewry, C.M.	Bdr	W	F	Dec 1881	19	S				MS	GA	GA	Chan.Ct.Clerk
	A.C.	Bdr	W	M	Feb 1879	21	S				GA	GA	GA	
	Whitesides, Mary	UN	B	F	UN UN	20	M	UN	1	6	MS	MS	MS	Cook
77	Haney, J.D.	H	W	M	Mar 1877	22	M	1			MS	SC	TN	Teacher
	Hassie	W	W	F	Sep 1879	20	M	1	1	1	MS	AL	SC	
	Rachel	D	W	F	Oct 1899	7/mo	S				MS	MS	MS	
	Little, C.N.	Bdr	W	M	Sep 1818	72	S				NC	NC	NC	Gsp.Minister
78	McKinney, ED	H	W	M	Aug 1870	29	M	4			MS	MS	TN	Merchant
	Anna T.	W	W	F	Mar 1874	26	M	4	2	2	TN	TN	TN	
	Martha	D	W	F	Nov 1897	2	S				MS	MS	TN	
	Elvina	D	W	F	Jan 1899	1	S				MS	MS	TN	
79	Ellis, Walter B.	H	W	M	Sep 1852	47	M	15			TN	VA	AL	Lawyer
	Sallie W.	W	W	F	Sep 1855	44	M	15	4	3	MS	AL	AL	
	B. Clopton	S	W	M	Feb 1888	12	S				MS	TN	MS	
	Marnie	D	W	F	Aug 1889	10	S				MS	TN	MS	
	Bruce	S	W	M	Jul 1891	8	S				MS	TN	MS	
80	Jourdan, Jno. W.	H	W	M	Jan 1858	42	M	18			MS	NC	MS	Bank Cashier
	Anna D.	W	W	F	Jan 1861	39	M	18	4	1	AL	UN	UN	
	Anna E.	D	W	F	Dec 1885	14	S				MS	MS	AL	
81	Curtin, Robert W.	H	W	M	Jun 1850	40	M	17			AL	VA	AL	Merchant
	Sallie V.	W	W	F	May 1859	41	M	17	5	5	MS	SC	MS	
	Ola D.	D	W	F	Jan 1884	16	S				MS	AL	MS	
	Sarah V.	D	W	F	Apr 1885	15	S				MS	AL	MS	
	Robert W.	S	W	M	Feb 1888	12	S				MS	AL	MS	

1	2	3	4	5	6	7	8	9	10	11	12	13	14	15
	Lucy W.	D	W	F	Sep 1892	7	S				MS	AL	MS	
	Sam Candler	S	W	M	May 1896	4	S				MS	AL	MS	
82	Parker, William	H	B	M	UN UN	UN	UN				MS	MS	MS	
	Martha	W	B	F	UN UN	28	M		5	3	MS	MS	MS	Laundress
	Pauline	D	B	F	UN UN	7	S				MS	MS	MS	
	Edward	S	B	M	UN UN	4	S				MS	MS	MS	
	Louverta	D	B	F	UN UN	2	S				MS	MS	MS	
	Harris, Mary	SiL	B	F	UN UN	28	Wd		3	3	MS	MS	MS	
83	Johnson, W.S.	H	W	M	Jul 1864	35	M	12			KY	UN	UN	R R Conductor
	J.E.	W	W	F	Oct 1866	33	M	12	3	3	TN	KY	KY	Kpg Boarders
	Henry	S	W	M	Dec 1888	11	S				TX	KY	TN	
	Lella C.	D	W	F	Jul 1891	8	S				MS	KY	TN	
	Mildred C.	D	W	F	Dec 1894	5	S				MS	KY	TN	
	Bridges, M.L.	MiL	W	F	Feb 1842	54	Wd		3	3	KY	VA	KY	
	Parnell, O. H.	Bdr	W	M	Dec 1871	28	S				AL	AL	AL	Dentistry
	Moore, George W.	Bdr	W	M	Jun 1841	58	Wd				MS	AL	TN	Farmer
	Oliver, J.M.	Bdr	W	M	Jun 1863	36	M	1			IL	TN	KY	Day Laborer
84	Leatherwood, W.B.	H	W	M	Sep 1853	46	M	20			MS	SC	GA	Prop. Hotel
	Ida A.	W	W	F	Sep 1862	37	M	20	2	2	MS	GA	GA	
	Walter S.	S	W	M	Dec 1883	16	S				MS	MS	MS	
	Paul	S	W	M	Jun 1886	13	S				MS	MS	MS	
	Buckinham, George	Bdr	B	M	Feb 1880	20	S				AL	AL	AL	Hotel porter
	Connell, V.L.	Bdr	W	F	Oct 1870	29	M	4	2	1	WI	VT	ME	Boarder
	Jefferson	Bdr	W	M	May 1899	1	S				MS	MS	UN	
85	McKinney, W.W.	H	W	M	Jul 1872	27	M	2			MS	MS	TN	Merchant
	Dizzie M.	W	W	F	Apr 1876	24	M	2	0	0	MS	Ire	MS	
86	Scruggs, A.T.	H	W	M	May 1845	55	M	17			MS	TN	UN	Farmer
	S.B.	W	W	F	Feb 1859	41	M	17	3	2	GA	MS	OH	
	Albert W.	S	W	M	Dec 1894	5	S				MS	MS	GA	
	Mary E.	D	W	F	Jan 1899	1	S				MS	MS	GA	
	Bell, Elizabeth	Aunt	W	F	Jan 1836	64	Wd				OH	OH	VA	
87	Candler, Milton	H	W	M	Aug 1879	20	M	0			MS	GA	FL	Clerk
	Lizzie	W	W	F	Aug 1880	19	M	0			MS	MS	TN	
88	Collin, Thomas L.	H	W	M	Nov 1824	75	Wd				NC	VA	NC	
89	Harris, Norman	H	B	M	UN UN	41	M	16			AL	UN	AL	Day Laborer
	Rebecca	W	B	F	Apr UN	38	M	16	6	5	AL	UN	AL	
	Dan	S	B	M	Jul UN	14	S				AL	Al	AL	
	Mary	D	B	F	UN UN	11	S				MS	AL	AL	
	George	S	B	M	UN UN	9	S				MS	AL	AL	
	John B.	S	B	M	UN UN	6	S				MS	AL	AL	
	Willard	S	B	F	UN UN	4	S				MS	AL	AL	
	Goodloe, Anna	Cou	B	F	UN UN	26	M	3			AL	AL	AL	Cook
	Warrine	Cou	B	M	UN UN	4	S				MS	UN	AL	
	Muson	Cou	B	M	UN UN	2	S				MS	UN	AL	
90	Ford, Ann	H	W	F	Apr 1835	65	S				AL	VA	NC	
91	Bailess, Jas. F.	H	W	M	Apr 1878	22	M	4			AL	UN	MS	Carpenter
	Lillie	W	W	F	Jun 1877	22	M	4	2	2	AL	AL	AL	
	Olive	D	W	F	Dec 1898	1	S				MS	AL	AL	
	Robert A.	S	W	M	Nov 1899	1/mo	S				AL	AL	AL	
92	Aldridge, Porter	H	B	M	UN UN	70	M	3			TX	UN	UN	Day Laborer
	Georgia Ann	W	B	F	UN UN	50	M	3	11	7	AL	UN	AL	Laundress
	Hamp	S	B	M	UN UN	17	S				MS	AL	AL	Day Laborer

1	2	3	4	5	6	7	8	9	10	11	12	13	14	15
	Clinton	SS	B	M	UN UN	14	S				MS	MS	AL	Day Laborer
	Dowdy	SS	B	M	UN UN	11	S				MS	MS	AL	
	Frada	SD	B	F	UN UN	10	S				MS	MS	AL	
93	Ricks, Minnie	H	B	F	UN UN	17	S		1	1	AL	UN	UN	Laundress
	Willie	S	B	M	UN UN	1	S				MS	MS	AL	
94	Mathews, D.O.	H	W	M	Mar 1868	31	M	5			AL	MS	MS	Merchant
	Florence A.	W	W	F	Feb 1876	24	M	5	1	1	MS	AL	MS	
	Edwin	S	W	M	Feb 1896	4	S				MS	AL	MS	
	Price, Mattie L.	Bdr	W	F	Feb 1855	45	Wd		0	0	MS	TN	TN	Prof. Nurse
95	Collin, Edie	H	B	F	UN UN	26	S		4	3	AL	UN	UN	Cook
	Sallie M.	D	B	F	Dec 1894	5	S				AL	UN	AL	
	Fred	D	B	F	Dec 1896	3	S				MS	UN	AL	
	Anna	D	B	F	Feb 1899	4/mo	S				MS	UN	AL	
96	Long, Henry	H	B	M	Feb 1876	24	M	4			MS	UN	AL	Cook
	Bulus	W	B	F	Mar 1880	20	M	4	3	3	AL	UN	AL	Cook
	Ben	S	B	M	Dec 1896	3	S				MS	MS	AL	
	Jake	S	B	M	May 1898	2	S				MS	MS	AL	
	Anna	D	B	M	Aug 1899	3/mo	S				MS	MS	AL	
97	Jordan, Ben	H	B	M	UN UN	31	M	9			MS	UN	UN	
	Fannie	W	B	F	Un Un	28	M	9	0	0	MS	VA	AL	
98	Brown, Thomas L.	H	W	M	Feb 1848	52	M	30			GA	TN	SC	Merchant
	Lucy A.	W	W	F	Oct 1848	51	M	30	3	2	MS	TN	TN	
	Emma	D	W	F	Sep 1872	28	S				MS	GA	MS	Clerk
	Will S.	S	W	M	Sep 1877	22	S				MS	GA	MS	Clerk
99	Pope, Will	H	B	M	UN UN	24	M	4			AL	UN	AL	Porter RR
	Anna	W	B	F	UN UN	25	M	4			MS	UN	UN	Laundress
100	Weaver, Idonia	H	W	F	Jul 1872	27	S				MS	VA	AL	Dress Maker
	Agnes	Sis	W	F	Jun 1878	21	S				MS	VA	AL	
	Bertia	Sis	W	F	Apr 1883	17	S				MS	VA	AL	
	Forest	Bro	W	M	Jan 1885	15	S				MS	VA	AL	Clerk
	Jessie	Sis	W	F	Mar 1887	13	S				MS	VA	AL	
101	Selman, Jack	H	B	M	Oct 1859	40	M	9			AL	UN	UN	RR Brakeman
	Emma	W	B	F	Mar 1861	39	M	9	1	0	AL	VA	AL	
102	Mars, James	H	W	M	Jan 1867	32	M	8			MS	TN	AL	RR Conductor
	Lida	W	W	F	Aug 1876	23	M	8	4	3	MS	KY	AL	
	Jimmie	S	W	M	Jul 1893	6	S				AL	MS	MS	
	Hettie May	D	W	F	Oct 1895	4	S				AL	MS	MS	
	Irene	D	W	F	Mar 1898	2	S				AL	MS	AL	
103	Reed, Isabelle	H	W	F	Feb 1849	51	Wd		5	5	MS	SC	SC	
	Carrie	D	W	F	Mar 1878	22	S				MS	AL	MS	Bank Bkkpr
	Anna Bell	D	W	F	Jun 1881	19	S				MS	AL	MS	
	Maud	D	W	F	Dec 1883	16	S				MS	AL	MS	
	Carmack	S	W	M	Jan 1886	14	S				MS	AL	MS	
104	Bean, C.A. Mrs	H	W	F	Jul 1840	70	Wd		4	4	TN	TN	TN	
	R.W.	S	W	M	Jan 1873	27	M	3			AL	TN	IL	Clerk
	S.C.	DiL	W	F	Mar 1886	19	M	3	2	2	AL	SC	AL	
	Anna May	D	W	F	Dec 1897	2	S				AL	AL	AL	
	Millie A.	D	W	F	Sep 1899	8/mo	S				MS	AL	AL	
105	Ervin, Minnie	H	W	F	Dec 1880	19	S				MS	AL	AL	
	Lillin	Sis	W	F	Jul 1884	15	S				MS	AL	AL	

1	2	3	4	5	6	7	8	9	10	11	12	13	14	15
	Oscar	Bro	W	M	May 1889	11	S				MS	AL	AL	
	Willie	Cou	W	F	Sep 1880	19	S				AL	AL	AL	
106	Deardolph, Kent	H	W	F	Aug 1837	62	Wd		2	1	TN	VA	VA	
	Mattie	D	W	F	Jun UN	37	S				TN	PA	TN	Dress Maker
107	Rutledge, R.T.	H	W	M	Mar 1856	44	M	17			MS	UN	UN	Clerk
	Dixie	W	W	F	Aug 1862	37	M	17	6	5	MS	VA	VA	
	Clara	D	W	F	Jul 1886	13	S				MS	MS	MS	
	Lillian	D	W	F	Oct 1889	10	S				MS	MS	MS	
	Velma	D	W	F	Sep 1891	8	S				MS	MS	MS	
	Terrell R.	S	W	M	Dec 1895	4	S				MS	MS	MS	
	Buell D.	S	W	M	Feb 1900	2/mo	S				MS	MS	MS	
108	Anderson, Nancy E.	H	W	F	Jan 1832	68	Wd		8	4	VA	VA	VA	
	Phelps, Carry	Bdr	W	F	Feb 1878	22	S				UN	TN	AL	Dress Maker
109	Williams, Jno. W.	H	W	M	Feb 1837	63	M	7			NC	NC	NC	Merchant
	M.E.	W	W	F	Mar 1845	56	M	7	6	6	MS	TN	SC	
	May Belle	D	W	F	Mar 1874	26	S				MS	NC	MS	Music Teacher
	Frank	S	W	M	Jan 1877	23	S				MS	NC	MS	Clerk
	Marcus	S	W	M	Mar 1889	20	S				MS	NC	MS	Clerk
	Lizzie	D	W	F	Apr 1882	18	S				MS	NC	MS	
	Eula	D	W	F	Mar 1884	15	S				MS	NC	MS	
110	Martin, Berry L.	H	W	M	Aug 1862	37	M	13			AL	AL	AL	RR Agent
	Mary P.	W	W	F	May 1865	35	M	13	1	1	AL	GA	AL	
	Berry L.	S	W	M	Nov 1887	12	S				AL	AL	AL	
111	Roberson, Jno. T.	H	W	M	Nov 1859	40	M	12			MS	UN	UN	Teacher
	Lizzie E.	W	W	F	Jun 1868	31	M	12	3	1	MS	SC	MS	
	Minnie L.	D	W	F	Sep 1889	10	S				MS	MS	MS	
	Brown, Middleton	Unc	W	M	May 1833	67	S				SC	SC	SC	Capitalist
112	Stephenson, M.S.	H	W	F	Sep 1839	60	Wd	1	0	0	MS	SC	TN	
	Miller, Fannie	Nce	W	F	Jul 1875	24	S				MS	NC	MS	
113	Jourdan, James C.	H	W	M	May 1870	30	M	11			MS	NC	MS	
	Ada	W	W	F	May 1868	28	M	11	5	1	MS	MS	MS	
	Talmer	S	W	M	Mar 1891	9	S				MS	MS	MS	
	Almer	D	W	F	Sep 1893	7	S				MS	MS	MS	
	Olen	S	W	M	Jan 1895	5	S				MS	MS	MS	
	Jimmie	S	W	M	Apr 1897	3	S				MS	MS	MS	
114	Rutledge, Lizzie	H	W	F	Sep 1852	47	S				MS	SC	SC	
	Jessie	Sis	W	F	Jan 1854	46	S				MS	SC	SC	
115	Ramsey, Sidney	H	W	M	Aug 1869	30	M	4			AL	AL	AL	RR Sect. Boss
	Ida	W	W	F	Jun 1871	28	M	4	1	1	KY	KY	GA	
	Milton	S	W	M	Jul 1899	10/mo	S				MS	AL	KY	
116	Sims, Mack	H	B	M	Jun 1843	56	M	31			TN	UN	NC	Day Laborer
	Hester A.	W	B	F	UN UN	47	M	31	10	8	AL	VA	AL	
	Lela	D	B	F	UN UN	18	S				AL	TN	AL	Cook
	Lily	S	B	F	UN UN	15	S				AL	TN	AL	Day Laborer
	Elizabeth	D	B	F	UN UN	14	S				AL	TN	AL	Nurse
117	Powell, J.D.	H	W	M	Aug 1861	38	M	13			MS	UN	MS	Merchant
	Julie	W	W	F	Jun 1868	31	M	13	6	4	MS	TN	MS	
	Nina	D	W	F	Feb 1890	10	S				MS	MS	MS	
	Tom W.	S	W	M	May 1895	5	S				MS	MS	MS	
	Christeen	D	W	F	Jun 1897	3	S				MS	MS	MS	
	Julia E.	D	W	F	May 1899	1	S				MS	MS	MS	

1	2	3	4	5	6	7	8	9	10	11	12	13	14	15
118	Mosier, Lee N.	H	W	M	Aug 1875	24	M	3			MS	MS	MS	Clerk
	Etta F.	W	W	F	Feb 1878	21	M	3	2	2	MS	MS	MS	
	Clio S.	D	W	F	Aug 1888	1	S				MS	MS	MS	
	Cecil	S	W	M	Nov 1899	6/mo	S				MS	MS	MS	
119	Archer, Mary	H	W	F	Mar 1870	30	Wd		3	2	MS	AL	MS	
	Ethel	D	W	F	Sep 1893	6	S				MS	AL	MS	
	Floyd	S	W	M	Dec 1896	3	S				MS	AL	MS	
	Woods, Sallie	Aunt	W	F	Jan 1824	76	Wd				TN	SC	AL	
120	Akers, Jeff	H	W	M	Sep 1841	58	M	32			GA	GA	VA	
	M.A.	W	W	F	Jan 1851	49	M	32	14	12	GA	GA	GA	
	Darling	S	W	M	Aug 1869	30	S				MS	GA	GA	Farmer
	Sallie	D	W	F	May 1871	28	S				MS	GA	GA	Teacher
	Bonnie	D	W	F	Jun 1875	24	S				AL	GA	GA	Teacher
	Jim	S	W	M	Sep 1877	22	S				AL	GA	GS	Drummer
	Jeffie	D	W	F	Nov 1879	20	S				AL	GA	GA	Teacher
	Charley	S	W	M	Apr 1882	18	S				AL	GA	GA	
	Myrtie	D	W	F	Feb 1884	16	S				AL	GA	GA	
	George	S	W	M	Feb 1886	14	S				AL	GA	GA	
	Twala	D	W	F	Jan 1888	12	S				AL	GA	GA	
	Millie	D	W	F	Jul 1871	9	S				AL	GA	GA	
	John	S	W	M	Feb 1893	7	S				AL	GA	GA	
	Tom	S	W	M	Jun 1895	4	S				MS	GA	GA	
121	Ross, Daniel S.	H	W	M	Nov 1866	33	M	3			MS	SC	TN	Teacher
	Elsie B.	W	W	F	Aug 1880	19	M	3	1	1	TN	SC	TN	
	Howard C.	S	W	M	Sep 1899	8/mo	S				MS	MS	TN	
122	Walker, Ed	H	B	M	Nov 1864	56	M	2			MS	MS	MS	Brick Mason
	Bell	W	B	F	UN 1874	24	M	2	3	3	MS	UN	UN	
	Eddie Bell	D	B	F	Sep 1898	1	S				MS	MS	MS	
	William C.	S	B	M	Dec 1899	7/mo	S				MS	MS	MS	
	Jones, Sam	SS	B	M	UN UN	5	S				TN	UN	MS	
123	Candler, E.S.	H	W	M	Dec 1838	61	M	40			GA	GA	GA	Lawyer
	Julia B.	W	W	F	Feb 1842	57	M	40	5	3	GA	GA	GA	
124	Dean, Sam M.	H	W	M	Oct 1826	73	M	44			SC	SC	SC	Merchant
	Millie	W	W	F	Apr 1839	61	M	44	11	10	MS	NC	TN	
	Whit W.	S	W	M	Sep 1873	26	S				MS	SC	TN	Telegraph Op.
	Lawrence L.	S	W	M	Apr 1875	25	S				MS	SC	TN	Farmer
	Orian O.	S	W	M	Feb 1880	20	S				MS	SC	TN	Farmer
	Gertrude	D	W	F	Jan 1882	18	S				MS	SC	TN	
	Swaine, Nels	Ser	B	M	UN UN	60	S				AL	UN	UN	Day Laborer
125	Wimbish, Jay	H	B	M	Apr 1865	35	M	13			MS	UN	AL	Day Laborer
	Martha	W	B	F	UN UN	28	M	13	4	4	MS	UN	UN	Laundress
	Clara	D	B	F	UN UN	8	S				MS	MS	AL	
	Ginnett	D	B	F	UN UN	5	S				MS	MS	MS	
	Jay	S	B	M	UN UN	3	S				MS	MS	MS	
	Mattie	D	B	F	UN UN	1	S				MS	MS	MS	
126	Patterson, Ben F.	H	W	M	Sep 1858	40	M	13			AL	GA	TN	Drummer
	Nettie	W	W	F	Feb 1868	32	M	13	4	4	MS	UN	MS	
	May	D	W	F	Oct 1888	11	S				MS	AL	MS	
	Blanche	D	W	F	Mar 1891	9	S				MS	AL	MS	
	Phillip	S	W	M	Feb 1894	6	S				MS	AL	MS	
	Arthur	S	W	M	Feb 1896	4	S				MS	AL	MS	
127	Whitworth, Ida	H	W	F	Aug 1858	41	Wd		3	1	MS	AL	AL	Millinery
	Shelby	S	W	M	Oct 1892	7	S				AL	AL	MS	

1	2	3	4	5	6	7	8	9	10	11	12	13	14	15
128	Hubbard, James B.	H	W	M	Oct 1860	39	M	9			MS	UN	GA	Farmer
	Anna B.	W	W	F	Oct 1860	39	M	9	4	4	MS	SC	MS	
	Grace V.	D	W	F	Sep 1892	7	S				MS	MS	MS	
	Cecil D.	S	W	M	Aug 1894	5	S				MS	MS	MS	
	Chester	S	W	M	Aug 1896	3	S				MS	MS	MS	
	John	S	W	M	Sep 1898	1	S				MS	MS	MS	
129	Carmack, Frank T.	H	W	M	Nov 1854	45	M	16			MS	AL	TN	Physician
	Willa	W	W	F	May 1868	32	M	16	3	2	MS	NC	MS	
	Dora	D	W	F.	Sep 1885	14	S				MS	MS	MS	
	Ruth	D	W	F	Dec 1887	12	S				MS	MS	MS	
130	Haney, Taswell	H	W	M	Jan 1868	32	M	8			TN	SC	SC	Teacher
	Mattie	W	W	F	Sep 1867	33	M	8	4	4	MS	TN	TN	
	Rhoda	D	W	F	Aug 1893	6	S				MS	TN	MS	
	Mary	D	W	F	Oct 1895	5	S				MS	TN	MS	
	Birdie	D	W	F	Aug 1896	3	S				MS	TN	MS	
	Taswell P.	S	W	M	Apr 1899	1	S				MS	TN	MS	
	Carpidge	Bdr	W	F	Dec 1836	63	Wd		1		MS	VA	NC	
131	Majors, Lany	H	B	F	UN UN	60	Wd		15	6	AL	UN	UN	Laundress
	Josie	D	B	F	UN UN	30	Wd		4	2	AL	UN	UN	
	Stalby, Sophia	D	B	F	UN UN	26	Wd		3	1	AL	UN	UN	
	Thompson, Mary	GD	B	F	UN UN	12	S				MS	UN	AL	
	Elma	GS	B	M	UN UN	7	S				MS	UN	AL	
	Stalby, Olivia	GD	B	F	UN UN	3	S				AL	UN	AL	
132	Barber, George A.	H	W	M	May 1825	75	M	49			TN	NC	VA	Farmer
	Virginia L.	W	W	F	Nov 1832	67	M	49	6	1	TN	UN	UN	
	Kemp, Wallis B.	GS	W	M	Dec 1887	15	S				MS	KY	TN	
	Robb M.	GS	W	M	Aug 1889	10	S				TN	KY	TN	
	Neblett, Horrace	Nep	W	M	UN UN	24	UN				MS	TN	TN	
133	McAlister, William	H	W	M	Feb 1856	44	M	16			SC	SC	SC	Farmer
	Lassie	W	W	F	Jan 1866	34	M	16	8	8	AL	GA	GA	
	Pauline	D	W	F	Apr 1885	15	S				AL	SC	GA	
	Dora	D	W	F	Jan 1887	13	S				AL	SC	AL	
	Gus	S	W	M	Mar 1889	11	S				MS	SC	AL	
	Hughie	S	W	M	Apr 1891	9	S				MS	SC	AL	
	William	S	W	M	Jun 1893	6	S				MS	SC	AL	
	Ward	S	W	M	Jan 1895	5	S				MS	SC	AL	
	Harry	S	W	M	Dec 1896	3	S				MS	SC	AL	
	Fannie	D	W	F	Oct 1899	7/mo	S				MS	SC	AL	
134	Smith, Lillie	H	B	F	May 1869	31	Wd				MS	UN	AL	Cook
	Bell, Dolly	Bdr	B	F	UN UN	70	Wd				UN	UN	UN	
135	Abanathy, Kate	H	B	F	Dec UN	29	Wd		4	3	MS	AL	MS	Cook
	Mary	D	B	F	Oct UN	13	S				AL	TN	MS	
	George	S	B	M	UN UN	6	S				MS	TN	MS	
	Ester	S	B	M	UN UN	5/mo	S				MS	TN	MS	
136	Johnson, Josie	H	W	F	Dec 1866	33	S				MS	AL	TN	
	Jennie	Sis	W	F	Dec 1864	35	S				MS	AL	TN	
	McCrackin, Alvin	Nce	W	F	Jun 1894	8	S				MS	AL	MS	
137	Davis, Sabry	H	B	F	UN UN	65	Wd		8	7	SC	UN	UN	Laundress
	Gussie	GD	B	F	UN UN	13	S				UN	UN	UN	
	Ida	GD	B	F	UN UN	10	S				UN	UN	UN	
138	Moody, Josephine	H	B	F	UN UN	55	Wd		3	2	TN	UN	VA	
	Marks, Hattie	GD	B	F	UN UN	13	S				MS	UN	UN	Laundress

1	2	3	4	5	6	7	8	9	10	11	12	13	14	15
139	Tumage, W.	H	W	M	Aug 1858	41	M	18			MS	UN	UN	Minister
	Mary A.	W	W	F	Apr 1866	31	M	18	12	4	TN	NC	SC	
	Mayoma	D	W	F	Sep 1887	12	S				TX	MS	TN	
	Lovie Lou	D	W	F	Jul 1894	5	S				AR	MS	TN	
	Myrtle Toland	D	W	F	Apr 1895	4	S				AR	MS	TN	
	Ruth C.	D	W	F	Sep 1897	2	S				MS	MS	TN	
140	Hamilton, Ida	H	W	F	May 1858	42	M		6	6	MS	PA	SC	
	Oscar	S	W	M	Mar 1882	17	S				MS	TN	MS	Farmer
	Ora	D	W	F	Feb 1885	15	S				MS	TN	MS	
	Albert	S	W	M	Dec 1887	12	S				MS	TN	MS	
	Laura	D	W	F	May 1890	10	S				MS	TN	MS	
	Susie	D	W	F	Jul 1892	7	S				MS	TN	MS	
	Luna	D	W	F	Oct 1894	5	S				MS	TN	MS	
141	Duggar, William J.	H	W	M	Mar 1833	67	M	44			TN	TN	TN	
	Mariah J.	W	W	F	Oct 1842	57	M	44	6	6	TN	TN	NC	
	Frank	S	W	M	Aug 1865	34	S				MS	TN	TN	
	Martha A	D	W	F	Jan 1868	33	S				MS	TN	TN	Dress Maker
	Fannie A.	D	W	F	Sep 1876	23	S				MS	TN	TN	
	Birdie A.	D	W	F	Sep 1881	18	S				MS	TN	TN	Music Teacher
	David A.	S	W	M	Jun 1883	16	S				MS	TN	TN	
	Felix W	S	W	M	Feb 1885	15	S				MS	TN	TN	
142	Cary, Jas. L.	H	W	M	Dec 1824	75	M	8			NC	MD	NC	Farmer
	Eliza	W	W	F	Aug 1827	72	M	8	1	0	TN	VA	TN	
	Phelps, Marguerett	Bdr	W	F	Apr 1839	60	Wd		2	1	AL	SC	SC	
143	Haney, M.J.	H	W	F	Apr 1851	49	Wd		2	2	TN	UN	AL	
	A.P.	D	W	F	Aug 1874	25	S				AL	MS	TN	
	Ed R.	S	W	M	Jan 1876	24	S				AL	MS	TN	
144	Adams, Lou	H	W	F	Feb 1859	41	Wd		1	1	MS	VA	NC	
	Tommie F.	S	W	M	Apr 1884	16	S				MS	MS	MS	
145	Smith, Thomas R.	H	W	M	UN UN	65	M	47			GA	SC	SC	RR Conductor
	Lou H.	W	W	F	Sep UN	72	M	47	5	5	NC	TN	TN	
	Wildes, Rhoda	Bdr	W	F	UN UN	80	Wd				VA	UN	UN	
146	Smith, Rube D.	H	W	M	Jun 1850	49	M	18			MS	GA	GA	Plasterer
	Callie	W	W	F	Jul 1856	43	M	18	2	1	GA	UN	UN	
	Cora E.	D	W	F	Jan 1875	24	S				TN	MS	AL	Teacher
	Elam R.	S	W	M	Jun 1887	17	S				MS	MS	AL	
147	Haney, W.W.	H	W	M	Dec 1840	59	M	34			MS	TN	TN	Farmer
	Sallie E.	W	W	F	Sep 1843	56	M	34	4	3	GA	SC	GA	
	Kate S.	D	W	F	Jun 1868	31	S				MS	MS	GA	Music Teacher
	Corrie	D	W	F	Nov 1873	26	S				MS	MS	GA	Music Teacher
	Virgie	Nce	W	F	Nov 1888	11	S				UN	UN	UN	
	Katie	Nce	W	F	Mar 1890	10	S				UN	UN	UN	
148	Brown, Elizabeth	H	W	F	May 1843	57	Wd		9	8	UN	UN	UN	
	Nina	D	W	F	Dec 1875	24	S				UN	UN	UN	
	Robert J.	S	W	M	Oct 1877	22	S				UN	UN	UN	
	Katie B.	D	W	F	Oct 1879	20	S				UN	UN	UN	
	Effie	D	W	F	Jul 1883	16	S				MS	SC	MS	Teacher
149	Luker, Sarah	H	W	F	Sep 1864	35	Wd		5	4	MS	SC	MS	Clerk
	Lizzie E.	D	W	F	Dec 1888	11	S				MS	MS	MS	
	Moses B.	S	W	M	Jun 1892	9	S				MS	MS	MS	
	Rachel P.	D	W	F	Apr 1895	5	S				MS	MS	MS	
	John R.	S	W	M	Aug 1897	2	S				TX	MS	MS	

1	2	3	4	5	6	7	8	9	10	11	12	13	14	15
150	Barnett, John T.	H	W	M	Dec 1842	57	M	33			TN	GA	GA	Post Master
	Sallie H.	W	W	F	Oct 1848	52	M	33	8	7	MS	AL	AL	
	Clifford M.	S	W	M	Sep 1882	17	S				MS	TN	AL	Asst. Pmaster
	Claud A.	S	W	M	Jan 1888	12	S				MS	TN	AL	
151	Hyatt, Ida Lee	H	W	F	Apr 1850	50	Wd		1	0	AL	AL	VA	Bank Cashier
	Anna	SD	W	F	Apr 1866	34	S				AL	AL	AL	
	Rosa F.	SD	W	F	Jun 1877	3	S				MS	AL	AL	Music Store Clerk
152	Hammerly, E. Terry	H	W	M	Feb 1870	30	M	1			MS	AL	AL	Merchant
	Pearl Rose	W	W	F	Oct 1877	22	M	1	1	1	MS	MS	MS	
	Tom Ross	S	W	M	Oct 1899	7/mo	S				MS	MS	MS	
153	Hammerly, G.P.	H	W	M	Aug 1829	70	M	42			AL	VA	NC	Merchant
	Martha A.	W	W	F	Oct 1836	63	M	42	11	4	AL	TN	NC	Cook
	Thompson, Violett	Ser	B	F	UN UN	60	Wd		0	0	NC	NC	NC	Cook
154	Ross, W.Tom	H	W	M	May 1851	49	M	15			MS	NC	MS	Merchant
	Mollie L.	W	W	F	Dec 1851	49	M	15	5	3	MS	GA	MS	
	Bertha R.	D	W	F	Jan 1880	20	S				MS	MS	MS	
	Will A.	S	W	M	Mar 1890	10	S				MS	MS	MS	
	Lock R.	D	W	F	Dec 1893	6	S				MS	MS	MS	
	Joe A.	S	W	M	Mar 1897	3	S				MS	MS	MS	
	Hunt, Dandy	Bdr	B	M	Feb 1881	19	S				MS	MS	MS	Servant
155	Haney, D. Thomas	H	W	M	Jul 1870	29	M	3			MS	MS	MS	Sheriff
	Mary	W	W	F	May 1875	25	M	3	2	2	MS	UN	MS	
	Mary	D	W	F	Oct 1897	2	S				MS	MS	MS	
	Emory P	S	W	M	May 1899	1	S				MS	MS	MS	
156	Gist, William	H	W	M	Dec 1834	65	M	40			TN	TN	TN	Mayor Iuka
	Mary	W	W	F	Mar 1828	72	M	40	6	4	TN	TN	TN	
	Burtie	D	W	F	Mar 1862	38	S				MS	TN	TN	
157	Glenn, Dave E.	H	W	F	Jan 1860	40	M	19			MS	SC	KY	Circuit Clerk
	Amanda L.	W	W	F	Oct 1859	40	M	19	3	1	MS	UN	UN	
	William Jesse	S	W	M	Dec 1881	18	S				MS	MS	MS	
158	Cummings, Henry	H	B	M	UN UN	Un	M	8			MS	MS	MS	Hotel Porter
	Sarah	W	B	F	UN UN	26	M	8	6		MS	MS	MS	
	Jimmie	D	B	F	Sep 1893	6	S				MS	MS	MS	
	Edwin	S	B	M	Jul 1894	5	S				MS	MS	MS	
	George	S	B	M	Jul 1896	3	S				MS	MS	MS	
	Sallie	D	B	F	Nov 1898	1	S				MS	MS	MS	
	Verberly	S	B	M	May 1900	0/mo	S				MS	MS	MS	
159	Dudley, George W.	H	W	M	May 1846	54	M	28			MS	UN	UN	Painter
	Georgia	W	W	F	Jun 1854	45	M	28	2	2	AL	GA	UN	
	Granville	S	W	M	Jul 1877	22	S				MS	MS	MS	BookKeeper
160	Bell, Emily	H	W	F	Feb 1837	63	Wd		9	3	TN	TN	UN	
	Katherine	D	W	F	Feb 1870	30	S				MS	TN	UN	
	Willie	D	W	F	Oct 1876	23	S				MS	TN	TN	
161	Enloe. John	H	W	M	Jun 1857	42	M	19			TN	UN	AL	Carpenter
	Susie	W	W	F	Jun 1861	38	M	19	7	5	MS	AL	NC	
	Ottie	D	W	F	Oct 1881	18	S				MS	TN	MS	
	Estele	D	W	F	Oct 1888	11	S				MS	TN	MS	
	Laura	D	W	F	Apr 1893	7	S				MS	TN	MS	
	Hugh	S	W	M	Mar 1896	4	S				MS	TN	MS	
	Emma	D	W	F	Apr 1899	1	S				MS	TN	MS	
	Rodgers, Elizabeth	MiL	W	F	Oct 1825	74	Wd		1	1	AL	UN	OH	
	Richard	Bro	W	M	Apr 1867	33	S				TN	SC	AL	Day Laborer

1	2	3	4	5	6	7	8	9	10	11	12	13	14	15
162	Goyer, James T.	H	W	M	Oct 1862	37	M	17			MS	PA	SC	Merchant
	Mary Alice	W	W	F	Jul 1854	45	M	17	6	2	TN	UN	TN	
	Homer	S	W	M	Sep 1885	14	S				MS	MS	TN	
	Allice	D	W	F	Apr 1892	8	S				MS	MS	TN	
163	Paden, Jesse	H	W	M	Aug 1843	56	M		7	4	MS	SC	GA	Teacher
	Liman	S	W	M	Jan 1879	21	S				MS	TN	MS	Clerk
	Lizzie	D	W	F	Sep 1881	18	S				MS	TN	MS	
	McRae, Mary	Ser	B	F	UN UN	10	S				MS	MS	MS	
164	Studivant, Nathan	H	W	M	Jan 1818	82	W				VA	VA	VA	
	Mollie R.	D	W	F	Aug 1846	53	S				AL	VA	AL	
	Bell, Dolly	Ser	B	F	UN UN	75	Wd				UN	UN	UN	
165	Goyer, Fannie	H	W	F	Jan 1859	41	Wd		5	4	MS	AL	TN	
	Winfield	S	W	M	Sep 1882	17	S				MS	AL	TN	
	Earl	S	W	M	Dec 1887	12	S				MS	AL	TN	
	James L.	S	W	M	Jul 1890	9	S				MS	AL	TN	
	Julian	S	W	M	Feb 1892	7	S				MS	AL	TN	
	Wilburn, Caroline	M	W	F	Sep 1836	63	Wd				TN	VA	VA	
166	Knowles, Fred	H	W	M	Mar 1851	49	M	27			MS	VA	MS	Farmer
	Harriett	W	W	F	Jul 1852	47	M	27	2	1	MS	AL	VA	
	Kittie L.	D	W	F	Oct 1876	25	S				MS	MS	MS	
	Nolan, Cara	Bd	W	F	May 1883	17	S				MS	MS	MS	
167	Castleberry, Nina	H	W	F	Dec 1836	64	S				GA	GA	GA	
	Walmesly, John	Nep	W	M	Feb 1878	22	S				MS	Ire	MS	
	James	Nep	W	M	Oct 1880	19	S				MS	Ire	MS	
	William	Nep	W	M	Oct 1883	16	S				MS	Ire	MS	
	Mary	Nce	W	F	Jul 1885	14	S				MS	Ire	MS	
	Hodges, Myrta	Nce	W	F	Feb 1874	26	M		1	0	MS	Ire	MS	
	Castleberry, Charley	Bro	W	M	Mar 1841	59	Wd				MS	GA	GA	
168	Gaines, Henry T.	H	W	M	Jan 1856	44	M	8			MS	TN	SC	Minister Gosp.
	Bettie	W	W	F	UN UN	UN	M	8	4	4	MS	MS	MS	
	Mary	D	W	F	Apr 1893	7	S				MS	MS	MS	
	Henry T.	S	W	M	Oct 1894	5	S				MS	MS	MS	
	John P.	S	W	M	Nov 1896	3	S				MS	MS	MS	
	James C.	S	W	M	Nov 1898	1	S				MS	MS	MS	
169	Shockley, Sam	H	W	M	Dec 1861	38	M	15			AR	GA	AR	Barber
	Anna E.	W	W	F	Jul 1864	35	M	15	3	3	MS	UN	GA	
	Sam	S	W	M	Jul 1867	12	S				MS	AR	MS	
	Ruth	D	W	F	Jun 1894	5	S				MS	AR	MS	
	Nell	D	W	F	Feb 1897	3	S				MS	AR	MS	
	Hughes, Sallie	MiL	W	F	UN UN	60	Wd				GA	SC	SC	
	Eccles, Arinlas	Unc	W	M	Aug 1824	75	Wd				NC	UN	UN	
170	Moss, H. Tom	H	W	M	Mar 1833	67	Wd				GA	NC	VA	Farmer
	Mollie	D	W	F	Jan 1867	32	S				MS	GA	AL	
	Doan	S	W	M	May 1860	31	S				MS	GA	AL	
	Robert	S	W	F	Aug 1872	28	S				MS	GA	AL	
	Coleman	S	W	M	Jan 1874	26	S				MS	GA	AL	
	Katie	D	W	F	Mar 1883	17	S				MS	GA	AL	
	Ida	Sil	W	F	Oct 1865	34	M	12	4	3	AL	VA	VA	
	Ernest	GS	W	M	Mar 1889	11	S				MS	AL	AL	
	James	GS	W	M	Jan 1893	7	S				TN	AL	AL	
	Ida Bell	GD	W	F	Sep 1899	8/mo	S				MS	AL	AL	
171	Reed, George W.	H	W	M	Sep 1849	50	M	17			MS	IN	TN	Painter
	Ada Lou	W	W	F	Sep 1859	40	M	17	4	4	MS	GA	GA	
	Talmadge	S	W	M	Oct 1884	15	S				MS	MS	MS	

1	2	3	4	5	6	7	8	9	10	11	12	13	14	15
	Pearl	D	W	F	Oct 1885	14	S				MS	MS	MS	
	Newton	S	W	M	May 1889	11	S				MS	MS	MS	
	Clifton	S	W	M	Sep 1897	2	S				MS	MS	MS	
	Reed, Matilda	MiL	W	F	May 1825	75	W				TN	GA	GA	
172	Harris, Will	H	W	M	Dec 1862	37	M	16			AL	UN	MS	Merchant
	M. Ida	W	W	F	Feb 1862	38	M	16	3	2	AL	TN	SC	
	Herbert	S	W	M	Mar 1885	15	S				AL	AL	AL	
	Otey	S	W	M	Sep 1887	12	S				AL	AL	AL	
173	Rowe, William	H	W	M	Feb 1846	54	M	4			Eng	Eng	Scot	Merchant
	Lizzie	W	W	F	Mar 1870	30	M	4	1	1	MS	VA	AL	
	Margaret	D	W	F	Jul 1897	2	S				TN	Eng	MS	
	Thomas, Patty	Bdr	W	F	Nov 1861	38	W				MS	MS	MS	Teacher
	Agnes	Bdr	W	F	Aug 1890	9	S				MS	MS	MS	
174	Thompson, Mattie	H	B	F	UN UN	21	UN		2	2	MS	UN	UN	Cook
	Ruth	D	B	F	UN UN	2	S				MS	MS	MS	
	Luellin	D	B	F	UN UN	10/mo	S				MS	MS	MS	
175	Milsaps, Humphrey	H	W	M	Jun 1843	56	M	31			GA	UN	GA	Carpenter
	Carrie	W	W	F	Nov 1845	54	M	31	5	4	MO	GA	MO	
	Allice	D	W	F	Jan 1879	21	S				MO	GA	MO	
	Susie	D	W	F	Jan 1883	17	S				MS	GA	MO	
	Sam	S	W	M	Sep 1884	15	S				MS	GA	MO	
176	Clement, William A.	H	W	M	Sep 1860	39	M	14			TN	NC	TN	Farmer
	Lilian	W	W	F	Dec 1859	40	M	14	5	4	TN	NC	TN	
	Hattie Lee	D	W	F	Jun 1889	10	S				TN	TN	TN	
	Ben E.	S	W	M	Sep 1882	7	S				TN	TN	TN	
	Jesse W.	S	W	M	Apr 1896	4	S				TN	TN	TN	
	William B.	S	W	M	May 1890	1	S				TN	TN	TN	
177	Creed, Nancy L.	H	W	F	Jul 1843	46	Wd				MS	MS	MS	Capitilist
178	Cogere, Tom	H	B	M	Jul 1871	27	M	4			MS	MS	MS	RR Brakeman
	Henryetta	W	B	F	UN UN	27	M	4	1	1	MS	MS	MS	
	Lida May	D	B	F	Apr 1892	8	S				MS	MS	MS	
	Frank	Bro	B	M	UN UN	18	S				MS	MS	MS	
179	Turner, Anna	H	B	F	UN UN	22	Wd		0	0	MS	MS	MS	Cook
	Mary	D	B	F	Jun 1894	5	S				MS	MS	MS	
	Counts, Sallie	Bdr	B	F	UN 1877	22	Wd				MS	MS	MS	Chamber Maid
180	Dean, Julius	H	B	M	UN UN	30	M	4			MS	MS	MS	Day Laborer
	Mattie	W	B	F	UN UN	27	M	4	1	1	MS	MS	MS	
	Minnie	D	B	F	Jul 1898	1	S				MS	MS	MS	
181	Bonds, Sonnie	H	B	M	UN 1874	26	M	4			MS	GA	UN	Day Laborer
	Mary	D	B	F	UN UN	22	M	4	4	2	MS	GA	UN	
	Onie	D	B	F	UN UN	4	S				MS	UN	UN	
	Selma	D	B	F	UN UN	1	S				MS	UN	UN	
	Turner, Susie	Bdr	B	F	Jan 1882	18	S				AL	AL	AL	Laundress
182	Rice, James	H	W	M	Aug 1880	19	M	3			TN	UN	UN	Day Laborer
	Mary	W	W	F	Aug 1880	19	M	3	1	1	TN	MS	MS	Laundress
	Ida May	D	W	F	May 1899	1	S				MS	UN	TN	
	Thompson, Nannie	MiL	W	F	Jul 1849	50	Wd		0	0	MS	MS	MS	
	William	BiL	W	M	UN UN	22	Wd				TN	UN	MS	Day Laborer
	Ella	UN	W	F	May 1885	15	S				TN	TN	MS	
183	Reed, Fannie V.	H	W	F	Jan 1836	64	Wd		3	2	TN	TN	MS	

1	2	3	4	5	6	7	8	9	10	11	12	13	14	15
184	Miller, Charles P.	H	W	M	Sep 1852	47	M	17			IN	UN	UN	Painter
	Mirisa F.	W	W	F	Oct 1863	36	M	17	4	4	MS	TN	TN	
	Katie	D	W	F	Jun 1885	14	S				MS	IN	MS	
	Mary Bell	D	W	F	Jun 1887	12	S				MS	IN	MS	
	Susie	D	W	F	Aug 1889	10	S				MS	IN	MS	
	Charles B.	S	W	M	Dec 1892	7	S				MS	IN	MS	
185	Thompson, Jerry	H	B	M	UN UN	60	M	6			GA	UN	UN	
	Jinnett	W	B	F	UN UN	40	M	6	1	1	GA	UN	UN	
	Walter	S	B	M	UN UN	19	S				MS	GA	GA	
186	Wells, Anna C.	H	W	F	Apr 1862	38	Wd		6	5	MS	TN	TN	
	James R.	S	W	M	Apr 1880	20	S				MS	MS	MS	
	Mattie G.	D	W	F	Mar 1884	16	S				MS	MS	MS	
	Kittie E.	D	W	F	Oct 1886	13	S				MS	MS	MS	
	Mary A.	D	W	F	Dec 1888	11	S				MS	MS	MS	
	Paul C.	S	W	M	Jan 1892	8	S				MS	MS	MS	
187	Thorne, Eugene	H	W	M	Apr 1861	39	M	16			AL	PA	KY	Drummer
	Lulu	W	W	F	UN UN	36	M	16	0	0	KY	MS	MS	
188	Thompson, Charley	H	B	M	UN UN	30	M	10			AL	UN	UN	Day Laborer
	Mary	W	B	F	UN UN	28	M	10	5	5	MS	UN	UN	
	Lucille	D	B	F	Jul 1891	8	S				MS	AL	MS	
	Claud	S	B	M	Mar 1893	7	S				MS	AL	MS	
	Ugene	S	B	M	Jul 1895	5	S				MS	AL	MS	
	Lany May	D	B	F	Aug 1897	2	S				MS	AL	MS	
	Otto	S	B	M	Mar 1899	1	S				MS	AL	MS	
189	Wilson, Zora	H	B	F	UN UN	32	Wd	UN	2	2	MS	MS	MS	Laundress
	Della	D	B	F	Mar 1888	12	S				MS	UN	MS	
	Freddie	S	B	M	Jul 1890	9	S				MS	UN	MS	
	Grizzard, Sid	Bdr	B	M	UN UN	3	S				TN	TN	SC	Day Laborer
190	Hogue, Vick	H	B	F	UN UN	44	Wd		7	7	MS	MS	UN	Laundress
	Girdie	D	B	F	UN UN	17	S				MS	MS	MS	
	Linda	D	B	F	UN UN	12	S				MS	MS	MS	
191	Gravett, Elijah	H	W	M	May 1854	46	M	24			AL	UN	AL	Carpenter
	Milly Jane	W	W	F	Nov 1859	40	M	24	10	4	TN	SC	SC	
	John Raymond	S	W	M	Aug 1877	22	S				MS	AL	TN	
	Elma	S	W	M	Aug 1888	11	S				MS	AL	TN	
	Bertha	D	W	F	Oct 1891	8	S				MS	AL	TN	
	Clara	D	W	F	Aug 1898	1	S				MS	AL	TN	
192	Bayless, Robert G.	H	W	M	Dec 1851	48	M	26			LA	UN	AL	Carpenter
	Elizabeth E.	W	W	F	Nov 1855	44	M	26	7	6	MS	GA	NC	
	Frances L.	D	W	F	Jun 1880	19	S				MS	LA	MS	
	Mary E.	D	W	F	Mar 1883	17	S				MS	LA	MS	
	Frank C.	S	W	M	Nov 1886	13	S				MS	LA	MS	
	Blanche	D	W	F	Nov 1891	8	S				MS	LA	MS	
	Julia C.	D	W	F	Aug 1893	7	S				MS	LA	MS	
193	Goode, E. Bell	H	W	F	Aug 1869	30	S				MS	AL	UN	Laundress
	Henry	S	W	M	May 1894	6	S				MS	MS	MS	
	Silas	S	W	M	Feb 1899	1	S				MS	MS	MS	
194	Carpenter, James	H	W	M	Oct 1844	55	M	33			MS	UN	UN	
	Mattie L.	W	W	F	Aug 1848	52	M	33	5	3	MS	SC	SC	
195	Carpenter, Will	H	W	M	Jan 1873	26	M	7			MS	MS	MS	Day Laborer
	Cora	W	W	F	Jan 1874	25	M	7	3	2	SC	SC	SC	
	J.B.	S	W	M	Dec 1894	5	S				TX	MS	SC	

1	2	3	4	5	6	7	8	9	10	11	12	13	14	15
	John William	S	W	M	Jun 1897	3	S				AR	MS	SC	
	Alice	D	W	F	Oct 1899	1	S				MS	MS	SC	
	Broadway, King	Bdr	B	M	UN UN	25	M				IA	UN	UN	Day Laborer
	Johnson, Arthur	Bdr	B	M	UN UN	22					TN	TN	KY	Day Laborer
	Crumb, Oliver	Bdr	B	M	UN UN	21					MS	UN	MS	Day Laborer
196	Harris, Clayborn	H	W	M	UN UN	45	M	15			TN	UN	UN	Drummer
	Carrie L.	W	W	F	Dec 1858	42	M	15			AL	PA	KY	
	Thorne, Anna	MiL	W	F	Dec 1827	73	Wd		1	1	KY	UN	UN	

1	2	3	4	5	6	7	8	9	10	11	12	13	14	15
1	Barnes, James	H	W	M	Dec 1824	75	M	20			MS	TN	TN	Farmer
	Barbara, L,	W	W	F	Mar 1845	57	M	20	1	1	MS	NC	NC	
2	Barnes, J.F.	H	W	M	Apr 1871	29	M	11			MS	MS	MS	Farmer
	Poley M.	W	W	F	Mar 1870	30	M	11	5	5	MS	MS	MS	
	Oscar L.	S	W	M	Jul 1890	9	S				MS	MS	MS	
	Dasey, P.	D	W	F	Apr 1892	8	S				MS	MS	MS	
	James	S	W	M	Aug 1894	5	S				MS	MS	MS	
	Joseph	S	W	M	Nov 1896	4	S				MS	MS	MS	
	Minnie	D	W	F	Mar 1899	1	S				MS	MS	MS	
3	Barnes, Thomas	H	W	M	Sep 1863	37	M				MS	TN	TN	Farmer
	Rosa	W	M	F	Jul 1861	39	M	18	7	4	TN	SC	SC	
	James C.	S	W	M	Sep 1885						MS	TN	TN	
	Jesse L.	S	W	M	Oct 1889	10	S				MS	TN	TN	Farm Laborer
	William A.	S	W	M	Mar 1891	9	S				MS	MS	TN	
	Levy L.	S	W	M	Aug 1897	3	S				MS	TN	TN	
	Davis, Margaret C.	MiL	W	F	Apr 1828	72	Wd		6	3	SC	NC	TN	
4	McDuffey, Jesse	H	W	M	Oct 1861	39	M	22			MS	AL	MS	Farmer
	Jemima	W	W	F	Mar 1855	45	M	22	10	8	MS	NC	NC	
	Martha L.	D	W	F	Oct 1880	19	S				MS	MS	MS	
	Georgia	D	W	F	Jan 1882	18	S				MS	MS	MS	
	James R.	S	W	M	Mar 1884	16	S				MS	MS	MS	Farm Laborer
	Effie M.	D	W	F	May 1886	14	S				MS	MS	MS	
	Sarah L.	D	W	F	Sep 1888	12	S				MS	MS	MS	
	Charley W.	S	W	M	Nov 1890	10	S				MS	MS	MS	Farm Laborer
	Jesse G.	S	W	M	Sep 1892	8	S				MS	MS	MS	
	Sina Jane	D	W	F	Oct 1878	21	Wd		1	0	MS	MS	MS	
5	Burney, Woodard	H	W	M	Sep 1872	27	M	4			AL	AL	AL	Farmer
	Ela	W	W	F	Jun 1876	24	M	4	1	1	AL	AL	AL	
	Mamie	D	W	F	Oct 1899	7/mo	S				MS	AL	AL	
6	Wood, Daniel	H	W	M	Nov 1868	31	M	5			TN	TN	TN	Farmer
	Joan	W	W	F	Mar 1869	31	M	5	2	2	MS	TN	MS	
	Ernest G.	S	W	M	Mar 1896	4	S				MS	TN	MS	
	Alonza B.	S	W	M	Apr 1898	2	S				MS	TN	MS	
	Wood, Charley A.	Rel	W	M	May 1870	30	S				TN	TN	TN	Farm Labor
7	Simpson, David	H	W	M	Dec 1880	19	M	3			AL	AL	AL	Farmer
	Francis	W	W	F	Jan 1879	21	M	3	2	1	AL	AL	AL	
8	Vinson, Hyram	H	W	M	Aug 1822	77	M	7			TN	GA	VA	Farmer
	Nancy	W	W	F	Aug 1847	52	M	7	0	0	NC	NC	NC	
9	Robinson, J.H.C.	H	W	M	Sep 1840	59	M	33			AL	SC	AL	Farmer
	Paralee	W	W	F	Feb 1850	50	M	33	4	4	AL	TN	AL	
	Harvey	S	W	M	Feb 1877	23	S				AL	AL	AL	Farm Laborer
	James	S	W	M	Feb 1882	18	S				AL	AL	AL	Farm Laborer
	Edward	S	W	M	Sep 1884	16	S				AL	AL	AL	Farm Laborer
	Fannie	D	W	F	Jul 1888	11	S				AL	AL	AL	Farm Laborer
10	Bates, James	H	W	M	Jun 1877	23	M	2			TN	NC	NC	Farmer
	Glena L.	W	W	F	Feb 1879	21	M	2	0	0	AL	AL	AL	
11	Morris, J.S.	H	W	M	Jul 1866	33	M	7			MS	MS	TN	Farmer
	S.E.	W	W	F	Sep 1872	27	M	7	4	2	MS	TN	TN	

1	2	3	4	5	6	7	8	9	10	11	12	13	14	15
	Ida	D	W	F	Jan 1896	4	S				MS	MS	MS	
	Minnie	D	W	F	Jan 1900	4/mo	S				MS	MS	MS	
12	Grisham, L.D.	H	W	M	Jun 1862	39	M	1			AL	AL	AL	Farmer
	Mary E.	W	W	F	Mar 1862	38	M	1	1	0	MS	AL	AL	
13	Miller, Synth A.	H	W	F	May 1836	64	Wd		5	3	MS	KY	KY	
	Morris, Fannie	Bdr	W	F	Jun 1861	39	Wd		2	2	MS	AL	AL	
	John N.	S	W	M	Jan 1891	9	S				MS	MS	MS	
	Grover	S	W	M	Jul 1892	7	S				MS	MS	MS	
14	Welch, Stephen	H	W	M	Feb 1852	48	M	5			MS	NC	AL	Farmer
	Mary E.	W	W	F	Mar 1860	40	M	5	9	5	MS	TN	AL	
	Jesse V.	SD	W	F	Nov 1884	15	S				AL	Ita	MS	
	Thornton, Buford W.	SS	W	M	Sep 1889	10	S				TN	TN	MS	Farm Laborer
	Thornton, Peter P.	SS	W	M	Sep 1892	7	S				TN	TN	MS	Farm Laborer
	Welch, Sally H.	D	W	F	Jul 1896	3	S				MS	MS	MS	
	Welch, Dollie A.	D	W	F	Oct 1898	1	S				MS	MS	MS	
15	Blakney, B.T.	H	W	M	Jun 1851	48	M	19			MS	MS	MS	
	Margret	W	W	F	Sep 1862	37	M	19	8	8	MS	UN	MS	
	Charley	S	W	M	Feb 1882	18	S				MS	MS	MS	Farm Laborer
	Dora	D	W	F	Jan 1884	16	S				MS	MS	MS	
	Docia V.	D	W	F	Jan 1886	14	S				MS	MS	MS	
	John H.	S	W	M	Oct 1888	11	S				MS	MS	MS	Farm Laborer
	Noria B.	D	W	F	Feb 1890	10	S				MS	MS	MS	
	Enry F.	S	W	M	Jun 1892	7	S				MS	MS	MS	
	Addie C.	D	W	F	Dec 1895	4	S				MS	MS	MS	
	Loureny	D	W	F	Sep 1898	1	S				MS	MS	MS	
16	Mosely, Joseph	H	W	M	Jul 1843	56	Wd				MS	NC	TN	Farmer
	Henry	S	W	M	Apr 1888	12	S				MS	MS	MS	Farm Laborer
	Frank	S	W	M	Jul 1890	9	S				MS	MS	MS	
	Sarah	D	W	F	Feb 1893	7	S				MS	MS	MS	
17	Mosley, Mansel	H	W	M	Mar 1872	28	S				MS	MS	MS	Day Laborer
18	Whitehurst, J.B.	H	W	M	Dec 1850	49	M	23			MS	NC	MD	Farmer
	Sarah	W	W	F	May 1860	40	M	23	8	8	MS	NC	MS	
	Amy	D	W	F	Feb 1883	17	S				MS	MS	MS	
	Carol Z.	S	W	M	Dec 1885	14	S				MS	MS	MS	Farm Laborer
	Ruba A.	D	W	F	May 1887	13	S				MS	MS	MS	
	Dasy C.	D	W	F	Jun 1890	9	S				MS	MS	MS	
	Mattie E.	D	W	F	Oct 1892	7	S				MS	MS	MS	
	James H.	S	W	M	Jan 1895	5	S				MS	MS	MS	
	Oscar E.	S	W	M	Aug 1898	1	S				MS	MS	MS	
	James	F	W	M	Dec 1822	78	M	1			NC	NC	NC	
19	Robinson, John	H	W	M	Jun 1862	37	M	5			MS	MS	MS	Farmer
	Josie C.	W	W	F	Oct 1860	39	M	5	4	3	MS	MS	MS	
	Sidney E.	S	W	M	Dec 1887	12	S				MS	MS	MS	
	Lena F.	D	W	F	Nov 1896	3	S				MS	MS	MS	
	James M.	S	W	M	Dec 1897	2	S				MS	MS	MS	
	Minnie	D	W	F	Oct 1899	7/mo	S				MS	MS	MS	
20	Young, Thomas	H	W	M	Oct 1827	72	M	50			MS	NC	NC	Farmer
	Sarah	W	W	F	Oct 1824	75	M	50	7	5	AL	NY	AL	
	Rebecca F.	D	W	F	Jan 1856	44	S				MS	NC	AL	
21	Phillips, James	H	W	M	Dec 1875	24	M	1			MS	MS	MS	Farm Laborer
	Minnie	W	W	F	Jun 1882	17	M	1	0	0	MS	MS	MS	
22	Phillips, Emma	H	W	F	Dec 1854	46	Wd		7	7	MS	NC	NC	

1	2	3	4	5	6	7	8	9	10	11	12	13	14	15
	Whitfield	S	W	M	Oct 1882	17	S				MS	MS	MS	Farm Labor
	Blanch	D	W	F	Dec 1883	16	S				MS	MS	MS	
	Viola	D	W	F	Aug 1886	13	S				MS	MS	MS	
	Izora	D	W	F	May 1891	9	S				MS	MS	MS	
23	Johnson, David	H	W	M	Nov 1851	48	M	23			MS	TN	TN	Farmer
	Mary	W	W	F	Mar 1853	47	M	23	9	6	MS	MS	IL	
	Jinnie L.	D	W	F	Mar 1885	15	S				MS	MS	MS	
	Dollie A.	D	W	F	Apr 1889	11	S				MS	MS	MS	
	Lillie H.	D	W	F	Apr 1891	9	S				MS	MS	MS	
	Deller P.	D	W	F	Jun 1894	5	S				MS	MS	MS	
	Rula E.	D	W	F	Aug 1896	3	S				MS	MS	MS	
24	Johnson, Rinal	H	W	M	Jan 1855	45	M	21			MS	TN	TN	Farmer
	Hyburney B.	W	W	F	Jun 1860	40	M	21	8	7	MS	MS	MS	
	Rufus A.	S	W	M	May 1882	18	S				MS	MS	MS	Farm Laborer
	Lou Ola	D	W	F	Jun 1884	15	S				MS	MS	MS	
	Pink G.	S	W	M	Apr 1886	14	S				MS	MS	MS	Farm Laborer
	Duthula J.	D	W	F	Apr 1888	12	S				MS	MS	MS	
	Daisy L.	D	W	F	Apr 1891	9	S				MS	MS	MS	
	Alice C.	D	W	F	Feb 1895	5	S				MS	MS	MS	
	William	S	W	M	Aug 1899	9/mo	S				MS	MS	MS	
25	Robinson, Jefferson	H	W	M	Mar 1873	27	M	1			MS	MS	MS	Day Laborer
	Rebecca E.	W	W	F	Feb 1870	30	M	1			MS	MS	MS	
	Smith, William R.	F	W	M	Jan 1833	77	Wd				TN	NC	NC	
26	Smith, Henry	H	W	M	Mar 1861	39	M	18			MS	NC	NC	Farmer
	M. C.	W	W	F	Dec 1861	38	M	18	8	8	MS	MS	SC	
	Lou E.	D	W	F	Dec 1882	17	S				MS	MS	MS	
	William L.	S	W	M	Jan 1884	16	S				MS	MS	MS	
	Maggie J.	D	W	F	Feb 1885	15	S				MS	MS	MS	
	Tolbert F.	S	W	M	Jun 1886	13	S				MS	MS	MS	Farm Laborer
	Luther E.	S	W	M	Mar 1888	12	S				MS	MS	MS	Farm Laborer
	Clarence D.	S	W	M	Oct 1889	10	S				MS	MS	MS	Farm Laborer
	Elbert B.	S	W	M	Dec 1894	5	S				MS	MS	MS	
	Elmer A.	D	W	F	Jan 1898	2	S				MS	MS	MS	
27	Smith, John W.	H	W	M	Aug 1871	28	M	6			TN	TN	TN	Farmer
	Lillie	W	W	F	May 1875	25	M	6	4	4	MS	MS	MS	
	Daisy	D	W	F	Jul 1894	5	S				MS	MS	MS	
	David	S	W	M	Dec 1896	3	S				MS	MS	MS	
	Looney	S	W	M	Nov 1897	2	S				MS	MS	MS	
	Doctor	S	W	M	Aug 1899	9/mo	S				MS	MS	MS	
28	Morris, James	H	W	M	Jan 1853	47	M	22			MS	TN	AL	Farmer
	Sinna	W	W	F	Jan 1852	48	M	22	0	0	TN	TN	TN	
29	Morris, Edgar	H	W	M	Aug 1880	19	M	1			TN	TN	TN	Farmer
	Rosetta	W	W	F	Dec 1876	23	M	1	0	0	MS	MS	MS	
30	Joslin, William	H	W	M	Oct 1853	46	M	26			MS	MS	MS	Farmer
	Nannie	W	W	F	Jan 1854	45	M	26	8	7	AL	AL	AL	
	Ina	D	W	F	Mar 1884	16	S				MS	MS	AL	
	Virgil	S	W	M	Jun 1886	13	S				MS	MS	AL	Farm Laborer
	Obie	S	W	M	Apr 1890	10	S				MS	MS	AL	Farm Laborer
	Elzonia	D	W	F	Jul 1892	7	S				MS	MS	AL	
	Joslin, Elmo	Rel	W	M	Jul 1877	22	S				MS	MS	AL	Day Laborer
31	Woodruff, A.	H	W	M	Jul 1860	39	M	11			MS	NC	AL	Farmer
	Ollie	W	W	F	Sep 1870	29	M	11	4	3	MS	KY	NC	
	Ed	S	W	M	Jun 1893	6	S				MS	MS	MS	
	Ester	D	W	F	Aug 1895	4	S				MS	MS	MS	

1	2	3	4	5	6	7	8	9	10	11	12	13	14	15
	Elva	S	W	M	May 1899	1	S				MS	MS	MS	
32	Holland, Lafayette	H	W	M	Apr 1878	22	S				AL	AL	AL	Farm Laborer
33	Morris, Jackson	H	W	M	Jan 1837	63	M	35			MS	AL	AL	Farmer
	Lucinda	W	W	F	Jan 1850	50	M	35	11	8	TN	TN	TN	
	Josie	D	W	F	Feb 1882	18	S				MS	MS	TN	
	Dorcey	S	W	M	Aug 1886	13	S				MS	MS	TN	Farm Laborer
	Mattie	D	W	F	Aug 1887	12	S				MS	MS	TN	
	Lonie	S	W	M	Feb 1890	10	S				MS	MS	TN	Farm Laborer
34	Holland, John	H	W	M	Apr 1876	24	M	3			AL	AL	AL	Farmer
	Etter	W	W	F	Apr 1878	22	M	3	1	1	MS	NC	AL	
	Ezra	S	W	M	Oct 1897	2	S				MS	AL	MS	
35	Joslin, Odis	H	W	M	Jan 1876	24	M	1			MS	MS	MS	Day Laborer
	Lizie	W	W	F	Jan 1873	27	M	1	1	1	MS	MS	MS	
36	Morris, William	H	W	M	Nov 1870	29	M	7			MS	MS	MS	Farmer
	Virda	W	W	F	May 1873	27	M	7	4	4	MS	MS	MS	
	Kenny W.	S	W	M	Feb 1895	5	S				MS	MS	MS	
	Buna V.	D	W	F	Mar 1896	4	S				MS	MS	MS	
	Loney C.	S	W	M	Mar 1898	2	S				MS	MS	MS	
	Tony C.	S	W	M	Aug 1899	9/mo	S				MS	MS	MS	
37	Young, George W.	H	W	M	Aug 1852	47	M	6			MS	MS	MS	Farmer
	Ellen M.	W	W	F	Apr 1861	39	M	6	3	3	MS	MS	MS	
	Thomas H.	S	W	M	May 1894	6	S				MS	MS	MS	
	Emma N.	D	W	F	Mar 1896	4	S				MS	MS	MS	
	William B.	S	W	M	Oct 1897	2	S				MS	MS	MS	
38	Bennett, James	H	W	M	Apr 1868	32	M	11			GA	GA	GA	Farm Laborer
	Jackalean	W	W	F	Aug 1864	35	M	11	5	5	TN	TN	TN	
	Walter	S	W	M	Jul 1882	17	S				TN	GA	TN	Day Laborer
	Eller	D	W	F	Oct 1889	10	S				TN	GA	TN	
	Maud	D	W	F	Jun 1891	8	S				TN	GA	TN	
	Charlie	S	W	M	Apr 1895	5	S				TN	GA	TN	
	Minnie	D	W	F	Jan 1900	3/mo	S				TN	GA	TN	
39	Jackson, Caroline	H	W	F	Oct 1871	28	UN				AL	AL	AL	
40	Tucker, Della	H	W	F	Jan 1883	17	UN				MS	AL	TN	
41	Castlebury, W.H.	H	W	M	Aug 1850	49	Wd				GA	GA	AL	Day Laborer
42	Odom, Thomas	H	W	M	Dec 1867	32	M	5			TN	TN	TN	Day Laborer
	Sarah	W	W	F	Dec 1876	35	M	5	4	3	TN	AL	AL	
	Magie	D	W	F	Sep 1895	4	S				TN	TN	AL	
	Robert	S	W	M	Sep 1897	2	S				TN	TN	AL	
	Floyd	S	W	M	Oct 1899	9/mo	S				TN	TN	AL	
43	Field, Robert	H	W	M	Oct 1872	27	M	3			TN	MS	AL	Day Laborer
	Ezella	W	W	F	Apr 1875	25	M	3	2	2	TN	TN	TN	
	Marry A.	D	W	F	Oct 1897	2	S				TN	TN	TN	
	Marna F.	D	W	F	Dec 1899	5/mo	S				TN	TN	TN	
44	Lutts, Jacobs	H	W	M	Jan 1839	61	M	35			NC	NC	SC	Saw Milling
	Malinda	W	W	F	Jan 1839	61	M	35	6	5	AL	KY	TN	
45	Coffman, Jesse	H	W	M	Jan 1875	25	S				TN	TN	TN	Day Laborer
46	Morris L.P.	H	W	M	Jan 1875	25	M	3			MS	MS	MS	
	Sarah	W	W	F	Oct 1878	21	M	3	2	2	AL	AL	AL	

1	2	3	4	5	6	7	8	9	10	11	12	13	14	15
	Lula	D	W	F	Apr 1898	2	S				MS	MS	AL	
	Bulah	D	W	F	Sep 1899	9/mo	S				MS	MS	AL	
47	Morris, John W.	H	W	M	Jan 1865	35	M	4			MS	MS	MS	Day Laborer
	Julia	W	W	F	Mar 1880	20	M	4	1	1	MS	MS	MS	
	Dona L.	D	W	F	Sep 1899	8/mo	S				MS	MS	MS	
	Malone, Thomas	Bd	W	M	Feb 1880	20	S				MS	MS	MS	Day Laborer
48	White, T. H.	H	W	M	Jan 1856	44	M	23			MS	TN	MS	Farmer
	Dona	W	W	F	Jul 1859	40	M	23	8	5	MS	MS	MS	
	Edgar	S	W	M	May 1883	17	S				MS	MS	MS	Farm Laborer
	Millard	S	W	M	Mar 1885	15	S				MS	MS	MS	Farm Laborer
	Geneva	D	W	F	Sep 1888	11	S				MS	MS	MS	
49	Marlar, J. R.	H	W	M	Feb 1858	42	M	19			MS	Ind	MS	Farmer
	Martha	W	W	F	Mar 1858	42	M	19	8	8	AL	SC	AL	
	Birtha	D	W	F	Jan 1882	18	S				MS	MS	AL	
	Eugene O.	S	W	M	Jan 1884	16	S				MS	MS	AL	
	Kenneth L.	S	W	M	Dec 1885	14	S				MS	MS	AL	
	Ida	D	W	F	Mar 1888	12	S				MS	MS	AL	
	Maud	D	W	F	May 1892	8	S				MS	MS	AL	
	William R.	S	W	M	Feb 1894	6	S				MS	MS	AL	
	Millard F.	S	W	M	Apr 1895	5	S				MS	MS	AL	
	Olen Dewey	S	W	M	Apr 1898	2	S				MS	MS	AL	
50	Holcomb, J.A.	H	W	M	Feb 1842	58	M	35			GA	SC	Ger	Farmer
	Sarah E.	W	W	F	Oct 1884	55	M	35	4	4	AL	TN	AL	
	Houston	S	W	M	Feb 1889	11	S				AL	GA	AL	Farm Laborer
51	Reynolds, G.W.	H	W	M	Mar 1843	57	M	10			MS	MS	MS	Farmer
	Rebecca	W	W	F	Dec 1852	47	M	10			MS	MS	MS	
	Millie	D	W	F	Apr 1887	13	S				MS	MS	MS	
52	Godwin, C. T.	H	W	M	Sep 1844	55	Wd				TN	GA	TN	
	Strom G.	S	W	M	Nov 1880	19	S				TN	TN	TN	Farm Laborer
	Estelle	D	W	F	Aug 1882	17	S				TN	TN	TN	
	Henry	S	W	M	Mar 1883	14	S				TN	TN	TN	Farm Laborer
53	Bingham, James	H	W	M	Mar 1850	50	M	30			MS	AL	TN	Farmer
	Susan	W	W	F	Jun 1840	59	M	30	7	4	TN	NC	NC	
54	Bingham, C.W.	H	W	M	Sep 1877	22	M	3			MS	MS	MS	Farmer
	Ida	W	W	F	May 1880	20	M	3	2	2	MS	MS	MS	
	Lesley D.	S	W	M	Sep 1898	1	S				MS	MS	MS	
	Leon	S	W	M	Jan 1900	4/mo	S				MS	MS	MS	
	Johnson, Sturt	Bdr	W	M	Jul 1880	19	S				GA	GA	GA	Farm Laborer
55	Johnson, William M.	H	W	M	Sep 1866	33	M	12			GA	GA	GA	Farmer
	Lou	W	W	F	Jul 1864	35	M	12	3	3	GA	GA	GA	
	Jessie	S	W	M	Oct 1888	11	S				GA	GA	GA	Farm Laborer
	James	S	W	M	Oct 1893	6	S				GA	GA	GA	
	Rina	D	W	F	Jan 1896	4	S				TN	GA	GA	
56	Jones, Ervin	H	W	M	Sep 1879	20	M	2			AL	AL	AL	Farmer
	Sarah	W	W	F	Aug 1879	20	M	2	1	0	AL	AL	AL	
57	Carroll, Ira M.	H	W	M	Aug 1879	33	M	11			TN	NC	MS	Farmer
	Rebecca	W	W	F	Mar 1868	32	M	11	6	5	TN	TN	TN	
	Forrest	S	W	M	Aug 1889	10	S				TN	TN	TN	Farm Laborer
	Ethel	D	W	F	Jun 1892	8	S				TN	TN	TN	
	Anna	D	W	F	Mar 1894	6	S				TN	TN	TN	
	Elbert	S	W	M	Feb 1897	3	S				TN	TN	TN	

1	2	3	4	5	6	7	8	9	10	11	12	13	14	15
	Avis	D	W	F	Oct 1899	7/mo	S				TN	TN	TN	
58	Buchannon, Joseph	H	W	M	Dec 1862	37	M	15			TN	TN	TN	Farmer
	A. L.	W	W	F	Feb 1870	29	M	15	7	6	TN	TN	TN	
	George	S	W	M	Jan 1886	14	S				TN	TN	TN	Farm Laborer
	Taylor	S	W	M	Nov 1887	12	S				TN	TN	TN	Farm Laborer
	Elizabeth	D	W	F	Jul 1891	8	S				TN	TN	TN	
	Lewis N.	S	W	M	Feb 1894	6	S				TN	TN	TN	
	Andy	S	W	M	Dec 1895	4	S				TN	TN	TN	
	May	D	W	F	Dec 1897	2	S				TN	TN	TN	
59	Sharp, Mrs. J.M.	H	W	F	Jun 1836	63	Wd		6	1	MS	MS	MS	Farmer
	Eler	D	W	F	Oct 1870	29	S				MS	MS	MS	
	Johnson, Andy	Bdr	W	M	Apr 1877	23	S				TN	TN	TN	Farm Laborer
	Godwin, Joseph	Bdr	W	M	UN 1874	25	S				TN	TN	TN	Farm Laborer
60	King, E.B.	H	W	M	Dec 1861	38	M	20			MS	SC	SC	Farmer
	B.M.	W	W	F	Jan 1876	24	M	20	11	11	TN	TN	TN	
	Adney	D	W	F	Feb 1882	18	S				MS	MS	MS	
	Harvey	S	W	M	Sep 1883	16	S				MS	MS	MS	Farm Laborer
	Lilley	D	W	F	Oct 1885	14	S				MS	MS	MS	
	Edmon	S	W	M	May 1887	13	S				MS	MS	MS	Farm Laborer
	Virda	D	W	F	Feb 1889	11	S				MS	MS	MS	
	Hubard	S	W	M	Feb 1891	9	S				MS	MS	MS	
	Elija	S	W	M	Nov 1894	5	S				MS	MS	MS	
	Myrtle	D	W	F	May 1898	2	S				MS	MS	MS	
	Flossey D.	D	W	F	Mar 1900	2mo	S				MS	MS	MS	
61	Carroll, Joseph	H	W	M	Mar 1872	28	M	7			TN	NC	TN	Farmer
	Fannie	W	W	F	Feb 1868	32	M	7	2	1	MS	NC	GA	
	Minnie	D	W	F	Dec 1898	1	S				MS	TN	MS	
62	Dethardge, J.N.	H	W	M	Mar 1833	67	M	1			TN	TN	TN	Farmer
	S.E.	W	W	F	May 1848	52	M	1	0	0	AL	AL	GA	
63	Buchanan, S.W.	H	W	M	Sep 1845	54	M	6			TN	TN	TN	Day Laborer
	Elizabeth	W	W	F	Dec 1844	55	M	6	0	0	TN	TN	TN	
	Avis	F	W	F	Jan 1888	12	S				TN	TN	TN	
	Richard P.	S	W	M	Dec 1889	10	S				TN	TN	TN	
	Johnson, J.L.	Bdr	W	M	Oct 1873	26	M	1			TN	TN	TN	Day Laborer
	Maud L.	W	W	F	Dec 1882	17	M	1	0	0	TN	TN	TN	
64	Sharp, M.D.	H	W	M	Jul 1840	59	M	22			TN	SC	NC	Farmer
	C.E.	W	W	F	Mar 1852	48	M	22	8	8	MS	KY	GA	
	S.E.	D	W	F	Jun 1878	22	S				MS	TN	MS	
	J.L.	S	W	M	Jan 1879	21	S				MS	TN	MS	Farm Laborer
	Anne D.	D	W	F	Dec 1882	17	S				MS	TN	MS	
	J.T.	S	W	M	Jun 1885	14	S				MS	TN	MS	Farm Laborer
	Molie	D	W	F	Jan 1888	11	S				MS	TN	MS	
	Kate	D	W	F	Jul 1890	9	S				MS	TN	MS	
	Samuel D.	S	W	M	Apr 1893	7	S				MS	TN	MS	
	Anah	D	W	F	Jan 1897	3	S				MS	TN	MS	
65	Edwards, G.R.	H	W	M	Mar 1861	39	M	14			GA	GA	GA	
	Rebecca	W	W	F	Oct 1860	39	M	14	7	5	MS	TN	TN	
	Walter	S	W	M	Nov 1887	12	S				TN	GA	MS	Farm Laborer
	Carroll	S	W	M	Mar 1889	11	S				TN	GA	MS	Farm Laborer
	Annie M.	D	W	F	Jan 1894	6	S				MS	GA	MS	
	Ethel	D	W	F	Oct 1896	3	S				MS	GA	MS	
	Robert	S	W	M	Mar 1899	1	S				MS	GA	MS	
66	Johnson, Y.T.	H	W	M	Mar 1850	50	Wd				MS	TN	NC	Farmer
	Roxey A.	D	W	F	Apr 1886	14	S				TN	MS	NC	

1	2	3	4	5	6	7	8	9	10	11	12	13	14	15
	Ada R.	D	W	F	Mar 1888	12	S				TN	MS	MS	
	Sarah H.	M	W	F	Jul 1823	77	Wd		1	1	NC	SC	NC	
67	Coln, J.T.	H	W	M	Dec 1856	43	M	20			TN	SC	TN	Farmer
	T.T.	W	W	F	May 1859	41	M	20	7	6	MS	AL	MS	
	W.R.	S	W	M	Jun 1882	17	S				TN	TN	MS	Farm Laborer
	J.M.	S	W	M	Feb 1884	16	S				TN	TN	MS	
	Mary E.	D	W	F	Jul 1889	10	S				TN	TN	MS	
	T.C.	S	W	M	May 1893	7	S				TN	TN	MS	
	M.O.	D	W	F	Feb 1895	5	S				TN	TN	MS	
	M.E.	D	W	F	Apr 1896	4	S				TN	TN	MS	
68	Utley, J.H.	H	W	M	Apr 1837	62	M	40			TN	VA	TN	Farmer
	Martha J.	W	W	F	Jan 1848	52	M	40	8	7	TN	AL	TN	
	Mary R.	D	W	F	Aug 1863	36	S				TN	TN	TN	
	Synthia	D	W	F	Sep 1881	18	S				TN	TN	TN	
	James D.	S	W	M	Nov 1883	16	S				TN	TN	TN	
69	Phelps, W.G.	H	W	M	Aug 1851	48	M	18			TN	GA	GA	Day Laborer
	H.G.	W	W	F	Jul 1859	40	M	18	5	4	MS	MS	AL	
	Nancy S.	D	W	F	Jan 1883	17	S				TN	TN	MS	
	William G.	S	W	M	Apr 1885	15	S				TN	TN	MS	Day Laborer
	Evaline O.	D	W	F	Sep 1887	12	S				TN	TN	MS	
	Mary M.	D	W	F	Dec 1889	11	S				TN	TN	MS	
	Synthia Zula	D	W	F	May 1891	9	S				TN	TN	MS	
	Phelps, Virginia	M	W	F	Sep 1838	61	Wd		1	1	AL	KY	KY	
70	Utley, William	H	W	M	Feb 1881	39	M	7			TN	TN	TN	Farmer
	Malinda	W	W	F	Apr 1877	23	M	7	5	2	TN	TN	TN	
	Treesse A.	D	W	F	Jan 1897	3	S				MS	TN	TN	
	Mattie G.	D	W	F	Feb 1899	1	S				MS	TN	TN	
	Utley, Sarah A.	M	W	F	Sep 1835	64	Wd		1	0	TN	TN	TN	
71	Utley, J.S.	H	W	M	Mar 1856	44	M	12			MS	TN	TN	Farmer
	Eliza	W	W	F	Mar 1871	29	M	12	7	5	TN	TN	TN	
	Norma G.	D	W	F	Sep 1888	11					MS	MS	TN	
	Nora R.	D	W	F	Feb 1890	10	S				MS	MS	TN	
	J.D.	S	W	M	Apr 1895	5	S				MS	MS	TN	
	M.A.	D	W	F	Oct 1897	2	S				MS	MS	TN	
	Lovy J.	D	W	F	Jul 1900	4/mo	S				MS	MS	TN	
72	Weathers, B.F.	H	W	M	Aug 1856	43	M	16			AL	AL	AL	Farmer
	S.V.A.	W	W	F	Mar 1867	33	M	16	4	4	MS	GA	GA	
	Alonza M.	S	W	M	Mar 1884	16	S				MS	AL	MS	Farm Laborer
	Earley	S	W	M	Mar 1886	14	S				MS	AL	MS	Farm Laborer
	Odel	S	W	M	Sep 1889	10	S				MS	AL	MS	Farm Laborer
	Carl R.	S	W	M	Jul 1894	5	S				MS	AL	MS	
73	Gray, Joseph	H	W	M	Oct 1875	24	M	1			MS	GA	GA	Day Laborer
	Linna	W	W	F	Nov 1880	19	M	1	0	0	MS	GA	GA	
74	Gray, David	H	W	M	Jul 1832	68	M	44			TN	TN	TN	Farmer
	Bethena	W	W	F	Jul 1834	65	M	44	8	5	TN	TN	TN	
	Abby	D	W	F	Sep 1862	37	5				MS	TN	TN	
75	Lamb, C.W.	H	W	M	Jul 1865	34	M	12			TN	TN	TN	Farmer
	Dollie	W	W	F	Jan 1870	30	M	12	6	5	MS	MS	TN	
	Dasie	D	W	F	Apr 1889	11	S				MS	TN	MS	
	Laticue	D	W	F	Aug 1891	8	S				MS	TN	MS	
	Katie	D	W	F	Sep 1894	5	S				MS	TN	MS	
	Luther	S	W	M	Jan 1897	3	S				MS	TN	MS	
	Lovie	D	W	F	Jul 1899	1	S				MS	TN	MS	

1	2	3	4	5	6	7	8	9	10	11	12	13	14	15
76	Gray, Hulda	H	W	F	Mar 1830	70	Wd		15	9	TN	TN	TN	Farmer
	Manda	D	W	F	Sep 1865	34	S				TN	TN	TN	
	Willis	S	W	M	Jul 1867	32	S				MS	TN	TN	
	Lewis	S	W	M	Jan 1870	30	S				MS	TN	TN	
	Joseph	S	W	M	Oct 1872	27	S				MS	TN	TN	
77	Gray, John	H	W	M	Jul 1848	51	M	4			MS	TN	TN	Farmer
	Gurtrue	W	W	F	Feb 1877	23	M	4	0	0	MS	TN	TN	
78	Gray, David	H	W	M	Jan 1854	46	M	22			MS	TN	TN	Farmer
	Jenny	W	W	F	Oct 1861	38	M	22	7	5	MS	MS	MS	
	Annie	D	W	F	May 1879	21	S				MS	MS	MS	
	Robert	S	W	M	Jun 1882	18	S				MS	MS	MS	Farm Laborer
	Isaac	S	W	M	Sep 1885	14	S				MS	MS	MS	Farm Laborer
	Joseph	S	W	M	May 1891	9	S				MS	MS	MS	
	Eller Lee	D	W	F	Jul 1894	5	S				MS	MS	MS	
79	Lamb, William	H	W	M	May 1862	38	M	18			TN	TN	TN	Farmer
	Matilda	W	W	F	Jul 1863	36	M	18			MS	TN	TN	
	Lamb, Andy J.	F	W	M	Feb 1832	68	Wd				TN	VA	VA	
80	McDuffie, J.W.	H	W	M	Mar 1865	35	M	17			MS	MS	MS	Day Laborer
	Mollie	W	W	F	Jun 1860	39	M	17	5	5	TN	TN	MS	
	Jernigan, Bessie	SD	W	F	Apr 1880	20	S				TN	MS	TN	
	McDuffie, Maud	D	W	F	Jul 1883	16	S				TN	MS	TN	
	Ellen	D	W	F	Dec 1884	15	S				TN	MS	TN	
	William	S	W	M	Oct 1889	10	S				TN	MS	TN	
	Millard	S	W	M	Mar 1892	8	S				TN	MS	TN	
81	Jernigan, W.C.	H	W	M	Jul 1842	57	M	38			MS	NC	AL	Farmer
	Nancy	W	W	F	Jan 1850	50	M	38	3	2	AL	AL	AL	
	Jernigan, Eller	GD	W	F	Nov 1891	8	S				MS	MS	MS	
	Lafeyette	GS	W	M	May 1892	8	S				TN	MS	MS	
	Marvin	GS	W	M	Nov 1893	6	S				TN	MS	MS	
82	Haynes, William	H	W	M	Aug 1854	45	M	27			AL	AL	AL	Farmer
	Mary E.	W	W	F	Jan 1849	51	M	27	10	4	AL	TN	AL	
	James A.	S	W	M	Mar 1882	18	S				MS	AL	AL	
	Alonzo	S	W	M	Apr 1884	16	S				MS	AL	AL	
	Katie	D	W	F	May 1889	11	S				MS	AL	AL	
	Frederick	S	W	M	Aug 1891	8	S				MS	AL	AL	
83	Gray, Isaac	H	W	M	Aug 1845	54	M	20			MS	MS	TN	Farmer
	Mary	W	W	F	May 1856	44	M	20	3	3	MS	MS	TN	
	Annie G.	D	W	F	Jan 1881	19	S				MS	MS	TN	
	Luelar	D	W	F	Sep 1885	14	S				MS	MS	TN	
84	Lamb, T.J.	H	W	M	Jan 1874	26	M	2			TN	VA	VA	Farmer
	Martha	W	W	F	Jan 1864	36	M	2	1	1	TN	TN	MS	
	L.M.	D	W	F	Jun 1899	11/mo	S				MS	TN	MS	
85	Whiticur, W.W.	H	W	M	Mar 1854	46	M	28			MS	MS	TN	Farmer
	L.T.	W	W	F	Jun 1875	24	M	28	7	7	MS	NC	MS	
	Suda	D	W	F	Jan 1879	21	S				MS	MS	MS	
	Ellis	S	W	M	Seo 1882	17	S				MS	MS	MS	Farm Laborer
	Marcus	S	W	M	Mar 1885	15	S				MS	MS	MS	Farm Laborer
	Lelza	D	W	F	Dec 1887	12	S				MS	MS	MS	
	Erwin	S	W	M	Mar 1890	10	S				MS	MS	MS	
	Opha	D	W	F	May 1896	4	S				MS	MS	MS	
	Cercy	S	W	M	Aug 1898	1	S				MS	MS	MS	
86	Gray, J.W.	H	W	M	Jan 1839	61	M	42			TN	AL	AL	Farmer
	Mary Jane	W	W	F	Jul 1835	64	M	42	10	7	TN	AL	SC	

1	2	3	4	5	6	7	8	9	10	11	12	13	14	15
87	Gray, D.L.	H	W	M	Feb 1869	31	M	1			MS	AL	SC	Farmer
	Sallie	W	W	F	Feb 1882	18	M	1	0	0	MS	MS	TN	
88	Gray, C.C.	H	W	M	Mar 1833	67	M	35			GA	GA	GA	Farmer
	Hannah	W	W	F	Oct 1844	55	M	35	9	9	GA	GA	GA	
	Henry	S	W	M	May 1881	19	S				MS	GA	GA	
89	Gray, George	H	W	M	Oct 1878	21	S				MS	GA	GA	Farmer
	Lovey	D	W	F	Feb 1889	11	S				MS	GA	GA	
90	Ward, C.F.	H	W	M	Apr 1866	34	M	11			IN	OH	OH	Farmer
	Mary	W	W	F	Jan 1866	34	M	11	5	5	TN	TN	TN	
	Charley	S	W	M	Dec 1890	9	S				MS	MS	MS	
	Nettie M.	D	W	F	May 1892	8	S				MS	MS	MS	
	Alley	S	W	M	Mar 1895	5	S				MS	MS	MS	
	Clifford	S	W	M	Mar 1897	3	S				MS	MS	MS	
	Robert L.	S	W	M	Mar 1900	2/mo	S				MS	MS	MS	
91	James, Thomas	H	W	M	Aug 1875	24	M	3			MS	Eng	MS	Day Laborer
	Maybell	W	W	F	Sep 1881	18	M	3	1	1	AL	AL	AL	
	James R.	S	W	M	Jun 1898	2	S				MS	AL	AL	
	Love, D.H.	F	W	M	Aug 1859	40	Wd				AL	NC	AL	
92	Gray, P.A.	H	W	M	Dec 1868	31	M	5			MS	GA	GA	Farmer
	Della	W	W	F	Jul 1876	23	M	5	2	2	MS	MS	MS	
	D.	D	W	F	Apr 1895	4					MS	MS	MS	
	Nelly	D	W	F	Dec 1898	1					MS	MS	MS	
93	Gray, James W.	H	W	M	Jul 1827	72	M	21			GA	GA	UN	Farmer
	Mary C.	W	W	F	Nov 1848	51	M	21	7	4	MS	TN	NC	
	Ezekiel G.	S	W	M	Oct 1883	16	S				MS	GA	MS	Farm Labor
	Sarah C.	D	W	F	Jan 1886	14	S				MS	GA	MS	
	Charles R.	S	W	M	Apr 1892	8	S				MS	GA	MS	
94	James, Thomas	H	W	M	Oct 1838	61	M	4			Eng	Eng	Eng	
	Mary E.	W	W	F	Aug 1876	23	M	4	2	2	AL	AL	AL	
	Cordelia	D	W	F	Aug 1872	27	S				MS	Eng	AL	
	Mary E.	D	W	F	Feb 1898	2	S				MS	Eng	AL	
	Minnie M.	D	W	F	Oct 1899	10/mo	S				MS	Eng	AL	
95	James, Thomas	H	W	M	May 1875	25	M	3			MS	Eng	AL	
	Mary	W	W	F	Aug 1881	18	M	3	1	1	MS	MS	AL	
	James B.	S	W	M	Jan 1897	2	S				MS	MS	AL	
96	Marlar, G.W.	H	W	M	Dec 1855	44	M	24			MS	AL	TN	Farmer
	Virginia	W	W	F	Jan 1844	56	M	24	5	4	AL	TN	AL	
	Anne	D	W	F	Apr 1878	22	S				MS	MS	AL	
	Louis	S	W	M	Apr 1880	20	S				MS	MS	AL	Farm Laborer
	Cora	D	W	F	Nov 1882	17	S				MS	MS	AL	
	A.P.Hill	S	W	M	Jan 1885	15	S				MS	MS	AL	Farm Laborer
97	Igo, John	H	W	M	Nov 1866	33	M	13			AL	AL	AL	
	Mary	W	W	F	Mar 1864	36	M	3	8	7	AL	AL	MS	
	Roda A.	Sd	W	F	Apr 1880	20	S				AL	AL	AL	
	Andrew	Ss	W	M	Nov 1882	17	S				AL	AL	AL	Farm Laborer
	Crickett	D	W	F	Dec 1890	9	S				AL	AL	AL	
	Iva	D	W	F	Jun 1892	7	S				AL	AL	AL	
	Josea	D	W	F	Oct 1894	6	S				TN	AL	AL	
	Lona	D	W	F	Sep 1899	8/mo	S				MS	AL	AL	
98	Gray, William	H	W	M	Nov 1819	80	M	40			GA	GA	GA	Farmer
	Mary	W	W	F	Aug 1840	59	M	40			TN	TN	TN	
	Shug	S	W	M	Nov 1883	16	S				MS	GA	TN	Farm Laborer

1	2	3	4	5	6	7	8	9	10	11	12	13	14	15
99	Gray, T.	H	W	M	Mar 1870	30	M	1			AL	GA	TN	Farmer
	Ollie	W	W	F	Feb 1882	18	M	1	0	0	MS	TN	MS	
	Reece	Rel	W	M	Apr 1878	22	S				MS	GA	TN	Farm Laborer
100	Gray, William	H	W	M	Jan 1874	26	M	5			MS	GA	TN	Day Laborer
	Jennie	W	W	F	Aug 1878	21	M	5	2	2	MS	MS	MS	
	Willie	S	W	M	Sep 1894	5	S				TN	MS	MS	
	Sallie	D	W	F	Dec 1897	2	S				TN	MS	MS	
101	Wilkins, W.J.	H	W	M	Jan 1852	48	M	3			GA	GA	GA	Farmer
	Rina	W	W	F	Jan 1877	23	M	3	2	2	TN	TN	TN	
	William F.	S	W	M	Oct 1898	2	S				MS	GA	TN	
	Troy W.	W	M	M	Dec 1899	5/mo	S				MS	GA	TN	
102	Marlar, Thomas	H	W	M	Apr 1817	83	M	18			AL	VA	AL	Farmer
	Elizabeth	W	W	F	Sep 1834	65	M	18	1	1	GA	GA	TN	
103	Sitton, Elizabeth	H	W	F	Feb 1848	52	Wd		10	8	MS	AL	MS	
	Perry, Fannie	D	W	F	Jan 1878	22	Wd		2	1	TX	AL	MS	
	Perry, Clidy	D	W	F	Jan 1897	3	S				TN	TX	TX	
104	Bray, J.G.	H	W	M	Sep 1850	49	M	30			GA	GA	GA	Farmer
	Louisa	W	W	F	Mar 1853	47	M	30	12	9	MS	MS	MS	
	T.G.	S	W	F	Mar 1879	21	S				MS	GA	MS	Farm Laborer
	Bird	S	W	M	Jun 1880	19	S				MS	GA	MS	Farm Laborer
	Benjamin	S	W	M	Jun 1883	16	S				MS	GA	MS	Farm Laborer
	John	S	W	M	Sep 1886	13	S				MS	GA	MS	Farm Laborer
	Archie	S	W	M	Jan 1890	10	S				MS	GA	MS	
	Calvin	S	W	M	Sep 1892	7	S				MS	GA	MS	
	Autrey	S	W	M	Mar 1895	5	S				MS	GA	MS	
105	Streetman, Joseph	H	W	M	Jul 1862	37	M	14			AL	AL	MS	Farmer
	Marcia	W	W	F	Jul 1866	33	M	14	6	6	MS	AL	MS	
	Cora P.	D	W	F	Aug 1887	12					MS	AL	MS	
	Lee	S	W	M	Oct 1891	8					MS	AL	MS	
	Dosia	D	W	F	Mar 1894	6					MS	AL	MS	
	Josia	D	W	F	Mar 1894	6					MS	AL	MS	
	Kenny	S	W	M	Sep 1896	3					MS	AL	MS	
	Charley	S	W	M	Jan 1898	1					MS	AL	MS	
106	Lambert, Charley	H	W	M	Jul 1855	44	M	19			MS	NC	MS	Farmer
	Martha	W	W	F	Oct 1855	44	M	19	2	1	MS	MS	AL	
	William T.	S	W	M	Feb 1882	18	S				MS	MS	MS	
107	Johnson, Betsey	H	W	F	May 1857	43	Wd		7	6	MS	NC	MS	
108	Lambert, Joseph	H	W	M	Feb 1863	37	M	8			MS	NC	MS	Farmer
	Ninia	W	W	F	Sep 1874	25	M	8	4	4	AL	AL	AL	
	Dollie	D	W	F	Sep 1884	15	S				MS	AL	MS	
	Robert F	S	W	M	Feb 1886	14	S				MS	AL	MS	
	William F.	S	W	M	Jun 1888	11	S				MS	AL	MS	
	Joseph B.	S	W	M	Jul 1893	6	S				MS	AL	MS	
	Ida P.	D	W	F	Jul 1895	4	S				MS	AL	MS	
	Ora J.	D	W	F	Feb 1897	3	S				MS	AL	MS	
	Millie E.	D	W	F	Sep 1898	1	S				MS	AL	MS	
109	Gann, T.J.	H	W	M	Oct 1850	49	M	11			MS	AL	AL	Farmer
	Lula M.	W	W	F	Jul 1868	32	M	11	7	7	MS	MS	MS	
	Cora D.	D	W	F	Oct 1889	10	S				MS	MS	MS	
	Luther	S	W	M	Dec 1890	9	S				MS	MS	MS	
	Maggie	D	W	F	Feb 1893	7	S				MS	MS	MS	
	Fannie	D	W	F	Dec 1894	5	S				MS	MS	MS	

1	2	3	4	5	6	7	8	9	10	11	12	13	14	15
	Minnie	D	W	F	Oct 1896	4	S				MS	MS	MS	
	Randle	S	W	M	Aug 1898	1	S				MS	MS	MS	
	James	S	W	M	Dec 1899	5/mo	S				MS	MS	MS	
110	Reynolds, J.W.	H	W	M	Mar 1869	31	M	5			MS	MS	MS	Farmer
	Mollie	W	W	F	Jul 1872	27	M	5	2	2	MS	MS	MS	
	Cuthbert	S	W	M	Jul 1896	4	S				MS	MS	MS	
	Vosta	D	W	F	Apr 1899	1	S				MS	MS	MS	
111	Grisham, Thomas	H	W	M	Apr 1832	68	M	7			TN	KY	VA	Farmer
	Martha	W	W	F	Feb 1870	30	M	7	1	1	MS	TN	GA	
	Esa	D	W	F	Feb 1893	7	S				MS	TN	MS	
112	Cole, A.J.	H	W	M	Apr 1848	53	Wd				MS	TN	AL	Farmer
	Fannie	D	W	F	Jan 1876	24	S				MS	MS	AL	
	John	S	W	M	May 1881	19	S				MS	MS	AL	Farm Laborer
	Eda	D	W	F	Feb 1885	15	S				MS	MS	AL	
113	McMeans, J.L.	H	W	M	Mar 1870	30	M	7			AL	AL	TN	Farmer
	M.D.	W	W	F	Feb 1873	27	M	7	4	2	MS	MS	MS	
	Alice	D	W	F	Feb 1895	5	S				MS	AL	MS	
	Carra	D	W	F	Oct 1899	7/mo	S				MS	AL	MS	
	Phillips, M.H.	Aunt	W	F	Feb 1841	59	S				MS	SC	GA	
114	Burney, James	H	W	M	May 1833	67	M	42			AL	NC	TN	
	Phoebea	W	W	F	Aug 1834	65	M	42	5	4	TN	TN	TN	
115	Fite, P.M.	H	W	M	Aug 1847	52	M	8			NC	NC	AL	Farmer
	Annie	W	W	F	May 1860	40	M	8			MS	NC	MS	
116	Marlar, Joseph	H	W	M	Mar 1860	40	M	19			MS	NC	MS	Farmer
	Mollie	W	W	F	Jul 1865	34	M	19	12	10	MS	MS	MS	
	James M.	S	W	M	Nov 1883	16	S				MS	MS	MS	
	Cona	S	W	M	May 1886	14	S				MS	MS	MS	
	Keltz	S	W	M	Apr 1888	12	S				MS	MS	MS	
	Pearl	D	W	F	Jul 1890	9	S				MS	MS	MS	
	Oscar	S	W	M	Feb 1892	8	S				MS	MS	MS	
	Kimbell C.	S	W	M	Dec 1893	6	S				MS	MS	MS	
	Bart	S	W	M	Apr 1895	5	S				MS	MS	MS	
	Luler	D	W	F	Jan 1897	3	S				MS	MS	MS	
	Earley	S	W	M	Oct 1898	1	S				MS	MS	MS	
	Dewy S.	S	W	M	Jan 1900	4/mo	S				MS	MS	MS	
117	Burney, A.F.	H	W	M	Sep 1859	40	M	17			AL	AL	TN	Farmer
	Ellen	W	W	F	May 1863	37	M	17	7	7	MS	AL	MS	
	R.V.	D	W	F	Jul 1885	14	S				MS	AL	MS	
	L.P.	D	W	F	Mar 1887	13	S				MS	AL	MS	
	L.A.	S	W	M	Jan 1899	11	S				MS	AL	MS	
	Stanley	S	W	M	Nov 1892	7	S				MS	AL	MS	
	Mary M.	D	W	F	Jan 1895	5	S				MS	AL	MS	
	Estell	D	W	F	Jan 1897	3	S				MS	AL	MS	
	Millie	D	W	F	Nov 1899	6/mo	S				MS	AL	MS	
	Welch, Mrs. J.W.	M	W	F	Nov 1828	71	Wd		5	5	AL	VA	KY	
	Welch, Mary	D	W	F	Jul 1860	39	S				MS	AL	NC	
	Welch, Lee	Rel	W	M	Feb 1870	30	S				MS	NC	AL	Farm Labor
118	Whiticur, T.L.	H	W	M	Mar 1874	26	M	4			MS	MS	MS	Farmer
	Eva	W	W	F	Mar 1878	22	M	4	2	2	MS	GA	MS	
	William L.	S	W	M	Oct 1896	3	S				MS	MS	MS	
	Bessie L.	D	W	F	Dec 1898	1	S				MS	MS	MS	
119	Whiticur, J.W.	H	W	M	Jan 1877	23	M	1			MS	MS	MS	Farmer
	Carrie N.	W	W	F	Jan 1884	16	M	1			MS	GA	GA	

1	2	3	4	5	6	7	8	9	10	11	12	13	14	15
	Hershel	S	W	M	Mar 1900	2/mo	S				MS	MS	MS	
120	Tucker, V.L.	H	W	M	Apr 1856	44	M	20			MS	GA	GA	Farmer
	L.D.	W	W	F	Mar 1858	42	M	20	8	7	MS	NC	TN	
	George	S	W	M	Dec 1884	15	S				MS	MS	MS	Farm Laborer
	Edgar	S	W	M	Apr 1887	13	S				MS	MS	MS	Farm Laborer
	Robert	S	W	M	Dec 1889	10	S				MS	MS	MS	Farm Laborer
	Ross	S	W	M	May 1891	9	S				MS	MS	MS	
	Lillie	D	W	F	Feb 1894	6	S				MS	MS	MS	
	Lucy	D	W	F	Aug 1898	1	S				MS	MS	MS	
	McMasters, J.	F	W	M	Feb 1819	81	M	49			NC	NC	NC	
	Eliza	M	W	F	Dec 1832	67	M	49	7	3	TN	TN	TN	
121	Lambert, G.W.	H	W	M	May 1854	46	M	22			NC	MS	MS	Farmer
	Mary	W	W	F	Jun 1855	44	M	22	7	7	TN	MS	AL	
	John W.	S	W	F	Apr 1881	19	S				MS	MS	MS	Farm Laborer
	Mollie	D	W	F	Jul 1883	16	S				MS	MS	MS	
	James E.	S	W	M	May 1886	14	S				MS	MS	MS	Farm Laborer
	Maggie	D	W	F	May 1889	11	S				MS	MS	MS	
	Oscar A.	S	W	M	Jan 1892	7	S				MS	MS	MS	
	Kinney	S	W	M	Jan 1896	4	S				MS	MS	MS	
	George W.	S	W	M	Apr 1898	2	S				MS	MS	MS	
122	Clark, William	H	W	M	Dec 1844	56	M	14			VA	VA	NC	Farmer
	Caroline	W	W	F	Feb 1855	45	M	14	0	0	MS	KY	TN	
123	Honeycutt, N.T.	H	W	M	Aug 1841	58	M	38			GA	SC	NC	Farmer
	Elizabeth	W	W	F	Jan 1840	60	M	38	10	8	MS	KY	TN	
	Ambrus	S	W	M	Sep 1881	18	S				TN	GA	MS	Farm Laborer
124	Lamb, Andy	H	W	M	UN 1875	25	M	2			TN	TN	TN	Farmer
	Barbe	W	W	F	Jan 1877	23	M	2	0	0	MS	GA	MS	
125	Honeycutt, D.W.	H	W	M	Jan 1870	30	M	6			MS	SC	NC	Farmer
	Lular	W	W	F	Mar 1872	28	M	6	2	2	MS	SC	MS	
	Lee	S	W	M	Feb 1895	5	S				MS	MS	MS	
	Minnie	D	W	F	May 1896	4	S				MS	MS	MS	
	Kendrick	S	W	M	Nov 1892	7	S				MS	MS	MS	
126	Honeycutt, George	H	W	M	Jan 1870	30	M	5			MS	GA	GA	Farmer
	Belmer	W	W	F	Feb 1879	21	M	5			MS	MS	MS	
	Ellis E.	S	W	M	May 1898	2	S				MS	MS	MS	
127	Marlar, J.W.	H	W	M	Oct 1860	39	M	10			MS	MS	MS	Farmer
	Nora	W	W	F	Sep 1869	30	M	10	6	4	MS	MS	MS	
	Loucinda	D	W	F	Aug 1890	9	S				MS	MS	MS	
	George	S	W	M	Apr 1893	7	S				MS	MS	MS	
	Henry	S	W	M	Mar 1894	6	S				MS	MS	MS	
	Bricey	S	W	M	May 1897	3	S				MS	MS	MS	
128	Feltman, Sam	H	W	M	Aug 1848	51	W		9	3	AL	KY	AL	
	Richard	S	W	M	May 1878	22	S				AL	AL	AL	Farm Laborer
129	Walker, Henry	H	W	M	Sep 1871	28	M	4			TN	TN	TN	Farmer
	Margaret	W	W	F	Jan 1873	27	M	4	0	0	MS	TN	TN	
130	Johnson, Lewis	H	W	M	Dec 1824	75	M	28			AL	NC	NC	Farmer
	Mary	W	W	F	Jan 1855	45	M	28	11	7	MS	MS	MS	
	Levy	S	W	M	Mar 1883	17	S				MS	AL	MS	Farm Laborer
	Ellen	D	W	F	Apr 1887	13	S				MS	AL	MS	
	Jessey	S	W	M	Jan 1888	12	S				MS	AL	MS	Farm Laborer
	Deely	D	W	F	Mar 1890	10	S				MS	AL	MS	

1	2	3	4	5	6	7	8	9	10	11	12	13	14	15
131	Johnson, Carroll	H	W	M	Jul 1877	22	M	1			MS	AL	SC	Farmer
	Belle	W	W	F	Sep 1875	24	M	1	1	1	MS	TN	MS	
	Alley M.	D	W	F	Nov 1899	6/mo	S				MS	MS	MS	
132	Honeycutt, Bud	H	W	M	Jul 1860	40	M	18			MS	MS	MS	Farmer
	Nancy	W	W	F	Apr 1863	37	M	18	6	3	MS	MS	MS	
	James D.	S	W	M	Dec 1883	16	S				MS	MS	MS	Farm Laborer
	Claudia	D	W	F	May 1889	11	S				TN	MS	MS	
	Doss	S	W	M	Apr 1898	2	S				MS	MS	MS	
133	Johnson, Mose	H	W	M	May 1876	24	M	0			MS	AL	MS	Farmer
	Daisey	W	W	F	UN 1884	16	M	0	0	0	MS	MS	MS	
134	Osborn, J.D.	H	W	M	Jul 1864	35	M	13			AL	SC	GA	
	Catherine	W	W	F	Oct 1867	32	M	13	3	2	MS	AL	MS	
	Charley L.	S	W	M	Dec 1893	6	S				TN	AL	MS	
	Callie M.	D	W	F	Jul 1900	0/mo	S				MS	AL	MS	
	Scott, J.W.	Bd	W	M	UN 1879	21	UN				MS	AL	AL	Farm Laborer
135	Willcutt, J. Kelly	H	W	M	Feb 1868	32	M	7			AL	AL	IN	Farmer
	Irna	W	W	F	Sep 1875	24	M	7	2	2	MS	AL	AL	
	Martha G.	D	W	F	Jan 1894	6	S				MS	AL	MS	
	James B.O.	S	W	M	Jul 1897	2	S				TN	AL	MS	
136	Stephens, William	H	W	M	Jan 1836	64	M	38			TN	TN	TN	Farmer
	Martha	W	W	F	Jan 1840	60	M	38	4	1	TN	TN	TN	
137	Pyron, William	H	W	M	Mar 1845	55	M	28			MS	TN	MS	Farmer
	Mary O.	W	W	F	Jan 1854	46	M	28	7	5	MS	GA	MS	
	Estes B.	S	W	M	Apr 1888	12	S				MS	MS	MS	
	O.B.	D	W	F	Oct 1890	9	S				MS	MS	MS	
138	Medley, B.B.	H	W	M	Mar 1852	48	M	24			MS	MS	MS	Farmer
	Sarah E.	W	W	F	Sep 1849	50	M	24	9	6	TN	NC	TN	
	Clyde	S	W	M	Apr 1885	15	S				TN	MS	TN	Farm Laborer
	Bart	S	W	M	Oct 1887	12	S				MS	MS	TN	Farm Laborer
	Bessie	D	W	F	Aug 1890	9	S				MS	MS	TN	
139	McMasters, James	H	W	M	Mar 1853	47	M	28			AL	NC	TN	Sawmill
	Bettie	W	W	F	Jul 1847	52	M	28	5	2	MS	TN	TN	
140	Johnson, C.C.	H	W	M	Jan 1867	33	M	8			MS	MS	MS	Dry Goods
	Serena	W	W	F	Jan 1874	25	M	8	6	4	MS	MS	MS	
	Luther A.	S	W	M	Jul 1894	5	S				MS	MS	MS	
	Bryant W.	S	W	M	Feb 1897	3	S				MS	MS	MS	
	Pearl	D	W	F	Oct 1898	1	S				MS	MS	MS	
	Bessie	D	W	F	Mar 1900	0/mo	S				MS	MS	MS	
	Rodgers, W.R.	Bdr	W	M	Jul 1857	63	W				AL	NC	AL	Farm Laborer
141	Rodgers, M.M.	H	W	M	Feb 1875	25	M	5			AL	AL	AL	Farm Laborer
	Julia	W	W	F	May 1878	22	M	5	2	2	TN	AL	AL	
	Ethel	D	W	F	Aug 1896	3	S				AL	AL	TN	
	Della	D	W	F	Mar 1897	2	S				AL	AL	TN	
142	Rodgers, J.M.	H	W	M	Nov 1878	21	M	3			AL	NC	AL	Farm Laborer
	L.E.	W	W	F	UN 1877	23	M	3	1	1	AL	AL	AL	
	L.E.	S	W	M	Oct 1898	1	S				AL	AL	AL	
143	Scruggs, P.T.	H	W	M	Feb 1857	43	M	17			MS	TN	AL	Farmer
	A.L.	W	W	F	Dec 1866	33	M	17	3	3	GA	AL	GA	
	John H.	S	W	M	Sep 1884	15	S				MS	MS	GA	Farm Laborer
	Henry G.	S	W	M	Jan 1890	10	S				MS	MS	GA	Farm Laborer
	J.W.	S	W	M	Jun 1892	7	S				MS	MS	GA	

1	2	3	4	5	6	7	8	9	10	11	12	13	14	15
144	Phelps, G.P.	H	W	M	Mar 1837	63	M	6			MS	VA	GA	
	Martha E.	W	W	F	Dec 1847	52	M	6	0	0	MS	TN	SC	
	Lottie	D	W	F	UN 1885	15	S				MS	MS	MS	
	Berty J.	D	W	F	Aug 1886	13	S				MS	MS	MS	
145	Reece, G.W.	H	W	M	Mar 1863	37	M	13			MS	AL	GA	Farmer
	M.A.	W	W	F	Jul 1867	32	M	13	7	5	AL	AL	AL	
	William H.	S	W	M	Dec 1888	11	S				MS	MS	AL	
	Hassie	D	W	F	Jun 1890	10	S				MS	MS	AL	
	James M.	S	W	M	Jun 1891	8	S				MS	MS	AL	
	John A.	S	W	M	Aug 1893	6	S				MS	MS	AL	
	Gustavy	D	W	F	May 1898	2	S				MS	MS	AL	
146	Donahoo, James	H	W	M	Feb 1868	32	M	8			MS	MS	AR	Farmer
	Dollie A.	W	W	F	Jan 1869	31	M	8	0	0	MS	MS	TN	
147	McMeans, C.B.	H	W	M	UN 1862	37	M	16			AL	AL	TN	Farmer
	Fannie	W	W	F	May 1870	30	M	16	6	6	TN	TN	MS	
	Arthur	S	W	M	Sep 1885	14	S				TN	AL	MS	Farm Laborer
	Oscar	S	W	M	Sep 1887	12	S				MS	AL	MS	Farm Laborer
	Mame	D	W	F	Apr 1891	9	S				TN	AL	MS	
	Mattie	D	W	F	Dec 1892	7	S				TN	AL	MS	
	Rena	D	W	F	Aug 1896	3	S				MS	AL	MS	
	Merrell	S	W	F	Aug 1898	1	S				MS	AL	MS	
148	Simmons, W.W.	H	W	M	Jun 1821	78	M	22			AL	NC	AL	Farmer
	Mary	W	W	F	Jan 1860	39	M	22	5	3	TN	TN	TN	
	William	S	W	M	Mar 1886	14	S				TN	AL	TN	Farm Laborer
	Thomas C.	S	W	M	Jun 1889	10	S				TN	AL	TN	
	Fannie	D	W	F	Nov 1896	3	S				MS	AL	TN	Farm Laborer
149	Adcock, J.C.	H	W	M	Feb 1834	66	Wd				NC	VA	Ire	Farmer
	N.M.	Sis	W	F	Apr 1860	40	S				TN	NC	Ire	
150	McMasters, S.A.	H	W	M	Jul 1870	29	S				MS	TN	TN	Farmer
	Guthrey, J.R.	Bdr	W	M	UN 1860	40	S				MS	NC	SC	Farm Laborer
151	Clement, J.W.	H	W	M	Sep 1821	78	M	7			SC	SC	AL	Farmer
	M.L.	W	W	F	UN 1850	50	M	7	0	0	MS	SC	AL	
	Barnett, M.A.	Sil	W	F	UN 1849	50	S				MS	SC	AL	
	Hannah, J.E.	Bdr	W	M	UN 1849	19	S				TN	MS	MS	Farm Laborer
152	Bray, Nancy	H	W	F	UN 1823	77	Wd		7	4	GA	SC	GA	
	Susan	D	W	F	May 1839	41	Wd		1	1	GA	GA	GA	
	Briny K.	D	W	F	UN UN	UN	UN				MS	AL	GA	
153	Bray, W.C.	H	W	M	Mar 1861	39	M	15			GA	GA	GA	Farmer
	Manetta	W	W	F	Jul 1869	30	M	15	6	6	TN	TN	SC	
	Walter	S	W	M	Sep 1885	14	S				TN	GA	TN	
	Alice	D	W	F	Dec 1887	12	S				MS	GA	TN	
	Sims	S	W	M	Aug 1889	10	S				MS	GA	TN	
	Sharp	S	W	M	Jul 1891	8	S				MS	GA	TN	
	Evia	D	W	F	Nov 1895	4	S				MS	GA	TN	
	Maggie	D	W	F	Jul 1897	2	S				MS	GA	TN	
154	Bumpass, J.	H	W	M	Jul 1857	61	S				AL	SC	NC	
	Allison	Sis	W	F	Jun 1831	69	S				TN	SC	NC	
	Ligen	Sis	W	F	Apr 1843	57	S				AL	SC	NC	
	Stanley, Arch	Bdr	W	M	Aug 1882	17	S				MS	MS	MS	Farm Laborer
155	Lock, D.C.	H	W	M	Jan 1860	40	M	15			MS	MS	MS	Farmer
	Lucy	W	W	F	Jan 1865	35	M	15	9	7	MS	MS	MS	

1	2	3	4	5	6	7	8	9	10	11	12	13	14	15
	Elmer	S	W	M	Aug 1886	14	S				MS	MS	MS	
	Lourene	D	W	F	Apr 1888	13	S				MS	MS	MS	
	Leroy	S	W	M	Feb 1897	4	S				MS	MS	MS	
156	Skinner, I.W.	H	W	M	Jan 1859	41	M	15			MS	AL	UN	Farmer
	W.R.	W	W	F	Jul 1862	37	M	15	8	6	MS	AL	MS	
	E.F.	D	W	F	Nov 1884	15	S				MS	MS	MS	
	L.M.	D	W	F	May 1886	14	S				MS	MS	MS	
	E.D.	D	W	F	Jan 1889	10	S				MS	MS	MS	
	A.B.	S	W	M	Jul 1891	8	S				MS	MS	MS	
	Lester	S	W	M	Jan 1896	4	S				MS	MS	MS	
	I.N.	S	W	M	Dec 1899	6/mo	S				MS	MS	MS	
157	Skinner, W.H.	H	W	M	Dec 1846	53	M	21			AL	AL	AL	
	E.A.	W	W	F	Sep 1853	46	M	21	6	6	AL	AL	AL	
	D.C.	D	W	F	Dec 1879	20	S				AL	AL	AL	
	R.A.	D	W	F	Jul 1881	18	S				MS	AL	AL	
	J.T.	S	W	M	Jun 1883	16	S				MS	AL	AL	
	H.L.	S	W	M	Jan 1886	13	S				MS	AL	AL	
	S.A.	D	W	F	Mar 1888	12	S				MS	AL	AL	
	W.J.	S	W	M	Sep 1893	6	S				MS	AL	AL	
158	Skinner, Jiddy	H	W	M	Jan 1824	76	M	56			AL	TN	NC	Farmer
	S.M.	W	W	F	Sep 1828	71	M	56	9	6	GA	GA	KY	
159	White, J.L.	H	W	M	Jan 1866	34	M	1			MS	TN	MS	
	Dona	W	W	F	Dec 1879	20	M	1	0	0	MS	MS	AL	
160	Wyoms, T.W.	H	W	M	Aug 1852	47	M	19			MS	TN	AL	Farmer
	Sallie	W	W	F	Dec 1863	36	M	19	7	7	MS	VA	MS	
	F.E.	D	W	F	Sep 1883	16	S				MS	MS	MS	
	E.I.	D	W	F	May 1885	15	S				MS	MS	MS	
	E.G.	D	W	F	Dec 1887	13	S				MS	MS	MS	
	E.B.	D	W	F	May 1890	10	S				MS	MS	MS	
	F.C.	S	W	M	Dec 1891	8	S				MS	MS	MS	
	R.C.	S	W	M	May 1894	6	S				MS	MS	MS	
	Edith R.	D	W	F	Jan 1896	4	S				MS	MS	MS	
161	Robinson, John A.	H	W	M	Mar 1870	30	M	4			MS	SC	AL	Farmer
	Clara	W	W	F	Sep 1881	18	M	4	3	3	MS	TN	AL	
	Lawrence	S	W	F	Dec 1896	3	S				MS	MS	MS	
	Kenny	S	W	M	Jan 1897	2	S				MS	MS	MS	
	Chester	S	W	M	Dec 1899	5/mo	S				MS	MS	MS	
	Robertson, William	F	W	M	Sep 1818	81	Wd		1	1	SC	SC	SC	
162	Robinson, Martha	H	W	F	Sep 1864	35	W		1	1	AL	SC	SC	
163	Flynt, W.A.	H	W	M	May 1839	61	W				MS	NC	TN	Farmer
	Robert	S	W	M	Sep 1882	17	S				MS	MS	SC	
	Eutake	D	W	F	Feb 1885	15	S				MS	MS	SC	
	Flynt, H.L.	Bdr	W	M	Nov 1875	24	S				MS	MS	SC	
164	Lambert, Wiley	H	W	M	Mar 1855	45	M	13			MS	MS	AL	Farmer
	Melissa A.	W	W	F	Jan 1863	37	M	13	4	4	AL	MS	AL	
	Milly J.	D	W	F	Aug 1888	11	S				MS	MS	AL	
	John	S	W	M	Mar 1891	9	S				MS	MS	AL	
	Edmond	S	W	M	Oct 1896	3	S				MS	MS	AL	
	Bessy	D	W	F	Jan 1900	5/mo	S				MS	MS	AL	
165	Lock, W. P.	H	W	M	Jan 1862	37	S				MS	AL	MS	Farmer
166	South, John B.	H	W	M	Oct 1841	58	M	35			TN	TN	TN	Farmer
	M.A.	W	W	F	Aug 1845	54	M	35	10	10	MS	NC	TN	
	J.D.	S	W	M	Mar 1880	19	S				MS	TN	MS	Farm Laborer

1	2	3	4	5	6	7	8	9	10	11	12	13	14	15
	Sallie	D	W	F	Mar 1884	16	S				MS	TN	MS	
	Willie	D	W	F	Mar 1886	14	S				MS	TN	MS	
	Julie	D	W	F	Jul 1890	9	S				MS	TN	MS	
	South, S.B.	Bdr	W	M	Dec 1875	24	S				MS	TN	MS	Farm Laborer
167	South, Robert B.	H	W	M	Jul 1870	29	M	3			MS	TN	MS	Farmer
	Mary	W	W	F	Jan 1878	22	M	3	1	1	MS	MS	MS	
	Itter	D	W	F	Aug 1889	10/mo	S				MS	MS	MS	
168	Kemp, Walter	H	W	M	May 1877	23	M	1			MS	MS	MS	Farmer
	Dasie	W	W	F	May 1878	22	M	1	0	0	MS	MS	MS	
169	South, Riley	H	W	M	Dec 1872	27	M	3			MS	MS	AR	Farmer
	Daisy	W	W	F	Oct 1881	18	M	3	2	2	MS	MS	MS	
	George	S	W	M	Jul 1898	1	S				MS	MS	MS	
	Burley	S	W	M	Jul 1898	1	S				MS	MS	MS	
170	Holder, B.A.	H	W	M	Nov 1863	37	M	18			MS	MS	MS	Farmer
	Rachel A.	W	W	F	Apr 1866	34	M	18	6	6	AL	MS	MS	
	C. L.	S	W	M	May 1883	17	S				MS	MS	MS	
	William D.	S	W	M	Nov 1884	15	S				MS	MS	MS	
	Coda A.	S	W	M	Dec 1886	13	S				MS	MS	AL	
	V.O.	D	W	F	Feb 1889	11	S				MS	MS	AL	
	Elmer	S	W	M	Mar 1891	9	S				MS	MS	AL	
	Elsa	D	W	F	Jan 1893	7	S				MS	MS	AL	
171	Robinson, Alf.	H	W	M	May 1855	45	M	26			AL	SC	SC	
	E.M.	W	W	F	Dec 1857	42	M	26	10	9	MS	AL	MS	
	Luler B.	D	W	F	Jan 1879	21	S				MS	AL	MS	
	Frances D.	D	W	F	Mar 1881	19	S				MS	AL	MS	
	Minnie L.	D	W	F	Aug 1884	15	S				MS	AL	MS	
	Willie H.	S	W	M	Jan 1886	14	S				MS	AL	MS	
	Shelly O.	D	W	F	Feb 1888	12	S				MS	AL	MS	
	Norma E.	D	W	F	Jun 1891	9	S				MS	AL	MS	
	E. G.	S	W	M	Jul 1895	4	S				MS	AL	MS	
	B. P.	D	W	F	Apr 1898	2	S				MS	AL	MS	
172	Barnes, John	H	W	M	May 1882	18	M	1			MS	MS	MS	
	Roxie	W	W	F	May 1882	18	M	1	0	0	MS	AL	MS	
173	McMasters, Uriah	H	W	M	Nov 1842	57	M	31			TN	NC	NC	Farmer
	Sarah	W	W	F	Jun 1844	55	M	31	8	8	TN	TN	TN	
	George	S	W	M	Jul 1882	17	S				MS	TN	TN	
	William L.	S	W	M	Dec 1886	13	S				MS	TN	TN	
	McMasters, John	Bdr	W	M	Nov 1878	21	S				MS	TN	TN	
174	Davis, James	H	W	M	Feb 1874	26	M	1			AL	AL	AL	Farmer
	Emma	W	W	F	Sep 1880	19	M	1	1	1	MS	MS	AL	
	Bessy L.	D	W	F	Dec 1889	6/mo	S				MS	AL	MS	
175	Brooks, W.D.	H	W	M	May 1861	39	M	20			AL	AL	AL	Farmer
	M.A.	W	W	F	Dec 1865	34	M	20	3	3	AL	AL	AL	
	J.E.	S	W	M	Sep 1881	18	S				MS	AL	AL	
	T.H.	S	W	M	Feb 1885	15	S				MS	AL	AL	
	Willie	S	W	M	Nov 1886	13	S				MS	AL	AL	
176	Sprouse, M.	H	W	M	Jul 1827	73	M	50			SC	SC	SC	Farmer
	C.	W	W	F	Mar 1831	69	M	50	13	3	NC	NC	NC	
	T. P.	S	W	M	Mar 1874	26	S				AL	SC	NC	
177	Hatcher, W.P.	H	W	M	Oct 1857	42	M	20			AL	GA	MS	Farmer
	S.J.	W	W	F	Jan 1865	35	M	20	6	6	AR	AL	AR	
	Ward	S	W	M	Mar 1883	17	S				MS	AL	AR	

1	2	3	4	5	6	7	8	9	10	11	12	13	14	15
	Gretna	D	W	F	Mar 1885	15	S				MS	AL	AR	
	Mattie	D	W	F	May 1887	13	S				MS	AL	AR	
	James	S	W	M	May 1888	12	S				MS	AL	AR	
	Minnie	D	W	F	Apr 1889	2	S				MS	AL	AR	
	Dempsey, James	OT	W	M	UN 1884	16	S				TN	TN	TN	
178	Wilson, S.T.	H	W	M	Aug 1860	39	M	16			MS	IL	SC	Farmer
	Hanner	W	W	F	Apr 1860	39	M	16	6	5	MS	AL	TN	
	W.D.G.	S	W	M	Sep 1885	14	S				MS	MS	MS	Farm Laborer
	Margaret J.	D	W	F	Sep 1887	12	S				MS	MS	MS	
	John T.	S	W	M	Feb 1892	8	S				MS	MS	MS	
	Robert P.	S	W	M	Feb 1892	8	S				MS	MS	MS	
	Rufus E.	S	W	M	Dec 1896	3	S				MS	MS	MS	
179	Rossur, C.B.	H	W	M	Aug 1830	69	M	40			Swit	Swit	Swit	Farmer
	S.H.	W	W	F	Feb 1838	62	M	40	15	10	Swit	Swit	Swit	
	Mabel	D	W	F	May 1882	18	S				IL	Swit	Swit	
180	Miller, James	H	W	M	Feb 1851	49	M	26			IN	Scot	Scot	Farmer
	Sarah	W	W	F	Oct 1859	40	M	26	7	6	KY	KY	KY	
	Viola	D	W	F	Jul 1875	24	S				IN	IN	KY	
	Mary E.	D	W	F	Jun 1880	19	S				TN	IN	KY	Farm Laborer
	Harvey C.	S	W	M	Jul 1890	10	S				MS	IN	KY	
	Clarinda	D	W	F	Sep 1888	11	S				MS	IN	KY	
181	Rodgers, C.W.	H	W	M	Sep 1859	40	M	15			GA	GA	GA	Farmer
	A.L.	W	W	F	Aug 1864	35	M	15	7	7	GA	GA	GA	
	Fred L.	S	W	M	Sep 1885	14	S				GA	GA	GA	
	Floyd H.	S	W	M	Mar 1887	13	S				GA	GA	GA	
	May	D	W	F	Jul 1890	9	S				GA	GA	GA	
	Mid C.	S	W	M	Dec 1892	7	S				GA	GA	GA	
	Maude L.	D	W	F	Dec 1894	5	S				GA	GA	GA	
	Carl D.	S	W	M	Jan 1897	3	S				MS	GA	GA	
	Ruth A.	D	W	F	Feb 1899	1	S				MS	GA	GA	
182	Armstrong, W.D.	H	W	M	Feb 1864	36	M	14			AL	AL	AL	Farmer
	Francis	W	W	F	Nov 1858	41	M	14	7	5	AL	AL	AL	
	Leoner	D	W	F	Jun 1882	17	S				AL	AL	AL	
	Earnest	S	W	M	Oct 1886	13	S				AL	AL	AL	
	Emit	S	W	M	May 1889	10	S				AL	AL	AL	
	Mattie M.	D	W	F	Jun 1893	6	S				AL	AL	AL	
	Ruda	D	W	F	Mar 1898	2	S				AL	AL	AL	
183	Lindsey, Robert	H	W	M	Apr 1870	30	M	9			AL	AL	AL	Farmer
	Dona	W	W	F	Feb 1880	20	M	9	4	4	MS	AL	MS	
	Magie B.	D	W	F	Aug 1892	7	S				MS	AL	MS	
	Maybell	D	W	F	May 1895	5	S				MS	AL	MS	
	R.	S	W	M	May 1897	3	S				MS	AL	MS	
	J.	S	W	M	Mar 1900	3/mo	S				MS	AL	MS	
184	Armstrong, Rubin	H	W	M	Dec 1844	55	M	22			AL	GA	AL	Day Laborer
	Martha	W	W	F	Jan 1854	46	M	22	8	6	AL	AL	AL	
	Andrew	S	W	M	Nov 1879	20	S				AL	AL	AL	Day Laborer
	Francis	D	W	F	Jan 1880	19	S				AL	AL	AL	
	James	S	W	M	Dec 1882	17	S				AL	AL	AL	Farm Laborer
	William	S	W	M	Jul 1885	14	S				AL	AL	AL	Farm Laborer
	Scott	S	W	M	Mar 1890	10	S				AL	AL	AL	Farm Laborer
	Julie	D	W	F	Sep 1892	7	S				AL	AL	AL	
185	Cay, William	H	W	M	Jan 1845	55	Wd				MS	SC	SC	Farmer
	O.D.	D	W	F	May 1877	23	S				MS	MS	MS	
	Luler	D	W	F	Jun 1880	19	S				MS	MS	MS	
	C. Everett	S	W	M	Jun 1883	16	S				MS	MS	MS	Farm Laborer

1	2	3	4	5	6	7	8	9	10	11	12	13	14	15
186	Moser, J.A.	H	W	M	Oct 1846	53	M	32			MS	TN	MS	Farmer
	Sarah J.	W	W	F	Sep 1844	55	m	32	7	7	MS	AL	SC	
	A.B.	S	W	M	Apr 1879	21	S				MS	AL	MS	Farm Laborer
	Ellis	S	W	M	Sep 1880	19	S				MS	AL	MS	Farm Laborer
	F.D.	D	W	F	Mar 1883	17	S				MS	AL	MS	
	Kate H.	D	W	F	Sep 1889	10	S				MS	AL	MS	
	George C.	S	W	M	Aug 1891	8	S				MS	AL	MS	
187	Provins, James	H	W	M	Jan 1872	28	Wd				KY	KY	KY	Farmer
	Elbert	S	W	M	May 1894	6	S				MS	KY	MS	
	Myrtle	D	W	F	Apr 1896	4	S				MS	KY	MS	
188	Ellis, L.A.	H	W	M	Dec 1860	39	M	20			TN	TN	TN	Farmer
	Nancy M.	W	W	F	May 1861	39	M	20	8	6	MS	TN	MS	
	Cora E.	D	W	F	Feb 1883	17	S				MS	TN	MS	
	Ora E.	D	W	F	May 1885	15	S				MS	TN	MS	
	Jesse L.	S	W	M	Jul 1887	12	S				MS	TN	MS	Farm Laborer
	Mary L.	D	W	F	Aug 1889	10	S				TN	TN	MS	
	Fannie E.	D	W	F	Aug 1891	8	S				MS	TN	MS	
	Martin E.	S	W	M	Jul 1898	1	S				MS	TN	MS	
189	Brown, Mrs. A.B.	H	W	F	May 1814	86	Wd		13	6	SC	SC	SC	Farmer
	Eliza	D	W	F	Nov 1844	55	S				SC	SC	SC	
	Narcis	D	W	F	Jun 1851	48	S				SC	SC	SC	
	Picken, Mary J.	Sis	W	F	Apr 1828	72	S				SC	SC	SC	
190	Flynt, Mrs. M.E.	H	W	F	Apr 1838	62	Wd				SC	SC	SC	
191	Lovelace, James	H	W	M	Jan 1860	40	M	16			TN	SC	TN	Blacksmith
	Francis	W	W	F	Jun 1857	42	M	16	8	8	MS	SC	SC	
	Eliza E.	D	W	F	Dec 1884	15	S				MS	TN	MS	
	Joseph D.	S	W	M	Aug 1886	13	S				MS	TN	MS	Farm Laborer
	Mary J.	D	W	F	Aug 1888	11	S				MS	TN	MS	
	John A.	S	W	M	Sep 1890	9	S				MS	TN	MS	
	James T.	S	W	M	Oct 1892	7	S				MS	TN	MS	
	Benjamin F.	S	W	M	Apr 1894	6	S				MS	TN	MS	
	George W.	S	W	M	Aug 1896	3	S				MS	TN	MS	
	Andrew	S	W	M	Oct 1899	7/mo	S				MS	TN	MS	
192	Dilworth, Henry	H	B	M	Sep 1872	22	M	2			MS	MS	MS	
	Lener	W	B	F	May 1883	17	M	2	0	0	MS	MS	MS	
193	Dilworth, Alex	H	B	M	Feb 1854	46	M	25			MS	IN	VA	
	Annie	W	B	F	May 1856	44	M	25	12	8	MS	MS	MS	
	David	S	B	M	Apr 1879	21	S				MS	MS	MS	Farm Laborer
	George	S	B	M	Jul 1884	16	S				MS	MS	MS	Farm Laborer
	Gensey	D	B	F	Mar 1886	14	S				MS	MS	MS	
	Coleman	S	B	M	May 1888	12	S				MS	MS	MS	Farm Laborer
	Daisy	D	B	F	Jun 1889	10	S				MS	MS	MS	
	Andrew	S	B	M	Jun 1894	5	S				MS	MS	MS	
	Mitchell, Mary A.	M	B	F	Jan 1820	80	Wd		1	1	VA	VA	VA	
194	Peal, November	H	B	M	Nov 1864	35	M	15			AL	VA	VA	Farmer
	Gemima	W	B	F	Nov 1876	23	M	15	4	4	MS	VA	VA	
	Roy	S	B	M	Mar 1888	12	S				MS	AL	MS	Farm Laborer
	Percy	S	B	M	Sep 1892	7	S				MS	AL	MS	
	James	S	B	M	Jun 1895	4	S				MS	AL	MS	
	Dealia	D	B	F	Mar 1896	4	S				MS	AL	MS	
	Peal, Dealia	M	B	F	May 1830	70	Wd		16	1	VA	VA	VA	
195	Parks, Wash	H	B	M	UN 1848	52	M	17			SC	SC	SC	Farmer
	Ida	W	B	F	May 1847	53	M	17	13	5	AL	VA	VA	

1	2	3	4	5	6	7	8	9	10	11	12	13	14	15
	Callie	D	B	F	Apr 1882	17	S				MS	SC	AL	
	Turner, Mary	Gd	B	F	May 1894	6	S				MS	SC	MS	
196	Joshlin, G.W.	H	W	M	Feb 1868	32	M	13			MS	SC	MS	Farmer
	Lottie	W	W	F	Jan 1870	30	M	13	6	3	MS	Ire	MS	
	John F.	S	W	M	Mar 1890	10	S				MS	MS	MS	Farm Laborer
	Edker	S	W	M	Oct 1896	3	S				MS	MS	MS	
	Louetta	D	W	F	Apr 1899	1	S				MS	MS	MS	
	Walters, Jacob	Bdr	W	M	UN 1876	24	S				MS	Ire	MS	RR Laborer
197	Brown, Ari	H	W	M	May 1834	66	M	42			SC	SC	SC	Farmer
	Margaret E.	W	W	F	Jan 1840	60	M	42	7	5	AL	TN	AL	
	James D.	S	W	M	Mar 1862	38	S				MS	SC	AL	Farm Laborer
	Minta J.	D	W	F	Jan 1877	23	S				MS	SC	AL	
198	Degraw, Sam	H	W	M	Aug 1876	23	M	3			MS	MS	AL	
	Sarah J.	W	W	F	Apr 1877	23	M	3	2	1	MS	SC	AL	
	Elmer A.	S	W	M	Mar 1899	1	S				MS	MS	MS	
199	Brown, Robert	H	W	M	May 1865	35	M	14			MS	SC	MS	Farm Laborer
	Sena	W	W	F	Jan 1873	27	M	14	4	3	MS	AL	AL	
	M.E.	D	W	F	Aug 1890	9	S				MS	MS	AL	
	S.L.	D	W	F	Oct 1893	6	S				MS	MS	AL	
	M.J.	D	W	F	Jan 1897	3	S				MS	MS	AL	
200	Brown, W.T.	H	W	M	Mar 1867	33	M	8			MS	SC	AL	Farmer
	M.L.	W	W	F	May 1875	25	M	8	4	4	MS	MS	MS	
	Willie F.	S	W	M	Apr 1893	7	S				MS	MS	MS	
	Annie B.	D	W	F	Jan 1895	5	S				MS	MS	MS	
	John H.	S	W	M	Jun 1897	2	S				MS	MS	MS	
	Sid A.	S	W	M	Aug 1899	9/mo	S				MS	MS	MS	
	Louis, Martha	Aunt	W	F	Aug 1825	74	Wd		3	2	AL	NC	NC	
201	Poole, William	H	W	M	Nov 1842	57	M	10			AL	AL	AL	Day Laborer
	Nancy E.	W	W	F	May 1872	28	M	10	1	1	AL	AL	AL	
	Lizea	D	W	F	Apr 1891	9	S				AL	AL	AL	
	C.B.	D	W	F	Mar 1879	21	S				AL	AL	AL	
202	Moser, Sarah	H	W	F	Apr 1836	63	Wd		8	5	AL	TN	AL	Farmer
	C.D.	S	W	M	Feb 1872	27	S				MS	TN	AL	Farm Laborer
	A.E.	S	W	M	Dec 1878	21	S				MS	TN	AL	Farm Laborer
203	Skelton, Mrs. Fannie	H	W	F	Jun 1850	49	Wd		9	7	AL	AL	AL	Farmer
	Victory	D	W	F	Apr 1881	19	S				MS	MS	AL	
	Eva	D	W	F	Jun 1885	14	S				MS	MS	AL	
	Annie	D	W	F	Oct 1887	12	S				MS	MS	AL	
	Tishie B.	D	W	F	Sep 1890	9	S				MS	MS	AL	
	Corbit J.	S	W	M	Oct 1895	4	S				MS	MS	AL	
204	Johnson, L.S.	H	W	M	Mar 1848	51	M	25			MS	NC	TN	
	Elizabeth	W	W	F	Aug 1850	49	M	25	6	4	AR	SC	TN	Day Laborer
	L.L.	S	W	M	Jan 1880	20	S				MS	MS	AR	Day Laborer
	Mandy E.	D	W	F	Feb 1885	15	S				MS	MS	AR	
	Mary M.	D	W	F	Oct 1887	12	S				MS	MS	MS	
205	Johnson, Hickman	H	W	M	Apr 1878	22	M	3			MS	MS	MS	Day Laborer
	Minie	W	W	F	Jul 1881	19	M	3	1	1	MS	MS	MS	
	Charley	S	W	M	Feb 1891	1	S				MS	MS	MS	
	Johnson, Joseph H.	Bdr	W	M	Jul 1887	23	S				TN	MS	MS	Day Laborer
206	Peterson, W.F.	H	W	M	May 1859	41	M	14			AL	SC	MS	Farmer
	C.C.	W	W	F	May 1858	42	M	14	6	6	MS	TN	TN	
	E.P.	D	W	F	Nov 1886	13	S				TN	AL	MS	

1	2	3	4	5	6	7	8	9	10	11	12	13	14	15
	S.B.	S	W	F	Mar 1889	11	S				MS	AL	MS	Farm Laborer
	M.B.	D	W	F	Feb 1891	9	S				MS	AL	MS	
	M.L.	D	W	F	Jul 1892	7	S				MS	AL	MS	
	T.C.	S	W	M	Mar 1895	5	S				MS	AL	MS	
	D.V.	S	W	M	Jan 1898	2	S				MS	AL	MS	
207	Marlar, R.L.	H	W	M	May 1863	37	M	18			MS	UN	UN	Farmer
	Martha	W	W	F	May 1866	34	M	18	7	7	MS	UN	UN	
	John W.	S	W	M	Feb 1884	16	S				MS	MS	MS	Farm Laborer
	Letha	D	W	F	Jan 1886	14	S				MS	MS	MS	
	Willie	S	W	M	Oct 1888	11	S				MS	MS	MS	Farm Laborer
	Reuben	S	W	M	Feb 1891	9	S				MS	MS	MS	
	Maggie	D	W	F	Dec 1893	6	S				MS	MS	MS	
	Nanie	D	W	F	Apr 1896	4	S				MS	MS	MS	
	Millie	D	W	F	Apr 1899	1	S				MS	MS	MS	
	Cathey, Mrs. Millie	Sis	W	F	Dec 1841	58	Wd				MS	KY	AL	
208	Jourdan, C.R.	H	W	M	Jun 1850	49	M	30			TN	VA	TN	Farmer
	Mary	W	W	F	Jun 1854	45	M	30	10	9	MS	TN	TN	
	M.D.	D	W	F	Dec 1880	19	S				MS	TN	TN	
	James C.	S	W	M	Nov 1885	14	S				MS	TN	TN	
	Irene	D	W	M	Jun 1891	8	S				MS	TN	TN	
	Ilean	D	W	F	Jun 1891	8	S				MS	TN	TN	
	Ivana	D	W	F	Jun 1891	8	S				MS	TN	TN	
	Luther M.	S	W	M	Nov 1894	5	S				MS	TN	TN	
209	Jourdan, B.F.	H	W	M	Feb 1872	28	M	1			MS	TN	MS	Farmer
	Emma	W	W	F	UN 1881	19	M	1	0	0	MS	GA	TN	
210	Whitehurst, C.	H	W	F	Mar 1825	75	Wd				SC	SC	SC	Farmer
	Lambert, Elizabeth	Bdr	W	F	Oct 1852	47	S				MS	MS	MS	
211	Smith, J.M.	H	W	M	Mar 1856	44	M	2			MS	TN	AL	Saw Mill
	Ida	W	W	F	Jul 1873	26	M	2	1	1	TN	Eng	AL	
	E.L.	D	W	F	Apr 1884	16	S				MS	MS	TN	
	M.E.	D	W	F	Apr 1888	12	S				MS	MS	TN	
	Q.D.	S	W	M	Apr 1900	2/mo	S				MS	MS	TN	
212	Ricks, Mrs. F.G.	H	W	F	Jan 1845	55	Wd		5	3	VA	VA	IL	
	John F.	S	W	M	Jul 1881	18	M	1			MS	MS	VA	Day Laborer
	Detishy	D	W	F	Jul 1882	17	M	1	0	0	MS	AL	MS	
213	Bain, Alford	H	W	M	Nov 1864	35	M	18			AL	AL	AL	Day Laborer
	Mary J.	W	W	F	Nov 1864	35	M	18	6	4	MS	NC	NC	
	John Henry	S	W	M	Feb 1883	17	S				AL	AL	MS	
	Nancy E.	D	W	F	Jul 1888	11	S				MS	AL	MS	
	Louetta	D	W	F	May 1894	6	S				MS	AL	MS	
	James C.	S	W	M	May 1896	4	S				MS	AL	MS	
214	Depoyster, Lafayette	H	W	M	Sep 1875	24	M	1			TN	TN	MS	RR Laborer
	I.	W	W	F	Aug 1884	15	M	1	0	0	MS	MS	MS	
215	Powell, John	H	B	M	Jan 1871	29	M	11			TN	TN	TN	RR Laborer
	L.	W	B	F	Jan 1863	37	M	11	1	1	TN	TN	MS	
216	Bain, John	H	W	M	Jul 1878	21	M	2			MS	AL	AL	RR Laborer
	Katie	F	W	F	Sep 1881	18	M	2	1	1	MS	AL	MS	
	Hendrix, Isaac	Bdr	W	M	Mar 1882	18	S				IL	IL	IL	Farm Laborer
217	Smith, W.R.	H	W	M	Jul 1827	72	M	43			TN	SC	TN	Farmer
	H.M.	W	W	F	Jun 1832	67	M	43	16	13	AL	AL	TN	
	Fannie V.	D	W	F	Mar 1874	26	S				MS	MS	AL	
	R.L.	S	W	M	May 1868	32	S				MS	MS	AL	

1	2	3	4	5	6	7	8	9	10	11	12	13	14	15
	Bulah	D	W	F	Mar 1876	23	S				MS	MS	AL	
	Gilbert, Lucinda M.	OT	W	F	Oct 1830	69	Wd				GA	GA	GA	
218	Waugh, Joseph	H	W	M	Jan 1873	27	M	7			AL	GA	GA	RR Laborer
	Anne	W	W	F	Jan 1878	22	M	7	4	3	MS	AL	MS	
	Gracy M.F.	D	W	F	May 1894	6	S				MS	AL	MS	
	Unice I.M.	D	W	F	Mar 1895	5	S				MS	AL	MS	
	Fred D.	S	W	M	Oct 1899	7/mo	S				MS	AL	MS	
	Waugh, Cora M.	Sis	W	F	May 1887	13	S				AL	AL	MS	
219	Depoyster, Lafayette	H	W	M	Sep 1875	24	M	1			MS	AL	MS	Farm Laborer
	Icy	W	W	F	Aug 1884	15	M	1	0	0	MS	AL	MS	
220	Holloway, Marsha	H	W	F	Sep 1842	57	Wd		10	7	MS	AL	NC	Farmer
221	Walden, J.P.	H	W	M	May 1849	51	Wd				MS	SC	SC	Farmer
	M.O.	Gd	W	F	Apr 1894	6	S				AR	MS	MS	
	M.G.L.T.	D	W	F	Jun 1874	25	S				MS	MS	AL	
	Holloway, I.C.	Mil	W	F	May 1818	82	Wd		8	0	AL	SC	TN	
222	Holloway, W.P.	H	W	M	Feb 1871	29	M	12			MS	MS	MS	Farm Laborer
	Fannie	W	W	F	Jul 1872	28	M	12	6	5	TN	AL	GA	
	Minnie	D	W	F	Mar 1892	8	S				MS	MS	TN	
	Annie	D	W	F	Jul 1889	10	S				MS	MS	TN	
	Sidney	S	W	M	Mar 1893	7	S				MS	MS	TN	
	Jessie	S	W	M	Aug 1894	5	S				MS	MS	TN	
	Stokley	S	W	M	Jul 1897	2	S				MS	MS	TN	
223	Ford, Joseph M.	H	W	M	Apr 1845	55	M	24			GA	GA	NC	Farmer
	Clista	W	W	F	Jul 1855	44	M	24	10	9	AL	SC	NC	
	Nina	D	W	F	Mar 1880	20	S				TN	GA	AL	
	Rosco	S	W	M	Nov 1881	18	S				TN	GA	AL	Farm Laborer
	Randle	S	W	M	Oct 1883	16	S				MS	GA	AL	
	Neal	S	W	M	Jan 1887	13	S				AL	GA	AL	
	J.A.	S	W	M	May 1882	17	S				MS	GA	AL	
	Myrtle	D	W	F	Feb 1890	10	S				MS	GA	AL	
	Paul	S	W	M	Nov 1894	5	S				MS	GA	AL	
	Myram	D	W	F	Feb 1897	3	S				MS	GA	AL	
	Ruby	D	W	F	Sep 1899	8/mo	S				MS	GA	AL	
224	Wilson, W.R	H	W	M	Aug 1868	32	M	9			KY	MS	IL	Farm Laborer
	Deller	W	W	F	Sep 1875	24	M	9	3	3	IL	IL	IL	Farm Laborer
	Bellvia	D	W	F	Oct 1893	6	S				IL	KY	IL	
	Ruda	S	W	M	Mar 1896	4	S				IL	KY	IL	
	Pearley	D	W	F	Oct 1898	1	S				IL	KY	IL	
225	Marlar, Joseph	H	W	M	Sep 183	6	M	20			MS	UN	UN	Farmer
	Ida	W	W	F	Apr 1857	43	M	20	8	8	MS	MS	MS	
	Daisy	D	W	F	Jun 1881	18	S				MS	MS	MS	
	Walter	S	W	M	Mar 1883	17	S				MS	MS	MS	
	Dollie	D	W	F	Jan 1885	15	S				MS	MS	MS	
	Minnie	D	W	F	Jan 1887	13	S				MS	MS	MS	
	John	S	W	M	Jan 1889	11	S				MS	MS	MS	
	Charley	S	W	M	Mar 1891	9	S				MS	MS	MS	
	Nora	D	W	F	Aug 1893	7	S				MS	MS	MS	
	W.J.	S	W	M	Mar 1895	5	S				MS	MS	MS	
226	Depoyster, A.	H	W	M	Sep 1851	48	M	26			TN	TN	TN	Farmer
	Sarah	W	W	F	Jul 1854	45	M	26	10	6	MS	MS	TN	
	G. Franklin	S	W	M	Jan 1880	20	S				MS	TN	MS	Farm Laborer
	James R.	S	W	M	Jan 1882	18	S				MS	TN	MS	Farm Laborer
	Levy	S	W	M	Mar 1885	15	S				MS	TN	MS	Farm Laborer
	Mahalia E.	D	W	F	Sep 1887	13	S				MS	TN	MS	

1	2	3	4	5	6	7	8	9	10	11	12	13	14	15
	John T.	S	W	M	Mar 1890	10	S				MS	TN	MS	Farm Laborer
227	Patrick, Thomas	H	W	M	Oct 1855	46	M	20			MS	MS	MS	Farmer
	Greely	W	W	F	Nov 1866	34	M	20	10	10	AL	AL	AL	
	Samuel A.	S	W	M	Feb 1884	16	S				MS	MS	AL	
	Sarah E.	D	W	F	Mar 1885	15	S				MS	MS	AL	
	Elsa A.	D	W	F	May 1887	13	S				MS	MS	AL	
	George A.	S	W	M	Dec 1889	10	S				MS	MS	AL	
	Thomas S.	S	W	M	Nov 1891	8	S				MS	MS	AL	
	Dosha L.	D	W	F	Oct 1892	7	S				MS	MS	AL	
	James C.	S	W	M	Sep 1895	5	S				MS	MS	AL	
	Henry C.	S	W	M	Feb 1896	4	S				MS	MS	AL	
	Helen	D	W	F	Apr 1898	2	S				MS	MS	AL	
	Walter	S	W	M	May 1900	1/mo	S				MS	MS	AL	
228	Morrow, Bruce	H	W	M	Dec 1858	51	M	18			AL	AL	AL	Farmer
	Malicus	W	W	F	Nov 1866	33	M	18	6	6	AL	AL	TN	
	Samantha S.	D	W	F	Mar 1883	17	S				AL	AL	AL	
	Nancy A.	D	W	F	Mar 1885	15	S				AL	AL	AL	
	Alex V.	S	W	M	Feb 1887	13	S				AL	AL	AL	
	John M.	S	W	F	Feb 1889	11	S				AL	AL	AL	
	Lenora	D	W	F	Feb 1891	9	S				AL	AL	AL	
	William W.	S	W	M	Mar 1893	7	S				AL	AL	AL	
229	Wilson, John R.	H	W	M	Jun 1845	54	M	7			MS	MS	MS	Farmer
	L.C.	W	W	F	Jul 1860	39	M	7	6	5	MS	NC	NC	
	M.E.	S	W	M	Dec 1881	18	S				MS	MS	MS	
	Francis I.	D	W	F	Mar 1893	7	S				MS	MS	MS	
	W.B.	D	W	F	Jul 1896	3	S				MS	MS	MS	
	Mary H.A.	D	W	F	Apr 1898	2	S				MS	MS	MS	
	Noah	S	W	M	May 1900	1/mo	S				MS	MS	MS	
230	Smith, George W.	H	W	M	Apr 1871	29	M	6			MS	TN	AL	Farmer
	Maggie	W	W	F	Sep 1871	28	M	6	2	2	AL	AL	AL	
	Eloyse	D	W	F	Jul 1895	5	S				MS	MS	AL	
	Ernest F.	S	W	M	Apr 1899	1	S				MS	MS	AL	
231	Lambert, W.H.	H	W	M	Sep 1864	36	M	13			MS	GA	AL	Farmer
	Mary	W	W	F	Jul 1870	30	M	13	5	5	MS	MS	MS	
	James	S	W	M	May 1889	11	S				MS	MS	MS	
	Leander	S	W	M	UN 1891	9	S				MS	MS	MS	
	Minnie	D	W	F	Mar 1894	6	S				MS	MS	MS	
	Lillie May	D	W	F	Aug 1895	4	S				MS	MS	MS	
	Luler G.	D	W	F	Jul 1898	1	S				MS	MS	MS	
232	Lambert J.	H	W	F	Mar 1876	24	Wd				MS	MS	TN	Farm Laborer
233	Marlar, George W.	H	W	M	Nov 1815	84	Wd				KY	VA	VA	Farmer
	Yates, Mary	Bdr	W	F	UN UN	40	M				MS	MS	UN	
	Patience	Bdr	W	F	UN UN	16	M				TX	MS	MS	
234	Lambert, Aron	H	W	M	Dec 1874	25	M	6			MS	MS	MS	Farmer
	Bulah	W	W	F	Oct 1879	20	M	6	1	1	MS	MS	MS	
	Lemuel G.	S	W	M	Aug 1895	4	S				MS	MS	MS	
235	Walker, John W.	H	W	M	Jan 1835	65	M	32			TN	TN	TN	Farmer
	Manda	W	W	F	Oct 1847	52	M	32	8	7	TN	NC	TN	
	Delila E.	D	W	F	Sep 1865	34	S				TN	TN	TN	
	James W.	S	W	M	Mar 1875	25	S				TN	TN	TN	Farm Laborer
	C.W.	S	W	M	Jul 1878	21	S				TN	TN	TN	Farm Laborer
	Mary E.	D	W	F	Sep 1881	18	S				TN	TN	TN	
236	Smith, V. W.	H	W	M	Aug 1831	68	Wd				SC	SC	SC	Farmer

1	2	3	4	5	6	7	8	9	10	11	12	13	14	15
237	Higgins, J.F.	H	W	M	Jul 1849	50	M	22			AL	AL	AL	Farmer
	Martha	W	W	F	Nov 1860	39	M	22	6	5	MS	AL	AL	
	Rubin	S	W	M	Nov 1877	22	S				MS	AL	MS	Farm Laborer
	Luler	D	W	F	Mar 1879	21	S				MS	AL	MS	
	John	S	W	M	Jan 1881	19	S				MS	AL	MS	Farm Laborer
	Bulah	D	W	F	Mar 1885	15	S				MS	AL	MS	
	Franklin	S	W	M	Jul 1887	13	S				MS	AL	MS	Farm Laborer
238	Gillian, John	H	W	M	Mar 1870	30	M	10			AL	MS	AL	Farmer
	Clemie	W	W	F	Dec 1873	26	M	10	4	2	MS	MS	MS	
	Kendrick	S	W	M	May 1896	3	S				MS	MS	MS	
	Desilas	S	W	M	May 1899	1	S				MS	MS	MS	
239	Gross, Frank	H	W	M	Apr 1883	17	M	0			MS	MS	MS	Farmer
	Mary	W	W	F	Jan 1881	19	M	0	0	0	MS	MS	MS	
240	Higginbottom, Massac	H	W	M	Jan 1875	22	M	0			MS	MS	MS	Farmer
	May	W	W	F	May 1875	22	M	0	1	1	MS	MS	MS	
	Irvin	S	W	M	Jul 1897	10/mo	S				MS	MS	MS	
241	George, Williams	H	W	M	Mar 1849	51	M	31			MS	MS	UN	Farmer
	Sarah	W	W	F	Sep 1848	51	M	31	7	7	MS	NC	TN	
	Sina U.	D	W	F	Jul 1871	28	S				MS	MS	MS	
	Oscar O.	S	W	M	May 1877	23	S				MS	MS	MS	Farm Laborer
	Luther D.	S	W	M	Jul 1879	20	S				MS	MS	MS	Farm Laborer
	Ona D.	S	W	M	Jul 1874	15	S				MS	MS	MS	Farm Laborer
	Lona A.	D	W	F	Jun 1886	13	S				MS	MS	MS	
	Stanley, William	Bdr	W	M	Mar 1881	19	S				MS	MS	MS	Farm Laborer
242	Barnes, Virginia	H	W	F	Aug 1861	38	Wd		6	6	MS	AL	AL	Farmer
	Minnie	D	W	F	Feb 1884	16	S				MS	MS	MS	
	James	S	W	M	Nov 1889	11	S				MS	MS	MS	Farm Laborer
	Lou Hattie	D	W	F	Nov 1890	9	S				MS	MS	MS	
	Cora Lee	D	W	F	Dec 1895	6	S				MS	MS	MS	
	Jesse J.	S	W	M	Apr 1896	4	S				MS	MS	MS	
243	Lambert, Dan	H	W	M	Aug 1854	45	Wd				MS	AL	AL	Farmer
	Marine	D	W	F	Oct 1885	16	S				MS	MS	AL	
	Lou F.	D	W	F	Nov 1885	14	S				MS	MS	MS	
	Joseph F.	S	W	M	Dec 1887	12	S				MS	MS	MS	Farm Laborer
	Olley B.	D	W	F	Mar 1889	11	S				MS	MS	MS	
	Barbara D.	D	W	F	Mar 1891	9	S				MS	MS	MS	
	Ideler	D	W	F	Jan 1893	6	S				MS	MS	MS	
	Ellen	D	W	F	Dec 1898	1	S				MS	MS	MS	
244	Blakney, Sam	H	W	M	May 1873	27	M	4			MS	TN	AL	Farmer
	Arvilla	W	W	F	Mar 1878	22	M	4	2	2	AL	AL	AL	
	Nellie	D	W	F	Apr 1897	3	S				MS	MS	AL	
	Edie	D	W	F	Dec 1896	1	S				MS	MS	AL	
245	Blakney, David	H	W	M	Apr 1827	73	M	45			TN	SC	SC	Farmer
	Clementine	W	W	F	May 1832	68	M	45	12	6	AL	SC	AL	
	Henry	S	W	M	Oct 1856	43	S				MS	TN	AL	
	Ballard	S	W	M	Nov 1861	38	S				MS	TN	AL	
	Grundy	S	W	F	UN 1868	32	S				MS	TN	AL	
	Joshlin, Catherine	SiL	W	F	UN 1830	70	S				MS	SC	AL	
246	Lambert, Lillie	H	W	F	Mar 1850	50	W		13	7	TN	AL	TN	Farmer
	Daniel	S	W	M	Jul 1882	18	S				MS	MS	TN	Farm Laborer
247	Gaines, James	H	W	M	Aug 1875	24	M	6			MS	MS	UN	Farmer
	Virda	W	W	F	Jan 1877	23	M	6	3	2	MS	MS	MS	

1	2	3	4	5	6	7	8	9	10	11	12	13	14	15
	Jeffie	D	W	F	Jul 1894	5	S				MS	TN	MS	
	Bessie	D	W	F	Mar 1898	2	S				MS	TN	MS	
248	Lambert, Hickman	H	W	M	Mar 1853	47	M	8			MS	MS	MS	
	Sarah	W	W	F	Mar 1860	40	M	8	1	1	MS	TN	TN	
	William	S	W	M	Apr 1894	6	S				MS	MS	MS	
	Lambert, Loucreacy	M	W	F	Mar 1823	77	Wd		13	8	TN	TN	TN	
249	Harris, M.L.	H	UN	UN	Oct 1861	38	M	18			MS	AL	MS	Farmer
	Luler	W	UN	UN	Nov 1865	34	M	18	6	6	MS	TN	AL	
	Kinney	S	UN	UN	Sep 1883	16	S				MS	MS	MS	Farm Laborer
	Minnie	D	UN	UN	Dec 1886	13	S				MS	MS	MS	
	Cleveland	S	UN	UN	May 1890	10	S				MS	MS	MS	
	Eda	D	UN	UN	Aug 1893	6	S				MS	MS	MS	
	Phil P.	S	UN	UN	Nov 1895	4	S				MS	MS	MS	
	Mamie	D	UN	UN	May 1897	3	S				MS	MS	MS	
250	Spoon, George	H	W	M	Apr 1867	3	M	6			TN	NC	TN	Farmer
	Mattie	W	W	F	May 1875	25	M	6	3	3	MS	MS	MS	
	Eva L.	D	W	F	Mar 1896	4	S				MS	TN	MS	
	John	S	W	M	Jan 1897	3	S				MS	TN	MS	
	Uley	D	W	F	Dec 1899	5/mo	s				MS	TN	MS	
251	Lambert, Joseph	H	W	M	Apr 1849	51	Wd				MS	TN	TN	Farmer
	Franklin	S	W	M	Dec 1882	17	S				MS	MS	AL	Farm Laborer
	Emma	D	W	F	Aug 1886	13	S				MS	MS	AL	
	Emmit	S	W	F	May 1889	11	S				MS	MS	AL	
	Julia	D	W	F	Dec 1894	5	S				MS	MS	AL	
252	Gurley, J.J.	H	W	M	Dec 1863	36	M	13			GA	GA	GA	Farmer
	Julia	W	W	F	Oct 1868	31	M	13	6	6	MS	MS	MS	
	Luther	S	W	M	Feb 1888	12	S				MS	GA	MS	
	May	D	W	F	Jun 1890	9	S				MS	GA	MS	
	Ruby	D	W	F	Jun 1892	7	S				MS	GA	MS	
	Hellen	D	W	F	Sep 1894	5	S				MS	GA	MS	
	Grace	D	W	F	Oct 1896	3	S				MS	GA	MS	
	Thomas	S	W	M	May 1899	1	S				MS	GA	MS	
253	Streetman, John	H	W	M	Dec 1827	72	M	50			GA	GA	GA	Farmer
	Elizabeth	W	W	F	Jun 1830	69	M	50	8	7	GA	GA	GA	
254	Harris, C.C.	H	W	M	Jun 1858	41	M	21			MS	AL	AL	Farmer
	Fannie	W	W	F	Oct 1864	35	M	21	12	9	KY	SC	AL	
	Harmon	S	W	M	Sep 1880	19	S				MS	MS	KY	
	Luther	S	W	M	Aug 1882	17	S				MS	MS	KY	
	Luler	D	W	F	Jul 1884	15	S				MS	MS	KY	
	Julius	S	W	M	Oct 1887	13	S				MS	MS	KY	
	Marcus	S	W	M	Oct 1889	10	S				MS	MS	KY	
	Kenny	S	W	M	Aug 1893	6	S				MS	MS	KY	
	Ethel	D	W	F	Apr 1896	4	S				MS	MS	KY	
	Lealier	D	W	F	Mar 1898	2	S				MS	MS	KY	
	Olen M.	S	W	M	Jan 1900	5/mo	S				MS	MS	KY	
255	Roach, J.W.W.	H	W	M	Jul 1870	29	M	8			TN	TN	GA	Farmer
	Francis	W	W	F	Oct 1875	24	M	8	5	4	MS	TN	MS	
	Lillie R.	D	W	F	Sep 1892	7	S				MS	TN	MS	
	Isaac E.	S	W	M	Dec 1893	6	S				MS	TN	MS	
	Jessie M.	S	W	M	Jun 1895	4	S				MS	TN	MS	
	Virginia M.	D	W	F	Jun 1898	2	S				MS	TN	MS	
256	Peterson, James	H	W	M	Jul 1856	43	M	15			AL	AL	AL	Farmer
	Francis M.	W	W	F	May 1870	30	M	15	8	4	AL	AL	AL	
	Claudy A.	S	W	M	Oct 1885	14	S				MS	AL	AL	Farm Laborer

1	2	3	4	5	6	7	8	9	10	11	12	13	14	15
	Nellie J.	D	W	F	Jul 1888	11	S				MS	AL	AL	
	Cora L.	D	W	F	Jul 1892	7	S				MS	AL	AL	
	Maud E.	D	W	F	Aug 1898	1	S				MS	AL	AL	
257	Roach, Henry	H	W	M	Nov 1828	71	M	31			SC	SC	SC	Farmer
	Mary	W	W	F	Jul 1838	61	M	31	6	1	NC	NC	NC	
258	Gross, L.A.	H	W	M	Feb 1875	25	M	4			TN	SC	AR	Farmer
	C.A.	W	W	F	Feb 1855	44	M	4	0	0	TN	SC	TN	
	Crossland, M.L.	M	W	F	Jul 1829	70	Wd				TN	VA	TN	
	Walker, George	Bdr	W	M	UN 1870	30	S				MS	UN	UN	
259	Dempsey, John	H	W	M	Feb 1877	23	M	0			MS	MS	MS	
	Sallie	W	W	F	May 1881	19	M	0	0	0	MS	MS	MS	
260	George, O.L.	H	W	M	Aug 1873	26	M	6			MS	MS	UN	
	Minnie	W	W	F	Apr 1879	21	M	6	1	1	KY	KY	KY	
	Earl N.	S	W	M	Aug 1899	9/mo					MS	MS	KY	
261	Davis, Oscar B.	H	W	M	Jan 1877	23	M	6			MS	TN	TN	Farmer
	Millie B.	W	W	F	Mar 1875	25	M	6	3	3	MS	MS	GA	
	Elsa	D	W	F	Nov 1894	5	S				MS	MS	MS	
	John W.	S	W	M	Dec 1896	3	S				MS	MS	MS	
	Loucina	D	W	F	Jan 1898	1	S				MS	MS	MS	
262	Harris, Albert	H	W	M	Oct 1850	49	M	28			AL	AL	AL	Farmer
	Mollie	W	W	F	Jan 1854	46	M	28	6	6	MS	AL	AL	
	Cora	D	W	F	Mar 1884	16	S				MS	AL	MS	
	Paul	S	W	M	Jul 1890	10	S				MS	AL	MS	
263	Stanley, Martin	H	W	M	Apr 1855	45	M	27			AL	VA	AL	Farmer
	Bettie	W	W	F	Mar 1855	45	M	27	10	10	MS	Belg	AL	
	Sallie P.	D	W	F	May 1888	12	S				MS	AL	MS	
	Grover	S	W	M	Mar 1890	10	S				MS	AL	MS	
	Lonnie	S	W	M	UN 1894	6	S				MS	AL	MS	
	Bird	D	W	F	UN 1892	8	S				MS	AL	MS	
	Charley M.	S	W	M	Jun 1900	10/mo	S				MS	AL	MS	
264	Harris, J.E.	H	W	F	Sep 1877	22	M	0			MS	MS	MS	Day Laborer
	Julia	W	W	F	May 1879	21	M	0	0	0	MS	MS	MS	
265	Reynolds, C.L.	H	W	M	Jun 1859	40	S				MS	TN	TN	Farmer
	Rapp	Bro	W	M	Feb 1868	32	S				MS	TN	TN	Farmer
	Leona	Sis	W	F	Jun 1856	43	S				MS	TN	TN	
266	Milton, Jacob	H	W	M	Nov 1856	43	M	22			TN	NC	TN	Farmer
	Sarah A.	W	W	F	May 1848	52	M	22	0	0	AL	TN	AL	
267	Woodley, J.S.	H	W	M	Feb 1865	35	M	15			MS	MS	MS	Farmer
	Katie	W	W	F	Feb 1863	37	M	15	6	3	MS	MS	MS	
	Birtha	D	W	F	Aug 1886	13	S				MS	MS	MS	
	Nora	D	W	F	Apr 1890	10	S				MS	MS	MS	
	Dalton	S	W	M	Oct 1892	7	S				MS	MS	MS	
268	Boothe, C.F.	H	W	M	May 1861	39	M	11			MS	VA	VA	Farmer
	A.F.	W	W	F	Aug 1867	37	M	11	6	4	MS	MS	MS	
	Eller	D	W	F	Aug 1891	9	S				MS	MS	MS	
	Claude C.	S	W	M	Apr 1893	7	S				MS	MS	MS	
	Lula F.	D	W	F	Nov 1895	4	S				MS	MS	MS	
	Mary Eva	D	W	F	Sep 1897	2	S				MS	MS	MS	
269	Davis, B.H.	H	W	M	Jun 1847	52	M	20			MS	SC	AL	Farmer
	E.B.	W	W	F	Apr 1854	46	M	20	4	4	MS	TN	AL	

1	2	3	4	5	6	7	8	9	10	11	12	13	14	15
	Willie A.	D	W	F	May 1885	17	S				MS	MS	MS	
	George H.	S	W	M	Jul 1884	15	S				MS	MS	MS	Farm Laborer
	Sallie	D	W	F	Oct 1887	12	S				MS	MS	MS	
270	Odom, Thomas	H	W	M	Sep 1851	48	M	23			MS	AR	AR	Farmer
	Mary A.	W	W	F	Feb 1856	44	M	23	11	8	MS	TN	SC	
	J.A.	S	W	M	Jan 1879	21	S				MS	MS	MS	Farm Laborer
	Laura J.	D	W	F	Oct 1880	19	S				MS	MS	MS	
	John R.	S	W	M	Dec 1882	17	S				MS	MS	MS	Farm Laborer
	Florence D.	D	W	F	Jan 1885	15	S				MS	MS	MS	
	James N.	S	W	M	Jan 1889	11	S				MS	MS	MS	Farm Laborer
	Eler	D	W	F	Jan 1893	7	S				MS	MS	MS	
	Leeona	D	W	F	Sep 1895	4	S				MS	MS	MS	
	Maudeen	D	W	F	Nov 1898	1	S				MS	MS	MS	
271	Osborn, G.W.	H	W	M	Oct 1827	72	M	31			GA	GA	GA	Farmer
	Sarah E.	W	W	F	Jul 1836	63	M	31	1	0	TN	TN	UN	
	Mary E.	D	W	F	May 1865	35	S				AL	GA	TN	
272	Osborn, G.W.S.	H	W	M	Feb 1872	28	M	5			AL	GA	TN	Farmer
	I.A.	W	W	F	Mar 1881	19	M	5	3	2	MS	AL	AL	
	Guy R.	S	W	M	Mar 1896	4	S				MS	AL	MS	
	E.M.	S	W	M	Jan 1899	1	S				MS	AL	MS	
273	Higginbottom,M.J.	H	W	M	Dec 1870	29	M	8			MS	MS	MS	Farmer
	Letha	W	W	F	May 1870	30	M	8	6	3	AL	GA	AL	
	J.T.G.	S	W	M	Jul 1892	7	S				MS	MS	AL	
	Lester Jane	D	W	F	Oct 1893	6	S				MS	MS	AL	
	Luther C.	S	W	M	Feb 1895	5	S				MS	MS	AL	
	Higginbottom, C.	M	W	F	Jun 1841	58	M	38	8	6	MS	MS	MS	
	Osborm, J.W.L.	Bdr	W	M	Aug 1877	22	S				MS	AL	GA	Farm Laborer
274	Williams, N.C.	H	W	M	Jul 1873	27	M	6			MS	NC	NC	Farmer
	Eliza	W	W	F	Jan 1875	25	M	6	4	4	MS	NC	NC	
	Jose	D	W	F	Mar 1895	5	S				MS	MS	MS	
	John H.	S	W	M	Mar 1895	5	S				MS	MS	MS	
	Olen	S	W	M	Oct 1897	2	S				MS	MS	MS	
	Effie L.	D	W	F	Sep 1899	8/mo	S				MS	MS	MS	
275	Williams, Martha	H	W	F	Sep 1835	64	Wd				MS	TN	TN	Farmer
	Mary	D	W	F	May 1855	45	S				MS	NC	TN	
	Harriett	D	W	F	Nov 1864	35	S				MS	NC	TN	
276	White, James	H	W	M	Mar 1853	47	M	5			MS	NC	MS	Farmer
	Nettie	W	W	F	Aug 1866	33	M	5	2	2	MS	NC	MS	
	Mary M.	D	W	F	Nov 1895	4	S				MS	MS	MS	
	John	S	W	M	Dec 1897	2	S				MS	MS	MS	
277	Whitfield, W.C.	H	W	M	Jun 1831	68	M	46			TN	NC	NC	Farmer
	E.J.	W	W	F	Feb 1838	62	M	46	8	6	TN	SC	TN	
	Nancy	M	W	F	Nov 1811	88	Wd		13	6	NC	NC	NC	
278	Gross, D.G.	H	W	M	Nov 1873	26	M	6			TN	AL	TN	Farmer
	Milly	W	W	F	Sep 1870	29	M	6	2	2	MS	MS	MS	
	Daisy	D	W	F	Nov 1894	5	S				MS	TN	MS	
	Irshell	S	W	M	Sep 1899	8/mo	S				MS	TN	MS	
279	Newcomb, J.E.	H	W	M	UN UN	25	M	1			MS	MS	MS	
	Minnie	W	W	F	UN UN	22	M	1	2	2	MS	MS	MS	
	Nora	D	W	F	UN UN	5	S				MS	MS	MS	
	Asberry	S	W	M	UN UN	2	S				MS	MS	MS	
280	McGaughy, P.T.	H	W	M	UN UN	28	M	4			MS	AL	AL	Farmer

1	2	3	4	5	6	7	8	9	10	11	12	13	14	15
	One	W	W	F	Dec 1881	19	M	4	2	2	MS	MS	MS	
	Ula	D	W	F	UN 1898	2	S				MS	TN	MS	
	Bulah	D	W	F	May 1900	0/mo	S				MS	TN	MS	
281	Hodges, C.M.	H	W	M	Oct 1861	38	M	13			AL	AL	TN	Farmer
	A.J.	W	W	F	May 1864	36	M	13	3	3	MS	TN	MS	
	Lillie	D	W	F	Jul 1888	11	S				MS	AL	MS	
	Osca M.	S	W	M	May 1892	8	S				MS	AL	MS	
	Sarah M.	D	W	F	May 1897	3	S				MS	AL	MS	
282	McGaughy, J.E.	H	W	M	May 1828	72	M	48			AL	TN	TN	Farmer
	S.A.	W	W	F	Apr 1832	68	M	48	13	8	AL	AL	AL	
283	Coker, Nancy	H	W	F	UN UN	50	W				MS	TN	TN	Farmer
	Clarence	S	W	M	UN UN	28	S				MS	TN	TN	Farm Laborer
284	Pace, Culin	H	W	M	Nov 1872	27	M	3			MS	MS	MS	
	Mary C.	W	W	F	Aug 1870	29	M	3	1	1	MS	MS	MS	
	Rufus C.	S	W	M	Sep 1897	2	S				MS	MS	MS	
285	Coker, William	H	W	M	Jul 1861	38	M	13			MS	GA	SC	Farmer
	Sallie	W	W	F	Feb 1872	28	M	13	5	5	MS	GA	NC	
	Maude	D	W	F	Nov 1887	12	S				MS	MS	MS	
	Elmer	S	W	M	Sep 1890	9	S				MS	MS	MS	
	John	S	W	M	Dec 1892	7	S				MS	MS	MS	
	Kelly	S	W	M	Jan 1894	6	S				MS	MS	MS	
	Arnie	S	W	M	Aug 1898	1	S				MS	MS	MS	
286	Hardwick, M.	H	W	M	Dec 1856	43	M	22			MS	TN	AL	Farmer
	N.C.	W	W	F	Jan 1862	38	M	22	11	10	MS	MS	GA	
	Julia E.	D	W	F	Jul 1882	18	S				MS	MS	MS	
	George A.	D	W	F	Nov 1883	16	S				MS	MS	MS	
	John L.	S	W	M	Nov 1885	14	S				MS	MS	MS	Farm Laborer
	Sarah L.	D	W	F	Mar 1881	12	S				MS	MS	MS	
	Lillie M.	D	W	F	Jun 1889	10	S				MS	MS	MS	
	Charley C.	S	W	M	Jun 1891	8	S				MS	MS	MS	
	William A.	S	W	M	Sep 1893	6	S				MS	MS	MS	
	Milton R.	S	W	M	Aug 1895	4	S				MS	MS	MS	
	Jesse D.	S	W	M	Jan 1897	3	S				MS	MS	MS	
	Fannie L.	D	W	F	Nov 1898	1	S				MS	MS	MS	
287	Whitfield, M.D.	H	W	M	Nov 1861	38	M	15			MS	TN	TN	Farmer
	D.B.	W	W	F	Aug 1867	32	M	15	7	6	MS	GA	MS	
	John K.	S	W	M	Dec 1886	13	S				MS	MS	MS	Farm Laborer
	Hattie L.	D	W	F	Oct 1888	11	S				MS	MS	MS	
	Janie L.	D	W	F	Aug 1889	10	S				MS	MS	MS	
	Clemie B.	D	W	F	Dec 1893	6	S				MS	MS	MS	
	Beulah P.	D	W	F	Dec 1895	4	S				MS	MS	MS	
	Willie Mae	D	W	F	Dec 1898	1	S				MS	MS	MS	
288	Strickland, A.J.	H	W	M	Aug 1842	57	M	38			GA	NC	SC	Farmer
	Mary	W	W	F	Sep 1841	58	M	38	6	4	NC	NC	NC	
289	Strickland, M.	H	W	M	Aug 1878	21	M	0			MS	GA	NC	Farmer
	Blanch	W	W	F	Sep 1881	18	M	0	0	0	MS	AL	MS	
290	Umphress, Jacob	H	W	M	Jul 1859	40	M	12			AL	GA	GA	Farmer
	Mary	W	W	F	Sep 1861	38	M	12	5	4	AL	AL	AL	
	Luler	D	W	F	Mar 1889	11	S				MS	AL	AL	
	Benj C.	S	W	M	Mar 1891	1	S				TN	AL	AL	
	Jesse C.	D	W	F	Aug 1893	6	S				TN	AL	AL	
	William P.	S	W	M	Jun 1898	1	S				MS	AL	AL	
291	Armstrong, J.A.	H	W	M	Sep 1860	39	M	23			AL	AL	MS	Farmer

1	2	3	4	5	6	7	8	9	10	11	12	13	14	15
	H.M.	W	W	F	Mar 1858	41	M	23	11	7	AL	NC	AL	
	C.O.	S	W	M	Jul 1878	21	S				AL	AL	AL	Farm Laborer
	Thomas H.	S	W	M	Jan 1884	16	S				AL	AL	AL	Farm Laborer
	Riley J.	S	W	M	Aug 1886	13	S				AL	AL	AL	Farm Laborer
	Mattie L.	D	W	F	Nov 1889	10	S				AL	AL	AL	
	Benj.H.	S	W	M	Jun 1892	7	S				AL	AL	AL	
	Houston G.	S	W	M	Sep 1896	3	S				AL	AL	AL	
	Jefferson	S	W	M	Jul 1898	1	S				AL	AL	AL	
292	Holder, B.A.	H	W	M	Mar 1836	64	M	1			AL	MO	AL	Farmer
	Amanda	W	W	F	UN 1857	43	M	1	0	0	MS	VA	VA	
	Province, F.J.	Bdr	W	M	UN UN	62	Wd				AL	TN	AL	Farm Laborer
293	Boothe, J.G.	H	W	M	Sep 1820	79	M	27			VA	VA	VA	Farmer
	Delpha	W	W	F	May 1837	63	M	27	3	2	TN	GA	AL	
294	Boothe, Walter	H	W	M	Mar 1880	20	M	2			MS	VA	VA	Farmer
	Julie	W	W	F	Feb 1882	18	M	2	1	1	MS	MS	MS	
	Lillie	D	W	F	Apr 1899	1	S				MS	MS	MS	
295	Boothe, John	H	W	M	Dec 1877	22	M	6			MS	VA	TN	Farmer
	Ida	W	W	F	UN 1878	21	M	6	4	1	MS	MS	MS	
	Leona	D	W	F	Apr 1897	3					MS	MS	MS	
296	Peterson, J.T.	H	W	M	Dec 1854	45	M	21			AL	AL	MS	Farmer
	Sallie	W	W	F	Feb 1859	41	M	21	10	6	MS	TN	MS	
	L.J.	D	W	F	Dec 1879	20	S				TN	AL	MS	
	Willie E.	D	W	F	Feb 1886	14	S				MS	AL	MS	
	Georgia M.	D	W	F	May 1891	9	S				MS	AL	MS	
	Cora Lee	D	W	F	Jul 1893	6	S				MS	AL	MS	
	Nora Lee	D	W	F	Jul 1893	6	S				MS	AL	MS	
	Dona H.	D	W	F	Mar 1897	3	S				MS	AL	MS	
297	Humble, Henry	H	W	M	Nov 1846	43	M	10			KY	KY	KY	Farmer
	Mary	W	W	F	Dec 1869	30	M	10	6	3	AL	AL	AL	
	Mollie E.	D	W	F	Dec 1891	8	S				AL	KY	AL	
	Martha A.	D	W	F	Oct 1892	7	S				AL	KY	AL	
	Thomas J.	S	W	M	Dec 1899	5/mo	S				AL	KY	AL	
	Peterson, Laura A.	D	W	F	Aug 1881	18	S				TN	AL	MS	
298	Holder, J.C.S.	H	W	M	Jan 1874	26	M	6			MS	MS	MS	Farmer
	Minnie	W	W	F	Dec 1873	26	M	6	4	4	MS	MS	MS	
	Dora B.	D	W	F	Oct 1894	5	S				MS	MS	MS	
	George A.	S	W	M	May 1896	4	S				MS	MS	MS	
	David O.	S	W	F	Mar 1898	2	S				MS	MS	MS	
	Berry L.	D	W	F	May 1900	1/mo	S				MS	MS	MS	
	Nagle, Emmett	Bdr	W	M	Dec 1881	18	S				MS	MS	MS	Farm Laborer
299	Burcham, Lucy	H	W	F	Oct 1812	87	Wd		4	3	TN	TN	TN	Farmer
	W.C.	S	W	M	UN UN	30	S				MS	TN	TN	Farm Laborer
300	Cox, I.F.	H	W	M	Nov 1869	30	M	7			TN	TN	TN	Farmer
	Ada	W	W	F	Aug 1877	22	M	7	4	4	MS	MS	MS	
	Eva	D	W	F	Sep 1894	5	S				MS	TN	MS	
	Luther	S	W	M	Feb 1896	4	S				MS	TN	MS	
	Sevilla	D	W	F	Jan 1898	2	S				MS	TN	MS	
	Oscar	S	W	M	Aug 1899	9/mo	S				MS	TN	MS	
301	Parsons, William	H	W	M	Apr 1880	20	M	1			MS	MS	MS	Farmer
	Laura	W	W	F	Nov 1875	24	M	1	0	0	MS	MS	MS	
302	Nixon, T.L.	H	W	M	Dec 1830	69	W				TN	TN	TN	Farmer
	Hattie Bell	D	W	F	May 1874	26	M	5	1	1	MS	TN	TN	

1	2	3	4	5	6	7	8	9	10	11	12	13	14	15
	Hatcher, John	GS	W	M	Un 1886	13	S				MS	TN	TN	
303	Ross, Nute	H	W	M	UN 1878	22	M	5			MS	MS	MS	
	Minnie	D	W	F	May 1897	3	S				MS	MS	MS	
	Brother	S	W	M	Mar 1899	1	S				MS	MS	MS	
	Frank	Rel	W	M	UN 1882	18	M				MS	MS	MS	
304	Grymes, H.Y.	H	W	M	Dec 1817	82	M	56			TN	TN	TN	
	Elizabeth	W	W	F	Apr 1820	80	M	56	8	7	TN	TN	TN	
	S.E.	D	W	F	Feb 1860	40	S				MS	TN	TN	Farmer
305	White, William	H	W	M	May 1859	40	M	15			MS	SC	TN	Farmer
	Mary	W	W	F	UN 1861	39	M	15	2	2	AL	AL	AL	
	Bertha C.	D	W	F	Dec 1883	16	S				MS	AL	TN	
	Robert G.	S	W	M	Sep 1860	9	S				MS	AL	MS	
306	Wadkins, A.S.	H	W	M	Mar 1865	35	M	7			AL	SC	GA	Farmer
	Dovie	W	W	F	Nov 1877	22	M	7	4	4	AL	AL	AL	
	Mincie A.	D	W	F	May 1894	6	S				AR	AL	AL	
	Robert L.	S	W	M	Jan 1896	4	S				AR	AL	AL	
	Almie	D	W	F	Jan 1898	2	S				AR	AL	AL	
	Henry G.	S	W	M	Feb 1900	4/mo	S				MS	AL	AL	
	Griffin, Deller	SiL	W	F	Jan 1886	14	S				AL	AL	AL	
	Griffin, Dessa	SiL	W	F	UN 1888	12	S				AL	AL	AL	
307	Whitfield, John	H	W	M	Dec 1842	58	M	33			MS	NC	NC	Farmer
	Emma	W	W	F	Dec 1841	58	M	33	6	5	AL	VA	VA	
	Mary J.	D	W	F	Jan 1877	23	S				MS	MS	AL	
	Georgia A.	D	W	F	Feb 1879	21	S				MS	MS	AL	
308	Coker, L.L.	H	W	M	UN 1862	32	M	UN			MS	MS	MS	Farmer
	Nora B.	W	W	F	UN 1872	27	M	UN	3	3	MS	MS	MS	
	Herbert	S	W	M	UN UN	7	S				MS	MS	MS	
	Hester	D	W	F	UN UN	5	S				MS	MS	MS	
	Homer	S	W	M	UN UN	2	S				MS	MS	MS	
309	Cooksey, Ed	H	W	M	UN UN	23	M				MS	MS	MS	Farmer
	Janey	W	W	F	UN UN	26	M		3	3	MS	MS	TN	
	Levy	S	W	M	UN UN	7	S				MS	MS	MS	
	John H.	S	W	M	UN UN	5	S				MS	MS	MS	
	William	S	W	M	UN UN	2	S				MS	MS	MS	
310	Harvill, Sam	H	W	M	UN UN	34	M				MS	MS	MS	Sawyer, Steam Mill
	Calley	W	W	F	UN UN	27	M		4	4	MS	MS	MS	
	Garland	S	W	M	UN UN	8	S				MS	MS	MS	
	Solon P.	S	W	M	UN UN	5	S				MS	MS	MS	
	Maud	D	W	F	UN UN	3	S				MS	MS	MS	
	Liner	D	W	F	UN UN	3	S				MS	MS	MS	
311	Strickland, J.H.	H	W	M	Oct 1857	42	M	14			MS	AL	TN	Farmer
	Mary A.	W	W	F	UN 1865	35	M	14	5	5	MS	MS	MS	
	Lehue	S	W	M	Nov 1887	12	S				MS	MS	MS	
	John C.	S	W	M	Mar 1890	10	S				MS	MS	MS	
	Henry C.	S	W	M	Jan 1893	7	S				TX	MS	MS	
	E.H.	S	W	M	May 1895	5	S				MS	MS	MS	
	Caledonia	D	W	F	Jun 1898	1	S				MS	MS	MS	
312	Browning, J.W.	H	W	M	Aug 1869	30	M	12			AL	AL	AL	Farmer
	Georgia	W	W	F	Dec 1870	29	M	12	5	5	MS	NC	MS	
	Henry F.	S	W	M	Jan 1892	8	S				MS	AL	MS	
	Martin	S	W	M	Feb 1894	6	S				MS	AL	MS	
	Lillie P.	D	W	F	Feb 1896	4	S				MS	AL	MS	
	William T.	S	W	M	Oct 1897	2	S				MS	AL	MS	

1	2	3	4	5	6	7	8	9	10	11	12	13	14	15
	Luther	S	W	M	Jan 1900	4/mo	S				MS	AL	MS	
313	Whitfield, J.T.	H	W	M	Mar 1847	53	M	26			MS	SC	MS	Farmer
	W. Ammie E.	W	W	F	Dec 1849	50	M	26	8	8	MS	GA	SC	
	Eller	D	W	F	May 1878	22	S				MS	MS	MS	
	William W.	S	W	M	May 1880	20	S				MS	MS	MS	
	Arthur D.	S	W	M	Feb 1883	17	S				MS	MS	MS	
	George W.	S	W	M	Mar 1884	16	S				MS	MS	MS	
	James H.	S	W	M	Mar 1886	14	S				MS	MS	MS	
	Manda L.	D	W	F	Feb 1888	12	S				MS	MS	MS	
	Samuel B.	S	W	M	Aug 1891	8	S				MS	MS	MS	
	Code D.	S	W	M	Jul 1897	2	S				MS	MS	MS	
314	Whitfield, G.W.	H	W	M	Jun 1858	41	M	13			MS	SC	MS	Farmer
	Mollie	W	W	F	Jan 1866	34	M	13	7	7	MS	TN	TN	
	Oscar	S	W	M	Dec 1887	12	S				MS	MS	MS	
	Maggie E.	D	W	F	Feb 1889	11	S				MS	MS	MS	
	Walter	S	W	M	Mar 1890	10	S				MS	MS	MS	
	William M.	S	W	M	Jan 1893	7	S				MS	MS	MS	
	Mattie M.	D	W	F	Jan 1894	6	S				MS	MS	MS	
	Josie J.	D	W	F	Apr 1897	3	S				MS	MS	MS	
	Onie May	D	W	F	May 1898	2	S				MS	MS	MS	
	Whitfield, Martha A.	M	W	F	Nov 1823	76	Wd		6	6	GA	SC	SC	
315	Lambert, C.R.	H	W	M	Nov 1877	22	M	4			MS	MS	MS	Farmer
	Sallie A.	W	W	F	Dec 1877	22	M	4	2	2	MS	AL	MS	
	Willie B.	D	W	F	Dec 1897	2	S				MS	MS	MS	
	Urskin	S	W	M	Sep 1899	7mo	S				MS	MS	MS	
	Ross, G.H.H.	Bdr	W	M	Feb 1841	58	Wd				AL	SC	SC	Farm Laborer
316	Woodley, J.H.	H	W	M	Jun 1833	67	M	4			MS	TN	TN	Farmer
	Sarah	W	W	F	Oct 1843	56	M	4	12	6	TN	PA	SC	
	Sallie R.	D	W	F	Oct 1876	23	S				MS	MS	MS	
	Laura E.	D	W	F	Oct 1881	18	S				MS	MS	MS	
	Hamilton, Oscar	Bdr	W	M	UN 1882	17	S				MS	TN	MS	
317	Woodley, A.E.	H	W	M	Aug 1874	25	M	4			MS	MS	TN	Farmer
	Annie L.	W	W	F	Feb 1875	25	M	4	2	1	MS	MS	TN	
	Minnie	D	W	F	Mar 1889	1	S				MS	MS	MS	
318	Wheeler, Charley	H	W	M	Fev 1847	53	M	3			TN	NC	TN	Farmer
	Julia	W	W	F	Nov 1871	28	M	3	2	2	MS	NC	AL	
	Lettie	D	W	F	Jun 1898	2	S				MS	TN	MS	
	Whitley	S	W	M	Nov 1899	1	S				MS	TN	MS	
	Britton, Mary J.	Aunt	W	F	Feb 1829	71	Wd				MS	NC	NC	
	Britton, Charley	Bdr	B	M	Oct 1881	18	S				MS	TN	TN	
319	Strickland, Henry	H	W	M	Dec 1855	44	M	22			MS	UN	UN	Farmer
	E.L.	W	W	F	Mar 1855	44	M	22	10	9	MS	NC	TN	
	Hattie L.	D	W	F	Jan 1879	21	S				MS	MS	MS	
	N. Elle	D	W	F	Jun 1880	19	S				MS	MS	MS	
	Minnie L.	D	W	F	Jan 1882	18	S				MS	MS	MS	
	George W.	S	W	M	Jan 1883	16	S				MS	MS	MS	Farm Laborer
	Nellie J.	D	W	F	Apr 1885	15	S				MS	MS	MS	
	Columbus J.	S	W	M	Jun 1886	13	S				MS	MS	MS	Farm Laborer
	Dora A.	D	W	F	Aug 1888	11	S				MS	MS	MS	
	Mattie E.	D	W	F	Mar 1890	10	S				MS	MS	MS	
	Pearl	D	W	F	Jul 1892	7	S				MS	MS	MS	
320	Bonds, Thomas	H	W	M	UN 1881	19	M	4			AL	AL	AL	Farmer
	Dealy	W	W	F	UN 1883	17	M	4	1	1	AL	AL	AL	
	Fred	S	W	M	Mar 1900	2/mo	S				MS	AL	AL	

1	2	3	4	5	6	7	8	9	10	11	12	13	14	15
321	Parsons, J.P.	H	W	M	Jun 1858	41	M	25			MS	AL	AL	Farmer
	Lucinda	W	W	F	UN 1855	45	M	25	10	10	AL	AL	AL	
	Pearl	D	W	F	Feb 1885	15	S				MS	MS	AL	
	Georgia	D	W	F	Oct 1887	12	S				MS	MS	AL	
	Marcus	S	W	M	Feb 1890	10	S				MS	MS	AL	Farm Laborer
	Burt	S	W	M	May 1892	8	S				MS	MS	AL	
	Paulean	D	W	F	Apr 1894	6	S				MS	MS	AL	
	Louetta	D	W	F	Feb 1896	4	S				MS	MS	AL	
	Guy	S	W	M	Feb 1900	3/mo	S				MS	MS	AL	
322	McCoy, J.C.	H	W	M	Sep 1871	28	M	7			MS	MS	MS	Farmer
	L.A.	W	W	F	Sep 1875	24	M	7	4	2	MS	MS	MS	
	Lena	D	W	F	Jul 1896	3	S				MS	MS	MS	
	Bulah	D	W	F	Jul 1889	11/mo	S				MS	MS	MS	
323	McCoy, Samuel	H	W	M	Feb 1864	36	M	2			MS	MS	MS	Farmer
	Jennie	W	W	F	UN 1879	21	M	2	1	1	MS	MS	MS	
	Dixie	D	W	F	Dec 1898	1	S				MS	MS	MS	
324	McCoy, L.A.	H	W	F	May 1838	62	Wd		10	8	AL	AL	AL	Farmer
	Vina	D	W	F	Jul 1867	32	S				MS	AL	AL	
	Luvicy E.	D	W	F	Jan 1878	22	S				MS	AL	AL	
	Oda L.	Gs	W	M	Jan 1900	5/mo	S				MS	MS	MS	
325	Parsons, Charley	H	W	M	Sep 1861	39	M	15			MS	MS	MS	Farm Laborer
	Mary J.	W	W	F	May 1862	38	M	15	9	9	MS	MS	MS	Farmer
	Minnie L.	D	W	F	Apr 1886	14	S				MS	MS	MS	
	Mary M.	D	W	F	Mar 1888	12	S				MS	MS	MS	
	James W.	S	W	M	Aug 1889	10	S				MS	MS	MS	Farm Laborer
	J.Tye	S	W	M	Jan 1891	9	S				MS	MS	MS	
	Synthia A.	D	W	F	Aug 1892	7	S				MS	MS	MS	
	Sarah A.	D	W	F	May 1894	6	S				MS	MS	MS	
	Georgia L.	D	W	F	Aug 1896	4	S				MS	MS	MS	
	Jessey	S	W	M	Apr 1898	2	S				MS	MS	MS	
	Janey E.	D	W	F	Mar 1900	2/mo	S				MS	MS	MS	
326	Lentz, J.M.	H	W	M	UN 1843	57	M	22			AL	AL	AL	Farmer
	E.E.	W	W	F	Jul 1860	39	M	22	9	9	AL	AL	AL	
	M.E.	D	W	F	Dec 1884	15	S				MS	AL	AL	
	James W.	S	W	M	Dec 1887	12	S				MS	AL	AL	Farm Laborer
	Alford B.	S	W	M	Mar 1890	10	S				MS	AL	AL	Farm Laborer
	S.U.	D	W	F	Sep 1893	6	S				MS	AL	AL	
	Hattie V.	D	W	F	Apr 1897	3	S				MS	AL	AL	
	Lee D.	S	W	M	Mar 1899	1	S				MS	AL	AL	
327	Bishop, W.G.	H	W	M	Oct 1851	48	M	28			MS	TN	TN	Farmer
	Mary F.	W	W	F	Apr 1853	47	M	28	0	0	AL	AL	AL	
	Music, Elmyra	M	W	F	May 1835	65	Wd		5	5	AL	AL	AL	
	Bishop, James	F	W	M	Feb 1828	72	Wd				TN	TN	TN	
328	Moor, W.R.	H	W	M	Oct 1878	21	M	3			MS	AL	MS	
	Ida P.	W	W	F	Oct 1880	19	M	3	1	1	MS	MS	MS	
329	McCoy, John B.	H	W	M	Mar 1860	40	M	10			MS	TN	TN	Farmer
	Liza	W	W	F	Sep 1869	30	M	10	4	4	MS	AL	AL	
	Noe	S	W	M	Aug 1890	9	S				MS	MS	MS	
	Flora	D	W	F	Sep 1893	6	s				MS	MS	MS	
	Oler	D	W	F	Apr 1895	5	S				MS	MS	MS	
	Nora	D	W	F	Jun 1899	11/mo	S				MS	MS	MS	
	McCoy, A.	Sis	W	F	Jul 1850	49	Wd				MS	MS	MS	
330	Hughes, J.C.	H	W	M	Feb 1836	64	M	12			AL	GA	AL	Farmer
	Columbia	W	W	F	Aug 1856	43	M	12	3	3	MS	AL	AL	

1	2	3	4	5	6	7	8	9	10	11	12	13	14	15
	Owen R.	S	W	M	Dec 1888	11	S				MS	AL	MS	
	Garvin C.	S	W	M	Aug 1890	9	S				MS	AL	MS	
	Nora H.	D	W	F	Apr 1893	7	S				MS	AL	MS	
331	Emry, George W.	H	W	M	Apr 1858	42	M	21			MS	MS	MS	Farmer
	Neely	W	W	F	Jul 1865	34	M	21	6	4	MS	MS	MS	
	William	S	W	M	Feb 1884	16	S				MS	MS	MS	Farm Laborer
	Cora	D	W	F	Oct 1886	13	S				MS	MS	MS	
	Nora	D	W	F	UN 1892	7	S				MS	MS	MS	
	Pearley	D	W	F	Sep 1896	3	S				MS	MS	MS	
332	Cummings, C.C.	H	W	M	Oct 1862	37	M	20			AL	AL	AL	Farmer
	Laura	W	W	F	Nov 1861	38	M	20	8	7	AL	AL	AL	
	Minnie	D	W	F	Apr 1884	16	S				MS	AL	AL	
	Columbus S.	S	W	M	Jan 1886	14	S				AL	AL	AL	Farm Laborer
	Willie J.	D	W	F	Mar 1890	10	S				AL	AL	AL	
	Arthur. F.	S	W	M	Oct 1892	7	S				AL	AL	AL	
	James L.	S	W	M	Jul 1895	4	S				MS	AL	AL	
	Goldie A.	D	W	F	May 1898	2	S				MS	AL	AL	
	Cummings, Elmina	M	W	F	Oct 1838	61	Wd		3	1	MS	AL	AL	
333	Taylor, A.J.	H	W	M	Sep 1828	71	M	46			AL	TN	TN	Farmer
	Hulda	W	W	F	Jan 1839	61	M	10	9		AL	KY	KY	
334	Taylor, J.H.	H	W	M	Aug 1866	33	M	14			MS	AL	UN	Farmer
	Sallie	W	W	F	Sep 1873	26	M	14	6	6	MS	KY	KY	
	Willie	S	W	M	Aug 1886	13	S				MS	MS	MS	Farm Laborer
	Daisy	D	W	F	UN 1888	12	S				MS	MS	MS	
	Franklin	S	W	M	Feb 1891	9	S				MS	MS	MS	
	John D.	S	W	M	Mar 1893	7	S				MS	MS	MS	
	Ida	D	W	F	Jan 1896	4	S				MS	MS	MS	
	Birtha	D	W	F	Jan 1898	2	S				MS	MS	MS	
335	Taylor, J.D.	H	W	M	Sep 1857	42	M	21			MS	AL	AL	Farmer
	Jane	W	W	F	UN 1869	31	M	21	5	4	MS	MS	MS	
	Effie	D	W	F	May 1887	13	S				MS	MS	MS	
	Willie	S	W	M	Sep 1893	6	S				MS	MS	MS	
336	Amerson, J.B.	H	W	M	Aug 1859	40	M	20			AL	AL	AL	Farmer
	Dora P.	W	W	F	May 1862	38	M	20	9	7	MS	AL	AL	
	Marion A.	S	W	M	Jan 1883	17	S				MS	AL	MS	Farm Laborer
	Andrew	S	W	M	Feb 1886	14	S				MS	AL	MS	Farm Laborer
	Virgie	D	W	F	Aug 1888	11	S				MS	AL	MS	
	Minnie B.	D	W	F	Nov 1890	9	S				MS	AL	MS	
	John W.	S	W	M	Jul 1892	7	S				MS	AL	MS	
	Sylvester	S	W	M	Apr 1895	5	S				MS	AL	MS	
	Dora P.	D	W	F	Oct 1898	2	S				MS	AL	MS	
	Hale, Kenny	Nep	W	M	Dec 1898	1	S				MS	AL	MS	
337	Wood, J.L.	H	W	M	Mar 1868	32	M	12			TN	TN	GA	Farmer
	Roda	W	W	F	Oct 1868	31	M	12	6	5	TN	TN	TN	
	Miller	S	W	M	Jan 1889	11	S				TN	TN	TN	
	Ora	D	W	F	Jan 1891	9	S				TN	TN	TN	
	Minda	D	W	F	Nov 1893	6	S				TN	TN	TN	
	Myrtle	D	W	F	Dec 1893	6	S				TN	TN	TN	
	Ida	D	W	F	Nov 1899	6/mo	S				TN	TN	TN	
338	Holder, J.O.	H	W	M	UN 1842	58	M	35			AL	AL	SC	Farmer
	F.M.	W	W	F	Nov 1847	52	M	35	12	8	MS	AL	SC	
	J.L.	S	W	M	Nov 1870	30	S				MS	AL	MS	Farm Laborer
	I.S.	D	W	F	Apr 1877	23	S				MS	AL	MS	
	Linda C.	D	W	F	Jan 1880	20	S				MS	AL	MS	
	Luler A.	D	W	F	Jan 1882	18	S				MS	AL	MS	

1	2	3	4	5	6	7	8	9	10	11	12	13	14	15
	Riley	S	W	M	Feb 1887	13	S				MS	AL	MS	
	Mattie	D	W	F	Jul 1892	7	S				MS	AL	MS	
339	Whitfield, Lee	H	W	M	Aug 1873	26	M	6			TN	TN	TN	Farmer
	Dora Ela	W	W	F	Apr 1878	22	M	6	2	2	MS	TN	MS	
	Benjamin Toy	S	W	M	Sep 1895	4	S				MS	TN	MS	
	Charley A.	S	W	M	Nov 1898	1	S				MS	TN	MS	
340	Glover, D.H.	H	W	M	Mar 1832	68	M	34			TN	TN	TN	Farmer
	Mattie	W	W	F	UN 1847	53	M	34	8	3	MS	GA	TN	
	George W.	S	W	M	Jun 1877	22	S				MS	TN	MS	Farm Laborer
	Minnie C.	D	W	F	Nov 1875	24	S				MS	TN	MS	
341	Kennedy, H.J.	H	W	M	Jul 1843	56	M	2			AL	SC	AL	Farmer
	E.B.	W	W	F	UN 1851	49	M	2	0	0	MS	TN	MS	
	Rener A.	D	W	F	UN 1893	6	S				MS	MS	MS	
342	Kennedy, S.G.	H	W	M	Mar 1857	43	S				MS	AL	AL	Farmer
	Kennedy, D.P.	Bro	W	M	Feb 1877	23	S				MS	AL	AL	Farm Laborer
	Margaret M.	M	W	F	UN 1835	65	Wd		1	1	Al	AL	AL	
343	Skelton, J.L.	H	W	M	Mar 1868	31	M	13			MS	MS	MS	Miller
	A.M.	W	W	F	Nov 1870	29	M	13	5	5	MS	MS	MS	
	Minie	D	W	F	Jan 1890	10	S				MS	MS	MS	
	Jessie	S	W	M	Nov 1891	8	S				MS	MS	MS	
	Frank	S	W	M	Sep 1893	6	S				MS	MS	MS	
	Fannie	D	W	F	Feb 1896	4	S				MS	MS	MS	
	Maud	D	W	F	Aug 1898	1	S				MS	MS	MS	
344	Maness, Maria	H	W	F	Jan 1882	18	S				MS	MS	MS	
345	Griffin, John	H	W	M	Jan 1878	22	M	1			MS	AL	MS	Farmer
	Liller	W	W	F	Jan 1883	17	M	1			MS	MS	MS	
346	Woodley, Narcissia	H	W	F	Oct 1825	74	Wd		9	6	SC	SC	SC	Farmer
	Mandie	D	W	F	Mar 1852	48	S				MS	AL	SC	
347	Woodley, James	H	W	M	May 1863	37	M	16			MS	TN	SC	Farmer
	Alice	W	W	F	Jul 1866	33	M	16	9	7	MS	MS	MS	
	Charley	S	W	M	Nov 1884	15	S				MS	MS	MS	
	Samuel	S	W	M	Jun 1885	14	S				MS	MS	MS	
	Annie	D	W	F	Jul 1888	11	S				MS	MS	MS	
	Annis	D	W	F	Jul 1888	11	S				MS	MS	MS	
	Elmer	S	W	M	May 1891	9	S				MS	MS	MS	
	Frank	S	W	M	Nov 1893	7	S				MS	MS	MS	
	Leola	D	W	F	Jan 1898	2	S				MS	MS	MS	
348	Bonds, Wesley	H	W	M	Feb 1864	36	M	8			MS	MS	MS	Farmer
	Calley	W	W	F	Sep 1859	40	M	8	3	3	MS	MS	MS	
	John Wesley	S	W	M	Sep 1894	5	S				MS	MS	MS	
	R.C.	S	W	M	Jun 1897	3	S				MS	MS	MS	
	Ada V.	D	W	F	May 1899	1	S				MS	MS	MS	
349	Skelton, Thomas	H	W	M	Mar 1851	49	M	27			MS	SC	SC	Farmer
	Telitha	W	W	F	UN 1860	40	M	27	5	5	MS	AL	AL	
	George	S	M	M	Oct 1878	21	S				MS	MS	MS	
	John W.	S	W	M	Dec 1888	11	S				MS	MS	MS	
	James T.	S	W	M	May 1896	4	S				MS	MS	MS	
350	Carpenter, Josh	H	W	M	Dec 1830	69	M	35			AL	SC	SC	Miller
	Flora	W	W	F	May 1850	50	M	35	2	2	MS	TN	TN	
	Manda E.	D	W	F	Jun 1881	18	S				MS	AL	MS	

1	2	3	4	5	6	7	8	9	10	11	12	13	14	15
351	Carpenter, W.R.	H	W	M	Jun 1835	64	M	6			MS	SC	SC	Farmer
	Susan	W	W	F	Jun 1877	22	M	6	3	2	MS	TN	AL	
	Dora	D	W	F	Feb 1884	16	S				MS	MS	MS	
	Uler	D	W	F	Jul 1895	4	S				MS	MS	MS	
	Lee	S	W	M	Aug 1899	9/mo	S				MS	MS	MS	
352	Carpenter, Elizabeth	H	W	F	UN 1799	100	M		3	3	SC	SC	SC	Farmer
	George	S	W	M	UN 1832	68	UN				SC	SC	SC	Farmer
	Elizabeth J.	D	W	F	UN 1850	50	UN				SC	SC	SC	
	Elisha	S	W	M	UN 1885	45	UN				SC	SC	SC	Farmer
	Griffin, Caroline	Sis	W	F	UN 1852	48	UN				SC	SC	SC	
	Griffin, Willie A.	GD	W	F	UN 1886	14	UN				MS	AL	MS	
353	Sego, L.D.	H	W	M	Jan 1874	26	M	6			MS	MS	MS	Farmer
	L.T.	W	W	F	Apr 1877	23	M	6	5	5	MS	MS	MS	
	Leona	D	W	F	Sep 1895	4	S				MS	MS	MS	
	Blanch	D	W	F	Feb 1897	3	S				MS	MS	MS	
	Georgia	D	W	F	Sep 1898	1	S				MS	MS	MS	
	Andy	S	W	M	Mar 1900	2/mo	S				MS	MS	MS	
	Frank	S	W	M	Mar 1900	2/mo	S				MS	MS	MS	
354	Hale, W.J.	H	W	M	Aug 1864	35	Wd				MS	PA	MS	Farmer
	Lucy C.	D	W	F	Nov 1888	11	S				MS	MS	MS	
	Georgia L.	D	W	F	Jul 1891	8	S				MS	MS	MS	
	Paul M.	S	W	M	Sep 1896	3	S				MS	MS	MS	
	Kenny A.	S	W	M	Dec 1898	1	S				MS	MS	MS	
355	Glascow, William	H	W	M	Mar 1840	60	M	8			AL	TN	TN	Farmer
	T.L.	W	W	F	Apr 1861	39	M	8	8	8	MS	PA	MS	
	M.J.	S	W	M	Aug 1883	16	S				TN	AL	MS	
	Daniel B.	S	W	M	Nov 1885	14	S				MS	AL	MS	
	John H.	S	W	M	Aug 1892	7	S				MS	AL	MS	
	George W.	S	W	M	Nov 1893	6	S				MS	AL	MS	
	J.N.	S	W	M	Jan 1895	5	S				MS	AL	MS	
	Arty L.	D	W	F	May 1897	3	S				MS	AL	MS	
	William R.	S	W	M	Oct 1898	1	S				MS	AL	MS	
	Virda M.	D	W	F	Apr 1900	2/mo	S				MS	AL	MS	
356	Gross, Henry F.	H	W	M	Aug 1849	50	M	27			AL	TN	GA	Farmer
	Synthia R.	W	W	F	Nov 1855	45	M	27	9	8	TN	TN	TN	
	Ozia L.	D	W	F	Mar 1877	23	S				TN	AL	TN	
	Charley W.	S	W	M	Jul 1882	17	S				AR	AL	TN	
	Pearl P.	D	W	F	Jan 1885	15	S				TN	AL	TN	
	Henry A.	S	W	M	Jul 1888	12	S				TN	AL	TN	
	Sylvester L.	S	W	M	Dec 1892	7	S				MS	AL	TN	
	Walter C.	S	W	M	May 1895	5	S				MS	AL	TN	
357	Broughton, W.A.	H	W	M	Aug 1866	33	M	12			MS	SC	AL	Farmer
	Laura B.	W	W	F	Jun 1870	30	M	12	4	4	MS	MS	MS	
	Clara G.	D	W	F	Feb 1891	9	S				MS	MS	MS	
	Betsy P.	D	W	F	Aug 1893	6	S				MS	MS	MS	
	James L.	S	W	M	Oct 1895	4	S				MS	MS	MS	
	Hattie	D	W	F	Sep 1898	1	S				MS	MS	MS	
358	Davis, J.H.	H	W	M	Aug 1869	30	M	15			MS	MS	MS	Farmer
	N.C.	W	W	F	Jan 1870	30	M	15	2	2	MS	MS	MS	
	Gracey	D	W	F	Dec 1886	13	S				MS	MS	MS	
	James E.	S	W	M	Dec 1888	11	S				MS	MS	MS	
359	Glenn, J.H.	H	W	M	Feb 1855	45	M	20			MS	SC	MS	Farmer
	M.L.	W	W	F	Nov 1859	40	M	20	6	6	MS	MS	AL	
	G.W.	S	W	M	Jan 1881	19	S				MS	MS	MS	
	Robert H.	S	W	M	Jul 1882	17	S				MS	MS	MS	

1	2	3	4	5	6	7	8	9	10	11	12	13	14	15
	Sylvester	S	W	M	Mar 1885	15	S				MS	MS	MS	
	John Riley	S	W	M	Dec 1886	13	S				MS	MS	MS	
	Kirby L.	S	W	M	Oct 1889	10	S				MS	MS	MS	
	Alford D.	S	W	M	Jan 1899	1	S				MS	MS	MS	
360 Sego, Nancy		H	W	F	Mar 1849	51	Wd		8	7	AL	AL	AL	Farmer
	William P.	S	W	M	Aug 1882	17	S				MS	MS	AL	
	Chester P.	S	W	M	Nov 1884	15	S				MS	MS	AL	
	Francis E.	D	W	F	Apr 1888	12	S				MS	MS	AL	
	Earley W.	S	W	M	Aug 1890	9	S				MS	MS	AL	
361 Deaton, J.E.W.		H	W	M	Oct 1869	30	M	8			MS	NC	MS	Farmer
	Mary E.	W	W	F	Jan 1875	25	M	8	5	5	MS	MS	MS	
	James C.	S	W	M	Jan 1893	7	S				MS	MS	MS	
	Minnie M.	D	W	F	Aug 1894	5	S				MS	MS	MS	
	Forest L.	S	W	M	Apr 1896	4	S				MS	MS	MS	
	Myrtle M.	D	W	F	Mar 1898	2	S				MS	MS	MS	
	William N.	S	W	M	Mar 1900	3/mo	S				MS	MS	MS	
362 Deaton, Lewis		H	W	M	Feb 1841	59	M	33			NC	SC	SC	Farmer
	Sallie	W	W	F	Jan 1851	49	M	33	8	6	MS	SC	SC	
	Cahoon	S	W	M	May 1881	19	S				MS	UN	MS	
	Sophia	D	W	F	Jul 1886	13	S				MS	NC	MS	
363 Robinson, R.		H	W	M	Jul 1833	66	M	43			TN	VA	TN	Farmer
	Nancy	W	W	F	Nov 1858	41	M	43	8	6	AL	AL	AL	
364 Hale, G.A.		H	W	M	Nov 1858	41	M	21			MS	PA	NC	Farmer
	M.J.	W	W	F	Jun 1858	41	M	21	11	7	MS	MS	SC	
	G.W.	S	W	M	Aug 1884	19	S				MS	MS	MS	
	Julie P.	D	W	F	Mar 1886	14	S				MS	MS	MS	
	Virgie M.	D	W	F	Dec 1887	12	S				MS	MS	MS	
	Dora E.	D	W	F	Aug 1891	9	S				MS	MS	MS	
	Cora E.	D	W	F	Dec 1893	6	S				MS	MS	MS	
	Lewis W.	S	W	M	Sep 1895	4	S				MS	MS	MS	
	Livia M.	D	W	F	Nov 1898	1	S				MS	MS	MS	
365 Moore, John E.		H	W	M	Mar 1820	80	M	45			TN	NC	NC	
	Nancy	W	W	F	Nov 1826	73	M	45	10	7	GA	SC	NC	
366 Moore, George		H	W	M	Jan 1871	29	M	8			MS	GA	SC	Farmer
	Elen	W	W	F	Oct 1874	25	M	8	4	4	MS	MS	MS	
	Homer	S	W	M	Oct 1892	7	S				MS	MS	MS	
	Hafford	S	W	M	Aug 1894	5	S				MS	MS	MS	
	Melva	D	W	F	Dec 1895	4	S				MS	MS	MS	
	Nora	D	W	F	Oct 1898	1	S				MS	MS	MS	
367 Moore, Robert		H	W	M	Mar 1863	37	M	16			MS	NC	NC	Farmer
	Josie	W	W	F	Aug 1869	30	M	16	4	4	MS	MS	MS	
	Charley	S	W	M	Dec 1885	14	S				MS	MS	MS	
	John	S	W	M	Dec 1887	12	S				MS	MS	MS	
	Oscar	S	W	M	Sep 1889	10	S				MS	MS	MS	
	Ester	D	W	F	Mar 1891	9	S				MS	MS	MS	
368 Sego, J.C.		H	W	M	Apr 1852	48	M	26			MS	NC	NC	Farmer
	Mary E.	W	W	F	Feb 1855	45	M	26	10	10	MS	MS	MS	
	Marcus	S	W	M	Oct 1884	15	S				MS	MS	MS	
	Martha J.	D	W	F	Feb 1887	13	S				MS	MS	MS	
	Oda E.	D	W	F	Jun 1889	10	S				MS	MS	MS	
	Luler P.	D	W	F	May 1891	9	S				MS	MS	MS	
	Minnie E.	D	W	F	May 1893	7	S				MS	MS	MS	
	William A.	S	W	M	Aug 1896	3	S				MS	MS	MS	

1	2	3	4	5	6	7	8	9	10	11	12	13	14	15
369	Adams, W.T.	H	W	M	Jul 1875	24	M	0			MS	MS	MS	Farmer
	Lara D.	W	W	F	Oct 1883	17	M	0	0	0	MS	MS	MS	
370	Bonds, J.D.	H	W	M	Jun 1870	29	M	3			MS	MS	MS	Farmer
	Mary E.	W	W	F	Mar 1875	25	M	3	2	2	MS	MS	MS	
	Clanch V.	S	W	M	Aug 1897	2	S				MS	MS	MS	
	Milton Ovel	S	W	M	Jul 1899	10/mo	S				MS	MS	MS	
371	Barnett, Nimrod	H	W	M	May 1851	49	Wd				AL	AL	AL	Farmer
	Mary J.	D	W	F	Oct 1875	24	Wd		0	0	AL	AL	AL	
	Charity A.	D	W	F	May 1882	18	S				AL	AL	AL	
	Jerush P.	D	W	F	Dec 1885	14	S				MS	AL	AL	
	Martesha R.	D	W	F	Mar 1890	10	S				MS	AL	AL	
372	Norris, D.M.	H	W	M	May 1858	48	M	15			GA	NC	NC	Farmer
	Parcella	W	W	F	May1864	36	M	15	8	8	AL	AL	AL	
	Domeo	S	W	M	Jan 1888	12	S				MS	GA	AL	
	Romeo	S	W	M	Nov 1889	10	S				MS	GA	AL	
	Virginia	D	W	F	Jul 1891	8	S				MS	GA	AL	
	Homer J.	S	W	M	May 1892	8	S				MS	GA	AL	
	Dona E.	D	W	F	Apr 1894	6	S				MS	GA	AL	
	Lula M.	D	W	F	Feb 1895	5	S				MS	GA	AL	
	Myrtle	D	W	F	Jan 1897	3	S				MS	GA	AL	
	Minnie P.	D	W	F	Mar 1899	1	S				MS	GA	AL	
373	Bonds, J.E.	H	W	M	Mar 1849	51	M	28			MS	AL	AL	Farmer
	Martha	W	W	F	Aug 1852	47	M	28	9	8	MS	TN	TN	
	John E.	S	W	M	Nov 1883	16	S				MS	MS	TN	
	Nancy J.	D	W	F	Jul 1886	13	S				MS	MS	TN	
	James L.	S	W	M	Nov 1888	11	S				MS	MS	TN	
	Joseph O.	S	W	M	Sep 1890	9	S				MS	MS	TN	
374	Bonds, William	H	W	M	Sep 1877	22	M	3			MS	MS	MS	Farmer
	Almer	W	W	F	Jun 1881	18	M	3	2	2	MS	MS	MS	
	Hellen H.	D	W	F	Jun 1898	1	S				MS	MS	MS	
	William L.	S	W	M	Nov 1899	6/mo	S				MS	MS	MS	
375	Bonds, William	H	W	M	Sep 1856	63	M	40			AL	TN	AL	Farmer
	Martha F.	W	W	F	Mar 1844	56	M	40	10	10	MS	SC	NC	
	Manda E.	D	W	F	Jul 1877	22	S				MS	AL	MS	
	James H.	S	W	M	Mar 1880	20	S				Ms	AL	MS	
	Francis L.	D	W	F	Sep 1882	17	S				MS	AL	MS	
	Walter R.	S	W	M	Apr 1885	15	S				MS	AL	MS	
376	Lewis, John	H	W	M	Mar 1854	46	M	20			MS	MS	MS	Farmer
	Ellener	W	W	F	Aug 1861	38	M	20	8	8	MS	MS	MS	
	Charley M.	S	W	M	Feb 1882	18	S				MS	MS	MS	
	Ada C.	D	W	M	May 1884	16	S				MS	MS	MS	
	Deller	D	W	F	Feb 1886	14	S				MS	MS	MS	
	Arthur	S	W	M	Dec 1888	11	S				MS	MS	MS	
	Maud	D	W	F	Feb 1891	9	S				MS	MS	MS	
	Cora	D	W	F	Mar 1894	6	S				MS	MS	MS	
	Edcar	S	W	M	May 1896	4	S				MS	MS	MS	
	Agnes	D	W	F	Mar 1889	1	S				MS	MS	MS	
377	McCullough, M.C.	H	W	M	Feb 1850	50	M	30			MS	AL	AL	Farmer
	M.L.	W	W	F	Mar 1853	47	M	30	9	8	AL	MS	AL	
	George W.	S	W	M	May 1885	15	S				MS	MS	AL	
	Nancy E.	D	W	F	Jan 1884	16	S				MS	MS	AL	
	James C.	S	W	M	Jul 1886	13	S				MS	MS	AL	
	Cerdeler	D	W	F	Feb 1889	11	S				MS	MS	AL	
	Odis L.	S	W	M	Jul 1891	8	S				MS	MS	AL	
	Luther A.	S	W	M	May 1897	13	S				MS	MS	AL	

1	2	3	4	5	6	7	8	9	10	11	12	13	14	15
378	Providence, J.W.	H	W	M	UN UN	44	M	15			MS	MS	MS	Farmer
	Sarah J.	W	W	F	UN UN	45	M	15	5	4	MS	MS	MS	
	John W.	S	W	M	Nov 1886	13	S				MS	MS	MS	
	M.E.	D	W	F	Feb 1891	9	S				MS	MS	MS	
	Mandy L.	D	W	F	Dec 1892	7	S				MS	MS	MS	
	Emmer C.	D	W	F	Mar 1896	4	S				MS	MS	MS	
379	Bishop, W.C.	H	W	M	Jan 1855	45	M	20			MS	TN	TN	Farmer
	Weathy A.	W	W	F	Apr 1854	46	M	20	5	3	MS	AL	AL	
	Marion	S	W	M	Sep 1884	15	S				MS	MS	AL	
	Georgia A.	D	W	F	Apr 1887	13	S				MS	MS	AL	
	Maggie	D	W	F	Apr 1870	10	S				MS	MS	MS	
	Walker, Mary E.	OT	W	F	Jul 1833	66	Wd				GA	Eng	Eng	
380	Ezell, David	H	W	M	Oct 1861	38	M	17			GA	SC	GA	
	Carol	W	W	F	Sep 1866	33	M	17	8	8	GA	GA	TN	
	Leander	S	W	M	Aug 1884	15	S				AL	GA	GA	
	Emer	D	W	F	Jul 1885	15	S				AL	GA	GA	
	Syler	D	W	F	Sep 1886	13	S				AL	GA	GA	
	Ideler	D	W	F	May 1892	8	S				AL	GA	GA	
	Susan J.	D	W	F	Nov 1892	7	S				AL	GA	GA	
	Lillie	D	W	F	Apr 1894	6	S				AL	GA	GA	
	Dona	D	W	F	Jul 1896	3	S				AR	GA	GA	
	Florence	D	W	F	Sep 1898	1	S				MS	GA	GA	
381	Bishop, G.W.	H	W	M	Sep 1849	50	M	27			MS	TN	TN	Farmer
	Drucilla	W	W	F	Nov 1853	46	M	27	2	2	MS	GA	GA	
	Yow, Catie	S	W	F	UN 1853	47	S				MS	TN	TN	
382	Bishop, J.L.	H	W	M	Nov 1873	27	M	9			MS	MS	GA	Farmer
	Bettie	W	W	F	Aug 1874	25	M	9	2	2	MS	MS	MS	
	Lillian	D	W	F	Jun 1896	3	S				MS	MS	MS	
	Vivian	D	W	F	May 1899	1	S				MS	MS	MS	
383	White, J.W.	H	B	M	Apr 1848	52	M	13			VA	VA	VA	Farmer
	Roxey	W	B	F	UN 1870	30	M	13	2	2	MS	MS	MS	
	Mary	D	B	F	Feb 1886	14	S				MS	VA	MS	
	Emma	D	B	F	Oct 1899	9/mo	S				MS	VA	MS	
	Adams, Bulah	Nce	B	F	UN 1888	12	S				AL	AL	AL	
384	Sey, Ned	H	B	M	UN UN	35	M				VA	VA	VA	Day Laborer
	Emeline	W	B	F	UN UN	35	M		0	0	MS	MS	MS	
385	Sea, John	H	B	M	Jun 1879	20	M	1			MS	VA	MS	Farmer,Day Laborer
	Bulah	W	B	F	UN 1885	15	M	1	1	1	TN	TN	TN	
	Carry	D	B	F	Jan 1900	4/mo	S				MS	MS	TN	
386	Harvey, Henry	H	B	M	UN 1850	50	M	23			MS	TN	TN	Farmer
	Bettie	W	B	F	UN 1850	50	M	23	2	2	MS	VA	VA	
387	Harvey, Frank	H	B	M	Sep 1874	25	M	0			MS	AL	AL	Day Laborer
	Lou	W	B	F	Sep 1877	22	M	0	0	0	AL	MS	MS	
388	McRee, James	H	B	M	UN 1866	34	M	12			MS	MS	MS	Farmer
	Emmer	W	B	F	UN 1865	35	M	12	4	3	TN	TN	TN	
	Charley	S	B	M	Oct 1881	18	S				MS	MS	TN	
	McRee, James	Nep	B	M	Oct 1880	19	S				MS	MS	MS	
	McRee, Willie	D	B	F	May 1890	10	S				MS	MS	MS	
	Oda	S	B	M	Jan 1898	2	S				MS	MS	MS	
	Roda	D	B	F	Jan 1898	2	S				MS	MS	MS	
389	Smith, W.T.	H	B	M	Jun 1865	35	M	7			MS	MS	MS	Day Laborer

1	2	3	4	5	6	7	8	9	10	11	12	13	14	15
	Ada	W	B	F	May 1874	26	M	7	1	1	MS	MS	MS	
	Viola	D	B	F	May 1889	11	S				MS	MS	MS	
390	Galyean, Martha	H	W	F	May 1840	60	W		6	4	MS	VA	SC	Farmer
	Robert	S	W	M	Jul 1878	21	S				TN	TN	MS	
	Georgia	D	W	F	Feb 1880	20	S				TN	TN	MS	
391	Emerson, H.R.	H	W	M	Jan 1862	38	M	8			AL	AL	AL	Farmer
	Minnie	W	W	F	Nov 1873	26	M	8	0	0	MS	MS	MS	
	Biggs, Arthur	Bro	W	M	Oct 1882	17	S				MS	MS	MS	
	Biggs, Armor	Bro	W	M	Oct 1895	4	S				MS	MS	MS	
	Biggs, Agnes	Sis	W	F	Nov 1886	3	S				MS	MS	MS	
392	Nixon, John	H	W	M	Aug 1868	31	M	10			MS	TN	MS	Drygds Salesman
	Hatta A.	W	W	F	Sep 1875	24	M	10	4	3	MS	MS	MS	
	Clarah L.	D	W	F	Sep 1892	7	S				MS	MS	MS	
	Olen S.	S	W	M	Mar 1896	4	S				MS	MS	MS	
	Viola	S	W	F	Oct 1899	9/mo	S				MS	MS	MS	
393	Gray, James	H	W	M	Dec 1846	53	M	4			GA	GA	GA	Drygds Salesman
	Allie	W	W	F	Aug 1876	23	M	4	4	3	MS	AL	MS	
	Eva	D	W	F	Nov 1886	13	S				MS	GA	MS	
	Alvis	S	W	M	Apr 1899	1	S				MS	GA	MS	
394	Smith, Mary A.	H	W	F	Jul 1836	63	Wd		6	5	AL	SC	GA	
395	Clemente, John E.	H	W	M	UN UN	40	M	5			KY	KY	KY	
	Eller	W	W	F	Feb 1876	24	M	5	2	2	MS	MS	TN	
	E. Kittie	D	W	F	Feb 1897	3	S				KY	MS	MS	
	Mildridge	D	W	F	Apr 1900	2/mo	S				MS	MS	MS	
396	Blakney, Thomas	H	W	M	Jan 1835	65	M	7			MS	MS	MS	
	Edna	W	W	F	Dec 1872	27	M	7	3	3	AR	VA	AR	
	Henry	S	W	M	Oct 1858	41					MS	MS	AR	
	Lester	S	W	M	Apr 1894	6					MS	MS	AR	
	Bessy	D	W	F	Aug 1895	4					MS	MS	AR	
	Dewey	S	W	M	Jul 1898	1					MS	MS	AR	
	Blakney, Bettie	Sis	W	F	Apr 1863	37	S				MS	MS	AR	
397	Counce, Melissa	H	B	F	UN UN	61	W		8	8	MS	MS	MS	
	Anner	D	B	F	UN UN	17	S				MS	MS	MS	
	Chester	S	B	M	UN UN	14	S				MS	MS	MS	
	Knot, Carthrin	D	B	F	Aug 1869	30	W				MS	MS	MS	
	Counce, Lottie M.	D	B	F	Mar 1898	2	S				MS	MS	MS	
398	Rodgers, Maggie	H	B	F	Apr 1880	20	Wd		1	1	MS	MS	MS	
399	Holder, Thomas	H	W	M	Sep 1860	39	M	10			MS	TN	SC	Drygds Salesman
	Minnie R.	W	W	F	Apr 1867	33	M	10	6	6	MS	SC	AL	
	Owen T.	S	W	M	Sep 1890	9	S				MS	MS	MS	
	Mabel S.	D	W	F	Jan 1892	8	S				MS	MS	MS	
	Fred K.	S	W	M	Aug 1893	6	S				MS	MS	MS	
	Charley U.	S	W	M	Aug 1895	5	S				MS	MS	MS	
	Clifford	S	W	F	Feb 1897	3	S				MS	MS	MS	
	Gladys	D	W	F	Jan 1899	1	S				MS	MS	MS	
400	Woodley, S.W.	H	W	M	Jan 1846	54	M	30			MS	TN	SC	Drygds Salesman
	Martha A.	W	W	F	Apr 1850	50	M	30	3	3	MS	NC	TN	
401	Dean, R.M.	H	W	M	Jul 1840	59	W				MS	SC	SC	Drygds Salesman
402	Manard, John	H	W	M	Mar 1844	56	M	33			Can	Can	Can	Farmer
	Margaret	W	W	F	Dec 1836	63	M	33	3	3	Can	Can	Can	

1	2	3	4	5	6	7	8	9	10	11	12	13	14	15
403	Jones, Sarah	H	W	F	Mar 1837	63	Wd		6	5	AL	TN	TN	
	A.H.	S	W	M	Feb 1867	33	S				TN	AL	AL	Farmer
	H.L.	S	W	M	Jul 1872	27	S				MS	AL	AL	Farmer
	Roy L.	S	W	M	Apr 1875	25	S				MS	AL	AL	Farmer
	W.C.	S	W	M	May 1878	22	S				MS	AL	AL	Farmer
404	Reeves, James	H	W	M	Dec 1856	43	M	14			AL	GA	TN	Day Laborer
	Rutha	W	W	F	Mar 1869	31	M	14	4	3	TN	AL	TN	
	Ora L.	D	W	F	Feb 1892	8	S				MS	AL	TN	
	James A.	S	W	M	Apr 1895	5	S				MS	AL	TN	
	Ema K.	D	W	F	Oct 1897	2	S				MS	AL	TN	
405	Sanders, Nancy	H	W	F	Jun 1828	71	Wd		7	4	GA	SC	SC	
	Montgomery, Rosa	D	W	F	Apr 1884	16	S				AR	MS	AL	
	Monrgomery, Viola	D	W	F	Jul 1886	13	S				TN	MS	AL	
	Montgomery, Georgia	D	W	F	Jul 1895	4	S				TN	MS	AL	
	Montgomery, Willie	S	W	M	Mar 1897	3	S				TN	MS	AL	
406	Hutton, G.W.	H	W	M	Mar 1847	53	M	30			AL	TN	TN	Physician
	N.L.	W	W	F	Jun 1850	49	M	30	10	9	MS	PA	MS	
	S.L.	S	W	M	Aug 1876	23	S				MS	AL	MS	Drugist
	W. Murry	S	W	M	Jul 1880	19	S				MS	AL	MS	Day Laborer
	J.M.	S	W	M	Mar 1881	18	S				MS	AL	MS	Day Laborer
	Virgie	D	W	F	Sep 1889	18	S				MS	AL	MS	
	Grace	D	W	F	Sep 1892	7	S				MA	AL	MS	
407	Smith, J.T.	H	W	M	Jan 1861	39	M	9			MS	SC	AL	Postmaster
	Lena	W	W	F	Apr 1871	29	M	9	4	4	MS	AL	MS	
	Kirby	S	W	M	Jan 1892	8	S				TX	MS	MS	
	Laura	D	W	F	Feb 1894	6	S				MS	MS	MS	
	Lillie	D	W	F	Aug 1896	3	S				MS	MS	MS	
	G. Milton	S	W	M	Nov 1898	1	S				MS	MS	MS	
408	Faust, John	H	W	M	UN 1861	39	M	15			MS	AL	MS	Idiot
	Katy	W	W	F	May 1864	36	M	15	2	2	MS	Ger	Ger	
	Rayford C.	S	W	M	Sep 1886	13	S				TN	MS	TN	Farm Laborer
	Girtree	D	W	F	May 1890	10	S				TN	MS	TN	
409	Skinner, Henry	H	W	M	Nov 1855	44	M	19			MS	SC	MS	Farmer
	Francis	W	W	F	May 1861	39	M	19	7	6	MS	MS	MS	
	Charley M.	S	W	M	Dec 1881	18	S				MS	MS	MS	Drygds Salesman
	John B.	S	W	M	Feb 1884	16	S				MS	MS	MS	Day Laborer
	Maud F.	D	W	F	Mar 1886	14	S				MS	MS	MS	
	Sarah M.	D	W	F	Dec 1891	8	S				MS	MS	MS	
	Katie L.	D	W	F	Mar 1895	5	S				MS	MS	MS	
	Samuel	S	W	M	May 1900	0/mo	S				MS	MS	MS	
410	Lindsey, W.T.	H	W	M	Aug 1857	42	M	17			AL	TN	AL	Physician
	Levina	W	W	F	Jun 1867	32	M	17	8	4	GA	GA	GA	
	Lizzie	D	W	F	Jan 1884	15	S				AL	AL	GA	
	Cleveland	S	W	M	Apr 1890	10	S				MS	AL	GA	Farm Laborer
	Maggie	D	W	F	Aug 1893	6	S				TN	AL	GA	
	Robert D.	S	W	M	Mar 1899	1	S				MS	AL	GA	
411	King, Samuel	H	W	M	Feb 1867	33	M	6			MS	TX	GA	Farmer
	Virginia	W	W	F	Sep 1880	19	M	6	3	3	MS	MS	MS	
	Luler P.	D	W	F	Jan 1896	4	S				MS	MS	MS	
	Minnie B.	D	W	F	Aug 1897	2	S				MS	MS	MS	
	Dewey	S	W	M	Oct 1899	4/mo	S				MS	MS	MS	
412	King, Sarah	H	W	F	Feb 1849	51	Wd		7	3	TN	NC	NC	
	Dock	S	W	M	Sep 1878	21	S				MS	TN	TN	Painter

1	2	3	4	5	6	7	8	9	10	11	12	13	14	15
413	Rodgers, S.L.	H	W	M	Feb 1833	67	M	45			TN	TN	VA	Teacher
	Emma	W	W	F	May 1837	63	M	45	10	7	GA	VA	VA	
	Mattie	D	W	F	Dec 1872	27	S				MS	TN	GA	
414	Akers, Thomas	H	W	M	Dec 1877	22	M	1			MS	MS	MS	Drygds Salesman
	Bertie	W	W	F	Oct 1880	19	M	1	0	0	MS	MS	MS	
415	Formby, J.T.	H	W	M	Nov 1833	66	M	36			GA	VA	GA	Farmer, former J.P.
	Nancy C.	W	W	F	Apr 1843	57	M	36	7	3	AL	AL	AL	
	Maryetta	D	W	F	Jun 1880	19	S				MS	GA	AL	
416	Faust, William	H	W	M	Dec 1864	35	M	11			MS	SC	SC	Farmer
	Florina	W	W	F	Jan 1874	26	M	11	4	4	TN	MS	MS	
	William N.	S	W	M	UN 1891	9	S				MS	MS	MS	
	Daniel E.	S	W	M	UN 1893	7	S				MS	MS	MS	
	Thester A.	S	W	M	UN 1895	5	S				MS	MS	MS	
	Bertha L.	D	W	F	UN 1898	2	S				MS	MS	MS	
417	Counce, Moses	H	B	M	Jan 1824	76	Wd				AL	VA	VA	Day Laborer
418	Phelps, W.H.	H	W	M	Sep 1840	59	M	32			TN	NY	TN	Farmer
	Matilda	W	W	F	Aug 1845	54	M	32	0	0	AL	SC	SC	
	Thomas, M.J.	Sis	W	F	Mar 1849	51	Wd		1	0	MS	NY	Ger	
419	Epperson, J.H.	H	W	M	Dec 1849	50	M	14			MS	VA	SC	Drygds Salesman
	Francis	W	W	F	Feb 1863	37	M	14	4	4	MS	TN	TN	
	Eullah	D	W	F	Aug 1886	13	S				MS	MS	MS	
	Luceal	D	W	F	Aug 1891	8	S				MS	MS	MS	
	Elia M.	D	W	F	Oct 1896	3	S				MS	MS	MS	
	Sherrill, J.T.	SS	W	M	Feb 1881	19	S				MS	MS	MS	
420	Epperson, David	H	W	M	Feb 1854	46	M	5			MS	VA	SC	Farmer
	Ida	W	W	F	Nov 1872	27	M	5	2	2	MS	MS	MS	
	John	S	W	M	Jun 1872	27	S				MS	MS	MS	
	Effie	D	W	F	Nov 1875	24	S				MS	MS	MS	
	Fannie	D	W	F	Feb 1882	18	S				MS	MS	MS	
	Olie	D	W	F	Feb 1896	4	S				MS	MS	MS	
	Charley	S	W	M	May 1898	2	S				MS	MS	MS	
421	Epperson, William	H	W	M	May 1846	54	Wd				MS	VA	SC	Farmer
	Francis	Sis	W	F	Mar 1844	56	S				MS	VA	SC	
422	Aldridge, A.J.	H	W	M	Feb 1829	71	M	30			Al	TN	AL	Drygds Salesman
	Nancy R.	W	W	F	Jul 1841	58	M	30	10	6	AL	TN	NC	
	Martha A.	D	W	F	Dec 1881	18	S				AL	TN	AL	
423	Lambert, George	H	W	M	Oct 1873	26	M	6			MS	MS	MS	Farmer
	Minnie	W	W	F	May 1875	25	M	6	3	0	MS	MS	MS	
424	Norman, William	H	W	M	Mar 1849	51	M	32			MS	SC	SC	Farmer
	Nettie	W	W	F	Dec 1848	51	M	32	4	4	MS	TN	TN	
	James C.	S	W	M	Nov 1884	16	S				MS	MS	MS	
	Willie	S	W	M	Jun 1887	12	S				MS	MS	MS	
	Katie	D	W	F	Jun 1887	12	S				MS	MS	MS	
425	Walker, Thomas	H	B	M	UN 1840	60	Wd				MS	VA	MS	
426	Searcy, Robert	H	W	M	Mar 1838	62	Wd				NC	NC	NC	Drygds Salesman
	Mattie	D	W	F	May 1883	17	S				MS	NC	GA	
	Rubin	S	W	M	Aug 1884	15	S				MS	NC	GA	
	Henry	S	W	M	Jul 1888	11	S				MS	NC	GA	
	Rally	S	W	M	Jul 1890	9	S				MS	NC	GA	

1	2	3	4	5	6	7	8	9	10	11	12	13	14	15
427	Skelton, Thomas	H	W	M	Jan 1876	24	M	4			MS	MS	MS	RR Laborer
	Julia	W	W	F	Dec 1876	23	M	4	1	1	MS	MS	MS	
	Anna	D	W	F	Sep 1898	1	S				MS	MS	MS	
428	Eldridge, M.O.	H	W	M	May 1848	52	M	28			SC	SC	SC	
	N.A.	W	W	F	Jul 1852	57	M	28	10	7	MS	VA	TN	
	W.L.	S	W	M	Feb 1882	18	S				MS	SC	MS	
	Jalie	D	W	F	Feb 1885	15	S				MS	SC	MS	
	Charley	S	W	M	Jun 1888	11	S				MS	SC	MS	
	Mary	D	W	F	Jul 1890	9	S				MS	SC	MS	
	Berthie	D	W	F	Feb 1893	6	S				MS	SC	MS	
429	Medows, T.C.	H	W	M	Nov 1834	65	M	34			AL	TN	TN	
	M.E.	W	W	F	Dec 1844	55	M	34	9	6	TN	TN	TN	
430	Eldridge, Henry	H	UN	UN	Mar 1876	24	M	1			MS	SC	MS	Day Laborer
	Annie	W	UN	UN	Nov 1889	19	M	1	1	1	MS	MS	MS	
	Ruth	D	UN	UN	Jan 1900	4/mo	S				MS	MS	MS	
431	Aldridge, R.	H	W	M	Nov 1878	21	M	1			AL	AL	AL	Farmer
	R.E.	W	W	F	Feb 1880	20	M	1	0	0	MS	MS	MS	
432	Grinder, George	H	B	M	Feb 1862	38	M	14			MS	TN	TN	Farmer
	Fannie	W	B	F	Jan 1863	37	M	14	10	7	MS	VA	TN	
	Lilian	D	B	F	Feb 1886	14	S				MS	MS	MS	
	Effie	D	B	F	Dec 1887	12	S				MS	MS	MS	
	Virgie	D	B	F	Dec 1889	10	S				MS	MS	MS	
	Nora	D	B	F	Sep 1892	7	S				MS	MS	MS	
	Jack	S	B	M	Feb 1894	6	S				MS	MS	MS	
	Hattie	D	B	F	Feb 1896	4	S				MS	MS	MS	
	Word	S	B	M	Mar 1898	2	S				MS	MS	MS	
433	Hines, Berry	H	B	M	Mar 1855	45	M	16			AL	VA	NC	Farmer
	Julia	W	B	F	Aug 1863	36	M	16	8	7	MS	MS	MS	
	Brinda L.	D	B	F	Apr 1884	16	S				MS	AL	MS	
	Rubin	S	B	M	Apr 1886	14	S				MS	AL	MS	
	Shurman	S	B	M	Jun 1888	11	S				MS	AL	MS	
	Willie M.	S	B	M	Apr 1890	10	S				MS	AL	MS	
	Ulalah	D	B	F	Sep 1893	7	S				MS	AL	MS	
	Odell	S	B	M	Jul 1895	4	S				MS	AL	MS	
	Clara	D	B	F	Dec 1899	5/mo	S				MS	AL	MS	
434	Welch, Peter	H	B	M	Dec 1832	67	Wd				AL	VA	SC	Farmer
435	Traylor, Malvina	H	B	F	UN 1855	45	Wd		6	5	MS	VA	SC	Farmer
	Sam	S	B	M	Aug 1874	25	S				MS	MS	MS	
	Emeline	D	B	F	Jul 1876	23	S				MS	MS	MS	
	Everett	S	B	M	Mar 1889	11	S				MS	MS	MS	
	Jennie	D	B	F	May 1896	4	S				MS	MS	MS	
	Carter, Jency	M	B	F	UN 1809	90	Wd		1	1	MS	VA	SC	
	Orr, John	Bdr	B	M	Mar 1870	30	S				AL	AL	AL	Day Laborer
436	Keith, Charley	H	B	M	UN 1868	32	M	5			GA	GA	GA	RR Laborer
	Safrona	W	B	F	Oct 1877	22	M	5	2	2	MS	MS	MS	
	Harry	S	B	M	Dec 1896	3	S				MS	GA	MS	
	Fred	S	B	M	Jan 1899	1	S				MS	GA	MS	
437	Joslin, Dick	H	B	M	UN 1863	37	M	3			MS	MS	MS	RR Laborer
	Annie	W	B	F	Mar 1868	32	M	3	0	0	MS	MS	MS	
	Thomas, Enoch	Nce	B	F	Apr 1884	16	S				MS	MS	MS	
438	Gross, Theodore	H	W	M	Jan 1844	56	M	5			VA	VA	VA	Carpenter
	Pemelia	W	W	F	Jul 1865	35	M	5	0	0	MS	MS	MS	

1	2	3	4	5	6	7	8	9	10	11	12	13	14	15
	Cora L.	D	W	F	Jul 1887	12	S				MS	VA	MS	
	Thomas J.	S	W	M	Aug 1891	8	S				AL	VA	MS	
	Charley A.	S	W	M	Dec 1893	6	S				MS	VA	MS	
439	Whitehurst, A.J.	H	W	M	Jul 1869	30	M	15			MS	MS	GA	Physician
	Lina	W	W	F	May 1872	28	M	15	0	0	MS	TN	TN	
440	Emmons, Hugh	H	B	M	UN 1879	22	M	4			MS	MS	MS	Day Laborer
	Cora	W	B	F	Apr 1879	21	M	4	1	1	MS	AL	TN	
	Elvis	S	B	M	Dec 1897	2	S				MS	MS	MS	
	Wimbush, Harriet	M	B	F	May 1836	64	Wd		7	5	TN	TN	TN	
441	Britton, Harry	H	B	M	May 1843	57	Wd				TN	TN	SC	Day Laborer
442	Counce, Zandy	H	B	M	Nov 1862	37	M	6			MS	VA	VA	
	Sarah	W	B	F	Jun 1875	24	M	6	3	2	MS	TN	MS	
	Dannie	D	B	F	Jul 1894	5	S				MS	MS	MS	
	Mary	D	B	F	Apr 1898	2	S				MS	MS	MS	
443	Smith, S.J.	H	W	M	Nov 1859	40	M	4			MS	SC	AL	Farmer
	Corra L.	W	W	F	Sep 1875	24	M	4	1	1	MS	MS	MS	
	C.C.	S	W	M	Oct 1896	3	S				MS	MS	MS	
444	Trotter, Mary A.	H	W	F	Mar 1845	55	M	25	4	4	TN	NC	NC	
	Jennie	D	W	F	May 1876	24	S				TN	TN	TN	
	Peyton	S	W	M	Nov 1879	20	S				TN	TN	TN	RR Agent
	Etter	D	W	F	Oct 1881	18	S				TN	TN	TN	
	James	S	W	M	Jun 1884	16	S				TN	TN	TN	
445	Medders, F.M.	H	W	M	May 1843	57	M	32			AL	TN	TN	Carpenter
	Susan N.	W	W	F	Aug 1845	54	M	32	8	6	MS	SC	GA	
	J.A.	S	W	M	Sep 1880	19	S				MS	AL	MS	
	Gertrude	D	W	F	Mar 1883	17	S				MS	AL	MS	
	Clyde	S	W	M	Apr 1885	15	S				MS	AL	MS	
	Nola	D	W	F	Mar 1887	13	S				MS	AL	MS	

End of Enumeration of District #2

1	2	3	4	5	6	7	8	9	10	11	12	13	14	15
1	Woodley, Robert V.	H	W	M	Jan 1870	30	M	8			MS	MS	UN	Farmer
	Leona C.	W	W	F	Jan 1876	24	M	8	4	3	MS	MS	MS	
	Ruby P.	D	W	F	Nov 1892	7	S				MS	MS	MS	
	Carlton L.	S	W	M	Oct 1896	4	S				MS	MS	MS	
	Lemay G.	D	W	F	Feb 1899	1	S				MS	MS	MS	
2	McNutt, William	H	W	M	Jan 1852	48	M	29			MS	NC	NC	Farmer
	Nancy E.	W	W	F	UN 1851	49	M	29	13	12	AL	NC	AL	
	Vonnie L.	D	W	F	Jan 1875	25	S				MS	MS	AL	
	Georgia E.	D	W	F	Dec 1879	20	S				MS	MS	AL	
	Thomas E.	S	W	M	UN 1881	18	S				MS	MS	AL	Farm Laborer
	James J.	S	W	M	UN 1883	17	S				MS	MS	AL	Farm Laborer
	Wiley C.	S	W	M	Dec 1885	15	S				MS	MS	AL	Farm Laborer
	Artie	D	W	F	Mar 1887	13	S				MS	MS	AL	
	Charles G.	S	W	M	UN 1891	10	S				MS	MS	AL	Farm Laborer
	Roy R.	S	W	M	UN 1892	8	S				MS	MS	AL	
3	Degraw, William	H	W	M	Feb 1872	28	M	10			MS	UN	AL	Farmer
	Marietta	W	W	F	Oct 1874	27	M	10	5	4	AL	AL	UN	
	Annie	D	W	F	Nov 1892	7	S				MS	MS	AL	
	Wiley	S	W	M	UN 1894	5	S				MS	MS	AL	
	Walter	S	W	M	UN 1896	4	S				MS	MS	AL	
	Lacy	S	W	M	Feb 1899	1	S				MS	MS	AL	
4	Moore, William H.	H	W	M	Jul 1879	20	M	1			MS	MS	MS	
	Docia	W	W	F	Jan 1878	18	M	1	0	0	MS	MS	MS	
5	Common, William	H	B	M	Jun 1844	56	M	24			GA	AL	AL	
	Mary	W	B	F	Aug 1849	51	M	24	8	4	MS	MS	UN	
	Ben F.	S	B	M	Jan 1883	17	S				MS	AL	MS	
	Mary L.	SD	B	F	Feb 1881	19	S				MS	AL	MS	
6	Haney, Ira T.	H	W	M	Jun 1832	67	M	49			TN	SC	SC	Farmer
	Rhoda	W	W	F	Apr 1836	64	M	49	14	9	SC	SC	SC	
	Louis R.	S	W	M	Jun 1879	21	M	0			MS	TN	SC	
	Maggie F.	DiL	W	F	Apr 1887	18	M	0	0	0	MS	GA	MS	
	Appleton, Ethel M.	GD	W	F	Jul 1880	19	S				TN	TN	TN	
7	Wimbish, George	H	W	M	May 1831	69	M	45			KY	VA	VA	Farmer
	Martha A.	W	W	F	Oct 1828	71	M	46	5	4	AL	IN	TN	
8	Moore, Calvin A.	H	W	M	Jul 1848	51	M	22			MS	TN	TN	Farmer
	Mary J.	W	W	F	Mar 1857	43	M	22	6	6	MS	KY	AL	
	Mary H.	D	W	F	Jan 1884	16	S				MS	MS	MS	
	Sue L.	D	W	F	Apr 1887	13	S				MS	MS	MS	
	Samuel M.	S	W	M	Aug 1889	10	S				MS	MS	MS	Farm Laborer
	Henry H.	S	W	M	Apr 1896	4	S				MS	MS	MS	
9	Epps, George F.	H	W	M	Oct 1853	44	M	19			AL	AL	AL	Farmer
	Martha C.	W	W	F	Dec 1861	38	M	19	5	3	MS	AL	AL	
	Ada L.	D	W	F	Jul 1881	18	S				MS	AL	MS	
	James R.	S	W	M	Jul 1885	14	S				MS	AL	MS	Farm Laborer
	David T.	S	W	M	Jul 1890	9	S				MS	AL	MS	
10	Gregson, Will F.	H		W	M	Aug 1868	31	M	0			TN	NC	NC	Farmer
	Mollie	W	W	F	Jan 1872	28	M	0	0	0	MS	MS	MS	
	Katie	D	W	F	Aug 1894	5	S				MS	TN	TN	

1	2	3	4	5	6	7	8	9	10	11	12	13	14	15
11	Bonds, David A.	H	W	M	Sep 1876	23	M	1			MS	MS	MS	Farmer
	Dora A.	W	W	F	May 1880	20	M	1	1	1	MS	MS	MS	
	Clifford	S	W	M	Apr 1899	1	S				MS	MS	MS	
12	Bonds, David E.	H	W	M	Jun 1851	48	M	27			MS	TN	TN	Farmer
	Mary E.	W	W	F	Mar 1853	47	M	27	6	6	MS	SC	AL	
	Robert G.	S	W	M	May 1884	16	S				MS	MS	MS	Farm Laborer
	William E.	S	W	M	Jun 1888	11	S				MS	MS	MS	Farm Laborer
	Nora L.	D	W	F	May 1892	8	S				MS	MS	MS	
	Mary	M	W	F	Mar 1811	89	Wd				TN	UN	UN	
13	Wimbish, Robert L.	H	W	M	May 1866	34	M	9			MS	KY	AL	Farmer
	Cora A.	W	W	F	Jan 1871	29	M	9	6	5	MS	MS	MS	
	William Ward	S	W	M	Feb 1892	8	S				MS	MS	MS	
	Ruby L.	D	W	F	Sep 1893	6	S				MS	MS	MS	
	Weda	D	W	F	Jan 1895	5	S				MS	MS	MS	
	Annie L.	D	W	F	Feb 1898	2	S				MS	MS	MS	
	No Name	D	W	F	May 1900	1/mo	S				MS	MS	MS	
14	West, James G.	H	W	M	Dec 1866	33	M	2			AL	MS	MS	Farmer
	Alta	W	W	F	UN 1877	23	M	2	0	0	AL	AL	AL	
15	Stubbs, ?	H	W	M	Mar 1851	49	M	0			MI	MI	MI	Farmer
	Mary E.	W	W	F	Nov 1852	47	M	0	5	1	MS	MS	KY	
16	White, Mary	H	W	F	Jan 1867	33	Wd		5	3	MS	TN	NC	Farm Laborer
	Virdie L.	D	W	F	Jan 1894	6	S				TN	TN	MS	
	Winona	D	W	F	Jan 1897	3	S				TN	TN	MS	
	Dewey A.	S	W	M	Jun 1898	1	S				TN	TN	MS	
17	Martin, Lee	H	W	M	Jan 1874	26	M	5			MS	MS	MS	Farmer
	Hattie A.	W	W	F	Oct 1876	23	M	5	1	0	MS	MS	MS	
18	Stanford, Charlie L.	H	W	M	Sep 1872	27	M	1			AL	AL	AL	Farmer
	Lular R.	W	W	F	Nov 1870	29	M	1	1	1	AL	AL	AL	
	Bulah L.	D	W	F	Dec 1899	5/mo	S				AL	AL	AL	
19	Wright, Robert P.	H	W	M	UN 1850	50	Wd				MS	MS	MS	Farmer
	Lenna W.	D	W	F	UN 1888	20	S				MS	MS	MS	
	Emma L.	D	W	F	May 1882	18	S				MS	MS	MS	
	Wesley H.	S	W	M	Aug 1883	16	S				MS	MS	MS	
	Lowery	S	W	M	UN 1887	13	S				MS	MS	MS	
	Nancy L.	D	W	F	Apr 1889	11	S				MS	MS	MS	
	Alta B.	D	W	F	UN 1892	8	S				MS	MS	MS	
	Henry L.	S	W	M	Aug 1893	6	S				MS	MS	MS	
20	Rutledge, John H.	H	W	M	Dec 1835	64	M	32			SC	SC	SC	Farmer
	Martha A.	W	W	F	Feb 1842	58	M	32	4	4	SC	SC	SC	
21	Rutledge, Charlie Oscar	H	W	M	Jun 1869	30	M	12			MS	SC	SC	Farmer
	Sarah A.	W	W	F	Sep 1869	30	M	12	5	4	MS	SC	AL	
	Ida B.	D	W	F	May 1889	11	S				MS	MS	MS	
	Samie E.	S	W	M	Mar 1891	9	S				MS	MS	MS	
	Charlie	S	W	M	Sep 1895	4	S				MS	MS	MS	
	Bruce	S	W	M	Jul 1897	2	S				MS	MS	MS	
22	Pannell, John A.	H	W	M	Nov 1851	49	M	27			MS	MS	MS	Farmer
	Mary	W	W	F	Jan 1846	54	M	27	5	5	MS	NC	NC	
	Richard J.	S	W	M	May 1880	20	S				MS	MS	MS	
	Luticia	D	W	F	Aug 1883	16	S				MS	MS	MS	
	Robert W.	S	W	M	May 1890	10	S				MS	MS	MS	
23	Hall, Thomas	H	W	M	Feb 1873	27	M	0			AL	AL	TN	Farmer

1	2	3	4	5	6	7	8	9	10	11	12	13	14	15
	Fannie	W	W	F	Jan 1871	29	M	0	0	0	MS	MS	AL	
24	Grimes, John F.	H	W	M	Aug 1846	53	M	30			MS	MS	TN	Farmer
	Sarah E.	W	W	F	Dec 1849	50	M	30	4	3	AL	NC	GA	
	Sarah C.	D	W	F	Sep 1872	27	S				MS	MS	AL	
	William B.	GS	W	M	Mar 1898	2	S				MS	MS	AL	
25	Fairless, Ben F.	H	W	M	Jul 1835	64	M	42			NC	NC	NC	Farmer
	Mandy E.	W	W	F	Feb 1837	62	M	42	4	2	GA	SC	SC	
26	Fairless, James D.	H	W	M	Apr 1863	37	M	13			MS	NC	GA	Farmer
	Georgia	W	W	F	Mar 1865	35	M	13	2	1	MS	AL	GA	
	Pearl S.	D	W	F	Jan 1890	10	S				MS	MS	MS	
27	Fairless, William	H	W	M	Jan 1861	39	M	14			MS	NC	GA	Farmer
	Alice	W	W	F	Jan 1867	38	M	14	0	0	MS	AL	AL	
	Holt, Mamie	Nce	W	F	Jan 1887	13	S				MS	MS	MS	
	Holt, Willie B.	Nce	W	F	Jan 1889	11	S				MS	MS	MS	
	Ellis, Luther J.	Bdr	W	M	Oct 1876	23	S				GA	GA	GA	Farm Laborer
	Willingham, George L.	Bdr	W	M	Sep 1881	18	S				AL	AL	AL	Farm Laborer
28	Enlow, James E.	H	W	M	Nov 1862	37	M	12			AL	TN	NC	Farmer
	Mandy H.	W	W	F	Sep 1865	34	M	12	7	7	KY	CA	AL	
	James Wheeler	S	W	M	Sep 1889	10	S				AL	AL	KY	Farm Laborer
	Jessie O.	D	W	F	Nov 1890	9	S				MS	AL	KY	
	Fred A.	S	W	M	Aug 1892	7	S				MS	AL	KY	
	Hallie	D	W	F	Jan 1894	6	S				MS	AL	KY	
	Burton F.	S	W	M	Nov 1895	4	S				MS	AL	KY	
	Alvin E.	S	W	M	Mar 1897	3	S				MS	AL	KY	
	Maggie R.	D	W	F	Dec 1898	1	S				MS	AL	KY	
29	Estes, Charlie	H	W	M	Aug 1846	53	M	27			GA	GA	GA	Farmer
	Nicey	W	W	F	Feb 1846	54	M	27	1	1	AL	SC	SC	
30	Estes, Henry A.	H	W	M	Jul 1878	21	M	2			MS	GA	AL	Farmer
	Alice	W	W	F	Mar 1877	23	M	2	1	1	MS	MS	TN	
	Norah	D	W	F	Aug 1898	1	S				MS	MS	MS	
31	Davis, James H.	H	W	M	Mar 1828	72	M	34			MS	AL	AL	Farmer
	Malisa H.	W	W	F	Nov 1849	50	M	34	4	4	AL	SC	SC	
32	Gattis, William	H	W	M	May 1840	60	M	40			MS	AL	TN	Farmer
	Senthie	W	W	F	Jul 1848	52	M				TN	NC	NC	
	William G.	S	W	M	Oct 1873	27	S				MS	MS	VA	Farm Laborer
	Jennie M.	D	W	F	Apr 1879	21	S				MS	MS	VA	
	George W.	S	W	M	Mar 1880	20	Wd				MS	MS	VA	Farm Laborer
33	Robinson, James	H	W	M	Jun 1862	39	M	8			MS	TN	AL	Farmer
	Laura J.	W	W	F	Dec 1871	28	M	8	1	1	MS	UN	AL	
	Annie W.	D	W	F	Sep 1897	2	S				MS	MS	MS	
	Charlie F.	Bro	W	M	Jun 1862	37	S				MS	TN	AL	Farmer
34	Davis, Joe	H	W	M	Jun 1872	26	M	1			MS	AL	AL	Farmer
	Dora T.	W	W	F	Jan 1880	20	M	1	1	1	MS	SC	AL	
	Earl C.	S	W	M	Dec 1899	5/mo	S				MS	MS	MS	
35	Edwards, Charlie	H	W	M	Feb 1867	33	M	7			MS	SC	MS	Farmer
	Catherine G.	W	W	F	Dec 1873	26	M	7	2	2	MS	MS	MS	
	Claire B.	D	W	F	Dec 1893	6	S				MS	MS	MS	
	William J.	S	W	M	Mar 1897	3	S				MS	MS	MS	
36	Long, Richard	H	W	M	Apr 1828	72	M	30			AL	VA	VA	Landlord
	Luticia H.	W	W	F	Jun 1837	62	M	30	3	3	TN	NC	NC	

1	2	3	4	5	6	7	8	9	10	11	12	13	14	15
	Jourdan, Katie	SiL	W	F	Mar 1835	65	S				TN	NC	NC	
37	Long, Adolphus B.	H	W	M	Dec 1874	25	M	1			MS	AL	VA	Farmer
	Melvie	W	W	F	Mar 1875	25	M	1	1	1	MS	MS	MS	
	Fred A.	S	W	M	Apr 1900	2/mo	S				MS	MS	MS	
38	Durham, John W.	H	W	M	Jun 1844	55	M	6			AL	KY	AL	Farmer
	Nancy E.	W	W	F	Feb 1857	43	M	6	1	1	MS	NC	AL	
	Francis M.	S	W	M	Jul 1866	33	Wd				MS	AL	TN	Farmer
39	Mitchel, Joe	H	B	M	UN 1830	70	M	23			MS	MS	MS	Farmer
	Rose	W	B	F	UN 1850	50	M	23	14	5	MS	MS	MS	
	James	S	B	M	Jun 1877	23	M	4			MS	MS	MS	Teamster
	Ben	S	B	M	Jan 1879	21	S				MS	MS	MS	Farm Laborer
	Wilson	S	B	M	Feb 1888	12	S				MS	MS	MS	Farm Laborer
	Lou	DiL	B	F	Feb 1877	23	M	4	3	2	MS	MS	MS	
	Tinie	GD	B	F	Dec 1893	6	S				MS	MS	MS	
	Rosa L.	GD	B	F	Apr 1900	1/mo	S				MS	MS	MS	
	Robinson, Nannie	Bdr	B	F	UN 1879	20	S				MS	MS	MS	
	Long, Anna	SD	B	F	Mar 1860	40	S				MS	MS	MS	
	Dulaney, Sam	GS	B	M	Sep 1881	18	S				MS	MS	MS	Farm Laborer
40	Vance, Manervie	H	B	F	UN 1830	70	Wd		6	3	SC	SC	SC	Farmer
	Mose H.	S	B	M	Apr 1879	21	S				MS	MS	SC	Farm Laborer
41	Burgess, George	H	B	M	Jan 1875	25	M	4			MS	MS	SC	Farmer
	Rachell	W	B	F	Jul 1875	24	M	4	3	3	MS	MS	MS	
	Viola	D	W	F	Feb 1897	3	S				MS	MS	MS	
	??	S	B	M	Jun 1898	1	S				MS	MS	MS	
	Clide	S	B	M	Jan 1900	4/mo	S				MS	MS	MS	
42	Aldrige, T.	H	W	M	Oct 1871	28	M	7			MS	MS	MS	Teamster
	Hattie	W	W	F	Jul 1874	25	M	7	5	1	MS	MS	TN	
	Lonnie F.	S	W	M	Jan 1900	5/mo	S				MS	MS	MS	
43	Sutton, John W.	H	W	M	Oct 1876	23	M	0			AL	TN	NC	Teamster
	Mary J.	W	W	F	Aug 1881	18	M	0	0	0	MS	MS	MS	
	John A.	F	W	M	May 1826	74	M	36			TN	NC	NC	
	Mary E.	M	W	F	Oct 1830	69	M	36	3	3	NC	NC	NC	
44	Edmondson, Charlie	H	W	M	Oct 1875	24	M	5			MS	MS	MS	Saw Mill Man
	Minnie	W	W	F	Jun 1877	22	M	5	2	2	MS	MS	MS	
	Annie	D	W	F	Sep 1896	3	S				MS	MS	MS	
	Margret	D	W	F	Dec 1898	1	S				MS	MS	MS	
	Murphy, Thomas	Bdr	W	M	UN 1877	23	S				MS	MS	AL	Laborer, Sawmill
45	Chenault, Lim C.	H	W	M	Jan 1863	37	M	2			MS	AL	GA	Farmer
	Mattie E.	W	W	F	Jun 1866	33	M	2	0	0	MS	AL	GA	
46	Webb, Thomas	H	W	M	Feb 1874	26	M	2			AL	VA	AL	Farmer
	Ethel J.	W	W	F	Nov 1878	21	M	2	0	0	MS	MS	MS	
47	Aldrige, John C.	H	W	M	Dec 1842	57	M	33			MS	Ind	TN	Farmer
	Ugenia	W	W	F	Dec 1842	58	M	33	9	8	MS	SC	SC	
	Gerdie	D	W	F	Jul 1884	15	S				MS	MS	MS	
	Hartman, Mattie	D	W	F	Sep 1867	32	Wd		3	2	MS	MS	MS	
	Hartman, Bessie	GD	W	F	Jan 1892	8	S				MS	Eng	MS	
	Hartman, Edwin	GS	W	M	Sep 1899	2	S				MS	Eng	MS	
	Wilson, Walter	Bdr	W	M	UN 1878	22	S				MS	TN	MS	Farm Laborer
48	Thomson Morgan	H	B	M	Apr 1862	38	M	21			MS	MS	MS	Farmer
	Tinie	W	B	F	UN 1866	34	M	21			MS	MS	MS	
	Marshal	S	B	M	Oct 1879	20	S				MS	MS	MS	Farm Laborer

1	2	3	4	5	6	7	8	9	10	11	12	13	14	15
	Robert	S	B	M	Jan 1884	16	S				MS	MS	MS	Farm Laborer
	Charlie	S	B	M	Feb 1889	11	S				MS	MS	MS	
	Hattie	D	B	F	Jul 1893	6	S				MS	MS	MS	
	Condry, Rachel	MiL	B	F	UN 1840	60	Wd				MS	MS	MS	
49	Coman, Willie	H	B	M	Mar 1878	22	M	1			MS	AL	MS	Farmer
	Minnie	W	B	F	Jan 1882	18	M	1	2	2	MS	MS	MS	
	Fairfoot	S	B	M	Aug 1897	2	S				MS	MS	MS	
	Pearl	D	B	F	Aug 1899	10/mo	S				MS	MS	MS	
50	Ellis, Samuel	H	W	M	Jun 1843	56	M	35			GA	NC	NC	Farmer
	Sarah A.	W	W	F	Jun 1844	55	M	35	8	8	GA	GA	GA	
	Augustia	D	W	F	Jul 1882	17	S				GA	GA	GA	
	Burton	S	W	M	Aug 1885	14	S				GA	GA	GA	
51	Robinson, Henry, Jr	H	W	M	Jan 1853	47	M	18			MS	MS	AL	Farmer
	Maggie A.	W	W	F	Jun 1852	49	M	18	7	4	MS	AL	AL	
	Henry O.	S	W	M	Feb 1884	16	S				MS	MS	MS	Farm Laborer
	Julia M.	D	W	F	Nov 1885	14	S				MS	MS	MS	
	Wesley B.	S	W	M	Sep 1887	12	S				MS	MS	MS	
	Maggie E.	D	W	F	Dec 1889	10	S				MS	MS	MS	
52	Long, Horace C.	H	W	M	Jul 1873	26	M	4			MS	AL	MS	Co. Supt.
	Mollie	W	W	F	May 1875	25	M	4	1	1	MS	TN	MS	
	Alvah C.	S	W	M	Dec 1896	3	S				MS	MS	MS	
	Myrics, Will P.	Bdr	W	M	Dec 1869	30	S				MS	TN	MS	Farm Laborer
53	Burnett, William B.	H	W	M	Nov 1826	73	M	13			TN	SC	GA	Farmer
	Elvira	W	W	F	Oct 1837	62	M	13	3	1	TN	VA	VA	
	Mares, Annie E.	D	W	F	Sep 1865	34	Wd		6	4	TN	TN	TN	
	Mares, Martha T.	GD	W	F	Apr 1889	11	S				AL	AL	TN	
	Mares, Raymond	GS	W	M	Jul 1892	8	S				TN	AL	TN	
	Mares, Crede Herbert	GS	W	M	Nov 1895	4	S				MS	AL	TN	
	Mares, Clifton H.	GS	W	M	Feb 1899	1	S				MS	AL	TN	
	Laffoon, George	SS	W	M	Sep 1877	22	S				MS	VA	TN	Farm Laborer
54	Hubbard, Thomas	H	W	M	Mar 1854	46	M	23			MS	SC	GA	Farmer
	Mary	W	W	F	Dec 1850	49	M	23	8	7	MS	NC	NC	
	Carrie	D	W	F	Nov 1879	20	S				MS	MS	MS	
	Glaucus	S	W	M	Apr 1881	19	S				MS	MS	MS	Farm Laborer
	Ione	D	W	F	Apr 1883	17	S				MS	MS	MS	
	Georgia	D	W	F	Dec 1885	14	S				MS	MS	MS	
	Lota	D	W	F	Mar 1889	11	S				MS	MS	MS	
	Alice	D	W	F	Apr 1873	7	S				MS	MS	MS	
	Gertrude	D	W	F	Feb 1897	3	S				MS	MS	MS	
55	Bumpass, James E.	H	W	M	Dec 1856	43	M	18			MS	MS	MS	Farmer
	Fannie	W	W	F	Mar 1862	38	M	18	8	8	MS	SC	SC	
	Velmer	D	W	F	Jul 1883	16	S				MS	MS	MS	
	Luther A.	S	W	M	May 1885	15	S				MS	MS	MS	Farm Laborer
	Louis C.	S	W	M	Aug 1887	12	S				MS	MS	MS	Farm Laborer
	Ollie V.	S	W	M	Mar 1890	10	S				MS	MS	MS	Farm Laborer
	Mary A.	D	W	F	Jun 1892	7	S				MS	MS	MS	
	Verdie D.	D	W	F	Aug 1894	5	S				MS	MS	MS	
	Cara	D	W	F	May 1897	3	S				MS	MS	MS	
	Audy	D	W	F	Jan 1900	4/mo	S				MS	MS	MS	
56	Williams, Soloman	H	W	M	Feb 1857	43	M	20			AL	TN	GA	Farmer
	Lovie L.	W	W	F	May 1857	43	M	20	8	7	MS	GA	GA	
	Mary E.	D	W	F	Feb 1887	19	S				AL	AL	MS	
	Perry J.	S	W	M	Nov 1882	17	S				MS	AL	MS	Farm Laborer
	Sam J.	S	W	M	Aug 1883	16	S				MS	AL	MS	Farm Laborer
	Ab L.	S	W	M	Aug 1884	15	S				MS	AL	MS	Farm Laborer

1	2	3	4	5	6	7	8	9	10	11	12	13	14	15
	Carlen	D	W	F	Aug 1888	11	S				MS	AL	MS	
	Katie	D	W	F	Oct 1890	9	S				MS	AL	MS	
	Euna	D	W	F	Aug 1893	6	S				MS	AL	MS	
57	Rowin, James	H	W	M	UN 1838	62	M	29			GA	GA	GA	Farmer
	Harriett	W	W	F	Nov 1846	53	M	29	2	2	AL	NC	GA	
	Frank F.	S	W	M	Dec 1879	20	S				AL	GA	AL	Farm Laborer
	James	S	W	M	Sep 1886	13	S				AL	GA	AL	Farm Laborer
58	Dennington, William	H	W	M	Nov 1852	47	M	1			GA	SC	SC	Farmer
	Marget	W	W	F	Sep 1852	48	M	1	4	2	MS	MS	MS	
	Clara B.	D	W	F	May 1885	15	S				MS	GA	MS	
	Louis	S	W	M	May 1889	10	S				MS	GA	MS	Farm Laborer
	Mattie	D	W	F	Sep 1893	6	S				MS	GA	MS	
	Silman, Ettea	SD	W	F	Jan 1893	7	S				TN	TN	TN	
	Baley, John B.	Bdr	W	M	Jan 1879	21	S				TN	UN	UN	Farm Laborer
59	Wilson, Silas A.	H	W	M	UN 1876	24	M	1			GA	GA	GA	Farm Laborer
	Willie G.	W	W	F	Jan 1878	22	M	1	1	1	MS	GA	MS	
	Neb	S	W	M	Dec 1798	1	S				MS	GA	MS	
60	Dees, Jemy T.	H	W	M	Feb 1867	33	M	13			MS	SC	SC	Farmer
	Mahalie C.	W	W	F	UN 1853	47	M	13	2	2	MS	AL	AL	
	Belle	D	W	F	Nov 1887	13	S				MS	MS	MS	
	Moses	S	W	M	Mar 1890	10	S				MS	MS	MS	
61	Wiley, William	H	W	M	UN 1833	67	Wd				TN	TN	AL	Farmer
	Tennessee	D	W	F	Mar 1889	21	S				MS	TN	AL	
62	Farris, James B.	H	W	M	Aug 1844	55	Wd				MS	TN	TN	Farmer
	Frank C.	S	W	M	Mar 1875	25	S				MS	MS	MS	Farm Laborer
	Charlie	S	W	M	Jun 1880	19	S				MS	MS	MS	Farm Laborer
	Ennis	D	W	F	May 1882	18	S				MS	MS	MS	
	Seilman, George	Cou	W	M	Jun 1878	21	S				MS	MS	MS	Farm Laborer
63	Murphy, George	H	W	M	Aug 1862	48	M	23			MS	TN	TN	Teamster
	Luddie	W	W	F	Mar 1845	45	M	23	1	1	AL	AL	AL	
	Thorn, Merl J.	D	W	F	Oct 1878	21	M	1	1	1	AL	MS	AL	
	Thorn, William	SiL	W	M	Mar 1878	22	M	1			AL	AL	AL	Farm Laborer
	Thorn, Elmer	GS	W	M	Aug 1899	8/mo	S				AL	AL	AL	
	Cagle, Elizabeth	MiL	W	F	Jun 1831	68	Wd		1	1	AL	GA	DC	
64	Stanford, Harvey A.	H	W	M	May 1852	48	M	24			TN	TN	TN	Farmer
	Amie E.	W	W	F	Jul 1858	41	M	24	8	6	AL	AL	AL	
	John	S	W	M	Dec 1878	21	S				MS	TN	AL	
	Mary E.	D	W	F	Mar 1880	20	S				MS	TN	AL	
	Lou A.	D	W	F	Nov 1886	13	S				MS	TN	AL	
	William H.	S	W	M	Aug 1889	10	S				MS	TN	AL	Farm Laborer
	George D.	S	W	M	Aug 1892	7	S				MS	TN	AL	
	Emmer L.	D	W	F	Apr 1896	4	S				MS	TN	AL	
65	Turner, James	H	W	M	Dec 1839	60	M	9			TN	VA	VA	Farmer
	Malina E.	W	W	F	Jul 1861	38	M	9	1	1	AL	GA	GA	
66	Nunley, John A.	H	W	M	May 1863	37	M	10			MS	TN	AL	Farmer
	Meredian C.	W	W	F	Sep 1870	29	M	10	4	4	MS	MS	AL	
	Lonnie F.	S	W	M	Oct 1890	9	S				AL	MS	MS	
	Orah E.	D	W	F	Apr 1892	7	S				MS	MS	MS	
	Delphia E.	D	W	F	Dec 1895	4	S				MS	MS	MS	
	Fernie N.	S	W	M	Sep 1898	1	S				MS	MS	MS	
67	Parsons, Nelson	H	W	M	Oct 1852	48	M	28			GA	NC	NC	Farmer
	Lou	W	W	F	Jun 1852	48	M	28	8	8	MS	AL	TN	

1	2	3	4	5	6	7	8	9	10	11	12	13	14	15
	James	S	W	M	Sep 1873	26	S				MS	GA	MS	Farm Laborer
	John	S	W	M	Dec 1875	24	S				MS	GA	MS	Farm Laborer
	Rosa A.	D	W	F	Jan 1878	22	S				MS	GA	MS	
	Emma	D	W	F	Jan 1882	18	S				MS	GA	MS	
	Robert L.	S	W	M	Mar 1884	16	S				MS	GA	MS	Farm Laborer
	Oscar E.	S	W	M	Jul 1890	9	S				MS	GA	MS	
68	Underwood, Henry	H	W	M	Oct 1860	39	M	12			TN	TN	GA	Farmer
	Julia C.	W	W	F	Mar 1875	25	M	12	6	6	AL	AL	AL	
	John F.	S	W	M	Oct 1890	9	S				MS	TN	AL	
	Lillie O.	D	W	F	Jun 1892	7	S				MS	TN	AL	
	William D.	S	W	M	Sep 1893	6	S				MS	TN	AL	
	Henry H.	S	W	M	Apr 1895	5	S				MS	TN	AL	
	Ida	D	W	F	Jan 1897	3	S				MS	TN	AL	
	Julia A.	D	W	F	Mar 1899	1	S				MS	TN	AL	
69	Williams, Joel W.	H	W	M	Apr 1829	72	Wd				TN	NC	NC	Farmer
	John	S	W	M	Jul 1851	40	S				AL	TN	GA	Farmer
	Robert	S	W	M	Oct 1866	33	S				AL	TN	GA	Blacksmith
70	Williams, Evert	H	W	M	UN 1871	29	M	10			AL	TN	GA	Farmer
	Lou	W	W	F	Sep 1873	26	M	10			MS	GA	MS	
	Joel	S	W	M	Sep 1892	7	S				AL	AL	MS	
	Nancy	D	W	F	Jan 1894	6	S				MS	AL	MS	
	William	S	W	M	Apr 1897	3	S				AL	AL	MS	
	Robert A.	S	W	M	Jan 1899	1	S				MS	AL	MS	
71	Faris, William	H	W	M	Sep 1870	29	S				MS	MS	MS	
72	Trumell, John	H	W	M	Feb 1828	72	Wd				GA	SC	SC	Farmer
73	Dees, William D.	H	W	M	Sep 1870	29	M	5			MS	SC	SC	Farmer
	Martha	W	W	F	Mar 1874	26	M	5	3	3	AL	AL	AL	
	John W.	S	W	M	Mar 1891	9	S				MS	MS	AL	
	Isic L.	S	W	M	Sep 1892	7	S				MS	MS	AL	
	Victoria	D	W	F	Sep 1895	4	S				MS	MS	AL	
	Harry/Henry	S	W	M	May 1897	3	S				MS	MS	AL	
	Harris S.	S	W	M	Feb 1899	1	S				MS	MS	AL	
74	Dees, John	H	W	M	Apr 1833	67	M	44			SC	SC	SC	Farmer
	Claire C.	W	W	F	Jan 1836	64	M	44	11	4	SC	SC	SC	
	? Remie E.	D	W	F	Nov 1856	43	M	17	0	0	SC	SC	SC	
75	Murphy, John	H	W	M	Jan 1849	50	M	23			AL	TN	AL	Farmer
	Malisia	W	W	F	Dec 1852	47	M	23	8	8	MS	MS	MS	
	James M.	S	W	M	Jul 1883	16	S				MS	MS	MS	Farm Laborer
	America E.	D	W	F	Aug 1888	11	S				MS	MS	MS	
	John A.	S	W	M	Jan 1890	10	S				MS	MS	MS	Farm Laborer
	Martha A.	D	W	F	Jun 1891	8	S				MS	MS	MS	
	Washington	S	W	M	Feb 1894	6	S				MS	MS	MS	
	Irene	D	W	F	Feb 1897	3	S				MS	MS	MS	
	Catherine	M	W	F	Nov 1818	81	Wd		8	8	TN	VA	NC	
76	Monroe, George W.	H	W	M	Feb 1848	52	M	22			MS	NC	VA	Farmer
	Mary A.	W	W	F	Apr 1852	48	M	22	6	4	MS	TN	KY	
	William W.	S	W	M	Jun 1878	21	S				MS	MS	MS	Farm Laborer
	Dora J.	D	W	F	Jun 1881	18	S				MS	MS	MS	
	Ida D.	D	W	F	Dec 1882	17	S				MS	MS	MS	
	Annie E.	D	W	F	May 1887	13	S				MS	MS	MS	
77	Rast, James A.	H	W	M	Dec 1846	53	M	14			MS	SC	AL	Farmer
	Emay E.	W	W	F	Nov 1865	45	M	14	8	7	MS	TN	GA	
	Hattie B.	D	W	F	Nov 1886	13	S				MS	MS	MS	

1	2	3	4	5	6	7	8	9	10	11	12	13	14	15
	Walter L.	S	W	M	Feb 1888	12	S				MS	MS	MS	Farm Laborer
	Oscar C.	S	W	M	May 1890	10	S				MS	MS	MS	Farm Laborer
	Charlie M.	S	W	M	Mar 1893	7	S				MS	MS	MS	
	Pearl	D	W	F	Mar 1895	5	S				MS	MS	MS	
	Lamar C.	S	W	M	Jun 1898	1	S				MS	MS	MS	
	Douglas, Edward	SS	W	M	Jun 1885	14	S				AL	TN	MS	Farm Laborer
78	Chambers, Jeffery	H	W	M	Nov 1848	51	M	34			TN	TN	UN	Farmer
	Lucy A.	W	W	F	Apr 1845	55	M	34	3	1	TN	NC	TN	
	Robert C.	S	W	M	Jan 1886	14	S				AL	TN	TN	Farm Laborer
79	Turner, John	H	W	M	Nov 1864	35	M	7			AL	AL	AL	Farmer
	Mary J.	W	W	F	Oct 1864	35	M	7	5	4	MS	AL	MS	
	Leland	S	W	M	Feb 1890	10	S				MS	MS	MS	Farm Laborer
	Mertie	D	W	F	Jul 1893	6	S				MS	MS	MS	
	George A.	S	W	M	Oct 1895	4	S				MS	MS	MS	
	Carrie A.	D	W	F	Dec 1897	3	S				MS	MS	MS	
80	Turner, Monroe	H	W	M	Jul 1847	52	W				AL	TN	TN	Farmer
	Parsons, Willie B.	Gd	W	F	Sep 1892	7	S				MS	MS	MS	
81	Thomson, Fannie	H	W	F	Feb 1840	60	Wd		2	2	MS	SC	SC	Farmer
	Robert	S	W	M	May 1877	23	S				MS	MS	MS	Farm Laborer
	Charlie	S	W	M	May 1877	23	S				MS	MS	MS	Farm Laborer
82	Floyd, John D.	H	W	M	Dec 1864	38	M	19			MS	SC	MS	Farmer
	Annie C.	W	W	F	Jan 1868	42	M	19	4	4	MS	MS	MS	
	Arlander J.	S	W	M	Aug 1884	15	S				MS	MS	MS	Farm Labor
	James D.	S	W	M	Dec 1886	14	S				MS	MS	MS	Farm Labor
	Virginia M.	D	W	F	Nov 1888	11	S				MS	MS	MS	
83	Rast, Thomas W.	H	W	M	Dec 1849	40	M	12			MS	SC	TN	Farmer
	Martha B.	W	W	F	Dec 1867	32	M	12	0	0	MS	TN	VA	
	Nancy	M	W	F	Feb 1820	80	Wd		9	6	TN	SC	TN	
	Annie	Sis	W	F	Feb 1850	50	S				AL	SC	TN	
84	Finch, James H.	H	W	M	Feb 1869	31 M	9					MS	MS	MS	Farmer
	Mary L.	W	W	F	Sep 1872	27	M	9	6	6	MS	MS	MS	
	Henry G.	S	W	M	Aug 1891	8	S				MS	MS	MS	
	Ada B.	D	W	F	Oct 1892	7	S				MS	MS	MS	
	Louis C.	S	W	M	Jul 1894	5	S				MS	MS	MS	
	Oma M.	D	W	F	Mar 1896	4	S				MS	MS	MS	
	Walace P.	S	W	M	Sep 1897	2	S				MS	MS	MS	
	Evie L.	D	W	F	Sep 1899	9/mo	S				MS	MS	MS	
	Southward, Perry	Ser	B	M	UN 1880	20	S				MS	MS	MS	Farm Laborer
85	Rutledge, Richard	H	W	M	Sep 1863	36	M	16			MS	SC	SC	Farmer
	Mary R.	W	W	F	Oct 1863	34	M	16	8	8	MS	GA	AL	
	Effie M.	D	W	F	Dec 1885	14	S				MS	MS	MS	
	Gene	S	W	M	UN 1887	13	S				MS	MS	MS	Farm Laborer
	Parahm	S	W	M	Jun 1899	10	S				MS	MS	MS	
	May	D	W	F	UN 1891	8	S				MS	MS	MS	
	William	S	W	M	Mar 1893	7	S				MS	MS	MS	
	Marvin W.	S	W	M	Feb 1895	5	S				MS	MS	MS	
	Mosley R.	S	W	M	UN 1897	3	S				MS	MS	MS	
	Eva	D	W	F	UN 1899	10/mo	S				MS	MS	MS	
86	Rutledge, Joe	H	W	M	UN 1830	70	M	43			SC	SC	SC	Farmer
	Nancy W.	W	W	F	UN 1830	69	M	43	6	5	AL	TN	GA	
87	Edmondson, Landry	H	W	M	Aug 1850	49	M	25			MS	TN	TN	Farmer
	Margie E.	W	W	F	Nov 1853	46	M	25	8	8	MS	AL	AL	
	Virginia P.	D	W	F	Sep 1877	22	S				MS	MS	MS	

1	2	3	4	5	6	7	8	9	10	11	12	13	14	15
	Roufus	S	W	M	Sep 1882	17	S				MS	MS	MS	Farm Laborer
	Walter	S	W	M	Oct 1883	16	S				MS	MS	MS	Farm Laborer
	R.C.	S	W	M	Nov 1885	14	S				MS	MS	MS	Farm Laborer
	William	S	W	M	Dec 1888	11	S				MS	MS	MS	Farm Laborer
	Henry O.	S	W	M	Mar 1892	8	S				MS	MS	MS	
	Velmer M.	D	W	F	Oct 1897	2	S				MS	MS	MS	
	Thompson, Joe	Bdr	W	M	UN 1835	65	S				AL	AL	AL	Carpenter
88	Davis, George	H	W	M	Aug 1867	32	M	12			MS	UN	AL	Farmer
	Nettie	W	W	F	Jul 1868	31	M	12	6	6	MS	AL	MS	
	Mary M.	D	W	F	Jan 1889	11	S				MS	MS	MS	
	Charlie	S	W	M	Aug 1891	8	S				MS	MS	MS	
	Pearly E.	D	W	F	Jul 1893	6	S				MS	MS	MS	
	Annie L.	D	W	F	Oct 1895	4	S				MS	MS	MS	
	Robert W.	S	W	M	Sep 1897	2	S				MS	MS	MS	
	Wallace	S	W	M	Sep 1899	10/m	S				MS	MS	MS	
	Hubbard, Cora	SiL	W	F	Jan 1875	25	S				MS	AL	MS	
89	Milford, Uriah W.	H	W	M	UN 1839	60	M	21			MS	SC	SC	Farmer
	Annie H.	W	W	F	Sep 1852	47	M	21	3	3	MS	TN	AL	
	Fannie	D	W	F	Jun 1881	18	S				MS	MS	MS	
	Archie	S	W	M	Jun 1884	15	S				MS	MS	MS	Farm Laborer
	Charlie J.	S	W	M	Feb 1889	11	S				MS	MS	MS	Farm Laborer
90	Milford, George	H	W	M	UN 1835	65	M	23			MS	SC	SC	Farmer
	Nancy E.	W	W	F	Dec 1838	61	M	23	4	4	AL	SC	AL	
	Nancy E.	Sis	W	F	Dec 1830	60	S				AL	SC	SC	
91	Blissit, James M.	H	W	M	Jun 1846	54	M	30			AL	GA	GA	Farmer
	Aramento A.	W	W	F	Jun 1846	53	M	30	8	8	AL	GA	AL	
	Bettie	D	W	F	Mar 1876	24	S				MS	AL	AL	
	James T.	S	W	M	Jan 1877	23	S				MS	AL	AL	Farmer
	Walter W.	S	W	M	Sep 1879	20	S				MS	AL	AL	Farm Laborer
	Preston	S	W	M	Sep 1883	16	S				MS	AL	AL	Farm Laborer
	Ester L.	D	W	F	Nov 1884	14	S				MS	AL	AL	
	Artie	D	W	F	May 1888	12	S				MS	AL	AL	
	George	S	W	M	Aug 1890	9	S				MS	AL	AL	
92	Wynn, Edward	H	W	M	Nov 1852	47	M	11			MS	TN	TN	Farmer
	Mary L.	W	W	F	Jul 1868	31	M	11	3	3	MS	AL	MS	
	Blanch O.	D	W	F	Feb 1891	9	S				MS	MS	MS	
	Orah E.	D	W	F	Feb 1894	6	S				MS	MS	MS	
	Walter R.	S	W	M	Jun 1897	2	S				MS	MS	MS	
	Milton L.	Bdr	W	M	Jul 1855	44	Wd				MS	TN	TN	Farmer
93	Wynn, Samuel	H	W	M	Nov 1852	47	Wd				MS	TN	TN	Farmer
94	Hubbard, Matthew	H	W	M	Aug 1866	33	M	10			MS	AL	MS	Farmer
	Ellen	W	W	F	Feb 1868	32	M	10	3	3	AL	AL	AL	
	Mamie	D	W	F	Feb 1892	8	S				MS	MS	AL	
	Ursley M.	D	W	F	Sep 1893	6	S				MS	MS	AL	
	Corrie	D	W	F	May 1896	4	S				MS	MS	AL	
95	Storment, Thomas	H	B	M	UN 1845	55	M	26			MS	SC	SC	Farmer
	Louisa W	B	B	F	UN 1852	48	M	26	10	7	MS	VA	SC	
	Rosey	D	B	F	Feb 1876	24	S				MS	MS	MS	
	Sarah A.	D	B	F	Sep 1882	17	S				MS	MS	MS	
	Mary C.	D	B	F	Jul 1885	14	S				MS	MS	MS	
	Owen	S	B	M	Sep 1890	9	S				MS	MS	MS	
	Willie C.	S	B	M	Oct 1894	6	S				MS	MS	MS	
	Norah C.	D	B	F	Jan 1896	4	S				MS	MS	MS	
	Vinah	D	B	F	May 1898	2	S				MS	MS	MS	
	Mary L.	GD	B	F	Jul 1896	3	S				AL	MS	MS	

1	2	3	4	5	6	7	8	9	10	11	12	13	14	15
	Johnnie C.	GS	B	M	Sep 1899		S				AL	MS	MS	
	Warren, Minnie	Bdr	B	F	UN 1884	16	S				MS	MS	MS	
96	Blissit, Millard	H	W	M	Nov 1858	41	M	7			AL	GA	AL	Farmer
	Nancy	W	W	F	Oct 1873	26	M	7	4	4	MS	AL	AL	
	Jerome M.	S	W	M	Oct 1894	5	S				MS	AL	MS	
	Orminn M.	S	W	M	Apr 1896	4	S				MS	AL	MS	
	Carrie H.	D	W	F	Jan 1898	2	S				MS	AL	MS	
	Clarrie E.	D	W	F	Dec 1899	5/mo	S				MS	AL	MS	
	Nancy J.	Sis	W	F	Nov 1853	46	S				AL	GA	AL	
	Herrone E.	Sis	W	F	Jun 1863	36	S				AL	GA	AL	
97	Rast, William	H	W	M	Jan 1868	32	M	12			MS	AL	TN	Farmer
	Malinda E.	W	W	F	Jul 1864	36	M	12	5	4	AL	AL	AL	
	Minnie D.	D	W	F	Jan 1889	11	S				MS	AL	MS	
	George W.	S	W	M	Sep 1891	8	S				MS	AL	MS	
	Mary R.	D	W	F	Apr 1894	6	S				MS	AL	MS	
	Fred E.	S	W	M	Jun 1899	1	S				MS	AL	MS	
98	Selby, Robert F.	H	W	M	Dec 1828	71	M	34			TN	OH	TN	Farmer
	Mary F.	W	W	F	Jul 1844	65	M	34	0	0	AL	AL	KY	
99	Rast, James D.	H	W	M	Jan 1847	53	M	28			MS	SC	TN	Farmer
	Sarah J.	W	W	F	Jun 1857	42	M	28	5	4	AL	AL	AL	
	Maggie O.	D	W	F	Dec 1876	23	S				MS	MS	AL	
	Filmore W.	S	W	M	Jun 1883	16	S				MS	MS	AL	Farm Laborer
	Earnest A.	S	W	M	Aug 1892	7	S				MS	MS	AL	
100	Rast, Monroe J.	H	W	M	Feb 1875	25	M	0			MS	TN	MS	Sawmill
	Cassie	W	W	F	Dec 1882	17	M	0	0	0	MS	MS	MS	
101	Gray, Simon P.	H	W	M	Mar 1872	28	M	4			MS	GA	TN	Farmer
	Annie M.	W	W	F	Apr 1869	31	M	4	3	3	AL	AL	VA	
	Beatrice P.	D	W	F	Sep 1896	3	S				AL	MS	AL	
	Earnest E.	S	W	M	Jan 1898	2	S				TN	MS	AL	
	Millie E.	D	W	F	Jan 1900		S				MS	MS	AL	
	Archie, Felix G.	FiL	W	M	Dec 1832	67	Wd				TN	TN	TN	Peddler
102	Blake, David	H	W	M	Nov 1872	28	M	3			OH	PA	OH	
	Martha C.	W	W	F	Jan 1874	26	M	3	2	2	MS	MS	AL	
	Mariland	D	W	F	Dec 1897	2	S				MS	OH	MS	
	Arrie E.	D	W	F	Apr 1900		S				MS	OH	MS	
103	Edmondson, Richard C.	H	W	M	Apr 1822	78	Wd				TN	VA	VA	
	Carrey B.	D	W	F	Aug 1891	8	S				MS	TN	MS	
	Panthie P.	D	W	F	Jul 1893	6	S				MS	TN	MS	
	James M.	S	W	M	Jan 1854	46	Wd				MS	TN	MS	Farmer
	Ugean F.	GS	W	M	Nov 1888	19	S				MS	MS	MS	Farm Laborer
	William	GS	W	M	Oct 1882	15	S				MS	MS	MS	Farm Laborer
	Virginia B.	GD	W	F	Jan 1889	11	S				MS	MS	MS	
	Jorah G.	GD	W	F	Dec 1893	6	S				MS	MS	MS	
	Ermer V.	GD	W	F	Jul 1896	3	S				MS	MS	MS	
104	Murphy, James R.	H	W	M	Oct 1867	37	M	10			MS	AL	AL	Farmer
	Mandy	W	W	F	UN 1876	24	M	10	0	0	MS	MS	MS	
	Parsons, John	Cou	W	M	UN 1876	24	S				MS	MS	MS	Farm Laborer
105	Underwood, Martin	H	W	M	Sep 1837	62	M	10			TN	TN	TN	Farmer
	Sarah E.	W	W	F	Dec 1852	47	M	10			TN	TN	NC	
	Martin Z.	S	W	M	Dec 1894	5	S				MS	TN	TN	
106	Cain, William	H	W	M	Jul 1824	76	Wd				AL	NC	NC	Farmer
	Harrison, Melvina	D	W	F	Nov 1863	36	Wd				AL	AL	AL	

1	2	3	4	5	6	7	8	9	10	11	12	13	14	15
	Harrison, Sidney C.	GS	W	M	Feb 1895	5	S				MS	AL	AL	
107	Belue, Thomas N.	H	W	M	Nov 1847	52	M	24			TN	NC	TN	
	Sarah J.	W	W	F	Sep 1853	46	M	24			MS	TN	AL	
	Davis, Misie I.	D	W	F	Jul 1877	22	Wd		1	1	MS	TN	AL	
	Belue, Nancy A.	D	W	F	Jun 1885	16	S				MS	TN	MS	
	Elsie W.	D	W	F	Oct 1888	11	S				MS	TN	MS	
	Thomas S.	S	W	M	Sep 1892	7	S				MS	TN	MS	
	David N.	S	W	M	Oct 1895	2	S				MS	TN	MS	
	Davis, Beulah D.	GD	W	F	Nov 1899	6/mo	S				MS	TN	AL	
108	Castleberry, Robert W.	H	W	M	Dec 1861	38	M	16			MS	GA	AL	Farmer
	Ofle F.	W	W	F	Oct 1863	36	M	16	6	5	AL	AL	AL	
	John F.	S	W	M	Aug 1882	15	S				AL	MS	AL	Farm Laborer
	Robert R.	S	W	M	Dec 1885	16	S				AL	MS	AL	Farm Laborer
	Enue	D	W	F	Aug 1891	9	S				MS	MS	AL	
	Sal	D	W	F	May 1894	6	S				MS	MS	AL	
	Katie A.	D	W	F	Jun 1900		S				MS	MS	AL	
109	Rast, John T.	H	W	M	Aug 1867	30	M	10			MS	MS	TN	Sawmill
	Nancy	W	W	F	Jan 1874	26	M	10	3	2	MS	TN	AL	
	Ambrose	S	W	M	Sep 1890	9	S				MS	MS	MS	
	David E.	S	W	M	Jul 1895	2	S				MS	MS	MS	
110	Rast, Mary J.	H	W	F	Dec 1827	57	Wd		7	6	TN	TN	TN	Farmer
	Aldridge Effie	D	W	F	Apr 1881	19	M	0	0	0	MS	MS	TN	
	Marshal	SiL	E	M	Jan 1870	30	M				MS	MS	MS	Sawmill
	Ethel	GD	W	F	Feb 1896	4	S				AR	MS	AR	
111	Rast, James E.	H	W	M	Jan 1872	29	M	7			MS	MS	TN	Sawmill
	Lizzie D.	W	W	F	Aug 1874	25	M	7	2	2	MS	MS	MS	
	Henry W.	S	W	M	Aug 1895	4	S				MS	MS	MS	
	Carrie	D	W	F	Feb 1898	2	S				MS	MS	MS	
112	Underwood, Charles	H	W	M	May 1883	17	M	0			MS	TN	MS	Sawmill
	Ada	W	W	F	Nov 1878	21	M	0	0	0	MS	MS	MS	
113	Page, William H.	H	W	M	Sep 1873	26	M	2			AL	AL	AL	Farmer
	May	W	W	F	Oct 1877	22	M	2	2	2	MS	MS	AR	
	Allie O.	D	W	F	Feb 1898	2	S				MS	MS	MS	
	George R.	S	W	M	Apr 1899	1	S				MS	MS	MS	
114	Dawson, George W.	H	W	M	Feb 1867	33	M	6			MS	MS	AL	Farmer
	Marthie A.	W	W	F	Jul 1879	20	M	6	1	1	MS	AL	AL	
	Carrie E.	D	W	F	Jul 1896	3	S				MS	MS	MS	
	Joe	F	W	M	Jan 1832	68	M	35			MS	TN	TN	Farmer
	Mary	M	W	F	UN 1840	60	M	35	2	2	AL	NC	SC	
115	Cothren, John W.	H	W	M	May 1856	44	M	13			TN	TN	TN	Farmer
	Ellen	W	W	F	Jan 1864	36	M	13	3	3	MS	SC	AL	
	James F.	S	W	M	Feb 1888	12	S				MS	TN	MS	Farm Laborer
	William T.	S	W	M	Jan 1890	10	S				MS	TN	MS	Farm Laborer
	Lillie E.	D	W	F	May 1898	2	S				MS	TN	MS	
116	Rast, James A.	H	W	M	Jun 1822	78	M	7			SC	Ger	Ger	Farmer
	Louisianna	W	W	F	Feb 1838	62	M	7	6	3	TN	SC	SC	
117	Claunch, George T.	H	W	M	Sep 1877	22	M	0			MS	MS	MS	Farmer
	Annie B.	W	W	F	Jul 1884	15	M	0	0	0	MS	VA	MS	
118	Dawson, Dee N.	H	W	M	Jun 1863	36	M	13			MS	MS	MS	Farmer
	Sarah H.	W	W	F	Apr 1866	34	M	13	2	2	MS	MS	MS	
	James S.	S	W	F	Feb 1890	10	S				MS	MS	MS	Farm Laborer

1	2	3	4	5	6	7	8	9	10	11	12	13	14	15
	William	S	W	M	Jan 1898	2	S				MS	MS	MS	
	Martin	Bdr	W	M	Apr 1859	41	Wd				MS	MS	MS	Farm Laborer
119	Belue, William	H	W	M	Jan 1878	22	M	0			MS	AL	AL	Farmer
	Mertie M.	W	W	F	Apr 1880	20	M	0	0	0	MS	MS	MS	
120	Cobb, William A.	H	W	M	Nov 1861	38	M	18			MS	NC	GA	Farmer
	Lizey	W	W	F	May 1864	36	M	18	5	4	AL	AL	AL	
	Lidia O.	D	W	F	Aug 1886	13	S				AR	MS	AL	
	Verdia E.	D	W	F	Apr 1889	11	S				MS	MS	AL	
	Ines	D	W	F	Jan 1892	8	S				MS	MS	AL	
	Callie E.	D	W	F	Oct 1896	3	S				TX	MS	AL	
121	Belue, Winnie A.	H	W	F	UN 1835	65	Wd		10	6	AL	AL	AL	Farmer
	Robert A.	S	W	M	Aug 1880	19	S				MS	AL	AL	Farm Laborer
	Livinia R.	D	W	F	Aug 1883	16	S				MS	AL	AL	
122	Montgomery, David M.	H	W	M	Feb 1848	52	M	6			MS	AL	AL	Farmer
	Artie E.	W	W	F	Sep 1855	44	M	6	2	0	MS	MS	MS	
123	Donaldson, William	H	W	M	May 1849	51	M	25			MS	SC	SC	Farmer
	Mary	W	W	F	Feb 1857	43	M	25	1	1	MS	AL	TN	
124	Mock, William	H	W	M	Apr 1854	46	M	25			MS	NC	GA	Farmer
	Margret L.	W	W	F	Jun 1858	41	M	25	8	5	AL	GA	GA	
	Lee P.	S	W	M	Dec 1878	21	S				MS	MS	AL	Farm Laborer
	Newton B.	S	W	M	Feb 1880	20	S				MS	MS	AL	Farm Laborer
	Belle C.	D	W	F	Mar 1884	16	S				MS	MS	AL	
	George A.	S	W	M	Oct 1885	14	S				MS	MS	AL	Farm Laborer
	Jessie E.	S	W	M	Jul 1889	10	S				MS	MS	AL	
125	Storment, Alex	H	W	M	Jul 1856	43	M	14			MS	SC	SC	Farmer
	Ellener W.	W	W	F	Jun 1855	45	M	14	8	8	MS	AL	TN	
	John B.	S	W	M	Dec 1886	13	S				MS	MS	MS	Farm Laborer
	Blanch	D	W	F	Mar 1892	8	S				MS	MS	MS	
	Jernigan, James R.	SS	W	M	Oct 1874	25	S				TN	TN	MS	Farm Laborer
126	Buchannan, Robert H.	H	W	F	Jan 1861	39	M	9			MS	AL	TN	Farmer
	Cora L.	W	W	F	Oct 1871	28	M	9	3	3	MS	MS	SC	
	Dwight M.	S	W	M	Mar 1892	8	S				MS	MS	MS	
	Burnia	D	W	F	Oct 1894	5	S				MS	MS	MS	
	Grace	D	W	F	Sep 1895	4	S				MS	MS	MS	
	Williams, Jane C.	Sis	W	F	Mar 1850	49	S				MS	TN	TN	
127	Belue, James	H	W	M	Aug 1824	25	M	6			MS	MS	AL	Farmer
	Lucinda A.	W	W	F	Jan 1878	22	M	6	3	2	MS	AL	AL	
	Virdie L.	D	W	F	Jan 1896	4	S				MS	MS	MS	
	Winnie F.	D	W	F	Dec 1898	1	S				MS	MS	MS	
128	Buchanan, Walter	H	W	M	Feb 1868	32	M	12			MS	AL	TN	Farmer
	Verdie	W	W	F	Aug 1871	28	M	12	7	6	MS	SC	MS	
	Artie	D	W	F	Apr 1891	9	S				MS	MS	MS	
	Lilan	D	W	F	May 1893	7	S				MS	MS	MS	
	Eunis	D	W	F	Dec 1894	5	S				MS	MS	MS	
	Ruth	D	W	F	Apr 1896	4	S				MS	MS	MS	
	Ednie	D	W	F	Feb 1898	2	S				MS	MS	MS	
	Almer	D	W	F	Mar 1900	S	S				MS	MS	MS	
	West, John	Bdr	W	M	Dec 1880	19	S				MS	MS	MS	Farm Laborer
129	McDougal, John	H	W	M	Sep 1870	29	M	4			MS	MS	MS	Farmer
	Minnie D.	W	W	F	Jul 1875	24	M	4	1	1	MS	MS	MS	
	Lilian C.	D	W	F	Sep 1896	3	S				MS	MS	MS	

1	2	3	4	5	6	7	8	9	10	11	12	13	14	15
130	Crisamore, William	H	W	M	UN 1855	45	M	17			MS	MS	MS	Farmer
	Mary	W	W	F	Aug 1868	32	M	17	4	4	AL	AL	AL	
	George A.	S	W	M	Apr 1886	14	S				MS	MS	AL	Farm Labor
	Lizzie M.	D	W	F	Mar 1890	10	S				MS	MS	AL	
	Vadie V.	D	W	F	May 1898	2	S				MS	MS	AL	
131	Nelson, William	H	W	M	May 1844	64	S	C						Farmer
	Carpenter, George		W	M	UN 1820	80	Wd	o	H					Pauper
	Lambert, David		W	M	UN 1865	35	S	u	o					Pauper
	Wingo, Lillie		W	F	UN 1868	32	S	n	m					Pauper
	Long, Tener		B	M	UN 1860	40		t	e					Pauper
	Bly, Shauet		B	F	UN 1840	60	Wd	y						Pauper
132	Hill, George L.	H	W	M	Sep 1866	33	M	11			MS	MS	MS	Farmer
	Elizabeth	W	W	F	Jan 1867	33	M	11	5	5	MS	MS	SC	
	Ida P.	D	W	F	Oct 1889	10	S				MS	MS	MS	
	Nora	D	W	F	UN 1891	8	S				MS	MS	MS	
	Margie E.	D	W	F	UN 1893	7	S				MS	MS	MS	
	Robert	S	W	M	May 1896	4	S				MS	MS	MS	
	Lida V.	D	W	F	Sep 1899	9/mo	S				MS	MS	MS	
133	Umbers, Robert F.	H	W	M	Apr 1846	54	M	33			AL	AL	TN	Farmer
	Rebecca E.	W	W	F	Jul 1849	50	M	33	8	6	AL	SC	TN	
	John W.	S	W	M	Aug 1880	19	S				AL	AL	AL	Farm Labor
	Sintria L.	D	W	F	Jul 1884	15	S				AL	AL	AL	
	Charles C.	S	W	M	Sep 1893	6	S				AL	AL	AL	
134	Millsaps, Mary J.	H	W	F	Sep 1836	63	Wd		12	4	TN	TN	TN	
	Sarah J.	Bdr	W	F	Feb 1834	66	S				AL	VA	VA	
135	Millsaps, Austin W.	H	W	M	Apr 1874	26	M	5			MS	GA	TN	Farmer
	Ethel	W	W	F	Aug 1880	19	M	5	2	2	MS	AL	AL	
	Minnie T.	D	W	F	Dec 1895	4	S				MS	MS	MS	
	Dorah L.	D	W	F	Jun 1898	2	S				TN	MS	MS	
136	Floyd, Robert H.	H	W	M	Nov 1847	52	M	31			MS	SC	SC	Farmer
	Mary A.	W	W	F	Mar 1852	48	M	31	0	0	SC	SC	SC	
	Mary A.	D	W	F	Jun 1892	8	S				MS	TN	SC	
137	Bodiford, Martha	H	W	F	Mar 1826	74	Wd		9	9	SC	SC	SC	Farmer
	Sarah E.	D	W	F	Mar 1868	32	S				MS	SC	SC	
138	Bryant, William	H	W	M	Feb 1861	39	M	14			MS	GA	GA	Farmer
	Martha J.	W	W	F	Mar 1862	38	M	14	3	3	MS	SC	SC	
	Thomas	S	W	M	Aug 1886	13	S				MS	MS	MS	Farm Labor
	Blanch	D	W	F	UN 1890	9	S				MS	MS	MS	
	Charlie F.													
139	Belue, Jesse P.	H	W	M	Aug 1863	44	M	21			MS	TN	TN	Farmer
	Elizer H.	W	W	F	Jul 1860	39	M	21	4	3	MS	TN	TN	
	James F.	S	W	M	Mar 1883	17	S				MS	MS	MS	
	Annie V.	D	W	F	Mar 1885	15	S				MS	MS	MS	
140	Bruton, Elisha L.	H	W	M	Jun 1876	29	M	1			MS	MS	MS	Farmer
	Ada	W	W	F	Feb 1876	24	M	1	0	0	TN	MS	MS	
141	Bruton, Elishia M.	H	W	M	UN 1834	66	M	40			AL	AL	AL	Farmer
	Mary	W	W	F	UN 1846	64	M	40			NC	NC	NC	
142	Floyd, James R.	H	W	M	May 1825	75	M	53			SC	SC	SC	Farmer
	Patsey	W	W	F	Apr 1822	78	M	53	0	0	TN	NC	NC	
143	Bruton, James W.	H	W	M	Nov 1862	37	M	15			MS	NC	AL	Farmer

1	2	3	4	5	6	7	8	9	10	11	12	13	14	15
	Marthia L.	W	W	F	Jan 1867	33	M	15	7	6	MS	SC	NC	
	Esther E.	D	W	F	Nov 1886	13	S				MS	MS	MS	
	Norah V.	D	W	F	Mar 1889	11	S				AR	MS	MS	
	Velmer L.	D	W	F	Sep 1891	8	S				MS	MS	MS	
	Ada O.	D	W	F	UN 1894	6	S				MS	MS	MS	
	Alfred C.	S	W	M	Sep 1897	2	S				MS	MS	MS	
	Worth J.	S	W	M	Feb 1900		S				MS	MS	MS	
144	Cadle, George W.	H	W	M	Apr 1861	39	M	16			MS	MS	AL	Farmer
	Louisa	W	W	F	Oct 1857	42	M	16	5	2	MS	AL	NC	
	George A.	S	W	M	Sep 1885	14	S				MS	MS	MS	Farm Labor
	Ola	D	W	F	Sep 1892	7	S				MS	MS	MS	
145	Walker, George W.	H	W	M	Jun 1860	39	M	19			MS	AL	TN	Farmer
	Sarah E.	W	W	F	Nov 1866	33	M	19	10	8	MS	PA	MS	
	John H.	S	W	M	May 1885	15	S				MS	MS	MS	Farm Labor
	Bulah I.	D	W	F	Jul 1886	13	S				MS	MS	MS	
	James D.	S	W	M	Jun 1890	10	S				MS	MS	MS	
	Mandy R.	D	W	F	Aug 1893	6	S				MS	MS	MS	
	George Jr.	S	W	M	Jun 1895	4	S				MS	MS	MS	
	Bessie I.	D	W	F	Aug 1898	1	S				MS	MS	MS	
	Firley A.	S	W	M	Feb 1900	3/mo	S				MS	MS	MS	
146	Reiche, Christina M.	H	W	F	Mar 1846	54	Wd		5	5	Ger	Ger	Ger	Farmer
	Joseph C.	S	W	M	Oct 1873	26	S				IN	OH	Ger	Farmer
	Hannah F.	D	W	F	Dec 1879	20	S				IN	OH	Ger	
	John H.	S	W	M	Jun 1882	18	S				IN	OH	Ger	Teacher
	David T.	S	W	M	Jan 1886	14	S				IN	OH	Ger	Farm Labor
147	Montgomery, Robert	H	W	M	Sep 1870	29	M	4			MS	AL	SC	Farmer
	Nancy J.	W	W	F	Dec 1878	21	M	4	0	0	MS	MS	MS	
	Robinson, Sallie	Aunt	W	F	Nov 1830	69	Wd		6	4	AL	TN	TN	
148	Kennedy, Jasper L.	H	W	M	UN 1862	38	M	17			MS	MS	MS	
	Millie A.	W	W	F	Dec 1852	47	M	17	6	6	MS	MS	MS	
	John S.	S	W	M	Oct 1882	17	S				MS	MS	MS	Farm Labor
	Marthie J.	D	W	F	UN 1886	14	S				MS	MS	MS	
	Dorah E.	D	W	F	Sep 1887	12	S				MS	MS	MS	
	Thomas G.	S	W	M	Sep 1891	8	S				MS	MS	NC	
	Julia A.	D	W	F	Mar 1894	6	S				MS	MS	MS	
	Humphres, James H.	S	W	M	Oct 1881	19	S				MS	MS	MS	Farm Labor
149	Grimes, George N.	H	W	M	Feb 1878	22	M	1			MS	MS	MS	Farmer
	Lou J.	W	W	F	Nov 1877	22	M	1	1	1	MS	NC	MS	
	Dewey L.	S	W	M	Aug 1899		S				MS	MS	MS	
150	Davenport, William	H	W	M	Jun 1859	40	M	19			MS	AL	UN	Farmer
	Sallie E.	W	W	F	UN UN	UN	M	19	8	7	MS	AL	UN	
	Mary N.	D	W	F	UN 1889	18	S				MS	MS	MS	
	Shelby	S	W	M	Mar 1886	14	S				MS	MS	MS	
	Robert G.	S	W	M	Oct 1888	11	S				MS	MS	MS	
	Eugean	S	W	M	UN 1891	9	S				MS	MS	MS	
	Edith	D	W	F	UN 1893	7	S				MS	MS	MS	
	Aileen	D	W	F	UN 1895	4	S				MS	MS	MS	
	Fredic	S	W	M	Nov 1897	3	S				MS	MS	MS	
151	Bell, James F.	H	W	M	Aug 1843	56	M	34			SC	SC	SC	Farmer
	Mary A.	W	W	F	Feb 1848	52	M	34	8	3	SC	SC	SC	
	Rodger L.	S	W	M	Dec 1873	26	S				SC	SC	SC	Farmer
	John W.	S	W	M	Feb 1880	20	S				SC	SC	SC	Farm Labor
152	Jourdan, William A.	H	W	M	UN UN	UN	M	30			TN	NC	NC	Farmer
	Rebecca	W	W	F	May 1849	51	M	30	8	8	MS	GA	GA	

1	2	3	4	5	6	7	8	9	10	11	12	13	14	15
	Louis	S	W	M	Jun 1878	21	S				MS	TN	MS	Farm Labor
	Sallie P.	D	W	F	Apr 1880	20	S				MS	TN	MS	
	Louis	D	W	F	Jul 1887	12	S				MS	TN	MS	
153	Martin, William	H	W	M	May 1848	52	M	30			MS	TN	TN	Farmer
	Bithie P.	W	W	F	Dec 1851	48	M	30	10	8	MS	TN	TN	
	Vergie M.	D	W	F	Dec 1881	19	S				TN	MS	MS	
	John D.	S	W	M	Aug 1883	16	S				TN	MS	MS	Farm Labor
	Marthie J.	D	W	F	Jan 1886	14	S				TN	MS	MS	
	Effie C.	D	W	F	Nov 1888	11	S				MS	MS	MS	
	Daisy P.	D	W	F	Aug 1891	8	S				MS	MS	MS	
	Hattie M.	D	W	F	Aug 1894	5	S				MS	MS	MS	
154	Snellins, John A.	H	W	M	May 1875	25	M	6			AL	AL	AL	Farmer
	Mary	W	W	F	Mar 1878	22	M	6	4	3	MS	AL	MS	
	Mary J.	D	W	F	Jun 1895	5	S				MS	AL	MS	
	Emma L.	D	W	F	Feb 1897	3	S				MS	AL	MS	
	Maudia V.	D	W	F	Apr 1900	2/mo	S				MS	AL	MS	
155	Hale, Henry D.	H	W	M	Sep 1868	31	M	4			MS	PA	MS	Farmer
	Jennie B.	W	W	F	Mar 1872	29	M	4	3	2	MS	MS	MS	
	Willie A.	D	W	F	Dec 1896	3	S				MS	MS	MS	
	Ione	D	W	F	Mar 1899	1	S				MS	MS	MS	
	Gortney, Claud J.	BiL	W	M	Feb 1881	19	S				MS	MS	MS	Farm Labor
	Gortney, Shelly A.	BiL	W	M	Dec 1885	14	S				MS	MS	MS	Farm Labor
	Gortney, Mertie	SiL	W	F	Feb 1888	12	S				MS	MS	MS	
156	Wright, Willie F.	H	W	M	Aug 1873	26	M	3			MS	MS	MS	Farmer
	Lizzie	W	W	F	Mar 1873	27	M	3	1	1	MS	MS	MS	
	Thomas L.	S	W	M	Aug 1898	1	S				MS	MS	MS	
157	Rumage, William B.	H	W	M	Apr 1875	25	M	6			AL	AL	AL	Farmer
	Sybil G.	W	W	F	UN 1876	24	M	6	2	2	MS	MS	MS	
	Mary	D	W	F	Apr 1897	3	S				MS	AL	MS	
	Belue, Raney	Bdr	W	M	Apr 1820	89	Wd				MS	?	?	Farm Labor
158	Hale, Jake	H	W	M	Feb 1817	83	M	2			PA	PA	PA	Farmer
	Fannie	W	W	F	Jan 1837	67	M	2	1	1	TN	TN	TN	
159	Floyd, Lois E.	H	W	F	Feb 1865	UN	Wd		6	6	MS	MS	MS	Farmer
	Lerther P.	D	W	F	Jan 1886	14	S				MS	MS	MS	
	Luther	S	W	M	Feb 1888	12	S				MS	MS	MS	Farm Labor
	Pinkie E.	D	W	F	Nov 1889	11	S				MS	MS	TN	
	Mary A.	D	W	F	Oct 1887	8	S				MS	MS	MS	
	Emmer R.	D	W	F	Jun 1894	6	S				MS	MS	MS	
	Lillie M.	D	W	F	Aug 1897	2	S				MS	MS	MS	
160	Glasgow, Calvin L.	H	W	M	Jun 1868	32	M	11			MS	MS	MS	Farmer
	Mary E.	W	W	F	Aug 1871	28	M	11	4	4	MS	MS	MS	
	Minnie L.	D	W	F	Mar 1890	10	S				MS	MS	MS	
	Lou J.	D	W	F	Feb 1892	8	S				MS	MS	MS	
	Tissie	D	W	F	Jun 1895	4	S				MS	MS	MS	
	Sydnie	S	W	M	Oct 1897	3	S				MS	MS	MS	
161	Oaks, James F.	H	W	M	Mar 1862	38	M	5			MS	UN	UN	Farmer
	Rosa L.	W	W	F	Jul 1876	23	M	5	2	2	MS	NC	TN	
	Owen C.	S	W	M	Sep 1896	3	S				MS	MS	MS	
	Dewey M.	D	W	F	Jul 1898	1	S				MS	MS	MS	
162	Massey, Joe R.	H	W	M	Feb 1849	51	M	9			GA	Eng	Scot	Farmer
	Susan N.	W	W	F	Feb 1865	35	M	9	0	0	MS	AL	TN	
163	Lovelace, Pinkney J.	H	W	M	Oct 1874	25	S				MS	AL	MS	

1	2	3	4	5	6	7	8	9	10	11	12	13	14	15
	Burt, Martha	A	W	F	UN 1833	67	Wd				MS	GA	GA	
164	Gray, Thomas N.	H	W	M	Dec 1870	29	M	8			MS	GA	GA	Farmer
	Eugenia M.	W	W	F	Oct 1877	22	M	8	3	3	MS	NC	MS	
	Essie L.	D	W	F	Jul 1895	4	S				MS	MS	MS	
	Cleo	D	W	F	Mar 1897	3	S				MS	MS	MS	
	Clarrie	D	W	F	Feb 1899	1	S				MS	MS	MS	
	Mock, Levi T.	Bdr	W	M	Oct 1875	24	S				MS	MS	GA	Farm Labor
165	Robinson, Al	H	W	M	Aug 1839	60	M	32			MS	SC	SC	Farmer
	Clemontine	W	W	F	Mar 1845	55	M	32	3	3	MS	AL	AL	
	Sydney E.	GS	W	M	Dec 1886	13	S				MS	MS	MS	Farm Labor
	Toles, Martin V.	Bdr	W	M	Dec 1886	13	S				MS	MS	MS	Farm Labor
	Barnes, Lum	Nep	W	M	UN 1878	25	S				MS	MS	MS	Farm Labor
166	Browning, Pernecia T.	H	W	F	Sep 1842	57	W		6	5	TN	TN	TN	Farmer
	Thomas L.	S	W	M	Mar 1874	26	S				MS	TN	TN	Farmer
167	McCoy, James	H	W	M	Nov 1840	59	M	11			MS	TN	TN	Farmer
	Charlotte	W	W	F	Jun 1846	53	M	11	1	1	AL	AL	AL	
	Louis	S	W	M	Dec 1879	20	S				MS	MS	AL	Farm Labor
	Robert L.	S	W	M	Aug 1890	9	S				MS	MS	AL	
168	Jones, Mary E.	H	W	F	Apr 1853	47	Wd		9	6	MS	NC	AL	Farmer
	Samuel	S	W	M	Nov 1878	21	S				MS	NC	MS	Farm Labor
	Flora D.	D	W	F	May 1889	11	S				MS	NC	MS	
	Terry, Jettie E.	D	W	F	May 1875	25	Wd		1	1	MS	NC	MS	Seamstress
	Terry, Alta P.	GD	W	F	Nov 1896	3	S				MS	AL	MS	
169	Bingham, William W.	H	W	M	Sep 1875	24	M	4			MS	MS	MS	Farmer
	Fannie J.	W	W	F	Jul 1879	21	M	4	2	2	MS	MS	MS	
	Homer C.	S	W	M	Nov 1896	3	S				MS	MS	MS	
	Clyde	S	W	M	Nov 1898	1	S				MS	MS	MS	
170	Roe, Sam N.	H	W	M	Nov 1877	22	M	3			TN	TN	TN	Farmer
	Alice I.	W	W	F	Aug 1871	28	M	3	1	1	MS	NC	MS	
171	Floyd, John F.	H	W	M	Dec 1857	42	M	20			MS	AL	AL	Farmer
	Rachel E.	W	W	F	Feb 1860	40	M	20	10	10	AL	AL	AL	
	Richard P.	S	W	M	Oct 1880	19	S				MS	MS	AL	Farm Labor
	Robert E.	S	W	M	Jan 1884	16	S				MS	MS	AL	Farm Labor
	Mary E.	D	W	F	Nov 1885	14	S				MS	MS	AL	
	Rachel L.	D	W	F	Oct 1887	12	S				MS	MS	AL	
	John	S	W	M	Jan 1890	10	S				MS	MS	AL	
	William A.	S	W	M	Mar 1892	8	S				MS	MS	AL	
	Ivey M.	D	W	F	Sep 1894	5	S				MS	MS	AL	
	Blanche I.	D	W	F	Apr 1896	4	S				MS	MS	AL	
	Elias A.	S	W	M	Jun 1898	2	S				MS	MS	AL	
172	Barnett, David R.	H	W	M	Aug 1851	48	M	24			SC	SC	SC	Farmer
	Annie H.	W	W	F	May 1854	46	M	24	6	6	MS	NC	AL	
	William A.	S	W	M	Feb 1880	20	S				MS	SC	MS	Farm Labor
	David P.	S	W	M	May 1883	17	S				MS	SC	MS	Farm Labor
	Jessie L.	D	W	F	Mar 1890	10	S				MS	SC	MS	
	Thomas W	S	W	M	May 1894	6	S				MS	SC	MS	
173	Bonds, George	H	W	M	Aug 1874	25	M	3			MS	AL	MS	Farmer
	Lula P.	W	W	F	May 1878	22	M	3	2	2	MS	SC	MS	
	Mamie L.	D	W	F	Mar 1898	2	S				MS	MS	MS	
174	Barnett, William	H	W	M	Aug 1867	32	M	12			MS	SC	SC	Farmer
	Cordie L.	W	W	F	Feb 1872	27	M	12	4	3	MS	MS	MS	
	William L.	S	W	M	Aug 1890	9	S				MS	MS	MS	

1	2	3	4	5	6	7	8	9	10	11	12	13	14	15
	Luther O.	S	W	M	Mar 1893	7	S				MS	MS	MS	
	James M.	S	W	M	Jun 1897	3	S				MS	MS	MS	
175	Barnett, Luther A.	H	W	M	Jun 1828	71	M	49			SC	SC	SC	Farmer
	Martha E.	W	W	F	Nov 1828	71	M	49	9	7	SC	SC	SC	
	Edwin L.	S	W	M	Sep 1874	25	M	5			MS	SC	SC	Farm Labor
	Virgie M.	DiL	W	F	Nov 1878	21	M	5	3	3	MS	MS	MS	
	Addie L.	GD	W	F	Feb 1900	3	S				MS	MS	MS	
	Mamie	GD	W	F	May 1898	2	S				MS	MS	MS	
176	Parsons, Mary A.	H	W	F	Sep 1834	65	Wd		9	6	TN	NC	TN	
	Mary L.	D	W	F	May 1873	27	S				MS	TN	TN	
177	Parsons, Newton H.	H	W	M	Apr 1870	30	M	2			MS	TN	TN	Farmer
	Fannie Mae	W	W	F	Sep 1879	20	M	2	2	2	MS	MS	MS	
	Oscar L.	S	W	M	Dec 1898	1	S				MS	MS	MS	
	Ward W.	S	W	M	Feb 1900	3/mo	S				MS	MS	MS	
178	Whitehurst, Delany	H	W	M	Apr 1832	68	M	2			NC	NC	NC	Farmer
	Nancy L.	W	W	F	Jun 1859	40	M	2	4	4	MS	TN	GA	
	Glenn, Maudie C.	SD	W	F	Dec 1885	14	S				MS	MS	MS	
179	Hubbard, Susan	H	W	F	Dec 1843	56	W		8	7	AL	SC	AL	Farmer
	Earnest	S	W	M	Jul 1881	18	M	2			MS	MS	MS	Farmer
	Marthia A.	DiL	W	F	Jun 1882	17	M	2	1	1	MS	MS	MS	
	Eulala P.	GD	W	F	Jul 1898	1	S				MS	MS	MS	
	Marona, America	DiL	W	F	Nov 1870	30	S				MS	AL	MS	
180	Barnes, James M.	H	W	M	UN 1869	31	M	2			MS	MS	MS	Farmer
	Nannie	W	W	F	UN 1874	26	M	2	1	1	AL	AL	AL	
	James E.	S	W	M	Aug 1899		S				MS	MS	AL	
181	Bishop, Joseph	H	W	M	Sep 1853	46	M	22			MS	MS	MS	Farmer
	Susan	W	W	F	Aug 1858	41	M	22	3	3	MS	UN	UN	
	Lillah	D	W	F	Nov 1882	17	S				MS	MS	MS	
	Eva L.	D	W	F	Nov 1884	15	S				MS	MS	MS	
182	Bishop, George E.	H	W	M	Apr 1879	21	M	1			MS	MS	MS	Farmer
	Leticia	W	W	F	Feb 1882	18	M	1	1	1	MS	MS	MS	
	Elton	S	W	M	Oct 1899		S				MS	MS	MS	
	Moore, Slatie	MiL	W	F	Sep 1852	47	Wd		4	4	MS	NC	GA	
183	Musick, James M.	H	W	M	Aug 1860	40	M	19			MS	MS	MS	Farmer
	Samantha A.	W	W	F	Jul 1861	38	M	19	3	2	MS	AL	GA	
	Lennar L.	D	W	F	May 1882	18	S				MS	MS	MS	
	Paul W.	S	W	F	Nov 1883	16	S				MS	MS	MS	
	Myrtle	D	W	F	Aug 1895	4	S				MS	MS	MS	
184	Holder, John W.	H	W	M	May 1858	42	M	22			MS	MS	UN	Farmer
	Nancy A.	W	W	F	Jan 1850	50	M	22	6	6	MS	SC	SC	
	Rufus P.	S	W	M	Oct 1878	21	S				MS	MS	MS	Farm Labor
	Ida L.	D	W	F	Mar 1882	18	S				MS	MS	MS	
	Alabama	D	W	F	Jul 1884	16	S				MS	MS	MS	
	George	S	W	M	UN 1886	14	S				MS	MS	MS	
185	Watkins, Nathaniel E.	H	W	M	Jan 1823	77	M	46			SC	SC	Ire	Farmer
	Sarah	W	W	F	Aug 1827	72	M	46	8	5	GA	SC	GA	
	Burt U.	S	W	M	Nov 1862	37	S				AL	SC	GA	Farm Labor
	Acia L.	GS	W	M	Dec 1878	21	S				TN	GA	TN	Farm Labor
186	Jourdan, John M.	H	W	M	May 1843	57	M	34			TN	NC	NC	Farmer
	Tennessee	W	W	F	Dec 1844	56	M	34	10		MS	TN	MS	
	Mollie	D	W	F	Nov 1874	25	S				MS	TN	MS	

1	2	3	4	5	6	7	8	9	10	11	12	13	14	15
	Claudis	S	W	M	Feb 1882	17	S				MS	TN	MS	Farm Labor
	Alice	D	W	F	Jun 1884	14	S				MS	TN	MS	
	John	S	W	M	Jun 1888	12	S				MS	TN	MS	
187	Bingham, George W.	H	W	M	Jul 1838	61	M	18			MS	TN	TN	Farmer
	Sarah E.	W	W	F	May 1839	61	M	18	0	0	TN	TN	TN	
	Mary A.	D	W	F	Mar 1876	24	S				MS	MS	MS	Seamstress
	Jennie	D	W	F	Jul 1878	21	S				MS	MS	MS	Seamstress
	George	S	W	M	Dec 1879	20	S				MS	MS	MS	Farm Labor
188	Stanley, John G.	H	W	M	Oct 1847	52	M	2			AL	VA	AL	Farmer
	Martha J.	W	W	F	Apr 1881	19	M	2	1	1	MS	GA	MS	
	George G.	S	W	M	Jul 1899	10/mo	S				MS	AL	MS	
189	Stanley, Sarah A.	H	W	F	Oct 1846	53	S				AL	VA	AL	Farmer
190	Moser, George W.	H	W	M	Dec 1824	75	M	45			AL	TN	TN	Farmer
	Synthia A.	W	W	F	Feb 1823	77	M	45	0	0	AL	AL	AL	
	James	S	W	M	Apr 1868	32	M	3			MS	AL	TN	Farm Labor
	Martha A.	D	W	F	Dec 1856	43	S				AL	AL	TN	
	Ada C.	DiL	W	F	Dec 1875	24	M	3	2	2	MS	TN	MS	
	Montia	GD	W	F	May 1899	1	S				MS	MS	MS	
	Leslie C	GS	W	M	May 1900		S				MS	MS	MS	
	Smith, Calvin L.	Bdr	W	M	Apr 1871	29	S				MS	MS	MS	Farm Labor
191	Davis, John A.	H	W	M	Sep 1854	45	M	15			MS	MS	MS	Farmer
	Lucendia A.	W	W	F	Apr 1859	41	M	15	1	1	MS	AL	TN	
	Leora	D	W	F	Jul 1886	13	S				MS	MS	MS	
192	White, James W.	H	W	M	Aug 1848	51	M	12			MS	KY	MS	Farmer
	Henretta	W	W	F	Apr 1845	55	M	12	4	4	MS	MS	MS	
	Lenah N.	D	W	F	Feb 1889	11	S				MS	MS	MS	
	Mollie J.	D	W	F	Apr 1890	10	S				MS	MS	MS	
	John H.	S	W	M	Jun 1892	8	S				MS	MS	MS	
	Victor W.	S	W	M	Feb 1896	4	S				MS	MS	MS	
193	Robinson, Ben F.	H	W	M	Oct 1823	76	M	35			AL	SC	AL	Farmer
	Elizabeth	W	W	F	UN 1838	62	M	35	10	5	AL	AL	NC	
194	Callicott, John A.	H	W	M	Jun 1853	46	M	28			MS	NC	TN	Farmer
	Susan V.	W	W	F	Mar 1854	46	M	28	9	9	MS	TN	TN	
	Cranee W.	S	W	M	Jul 1880	19	S				MS	MS	MS	Farm Labor
	Hattie L.	D	W	F	Mar 1882	18	S				MS	MS	MS	
	Martha E.	D	W	F	Nov 1888	11	S				MS	MS	MS	
	Mollie L.	D	W	F	Nov 1890	9	S				MS	MS	MS	
	Jessie J.	S	W	M	Nov 1892	7	S				MS	MS	MS	
	Alta D.	D	W	F	Feb 1895	5	S				MS	MS	MS	
195	Carpenter, John	H	W	M	Jan 1872	28	M	6			MS	GA	MS	Farm Labor
	Eunice	W	W	F	May 1877	28	M	6	2	1	MS	MS	MS	
	Joshuah P.	S	W	M	Aug 1899	8/mo	S				MS	MS	MS	
196	Strickland, John	H	W	M	Oct 1877	22	M	1			MS	MS	MS	Farmer
	Desia J.	W	W	F	Jan 1885	15	M	1	0	0	TN	TN	MS	
	Fields, Elizabeth	MiL	W	F	Oct 1866	33	Wd		1	1	MS	MS	MS	
197	Helton, Henry H.	H	W	M	Nov 1843	56	M	22			MS	TN	TN	Farmer
	Caroline	W	W	F	Jun 1856	44	M	22	11	9	MS	AL	AL	
	William	S	W	M	Oct 1879	20	S				MS	MS	MS	Farm Labor
	Hattie	D	W	F	UN 1884	16	S				MS	MS	MS	
	Odina	D	W	F	Mar 1886	14	S				MS	MS	MS	
	Carrie	D	W	F	Mar 1888	12	S				MS	MS	MS	
	Mirtie	D	W	F	Oct 1890	10	S				MS	MS	MS	

1	2	3	4	5	6	7	8	9	10	11	12	13	14	15
	Robert L.	S	W	M	Feb 1893	7	S				MS	MS	MS	
	Coleman	S	W	M	Sep 1894	5	S				MS	MS	MS	
	Hill	S	W	M	Dec 1896	3	S				MS	MS	MS	
	Alice	D	W	F	Dec 1898	1	S				MS	MS	MS	
198	Callicott, William	H	W	M	Oct 1873	26	M	4			MS	MS	MS	Farmer
	Julia	W	W	F	Jan 1879	21	M	4	2	2	MS	MS	MS	
	Claira L.	D	W	F	Jun 1896	4	S				MS	MS	MS	
	Milton B.	S	W	M	Dec 1897	2	S				MS	MS	MS	
199	Kennedy, Danniel	H	W	M	Mar 1826	74	M	26			AL	AL	AL	Farmer
	Mandia	W	W	F	Oct 1853	46	M	26	10	6	MS	AL	AL	
	Georgia A.	D	W	F	Dec 1880	19	S				MS	AL	MS	
	Joseph F.	S	W	M	Apr 1884	16	S				MS	AL	MS	Farm Labor
	Mary C.	D	W	F	May 1888	12	S				MS	AL	MS	
	Nancy N.	D	W	F	May 1891	9	S				MS	AL	MS	
	Walter	S	W	M	Nov 1878	21	S				MS	AL	MS	Farm Labor
200	Robinson William	H	W	M	UN 1849	50	M	22			MS	SC	SC	Farmer
	Sarah H.	W	W	F	May 1857	43	M	22	9	9	MS	SC	TN	
	Lillian C.	D	W	F	Oct 1879	20	S				MS	MS	MS	
	Martha L.	D	W	F	Sep 1881	18	S				MS	MS	MS	
	Willie E.	S	W	M	Apr 1883	17	S				MS	MS	MS	Farm Labor
	John W.	S	W	M	Aug 1885	14	S				MS	MS	MS	Farm Labor
	Hattie V.	D	W	F	Nov 1887	12	S				MS	MS	MS	
	Colman R.	S	W	M	Nov 1889	10	S				MS	MS	MS	Farm Labor
	Bettie C.	D	W	F	Mar 1892	8	S				MS	MS	MS	
	Maggie B.	D	W	F	UN 1894	5	S				MS	MS	MS	
	Ezekial C.	S	W	M	Mar 1897	3	S				MS	MS	MS	
201	Holder, James E.	H	W	M	Mar 1856	44	M	2			MS	AL	AL	Farmer
	Annie	W	W	F	UN 1867	33	M	2			MS	MS	MS	
	Mandie E.	D	W	F	May 1882	17	S				MS	MS	MS	
	John H.	S	W	M	Feb 1883	17	S				MS	MS	MS	Farm Labor
	Maggie	D	W	F	Nov 1884	15	S				MS	MS	MS	
	George A.	S	W	M	May 1887	12	S				MS	MS	MS	Farm Labor
	Wesley	S	W	M	Mar 1889	11	S				MS	MS	MS	Farm Labor
	Claud C.	S	W	M	UN 1893	7	S				MS	MS	MS	
	Sallie	D	W	F	May 1899	1	S				MS	MS	MS	
	Anglin, Martha J.	SD	W	F	UN 1887	12	S				MS	MS	MS	
	Anglin, Leander	SS	W	M	UN 1889	10	S				MS	MS	MS	Farm Labor
	Anglin, Austin	SS	W	M	UN 1892	7	S				MS	MS	MS	
202	Howard, Oliver L.	H	W	M	Jul 1848	51	M	29			MS	SC	TN	Farmer
	Emley	W	W	F	Jun 1848	51	M	29	9	8	MS	MS	MS	
	Mary A.	D	W	F	Jul 1872	27	S				MS	MS	MS	
	Willie L.	D	W	F	Oct 1880	19	S				MS	MS	MS	
	Walter B.	S	W	M	Mar 1885	15	S				MS	MS	MS	Farm Labor
	James R.	S	W	M	UN 1888	12	S				MS	MS	MS	Farm Labor
	Cora S.	D	W	F	Oct 1890	9	S				MS	MS	MS	
203	McNeil, William	H	W	M	Oct 1859	40	M	20			MS	UN	TN	Farmer
	Arlie	W	W	F	UN 1862	38	M	20	10	10	AL	AL	MS	
	Willie L.	S	W	M	Apr 1883	17	S				MS	MS	AL	Farm Labor
	Norah	D	W	F	Feb 1885	15	S				MS	MS	AL	
	John	S	W	M	UN 1886	14	S				MS	MS	AL	Farm Labor
	Mandy M.	D	W	F	Oct 1887	12	S				MS	MS	AL	
	Lenord	S	W	M	Nov 1889	10	S				MS	MS	AL	Farm Labor
	Bivon F.	D	W	F	Dec 1891	8	S				MS	MS	AL	
	Sam F.	S	W	M	Oct 1893	6	S				MS	MS	AL	
	Lina	D	W	F	Jun 1895	4	S				MS	MS	AL	
	Eddie F.	S	W	M	Apr 1898	3	S				MS	MS	AL	
	Laney	S	W	M	Feb 1899	1	S				MS	MS	AL	

1	2	3	4	5	6	7	8	9	10	11	12	13	14	15
204	Barnes, George W.	H	W	M	Dec 1847	53	Wd				MS	GA	UN	Farmer
	Liddie	D	W	F	Oct 1879	20	S				MS	MS	MS	
	George W.	S	W	M	Jan 1887	13	S				MS	MS	MS	Farm Labor
	Norah H.	D	W	F	Nov 1889	10	S				MS	MS	MS	
	Leonard	D	W	F	Feb 1893	7	S				MS	MS	MS	
205	Rumage, Francis L.	H	W	M	Feb 1844	56	M	32			TN	TN	TN	Farmer
	Beaty J.	W	W	F	Apr 1848	32	M	32	5	4	AL	SC	AL	
	Marthia J.	D	W	F	Jul 1879	20	S				AL	TN	AL	
206	Martin, William L.	H	W	M	Dec 1876	23	M	1			MS	MS	MS	Farmer
	Eliza E.	W	W	F	Sep 1881	18	M	1	1	1	MS	MS	MS	
	Eva M.	D	W	F	Oct 1899		S				MS	MS	MS	
207	Barnett, Richard L.	H	W	M	Dec 1824	75	M	50			SC	SC	SC	Farmer
	Sallie C.	W	W	F	Mar 1834	66	M	50	5	3	SC	SC	SC	
	John W.	S	W	M	Sep 1865	34	S				MS	SC	SC	Farm Labor
208	Gortney, Kine L.	H	W	M	Feb 1876	24	M	3			MS	MS	MS	Farmer
	Mandy L.	W	W	F	Dec 1877	22	M	3	1	1	MS	SC	MS	
	William G.	S	W	M	Jun 1899	1	S				MS	MS	MS	
209	Martin, John W.	H	W	M	Jan 1850	50	M	26			MS	TN	GA	Farmer
	Susan J.	W	W	F	Sep 1852	47	M	26	3	2	SC	SC	SC	
	Elsie E.	D	W	F	Nov 1882	17	S				MS	MS	SC	
	William	Bdr	W	M	Feb 1871	27	M	2			AL	AL	AL	Farm Labor
210	Claunch, William R.	H	W	M	Feb 1876	24	M	2			MS	AL	MS	
	Flora B.	W	W	F	Dec 1878	21	M	2	1	1	MS	MS	SC	
	Oma	D	W	F	Aug 1898	1	S				MS	MS	MS	
211	McAnnally, John	H	W	M	UN 1852	48	M				MS	MS	MS	Farmer
	Belle	W	W	F	Dec 1863	36	M	16	9	7	MS	MS	MS	
	Henry T.	S	W	M	Aug 1882	17	S				MS	MS	MS	Farm Labor
	Lula	D	W	F	Jun 1886	13	S				MS	MS	MS	
	Bahney	D	W	F	Sep 1887	12	S				MS	MS	MS	
	James W.	S	W	M	Aug 1891	8	S				MS	MS	MS	
	John T.	S	W	M	Feb 1894	6	S				MS	MS	MS	
	Lennie L.	S	W	M	Jun 1895	5	S				MS	MS	MS	
	Norah E.	D	W	F	Dec 1898	1	S				MS	MS	MS	
212	Felker, John R.	H	W	M	Nov 1868	30	M	10			MS	NC	NC	Farmer
	Martha	W	W	F	Feb 1869	31	M	10	4	4	MS	MS	MS	
	Bertrie C.	D	W	F	Apr 1891	9	S				MS	MS	MS	
	Charlie M.	S	W	M	Nov 1893	7	S				MS	MS	MS	
	Elvie R.	S	W	M	Mar 1895	5	S				MS	MS	MS	
	William A.	S	W	M	May 1898	2	S				MS	MS	MS	
213	Felker, John C.	H	W	M	Jun 1829	71	M	40			NC	NC	NC	Farmer
	Lucindia	W	W	F	Nov 1838	61	M	40	8	8	SC	SC	SC	
	Marvinia	D	W	F	Apr 1874	26	S				MS	NC	SC	
	Caroline	D	W	F	Jan 1876	24	S				MS	NC	SC	
	Sara	D	W	F	Nov 1879	21	S				MS	NC	SC	
214	Strickland, William	H	W	M	Sep 1857	43	M	24			GA	GA	GA	Farmer
	Lou D.	W	W	F	Jan 1838	42	M	24	9	8	MS	NC	VA	
	Walter B.	S	W	M	Mar 1881	19	S				MS	GA	MS	Farm Labor
	Martha C.	D	W	F	Sep 1882	17	S				MS	GA	MS	
	Rosa L.	D	W	F	Dec 1884	15	S				MS	GA	MS	
	Thomas	S	W	M	Mar 1890	10	S				MS	GA	MS	
	Mary L.	D	W	F	Sep 1892	7	S				MS	GA	MS	
	James	S	W	M	Jun 1895	5	S				MS	GA	MS	

1	2	3	4	5	6	7	8	9	10	11	12	13	14	15
	Jessie L.	S	W	M	May 1898	2	S				MS	GA	MS	
215	Strickland, William	H	W	M	Jan 1857	43	M	22			MS	GA	GA	Farmer
	Loretta H.	W	W	F	Jul 1863	36	M	22	7	6	AL	AL	AL	
	Joseph C.	S	W	M	Dec 1884	15	S				MS	MS	AL	Farm Labor
	Henry S.	S	W	M	Sep 1889	10	S				MS	MS	AL	
	James R.	S	W	M	Mar 1893	7	S				MS	MS	AL	
	Hattie R.	D	W	F	Jan 1896	4	S				MS	MS	AL	
	Lenory B.	D	W	F	Dec 1898	1	S				MS	MS	AL	
216	Strickland, Thomas	H	W	M	Oct 1859	40	M	13			MS	GA	GA	Farmer
	Mattie R.	W	W	F	Apr 1869	31	M	13	7	5	MS	Eng	MS	
	Andrew N.	S	W	M	Apr 1888	12	S				MS	MS	MS	Farm Labor
	Norah E.	D	W	F	Apr 1892	8	S				MS	MS	MS	
	Oscar L.	S	W	M	Jan 1895	5	S				MS	MS	MS	
	Elmer	S	W	M	Jul 1898	1	S				MS	MS	MS	
	Lillie M.	D	W	F	Feb 1900	2/mo	S				MS	MS	MS	
217	Strickland, John	H	W	M	Nov 1870	29	M	10			MS	GA	GA	Farmer
	Georgia A.	W	W	F	Mar 1871	29	M	10	4	4	AL	SC	NC	
	Andrew J.	S	W	M	Mar 1891	9	S				MS	MS	AL	
	Josie F.	D	W	F	Nov 1892	7	S				MS	MS	AL	
	Grover E.	S	W	M	Apr 1896	4	S				MS	MS	AL	
	Simon	S	W	M	Feb 1899	1	S				MS	MS	AL	
218	Strickland, Simon	H	W	M	Mar 1834	66	M	22			GA	GA	GA	Farmer
	Sarah M.	W	W	F	Sep 1839	60	M	22	9	4	AL	GA	GA	
	Hattie	D	W	F	May 1881	19	S				MS	GA	AL	
	Kennedy, Joe	Bdr	W	M	UN 1883	17	S				MS	AL	MS	Farm Labor
219	Tucker, Francis M.	H	W	M	Apr 1861	39	M	19			MS	MS	GA	
	Malissia P.	W	W	F	May 1867	33	M	17	7	7	MS	MS	MS	
	Rosella	D	W	F	Feb 1884	16	S				MS	MS	MS	
	George W.	S	W	M	Dec 1885	14	S				MS	MS	MS	
	Virgie L.	D	W	F	Mar 1888	12	S				MS	MS	MS	
	William V.	S	W	M	Sep 1890	9	S				MS	MS	MS	
	Joseph M.	S	W	M	Jan 1893	7	S				MS	MS	MS	
	Altie G.	D	W	F	Oct 1895	4	S				MS	MS	MS	
	Adis	D	W	F	Jul 1898	1	S				MS	MS	MS	
220	Browning John A.	H	W	M	Jul 1871	28	M	7			MS	MS	TN	Farmer
	Dora E.	W	W	F	Feb 1876	24	M	7	2	2	MS	MS	MS	
	Ruth L.	D	W	F	Sep 1894	5	S				MS	MS	MS	
	Howard E.	S	W	M	Jan 1898	2	S				MS	MS	MS	
221	Nickelson, William	H	W	M	Sep 1874	25	M	2			MS	TN	MS	Farmer
	Virginia P.	W	W	F	Feb 1878	22	M	2	1	1	MS	MS	MS	
	Lester S.	S	W	M	Aug 1898	2	S				MS	MS	MS	
222	Nickelson, Anna	H	W	F	Sep 1855	44	Wd		9	7	MS	VA	GA	Farmer
	Walter F.	S	W	M	Mar 1877	23	S				MS	TN	MS	Farm Labor
	Porter D.	S	W	M	Apr 1878	22	S				MS	TN	MS	Farm Labor
	Emmett J.	S	W	M	Jun 1880	20	S				MS	TN	MS	Farm Labor
	Oscar J.	S	W	M	Dec 1882	17	S				MS	TN	MS	Farm Labor
	Minnie B.	D	W	F	Oct 1882	15	S				MS	TN	MS	
	Ora E.	D	W	F	Sep 1888	11	S				MS	TN	MS	
223	Bellamy, Lude H.	H	W	M	Sep 1852	47	M	6			MS	GA	TN	Farmer
	Rhoda B.	W	W	F	Mar 1856	44	M	6	3	3	MS	AL	TN	
	Eugenia H.	D	W	F	Dec 1882	15	S				MS	MS	MS	
	Jessie L.	D	W	F	Nov 1894	5	S				MS	MS	MS	
	Bogley, Rusel A.	SS	W	M	Sep 1881	18	S				MS	AL	MS	Farm Labor

1	2	3	4	5	6	7	8	9	10	11	12	13	14	15
224	Phifer, Jacob W.	H	W	M	Feb 1851	49	M	16			MS	NC	GA	Farmer
	Mary C.	W	W	F	Jul 1859	40	M	16	10	9	MS	MS	SC	
	Ella C.	D	W	F	Jun 1885	14	S				MS	MS	MS	
	Nancy A.	D	W	F	Oct 1886	13	S				MS	MS	MS	
	Laura B.	D	W	F	Feb 1890	10	S				MS	MS	MS	
	Mary B.	D	W	F	Mar 1891	9	S				MS	MS	MS	
	Tersey L.	D	W	F	Mar 1892	8	S				MS	MS	MS	
	John W.	S	W	M	Jul 1893	6	S				MS	MS	MS	
	Leona	D	W	F	Aug 1895	4	S				MS	MS	MS	
	Modenia	D	W	F	Nov 1896	3	S				MS	MS	MS	
	James M.	S	W	M	Jan 1898	2	S				MS	MS	MS	
	Mandia C.	D	W	F	Nov 1899	5/mo	S				MS	MS	MS	
	Lidda H.	M	W	F	Jan 1831	69	Wd				GA	GA	GA	
225	Bruton, John A.	H	W	M	Feb 1864	36	M	7			MS	AL	NC	Farmer
	Nancy N.	W	W	F	Jul 1860	39	M	7	3	2	AR	SC	SC	
	Estes M.	S	W	M	Feb 1896	4	S				MS	MS	AR	
	Donald L.	S	W	M	Apr 1898	2	S				MS	MS	AR	
226	Nagle, John S.	H	W	M	Feb 1853	47	M	1			GA	Ire	GA	Sawmill
	Ellen	W	W	F	Nov 1862	37	M	1	0	0	MS	TN	MS	
	Hattie J.	D	W	F	Oct 1883	16	S				MS	GA	AL	
	Simmons F.	S	W	M	Nov 1898	1	S				MS	GA	MS	
	Emilia	M	W	F	Sep 1828	71	Wd	8	5		GA	GA	GA	
	Cain, Emma L.	SD	W	F	Apr 1872	8	S				MS	MS	MS	
227	Pace, David N.	H	W	M	Oct 1855	44	M	22			MS	MS	MS	Farmer
	Martha A.	W	W	F	Nov 1860	39	M	22	6	6	MS	TN	GA	
	Robert V.	S	W	M	Dec 1883	16	S				MS	MS	MS	Farm Labor
	Luther K.	S	W	M	Apr 1886	14	S				MS	MS	MS	Farm Labor
	Lester E.	S	W	M	Aug 1891	8	S				MS	MS	MS	
	Ira G.	S	W	M	Mar 1895	5	S				MS	MS	MS	
	Sybel G.	D	W	F	Jun 1898	2	S				MS	MS	MS	
	Martin, Selina J.	MiL	W	F	Sep 1831	68	Wd		5	4	GA	SC	GA	
228	Moore, William	H	W	M	Mar 1870	30	M	0			MS	MS	MS	Farmer
	Sallie E.	W	W	F	Jul 1875	24	M	0	0	0	MS	MS	MS	
229	McAnally, Walter	H	W	M	Apr 1879	21	M	2			MS	MS	MS	Farmer
	Puldy J.	W	W	F	Oct 1879	20	M	2	0	0	MS	MS	MS	
230	Bryant, Steve	H	W	M	Oct 1853	46	M	20			GA	SC	SC	Farmer
	Julia E.	W	W	F	Jun 1858	42	M	20	3	3	MS	MS	MS	
	William J.	S	W	M	Sep 1878	21	S				MS	GA	MS	Farm Labor
	Ellen	D	W	F	Sep 1889	19	S				MS	GA	MS	
	John B.	S	W	M	Aug 1883	16	S				MS	GA	MS	Farm Labor
	Joseph H.	S	W	M	May 1882	8	S				MS	GA	MS	
231	Pannel, James	H	W	M	Dec 1873	26	M	4			MS	MS	MS	Farmer
	Slatie R.	W	W	F	Mar 1878	22	M	4	0	0	MS	AL	NC	
	David	Bro	W	M	Oct 1877	22	S				MS	MS	MS	Farm Labor
232	Mock, John T.	H	W	M	Feb 1847	53	M	29			MS	NC	SC	Farmer
	Mary K.	W	W	F	Nov 1848	51	M	29	7	6	GA	NC	SC	
	Mary E.	D	W	F	Nov 1878	21	S				MS	MS	GA	
	Millie P.	D	W	F	May 1882	18	S				MS	MS	GA	
	Dillie E.	D	W	F	May 1882	18	S				MS	MS	GA	
	Samuel P.	S	W	M	Aug 1884	15	S				MS	MS	GA	Farm Labor
	Henry J.	S	W	M	Apr 1888	12	S				MS	MS	GA	Farm Labor
	Martha A.	M	W	F	Nov 1822	77	Wd		4	3	SC	VA	SC	
	Silas F.	Bro	W	M	Aug 1868	39	S				MS	NC	SC	Farmer
	Bodiford, Annie G.	Aunt	W	F	Feb 1813	87	Wd		0	0	SC	VA	SC	

1	2	3	4	5	6	7	8	9	10	11	12	13	14	15
233	Martin, Ambrose	H	W	M	Jul 1838	61	M	5			TN	NC	NC	Farmer
	Catherine	W	W	F							MS	NC	NC	
	Ida R.	D	W	F	Feb 1882	18	S				MS	TN	AL	
234	Cobb, Charles D.	H	W	M	Oct 1860	39	M	9			GA	GA	GA	Farmer
	Georgia A.	W	W	F	May 1871	29	M	9	2	2	MS	SC	SC	
	Odis	S	W	M	Feb 1892	8	S				MS	GA	MS	
	Archie F.	S	W	M	Jul 1897	1	S				MS	GA	MS	
235	Felker, Lucinda	H	W	F	Nov 1841	68	Wd		0	0	NC	NC	NC	Farmer
	James A.	Ss	W	M	Jun 1854	45	S				MS	NC	NC	Farmer
236	Bruton, Thomas	H	W	M	Nov 1859	40	M	17			MS	AL	NC	Farmer
	Tennie G.	W	W	M	Jun 1864	36	M	17	9	7	MS	NC	NC	
	Theron O.	S	W	M	Dec 1883	16	S				MS	MS	MS	Farm Labor
	Thadious F.	S	W	M	May 1887	13	S				MS	MS	MS	Farm Labor
	Dexter E.	S	W	M	May 1887	11	S				MS	MS	MS	Farm Labor
	Lester B.	S	W	M	Jul 1891	6	S				MS	MS	MS	
	Dewitt	S	W	M	Mar 1895	5	S				MS	MS	MS	
	Joseph M.	S	W	M	Mar 1897	3	S				MS	MS	MS	
	Daisy M.	D	W	F	Aug 1899		S				MS	MS	MS	
237	McKee, William	H	W	M	Feb 1862	38	M	19			MS	GA	MS	Farmer
	Georgia	W	W	F	May 1862	33	M	19	6	6	MS	GA	AL	
	William H.	S	W	M	Aug 1882	17	S				MS	MS	MS	Farm Labor
	Marandia B.	D	W	F	Nov 1884	15	S				MS	MS	MS	
	John R.	S	W	M	Jun 1888	12	S				MS	MS	MS	
	Marshel P.	S	W	M	May 1891	9	S				MS	MS	MS	
	Owen F.	S	W	M	May 1896	4	S				MS	MS	MS	
	Elsie C.	S	W	M	Apr 1899	1	S				MS	MS	MS	

End of Enumeration of District #3

1	2	3	4	5	6	7	8	9	10	11	12	13	14	15
1	Reno, Sam D.	H	W	M	Sep 1866	33	M	12			MS	IN	AL	Farmer
	Ludora	W	W	F	Nov 1870	29	M	12	7	6	MS	VA	VA	
	Earnest C.	S	W	M	Nov 1888	11	S				MS	MS	MS	Farm Laborer
	Lila V.	D	W	F	Feb 1890	10	S				MS	MS	MS	House Work
	Marshall C.	S	W	M	Aug 1893	6	S				MS	MS	MS	
	William L.	S	W	M	Jan 1895	5	S				MS	MS	MS	
	Reba C.	D	W	F	Apr 1897	3	S				MS	MS	MS	
	Lou O.	D	W	F	Dec 1898	1	S				MS	MS	MS	
2	Gardner, Pemia J.	H	W	M	Jan 1824	76	Wd		5	2	NC	NC	NC	
	Sarah J.	D	W	F	Aug 1854	45	S				MS	NC	NC	
3	McRae, Nancy C.	H	W	F	Jun 1861	38	M	20	3	3	MS	AL	VA	House Work
	McRae, Daniel P.	H	W	M	Aug 1855	44	M	20			MS	SC	SC	Farmer
	Henry K.	S	W	M	Jul 1880	19	S				MS	MS	MS	Farm Laborer
	Allen P.	S	W	M	Aug 1884	15	S				MS	MS	MS	Farm Laborer
	Affie B.	D	W	F	Sep 1891	8	S				MS	MS	MS	
4	Gardner, Gray T.	H	W	M	Jun 1857	42	M	20			MS	NC	NC	Farmer
	Mary G.	W	W	F	Jan 1860	40	M	20	8	5	MS	MS	MS	
	Nora B.	D	W	F	May 1881	19	S				MS	MS	MS	
	James R.	S	W	M	Apr 1882	18	S				MS	MS	MS	Farm Laborer
	Rosa E.	D	W	F	Jul 1883	16	S				MS	MS	MS	
	Frank B.	S	W	M	Dec 1884	15	S				MS	MS	MS	Farm Laborer
	Charley L.	S	W	M	Jul 1897	2	S				MS	MS	MS	
5	Duke, Lewis	H	B	M	May 1850	50	M	25			MS	MS	VA	Farmer
	Mealy	W	B	F	Jan 1850	50	M	25	12	10	TN	TN	TN	
	Soloman	S	B	M	May 1877	23	S				AL	MS	TN	
	Lewis A.	S	B	M	Jun 1878	21	S				MS	MS	TN	Farm Laborer
	Mealy A.	D	B	F	Oct 1879	20	S				MS	MS	TN	
	Hally	S	B	M	Mar 1886	14	S				MS	MS	TN	Farm Laborer
	Lesy	D	B	F	Apr 1888	12	S				MS	MS	TN	
	Noah	S	B	M	May 1890	10	S				MS	MS	TN	Farm Laborer
	Roy	S	B	M	Mar 1892	8	S				MS	MS	TN	
6	Rawson, May	H	W	F	Jan 1820	80	Wd		3	2	VA	VA	VA	
7	Hill, John T.	H	W	M	Jan 1844	56	M	12			NC	NC	NC	Farmer
	Mollie H.	W	W	F	Nov 1862	37	M	12	6	6	MS	MS	MS	
	Virdie L.	D	W	F	Mar 1882	18	S				MS	MS	MS	
	Martha L.	D	W	F	Nov 1889	10	S				MS	NC	MS	
	John A.	S	W	M	Jun 1891	8	S				MS	NC	MS	
	Myrtie L.	D	W	F	Jan 1893	7	S				MS	NC	MS	
	Connie E.	D	W	F	Mar 1895	5	S				MS	NC	MS	
	Annie E.	D	W	F	Jul 1896	3	S				MS	NC	MS	
	Thomas G.	S	W	M	Dec 1899	5/mo	S				MS	NC	MS	
8	Dean, John C.	H	W	M	Jul 1841	58	M	41			MS	GA	GA	Farmer
	Mary S.	W	W	F	Apr 1843	57	M	41	8	8	TN	SC	SC	
	Evie L.	D	W	F	Jun 1881	18	S				MS	MS	TN	
	Jones, M.D.	Ser	W	M	Dec 1880	19	S				MS	MS	TN	Day Laborer
	Dean, Thomas	S	W	M	Mar 1884	16	S				MS	MS	TN	Farm Laborer
9	Tittle, James	H	W	M	Sep 1855	44	M	8			AL	AL	AL	Farmer
	Nancy M.	W	W	F	Jul 1868	31	M	8	3	3	AL	AL	AL	
	Olivar A.	S	W	M	Mar 1883	17	S				MS	AL	AL	Farm Laborer
	Anderson W.	S	W	M	Feb 1886	14	S				MS	AL	AL	Farm Laborer

1	2	3	4	5	6	7	8	9	10	11	12	13	14	15
	Geneva C.	D	W	F	Jun 1889	10	S				MS	AL	AL	
	Luster D.	S	W	M	Apr 1893	7	S				MS	AL	AL	
	Loula B.	D	W	F	Mar 1895	5	S				MS	AL	AL	
	Emma J.	D	W	F	Jan 1889	1	S				MS	AL	AL	
	Maria	MiL	W	F	Oct 1822	72	Wd				AL	AL	AL	
10	Dean, James D.	H	W	M	Jul 1873	26	M	2			MS	MS	TN	Farmer
	Angelina	W	W	F	May 1876	24	M	2	1	1	AL	AL	AL	
	Roxie M.	D	W	F	Nov 1895	4	S				MS	MS	MS	
	Mary L.	D	W	F	Aug 1899	8/mo	S				MS	MS	MS	
11	Slack, Charles A.	H	W	M	Mar 1873	27	M	6			TN	TN	TN	Farmer
	Callie H.	W	W	F	Apr 1872	28	M	6	2	2	MS	MS	TN	
12	Trim, Sam C.	H	W	M	Dec 1869	30	M	8			MS	AL	GA	Teacher
	Kattie E.	W	W	F	Apr 1874	26	M	8	4	4	MS	MS	GA	
	Ruth V	D	W	F	Jul 1892	7	S				MS	MS	MS	
	Harry T.	S	W	M	Jan 1894	6	S				MS	MS	MS	
	Charles L.	S	W	M	Nov 1896	3	S				MS	MS	MS	
	Esther	D	W	F	Sep 1899	8/mo	S				MS	MS	MS	
	Nichols, Martha R.	MiL	W	F	Sep 1841	58	S		1	1	GA	GA	SC	
13	Trim, James L.	H	W	M	May 1833	67	M	34	9	7	GA	SC	SC	Farmer
	Rosa A.	W	W	F	Apr 1840	60	M	34	9	7	GA	GA	SC	
	Emma F.	D	W	F	Dec 1870	29	S		1	1	MS	GA	GA	
	Hattie N.	Nce	W	F	Jun 1896	3	S				MS	MS	MS	
14	Trim, Osborn P.	H	W	M	Sep 1878	21	M	2			MS	GA	GA	Farmer
	Velia	W	W	F	Nov 1876	23	M	2	1	1	TN	AL	GA	
	John W.	S	W	M	Nov 1898	1	S				MS	MS	TN	
15	Wigginton, F.	H	W	M	Apr 1856	44	M	23			AL	AL	AL	Farmer
	Sarah R.	W	W	F	Mar 1851	49	M	23	5	4	AL	AL	AL	
	Simon	S	W	M	Dec 1878	21	S				AL	AL	AL	Farm Laborer
	William J.	S	W	M	Jan 1883	17	S				MS	AL	AL	Farm Laborer
	Annty	S	W	M	Nov 1884	15	S				MS	AL	AL	Farm Laborer
	Lidda M.	D	W	F	Mar 1887	13	S				MS	AL	AL	
16	Tidwell, John R.	H	W	M	Jan 1873	26	M	6			AL	AL	AL	Farmer
	N.C.	W	W	F	Apr 1878	22	M	6	3	3	MS	SC	MS	
	Ruth B.	D	W	F	Oct 1895	4	S				MS	AL	MS	
	Ruby A.	D	W	F	Sep 1897	2	S				MS	AL	MS	
	Rufus L.	S	W	M	Mar 1899	1	S				MS	AL	MS	
17	Reynolds, P.M.	H	W	M	Jul 1837	62	M	39			AL	GA	GA	Farmer
	Mary J.	W	W	F	Apr 1850	50	M	39	9	9	MS	MS	MS	
	Lou Q.	D	W	F	Oct 1882	17	S				MS	AL	MS	
	Ned W.	S	W	M	Apr 1884	16	S				MS	AL	MS	Farm Laborer
	Fannie E.	D	W	F	Sep 1886	13	S				MS	AL	MS	
	Lee O.	D	W	F	Sep 1888	11	S				MS	AL	MS	
	Kennedy, Lou V.	D	W	F	Sep 1867	37	Wd		0	0	MS	AL	MS	
18	Hill, G.M.	H	W	M	Feb 1851	49	M	17			TN	NC	SC	Farmer
	C.D.	W	W	F	Oct 1867	32	M	17	7	7	MS	MS	MS	
	M.D.	D	W	F	Nov 1883	16	S				MS	TN	MS	
	I.B.	S	W	M	Jan 1886	14	S				MS	TN	MS	
	Burton	S	W	M	Mar 1889	11	S				MS	TN	MS	
	P.D.	D	W	F	Oct 1891	8	S				MS	TN	MS	
	Offie	D	W	F	Oct 1892	7	S				MS	TN	MS	
	Nullie C.	D	W	F	Jun 1893	6	S				MS	TN	MS	
	Nesie	D	W	F	Nov 1897	2	S				MS	TN	MS	
19	Hill, M.C.	H	W	M	Mar 1818	82	Wd				NC	NC	NC	Farmer

1	2	3	4	5	6	7	8	9	10	11	12	13	14	15
20	Dean, Ned C.	H	W	M	Jan 1870	30	M	8			MS	MS	TN	Farmer
	Nancy C.	W	W	F	Apr 1873	27	M	8	3	2	MS	NC	TN	
	Willie L.	D	W	F	Oct 1897	2	S				MS	MS	MS	
	Sydney G.	S	W	M	Jun 1898	1	S				MS	MS	MS	
	Hill, Sydney M.	Ser	W	M	Apr 1826	24	S				MS	NC	NC	Farmer
21	Tipton, H.T.	H	W	M	Mar 1871	29	M	7			MS	AL	NC	Farmer
	Marget A.	W	W	F	May 1877	23	M	7	2	2	MS	AL	AL	
	John R.	S	W	M	Mar 1896	4	S				MS	MS	AL	
	Charley, L.	S	W	M	Jun 1898	1	S				MS	MS	AL	
22	Tipton, G.W.	H	W	M	Aug 1881	18	M	0			MS	AL	TN	Farmer
	Sarah A.	W	W	F	Jun 1884	15	M	0	0	0	AL	AL	AL	
23	Osborn, Emolin	H	W	M	Feb 1838	62	Wd		0	0	GA	SC	SC	Farmer
	Flemmings, Lou	M	W	F	May 1820	80	Wd		2	1	SC	SC	SC	
24	Oaks, Stafford	H	W	M	Oct 1859	40	M	18			MS	TN	TN	Farmer
	Susan M.	W	W	F	Feb 1854	46	M	18	6	6	MS	TN	AL	
	Oliver O.	S	W	M	Jun 1884	15	S				MS	MS	MS	
	James A.	S	W	M	Jul 1886	13	S				MS	MS	MS	
	Ellen V.	D	W	F	Jul 1888	11	S				MS	MS	MS	
	Wallis F.	S	W	M	Jul 1889	10	S				MS	MS	MS	
	Lilly B.	D	W	F	Sep 1894	5	S				MS	MS	MS	
	Orim C.	D	W	F	Mar 1896	4	S				MS	MS	MS	
25	Short, B.L.	H	W	M	Sep 1836	73	M	2			TN	TN	TN	Farmer
	Jane T.	W	W	F	Apr 1861	39	M	2	7	6	MS	TN	TN	
	Allen, Clark	SS	W	M	Mar 1883	18	S				MS	TN	MS	
	Allen, Marion	SS	W	M	Mar 1886	14	S				MS	TN	MS	
	Mason, Edgar E.	SS	W	M	Oct 1888	11	S				MS	TN	MS	
	Mason, Alvin B.	SS	W	M	Oct 1891	8	S				MS	TN	MS	
	Short, Henry L.	SS	W	M	Mar 1898	2	S				MS	TN	MS	
26	Short, Robert L.	H	W	M	Dec 1871	28	M	9			MS	TN	TN	
	Amandie	W	W	F	Mar 1875	25	M	9	4	3	AL	AL	AL	
	Amanda E.	D	W	F	Dec 1893	6	S				MS	MS	AL	
	Henry D.	S	W	M	Nov 1895	4	S				MS	MS	AL	
	Markus L.	S	W	M	Mar 1900	2/mo	S				MS	MS	AL	
27	Lancaster, Harvy	H	W	M	Aug 1860	39	M	9			MS	NC	GA	Farmer
	Belle	W	W	F	May 1864	36	M	9	4	4	MS	MS	MS	
	Hardin N.	S	W	M	Jul 1893	6	S				MS	MS	MS	
	Lyman	S	W	M	Mar 1895	5	S				MS	MS	MS	
	Annie	D	W	F	Feb 1897	3	S				MS	AL	MS	
	Berta	D	W	F	Dec 1898	1	S				MS	MS	MS	
	Dean, K.A.	MiL	W	F	May 1828	72	Wd		1	1	MS	GA	GA	
	Gunn, Molise	Ser	W	F	Mar 1873	27	S				MS	AL	AL	
	Gunn, Andrew	Ser	W	M	Jul 1891	8	S				MS	MS	MS	
	Hill, W.A.	Ser	W	M	Oct 1877	22	Wd				MS	NC	TN	Farm Laborer
	Deaton, Dock	Bdr	W	M	May 1855	45	M	5			MS	MS	GA	Farm Laborer
	Ella	Bdr	W	F	Feb 1865	35	M	5	2	2	MS	TN	TN	
	John R.	Bdr	W	M	Oct 1897	2	S				MS	MS	MS	
	Walis	Bdr	W	M	Aug 1890	2/mo	S				MS	MS	MS	
28	Kennedy, Doctor R.	H	W	M	Jan 1850	50	M	32			AL	KY	VA	Farmer
	Jane S.	W	W	F	Oct 1855	45	M	32	13	12	MS	AL	AL	
	Cau J.	D	W	F	Nov 1879	20	S				AL	AL	MS	
	James G.	S	W	M	Jun 1882	18	S				MS	AL	MS	Farm Laborer
	Emma J.	D	W	F	Jul 1886	13	S				MS	AL	MS	
	Mary D.	D	W	F	Mar 1888	12	S				MS	AL	MS	
	Thur W.	S	W	M	Aug 1893	6	S				MS	AL	MS	

1	2	3	4	5	6	7	8	9	10	11	12	13	14	15
	Kizzie	D	W	F	Jan 1894	6	S				MS	AL	MS	
	Jessie D.	S	W	M	Jul 1899	10/mo	S				MS	AL	MS	
29	Tipton, Charley	H	W	M	Oct 1865	34	M				MS	AL	NC	Farmer
	Michie A.	W	W	F	May 1867	33	M				AL	SC	AL	
30	Paden, Martha	H	W	F	Oct 1839	60	Wd		9	6	MS	AL	AL	Landlord
31	Slack, Marget I.	H	W	F	Dec 1867	32	Wd				MS	SC	MS	Farmer
	Amus	SS	W	M	Sep 1883	16	S				MS	TN	TN	Farm Laborer
	John W.	S	W	M	May 1889	11	S				MS	TN	MS	Farm Laborer
	Henry D.	S	W	M	Jan 1891	9	S				MS	TN	MS	
	Rufus, O.	S	W	M	Jan 1892	8	S				MS	TN	MS	
	Georgia M.	D	W	F	Dec 1893	6	S				MS	TN	MS	
	Mary	D	W	F	Jun 1895	4	S				MS	TN	MS	
32	Britnell, Joseph W.	H	W	M	Jan 1865	35	M	3			AL	AL	AL	Farmer
	Tennessee E.	W	W	F	Oct 1870	29	M	3	2	2	MS	MS	MS	
	Ollie E.	D	W	F	Nov 1897	2	S				MS	AL	MS	
	Oren L.	S	W	M	Mar 1900	2/mo	S				MS	AL	MS	
33	Oaks, James F.	H	W	M	Feb 1826	74	M	49			TN	NC	NC	Farmer
	Rachel A.	W	W	F	Aug 1828	71	M	49	5	5	TN	NC	NC	
	Mary E.	D	W	F	Apr 1853	47	S				TN	TN	TN	
	Storment, Walter L.	Bdr	W	M	Apr 1874	26	S				MS	SC	MS	Teacher
34	Paden, Robert W.	H	W	M	Apr 1863	37	M	8			MS	SC	MS	Farmer
	Weby V.	W	W	F	May 1869	31	M	8	4	3	MS	SC	MS	
	Luke	Cou	W	M	May 1872	28	S				MS	SC	MS	Farmer
	Mattie P.	D	W	F	Oct 1892	7	S				MS	SC	AL	
	Annie L.	D	W	F	Aug 1893	6	S				MS	MS	AL	
	Flora B.	D	W	F	Apr 1898	2	S				MS	MS	AL	
35	Duboise, William T.	H	W	M	Mar 1849	51	M	9			MS	MS	MS	Farmer
	Lou E.	W	W	F	Oct 1865	34	M	9	6	3	MS	NC	MS	
	Mayo, Lou C.	SiL	W	F	Jun 1843	56	S				SC	SC	SC	
	Duboise, Alice C.	D	W	F	Jul 1882	17	S				MS	MS	MS	
	Sarah E.	D	W	F	Jul 1885	14	S				MS	MS	MS	
	William M.	S	W	M	Feb 1893	7	S				MS	MS	MS	
	Daniel H.	S	W	M	Jan 1895	5	S				MS	MS	MS	
	Thomas W.	S	W	M	Jul 1899	10/mo	S				MS	MS	MS	
36	Hall, William	H	W	M	May 1872	28	M	3			AL	AL	AL	Farmer
	Tilda P.	W	W	F	Dec 1872	27	M	3	1	1	MS	TN	MS	
	Stella	D	W	F	Dec 1898	1	S				MS	TN	MS	
37	Pitts, Charles F.	H	W	M	Mar 1856	44	Wd				MS	AL	AL	Farmer
	William C.	F	W	M	Mar 1827	73	Wd				AL	GA	GA	Farmer
	Joseph A.	S	W	M	Sep 1882	17	S				MS	MS	MS	Farm Laborer
	Emma T.	D	W	F	Dec 1883	16	S				MS	MS	MS	
	Leondis L.	S	W	M	May 1887	13	S				MS	MS	MS	Farm Laborer
	Annie E.	D	W	F	Jun 1891	8	S				MS	MS	MS	
38	Paden, David D.	H	W	M	Oct 1860	39	M	18			MS	SC	MS	Farmer
	Phoebia E.	W	W	F	Apr 1855	45	M	18	4	4	GA	GA	SC	
	John W.	S	W	M	Jan 1885	15	S				MS	MS	GA	
	Colonel C.	S	W	M	Nov 1887	12	S				MS	MS	GA	
	Robert H.	S	W	M	Jun 1890	9	S				MS	MS	GA	
	Bertie A.	D	W	F	Mar 1893	7	S				MS	MS	GA	
39	Flurry, John T.	H	W	M	Jul 1861	38	M	15			MS	AL	GA	Farmer
	Vinettie V.	W	W	F	Oct 1867	32	M	15	7	5	MS	MS	MS	
	Richard A.	S	W	M	Sep 1886	13	S				MS	MS	MS	

1	2	3	4	5	6	7	8	9	10	11	12	13	14	15
	Laura B.	D	W	F	Mar 1890	10	S				MS	MS	MS	
	Thomas O.	S	W	M	Dec 1891	8	S				MS	MS	MS	
	Eugene	D	W	F	Mar 1896	4	S				MS	MS	MS	
	Lawrence O.	S	W	M	Feb 1899	1	S				MS	MS	MS	
40	Frederick, John A.	H	W	M	Oct 1864	35	M	16			AL	AL	AL	Farmer
	Nancy A.	W	W	F	Mar 1867	33	M	16	5	4	MS	MS	MS	
	Emma E.	D	W	F	Nov 1887	12	S				MS	AL	MS	
	Joseph A.	S	W	M	Feb 1890	10	S				MS	AL	MS	
	William J.	S	W	M	Dec 1897	6	S				MS	AL	MS	
	Minnie B.	D	W	F	Aug 1896	5	S				MS	AL	MS	
41	Frederick, Mary P.	H	W	F	May 1834	66	Wd		5	4	AL	AL	AL	Farmer
	Harriet J.	D	W	F	Sep 1859	40	S				AL	AL	AL	
	Alice A.	D	W	F	Jul 1861	38	S				AL	AL	AL	
42	Gurley, Mattie M.	H	W	F	Jul 1865	34	Wd	11	7		TN	TN	TN	Housework
	Charley O.	S	W	M	Oct 1895	4	S				MS	MS	TN	
	Mattie P.	D	W	F	Apr 1899	8/mo	S				MS	MS	TN	
43	Wann, James R.	H	W	M	Nov 1833	67	M	42			SC	SC	SC	Farmer
	Martha R.	W	W	F	Nov 1831	68	M	42	2	1	SC	SC	SC	
	Burgess, Ellic	Ser	B	M	Mar 1880	20	S				MS	MS	MS	Farm Laborer
44	Hampton, Will	H	W	M	Jun 1886	33	M	10			TN	TN	TN	Farmer
	Mary E.	W	W	F	Mar 1866	34	M	10	4	4	MS	AL	MS	
	Charles C.	S	W	M	Nov 1890	9	S				MS	TN	MS	
	Samuel E.	S	W	M	Dec 1892	7	S				MS	TN	MS	
	William D.	S	W	M	Feb 1895	5	S				MS	TN	MS	
	Maud I.	D	W	F	Dec 1896	3	S				MS	TN	MS	
45	Carr, James	H	W	M	Jul 1849	50	Wd				GA	SC	SC	Farmer
	Walker P.	S	W	M	Jan 1878	22	S				AL	GA	AL	Farmer
	James T.	S	W	M	Mar 1879	21	S				AL	GA	AL	Farm Labor
	Walter M.	S	W	M	Jul 1882	17	S				AL	GA	AL	Farm Labor
	Monroe M.	S	W	M	Nov 1885	15	S				AL	GA	AL	Farm Labor
	Sylvester W.	S	W	M	Jan 1890	10	S				AL	GA	AL	
	Claudy N.	S	W	M	Mar 1892	8	S				AL	GA	AL	
	Grover J.	S	W	M	Apr 1894	6	S				MS	GA	AL	
	Hill K.	S	W	M	Feb 1896	4	S				MS	GA	AL	
46	Dean, Joseph	H	W	M	Dec 1858	41	M	20			MS	MS	MS	Farmer
	Mary E.	W	W	F	Aug 1860	39	M	20	4	4	AL	AL	AL	
	Bertha	D	W	F	Jan 1881	18	S				MS	MS	AL	
	Hattie S.	D	W	F	Apr 1884	15	S				MS	MS	AL	
	Lonia L.	D	W	F	Apr 1888	12	S				MS	MS	AL	
	Jessie L.	D	W	F	Jun 1893	6	S				MS	MS	AL	
47	Paden, Leroy M.	H	W	M	Aug 1853	46	M	8			MS	SC	MS	Farmer
	Syntha A.	W	W	F	Feb 1849	51	M	8	0	0	MS	MS	AL	
	Robert A.	S	W	M	Apr 1875	25	S				MS	MS	AL	Farmer
	John D.	S	W	M	Jan 1877	22	S				MS	MS	AL	Farm Labor
	Marget M.	D	W	F	May 1879	21	S				MS	MS	AL	
48	Neal, James	H	W	M	Mar 1865	35	M	6			MS	SC	SC	Farmer
	Georgia	W	W	F	Sep 1871	28	M	6	2	2	MS	AL	MS	
	Fannie May	D	W	F	Mar 1895	5	S				MS	MS	MS	
	Alma	D	W	F	Dec 1898	1	S				MS	MS	MS	
49	Neal, Mary	H	W	F	Dec 1829	70	Wd		7	4	SC	SC	SC	Landlord
	Mary E.	D	W	F	Mar 1865	35	S				MS	SC	SC	
	Mallie F.	GS	W	M	Mar 1885	15	S				MS	MS	MS	
	Luther R.	GS	W	M	Apr 1889	11	S				MS	MS	MS	

1	2	3	4	5	6	7	8	9	10	11	12	13	14	15
50	Flurry, William A.	H	W	M	Sep 1861	38	M	16			AL	GA	GA	Farmer
	Minnie L.	W	W	F	Oct 1865	34	M	16	7	6	MS	AL	AL	
	Mary L.	D	W	F	Jul 1886	13	S				MS	AL	MS	
	James G.	S	W	M	Sep 1888	11	S				MS	AL	MS	
	Ennis I.	D	W	F	Dec 1889	10	S				MS	AL	MS	
	Eula B.	D	W	F	Mar 1892	8	S				MS	AL	MS	
	William W.	S	W	M	Sep 1894	5	S				MS	AL	MS	
	Sallie A.	D	W	F	Jan 1898	2	S				MS	AL	MS	
51	Reno, Everette	H	W	M	Oct 1834	69	M	44			AL	TN	NC	Farmer
	Sarah J.	W	W	F	Jun 1839	60	M	44	7	7	AL	TN	NC	
	Margaret B.	D	W	F	Aug 1877	22	S				MS	AL	AL	
52	Cagle, James	H	W	M	Jun 1865	34	M	13			AL	AL	AL	Farmer
	Prudence C.	W	W	F	Jan 1870	30	M	13	6	5	AL	TN	AL	
	Irene E.	D	W	F	Jan 1888	12	S				AL	AL	AL	
	James T.	S	W	M	Jan 1890	10	S				AL	AL	AL	
	Martin L.	S	W	M	Nov 1891	8	S				MS	AL	AL	
	Benjamin F.	S	W	M	Feb 1894	6	S				MS	AL	AL	
	Effie A.	D	W	F	May 1898	2	S				MS	AL	AL	
53	Bottoms, Thomas	H	W	M	Dec 1848	51	M	31			TN	AL	TN	Farmer
	Elizabeth A.	W	W	F	Jan 1848	52	M	31	2	1	AL	AL	AL	
54	Burgess, Taylor	H	B	M	Jun 1874	25	M	6			MS	MS	MS	Farmer
	Susan S.	W	B	F	Jul 1873	26	M	6	4	4	MS	GA	GA	
	Flora	D	B	F	Nov 1892	7	S				MS	MS	MS	
	Neblet	S	B	M	Mar 1896	4	S				MS	MS	MS	
	Annie	D	B	F	Jul 1897	2	S				MS	MS	MS	
	Harriet	S	B	M	Apr 1899	1	S				MS	MS	MS	
55	Pitts, Columbus	H	W	M	Jan 1857	43	M	20			MS	AL	VA	Farmer
	Mary L.	W	W	F	Feb 1860	40	M	20			MS	AL	AL	
	Addie R.	D	W	F	Mar 1880	20	S				MS	MS	MS	
56	Paden, Leroy	H	W	M	May 1875	25	M	2			MS	SC	MS	Farmer
	Lou R.	W	W	F	Feb 1881	19	M	2	1	1	AL	AL	AL	
	Willie A.	D	W	F	Jul 1899	10/mo	S				MS	MS	AL	
57	Paden, Frank	H	W	M	Jul 1866	33	M	12			MS	SC	MS	Farmer
	Margret J.	W	W	F	Dec 1867	32	M	12	5	2	AL	AL	AL	
	Rosa A.	D	W	F	Feb 1893	7	S				MS	MS	AL	
	Gerty B.	D	W	F	Aug 1895	4	S				MS	MS	AL	
58	Hill, Allen	H	W	M	Sep 1856	43	M	15			AL	SC	NC	Farmer
	Sallie L.	W	W	F	Jun 1862	37	M	15	5	5	MS	MS	NC	
	Willie N.	D	W	F	Jan 1886	14	S				MS	GA	MS	
	Jessie L.	D	W	F	Jan 1887	13	S				MS	GA	MS	
	Minnie May	D	W	F	Feb 1889	11	S				MS	GA	MS	
	Mary D.	D	W	F	Aug 1891	8	S				MS	GA	MS	
	Horace. H.	S	W	M	Nov 1896	3	S				MS	GA	MS	
59	Robinson, William	H	B	M	Mar 1875	25	M	4			MS	MS	MS	Farmer
	Cathern	W	B	F	Apr 1876	24	M	4	2	2	MS	MS	MS	
	Decille	Cou	B	F	Apr 1885	15	S				MS	MS	MS	
	Melton	S	B	M	Apr 1898	2	S				MS	MS	MS	
	Zora	D	B	F	Jan 1900	4/mo	S				MS	MS	MS	
60	Robinson, Bales	H	B	M	Jul 1849	50	M	29			MS	MS	MS	Farmer
	Medy A.	W	B	F	Oct 1851	48	M	29	9	7	MS	MS	MS	
	Henry E.	D	B	F	Apr 1881	19	S				MS	MS	MS	
	Rosa	D	B	F	Jan 1883	17	S				MS	MS	MS	

1	2	3	4	5	6	7	8	9	10	11	12	13	14	15
	Emma	D	B	F	Oct 1885	14	S				MS	MS	MS	
	Roxie A.	D	B	F	Dec 1888	11	S				MS	MS	MS	
	Marshall	S	B	M	Nov 1891	8	S				MS	MS	MS	
61	King, Thomas J.	H	W	M	Jan 1868	32	M	8			MS	MS	MS	Ginner (Cotton)
	Sofa M.	W	W	F	Jan 1871	29	M	8	3	2	MS	MS	TX	
	Neeley E.	Bro	W	M	Oct 1882	17	S				MS	MS	MS	Farm Laborer
	William C.	S	W	M	Jul 1895	4	S				MS	MS	MS	
	James M.	S	W	M	Jan 1898	2	S				MS	MS	MS	
62	Sappington, James	H	W	M	Jul 1820	80	M	56			TN	TN	TN	Farmer
	Mary B.	W	W	F	Jul 1831	69	M	56	14	11	AL	AL	AL	
63	Sappington, Robert	H	W	M	Mar 1871	29	M	8			MS	TN	AL	Farmer
	Annie	W	W	F	May 1870	26	M	8	5	3	MS	AL	AL	
	Cloudz L.	D	W	F	Oct 1893	6	S				MS	MS	MS	
	Ilor B.	D	W	F	Oct 1895	4	S				MS	MS	MS	
	Mattie	D	W	F	Sep 1898	1	S				MS	MS	MS	
64	Butler, William	H	W	M	Feb 1866	34	M	14			MS	MS	MS	Farmer
	Landa B.	W	W	F	Jan 1867	33	M	14	13	12	MS	MS	TN	
	Calvin	S	W	M	Jan 1885	15	S				MS	MS	MS	
	Mary	D	W	F	Dec 1887	14	S				MS	MS	MS	
	Charles	S	W	M	Oct 1886	13	S				MS	MS	MS	
	Belie	D	W	F	Apr 1888	12	S				MS	MS	MS	
	Ermma	D	W	F	Apr 1889	11	S				MS	MS	MS	
	George A.	S	W	M	Nov 1890	10	S				MS	MS	MS	
	Dovie	D	W	F	Dec 1891	8	S				MS	MS	MS	
	Minnie	D	W	F	Jun 1892	8	S				MS	MS	MS	
	Lilly	D	W	F	Jun 1893	6	S				MS	MS	MS	
	Edna	D	W	F	Feb 1895	5	S				MS	MS	MS	
	Alda	D	W	F	Jun 1896	3	S				MS	MS	MS	
	Infant	D	W	F	Nov 1899	5/mo	S				MS	MS	MS	
65	Paden, Thomas G.	H	W	M	Aug 1844	55	M	26			TN	SC	SC	Physician
	Eusebiua	W	W	F	May 1847	53	M	26	4	4	MS	AL	TN	
	David W.	S	W	M	Aug 1875	24	S				MS	TN	MS	Grist Mill
	Sallie	D	W	F	Jul 1880	19	S				MS	TN	MS	
	Charley	S	W	M	Nov 1882	17	S				MS	TN	MS	Farm Laborer
	John	S	W	M	Nov 1886	13	S				MS	TN	MS	Farm Laborer
66	Brumley, William L.	H	W	M	Oct 1841	58	M	35			AL	AL	NC	Miller (Grist)
	Rebecca E.	W	W	F	Apr 1842	58	M	35			AL	KY	AL	
	Carr, Ida	Ser	W	F	Apr 1879	21	UN				MS	MS	AL	Servant
	Lou G.	Ser	W	F	Mar 1890	10	S				MS	MS	AL	Servant
67	Harp, John H.	H	W	M	Apr 1855	45	M	19			MS	MS	MS	Farmer
	Mary C.	W	W	F	Nov 1859	40	M	19	8	8	MS	MS	MS	
	James E.	S	W	M	Nov 1881	18	S				MS	MS	MS	Farm Laborer
	Hattie V.	D	W	F	Oct 1884	15	S				MS	MS	MS	
	Henry W.	S	W	M	Aug 1887	12	S				MS	MS	MS	
	Lee	S	W	M	Dec 1889	10	S				MS	MS	MS	
	Benjamin	S	W	M	Jun 1892	8	S				MS	MS	MS	
	William C.	S	W	M	Jul 1894	5	S				MS	MS	MS	
	Robert V.	S	W	M	Nov 1896	3	S				MS	MS	MS	
	Malissa	D	W	F	Jul 1899	10/mo	S				MS	MS	MS	
68	Green, Pleasant	H	W	M	Mar 1873	27	M	8			AL	AL	AL	Farmer
	Nancy L.	W	W	F	Apr 1870	30	M	8	3	1	MS	MS	MS	
	Olen B.	S	W	M	Sep 1895	4	S				MS	AL	MS	
69	Green, P.S.	H	W	M	Feb 1875	25	M	6			AL	AL	AL	Farmer
	Annah C.	W	W	F	Feb 1873	27	M	6	4	3	MS	MS	MS	

1	2	3	4	5	6	7	8	9	10	11	12	13	14	15
	Minnie R.	D	W	F	Jan 1896	4	S				MS	MS	MS	
	Tennie	D	W	F	Apr 1897	3	S				MS	MS	MS	
	William S.	S	W	M	Jan 1899	1	S				MS	MS	MS	
70	Shackleford, Will	H	W	M	Feb 1867	33	M	13			MS	MS	MS	Farmer
	Nancy A.	W	W	F	May 1865	35	M	13	3	3	MS	AL	GA	
	Lizza	D	W	F	Oct 1891	9	S				MS	MS	MS	
	Mattie B.	D	W	F	Jan 1895	5	S				MS	MS	MS	
	William D.	S	W	M	Aug 1898	1	S				MS	MS	MS	
71	Chase, John	H	W	M	Jul 1877	22	M	1			MS	MS	MS	Off bearer, Saw Mill
	Della	W	W	F	Sep 1880	19	M	1	1	1	MS	MS	AL	
	Dona	D	W	F	Feb 1900	0/12	S				MS	MS	MS	
72	Breadlove, T.F.	H	W	M	Apr 1858	42	M	16			MS	MS	MS	Teamster
	Beckie	W	W	F	Mar 1871	29	M	16	1	1	MO	AL	AL	
	Pearl	D	W	F	Mar 1893	7	S				MS	AL	MO	
73	Hellums, E.W.	H	W	M	Oct 1831	68	M	49			NC	NC	NC	Sawyer
	E.J.	W	W	F	Nov 1832	67	M	49	11	9	AL	VA	TN	
	McAnnally, B.	Bdr	W	M	UN UN	UN	UN				UN	UN	UN	Lever setter, Saw Mill
	Belue, William	Bdr	W	M	UN UN	UN	UN				UN	UN	UN	Off bearer, Saw Mill
74	Pounds, B.F.	H	W	M	Sep 1855	44	M	22			AL	AL	AL	Farmer
	Mary A.	W	W	F	Sep 1858	41	M	22	11	10	AL	AL	AL	
	Janie	D	W	F	Mar 1879	21	S				AL	AL	AL	
	Martha A.	D	W	F	Apr 1881	19	S				AL	AL	AL	
	Minnie	D	W	F	May 1884	16	S				MS	AL	AL	
	Emma	D	W	F	Oct 1886	13	S				MS	AL	AL	
	Ida	D	W	F	Jun 1889	11	S				MS	AL	AL	
	Thomas	S	W	M	Mar 1891	9	S				MS	AL	AL	
	Lee A.	S	W	M	Jun 1893	6	S				MS	AL	AL	
	Maudy	D	W	F	Feb 1895	5	S				MS	AL	AL	
	Blanche	D	W	F	Jan 1900	4/mo	S				MS	AL	AL	
75	Bryant, G.H.	H	W	M	Apr 1874	26	M	6			MS	MS	MS	Farmer
	Sallie	W	W	F	Jun 1879	20	M	6	2	2	MS	MS	MS	
	Lilly M.	D	W	F	Jun 1896	3	S				MS	MS	MS	
	John R.	S	W	M	Feb 1900	0/mo	S				MS	MS	MS	
76	Beard, William H.	H	W	M	May 1879	20	M	3			MS	MS	MS	Farmer
	Fannie L.	W	W	F	Sep 1876	23	M	3			MS	MS	MS	
77	Chunn, Lawrence	W	W	M	Nov 1880	19	M	2			MS	MS	MS	Off bearer, Saw Mill
	Mattie	W	W	F	Feb 1882	18	M	2	1	1	MS	MS	MS	
	Annie B.	D	W	F	Oct 1897	2	S				MS	MS	MS	
78	South, Jon	H	W	M	Aug 1848	51	M	30			TN	TN	TN	Farmer
	Mary	W	W	F	Sep 1847	52	M	30	10	8	TN	TN	NC	
	Arvy E.	D	W	F	May 1881	19	S				MS	TN	TN	
	John W.	S	W	M	Dec 1883	16	S				MS	TN	TN	
	Willis B.	S	W	M	Sep 1890	9	S				MS	TN	TN	
	William	S	W	M	Oct 1870	29	Wd				MS	TN	TN	Farmer
	Rosa L.	GD	W	F	Jan 1893	7	S				TX	MS	MS	
	Thomas L.	GS	W	M	May 1895	5	S				TX	MS	MS	
	Mary N.	GD	W	F	Mar 1898	2	S				TX	MS	MS	
	Joseph H.	S	W	M	Apr 1879	21	M	0			MS	TN	TN	Farmer
	Florence A.	DiL	W	F	Mar 1882	18	M	0	0	0	MS	MS	AL	
79	Millsaps, E.T.	H	W	M	Mar 1827	73	M	9			NC	NC	NC	Farmer
	Margaret A.	W	W	F	Sep 1862	37	M	9	3	2	MS	NC	AL	
	Billy	S	W	M	May 1852	48	S				MS	NC	NC	
	John P.	S	W	M	Jun 1894	5	S				MS	NC	MS	

1	2	3	4	5	6	7	8	9	10	11	12	13	14	15
	Essie M.	D	W	F	May 1899	1	S				MS	NC	MS	
80	Belue, William	H	W	M	Jun 1839	60	M	35			TN	SC	TN	Farmer
	Anna N.	W	W	F	Sep 1841	58	M	35	7	4	WV	WV	WV	
	Mattie	D	W	F	Apr 1882	18	S				MS	TN	WV	
81	Tucker, James A.	H	W	M	Aug 1865	34	M	8			MS	TN	GA	Farmer
	Mattie N.	W	W	F	Jul 1876	23	M	8	4	4	MS	AL	MS	
	Levi G.	S	W	M	May 1893	7	S				MS	MS	MS	
	Tennie E.	D	W	F	Jul 1894	5	S				MS	MS	MS	
	Forrest L.	S	W	M	Jul 1896	3	S				MS	MS	MS	
	Zulla	D	W	F	Apr 1900	3mo	S				MS	MS	MS	
82	Tucker, J.A.	H	W	M	May 1831	69	M	45			TN	TN	TN	
	Catherine	W	W	F	Aug 1837	62	M	45	3	3	GA	GA	GA	
83	Donaldson, J.	H	W	M	Apr 1851	49	M	22			MS	MS	SC	Farmer
	Martha A.	W	W	F	Sep 1861	38	M	22	5	5	MS	MS	TN	
	Paul	S	W	M	Sep 1879	20	S				MS	MS	TN	
	Willie E.	D	W	F	Sep 1881	18	S				MS	MS	TN	
	Oscar	S	W	M	Jun 1886	13	S				MS	MS	TN	
	Edgar	S	W	M	Dec 1895	6	S				MS	MS	TN	
	Walter	S	W	M	Aug 1897	2	S				MS	MS	MS	
	Harp, Rebecca	MiL	W	F	Aug 1834	65	Wd		3	3	TN	NC	NC	
84	Mayo, William J.	H	W	M	Jun 1848	51	M	26			AL	SC	GA	
	Sarah M.	W	W	F	Aug 1850	49	M	26	4	2	GA	SC	SC	
	South, Nancy J.	D	W	F	Sep 1874	25	Wd		2	1	MS	AL	GA	
	Altie B.	GD	W	F	Mar 1896	4	S				MS	MS	MS	
85	Mayo, William H.	H	W	M	Dec 1876	23	M	0			MS	MS	MS	Farmer
	Sarah A.	W	W	F	May 1882	18	M	0	0	0	MS	MS	MS	
86	Robinson, Lovin	H	W	M	May 1839	61	M	12			TN	VA	GA	Farmer
	Aulenia	W	W	F	Apr 1854	46	M	12	1	1	MS	MS	MS	
	Joseph H.	S	W	M	Sep 1875	24	S				MS	TN	GA	
	Russ S.	S	W	M	Jun 1894	6	S				MS	TN	MS	
87	Tucker, T.J.	H	W	M	Sep 1854	45	M	27			MS	MS	MS	Day Laborer
	Martha J.	W	W	F	Jan 1851	49	M	27	1	1	MS	SC	SC	
	Elizabeth	D	W	F	Jul 1874	25	S				MS	MS	MS	
	Orr, Lee O.	D	W	F	Dec 1877	22	M	7	1	1	MS	MS	MS	
	Tucker, Ed F.	GS	W	M	Jun 1894	5	S				MS	MS	MS	
88	Belue, Robert	H	W	M	Mar 1845	55	M	35			MS	TN	TN	Farmer
	Mary A.	W	W	F	Jan 1847	53	M	35	10	5	MS	GA	GA	
	Georgia	D	W	F	Jan 1875	25	S				MS	MS	MS	
	James	S	W	M	Mar 1879	21	S				MS	MS	MS	
89	Slack, Albert	H	W	M	Jun 1875	24	M	2			MS	MS	TN	Farmer
	Verdie	W	W	F	Jul 1882	17	M	2	0	0	MS	MS	MS	
90	Greene, Samuel	H	W	M	Jan 1863	37	M	16			AL	AL	AL	Farmer
	Amanda E.	W	W	F	Oct 1862	37	M	16	5	5	MS	TN	SC	
	Lennie A.	S	W	M	Jul 1884	15	S				MS	AL	MS	Farm Laborer
	Riley B.	S	W	M	Nov 1886	13	S				MS	AL	MS	Farm Laborer
	Lou V.	D	W	F	Apr 1890	10	S				MS	AL	MS	
	Eva	D	W	F	Mar 1896	4	S				MS	AL	MS	
	Dovie J.	D	W	F	Feb 1898	2	S				MS	AL	MS	
91	Parker, John	H	W	M	Feb 1856	44	M	2			MS	TN	AL	Farmer
	Addie	W	W	F	Apr 1867	33	M	2	3	3	TN	TN	TN	
	Thomas H.	S	W	M	Oct 1882	17	S				MS	MS	MS	Farm Laborer

1	2	3	4	5	6	7	8	9	10	11	12	13	14	15
	James T.	S	W	M	Dec 1886	13	S				MS	MS	MS	
	Edwin E.	S	W	M	Aug 1890	9	S				MS	MS	MS	
	John W.	S	W	M	Apr 1894	6	S				MS	MS	MS	
	Charley, E.	S	W	M	Apr 1899	1	S				MS	MS	MS	
	Belue, Allie	SD	W	F	Sep 1889	10	S				MS	MS	MS	
	Belue, Ned	SS	W	M	Mar 1892	8	S				MS	MS	TN	
92	Wright, William	H	W	M	Jun 1823	76	M	30			SC	SC	SC	Farmer
	Keedie M.	W	W	F	Oct 1826	63	M	30	4	4	TN	TN	TN	
	Emelie	D	W	F	Jul 1873	26	S				MS	SC	TN	
	Emellin	D	W	F	May 1875	25	S				MS	SC	TN	
93	Wright, Walter	H	W	M	Mar 1878	22	M	2			MS	SC	TN	
	Loula	W	W	F	Dec 1879	20	M	2	0	0	MS	MS	MS	
	Amanda	Sis	W	F	Mar 1879	21	S				MS	SC	SC	
	Hattie	Sis	W	F	May 1895	5	S				MS	MS	MS	
	Halman, James	Ser	W	M	Jan 1885	15	S				MS	MS	MS	Servant
94	Beard, J.B.	H	W	M	Jun 1849	50	M	25			GA	GA	GA	Farmer
	Sarah A.	W	W	F	Jan 1852	48	M	25	4	4	MS	SC	SC	
	Lou A.	D	W	F	Feb 1882	18	S				MS	GA	MS	
	David H.	S	W	M	Aug 1884	15	S				MS	GA	MS	
	Rosie M.	D	W	F	Jan 1886	14	S				MS	GA	MS	
	James O.	S	W	M	Sep 1891	8	S				MS	GA	MS	
95	Claunch, L.C.	H	W	M	Apr 1840	60	M	40			AL	NC	NC	Farmer
	Nancy L.	W	W	F	Sep 1845	55	M	40	10	8	AL	AL	TN	
	Morgan H.	S	W	M	Dec 1879	20	S				MS	AL	AL	Farmer
	James T.	S	W	M	Aug 1882	17	S				MS	AL	AL	Farm Hand
96	Claunch, John	H	W	M	Oct 1872	27	M	6			MS	AL	AL	Farmer
	Elzetta J.	W	W	F	Jan 1875	25	M	6	3	3	MS	MS	MS	
	Essie M.	D	W	F	Jul 1894	5	S				MS	MS	MS	
	Oscar L.	S	W	M	Feb 1897	3	S				MS	MS	MS	
	Sylvester	S	W	M	Apr 1900	1/mo	S				MS	MS	MS	
97	Gibson, Nancy I.	H	W	F	Oct 1848	51	Wd		6	4	MS	TN	MS	Farmer
	W.D.	S	W	M	Dec 1880	19	S				MS	MS	MS	Farm Laborer
	M.C.	D	W	F	May 1883	17	S				MS	MS	MS	
	H.L.	D	W	F	Sep 1887	12	S				MS	MS	MS	
98	Hart, W.J.	H	W	M	May 1829	71	M	22			TN	NC	SC	Farmer
	Isabella	W	W	F	Jun 1839	60	M	22	2	2	AL	TN	TN	
	Key, Sallie	Sis	W	F	Dec 1833	66	Wd		3	3	AL	TN	TN	
99	Bonds, C.W.	H	W	M	Sep 1861	38	M	12			MS	AL	AL	Farmer
	Fannie	W	W	F	Apr 1874	26	M	12			MS	AL	AL	
	Ozella	D	W	F	Nov 1888	11	S				MS	MS	MS	
	Herbit	S	W	M	Aug 1890	9	S				MS	MS	MS	
	Maxie	S	W	M	May 1899	1	S				MS	MS	MS	
100	Lawry, Samuel A.	H	W	M	Feb 1875	25	M	3			AL	AL	AL	Day Laborer
	Nellie	W	W	F	Dec 1874	25	M	3	1	1	AL	AL	AL	
	William A.	S	W	M	Sep 1898	1	S				AL	AL	AL	
101	Eaton, E.C.	H	W	M	Mar 1845	55	Wd		7	5	MS	TN	TN	Farmer
	Henry W.	S	W	M	Jul 1880	19	S				MS	AL	TN	Farm Laborer
	Broadwick, Rosco	GS	W	M	Feb 1888	12	S				MS	AL	TN	
102	Eaton, William B.	H	W	M	Feb 1875	25	M	3			MS	TN	TN	School Teacher
	Allena P.	W	W	F	Dec 1879	20	M	3	1	1	Ms	GA	TN	
	Bolivar M.	S	W	M	Jun 1898	1	S				MS	MS	GA	

1	2	3	4	5	6	7	8	9	10	11	12	13	14	15
103	Adams, Willie A.	H	W	M	Apr 1849	51	M	30			MS	MS	MS	Farmer
	Liza J.	W	W	F	Feb 1848	52	M	30	1	1	AL	AL	MS	
	Liza P.	D	W	F	Jan 1885	15	S				MS	MS	MS	
104	Breadlove, John S.	H	W	M	Sep 1855	44	M	23			GA	GA	GA	Farmer
	Martha A.	W	W	F	Nov 1856	43	M	23	7	5	MS	MS	MS	
	John W.	S	W	M	Sep 1883	16	S				MS	GA	MS	Farm Laborer
	William H.	S	W	M	Jul 1888	11	S				MS	GA	MS	
	Mary D.	D	W	F	Jul 1892	7	S				MS	GA	MS	
	Kizzie M.	D	W	F	Jul 1895	4	S				MS	GA	MS	
105	Ardis, David	H	W	M	Mar 1834	66	M	0			AL	AL	AL	Farmer
	Elizabeth	W	W	F	Apr 1839	61	M	0	2	1	TN	TN	TN	
106	Lee, James	H	W	M	Dec 1857	42	S				MS	AL	AL	Farmer
	E.A.	M	W	F	Jun 1836	63	Wd		3	1	AL	AL	AL	
	Whitehead, Mary J.	Ser	W	F	May 1885	15	S				AL	AL	AL	
107	Smith, J.	H	W	M	Dec 1851	48	M	28			MS	GA	MS	Farmer
	Harriett M.	W	W	F	Jun 1852	47	M	28	11	11	MS	AL	TN	
	Marcus R.	S	W	M	Apr 1877	23	S				MS	MS	MS	Farmer
	Elliot L.	S	W	M	Feb 1879	21	S				MS	MS	MS	Farmer
	Andrew L.	S	W	M	Jan 1881	19	S				MS	MS	MS	Farm Laborer
	Oscor H.	S	W	M	Jan 1883	17	S				MS	MS	MS	Farm Laborer
	David G.	S	W	M	Jan 1885	15	S				MS	MS	MS	Farm Laborer
	Doctor W.	S	W	M	Jan 1887	13	S				MS	MS	MS	
	Melly B.	D	W	F	Sep 1889	10	S				MS	MS	MS	
	Rily B.	S	W	M	Dec 1891	8	S				MS	MS	MS	
	Harriett L.	D	W	F	Feb 1894	6	S				MS	MS	MS	
108	Shackelford, W.	H	W	M	Oct 1819	80	M	9			MS	AL	TN	Farmer
	Lou I.	W	W	F	Dec 1836	65	M	9			AL	NC	TN	
109	Shackelford, William	W	W	M	Dec 1848	51	M	35			MS	AL	TN	Farmer
	Mary B.	W	W	F	Dec 1842	57	M	35	6	6	AL	SC	SC	
	Sarah K.	D	W	F	Feb 1874	26	S				MS	MS	AL	
	Willie I.	D	W	F	Jul 1875	24	S				MS	MS	AL	
	Richard P.	S	W	M	Aug 1878	21	S				MS	MS	AL	Farmer
	Thomas R.	S	W	M	Dec 1882	17	S				MS	MS	AL	
110	Duboise, John	H	W	M	Mar 1845	55	M	37			AL	AL	AL	Farmer
	Mary F.	W	W	F	Nov 1847	52	M	37	10	5	AL	AL	AL	
	Martha C.	D	W	F	Mar 1883	17	S				AL	AL	AL	
	Harriett C.	D	W	F	Mar 1883	17	S				AL	AL	AL	
	Sarah A.	D	W	F	Jul 1886	13	S				AL	AL	AL	
111	Crawley, L.D.	H	W	M	Aug 1860	39	M	12			MS	TN	MS	Farmer
	Dollie A.	W	W	F	Oct 1870	29	M	12	5	4	MS	MS	MS	
	Lucille	D	W	F	Dec 1887	12	S				MS	MS	MS	
	Rachel P.	D	W	F	Sep 1890	9	S				MS	MS	MS	
	Loyd E.	S	W	M	Aug 1893	6	S				MS	MS	MS	
	Myrtle	D	W	F	Jan 1898	2	S				MS	MS	MS	
112	Wileman, James C.	H	W	M	Jan 1870	30	M	5			MS	AL	MS	Farmer
	Roxie C.	W	W	F	Mar 1877	23	M	5	3	3	MS	AL	AL	
	Mattie L.	D	W	F	Aug 1896	3	S				MS	MS	MS	
	James A.	S	W	M	Apr 1898	2	S				MS	MS	MS	
	Silas	S	W	M	May 1900	2/mo	S				MS	MS	MS	
113	Wileman, John	H	W	M	Jun 1864	35	Wd				MS	AL	AL	Farmer
	Tilda	SiL	W	F	Mar 1877	23	S				MS	MS	MS	
	Dona	D	W	F	Feb 1892	8	S				MS	MS	MS	
	Annie B.	D	W	F	Aug 1894	5	S				MS	MS	MS	

1	2	3	4	5	6	7	8	9	10	11	12	13	14	15
	William H.	SiL	W	M	Jul 1897	2	S				MS	MS	MS	
114	Shackelford, L.C.	H	W	M	Feb 1860	40	M	4			MS	AL	TN	Farmer
	Annie L.	W	W	F	Apr 1867	33	M	4	2	1	MS	MS	MS	
	Maggie L.	D	W	F	Dec 1880	18	S				MS	MS	MS	
	John A.	S	W	M	Aug 1882	17	S				MS	MS	MS	
	Mattie B.	D	W	F	Aug 1884	15	S				MS	MS	MS	
	Charley R.	S	W	M	Apr 1886	12	S				MS	MS	MS	
	Jeffie A.	D	W	F	Mar 1870	10	S				MS	MS	MS	
	Sallie E.	D	W	F	Jan 1873	7	S				MS	MS	MS	
	Bennet F.	S	W	M	Feb 1895	5	S				MS	MS	MS	
	Winnie P.	D	W	F	Nov 1899	9/mo	S				MS	MS	MS	
115	Riddle, William	H	W	M	May 1854	46	M	24			MS	TN	IL	Farmer
	Mary D.	W	W	F	Aug 1859	40	M	24	10	8	MS	GA	AL	
	Minter V.	S	W	M	Dec 1880	19	S				MS	MS	MS	Farm Labor
	William M.	S	W	M	Mar 1882	18	S				MS	MS	MS	
	Ezra W.	S	W	M	Oct 1883	16	S				MS	MS	MS	
	Junior S.	S	W	M	Mar 1886	14	S				MS	MS	MS	
	Abner S.	S	W	M	Feb 1892	8	S				MS	MS	MS	
	Albert L.	S	W	M	Feb 1895	5	S				MS	MS	MS	
	Eliza G.	D	W	F	Jun 1896	3	S				MS	MS	MS	
	Martha E.	D	W	F	Feb 1898	2	S				MS	MS	MS	
116	Bellamy, R.	H	W	M	Oct 1856	43	M	23			MS	GA	MS	Farmer
	Nancy E.	W	W	F	Jul 1861	38	M	23	7	7	MS	GA	MS	
	Sidney W.	S	W	M	Jan 1879	21	S				MS	MS	MS	
	Robert E.	S	W	M	Feb 1881	19	S				MS	MS	MS	
	Finis W.	S	W	M	Feb 1882	17	S				MS	MS	MS	
	Oliver F.	S	W	M	Aug 1888	11	S				MS	MS	MS	
	Landa	S	W	M	Apr 1892	8	S				MS	MS	MS	
	Homer R.	S	W	M	Mar 1895	5	S				MS	MS	MS	
	Pearl N.	D	W	F	Mar 1895	5	S				MS	MS	MS	
117	Carter, Lucy C.	H	W	F	Feb 1840	60	Wd		10	4	AL	AL	AL	Farmer
	Sarah	D	W	F	Jun 1860	39	S				MS	TN	AL	
	Berry A.	S	W	M	Dec 1871	28	S				MS	TN	AL	Farm Laborer
	George P.	S	W	M	Aug 1878	21	S				MS	TN	AL	Farm Laborer
	Shackelford, Ruby	D	W	F	Jul 1870	29	Wd		3	1	MS	TN	AL	
	R. C.	GS	W	M	Oct 1896	3	S				MS	MS	MS	
118	Calton, T.W.	H	W	M	Mar 1870	30	M	9			AL	AL	AL	Farmer
	Mary O.	W	W	F	May 1871	29	M	9	2	2	MS	MS	MS	
	James	S	W	M	Dec 1892	7	S				MS	MS	MS	
	Clinton	S	W	M	Jul 1899	10/mo	S				MS	MS	MS	
119	Barnette, J.W.	H	W	M	Jan 1835	65	M	31			TN	SC	NC	Farmer
	M.J.	W	W	F	Aug 1841	58	M	31			TN	AL	TN	
	Eliza M.	D	W	F	Oct 1881	18	S				MS	TN	TN	
120	Ramsey, James	H	W	M	Feb 1867	33	Wd				AL	AL	MS	Farmer
	Mary E.	M	W	F	Apr 1843	57	Wd		3	2	MS	MS	MS	
	William A.	S	W	M	May 1893	7	S				MS	MS	MS	
	Minnie M.	D	W	F	Feb 1895	5	S				MS	MS	MS	
	Kellis S.	S	W	M	May 1897	3	S				MS	MS	MS	
	Owens, J.F.	Ser	W	M	Dec 1871	23	S				MS	MS	MS	Farm Laborer
121	Sanford, Henry	H	W	M	Jun 1875	24	M	0			AL	AL	AL	Farmer
	Doxie A.	W	W	F	Nov 1875	24	M	0	0	0	MS	MS	MS	
122	Shackelford, J.	H	W	M	Sep 1853	46	M	30			AL	AL	AL	Farmer
	Mary Jane	W	W	F	Oct 1856	43	M	30	10	10	MS	MS	MS	
	Minnie B.	D	W	F	Oct 1875	24	S				MS	MS	MS	

1	2	3	4	5	6	7	8	9	10	11	12	13	14	15
	Robert R.	S	W	M	Jan 1881	19	S				MS	MS	MS	Farm Laborer
	Miza M.	D	W	F	Jan 1893	17	S				MS	MS	MS	
	Fannie R.	D	W	F	Nov 1886	13	S				MS	MS	MS	
	Sydney M.	S	W	M	Feb 1889	11	S				MS	MS	MS	
	Mattie O.	D	W	F	Oct 1890	9	S				MS	MS	MS	
	Mary C.	D	W	F	Aug 1845	4	S				MS	MS	MS	
	William M.	S	W	M	Apr 1900	2/mo	S				MS	MS	MS	
123	Owens, Russell B.	H	W	M	Sep 1850	49	M	30			MS	TN	TN	Farmer
	Laura A.	W	W	F	Sep 1851	48	M	30	12	9	MS	NC	NC	
	Robert W.	S	W	M	Aug 1875	24	S				MS	MS	MS	Farmer
	William A.	S	W	M	May 1884	16	S				MS	MS	MS	
	Viola	D	W	F	Feb 1886	14	S				MS	MS	MS	
	Eva C.	D	W	F	May 1888	12	S				MS	MS	MS	
	Luther	S	W	M	Dec 1891	8	S				MS	MS	MS	
124	Wright, Molly A.	H	W	F	Dec 1848	51	Wd		6	4	AL	TN	TN	Farmer
	Eddy W.	S	W	M	Jun 1889	16	S				MS	MS	AL	Farm Laborer
	Hattie M.	D	W	F	Oct 1886	12	S				MS	MS	AL	
	Thomas L.	S	W	M	Jan 1880	10	S				MS	MS	AL	
125	Sandford, H.	H	W	M	Nov 1845	54	M	30			GA	GA	GA	Farmer
	S.J.	W	W	F	Dec 1846	53	M	30	6	4	GA	GA	GA	
	Minnie L.	D	W	F	Apr 1886	14	S				AL	GA	GA	
126	Glasgow, Thomas E.	H	W	M	Dec 1875	26	M	8			MS	MS	MS	Farmer
	Lou E.	W	W	F	Feb 1876	24	M	8	0	0	MS	AL	MS	
127	Dean, W.C.	H	W	M	Mar 1867	33	M	10			MS	MS	TN	Farmer
	Armenda C.	W	W	F	Aug 1872	27	M	10	4	4	MS	SC	MS	
	Edgar H.	S	W	M	Jan 1891	9	S				MS	MS	MS	
	Alfa P.	D	W	F	Aug 1896	3	S				MS	MS	MS	
	Ward T.	S	W	M	Mar 1898	2	S				MS	MS	MS	
	Walter H.	S	W	M	Mar 1898	2	S				MS	MS	MS	
128	Smith, James O.	H	W	M	Feb 1860	40	M	20			AL	AL	TN	Farmer
	C.C.	W	W	F	Dec 1860	39	M	20	8	8	MS	AL	GA	
	Flora L.	D	W	F	Dec 1881	18	S				MS	AL	MS	
	Walter C.	S	W	M	Nov 1883	16	S				MS	AL	MS	
	Rosco	S	W	M	Dec 1886	14	S				MS	AL	MS	
	Charley I.	S	W	M	Jun 1889	10	S				MS	AL	MS	
	Belvia A.	D	W	F	May 1891	9	S				MS	AL	MS	
	Alexandria	D	W	F	Nov 1892	7	S				TX	AL	MS	
	Arthur J.	S	W	F	Jul 1895	4	S				MS	AL	MS	
	William J.	S	W	M	Oct 1898	2	S				MS	AL	MS	
129	McNatt, T.L.	H	W	M	Sep 1863	36	M	13			AL	AL	AL	Farmer
	Annie	W	W	F	May 1870	30	M	13	5	4	AL	AL	AL	
	Jesse O.	S	W	M	Dec 1887	12	S				MS	AL	AL	
	Lesley	S	W	M	Aug 1891	8	S				MS	AL	AL	
	Robert C.	S	W	M	Jul 1893	6	S				MS	AL	AL	
	Thomas C.	S	W	M	May 1900	0/mo	S				MS	AL	AL	
130	McNatt, M.J.	H	W	F	Jul 1832	67	Wd		7	5	AL	AL	AL	Farmer
	Hamilton, Wesley	Bro	W	M	Jan 1842	58	S				AL	AL	AL	Farm Laborer
	Neal, Jessie	D	W	F	Jul 1871	28	Wd		4	4	AL	AL	AL	
	Daniel J.	S	W	M	Nov 1893	6	S				MS	MS	AL	
	Mary A.	D	W	F	Jul 1895	4	S				MS	MS	AL	
	Rosie P.	D	W	F	Jan 1897	3	S				MS	MS	AL	
	John C.	S	W	M	Jun 1883	17/mo	S				MS	MS	AL	
131	Howell, C.L.	H	W	M	Jun 1883	26	M	7			AL	MS	AL	Farmer
	Leanna B.	W	W	F	Nov 1871	28	M	7	5	5	MS	MS	MS	

1	2	3	4	5	6	7	8	9	10	11	12	13	14	15
	Lourie E.	D	W	F	Jan 1894	6	S				MS	MS	MS	
	John W.	S	W	M	Feb 1895	5	S				MS	MS	MS	
	Laura H.	D	W	F	Oct 1896	3	S				MS	MS	MS	
	Oliver B.	S	W	M	Mar 1898	2	S				MS	MS	MS	
	Zelma C.	D	W	F	Jan 1900	5/mo	S				MS	MS	MS	
132	Johnson, G.T.	H	W	M	Sep 1852	47	Wd				MS	MS	MS	Farmer
	Ova C.	D	W	F	Jun 1886	13	S				MS	MS	MS	
	Luther C.	S	W	F	Feb 1891	9	S				MS	MS	MS	
133	Choate, Rosa	H	W	F	Sep 1866	34	Wd		2	2	MS	AL	AL	Farmer
	Ida L.	D	W	F	Dec 1881	18	S				MS	MS	MS	
	Alfred E.	S	W	M	Nov 1883	16	S				MS	MS	MS	Farm Laborer
134	Harp, Thomas	H	W	M	Jul 1865	34	M	0			MS	TN	TN	Farmer
	Kate	W	W	F	May 1882	18	M	0	0	0	MS	AL	AL	
	Lewis E.	S	W	M	Jul 1889	11	S				MS	MS	MS	
	? , B	D	W	F	Jul 1892	8	S				MS	MS	MS	
	James A.	S	W	F	May 1896	4	S				MS	MS	AL	
135	Sanford, M.L.	H	W	M	Oct 1871	28	M	6			AL	AL	AL	Farmer
	Alice J.	W	W	F	Jun 1872	27	M	6	3	2	AL	AL	AL	
	Alley M.	D	W	F	Oct 1896	3	S				AL	AL	AL	
	Charley C.	S	W	M	Feb 1899	4/mo	S				MS	AL	AL	
136	Holley, W.S.	H	W	M	Feb 1850	50	M	17			MS	NC	NC	Farmer
	J.C.	W	W	F	Aug 1847	52	M	17	10	6	MS	GA	TN	
	Claudy C.	S	W	M	Feb 1884	16	S				MS	MS	MS	
	Jack H.	S	W	M	Apr 1886	14	S				MS	MS	MS	
	Glasgow, W.M.	SS	W	M	Dec 1878	21	S				MS	MS	MS	School Teacher
	Gurley, Myrtie	Nce	W	F	Jun 1889	10	S				MS	MS	TN	
137	Stephens, Nancy C.	H	W	F	Jun 1843	57	Wd		4	3	AL	AL	AL	Farmer
	Joe P.	S	W	M	Jan 1877	22	S				MS	AL	AL	
138	Stephens, A.C.	H	W	M	Jun 1848	51	M	8			MS	AL	TN	Farmer
	Sarah M.	W	W	F	Jan 1865	34	M	8	3	1	MS	NC	AL	
	J.H.	S	W	M	Apr 1881	19	S				MS	MS	MS	
	Kizzie	D	W	F	Oct 1882	17	S				MS	MS	MS	
	Roxie	D	W	F	Dec 1886	13	S				MS	MS	MS	
	Joe	S	W	M	Nov 1893	6	S				MS	MS	MS	
139	Goddard, C.T.	H	W	M	Apr 1875	25	M	4			MS	MS	MS	Farmer
	Carrie	W	W	F	Feb 1876	24	M	4	2	2	MS	MS	MS	
	Audie M.	D	W	F	Sep 1897	2	S				MS	MS	MS	
	Willie B.	S	W	M	Sep 1899	4/mo	S				MS	MS	MS	
140	Kennedy, Robert R.	H	W	M	Jul 1848	51	M	32			AL	KY	VA	Farmer
	Marget M.	W	W	F	Apr 1851	49	M	32	11	10	AL	AL	SC	
	Mary A.	D	W	F	Aug 1871	27	S				AL	AL	AL	
	Jane	D	W	F	Jun 1873	26	S				AL	AL	AL	
	Bashaw	S	W	M	Sep 1883	16	S				AL	AL	AL	Farm Laborer
	James H.	S	W	M	Aug 1886	13	S				MS	AL	AL	Farm Laborer
	Malinda	D	W	F	May 1889	10	S				MS	AL	AL	
	Geneva	D	W	F	Sep 1891	8	S				MS	AL	AL	
141	Smith, George T.	H	W	M	Dec 1866	33	M	10			MS	MS	MS	Farmer
	Elizabeth E.	W	W	F	Sep 1868	31	M	10	5	4	MS	MS	MS	
	Sarah E.	D	W	F	Dec 1890	9	S				MS	MS	MS	
	Conie L.	D	W	F	Feb 1894	6	S				MS	MS	MS	
	Fannie E.	D	W	F	Oct 1895	4	S				MS	MS	MS	
	Maury D.	S	W	M	Feb 1899	1	S				MS	MS	MS	

1	2	3	4	5	6	7	8	9	10	11	12	13	14	15
142	Stephens, John W.	H	W	M	May 1850	49	M	28			MS	NC	TN	Farmer
	E.P.	W	W	F	Mar 1853	47	M	28	6	6	MS	TN	TN	
	Emma	D	W	F	Jan 1875	25	S				MS	MS	MS	
	Charley B.	S	W	M	Jul 1883	16	S				MS	MS	MS	School Teacher
	John E.	S	W	M	Jul 1886	13	S				MS	MS	MS	
	Oscar	S	W	M	Dec 1887	12	S				MS	MS	MS	
	Anna	D	W	M	Mar 1890	10	S				MS	MS	MS	
	Alie	D	W	F	May 1892	8	S				MS	MS	MS	
143	Goddard, George T.	H	W	M	Jul 1845	54	M	33			GA	SC	SC	Farmer
	Sarah F.	W	W	F	Mar 1848	52	M	33	8	6	MS	AL	TN	
	Jennie	D	W	F	Oct 1879	20	S				MS	GA	MS	At School
	Sibbie	D	W	F	Jun 1880	19	S				MS	GA	MS	At School
	Luther	S	W	M	Mar 1892	8	S				MS	GA	MS	
144	Kennedy, Joseph D.	H	W	M	Jul 1868	31	M	11			AL	AL	AL	Farmer
	Nancy E.	W	W	F	May 1867	33	M	11	5	5	AL	AL	AL	
	Benjamin H.	S	W	M	Aug 1889	10	S				MS	AL	Al	
	Mary V.	D	W	F	Jun 1892	7	S				MS	AL	AL	
	Sarah A.	D	W	F	Dec 1894	5	S				MS	AL	AL	
	Marget M.	D	W	F	Mar 1897	3	S				MS	AL	AL	
	John B.	D	W	F	May 1899	1	S				MS	AL	AL	
145	Simpson, John D.	H	W	M	Jun 1866	33	M	10			MS	TN	TN	Meth. Preacher
	Mamie	W	W	F	Aug 1874	26	M	10	6	6	MS	VA	MS	
	Hugh W.	S	W	M	Jan 1891	9	S				MS	MS	MS	
	Herman R.	S	W	M	Dec 1891	8	S				MS	MS	MS	
	Ethel I.	D	W	F	Jul 1892	7	S				MS	MS	MS	
	Vestra V.	D	W	F	Feb 1895	5	S				MS	MS	MS	
	Audry P.	D	W	F	Dec 1896	3	S				MS	MS	MS	
	Ruth G.	D	W	F	Jan 1899	1	S				MS	MS	MS	
146	McClure, Margret C.	H	W	F	Nov 1858	41	Wd		5	4	AL	AL	NC	Farmer
	Thomas L.	S	W	M	Jul 1878	21	S				MS	MS	AL	Farmer
	John A.	S	W	M	Aug 1880	19	S				MS	MS	AL	Farm Laborer
	Finis O.	S	W	M	Jan 1886	14	S				AL	MS	AL	
	Ollie M.	D	W	F	Jun 1890	10	S				MS	MS	AL	
147	Britnell, M.D.	H	W	M	Jun 1850	50	M	28			AL	AL	AL	Farmer
	Viney	W	W	F	Feb 1855	45	M	28	11	9	AL	SC	AL	
	David B.	S	W	M	May 1876	24	S				AL	AL	AL	Farmer
	Lou I.	D	W	F	Jul 1879	20	S				AL	AL	AL	
	Tammy N.	D	W	F	Aug 1891	18	S				AL	AL	AL	
	Taylor T.	S	W	M	Jun 1884	16	S				AL	AL	Al	
	William M.	S	W	M	Mar 1887	13	S				MS	AL	AL	
	Viola E.	D	W	F	Jul 1889	10	S				MS	AL	AL	
	Ward S.	S	W	M	Apr 1892	8	S				MS	AL	AL	
	Olen A.	S	W	M	Jun 1894	5	S				MS	AL	AL	
	Charles C.	S	W	M	Apr 1897	3	S				MS	AL	AL	
	Green, Riley J.	SiL	W	M	Apr 1871	28	Wd				AL	AL	AL	Farmer
	Fannie B.	GD	W	F	Feb 1894	6	S				MS	AL	AL	
	Theoffis C.	GS	W	M	Mar 1898	2	S				MS	AL	AL	
148	Butler, J.T.	H	W	M	Dec 1859	45	M	23			MS	MS	MS	Farmer
	Marget	W	W	F	Feb 1839	41	M	23	5	5	MS	MS	MS	
	Annie	D	W	F	Sep 1877	22	S				MS	MS	MS	
	Mittie B.	D	W	F	Mar 1881	18	S				MS	MS	MS	
	Sydney	S	W	M	Dec 1879	20	S				MS	MS	MS	
	Elva	S	W	M	Feb 1889	11	S				MS	MS	MS	
	Maggie	D	W	F	Feb 1894	6	S				MS	MS	MS	
149	Stephens, George C.	H	W	M	May 1877	23	M	0			MS	MS	MS	Farmer
	Annie	W	W	F	Oct 1878	21	M	0	0	0	MS	MS	MS	

1	2	3	4	5	6	7	8	9	10	11	12	13	14	15
150	Panell, J.W.	H	W	M	Sep 1859	40	M	19			MS	MS	MS	Farmer
	Sarah S.	W	W	F	Apr 1866	34	M	19	0	0	MS	GA	GA	
	Davison, Margret	Sis	W	F	Feb 1869	31	Wd		2	1	MS	GA	GA	
	Thomas	Nep	W	M	May 1884	6	S				MS	MS	GA	
151	Stephens, William	H	W	M	Jan 1873	27	M	8			MS	MS	MS	Farmer
	Mollie	W	W	F	Feb 1875	25	M	8	4	3	MS	AL	AL	
	Thomas P.	S	W	M	Nov 1892	7	S				MS	MS	MS	
	Germany C.	S	W	M	Aug 1894	5	S				MS	MS	MS	
	Bolivar B.	S	W	M	Mar 1899	1	S				MS	MS	MS	
152	Adams, J.	H	W	M	Feb 1856	44	M	28			MS	GA	GA	Farmer
	Nancy	W	W	F	Jan 1852	48	M	28	9	8	MS	TN	TN	
	Gerile	S	W	M	Jun 1877	23	S				MS	MS	MS	Farmer
	Arden	S	W	M	Mar 1879	21	S				MS	MS	MS	Farmer
	Dana	D	W	F	Dec 1880	19	S				MS	MS	MS	
	Pearl	D	W	F	Feb 1884	16	S				MS	MS	MS	
	James	S	W	M	Apr 1888	12	S				MS	MS	MS	
	Mealy	D	W	F	May 1892	9	S				MS	MS	MS	
	Lily	D	W	F	Apr 1895	5	S				MS	MS	MS	
153	Kennedy, W.R.	H	W	M	Jan 1878	21	M	2			AL	AL	AL	Farmer
	Matilda	W	W	F	Aug 1875	24	M	2	1	1	MS	AL	AL	
	Laura B.	D	W	F	Apr 1898	1	S				MS	AL	MS	
154	Harp, J.W.	H	W	M	Oct 1847	52	S				TN	TN	TN	Farmer
	Mary J.	Sis	W	F	Aug 1850	48	S				MS	TN	TN	
155	Brazzle, R.L.	H	W	M	Dec 1862	37	M	12			AL	GA	GA	Farmer
	M.L.	W	W	F	Dec 1867	32	M	12	4	2	MS	TN	TN	
	Forest C.	S	W	M	Apr 1896	4	S				MS	AL	MS	
	Olen D.	S	W	M	May 1899	1	S				MS	AL	MS	
156	Oaks, L.M.	H	W	M	Jun 1857	42	M	17			MS	TN	TN	School Teacher
	Annie	W	W	F	Dec 1866	33	M	17	8	6	MS	NC	MS	
	Birtha	D	W	F	Sep 1887	12	S				MS	MS	MS	
	Grady	S	W	M	Oct 1889	10	S				MS	MS	MS	
	Greeley	S	W	M	May 1891	9	S				MS	MS	MS	
	Bula	D	W	F	Jul 1893	6	S				MS	MS	MS	
	Myrtle	D	W	F	Jul 1895	4	S				MS	MS	MS	
	Viola	D	W	F	Aug 1899	6/mo	S				MS	MS	MS	
157	Robinson, L.E.	H	W	F	Nov 1866	33	Wd		6	0	AL	AL	AL	Farmer
	Virginia P.	D	W	F	Apr 1884	16	S				MS	AL	AL	
	May B.	D	W	F	Jun 1886	13	S				MS	AL	AL	
	Frank M.	S	W	M	Jun 1891	8	S				MS	AL	AL	
	Mandy	D	W	F	Feb 1894	6	S				MS	AL	AL	
	Lela	D	W	F	Jun 1898	2	S				MS	AL	AL	
158	Perry, R.M.	H	W	M	Dec 1834	65	M	46			SC	SC	SC	Farmer
	Mary I.	W	W	F	May 1835	65	M	46	4	6	SC	SC	SC	
159	Blount, W.A.	H	W	M	Jun 1876	24	M	0			MS	TX	AL	Farmer
	Ada V.	W	W	F	Sep 1879	20	M	0	0	0	MS	MS	MS	
160	McRae, William A.	H	W	M	Sep 1841	58	M	34			AL	NC	NC	Farmer
	Lou J.	W	W	F	Sep 1840	59	M	34	7	7	NC	NC	NC	
	John F.	S	W	M	Jun 1871	29	S				MS	AL	NC	Farmer
	W.B.	S	W	M	Jan 1873	27	S				MS	AL	NC	
	Sallie	D	W	F	May 1875	25	S				MS	AL	NC	
	Charley	S	W	M	Feb 1885	15	S				MS	AL	NC	

1	2	3	4	5	6	7	8	9	10	11	12	13	14	15
161	Gurley, J.E.	H	W	M	Jul 1871	28	M	5			AL	AL	AL	Farmer
	Annie L.	W	W	F	Jun 1872	27	M	5	3	2	TN	TN	TN	
	Bula L.	D	W	F	Aug 1896	3	S				AL	AL	TN	
	Nellie C.	D	W	F	Nov 1898	2	S				MS	AL	TN	
162	Gardner, Nancy	H	W	F	Aug1857	42	Wd		6	5	MS	MS	MS	Merchant
	Hattie	D	W	F	Jul 1876	23	S				MS	MS	MS	
	A.V.	D	W	F	Oct 1878	21	S				MS	MS	MS	
	Mandy	D	W	F	Mar 1882	18	S				MS	MS	MS	
	Ocenia	D	W	F	Sep 1884	15	S				MS	MS	MS	
	Robert B.	S	W	M	Mar 1887	13	S				MS	MS	MS	
163	Bickerstaff, Mary	H	W	F	Mar 1838	62	Wd		5	5	MS	SC	SC	Farmer
	Alice	D	W	F	Jan 1865	35	S				MS	AL	AL	
	A.T.	S	W	M	Jun 1871	28	S				MS	AL	MS	Farmer
	Mary A.	Sis	W	F	Jan 1826	74	S				AL	AL	AL	
164	Abbott, Martha	H	W	F	Jan 1859	41	Wd		4	3	MS	AL	MS	Farmer
	Mary A.	D	W	F	Jan 1885	15	S				MS	AL	MS	
	Annie M.	D	W	F	May 1888	12	S				MS	AL	MS	
	Iva L.	D	W	F	Aug 1892	7	S				MS	AL	MS	
165	Gardner, G.L.	H	W	M	May 1828	72	M	33			NC	NC	NC	Farmer
	Jennie	W	W	F	May 1843	57	M	33	4	4	MS	TN	TN	
	Myrtle	D	W	F	Aug 1877	22	S				MS	NC	MS	
166	Gardner, E.N.	H	W	M	Nov 1870	29	M	5			MS	NC	MS	Farmer
	Sallie W.	W	W	F	Nov 1874	25	M	5	2	2	MS	MS	TX	
	Gerty	D	W	F	May 1897	3	S				MS	MS	MS	
	Forest A.	S	W	M	Dec 1899	5/mo	S				MS	MS	MS	
167	Bickerstaff, J.H.	H	W	M	Sep 1861	38	M	10			MS	AL	AL	Farmer
	Mary T.	W	W	F	Dec 1868	31	M	10	5	5	MS	AL	AL	
	Dovie L.	D	W	F	Oct 1890	9	S				MS	MS	MS	
	Henry R.	S	W	M	Mar 1892	8	S				MS	MS	MS	
	William A.	S	W	M	Sep 1893	6	S				MS	MS	MS	
	Bonnie E.	D	W	F	Oct 1895	4	S				MS	MS	MS	
	Thomas T.	S	W	M	Jun 1898	2	S				MS	MS	MS	
168	Blount, F.M.	H	W	M	Aug 1854	46	M	29			TX	MS	SC	Farmer
	Margaret	W	W	F	Oct 1849	50	M	29	6	6	AL	NC	NC	
	Altie	D	W	F	Sep 1879	20	S				MS	TX	AL	
	Edna	D	W	F	Oct 1883	17	S				MS	TX	AL	
	Frank	S	W	M	Apr 1886	14	S				MS	TX	AL	
	Tankersley, Sam	Ser	B	M	May 1830	70	Wd				VA	VA	VA	Farm Laborer
169	Bickerstaff, J. N.	H	W	M	Feb 1868	32	M	6			MS	AL	AL	Farmer
	Mary J.	W	W	F	Sep 1871	28	M	6	4	4	MS	TX	AL	
	Guy	S	W	M	Nov 1894	5	S				MS	MS	MS	
	Reece	S	W	M	May 1896	4	S				MS	MS	MS	
	Audry	D	W	F	Sep 1898	1	S				MS	MS	MS	
	Mammie	D	W	F	Jan 1900	4/mo	S				MS	MS	MS	
170	Blount, T.	H	W	M	Feb 1875	25	M	3			MS	TX	AL	Farmer
	J.A.	W	W	F	Apr 1877	23	M	3	1	1	MS	MS	MS	
	Ethel	D	W	F	Jun 1899	11/mo	S				MS	MS	MS	
171	Blount, W.N.	H	W	M	Jan 1839	61	M	9			AL	MS	NC	Farmer
	Nonnie	W	W	F	Oct 1867	33	M	9	2	2	AL	GA	GA	
	Ruby	D	W	F	Apr 1892	8	S				MS	AL	AL	
	Mattie	D	W	F	Oct 1895	4	S				MS	AL	AL	
172	Blount, J.S.	H	W	M	Nov 1840	59	M	38			AL	MO	SC	Farmer

1	2	3	4	5	6	7	8	9	10	11	12	13	14	15
	A.D.	W	W	F	Jan 1836	54	M	38	0	0	AL	IN	SC	
	Liza	Sis	W	F	May 1837	63	S				AL	MO	SC	
173	Cornelius, M.	H	W	M	Apr 1859	41	M	19			MS	TN	TN	Farmer
	?	W	W	F	Jan 1861	39	M	19	4	3	MS	MS	AL	
	Florence	D	W	F	May 1892	8	S				MS	MS	MS	
	I.C.	D	W	F	Sep 1896	4	S				MS	MS	MS	
	Alma	D	W	F	Apr 1897	3	S				MS	MS	MS	
174	Russle, B.B.	H	W	M	Aug 1857	42	M	17			MS	TN	TN	Farmer
	E.E.	W	W	F	Feb 1855	45	M	17	2	1	MS	MS	AL	
	Dink	S	W	M	Mar 1888	12	S				MS	MS	MS	
175	Nagle, Charley	H	W	M	Nov 1874	26	M	0			MS	MS	MS	Sawer, Saw Mill
	Rilla	W	W	F	Nov 1881	19	M	0	0	0	MS	MS	MS	
	Johnny	Bro	W	M	May 1882	18	S				MS	MS	MS	
176	Flanigan, Green	H	W	M	Nov 1873	27	M	7			MS	MS	MS	Lumber Hand
	Cynthia	W	W	F	Aug 1872	27	M	7	3	3	MS	MS	MS	
	Luther	S	W	M	Dec 1892	7	S				MS	MS	MS	
	Mandy	D	W	F	Mar 1896	4	S				MS	MS	MS	
	Pearl	D	W	F	Aug 1898	1	S				MS	MS	MS	
177	Lancaster, Thomas	H	W	M	Aug 1864	35	M	11			AL	AL	AL	Sawer, Saw Mill
	Nellie	W	W	F	Nov 1872	27	M	11	6	4	AL	AL	AL	
	Tonny	S	W	M	Nov 1888	11	S				AL	AL	AL	
	Any	S	W	M	Jan 1891	9	S				AL	AL	AL	
	Luther	S	W	M	Jun 1898	2	S				MS	AL	AL	
	Grover	S	W	F	Apr 1899	1	S				MS	AL	AL	
178	Whitfield, John	H	W	M	Mar 1867	33	M	3			MS	MS	MS	Log Hauler, Saw Mill
	Orna	W	W	F	Mar 1880	20	M	3	1	0	AL	AL	AL	
179	Nunnley, R.L.	H	W	M	Mar 1871	30	M	10			MS	MS	MS	Fireman, Saw Mill
	Bettie	W	W	F	Sep 1869	30	M	10	5	4	MS	MS	MS	
	John	S	W	M	Apr 1891	8	S				MS	MS	MS	
	Willis	S	W	M	Feb 1893	7	S				MS	MS	MS	
	Dee	S	W	M	Aug 1896	3	S				MS	MS	MS	
	Ellmond	S	W	M	Dec 1898	1	S				MS	MS	MS	
180	Searcy, Daniel W.	H	W	M	May 1874	26	M	7			MS	MS	MS	School Teacher
	Kate L.	W	W	F	Feb 1873	27	M	7	4	3	MS	AL	GA	
	Roxie M.	D	W	F	Dec 1894	5	S				TX	MS	MS	
	Ora R.	D	W	F	Jul 1896	3	S				MS	MS	MS	
	Travis H.	S	W	M	Apr 1900	4/mo	S				MS	MS	MS	
181	Bennett, George	H	B	M	Jun 1877	22	M	4			MS	MS	AL	Farmer
	Mollie	W	B	F	Sep 1880	19	M	4	2	1	MS	AL	AL	
	Webster	S	B	M	Sep 1898	1	S				MS	MS	MS	
182	Barnett, S.T.	H	W	M	Mar 1856	44	M	14			MS	MS	MS	Farmer
	Nancy A.	W	W	F	May 1855	45	M	14	2	2	MS	AL	MS	
	Mary M.	D	W	F	Dec 1885	14	S				MS	MS	MS	
	Mandemia	D	W	F	Mar 1887	12	S				MS	MS	MS	
	Robinson, Jim	Ser	B	M	Feb 1882	22	S				MS	MS	MS	
183	Nickolson, Frank	H	W	M	Aug 1881	18	M	0			MS	MS	MS	Day Laborer
	Ruby	W	W	F	Sep 1878	21	M	0	0	0	MS	MS	MS	
184	Holder, Thomas M.	H	W	M	Dec 1865	34	M	14			MS	TN	MS	Farmer
	Miney	W	W	F	Oct 1864	35	M	14	6	6	MS	MS	MS	
	Allen	S	W	M	Jan 1887	12	S				MS	MS	MS	
	Alva	S	W	M	May 1890	10	S				MS	MS	MS	

1	2	3	4	5	6	7	8	9	10	11	12	13	14	15
	Clora	D	W	F	Mar 1891	9	S				MS	MS	MS	
	Milton	S	W	M	May 1893	7	S				MS	MS	MS	
	Alan	S	W	M	Aug 1895	4	S				MS	MS	MS	
	Eddy	S	W	M	Mar 1898	2	S				MS	MS	MS	
	Page, Jim	Ser	W	M	Jul 1881	18	S				MS	MS	MS	Farm Laborer
185	Champion, John	H	W	M	May 1860	40	M	12			AL	AL	AL	Farmer
	Annie	W	W	F	Mar 1870	30	M	12	4	2	AL	AL	AL	
	Sarah J.	D	W	F	Jan 1891	9	S				MS	MS	MS	
	Robert I.	S	W	M	Feb 1897	3	S				MS	MS	MS	
186	Warren,Landa	H	B	M	Mar 1870	30	M	6			AL	AL	AL	Farmer
	Callie	W	B	F	Feb 1881	21	M	6	3	3	AL	AL	AL	
	Esria	D	B	F	Sep 1894	5	S				AL	AL	AL	
	Edgar	S	B	M	Nov 1898	2	S				TN	AL	AL	
	R.D.	S	B	M	May 1899	1	S				TN	AL	AL	
	Robert	Bro	B	M	Feb 1875	25	S				AL	AL	AL	Farm Laborer
187	Burns, William	H	W	M	May 1855	45	M	10			MS	MS	MS	Farmer
	Mary	W	W	F	Jan 1865	35	M	10	7	5	AL	AL	AL	
	Hassie	D	W	F	Feb 1885	15	S				AL	MS	AL	
	John	S	W	M	Sep 1887	12	S				AL	MS	AL	
	Morgan	S	W	M	Jan 1890	10	S				AL	MS	AL	
	Marchell	S	W	M	Jan 1895	5	S				AL	MS	AL	
	Mattie	D	W	F	Feb 1898	2	S				AL	MS	AL	
188	Hunt, C.W.	H	W	M	Sep 1855	44	M	20			AL	AL	AL	Farmer
	N.M.	W	W	F	Aug 1856	43	M	20	0	0	AL	AL	AL	
189	Kay, Ed	H	W	M	May 1872	28	M	2			AL	AL	AL	Farmer
	Hettie	W	W	F	Nov 1870	29	M	2	1	1	AL	AL	AL	
	Lillian	D	W	F	Oct 1899	7/mo	S				MS	AL	AL	
190	Burns, F.M.	H	W	M	Jan 1853	45	M	17			AL	SC	AL	Farmer
	Mattie	W	W	F	Dec 1861	38	M	17	6	5	MS	VA	MS	
	Carrie	D	W	F	Apr 1887	13	S				MS	AL	MS	
	Ben	S	W	M	Mar 1890	10	S				MS	AL	MS	
	Tay	S	W	M	Oct 1891	8	S				MS	AL	MS	
	Bessie	D	W	F	Aug 1894	5	S				MS	AL	MS	
	Ettie	D	W	F	Jan 1897	3	S				MS	AL	MS	
	Lee, J.D.	Bdr	W	M	Oct 1876	23	S				AL	AL	AL	Physician
191	Gillimon, J.B.	H	W	M	Feb 1856	44	M	18			MS	NC	NC	Farmer
	M.E.	W	W	F	Feb 1858	42	M	18	6	5	MS	TN	TN	
	Mary L.	D	W	F	Sep1885	14	S				MS	MS	MS	
	J.R.	S	W	M	Aug 1888	11	S				MS	MS	MS	
	John G.	S	W	M	Sep 1890	9	S				MS	MS	MS	
	James E.	S	W	M	Sep 1892	7	S				MS	MS	MS	
	Mattie	D	W	F	Oct 1894	5	S				MS	MS	MS	
192	Wrenn, W.F.	H	W	M	Aug 1857	42	M	11			SC	SC	SC	Farmer
	Ethel	W	W	F	Jun 1865	35	M	11	5	4	MS	SC	AL	
	Annie M.	D	W	F	Oct 1889	10	S				MS	SC	MS	
	Lida A.	D	W	F	Sep 1891	8	S				MS	SC	MS	
	William E.	S	W	M	May 1896	4	S				MS	SC	MS	
	Mattie W.	D	W	F	Oct 1898	1	S				MS	SC	MS	
193	Kay, W.P.	H	W	M	Apr 1870	29	M	9			AL	AL	AL	Farmer
	Georgia	W	W	F	Jun 1870	30	M	9	4	4	AL	AL	AL	
	Ellis	S	W	M	Jun 1891	9	S				AL	AL	AL	
	Ethel	D	W	F	Aug 1892	7	S				AL	AL	AL	
	Emmends	S	W	M	Aug 1895	4	S				MS	AL	AL	
	Bonnie	D	W	F	Mar 1899	1	S				MS	AL	AL	

1	2	3	4	5	6	7	8	9	10	11	12	13	14	15
194	Alexander, Joe	H	B	M	Mar 1855	45	M	30			MS	AL	AL	Farmer
	Betty	W	B	F	Apr 1855	45	M	30	11	8	MS	MS	MS	
	Ed	S	B	M	Mar 1878	22	S				MS	MS	MS	Farm Laborer
	Gus	S	B	M	Apr 1881	19	S				MS	MS	MS	Farm Laborer
	Joe	S	B	M	Aug 1882	17	S				MS	MS	MS	
	Thomas	S	B	M	Jul 1886	13	S				MS	MS	MS	
	Loula	D	B	F	Jan 1892	8	S				MS	MS	MS	
	Carrie	D	B	F	Oct 1893	6	S				MS	MS	MS	
	Mattie	D	B	F	Nov 1897	2	S				MS	MS	MS	
195	Smith, Marion	H	B	M	Mar 1858	42	M	10			AL	AL	AL	Farmer
	Tilda	W	B	F	Jan 1875	25	M	10	6	5	AL	AL	AL	
	Lida	D	B	F	Sep 1891	8	S				MS	AL	AL	
	Mollie	D	B	F	Nov 1892	7	S				MS	AL	AL	
	Londa	S	B	M	Dec 1894	5	S				MS	AL	AL	
	Gurn	S	B	M	Nov 1896	3	S				MS	AL	AL	
	Modenia	D	B	F	Feb 1899	1	S				MS	AL	AL	
196	Johnson, John	H	B	M	Jun 1869	40	M	3			AL	AL	AL	Day Laborer
	Indiana	W	B	F	May 1875	25	M	3	3	2	AL	AL	AL	
197	Savington, C.	H	W	M	May 1871	29	M	11			AL	AL	AL	Farmer
	Bima	W	W	F	Dec 1871	28	M	11	4	3	MS	AL	IL	
	William H.	S	W	M	Jan 1890	10	S				MS	AL	MS	
	James W.	S	W	M	Jul 1895	4	S				MS	AL	MS	
	Emma J.	D	W	F	Jun 1897	2	S				MS	AL	MS	
198	Bennett, AL	H	B	M	May 1850	50	M	30			AL	AL	AL	Farmer
	Emeline	W	B	F	Jan 1855	45	M	30	10	8	AL	AL	AL	
	Andrew	S	B	M	Oct 1880	19	S				MS	AL	AL	
	Charley	S	B	M	Dec 1882	17	S				MS	AL	AL	
	Savanah	D	B	F	Aug 1886	13	S				MS	AL	AL	
	Eva	D	B	F	May 1888	12	S				MS	AL	AL	
	Riley	S	B	M	Dec 1894	5	S				MS	AL	AL	
199	Lambert, Lou	H	W	F	Feb 1865	35	Wd		7	6	MS	AL	AL	
	Frank	S	W	M	Jan 1886	14	S				MS	MS	AL	
	Lizzie	D	W	F	May 1888	12	S				MS	MS	AL	
	Mattie	D	W	F	Mar 1890	10	S				MS	MS	AL	
	Nina	D	W	F	Jun 1891	8	S				MS	MS	AL	
	Eddy	D	W	F	Feb 1900	3/mo	S				MS	MS	AL	
200	Bennett, John	H	B	M	May 1877	23	M	5			MS	AL	AL	Farmer
	Mattie B.	W	B	F	Jan 1878	22	M	5	1	3	MS	MS	MS	
	Alford	S	B	M	Nov 1894	5	S				MS	MS	MS	
	Eva	D	B	F	Feb 1898	2	S				MS	MS	MS	
	Andrew	S	B	M	Jan 1900	0/mo	S				MS	MS	MS	
201	Southward, Alice	H	B	M	Jan 1850	50	M	30			MS	MS	MS	Farmer
	Disay	W	B	F	Mar 1855	45	M	30	13	8	MS	MS	MS	
	George	S	B	M	Jun 1879	20	M	0			MS	MS	MS	Farm Laborer
	Lucy	DiL	B	F	Oct 1882	18	M	0	0		MS	MS	MS	
	Eddy	S	B	M	Oct 1881	18	S				MS	MS	MS	Farm Laborer
	Sammy	S	B	M	Sep 1883	16	S				MS	MS	MS	
	James	S	B	M	Aug 1888	11	S				MS	MS	MS	
	Pearl	D	B	F	May 1891	9	S				MS	MS	MS	
	Etta	D	B	F	Mar 1896	4	S				MS	MS	MS	
	Maidy	D	B	F	Jul 1899	10/mo	S				MS	MS	MS	
202	Martin, Jake	H	B	M	Aug 1862	37	M	13			AL	AL	AL	Farmer
	Dilla	W	B	F	May 1865	35	M	13	8	8	MS	AL	AL	
	Sallie	D	B	F	Apr 1883	17	S				MS	AL	AL	

1	2	3	4	5	6	7	8	9	10	11	12	13	14	15
	Florence	D	B	F	May 1884	16	S				MS	AL	AL	
	Winston	S	B	M	Apr 1885	15	S				MS	AL	AL	
	Alice	D	B	F	Jun 1886	13	S				MS	AL	AL	
	Finis	S	B	M	Mar 1889	11	S				MS	AL	AL	
	Glensy	S	B	M	Jan 1891	9	S				MS	AL	AL	
	Myrtie	D	B	F	Oct 1892	7	S				MS	AL	AL	
	Edgar	S	B	M	Dec 1895	4	S				MS	AL	AL	
	Homer	S	B	M	May 1899	1	S				MS	AL	AL	
203 Rutherford, R.H.		H	W	M	Jan 1877	23	M	0			MS	AL	MS	Farmer
	Martha	W	W	F	Aug 1882	17	M	0	0	0	AL	AL	GA	
204 Rutherford, Harriett		H	W	F	May 1840	60	Wd		7	5	MS	GA	NC	
	J.N.	S	W	M	Feb 1873	27	S				MS	AL	MS	Farm Laborer
205 Jourdan, S.A.		H	W	M	Sep 1876	23	M	5			AL	AL	AL	Farmer
	Mamie	W	W	F	Jun 1876	23	M	5	2	2	MS	MS	MS	
	John	S	W	M	May 1897	3	S				MS	AL	MS	
	Maud	D	W	F	Oct 1899	7/mo	S				MS	AL	MS	
206 Gable, J.H.		H	W	M	May 1860	40	M	21			MS	GA	GA	Farmer
	Terressie	W	W	F	Mar 1864	36	M	21	6	6	AL	AL	AL	
	Mattie	D	W	F	Oct 1880	19	S				MS	MS	AL	
	Gus	S	W	M	Nov 1884	15	S				AL	MS	AL	
	Eva	D	W	F	Oct 1889	10	S				MS	MS	AL	
	Clara	D	W	F	Dec 1891	8	S				MS	MS	AL	
	Pearcey	S	W	M	Dec 1894	5	S				MS	MS	AL	
	Elona	D	W	F	Apr 1898	2	S				MS	MS	AL	
207 Kay, Joe M.		H	W	M	Feb 1863	37	M	13			AL	SC	AL	School Teacher
	M.E.	W	W	F	Nov 1863	36	M	13	4	3	AL	SC	SC	
	Grady T.	S	W	M	Sep 1892	7	S				AL	AL	AL	
	J.A.	D	W	F	Dec 1893	6	S				AL	AL	AL	
	J.C.	S	W	M	Dec 1899	0/mo	S				MS	AL	AL	
	Martin, C.M.	Ser	B	M	Apr 1879	21	S				MS	AL	AL	Farm Laborer
208 Burns, L.M.		H	W	M	Jan 1876	24	M	1			AL	AL	AL	Farmer
	Della	W	W	F	Oct 1883	16	M	1	0	0	AL	AL	AL	
	Josephine	M	W	F	Feb 1832	68	Wd		12	11	AL	AL	AL	
209 Cornelison, I.H.		H	W	M	Jan 1876	24	M	2			MS	MS	MS	Farm Laborer
	Josephine	W	W	F	Jan 1879	21	M	2	1	0	AL	AL	AL	
210 Rutherford, A.H.		H	W	M	Nov 1866	33	M	9			MS	NC	MS	Farmer
	Willie	W	W	F	Feb 1875	25	M	9	4	4	MS	MS	MS	
	James E.	S	W	M	Jul 1891	8	S				AL	MS	MS	
	Flora B.	D	W	F	Dec 1894	5	S				AL	MS	MS	
	Andy E.	S	W	M	Feb 1897	3	S				AL	MS	MS	
	Elbert L.	S	W	M	Nov 1899	6/mo	S				MS	MS	MS	
211 Twillin, J.W.		H	W	M	Mar 1866	34	M	11			AL	AL	AL	Farmer
	Olie	W	W	F	Dec 1872	27	M	11	4	3	MS	MS	MS	
	Forest	S	W	M	Jun 1890	9	S				MS	AL	MS	
	Earnest	S	W	M	Sep 1892	7	S				MS	AL	MS	
	Sydney	S	W	M	Apr 1896	4	S				MS	AL	MS	
212 Mann, W.A.		H	W	M	Jun 1864	35	M	2			AL	AL	AL	Farmer
	Mary	W	W	F	Oct 1872	27	M	2	0	0	MS	TN	MS	
	Richard	S	W	M	Apr 1888	12	S				MS	AL	MS	
	Shellie	S	W	M	Mar 1890	10	S				MS	AL	MS	
	Horace	S	W	M	Jan 1892	8	S				MS	AL	MS	
	Mary	D	W	F	Oct 1893	6	S				MS	AL	MS	

1	2	3	4	5	6	7	8	9	10	11	12	13	14	15
213	Nelson, J.J.	H	W	M	Apr 1862	38	M	16			AL	SC	TN	Farmer
	Alice C.	W	W	F	Jan 1867	33	M	16	9	7	AL	GA	TN	
	Jessie L.	D	W	F	Sep 1884	15	S				MS	AL	AL	
	Minnie E.	D	W	F	May 1886	14	S				MS	AL	AL	
	Sarah C.	D	W	F	Mar 1888	12	S				MS	AL	AL	
	Oscar	S	W	M	Jun 1890	10	S				MS	AL	AL	
	Omer	S	W	M	Sep 1891	9	S				MS	AL	AL	
	Marshall	S	W	M	Jan 1896	4	S				MS	AL	AL	
	Eular	D	W	F	Sep 1898	1	S				MS	AL	AL	
214	Savington, R.S.	H	W	M	Mar 1856	44	M	17			AL	GA	TN	Farmer
	Annie	W	W	F	Dec 1861	38	M	17	6	4	MS	AL	MS	
	Mattie	D	W	F	Jun 1883	17	S				MS	AL	MS	
	Neppie	D	W	F	Jun 1886	13	S				MS	AL	MS	
	James	S	W	M	Feb 1889	11	S				MS	AL	MS	
	Jodie	S	W	M	Aug 1897	2	S				MS	AL	MS	
	Brandson, Frank	Ser	W	M	Mar 1885	15	S				MS	AL	MS	
215	Sanders, T.M.	H	W	M	Oct 1872	27	M	5			MS	MS	MS	Farmer
	Ester	W	W	F	Nov 1880	19	M	5	2	2	MS	MS	MS	
	Willie	D	W	F	Jan 1898	2	S				MS	MS	MS	
	Virdie	D	W	F	Jan 1900	4/mo	S				MS	MS	MS	
216	Wallis, P.B.	H	W	M	Jun 1852	47	M	20			GA	GA	GA	Farmer
	Mary F.	W	W	F	Apr 1847	53	M	20			AL	AL	GA	
	Brown, James	FiL	W	M	Sep 1819	80	Wd				TN	KY	NC	
217	Brown, J.C.	H	W	M	Sep 1850	49	M	13			AL	TN	NC	Farmer
	Mallie	W	W	F	Oct 1863	36	M	13	7	6	AL	AL	GA	
	Lester	S	W	M	Jul 1883	16	S				MS	AL	AL	
	Molly D.	D	W	F	Feb 1888	12	S				MS	AL	AL	
	Snulphus F.	S	W	M	Sep 1889	10	S				MS	AL	AL	
	Ila B.	D	W	F	Sep 1891	8	S				MS	AL	AL	
	Nillie B.	D	W	F	Oct 1893	6	S				MS	AL	AL	
	Lizzie	D	W	F	Sep 1897	2	S				MS	AL	AL	
	Tillie	D	W	F	Jun 1899	10/mo	S				MS	AL	AL	
218	Twitty, R.B.	H	W	M	Apr 1863	37	M	18			AL	SC	TN	Farmer
	Fannie	W	W	F	Apr 1864	36	M	18	7	7	AL	AL	TN	
	Willie	S	W	M	Jan 1886	14	S				AL	AL	AL	
	Lillian	D	W	F	Sep 1889	10	S				AL	AL	AL	
	Henry	S	W	M	Apr 1892	8	S				MS	AL	AL	
	Omer	S	W	M	Mar 1895	5	S				MS	AL	AL	
	Fred	S	W	M	Jan 1897	3	S				MS	AL	AL	
	May B.	D	W	F	May 1899	1	S				MS	AL	AL	
	Twitty, Hannah	M	W	F	May 1825	75	Wd		5	4	TN	TN	AL	
219	Buchanan, R.W.	H	W	M	Jan 1836	64	M	11			AL	NC	NC	Farmer
	Belle G.	W	W	F	Aug 1865	34	M	11	1	1	AL	GA	GA	
	Grover	S	W	M	Dec 1892	7	S				MS	AL	AL	
	Robinson, Mary	MiL	W	F	Apr 1834	66	Wd		5	5	GA	SC	SC	
220	West, J.J.	H	W	M	Mar 1854	46	M	25			MS	TN	MS	Farmer
	H.P.	W	W	F	May 1852	48	M	25	5	4	MS	AL	MS	
	William T.	S	W	M	Mar 1882	18	S				MS	MS	MS	Farm Laborer
	Ada M.	D	W	F	May 1889	11	S				MS	MS	MS	
221	Standley, W.F.	H	W	M	May 1877	23	M	5			MS	MS	MS	Farmer
	Nora	W	W	F	Oct 1877	23	M	5	2	1	MS	MS	MS	
	Mandy	D	W	F	Aug 1896	3	S				MS	MS	MS	
222	Williams, S.R.	H	W	M	Aug 1837	62	M	29			AL	AL	AL	Farmer
	Emily	W	W	F	Apr 1846	54	M	29	7	7	AL	AL	AL	

1	2	3	4	5	6	7	8	9	10	11	12	13	14	15
	J.B.	S	W	M	Oct 1886	23	S				AL	AL	AL	Farmer
	Bertha	D	W	F	Mar 1880	20	S				AL	AL	AL	
	Lucy	D	W	F	Feb 1882	18	S				AL	AL	AL	
223	Beard, I.S.	H	W	M	Apr 1841	59	M	18			GA	GA	GA	Farmer
	Liza J.	W	W	F	Jun 1853	46	M	18	1	1	MS	MS	MS	
	West, Martha	MiL	W	F	Aug 1823	76	Wd		7	3	MS	MS	MS	
224	Hamiel, James J.	H	W	M	Nov 1859	40	Wd				MS	GA	AL	Farmer
	Mady E.	D	W	F	Oct 1891	8	S				MS	MS	MS	
	John W.	S	W	M	Oct 1891	8	S				MS	MS	MS	
	Oscar L.	S	W	M	Sep 1892	7	S				MS	MS	MS	
	Thomas C.	S	W	M	Oct 1895	4	S				MS	MS	MS	
225	Hale, D.M.	H	W	M	Aug 1870	29	M	10			MS	MS	MS	Farmer
	N.M.	W	W	F	Mar 1873	27	M	10	3	1	AL	AL	GA	
	A.L.	D	W	F	Nov 1894	5	S				MS	MS	AL	
	Martin, John	Bdr	W	M	Mar 1878	22	S				MS	MS	MS	Off bearer, Saw Mill
226	Medley, D.C.	H	W	M	Feb 1848	52	M	29			MS	MS	MS	Black Smith
	Malisa E.	W	W	F	Apr 1854	46	M	29	9	8	AL	SC	AL	
	Tilman C.	S	W	M	Feb 1882	18	S				MS	MS	AL	Day Laborer
	Robert D.	S	W	M	Dec 1883	16	S				MS	MS	AL	Day Laborer
	Lizz E.	D	W	F	Mar 1885	15	S				MS	MS	AL	
	Milley E.	D	W	F	May 1887	13	S				MS	MS	AL	
	Henry O.	S	W	M	Jul 1891	8	S				MS	MS	AL	
	Oen E.	S	W	M	Oct 1893	6	S				MS	MS	AL	
	Patterson, William	Bdr	W	M	Jan 1879	21	S				MS	AL	GA	Leversetter, Saw Mill
227	Sparks, J.S.	H	W	M	Oct 1864	35	M	11			MS	MS	MS	Farmer
	Mary E.	W	W	F	Mar 1870	30	M	11	6	5	TN	GA	MS	
	James C.	S	W	M	oct 1889	10	S				MS	MS	MS	
	Lewis J.	S	W	M	May 1891	9	S				MS	MS	TN	
	Marian E.	D	W	F	Feb 1895	5	S				MS	MS	TN	
	Quiny V.	D	W	F	Dec 1896	3	S				MS	MS	TN	
	James V.	S	W	M	Jan 1899	1	S				MS	MS	TN	
228	Waters, M.C.	H	W	M	Feb 1866	34	M	10			AL	AL	GA	Sawyer, Saw Mill
	Janie	W	W	F	Nov 1874	34	M	10	3	3	MS	MS	AL	
	James	S	W	M	Feb 1891	9	S				MS	AL	MS	
	Robert	S	W	M	Feb 1893	7	S				MS	AL	MS	
	Addie	D	W	F	Oct 1895	4	S				MS	AL	MS	
	Sanders, Robert	Bdr	W	M	May 1884	16	S				MS	MS	MS	Saws logs, Saw Mill
229	Gray, John	H	W	M	May 1877	23	M	2			MS	AL	MS	Off bearer, Saw Mill
	Hannah	W	W	F	Feb 1884	16	M	2	0	0	MS	MS	MS	
230	McAnally, R.B.	H	W	M	Jul 1869	30	M	11			MS	MS	MS	Leversetter, Saw Mill
	Etta	W	W	F	Apr 1869	30	M	11	5	4	MS	MS	MS	
	Sam	S	W	M	May 1891	9	S				MS	MS	MS	
	Alva	S	W	M	Oct 1894	5	S				MS	MS	MS	
	Cora	D	W	F	Mar 1897	3	S				MS	MS	MS	
	Rufus	S	W	M	Jan 1899	1	S				MS	MS	MS	
231	Hellums, H.J.	H	W	M	Jan 1868	32	M	3			MS	MS	MS	Sawyer, Saw Mill
	J.E.	W	W	F	Oct 1876	23	M	3	3	2	MS	MS	MS	
	James	S	W	M	Nov 1897	2	S				MS	MS	MS	
	Mattie	D	W	F	Mar 1893	7	S				MS	MS	MS	
	Sanders, W.L.	Bdr	W	M	Jul 1872	27	S				MS	MS	MS	Fireman, Saw Mill
	Wadkins, B.W.	Bdr	W	M	Oct 1862	37	S				MS	MS	MS	Sawyer, Saw Mill
232	Wright, Wesley F.	H	W	M	Feb 1859	41	M	11			MS	TN	TN	Farmer
	Ella	W	W	F	Oct 1871	28	M	11	3	3	MS	MS	MS	

1	2	3	4	5	6	7	8	9	10	11	12	13	14	15
	Thomas O.	S	W	M	Aug 1889	10	S				MS	MS	MS	
	Kizzie W.	D	W	F	Aug 1892	7	S				MS	MS	MS	
	May B.	D	W	F	Aug 1897	2	S				MS	MS	MS	
233	Gober, A.J.	H	W	M	Oct 1859	40	M	24			AL	AL	AL	Farmer
	Rachel	W	W	F	Jul 1858	41	M	24			AL	AL	AL	
	James W.	S	W	M	Jun 1876	23	S				AL	AL	AL	Farmer
	Mattie T.	D	W	F	Aug 1879	20	S				AL	AL	AL	
	George N.	S	W	M	Jan 1882	18	S				AL	AL	AL	Farm Laborer
	Elbert W.	S	W	M	Mar 1884	16	S				AL	AL	AL	
	Mel V.	D	W	F	Jul 1886	13	S				AL	AL	AL	
	Edgar B.	S	W	M	Mar 1889	11	S				AL	AL	AL	
	Susan R.	D	W	F	Aug 1891	8	S				AL	AL	AL	
	Maurine D.	D	W	F	Apr 1894	6	S				AL	AL	AL	
	Audry O.	D	W	F	Jan 1898	2	S				AL	AL	AL	
234	Pace, A.G.	H	W	M	Jun 1826	73	M	45			TN	NC	NC	Farmer
	Mary A.	W	W	F	May 1839	61	M	45	6	2	MS	NC	TN	
	Ben C.	S	W	M	Mar 1878	22	S				MS	TN	MS	School Teacher
235	Pace, Sign	H	W	M	Dec 1880	19	M	1			MS	TN	MS	Farmer
	Ada	W	W	F	Sep 1880	19	M	1	1	1	MS	MS	MS	
	Cecil B.	S	W	M	Feb 1900	3/mo	S				MS	MS	MS	
236	Page, W.D.	H	W	M	Mar 1847	53	M	11			AL	AL	AL	Farmer
	Martha A.	W	W	F	Apr 1844	56	M	11	0	0	MS	MS	MS	
	R.B.	S	W	M	Feb 1887	12	S				MS	AL	AL	
237	Montgomery, J.C.	H	W	M	Feb 1853	57	M	30			AL	KY	TN	Farmer
	Mary S.	W	W	F	Dec 1846	53	M	30	10	8	SC	SC	SC	
	Cleo P.	D	W	F	Nov 1880	19	S				MS	AL	SC	
	D.W.	S	W	M	Jun 1871	28	S				MS	AL	SC	Farmer
	A.H.	S	W	M	Nov 1874	26	S				MS	AL	SC	Day Laborer
	W.A.	S	W	M	Nov 1884	16	S				MS	AL	SC	Farm Laborer
	Thomas L.	S	W	M	Nov 1886	14	S				MS	AL	SC	Farm Laborer
238	Allen, D.W.	H	W	M	Apr 1822	78	M	50			SC	SC	SC	Farmer
	Catherine	W	W	F	Nov 1820	80	M	50	2	1	SC	SC	SC	
239	Underwood, D.R.	H	W	M	Oct 1866	33	M	12			TN	TN	TN	Farmer
	Lou	W	W	F	Jun 1867	32	M	12	5	5	AL	AL	AL	
	Berdie	D	W	F	Jul 1889	10	S				MS	TN	AL	
	Ada	D	W	F	Dec 1891	8	S				MS	TN	AL	
	Mammie	D	W	F	Dec 1893	6	S				MS	TN	AL	
	Mattie	D	W	F	Jul 1895	4	S				MS	TN	AL	
	James	S	W	M	Feb 1899	1	S				MS	TN	AL	
240	Storment, D.W.	H	W	M	Nov 1861	38	M	6			MS	TN	TN	Farmer
	Sallie	W	W	F	Mar 1863	37	M	6	2	2	MS	AL	SC	
	Arvilla	D	W	F	Feb 1896	4	S				MS	MS	MS	
	Lunsford	S	W	M	Sep 1897	2	S				MS	MS	MS	
241	Pace, R.A.	H	W	M	Mar 1860	40	M	19			MS	TN	TN	Farmer
	Amanda	W	W	F	Jul 1859	40	M	19	3	2	MS	AL	TN	Farmer
	Cora	D	W	F	Aug 1885	14	S				MS	MS	MS	
	Della	D	W	F	Jul 1892	7	S				MS	MS	MS	
242	Storment, T.J.	H	W	M	Aug 1858	41	S				MS	SC	SC	Farmer
	Sarah	Sis	W	F	Apr 1838	62	S				SC	SC	SC	
	Montgomery, J.P.	Bdr	W	M	Mar 1846	54	W				MS	GA	GA	Farmer
243	Riggs, J.M.	H	W	M	Dec 1852	42	M	20			AL	AL	MS	Farmer
	Sarah R.	W	W	F	Jan 1857	43	M	20	5	5	AL	AL	AL	

1	2	3	4	5	6	7	8	9	10	11	12	13	14	15
	Ermine	D	W	F	Oct 1885	14	S				AL	AL	AL	
	Sarah N.	D	W	F	Feb 1893	7	S				AL	AL	AL	
	William R.	S	W	M	Nov 1894	5	S				TX	AL	AL	
	John I.	S	W	M	Jun 1897	2	S				AL	AL	AL	
	Steward, Sarah	MiL	W	F	Dec 1832	67	Wd		11	3	AL	AL	AL	
244	Hill, Mary J.	H	W	F	Mar 1852	48	S				MS	NC	TN	Farmer
	Sarah L.	Sis	W	F	Jul 1854	45	S				MS	NC	TN	
245	Hill, M.C.	H	W	M	Mar 1839	61	M	36			MS	NC	TN	Farmer
	I.J.	W	W	F	Jun 1849	57	M	36	12	12	MS	TN	TN	
	Charley	S	W	M	Nov 1877	22	S				MS	MS	MS	Farmer
	Hester F.	D	W	F	Apr 1881	19	S				MS	MS	MS	
	Walter N.	S	W	M	Nov 1882	18	S				MS	MS	MS	
	Perry T.	S	W	M	Jun 1884	16	S				MS	MS	MS	
	Kizzie	D	W	F	Feb 1888	12	S				MS	MS	MS	
	Tinnie	D	W	F	Oct 1890	9	S				MS	MS	MS	
246	Hill, J.W.	H	W	M	Nov 1874	25	M	0			MS	MS	MS	Farmer
	Allie B.	W	W	F	Mar 1877	23	M	0	0	0	MS	MS	MS	
247	Hill, J.C.	H	W	M	Oct 1871	28	M	6			MS	MS	MS	Farmer
	M.J.	W	W	F	Nov 1869	30	M	6	3	3	MS	MS	MS	
	Virdie N.	D	W	F	Dec 1894	5	S				MS	MS	MS	
	Pearl	D	W	F	Mar 1897	3	S				MS	MS	MS	
	Exford	S	W	M	Aug 1899	9/mo	S				MS	MS	MS	
248	Gray, W.P.	H	W	M	Jul 1865	34	M	15			MS	MS	MS	Farmer
	Ellen	W	W	F	Jan 1865	35	M	15	7	7	MS	MS	MS	
	Jesse	S	W	M	Mar 1885	15	S				MS	MS	MS	
	Effie J.	D	W	F	Dec 1886	13	S				MS	MS	MS	
	Burton	S	W	M	Jan 1887	11	S				MS	MS	MS	
	Illa	D	W	F	Apr 1891	9	S				MS	MS	MS	
	Oma	D	W	F	May 1892	8	S				MS	MS	MS	
	Lilly	D	W	F	Jul 1893	6	S				MS	MS	MS	
	Altie	D	W	F	Jul 1896	3	S				MS	MS	MS	
249	Gober, G.W.	H	W	M	Oct 1851	48	M	28			AL	AL	AL	Farmer
	Mary	W	W	F	Mar 1857	49	M	28	10	10	AL	AL	AL	
	Alma	D	W	F	Apr 1878	22	S				AL	AL	AL	
	Harvey	S	W	M	Feb 1880	20	S				AL	AL	AL	Farm Laborer
	Alice	D	W	F	Jul 1885	14	S				AL	AL	AL	
	Ora	D	W	F	Sep 1887	12	S				AL	AL	AL	
	Georgie	D	W	F	Apr 1890	10	S				AL	AL	AL	
	Flora	D	W	F	Oct 1892	7	S				AL	AL	AL	
	Eva	D	W	F	Apr 1897	3	S				AL	AL	AL	
	Dobbs, Susan	M	W	F	Oct 1822	72	Wd		10	9	AL	AL	AL	
250	Hundley, W.M.	H	W	M	Feb 1845	55	M	29			AL	AL	AL	Farmer
	Callie	W	W	F	Nov 1850	49	M	29	3	3	MS	MS	MS	
	Mandy	D	W	F	Sep 1882	17	S				MS	AL	MS	
	Willie	S	W	M	May 1886	14	S				MS	AL	MS	
251	Storment, G.W.	H	W	M	Oct 1857	42	M	19			MS	MS	MS	Farmer
	Mattie	W	W	F	Jan 1864	36	M	19	5	5	MS	MS	MS	
	Craig	S	W	M	May 1883	17	S				MS	MS	MS	
	Bula	D	W	F	Jan 1886	14	S				MS	MS	MS	
	Claudy	D	W	F	Sep 1887	12	S				MS	MS	MS	
	Seth	S	W	M	Jul 1891	8	S				MS	MS	MS	
	Allie	D	W	F	Nov 1893	6	S				MS	MS	MS	
252	Elliott, J.W.	H	W	M	Nov 1852	47	M	27			AL	AL	AL	Farmer
	Penelopia	W	W	F	May 1855	45	M	27	9	7	AL	AL	AL	

1	2	3	4	5	6	7	8	9	10	11	12	13	14	15
	Charles I	S	W	M	Jun 1879	20	M	0			AL	AL	AL	Farm Laborer
	Dena	DiL	W	F	Feb 1884	16	M	0	0		AL	AL	AL	
	Thomas J.	S	W	M	May 1886	14	S				AL	AL	AL	
	George W.	S	W	M	Jul 1889	11	S				AL	AL	AL	
	Lomy O.	D	W	F	Jul 1891	8	S				AL	AL	AL	
253	Storment, W.T.	H	W	M	Jun 1848	51	M	12			MS	MS	MS	Farmer
	Tinnie	W	W	F	May 1850	50	M	12	0	0	MS	MS	MS	
	Sallie	Sis	W	F	Jul 1847	52	S				SC	SC	SC	
	Morrison, Andrew	Ser	B	M	Mar 1883	17	S				MS	MS	MS	Farm Laborer
	Rufus	Ser	B	M	Mar 1887	13	S				MS	MS	MS	Farm Laborer
254	Robinson, D.	H	B	M	Mar 1852	48	M	26			MS	MS	MS	Farmer
	Polly	W	B	F	Jan 1856	44	M	26	9	5	AL	AL	AL	
	July	D	B	F	Sep 1879	20	S				AL	MS	AL	
	Mary	D	B	F	Feb 1882	18	S				AL	MS	AL	
	Gib	S	B	M	Mar 1889	11	S				AL	MS	AL	At School
	Modenia	D	B	F	Jan 1896	4	S				MS	MS	AL	
255	Martin, Tom	H	B	M	Jan 1845	55	M	21			MS	AL	MS	Farmer
	Catherine	W	B	F	Feb 1855	45	M	21	7	6	AL	AL	AL	
	Margaret	D	B	F	Mar 1880	20	S				AL	MS	AL	
	John	S	B	M	Jul 1881	18	S				AL	MS	AL	
	James	S	B	M	Jul 1883	16	S				AL	MS	AL	
	Hose	S	B	M	Aug 1885	14	S				AL	MS	AL	
	Josie	D	B	F	Mar 1894	6	S				MS	MS	AL	
	Bertie	D	B	F	May 1896	4	S				MS	AL	MS	
256	Findley, Jim	H	B	M	May 1873	27	M	4			AL	AL	AL	Farmer
	Lee	W	B	F	Mar 1879	21	M	4	2	2	MS	AL	AL	
	Lilly	D	B	F	May 1897	3	S				MS	AL	MS	
	Ervine	S	B	M	May 1899	1	S				MS	AL	MS	
257	Burgess, Bill	H	B	M	Mar 1850	50	M	30			AL	AL	AL	Farmer
	Rendia	W	B	F	Apr 1850	50	M	30			AL	AL	AL	
	Willie	D	B	F	Jul 1867	32	M	7	1	1	AL	AL	AL	
	Harden, Coy	SiL	B	M	May 1870	30	M	7			MS	MS	MS	Day Laborer
	Burgess, Wesley	SiL	B	M	Feb 1874	26	Wd				MS	AL	AL	Farmer
	Frank	SiL	B	M	Mar 1883	17	S				MS	AL	AL	Farm Laborer
	Modenia	GD	B	F	May 1887	13	S				MS	AL	AL	
	Coy	GS	B	M	Aug 1874	5	S				MS	AL	AL	
258	Burgess, T.	H	B	M	Mar 1840	60	Wd		10	7	AL	AL	AL	Farmer
	Walter	S	B	M	May 1877	23	S				MS	MS	AL	Farm Laborer
	Delphia	D	B	F	Mar 1885	15	S				MS	MS	AL	
	Ezekiel	S	B	M	Feb 1888	12	S				MS	MS	AL	
	Dock	S	B	M	Apr 1890	10	S				MS	MS	AL	
259	Paden, Hann	H	B	F	Sep 1828	71	Wd		13	8	MS	MS	MS	Farmer
	John	S	B	M	Dec 1880	19	S				MS	MS	MS	Farm Laborer
	Wilson, Lum	GS	B	M	Jun 1873	26	Wd				MS	MS	MS	Day Laborer
260	McRae, W.D.	H	B	M	Aug 1851	48	M	30			NC	NC	NC	Farmer
	Belle	W	B	F	May 1848	52	M	30	13	8	MS	MS	MS	
	Sallie	D	B	F	Feb 1874	26	S				MS	NC	MS	
	Rosa	D	B	F	Jan 1883	17	S				MS	NC	MS	
	Oscar	S	B	M	May 1884	16	S				MS	NC	MS	
	Dana	GD	B	F	May 1899	1	S				MS	MS	MS	
261	McDougal, J.W.	H	W	M	Apr 1840	60	Wd				MS	NC	TN	Farmer
	E.A.	D	W	F	Aug 1868	31	S				MS	MS	NC	
	L.L.	S	W	M	Sep 1877	22	S				MS	MS	MS	School Teacher
	Lawrence	GS	W	M	Sep 1882	17	S				MS	MS	MS	Farm Laborer

1	2	3	4	5	6	7	8	9	10	11	12	13	14	15
	Lloyd	GS	W	M	Dec 1885	14	S				MS	MS	MS	
262	Savage, J.R.	H	W	M	Jan 1836	64	M	12			SC	SC	SC	Farmer
	Bertie	W	W	F	Apr 1858	42	M	12	4	3	SC	SC	SC	
	J.B.	S	W	M	Oct 1873	26	S				MS	AL	MS	
	Flora	D	W	F	Jan 1877	23	S				MS	SC	MS	
	Ward	S	W	M	Aug 1892	7	S				MS	SC	MS	
	John	S	W	M	Aug 1894	5	S				MS	SC	MS	
	Sibbie	D	W	F	Mar 1898	2	S				MS	SC	MS	
	Paden, R.W.	BiL	W	M	Sep 1835	64	S				SC	SC	SC	Farm Laborer
263	Long, Charlie	H	B	M	May 1860	40	Wd				MS	MS	MS	Farmer
	Annie	Sis	B	F	Jan 1875	25	S				MS	MS	MS	
	Lou	Nce	B	F	Jan 1900	5/mo	S				MS	MS	MS	
264	Paden, D.L.	H	W	M	Jan 1862	37	M	6			MS	SC	MS	Farmer
	Minnie	W	W	F	Dec 1872	27	M	6	2	2	MS	SC	MS	
	Obrien W.	S	W	M	Jul 1894	5	S				MS	MS	MS	
	Mary B.	D	W	F	Mar 1897	3	S				MS	MS	MS	
265	Gardner, A.C.	H	W	M	Oct 1870	29	M	7			MS	SC	MS	Farmer
	Lou	W	W	F	Aug 1872	27	M	7	2	2	MS	MS	AL	
	Clarence	S	W	M	May 1895	5	S				MS	MS	MS	
	Orien	S	W	M	Mar 1898	2	S				MS	MS	MS	
	King, B.B.	Ser	W	M	Nov 1874	25	S				MS	MS	MS	Farm Laborer
266	McDougal, J.T.	H	W	M	Jun 1851	48	M	30			MS	NC	TN	Farmer
	M.L.	W	W	F	May 1845	57	M	30	9	7	AL	GA	MS	
	Mary	D	W	F	Mar 1877	23	S				MS	MS	AL	
	Oscar	S	W	M	Jan 1881	19	S				MS	MS	AL	
	Steve	S	W	M	Apr 1883	17	S				MS	MS	AL	
267	Storment, A.J.	H	W	M	Nov 1852	47	M	23			MS	NC	TN	Farmer
	Synthia	W	W	F	Nov 1858	41	M	23	7	6	MS	MS	MS	
	Sam	S	W	M	Sep 1878	21	S				MS	MS	MS	Farm Laborer
	Annie	D	W	F	Feb 1881	19	S				MS	MS	MS	
	Francis	D	W	F	Jun 1883	16	S				MS	MS	MS	
	Ida	D	W	F	Jan 1887	13	S				MS	MS	MS	
	James	S	W	M	Feb 1893	7	S				MS	MS	MS	
	Josia	D	W	F	Jan 1896	4	S				MS	MS	MS	
268	Page, John	H	W	M	Jan 1873	27	M	7			MS	AL	AL	Saw Mill
	Lilly	W	W	F	May 1876	24	M	7	4	3	MS	TN	AL	
	Willie	S	W	M	Nov 1894	5	S				MS	MS	MS	
	Tom	S	W	M	Jul 1897	2	S				MS	MS	MS	
	Ninnie	D	W	F	Oct 1899	7/mo	S				MS	MS	MS	
269	Boggs, J.D.	H	W	M	Mar 1861	37	M	15			TX	AL	TN	Meth. Preacher
	Margaret	W	W	F	Oct 1853	46	M	15	4	4	MS	NC	TN	
	Sofa	D	W	F	Oct 1885	14	S				MS	TX	MS	
	Rosa	D	W	F	Feb 1888	12	S				MS	TX	MS	
	Sydney	S	W	M	Jan 1890	10	S				MS	TX	MS	
	Ruth	D	W	F	Mar 1894	6	S				MS	TX	MS	
270	Gurley, J.S.	H	W	M	Mar 1833	67	M	20			AL	SC	NC	Farm Laborer
	Mary	W	W	F	Nov 1853	46	M	20	1	1	MS	SC	SC	
	William F.	S	W	M	Mar 1886	14	S				MS	AL	MS	
271	Gurley, J.W.	H	W	M	Jun 1869	30	M	6			MS	AL	MS	Farmer
	Lizzie	W	W	F	Oct 1874	25	M	6	2	2	MS	MS	AL	
	Owen	S	W	M	Jul 1896	3	S				MS	MS	MS	
	Quinton	S	W	M	Aug 1898	1	S				MS	MS	MS	

1	2	3	4	5	6	7	8	9	10	11	12	13	14	15
272	Southward, Mat	H	B	M	Mar 1850	50	M	25			AL	AL	AL	Farmer
	Melia	W	B	F	Jan 1855	45	M	25	8	7	AL	AL	AL	
	Roda	D	B	F	Feb 1881	19	S				MS	AL	AL	
	Laura	D	B	F	Jul 1882	17	S				MS	AL	AL	
	Emma	D	B	F	Oct 1884	15	S				MS	AL	AL	
	Eddy	D	B	F	Dec 1890	9	S				MS	AL	AL	
	John	S	B	M	Jan 1893	7	S				MS	AL	AL	
	Luther	S	B	M	Feb 1895	5	S				MS	AL	AL	
	Susie	D	B	F	Mar 1897	3	S				MS	AL	AL	
273	Burgess, Jule	H	B	F	Mar 1877	23	Wd		3	3	MS	AL	AL	Day Laborer
	Earnest	S	B	M	Jan 1893	7	S				MS	MS	MS	
	Callie	D	B	F	Oct 1894	5	S				MS	MS	MS	
	Alice	D	B	F	Dec 1897	2	S				MS	MS	MS	
274	Anderson, Dock	H	B	M	Mar 1864	36	M	15			AL	AL	AL	Farmer
	Ella	W	B	F	Jan 1874	26	M	15	7	7	AL	AL	AL	
	Abe	S	B	M	Jun 1888	12	S				MS	AL	AL	
	Richard	S	B	M	Feb 1891	9	S				MS	AL	AL	
	Prince	S	B	M	Apr 1893	7	S				MS	AL	AL	
	Andy	D	B	F	May 1894	6	S				MS	AL	AL	
	Pearl	D	B	F	Oct 1895	4	S				MS	AL	AL	
	Crystial	S	B	M	Dec 1896	3	S				MS	AL	AL	
	James	S	B	M	Jan 1900	4/mo	S				MS	AL	AL	
275	McRae, George	H	B	M	May 1875	25	M	3			MS	AL	AL	Farmer
	Belle	W	B	F	Feb 1878	22	M	3	1	1	AL	MS	MS	
	Rose	S	B	M	Jan 1898	2	S				MS	MS	AL	
276	Inlow, R.F	H	W	M	Mar 1845	55	M	35			AL	AL	AL	Farmer
	M.J.	W	W	F	Sep 1845	54	M	35	9	8	AL	AL	AL	
	J.B.	S	W	M	Dec 1876	23	S				AL	AL	AL	
	Emma	D	W	F	May 1885	15	S				AL	AL	AL	
	Oscar	S	W	M	Sep 1887	12	S				MS	AL	AL	
	Ethel	D	W	F	May 1890	10	S				MS	AL	AL	
	Suttan, Ellen	D	W	F	Feb 1875	25	Wd		2	1	MS	AL	AL	
	Mary	GD	W	F	Mar 1900	2/mo	S				MS	AL	AL	
	Denton, Ethel	MiL	W	F	May 1826	74	Wd		5	5	AL	AL	AL	
277	Starky, J.F.	H	W	M	Dec 1864	35	M	13			AL	AL	AL	Farmer
	Delia	W	W	F	Nov 1866	33	M	13	5	5	AL	AL	AL	
	Callie	D	W	F	Dec 1887	12	S				AL	AL	AL	
	Homer	S	W	M	Feb 1890	10	S				AL	AL	AL	
	Dee	S	W	F	Feb 1892	8	S				AL	AL	AL	
	Mannine	D	W	F	Mar 1894	6	S				Al	AL	AL	
	Lee	S	W	M	Jan 1897	3	S				AL	AL	AL	
	Tifton, Frank	Ser	B	M	Apr 1875	25	S				AL	AL	AL	
278	Rutherford, R.W.	H	W	M	Feb 1870	30	M	2			AL	AL	AL	Farmer
	Addie	W	W	F	Dec 1874	25	M	2	1	1	AL	AL	AL	
	Myrtie	D	W	F	Jan 1900	3/mo	S				MS	AL	AL	
279	Commons, H.C.	H	B	M	Apr 1872	28	M	0			MS	AL	AL	Farmer
	Della	W	B	F	Mar 1874	26	M	0	4	4	MS	AL	AL	
	John E.	S	B	M	Mar 1888	12	S				MS	MS	MS	
	Nannie	D	B	F	May 1890	10	S				MS	MS	MS	
	Fred	S	B	M	May 1892	8	S				MS	MS	MS	
	Andy	D	B	F	May 1896	4	S				MS	MS	MS	
280	Martin, Charles	H	B	F	Jan 1845	55	S		10	10	AL	AL	AL	Farmer
	Willie	S	B	M	Oct 1871	28	Wd				AL	AL	AL	Farmer
	Jessie	D	B	F	Dec 1882	17	S				MS	AL	AL	
	William	S	B	M	Nov 1883	16	S				MS	AL	AL	Farm Laborer

1	2	3	4	5	6	7	8	9	10	11	12	13	14	15
	Maggie	D	B	F	Nov 1884	15	S				MS	AL	AL	
	Oscar	S	B	M	Mar 1888	12	S				MS	AL	AL	
	Estella	GD	B	F	Apr 1892	8	S				MS	MS	MS	
	Adus	GS	B	M	May 1899	1	S				MS	MS	MS	
281	Southward, Jesse	H	B	M	May 1858	47	M	20			AL	AL	AL	Farmer
	Marget	W	B	F	Apr 1860	40	M	20	9	5	AL	AL	GA	
	Sam	S	B	M	Mar 1883	17	S				MS	AL	AL	Farmer
	Willie	S	B	M	Oct 1884	15	S				MS	AL	AL	Farm Laborer
	James	S	B	M	Jun 1888	12	S				MS	AL	AL	
	David	S	B	M	Mar 1891	9	S				MS	AL	AL	
282	Mann, Joe	H	B	M	Mar 1845	55	M	30			AL	AL	AL	Farmer
	Hattie	W	B	F	May 1845	55	M	30	6	4	AL	AL	AL	
	Sam	S	B	M	Feb 1874	26	S				MS	AL	AL	Farmer
	Mattie	D	B	F	May 1880	20	S				MS	AL	AL	Farm Laborer
	Lucy	D	B	F	Apr 1884	16	S				MS	AL	AL	
283	Alexander, Pete	H	B	M	Apr 1816	84	Wd				VA	VA	VA	
284	Richardson, John	H	B	M	May 1860	40	M	18			AL	AL	AL	Farmer
	Lee	W	B	F	Jan 1860	40	M	18	3	3	AL	AL	AL	
	Peter	S	B	M	Jan 1885	15	S				MS	AL	AL	
	Alice	D	B	F	May 1892	8	S				MS	AL	AL	
	Porter	S	B	M	Apr 1894	6	S				MS	AL	AL	
285	Alexander, Edy	H	B	M	Mar 1862	38	Wd		3	3	AL	AL	AL	Farmer
	Morgan	D	B	F	Sep 1880	19	S				MS	AL	AL	At School
	Hardy	D	B	F	Oct 1885	14	S				MS	AL	AL	
	Fanny	D	B	F	May 1890	10	S				MS	AL	AL	
	Southward, Lucy	M	B	F	Mar 1830	70	Wd		6	4	AL	GA	GA	
286	Stanford, C.C.	H	W	M	Apr 1845	55	M	22			AL	AL	AL	Farmer
	E.J.	W	W	F	Nov 1838	61	M	22	2	2	SC	SC	SC	
	John F.	S	W	M	Apr 1879	21	S				MS	AL	SC	Farm Laborer
	Ada E.	D	W	F	Aug 1882	17	S				MS	AL	AL	
287	Southward, Ruffus	H	B	M	Mar 1846	54	Wd				AL	AL	AL	Farmer
	R.S.	S	B	M	May 1877	23	S				AL	AL	AL	Farm Laborer
	Perry	S	B	M	Jan 1882	18	S				MS	AL	AL	Farm Laborer
	Emma	D	B	F	Feb 1884	16	S				MS	AL	AL	
	Laula	D	B	F	Oct 1887	12	S				MS	AL	AL	
	Oscar	S	B	M	Feb 1892	8	S				MS	AL	AL	
	Frances	M	B	F	Mar 1815	85	Wd		10	1	VA	VA	VA	
288	Milford, J.H.	H	W	M	Oct 1841	58	M	25			MS	SC	GA	Farmer
	Lucy	W	W	F	Sep 1852	47	M	25	5	5	AL	AL	AL	
	Thomas	S	W	M	Jun 1877	22	S				MS	MS	AL	Farmer
	Olivar	S	W	M	Dec 1882	17	S				MS	MS	AL	
	Bernard	S	W	M	Apr 1889	11	S				MS	MS	AL	
	Eugenia	D	W	F	Jan 1893	7	S				MS	MS	AL	
289	Underwood, S.H.	H	W	M	Sep 1869	30	M	12			TN	TN	TN	Farmer
	Annie	W	W	F	Jul 1872	27	M	12	4	3	AL	AL	AL	
	Lizza	D	W	F	Nov 1889	10	S				MS	TN	AL	
	Willie	S	W	M	Aug 1890	9	S				MS	TN	AL	
	Fannie	D	W	F	Dec 1894	5	S				MS	TN	AL	
290	White, Miller	H	W	M	May 1839	61	M	11			MO	MO	MO	Farmer
	Demia	W	W	F	Dec 1867	32	M	11	6	6	AL	AL	AL	
	Willie	D	W	F	Dec 1888	11	S				AL	MO	AL	
	Dock	S	W	M	Jul 1890	9	S				AL	MO	AL	
	Joe	S	W	M	Jun 1891	8	S				AL	MO	AL	

1	2	3	4	5	6	7	8	9	10	11	12	13	14	15
	Ben	S	W	F	Aug 1894	5	S				AL	MO	AL	
	Lena	D	W	F	Aug 1897	2	S				AL	MO	AL	
	Rosa	D	W	F	Apr 1899	1	S				AL	MO	AL	
291	Rast, J.S.	H	W	M	Oct 1863	36	M	11			MS	MS	TN	Fireman, Saw Mill
	Mary	W	W	F	May 1873	27	M	11	5	4	MS	AL	TN	
	Lee	D	W	F	Sep 1890	9	S				MS	MS	MS	
	Lizzie	D	E	F	Dec 1891	8	S				MS	MS	MS	
	Arry	D	W	F	Jan 1894	6	S				MS	MS	MS	
	Willie	D	W	F	Mar 1897	3	S				MS	MS	MS	
292	Cox, Will	H	W	M	May 1872	28	M	12			TN	TN	TN	Farmer
	Mallie	W	W	F	Feb 1872	28	M	12	5	4	MS	MS	MS	
	Annie	D	W	F	Jan 1890	10	S				MS	TN	MS	
	Cornelia	D	W	F	Oct 1893	6	S				MS	TN	MS	
	Grady	S	W	M	Mar 1895	5	S				MS	TN	MS	
	Verdie	D	W	F	Apr 1898	2	S				MS	TN	MS	
293	Tankersley, G.P.	H	W	M	May 1832	68	M	45			SC	SC	SC	Farmer
	M.J.	W	W	F	Mar 1840	60	M	45	4	4	AL	AL	AL	
	Mammie	D	W	F	Apr 1871	29	S				MS	SC	AL	
294	Lawry, W. M.	H	W	M	Jan 1871	29	M	5			MS	MS	MS	Farmer
	Mary	W	W	F	Jun 1869	31	M	5	3	2	MS	SC	MS	
	Nancy B.	D	W	F	Jun 1896	3	S				MS	MS	MS	
	Charley	S	W	M	Jul 1899	10/mo	S				MS	MS	MS	
295	Tankersley, G.J.	H	W	M	May 1859	41	M	12			MS	SC	MS	Farmer
	L.E.	W	W	F	Jun 1862	37	M	12	2	2	MS	SC	SC	
	Homer	S	W	M	Nov 1888	11	S				MS	MS	MS	
	Alma	D	W	F	Oct 1894	5	S				MS	MS	MS	
	Gable, Henry	FiL	W	M	Feb 1823	78	Wd				SC	SC	SC	
296	Southward, Bud	H	B	M	Mar 1865	35	M	12			AL	AL	AL	Farmer
	Silvia	W	B	F	May 1870	30	M	12	4	3	MS	AL	AL	
	Myrtie	D	B	F	Feb 1895	5	S				MS	AL	MS	
	Fred	S	B	M	Jan 1897	3	S				MS	AL	MS	
	Eugenia	D	B	F	Jul 1899	10/mo	S				MS	AL	MS	
297	Lovelell, J.J.	H	W	M	Apr 1855	45	S				AL	AL	AL	Farmer
	Thomas	Bro	W	M	Jan 1857	43	S				AL	AL	AL	Farm Laborer
298	Hodge, J.L.	H	W	M	Nov 1861	38	M	17			AL	AL	AL	Farmer
	Ellie	W	W	F	Jun 1866	35	M	17	7	6	AL	MS	AL	
	Ida	D	W	F	Nov 1883	16	S				AL	AL	MS	
	Cora	D	W	F	Mar 1886	14	S				AL	AL	MS	
	Terresie	D	W	F	Aug 1889	10	S				AL	AL	MS	
	Lester	S	W	M	May 1894	6	S				AL	AL	MS	
	Mandy	D	W	F	Nov 1895	4	S				AL	AL	MS	
	Infant	D	W	F	Jan 1900	4/mo	S				MS	AL	MS	
	Hammon, Bertie	MiL	W	F	Oct 1846	53	Wd		1	1	MS	AL	GA	
299	Cornelison, A.J.	H	W	M	Oct 1877	22	M	1			MS	TN	TN	Farmer
	Annie	W	W	F	Sep 1880	19	M	1	0	0	MS	MS	MS	
300	Underwood, W.R.	H	W	M	Jan 1858	42	M	16			MS	NC	TN	Farmer
	Sarah E.	W	W	F	Feb 1862	38	M	16	5	5	AL	NC	TN	
	Emma	D	W	F	Nov 1885	14	S				MS	MS	AL	
	Nannie	D	W	F	Jun 1887	12	S				MS	MS	AL	
	William R.	S	W	M	Nov 1889	10	S				MS	MS	AL	
	Carrie E.	D	W	F	Oct 1890	9	S				MS	MS	AL	
	Robert B.	S	W	M	Mar 1893	7	S				MS	MS	AL	
	Hale, George	Ser	B	M	Dec 1875	24	S				AL	AL	MS	Farm Laborer

1 2	3	4	5	6	7	8	9	10	11	12	13	14	15
301 Russell, W.O.	H	W	M	Jan 1851	49	M	19			MS	VA	TN	Farmer
Marget E.	W	W	F	Dec 1863	36	M	19	5	4	AL	TN	TN	
Edmond	S	W	M	May 1882	18	S				MS	MS	AL	Farm Laborer
Charles	S	W	M	Aug 1885	14	S				MS	MS	AL	Farm Laborer
Sarah	D	W	F	Oct 1888	11	S				MS	MS	AL	
Carrie A.	D	W	F	Mar 1893	7	S				MS	MS	AL	
302 Southward, James	H	B	M	Feb 1867	33	M	11			MS	AL	AL	Farmer
Alice	W	B	F	Mar 1868	32	M	11	5	5	MS	AL	AL	
Claudy	D	B	F	Sep 1889	10	S				MS	MS	AL	
Candy	S	B	M	Sep 1891	8	S				MS	MS	MS	
James	S	B	M	Dec 1893	6	S				MS	MS	MS	
Maggie	D	B	F	Jul 1897	3	S				MS	MS	MS	
Modenia	D	B	F	Nov 1898	1	S				MS	MS	MS	
303 Puckett, M.G.	H	W	M	Feb 1862	38	M	20			MS	AL	AL	Farmer
Mary A.	W	W	F	Oct 1862	37	M	20	7	7	AL	AL	AL	
Miggie M	D	W	F	Oct 1883	16	S				MS	MS	AL	
Mammie	D	W	F	Aug 1887	12	S				MS	MS	AL	
Ben F.	S	W	M	May 1890	10	S				MS	MS	AL	
Ugenia	D	W	F	Nov 1893	6	S				MS	MS	AL	
Ezra	S	W	M	May 1895	5	S				MS	MS	AL	
Nathan	S	W	M	Nov 1897	2	S				MS	MS	AL	
Bryan	S	W	M	Jul 1899	8/mo	S				MS	MS	AL	
304 Puckett, B.F.	H	W	M	Sep 1833	66	M	49			TN	VA	VA	Farmer
Lucy J.	W	W	F	Sep 1837	62	M	49	9	8	TN	VA	TN	
Martha A.	D	W	F	Nov 1865	34	S				MS	TN	TN	
305 Talens, W.M.	H	W	M	Mar 1849	51	M	31			MS	MS	MS	Farmer
Susan	W	W	F	Jul 1849	50	M	31	5	5	MS	MS	MS	
Alley	D	W	F	Nov 1870	29	S				MS	MS	MS	
Emma	D	W	F	Aug 1876	23	S				MS	MS	MS	
James	S	W	M	May 1884	16	S				MS	MS	MS	
Mary	D	W	F	Nov 1888	11	S				MS	MS	MS	
Leasie	D	W	F	Mar 1898	2	S				MS	MS	MS	
Nancy A.	M	W	F	Feb 1822	78	Wd		8	5	GA	SC	SC	
306 Leatherwood, W.W.	H	W	N	Jul 1874	25	M	7			MS	AL	AL	Farmer
Carrie	D	W	F	Aug 1894	5	S				MS	MS	MS	
Allie	D	W	F	Jul 1896	3	S				MS	MS	MS	
Garvin	S	W	M	Jul 1898	1	S				MS	MS	MS	
307 Leatherwood, W.A.	H	W	M	Dec 1850	49	M	27			AL	GA	GA	Farmer
Mary	W	W	F	Nov 1858	41	M	27	11	6	AL	AL	AL	
Ella	D	W	F	May 1877	23	S				MS	AL	AL	
Lillly	D	W	F	Oct 1878	21	S				MS	AL	AL	
Ila	D	W	F	Feb 1880	20	S				MS	AL	AL	
Loula	D	W	F	Jun 1885	14	S				MS	AL	AL	
308 Upton, W.D.	H	W	M	Sep 1867	32	M	11			AL	AL	AL	Farmer
Catherine	W	W	F	Nov 1871	28	M	11	5	5	AL	AL	AL	
T.M.	S	W	M	Sep 1889	10	S				AL	AL	AL	
John W.	S	W	M	Oct 1891	8	S				AL	AL	AL	
James N.	S	W	M	Aug 1894	5	S				AL	AL	AL	
Sarah C.	D	W	F	Jul 1897	3	S				AL	AL	AL	
Richard	S	W	M	Mar 1900	2/mo	S				MS	AL	AL	
John	Cou	W	M	Mar 1890	10	S				MS	MS	MS	
309 Russell, W.P.	H	W	M	Sep 1845	54	M	32			TN	VA	TN	Farmer
R.J.	W	W	F	Aug 1846	53	M	32	8	5	MS	TN	MS	
Charley P.	S	W	M	Aug 1882	17	S				MS	TN	MS	Farm Laborer
Sydney, A.	S	W	M	Apr 1885	15	S				MS	TN	MS	Farm Laborer

1	2	3	4	5	6	7	8	9	10	11	12	13	14	15
	Aulty L.	D	W	F	Apr 1890	10	S				MS	TN	MS	
310	Russell, W.A.	H	W	M	Apr 1877	23	M	1			MS	TN	MS	Farmer
	Marget	W	W	F	Feb 1884	16	M	1	0	0	AL	AL	MS	
311	Nickelson, A.	H	W	F	Mar 1860	40	S		1	1	MS	AL	AL	Farmer
	Betie	D	W	F	Jan 1900	4/mo	S				MS	MS	AL	
312	Puckett, J.C.	H	W	M	Aug 1855	44	M	28			MS	GA	TN	Farmer
	M.A.	W	W	F	Nov 1861	38	M	28	10	9	MS	MS	MS	
	Nora	D	W	F	Oct 1881	18	S				MS	MS	MS	
	W.J.	S	W	M	Dec 1884	15	S				MS	MS	MS	
	Mary L.	D	W	F	Dec 1886	13	S				MS	MS	MS	
	Edgar	S	W	M	Jan 1889	11	S				MS	MS	MS	
	Frana	D	W	F	Jan 1891	9	S				MS	MS	MS	
	Yettie	D	W	F	Jul 1893	6	S				MS	MS	MS	
	Eugene	D	W	F	Sep 1897	2	S				MS	MS	MS	
313	Puckett, Oscar	H	W	M	Mar 1870	30	M	5			MS	GA	TN	Farmer
	Dizy	W	W	F	Apr 1869	31	M	5	4	3	AL	AL	AL	
	Charley	S	W	M	Jun 1894	5	S				MS	MS	AL	
	Horace	S	W	M	Jan 1897	3	S				MS	MS	AL	
	Sarah	D	W	F	Apr 1899	1	S				MS	MS	AL	
314	Twitty, J.M.	H	W	M	Jan 1858	42	Wd				AL	AL	AL	Farmer
	Edgar	D	W	F	Feb 1885	15	S				MS	AL	AL	
	Lindsay	D	W	F	Aug 1887	12	S				MS	AL	AL	
	Virginia	D	W	F	Jun 1888	11	S				MS	AL	SL	
	Lee	D	W	F	Apr 1893	7	S				MS	AL	AL	
315	Wallis, Rat	H	W	M	May 1865	35	M	21			AL	AL	AL	Farmer
	Nancy	W	W	F	Feb 1855	45	M	21	7	6	AL	AL	AL	
	Elnor	D	W	F	Mar 1880	20	S				MS	AL	AL	
	Cleo	D	W	F	Feb 1882	18	S				MS	AL	AL	
	Mary	D	W	F	Oct 1884	15	S				MS	AL	AL	
	John	S	W	M	Sep 1890	9	S				MS	AL	AL	
	Jim	S	W	M	Dec 1892	7	S				MS	AL	AL	
	Sarah	D	W	F	Aug 1895	4	S				MS	AL	AL	
316	Upton, N.R.	H	W	M	Nov 1869	30	M	7			AL	AL	AL	Farmer
	Janie	W	W	F	Jul 1874	25	M	7	4	3	AL	AL	AL	
	Donnie	D	W	F	Mar 1893	7	S				AL	AL	AL	
	Leone	D	W	F	Dec 1894	5	S				MS	AL	AL	
	Sarah E.	D	W	F	May 1898	2	S				MS	AL	AL	
317	Hughes, J.P.	H	W	M	Jul 1871	28	M	1			AL	AL	AL	Farmer
	Maggie	W	W	F	Sep 1871	28	M	1	1	1	AL	AL	AL	
	Unis	D	W	F	Jan 1900	4/mo	S				MS	AL	AL	
318	Russell, J.H.	H	W	M	Feb 1848	52	M	29			AL	TN	AL	Farmer
	Susan C.	W	W	F	Mar 1849	51	M	29	8	4	AL	AL	AL	
	Carrie A.	D	W	F	Jan 1879	21	S				MS	AL	AL	
	Viola F.	D	W	F	Dec 1881	18	S				MS	AL	AL	
	Issac F	S	W	M	Jan 1884	16	S				MS	AL	AL	
319	Hunt, E.J.	H	W	M	Jan 1850	50	M	30			AL	AL	AL	Farmer
	R.C.	W	W	F	Aug 1850	49	M	30	9	9	MS	AL	AL	
	Lilly M.	D	W	F	Jan 1882	18	S				MS	AL	MS	
	Alvira	D	W	F	Dec 1883	16	S				MS	AL	MS	
	John E.	S	W	M	Sep 1885	14	S				MS	AL	MS	
	William E.	S	W	M	Aug 1889	10	S				MS	AL	MS	
	Pearl L.	D	W	F	Aug 1889	10	S				MS	AL	MS	
	Stella E.	D	W	F	Sep 1883	6	S				MS	AL	MS	

1	2	3	4	5	6	7	8	9	10	11	12	13	14	15
	Hatcher, A.	Ser	W	M	Mar 1883	17	S				AL	AL	AL	Farm Laborer
320	Moody, Lee	H	W	M	Feb 1850	50	M	20			AL	AL	AL	Farmer
	Mary A.	W	W	F	Feb 1839	61	M	20	6	4	NC	NC	NC	
	Clay, Nannie	Ser	W	F	Feb 1879	21	S		1	1	MS	MS	MS	
	Pearly	Ser	W	F	Jul 1893	6	S				MS	MS	MS	
321	Nunley, John	H	W	M	Mar 1866	34	M	14			MS	MS	MS	Farmer
	Jane	W	W	F	Dec 1866	33	M	14	6	6	AL	AL	AL	
	Robert L.	S	W	M	Sep 1888	11	S				AL	AL	MS	
	Willis	S	W	M	Feb 1890	10	S				MS	MS	AL	
	Belle	D	W	F	Dec 1891	8	S				MS	MS	AL	
	Mahayley	D	W	F	Feb 1894	6	S				MS	MS	AL	
	Mary L.	D	W	F	Sep 1897	2	S				MS	MS	AL	
	Correlia	D	W	F	Mar 1900	2/mo	S				MS	MS	AL	
	Lambert, Mattie	Nce	W	F	Feb 1885	15	S				AL	AL	AL	
	Myrtie	Nce	W	F	Aug 1886	13	S				AL	AL	AL	
	Willie	Nce	W	F	Aug 1889	10	S				AL	AL	AL	
322	Burns, Guss	H	W	M	Sep 1852	47	M	15			AL	AL	GA	Farmer
	Cassie	W	W	F	Feb 1865	35	M	15	3	3	AL	TN	AL	
	Ednor	D	W	F	Sep 1886	13	S				MS	AL	AL	
	Alice	D	W	F	Jun 1890	9	S				MS	AL	AL	
	Fred	S	W	M	May 1892	8	S				MS	AL	AL	
323	Martin, W.M.	H	B	M	Oct 1865	34	M	4			MS	AL	AL	Farmer
	Ella	W	B	F	Mar 1869	31	M	4	3	2	MS	AL	AL	
	Elvester	S	B	M	Nov 1887	12	S				MS	AL	MS	
	Bessie	D	B	F	Jul 1897	2	S				MS	MS	MS	
324	Mann, Asa	H	W	M	Aug 1866	33	M	13			MS	VA	SC	Farmer
	Alice	W	W	F	Sep 1867	32	M	13	7	7	AL	AL	AL	
	Ola	D	W	F	May 1887	13	S				MS	MS	AL	
	Clidy	D	W	F	Jan 1888	12	S				MS	MS	AL	
	Ada	D	W	F	Oct 1892	7	S				MS	MS	AL	
	Maude	D	W	F	Jul 1893	6	S				MS	MS	AL	
	Alma	D	W	F	Sep 1895	4	S				MS	MS	AL	
	Wyley	S	W	M	Nov 1897	2	S				MS	MS	AL	
	Ethel M.	D	W	F	Sep 1899	8/mo	S				MS	MS	AL	
325	Johnson, Jack	H	B	M	Nov 1879	60	M	16			AL	AL	AL	Farmer
	Lucy	W	B	F	Mar 1865	35	M	16	7	5	AL	AL	AL	
	Lum	S	B	M	Feb 1882	18	S				MS	AL	AL	Farm Laborer
	Mattie	D	B	F	Feb 1885	15	S				MS	AL	AL	
	Alford	S	B	M	Apr 1890	10	S				MS	AL	AL	
	Lilly	D	B	F	May 1892	8	S				MS	AL	AL	
	George	S	B	M	Oct 1894	5	S				MS	AL	AL	
	Minnie	GD	B	F	Aug 1897	2	S				MS	MS	MS	
326	Harvey, J.W.	H	W	M	Dec 1840	69	M	13			MS	SC	SC	Farmer
	Margaret	W	W	F	May 1848	52	M	13	0	0	MS	VA	VA	
	Mary	D	W	F	Sep 1873	26	S				MS	MS	MS	
	Mattie	D	W	F	Sep 1873	26	S				MS	MS	MS	
	Jeff	S	W	M	Sep 1875	24	S				MS	MS	MS	Farmer
	Bailey, Thomas	Ser	B	M	Nov 1882	17	S				MS	AL	AL	Farm Laborer
327	Southward, W.A.	H	W	M	Sep 1840	59	M	27			AL	VA	VA	Farmer
	O.H.	W	W	F	Mar 1853	47	M	27	8	8	MS	AL	AL	
	Malle	D	W	F	Sep 1875	24	S				MS	AL	MS	
	Claudy	D	W	F	Nov 1877	22	S				MS	AL	MS	
	Charley	S	W	M	Jun 1879	20	S				MS	AL	MS	
	Ten	S	W	M	Jul 1882	17	S				MS	AL	MS	
	Hauty	D	W	F	Feb 1885	15	S				MS	AL	MS	

1	2	3	4	5	6	7	8	9	10	11	12	13	14	15
	John O.	S	W	M	Sep 1887	12	S				MS	AL	MS	
	Ben G.	S	W	M	Mar 1890	10	S				MS	AL	MS	
	James W.	S	W	M	Jun 1891	8	S				MS	AL	MS	
328	Boyd, J.E.	H	W	M	Jun 1850	49	M	17			AL	AL	AL	Farmer
	Mattie J.	W	W	F	Oct 1859	40	M	17	1	1	MS	MS	MS	
	James A.	S	W	M	May 1883	17	S				MS	AL	MS	Farm Laborer
329	Clifton, J.B.	H	W	M	Dec 1841	58	M	20			NC	NC	NC	Farmer
	Annie	W	W	F	Oct 1850	49	M	20	6	5	SC	Ger	SC	
	Belle	D	W	F	Oct 1882	17	S				MS	NC	SC	
	George	S	W	M	Jun 1885	14	S				MS	NC	SC	
	Willie	D	W	F	Aug 1886	13	S				MS	NC	SC	
	Fannie	D	W	F	Mar 1890	10	S				MS	NC	SC	
	Ward	S	W	M	Apr 1893	7	S				MS	NC	SC	
330	Finch, Paul	H	W	M	Dec 1839	60	M	30			MS	TN	TN	Farmer
	Eveline	W	W	F	Jan 1839	61	M	30	4	4	SC	SC	SC	
	R.C.	S	W	M	Nov 1874	25	S				MS	MS	SC	Farm Laborer
	Pearl	D	W	F	Oct 1878	21	S				MS	MS	SC	
	Cody, Pat	Ser	W	M	Nov 1880	19	S				AL	AL	AL	Farm Laborer
331	Maulding, J.A.	H	W	M	Feb 1878	22	M	2			MS	AL	AL	Farmer
	Mary A.	W	W	F	Oct 1879	20	M	2	2	2	AL	AL	AL	
	John H.	S	W	M	May 1898	2	S				AL	AL	AL	
	James D.	S	W	M	Mar 1900	2/mo	S				MS	MS	AL	
332	Maulding, John	H	W	M	Feb 1838	62	M	40			AL	AL	AL	Farmer
	Martha	W	W	F	Jan 1848	52	M	40	7	7	MS	AL	AL	
	Smith, Melvy	Ser	W	M	Feb 1882	18	S				AL	AL	AL	Farm Laborer
333	Cornelison, Mary J.	H	W	F	Jul 1838	61	Wd		13	8	TN	GA	OH	Farmer
	Morgan	S	W	M	Jul 1862	37	S				MS	TN	TN	Farm Laborer
334	Haygood, O.W.	H	W	M	Jan 1865	35	M	13			AL	AL	AL	Farmer
	A.A.	W	W	F	Dec 1871	28	M	13	6	5	AL	AL	AL	
	Bertha	D	W	F	Mar 1889	11	S				AL	AL	AL	
	Charley	S	W	M	Aug 1890	9	S				AL	AL	AL	
	Robert	S	W	M	Nov 1892	7	S				AL	AL	AL	
	Henry W.	S	W	M	Mar 1896	4	S				AL	AL	AL	
	Belle	D	W	F	Mar 1898	2	S				MS	AL	AL	
	Newt	Cou	W	M	Mar 1887	13	S				AL	AL	AL	
	Cummins, M.E.	MiL	W	F	Mar 1829	71	Wd		9	8	AL	AL	AL	
335	Alley, J.H.	H	W	M	Sep 1842	57	M	32			TN	TN	TN	Farmer
	Safrona	W	W	F	Jul 1841	58	M	32	4	3	TN	GA	VA	
	T.H.	S	W	M	Aug 1872	27	S				TN	TN	TN	Farm Laborer
336	McRae, J.D.	H	W	M	Apr 1848	52	M	27			MS	NC	TN	Farmer
	Margaret	W	W	F	Oct 1853	46	M	27	6	6	MS	AL	AL	
	Annah	D	W	F	Jul 1875	24	S				MS	MS	MS	School Teacher
	John B.	S	W	M	May 1878	22	S				MS	MS	MS	School Teacher
	Frank K.	S	W	M	Mar 1880	20	S				MS	MS	MS	School Teacher
	Lawrence J,	S	W	M	Sep 1882	17	S				MS	MS	MS	School Teacher
	Charley C.	S	W	M	Aug 1885	14	S				MS	MS	MS	
337	Green, M.B.	H	W	M	Jul 1840	59	M	39			AL	SC	SC	Farmer
	Martha	W	W	F	Oct 1839	60	M	39	11	10	MS	TN	TN	
	L.S.	S	W	M	Jan 1877	22	M	0			AL	AL	MS	Farm Laborer
	Dora	D	W	F	Feb 1880	20	S				MS	AL	MS	
	Green, J.E.	S	W	M	Sep 1866	33	Wd				AL	AL	MS	Farmer
	Amanda	Nce	W	F	Jan 1894	6	S				MS	AL	MS	
	E.B.	GS	W	M	Jan 1897	3	S				MS	AL	MS	

1	2	3	4	5	6	7	8	9	10	11	12	13	14	15
	Frederick, James	Ser	W	M	Aug 1880	19	S				MS	MS	AL	Farm Laborer
338	Bryant, Jack	H	W	M	May 1860	40	M	20			MS	MS	AL	Farmer
	Mary	W	W	F	Feb 1863	38	M	20	6	6	MS	MS	AL	
	Charley	S	W	M	Oct 1881	18	S				MS	MS	MS	
	Mandy	D	W	F	May 1888	12	S				MS	MS	MS	
339	Gortney, R.	H	W	M	Sep 1875	24	M	3			MS	AL	AL	Farmer
	Fannie	W	W	F	Oct 1878	21	M	3	0	0	MS	MS	MS	

End of Enumeration of District #4

1	2	3	4	5	6	7	8	9	10	11	12	13	14	15
1	Vaughn, Geo. W.	H	W	M	Jun 1820	79	M	60			TN	VA	VA	
	Mary J.	W	W	F	May 1818	82	M	60	9	3	TN	VA	VA	
	George H.	S	W	M	Apr 1847	53	D				TN	TN	TN	Teacher/Enumerator
	Campbell, Willie E.	Nce	W	F	Apr 1864	36	Wd		4	1	TN	TN	TN	
	Essie B.	D	W	F	Feb 1893	7	S				MS	MS	TN	
2	Fowler, Robert	H	W	M	Aug 1857	43	M	14			GA	SC	MS	Farmer
	Amelia A.	W	W	F	Apr 1864	36	M	14	6	5	GA	NC	NC	
	Senith D	D	W	F	Dec 1884	15	S				AL	GA	AL	
	Margaret E.	D	W	F	Nov 1888	11	S				MS	GA	GA	
	Amelia N.	D	W	F	Feb 1891	9	S				MS	GA	GA	
	William T.	S	W	M	Jan 1894	6	S				MS	GA	GA	
	Nathan M.	S	W	M	May 1896	4	S				MS	GA	GA	
	Ethel M.	D	W	F	Feb 1899	1	S				MS	GA	GA	
3	Harris, Ferrell	H	W	M	Dec 1820	79	M	46			NC	NC	NC	Farmer
	Margaret E.	W	W	F	Jun 1833	66	M	46	7	2	NC	NC	NC	
4	Tipton, William	H	W	M	Jan 1862	38	M	8			MS	AL	GA	Farmer
	Mary M.	W	W	F	Oct 1875	24	M	8	3	3	MS	AL	NC	
	William E.	S	W	M	Oct 1892	7	S				MS	MS	MS	
	Fannie B.	D	W	F	Aug 1892	4	S				MS	MS	MS	
	Henry T.	S	W	M	Mar 1897	2	S				MS	MS	MS	
	Tipton, Catherine	M	W	F	May 1836	63	Wd		12	11	NC	NC	NC	
	Dovie	Sis	W	F	Jan 1879	21	S				MS	MS	NC	
5	Davis, Mary J.	H	W	F	Oct 1857	42	Wd		6	6	MS	NC	NC	Farmer
	Reece C.	S	W	M	Oct 1882	17	S				MS	MS	MS	Farm Laborer
	James G.	S	W	M	Jul 1884	15	S				MS	MS	MS	Farm Laborer
	Rena B.	D	W	F	May 1887	13	S				MS	MS	MS	
	Walter T.	S	W	M	May 1888	11	S				MS	MS	MS	Farm Laborer
	Georgia A.	D	W	F	Mar 1890	9	S				MS	MS	MS	
	Lillie C.	D	W	F	Mar 1893	7	S				MS	MS	MS	
6	Oneal, John F.	H	W	M	Nov 1830	69	M	43			GA	GA	SC	Farmer
	Mary B.	W	W	F	Jul 1830	69	M	43	7	6	SC	SC	SC	
	Marery E.	D	W	F	Apr 1862	28	S				AL	GA	SC	
	John H.	GS	W	M	Jul 1891	9	S				MS	MS	AL	
7	Gable, Henry O.	H	W	M	Jan 1854	45	M	21			MS	SC	SC	Farmer
	Sarah M.	W	W	F	Dec 1854	45	M	21	6	5	AL	SC	SC	
	Thomas J.	S	W	M	Oct 1884	15	S				MS	MS	AL	Farm Laborer
	Mary E.	D	W	F	May 1887	13	S				MS	MS	AL	
	James W.	S	W	M	May 1891	9	S				MS	MS	AL	
	Henry P.	S	W	F	Sep 1893	6	S				MS	MS	AL	
	Andy S.	S	W	M	Feb 1897	3	S				MS	MS	AL	
8	Gable, Robert L.	H	W	M	Feb 1866	34	M	11			MS	SC	AL	Farmer
	Rebecca J.	W	W	F	Nov 1863	36	M	11	5	5	MS	SC	SC	
	Florence J.	S	W	M	Feb 1890	10	S				MS	MS	MS	
	Flora B.	D	W	F	May 1892	8	S				MS	MS	MS	
	Luther Y.	S	W	M	Nov 1894	5	S				MS	MS	MS	
	Sallie E.	D	W	F	Feb 1897	3	S				MS	MS	MS	
	Clarice W.	D	W	F	Nov 1899	6/mo	S				MS	MS	MS	
	James	F	W	M	Jul 1820	79	Wd				SC	VA	VA	Farmer
9	Tidwell, Mark J.	H	W	M	Nov 1851	48	M	30			AL	AL	AL	Farmer
	Nacy P.	W	W	F	Jun 1858	41	M	30	13	10	MS	AL	AL	

1	2	3	4	5	6	7	8	9	10	11	12	13	14	15
	Sallie L.	D	W	F	Oct 1879	20	S				AL	AL	AL	
	James W.	S	W	M	Apr 1881	19	S				MS	AL	AL	
	David R.	S	W	M	Dec 1882	17	S				MS	AL	AL	
	Henry W.	S	W	M	Dec 1884	15	S				MS	AL	AL	
	Levy H.	S	W	M	Dec 1886	13	S				MS	AL	AL	
	Bertha M.	D	W	F	Feb 1889	11	S				AL	AL	AL	
	Birtha A.	D	W	F	Aug 1893	9	S				AL	AL	AL	
10	Trollinger, Thomas J.	H	W	M	Mar 1865	35	M	4			AL	SC	TN	Farmer
	Lucy C.	W	W	F	Jan 1873	27	M	4	0	0	MS	AL	GA	
11	Oneal, John W.	H	W	M	Sep 1861	38	M	12			AL	GA	GA	Farmer
	Mary J.	W	W	F	Oct 1865	34	M	12	7	5	MS	AL	NC	
	Julia A.	D	W	F	Oct 1888	11	S				MS	AL	MS	
	Charles T.	S	W	M	Jun 1892	7	S				MS	AL	MS	
	Myrtle C.	D	W	F	Jan 1895	5	S				MS	AL	MS	
	Bradie D.	S	W	M	Oct 1897	2	S				TX	AL	MS	
	Henry O.	S	W	M	Jan 1900	4/mo	S				MS	AL	MS	
12	Tipton, James Jr	H	W	M	Nov 1875	23	M	1			MS	AL	NC	Farmer
	Vennie B.	W	W	F	Jan 1878	22	M	1	1	1	MS	AL	GA	
	William L.	S	W	M	Mar 1900	2/mo	S				MS	MS	MS	
13	Taylor, Lewis C.	H	W	M	Dec 1862	37	M	19			MS	MS	MS	Farmer
	Virginia F.	W	W	F	Dec 1863	36	M	19	8	7	MS	AL	AL	
	James A.	S	W	M	Mar 1882	18	S				MS	MS	MS	Farm Laborer
	Sidney R.	S	W	M	Feb 1885	15	S				MS	MS	MS	Farm Laborer
	William D.	S	W	M	Jan 1889	11	S				MS	MS	MS	Farm Laborer
	Nathan S.	S	W	M	Jan 1891	9	S				MS	MS	MS	
	Lewis E.	S	W	M	Apr 1893	7	S				MS	MS	MS	
	Elma	D	W	F	Mar 1895	5	S				MS	MS	MS	
	George W.	S	W	M	Feb 1888	2	S				MS	MS	MS	
14	Trollinger, Lemuel	H	W	F	Jul 1837	62	M	38			SC	VA	VA	Farmer
	Cintha R.	W	W	F	Dec 1839	60	M	38	1	1	GA	SC	SC	
	Lum S.	S	W	M	Jun 1875	24	M	0			AL	SC	TN	Farmer
	Julia A.	DiL	W	F	Nov 1878	21	M	0	0	0	AL	GA	SC	
	Weems, Marvin J.	SS	W	M	Mar 1865	35	S				AL	AL	GA	Crippled
15	Mauldin, James M.	H	W	M	Apr 1840	60	M	36			AL	SC	SC	Farmer
	Elizabeth	W	W	F	Feb 1842	58	M	36	5	3	AL	SC	SC	
	Sarah A.	GD	W	F	Jun 1890	9	S				MS	MS	AL	
	Lee R.	GS	W	M	Jan 1891	8	S				MS	MS	AL	
16	Mauldin, Robert	H	W	M	Dec 1869	30	M	4			MS	AL	AL	Farmer
	Ada	W	W	F	Jun 1880	19	M	4	2	1	MS	MS	MS	
	Lillie E.	D	W	F	Apr 1897	3	S				MS	MS	MS	
17	Dickinson, Wm. H.	H	W	M	Jun 1855	54	M	12			AL	GA	GA	Farmer
	Martha J.	W	W	F	Aug 1867	33	M	12	7	6	GA	GA	GA	
	Charles L.	S	W	M	Feb 1882	17	S				AL	AL	GA	Farm Laborer
	Neoma V.	D	W	F	Dec 1885	14	S				AL	AL	GA	
	Lavada C.	S	W	M	Aug 1889	10	S				MS	AL	GA	Farm Laborer
	Myrtle V.	D	W	F	Feb 1892	8	S				MS	AL	GA	
	Franklin G.	S	W	M	Mar 1894	6	S				MS	AL	GA	
	Grover T.	S	W	M	Jan 1896	4	S				MS	AL	GA	
	Maggie D.	D	W	F	Jan 1898	2	S				MS	AL	GA	
	Lillie L.	D	W	F	Feb 1900	4/mo	S				MS	AL	GA	
18	Harris, William R.	H	W	M	Nov 1869	30	M	10			MS	AL	MS	Farmer
	Mary I.	W	W	F	Jan 1871	29	M	10	5	4	MS	SC	SC	
	John F.	S	W	M	May 1892	8	S				MS	MS	MS	
	Mary J.	D	W	F	Mar 1894	6	S				MS	MS	MS	

1	2	3	4	5	6	7	8	9	10	11	12	13	14	15
	Rockford A.	S	W	M	Feb 1896	4	S				MS	MS	MS	
	Della C.	D	W	F	Jul 1898	1	S				MS	MS	MS	
19	Davis, George W.	H	W	M	Feb 1854	46	S				MS	AL	AL	Farmer
	Aldridge, Mary B.	Ser	W	F	May 1861	38	Wd		6	4	MS	AL	TN	Keeps House
	Jessy S.	S	W	M	Sep 1882	17	S				MS	AL	MS	Farm Laborer
	Hubert R.	S	W	M	Oct 1887	12	S				MS	MS	MS	Farm Laborer
	Mack G.	S	W	M	Jun 1890	9	S				MS	MS	MS	
	Salan, D.	HH	W	M	Nov 1883	16	S				MS	MS	MS	Day Laborer
20	Morgan, Nancy P.	H	W	F	May 1841	59	Wd		5	4	MS	AL	TN	Farmer
	Florence V.	D	W	F	Feb 1865	35	UN		3	2	MS	NC	MS	
	Mary E.	D	W	F	Aug 1878	21	S				MS	MS	MS	
	Mattie B.	GD	W	F	Aug 1886	13	S				MS	MS	MS	
	Minnie L.	GD	W	F	Oct 1892	7	S				MS	MS	MS	
21	Harris, Hop T.	H	W	M	Jul 1833	66	M	24			TN	GA	TN	Farmer
	Mary I.	W	W	F	Oct 1851	48	M	24	10	8	MS	AL	TN	
	Annie L.	D	W	F	Nov 1876	22	S				MS	TN	MS	
	Cora L.	D	W	F	Feb 1878	22	S				MS	TN	MS	
	James G.	S	W	M	Apr 1891	19	S				MS	TN	MS	Farm Laborer
	Thomas J.	S	W	M	Nov 1883	16	S				MS	TN	MS	Farm Laborer
	Myrtle L.	D	W	F	May 1886	14	S				MS	TN	MS	
	George F.	S	W	M	May 1886	14	S				MS	TN	MS	Farm Laborer
	Belvy E.	D	W	F	Dec 1890	9	S				MS	TN	MS	
22	Trolinger, Maury	H	W	M	Dec 1863	36	M	3			AL	SC	TN	Farmer
	Sarah R.	W	W	F	May 1863	37	M	3	2	1	MS	NC	NC	
	John T.	S	W	M	Oct 1899	7/mo	S				MS	AL	MS	
23	Aldridge, John J.	H	W	M	Sep 1872	27	S				MS	TN	MS	Farmer
	Sarah J.	Aunt	W	F	Jan 1842	58	UN		1	1	AL	MS	TN	
	James O.	Cou	W	M	Sep 1886	13	S				MS	MS	AL	Farm Laborer
24	Aldridge, Joseph F.	H	W	M	Nov 1876	23	M	3			MS	MS	MS	Farmer
	Cintha L.	W	W	F	Nov 1876	23	M	3	3	3	AL	AL	AL	
	Belle T.	D	W	F	Nov 1897	2	S				MS	MS	AL	
	Ora V.	D	W	F	Mar 1899	1	S				MS	MS	AL	
	Andrew J.	S	W	M	Mar 1900	2 mo	S				MS	MS	AL	
	Celie	Aunt	W	F	UN UN	UN	S				MS	AL	TN	
	Sell	Cou	W	M	UN UN	UN	S				MS	MS	MS	Farm Laborer
25	Harris, Agnes R.	H	W	F	Jan 1861	39	M	18	9	6	MS	TN	MS	Farmer
	Bonnie O.	D	W	F	Jun 1882	17	S				MS	MS	MS	
	Margie	D	W	F	Jan 1883	16	S				MS	MS	MS	
	Dalton	S	W	M	Nov 1885	14	S				MS	MS	MS	Farm Laborer
	Claudie	S	W	M	Feb 1890	10	S				MS	MS	MS	Farm Laborer
	Mattie C.	D	W	F	May 1892	8	S				MS	MS	MS	
	Bessie E.	D	W	F	Nov 1893	6	S				MS	MS	MS	
26	Hill, Mike C.	H	W	M	Apr 1853	47	M	27			GA	NC	NC	Farmer
	Amanda C.	W	W	F	Apr 1854	46	M	27	8	7	MS	GA	TN	
	Ina E.	D	W	F	Aug 1878	21	S				MS	GA	TN	
	Ward P.	S	W	M	Dec 1881	18	S				MS	GA	TN	Farm Laborer
	Charles A.	S	W	M	Sep 1884	15	S				MS	GA	TN	
	Junior D.	D	W	F	Feb 1888	12	S				MS	GA	TN	
	Belvy D.	D	W	F	Oct 1890	9	S				MS	GA	TN	
	Myrtle L.	D	W	F	Dec 1893	6	S				MS	GA	TN	
27	Pardue, Henry O.	H	W	M	May 1862	37	M	15			MS	TN	AL	Farmer
	Nancy P.	W	W	F	Dec 1873	26	M	15	7	5	MS	MS	MS	
	Eliza A.	D	W	F	Nov 1886	13	S				MS	MS	MS	
	David G.	S	W	M	Apr 1889	11	S				MS	MS	MS	Farm Laborer

1	2	3	4	5	6	7	8	9	10	11	12	13	14	15
	Bolivar R.	S	W	M	Jan 1891	9	S				MS	MS	MS	
	Felix O.	S	W	M	Mar 1893	7	S				MS	MS	MS	
	Captain D.	S	W	M	Feb 1896	4	S				MS	MS	MS	
28	McDougal, Sam	H	W	M	Sep 1875	24	M	3			MS	MS	MS	Farmer
	Birtie L.	W	W	F	Jul 1875	24	M	3	2	2	MS	GA	MS	
	Willie E.	D	W	F	Dec 1897	2	S				MS	MS	MS	
	Winnie E.	D	W	F	Nov 1899	7/mo	S				MS	MS	MS	
29	Frederick, Nathaniel H.	H	W	M	Sep 1859	40	M	2			MS	AL	MS	Farmer
	Sarah E.	W	W	F	Aug 1860	39	M	2	0	0	MS	AL	MS	
	Munro C.	S	W	M	Oct 1883	16	S				MS	MS	MS	Farm Laborer
	Walter G.	S	W	M	Jan 1886	14	S				MS	MS	MS	Farm Laborer
	Sarah J.	D	W	F	Sep 1889	11	S				MS	MS	MS	
	Joseph H.	S	W	M	Sep 1891	8	S				MS	MS	MS	
30	Gurley, William H.	H	W	M	Apr 1875	25	M	6			MS	AL	MS	Farmer
	Ellen V.	W	W	F	Jan 1876	24	M	6	3	3	MS	AL	MS	
	Alice G.	D	W	F	Oct 1895	4	S				MS	MS	MS	
	Disie M.	D	W	F	May 1897	3	S				MS	MS	MS	
	Curtis D.	S	W	M	Apr 1899	1	S				MS	MS	MS	
31	Gurley, William H.	H	W	M	Oct 1830	69	Wd				AL	NC	NC	Farmer
	Margaret, M.	D	W	F	Oct 1877	22	S				MS	AL	AL	
	James W.	S	W	M	Mar 1881	19	S				MS	AL	AL	Farmer
32	Davis, Lafayette R.	H	W	M	Oct 1855	44	M	23			MS	AL	AL	Gen.merchant
	Isabella	W	W	F	Dec 1855	44	M	23	7	7	MS	AL	AL	
	John R.	S	W	M	Nov 1880	19	S				MS	AL	AL	At School
	Dalton B.	S	W	M	Feb 1883	17	S				MS	AL	AL	Salesman
	Samuel J.	S	W	M	May 1885	15	S				MS	AL	AL	Farm Laborer
	Author	S	W	M	Jan 1888	11	S				MS	AL	AL	Farm Laborer
	Effie B.	D	W	F	Oct 1892	7	S				MS	AL	AL	
	Ioma J.	D	W	F	Jun 1895	4	S				MS	AL	AL	
	Byram, John	FiL	W	M	Jun 1817	82	Wd				AL	TN	SC	
	Tidwell, Ransom S.	HH	W	M	Nov 1878	21	S				AL	AL	AL	Day Laborer
33	Harrison, George M.	H	W	M	Sep 1869	30	M	9			MS	MS	MS	Farmer
	Lanora J.	W	W	F	Aug 1873	26	M	9	3	1	MS	MS	MS	
	Robert L.	S	W	M	Mar 1897	3	5				MS	MS	MS	
34	Phillips, John O.	H	W	M	Oct 1873	26	M	1			MS	TN	AL	Farmer
	Mollie L.	W	W	F	Sep 1877	22	M	1	0	0	AL	MS	MS	
35	Ardis, David D.	H	W	M	Jan 1865	35	M	9			MS	AL	AL	Farmer
	Amanda S.	W	W	F	Jul 1870	29	M	9	3	2	MS	AL	TN	
	Minnie I.	D	W	F	Sep 1893	7	S				MS	MS	MS	
	Ollie H.	D	W	F	May 1898	2	S				MS	MS	MS	
36	Phillips, David F.	H	W	M	Sep 1877	22	M	1			MS	TN	AL	Farmer
	Sarah D.	W	W	F	Dec 1877	22	M	1	0	0	MS	AL	MS	
37	Davis, Napoleon	H	W	M	Jun 1858	41	M	10			MS	AL	AL	Merchant
	Martha J.	W	W	F	May 1864	36	M	10	0	0	MS	AL	AL	
	Jessie E.	Adp S	W	M	Oct 1895	4	S				AR	AR	AL	
	Catherine R.	Aunt	W	F	Aug 1848	51	S				AL	AL	AL	
38	Hogeland, James T.	H	W	M	Nov 1869	30	M	10			AL	AL	AL	Farmer
	Jennie C.	W	W	F	Jun 1868	31	M	10	0	0	MS	MS	AL	
39	Harrison, Carroll	H	W	M	Mar 1853	47	M	18			AL	NC	NC	Farmer
	Amanda B.	W	W	F	Apr 1872	28	M	18	8	7	MS	TN	TN	
	James W.	S	W	M	Jul 1885	14	S				MS	AL	MS	Farm Laborer

1	2	3	4	5	6	7	8	9	10	11	12	13	14	15
	Richard G.	S	W	M	Aug 1888	10	S				MS	AL	MS	Farm Laborer
	Samantha	D	W	F	Sep 1891	8	S				MS	AL	MS	
	Geneva	D	W	F	Dec 1893	6	S				MS	AL	MS	
	Wallis	S	W	M	Feb 1896	4	S				MS	AL	MS	
	Audia	S	W	M	Feb 1898	2	S				MS	AL	MS	
	Olivia	D	W	F	Mar 1900	2/mo	S				MS	AL	MS	
40	Miller, James A.	H	W	M	Jul 1873	26	M	7			AL	MS	TN	Farmer
	Mary E.	W	W	F	Jan 1875	25	M	7	1	1	MS	GA	AL	
	Bertha L.	D	W	F	Jul 1895	4	S				AL	AL	MS	
41	Miller, John	H	W	M	Jul 1810	28	M	10			AL	AL	TN	Farmer
	Mary J.	W	W	F	Apr 1876	24	M	10	3	3	MS	MS	MS	
	Oscar A.	S	W	M	Aug 1892	7	S				MS	AL	MS	
	Olen C.	S	W	M	Jan 1896	4	S				MS	AL	MS	
	Margaret S.	D	W	F	Aug 1898	1	S				MS	AL	MS	
42	Jones, Luke	H	W	M	Mar 1856	44	M	13			AL	TN	AL	Farmer
	Dirotha	W	W	F	Jan 1859	41	M	13	8	5	AL	AL	TN	
	Atha C.	D	W	F	Jan 1889	11	S				MS	AL	AL	
	Luke Z.	S	W	M	Jan 1889	8	S				MS	AL	AL	
	William H.	S	W	M	Oct 1893	6	S				MS	AL	AL	
	Benjamin R.	S	W	M	Oct 1895	4	S				MS	AL	AL	
	James A.	S	W	M	Mar 1899	1	S				MS	AL	AL	
43	Harrison, Jasper M.	H	W	M	Mar 1848	52	M	32			MS	TN	MS	Farmer
	Elizabeth	W	W	F	Sep 1846	54	M	32	6	6	MS	TN	TN	
	Mattie S.	D	W	F	Sep 1862	37	S				MS	MS	MS	
	Nancy L.	D	W	F	Feb 1872	28	S				MS	MS	MS	
	William J.	S	W	M	Aug 1878	21	S				MS	MS	MS	
44	Tidwell, Stoke S.	H	W	M	Jan 1877	23	M	1			AL	AL	AL	Farmer
	Bettie	W	W	F	UN UN	24	M	1	1	1	AL	AL	AL	
45	Brown, William	H	W	M	Sep 1875	24	M	1			AL	AL	AL	Farmer
	Maranda N.	W	W	F	Sep 1872	27	M	1	0	0	MS	AL	AL	
46	Byram, John J.	H	W	M	Jan 1866	34	M	11			AL	GA	AL	Farmer
	Sarah J.	W	W	F	Oct 1871	28	M	11	5	4	MS	MS	AL	
	Charles S.	S	W	M	Feb 1890	10	S				MS	AL	MS	Farm Laborer
	Minnie U.	D	W	F	Aug 1891	8	S				MS	AL	MS	
	Archie G.	S	W	M	Sep 1895	4	S				MS	AL	MS	
	Arrie V.	D	W	F	Jan 1898	2	S				MS	AL	MS	
47	Hopkins, Benjamin	H	W	M	Apr 1835	65	M	44			KY	NC	KY	Farmer
	Mary E.	W	W	F	Dec 1840	58	M	44	9	8	MS	AL	AL	
	Orlander R.	S	W	M	Jul 1875	24	S				MS	KY	MS	Farmer
	Arthur C.	S	W	M	Jan 1883	17	S				MS	KY	MS	Farm Laborer
48	Deaton, John W.	H	W	M	Mar 1871	29	M	4			MS	SC	MS	Farmer
	Sarah A.	W	W	F	Mar 1878	22	M	4	0	0	MS	KY	MS	
49	Collums, Sarah D.	H	W	F	Jun 1854	45	Wd		2	2	AL	SC	AL	Farmer
	Laura A.	D	W	F	Oct 1890	9	S				MS	MS	TN	
50	Phillips, Oran	H	W	M	Jul 1844	55	Wd				TN	SC	AL	Farmer
	Lafayitt N.	W	W	F	Dec 1871	28	S				MS	TN	AL	Teacher
	Richard K.	S	W	M	Dec 1881	18	S				MS	TN	AL	Farm Laborer
	Adolphry	S	W	M	Sep 1886	13	S				MS	MS	GA	Farm Laborer
	Nancy L.	D	W	F	Sep 1875	24	S				MS	TN	AL	
	Gurley, Authur S.	HH	W	M	Nov 1880	19	S				MS	MS	TN	Day Laborer
51	Burlison, Calvin	H	W	M	Sep 1855	44	M	24			AL	TN	NC	Farmer

1	2	3	4	5	6	7	8	9	10	11	12	13	14	15
	Mary E.	W	W	F	Jul 1855	44	M	24	12	9	MS	MS	MS	
	Calvin D	S	W	M	Feb 1881	19	S				AL	AL	MS	Farm Laborer
	Rhoda J.	D	W	F	Apr 1882	18	S				AL	AL	MS	
	Crastis F.	S	W	M	Feb 1884	16	S				AL	AL	MS	Farm Laborer
	Charles J.	S	W	M	Mar 1892	8	S				MS	AL	MS	
	Etta L.	D	W	F	Mar 1894	6	S				MS	AL	MS	
	James M.	S	W	M	Aug 1896	3	S				MS	AL	MS	
52	Byram, Hiton P.	H	W	M	Feb 1875	25	M	2			MS	MS	MS	Farmer
	Emla A.	W	W	F	Oct 1879	20	M	2	1	1	AL	AL	MS	
	Ethie L.	D	W	F	Aug 1899	1	S				MS	MS	AL	
53	Deaton, George R.	H	W	M	Mar 1879	21	M	0			MS	NC	MS	Farmer
	Mary V.	W	W	F	Dec 1877	22	M	0	0	0	AL	AL	MS	
54	Cornelius, Eliza	H	W	F	Apr 1870	30	Wd		4	4	MS	GA	AL	Farmer
	John R.	S	W	M	Sep 1885	14	S				MS	AL	MS	Farm Laborer
	Mary L.	D	W	F	Dec 1888	11	S				MS	AL	MS	
	Birthie O.	D	W	F	Oct 1892	8	S				MS	AL	MS	
	Norah B.	D	W	F	Oct 1895	4	S				MS	AL	MS	
55	Flurry, Charles	H	W	M	Apr 1876	24	M	2			MS	GA	AL	School Teacher
	Lillie C.	W	W	F	May 1878	22	M	2	1	1	MS	AL	MS	
	Earnie P.	S	W	M	Nov 1898	1	S				MS	MS	MS	
	Mary J.	M	W	F	Nov 1834	65	Wd		4	3	AL	AL	AL	
	Paden, Sofa	Sis	W	F	Oct 1856	43	S				MS	TN	AL	
	Slack, Thomas C.	HH	W	M	Feb 1887	13	S				MS	AL	AL	Farm Laborer
56	Davis, David M.	H	W	M	Jan 1877	23	M	2			MS	AL	IL	Farmer
	Ella L.	W	W	F	Aug 1881	18	M	2	1	1	MS	KY	MS	
	Radia M.	D	W	F	May 1899	1	S				MS	MS	MS	
57	Campbell, Larance	H	W	M	Nov 1876	23	M	0			MS	MS	MS	Farmer
	Cora B.	W	W	F	Sep 1873	26	M	0	0	0	MS	AL	AL	
58	Flurry, Richard H.	H	W	M	May 1856	34	M	14			AL	GA	AL	Farmer
	Mary A.	W	W	F	Apr 1861	39	M	14	6	5	MS	AL	AL	
	Cilibie	D	W	F	Sep 1886	13	S				MS	MS	MS	
	Lizza M.	D	W	F	May 1856	12	S				MS	MS	MS	
	Richard E.	S	W	M	Mar 1890	10	S				MS	MS	MS	
	Charley E.	S	W	F	Jun 1893	6	S				MS	MS	MS	
	Katie A.	D	W	F	Aug 1894	5	S				MS	MS	MS	
59	Sartain, Lee F.	H	W	M	Feb 1873	27	M	4			AL	AL	AL	Farmer
	Lucy R.	W	W	F	Dec 1881	18	M	4	2	2	MS	MS	MS	
	Reatey, A.	S	W	M	Nov 1896	3	S				MS	AL	MS	
	Dewey S.	S	W	M	Jun 1898	1	S				MS	AL	MS	
60	Byram, Green	H	W	M	Feb 1871	29	M	9			MS	AL	AL	Farmer
	Malinda	W	W	F	May 1873	27	M	9	3	3	MS	MS	AL	
	Girittia G.	D	W	F	Sep 1892	7	S				MS	MS	MS	
	William O.	S	W	M	Nov 1894	5	S				MS	MS	MS	
	Clara A.	D	W	F	Apr 1897	3	S				MS	MS	MS	
61	Hughes, Thomas B.	H	W	M	Dec 1869	30	M	6			AL	AL	AL	Farmer
	Etta M.	W	W	F	Dec 1869	30	M	6	4	3	AL	MS	AL	
	Refus O.	S	W	M	Sep 1894	5	S				MS	AL	AL	
	Ola M.	D	W	F	Jan 1896	4	S				MS	AL	AL	
	Samantha J.	D	W	F	May 1899	1	S				MS	AL	AL	
62	Patterson, Charles W.	H	W	M	Jan 1855	45	M	28			MO	NC	NC	Farmer
	Josephine M.	W	W	F	Dec 1855	44	M	28	13	10	AL	AL	AL	
	Leora D.	D	W	F	May 1880	20	S				MS	MO	AL	

1	2	3	4	5	6	7	8	9	10	11	12	13	14	15
	Rilla P.	D	W	F	Apr 1882	18	S				MS	MO	AL	
	Josie A.	D	W	F	Jul 1887	12	S				MS	MO	AL	
	Charles W.	S	W	M	Feb 1890	10	S				MS	MO	AL	
	Bettie C.	D	W	F	May 1892	8	S				MS	MO	AL	
	Benjamin R.	S	W	M	Feb 1893	7	S				MS	MO	AL	
	John T.	S	W	M	Jul 1898	5	S				MS	MO	AL	
	Idela D	D	W	F	Aug 1899	9/mo	S				MS	MO	AL	
63	Lindsey, Thomas	H	W	M	May 1843	57	Wd				MS	KY	AL	Gen. Merchant
	Thomas O.	S	W	M	Nov 1887	12	S				MS	MS	AL	Farm Laborer
64	Shook, William	H	W	M	Jan 1874	26	M	0			MS	AL	MS	Farmer, Teacher
	Martha I.	W	W	F	Oct 1876	23	M	0	0	0	MS	MS	AL	
65	Shook, Robert	H	W	M	Dec 1870	29	M	6			MS	AL	MS	Farmer, Teacher
	Mary A.	W	W	F	Sep 1871	28	M	6	0	0	MS	MS	AL	
	Gurley, James A.	HH	W	M	Sep 1882	17	S				MS	MS	TN	Day Laborer
66	Shook, Columbus C.	H	W	M	Jan 1846	54	M	34			AL	NC	NC	Farmer
	Mary E.	W	W	F	Oct 1848	52	M	34	10	7	MS	MS	MS	
	Lottie V.	D	W	F	Dec 1881	18	S				MS	AL	MS	
	Hatta M.	S	W	M	Jul 1884	15	S				MS	AL	MS	Farm Laborer
	Laura J.	D	W	F	Oct 1886	13	S				MS	AL	MS	
	Marcus A.	S	W	M	Sep 1891	8	S				MS	AL	MS	
67	Hale, Allen P.	H	W	M	Jul 1869	30	M	10			MS	AL	NC	Farmer
	Annie I.	W	W	F	Mar 1872	28	M	10	4	4	MS	AL	MS	
	Earnest A.	S	W	M	Jan 1891	9	S				MS	MS	MS	
	Etha M.	D	W	F	Aug 1894	7	S				MS	MS	MS	
	Ara	D	W	F	Aug 1894	5	S				MS	MS	MS	
	Oscar O.	S	W	M	Aug 1898	2	S				MS	MS	MS	
68	Sartain, John M.	H	W	M	Mar 1869	31	M	7			AL	AL	GA	Farmer
	Josephen	W	W	F	Aug 1870	29	M	7	3	1	MS	MS	AL	
	Benjamin F.	S	W	M	Sep 1898	1	S				MS	AL	MS	
69	Byram, Carie	H	W	M	Oct 1830	69	M	50			AL	TN	TN	
	Lucinda	W	W	F	Mar 1830	70	M	50	10	8	AL	GA	GA	
70	Cornelius, George J.	H	W	M	Sep 1850	49	M	30			AL	AL	TN	Farmer
	Sarah H.	W	W	F	Apr 1853	47	M	30	6	6	MS	AL	GA	
	James F.	S	W	M	Apr 1882	18	S				MS	AL	MS	Farm Laborer
	Silas	S	W	M	May 1886	14	S				MS	AL	MS	Farm Laborer
	Lydia B.	D	W	F	May 1890	10	S				MS	AL	MS	
	Pollie	Sis	W	F	Jan 1828	72	Wd		8	4	TN	IL	IL	
71	Cornelius, Eliza	H	W	F	Jan 1882	38	Wd		8	6	MS	AL	AL	Farmer
	Cida V.	S	W	F	Feb 1882	18	S				MS	AL	MS	Farm Laborer
	Ema J.	D	W	F	Apr 1884	16	S				MS	AL	MS	
	Annie L.	D	W	F	Oct 1886	13	S				MS	AL	MS	
	George T.	S	W	M	Jul 1890	9	S				MS	AL	MS	
72	Robinson, Isaac L.	H	W	M	Sep 1845	54	M	29			AL	AL	AL	Farmer
	Mary E.	W	W	F	Mar 1851	49	M	29	5	4	SC	SC	SC	
	Nancy A.	D	W	F	Dec 1871	28	S				MS	AL	SC	
	Albert M.	S	W	M	Oct 1877	22	S				MS	AL	SC	Farm Laborer
	William M.	S	W	M	Jul 1882	17	S				MS	AL	SC	Farm Laborer
73	Lindsey, Elizabeth	H	W	F	May 1840	60	Wd				AL	NC	TN	Farmer
	Davis, Mary A.	Nce	W	F	Nov 1862	37	S				MS	AL	NC	
74	Phillips, Dixon C.	H	W	M	Mar 1847	53	S				TN	TN	TN	Farmer
	Lee N.	Sis	W	F	Jan 1860	40	S				MS	TN	TN	

1	2	3	4	5	6	7	8	9	10	11	12	13	14	15
	Elmira	Sis	W	F	Jan 1860	40	S				MS	TN	TN	
75	Rutherford, Verina D.	H	W	F	May 1864	36	S				AL	AL	AL	Farmer
	Edward C.	S	W	M	Feb 1884	16	S				MS	MS	AL	Farm Laborer
	Minnie L.	D	W	F	Sep 1891	8	S				MS	MS	AL	
	Nancy J.	D	W	F	Mar 1895	5	S				MS	MS	AL	
76	Chadwick, James M.	H	W	M	May 1836	64	M	30			GA	GA	GA	Farmer
	Margaret	W	W	F	Jan 1854	46	M	30	2	1	AL	AL	AL	
	Mary E.	D	W	F	Feb 1876	24	S				AL	GA	AL	
77	Pair, Richard H.	H	W	M	May 1831	69	M	29			GA	SC	SC	Farmer
	Parthenia J.	W	W	F	Jan 1854	40	M	29	2	1	GA	GA	AL	
78	Lindsey, Sidney M.	H	W	M	Dec 1877	22	M	0			MS	AL	AL	Farmer
	Peneley	W	W	F	Jun 1883	16	M	0	0	0	MS	MS	MS	
79	Lindsey, Matthew R.	H	W	M	Apr 1836	64	M	42			AL	KY	AL	Farmer
	Sarah L.	W	W	F	Aug 1838	61	M	42	10	3	AL	AL	AL	
	James P.	S	W	M	Apr 1880	20	S				MS	AL	AL	Farmer
	Matthew O.	S	W	M	Apr 1883	17	S				MS	AL	AL	Farm Laborer
80	Byram, Virginia P.	H	W	F	Aug 1867	32	Wd		4	3	MS	AL	AL	Farmer
	Emma V.	D	W	F	Dec 1887	12	S				MS	MS	MS	
	Ednar M.	D	W	F	Sep 1889	10	S				MS	MS	MS	
	Freddie S.	S	W	M	Jul 1893	6	S				MS	MS	MS	
81	Byram, James A.	H	W	M	Oct 1852	47	M	28			MS	TN	TN	Farmer
	Sarah M.	W	W	F	Jan 1858	42	M	28	12	8	MS	AL	AL	
	Orlander H.	S	W	M	Jun 1882	17	S				TX	MS	MS	Farm Laborer
	Grover C.	S	W	M	Sep 1884	15	S				MS	MS	MS	Farm Laborer
	Ella P.	D	W	F	Aug 1886	13	S				AR	MS	MS	
	Maud M.	D	W	F	Dec 1892	7	S				AR	MS	MS	
	Alva L.	S	W	M	Aug 1895	4	S				MS	MS	MS	
82	Perry, George W.	H	W	M	Nov 1857	42	M	21			FL	SC	SC	Farmer
	Tabitha J.	W	W	F	Mar 1861	39	M	21	10	7	MS	MS	MS	
	Gernal L.	S	W	M	May 1881	19	S				MS	FL	MS	Farm Laborer
	James O.	S	W	M	Jun 1883	16	S				MS	FL	MS	Farm Laborer
	Columbus C.	S	W	M	Jan 1886	14	S				MS	FL	MS	Farm Laborer
	Hester L.	D	W	F	Dec 1887	12	S				MS	FL	MS	
	Joseph J.	S	W	M	Sep 1889	10	S				MS	FL	MS	Farm Laborer
	Mary E.	D	W	F	Jun 1892	8	S				MS	FL	MS	
	Richard F.	S	W	M	Nov 1893	6	S				MS	FL	MS	
83	Patterson, James A.	H	W	M	Mar 1875	25	M	0			AL	MS	AL	Farmer
	Altha C.	W	W	F	Jan 1877	23	M	0	0	0	AL	AL	TN	
	Mary A.	D	W	F	Jan 1892	8	S				MS	MS	AL	
84	Mitchell, Dawson	H	W	M	Dec 1849	50	M	15			AL	SC	SC	Farmer
	Rebecca E.	W	W	F	Oct 1860	39	M	15	3	2	MS	TN	TN	
	Grover D.	S	W	M	Nov 1898	1	S				MS	AL	MS	
	Green, Lou B.	SD	W	F	Apr 1888	12	S				MS	AL	MS	
85	Crane, Aaron J.	H	W	M	May 1873	27	M	8			AL	AL	AL	Farmer
	Malinda V.	W	W	F	Jul 1873	26	M	8	5	3	MS	MS	MS	
	Sarah E.	D	W	F	Oct 1893	6	S				MS	MS	MS	
	Effie V.	D	W	F	Jun 1896	3	S				MS	MS	MS	
	Jettie E.	D	W	F	Jan 1900	5/mo	S				MS	MS	MS	
86	Sartain, John T.	H	W	M	May 1873	26	M	6			MS	AL	AL	Farmer
	Alice E.	W	W	F	May 1871	29	M	6	3	3	MS	MS	AR	
	Ora B.	D	W	F	Oct 1894	5	S				MS	MS	MS	

1	2	3	4	5	6	7	8	9	10	11	12	13	14	15
	Minnie M.	D	W	F	Sep 1896	3	S				MS	MS	MS	
	James W.	S	W	M	Jan 1899	1	S				MS	MS	MS	
87	Sartain, Thomas J.	H	W	M	Dec 1878	21	M	4			AL	AL	MS	Farmer
	Mary J.	W	W	F	Jan 1883	17	M	4	2	2	MS	MS	MS	
	Lee	S	W	M	Feb 1897	3	S				MS	AL	MS	
	George Davey	S	W	M	Feb 1899	1	S				MS	AL	MS	
88	Shook, John A.	H	W	M	Nov 1861	38	M	15			MS	AL	MS	Farmer
	Tesora B.	W	W	F	Nov 1872	27	M	15	6	6	MS	GA	MS	
	Marcus L.	S	W	M	Sep 1885	14	S				MS	MS	MS	Farm Laborer
	Georgia A.	D	W	F	Oct 1887	12	S				TX	MS	MS	
	Ida E.	D	W	F	Dec 1891	9	S				TX	MS	MS	
	Nancy E.	D	W	F	Sep 1893	6	S				TX	MS	MS	
	Gracie C.	D	W	F	Feb 1896	4	S				TX	MS	MS	
	Edith	D	W	F	Jul 1898	1	S				TX	MS	MS	
89	Moody, John A.	H	W	M	Jan 1862	38	M	15			AL	GA	AL	Farmer
	Mary C.	W	W	F	Mar 1860	40	M	15	11	9	MS	AL	MS	
	Walter L.	S	W	M	Apr 1886	14	S				TX	AL	MS	Farm Laborer
	Lottie	D	W	F	Mar 1888	12	S				TX	AL	MS	
	Texie K.	D	W	F	May 1891	9	S				MS	AL	MS	
	Maggie E.	D	W	F	Sep 1892	7	S				MS	AL	MS	
	Olen V.	S	W	M	Feb 1896	4	S				MS	AL	MS	
	Haden M.	S	W	M	Feb 1898	2	S				MS	AL	MS	
	Dersey A.	D	W	F	Feb 1900	3/mo	S				MS	AL	MS	
	Wembs, Sarah A.	SD	W	F	Aug 1879	20	S				MS	AL	MS	
	Wembs, Malida	SD	W	F	Apr 1880	19	S				MS	AL	MS	
90	Kennedy, Nathan M.	H	W	M	Sep 1864	35	M	19			TN	AL	GA	
	Sarah A.	W	W	F	Aug 1863	36	M	19	8	6	AL	SC	SC	
	Lucy J.	D	W	F	Jan 1883	17	S				AL	TN	AL	
	Louella G.	D	W	F	Aug 1886	13	S				AL	TN	AL	
	Mary E.	D	W	F	Apr 1889	11	S				AL	TN	AL	
	Lemiel L.	S	W	M	Sep 1891	8	S				AL	TN	AL	
	Arthur N.	S	W	M	Jan 1896	4	S				AL	TN	AL	
	Refus A.	S	W	M	Jan 1899	1	S				AL	TN	AL	
91	Fuller, Elmond	H	W	M	Jul 1877	22	M	0			AL	AL	AL	
	Emma E.	W	W	F	Apr 1880	20	M	0	0	0	MS	MS	MS	
92	Kennedy, Asberry P.	H	W	M	Jun 1871	28	M	8			AL	TN	GA	Farmer
	Amand J.	W	W	F	Aug 1874	25	M	8	4	3	MS	MS	MS	
	Ora F.	D	W	F	Jun 1893	6	S				MS	TN	MS	
	Dosia A.	D	W	F	Oct 1894	5	S				MS	TN	MS	
	Pearlie	D	W	F	May 1898	2	S				MS	TN	MS	
93	Campbell, Samantha	H	W	F	Nov 1855	44	Wd		8	5	MS	TN	TN	Farmer
	Roy O.	S	W	M	Dec 1878	21	S				MS	MS	MS	Farm Laborer
	Alex G.	S	W	M	Feb 1881	19	S				MS	MS	MS	
94	Sartain, William	H	W	M	Jun 1844	55	M	27			AL	SC	SC	Farmer
	Mary A.	W	W	F	Mar 1858	42	M	27	11	8	GA	GA	NC	
	Lottie L.	D	W	F	May 1884	16	S				MS	AL	GA	
	Mattie R.	D	W	F	Apr 1886	14	S				MS	AL	GA	
	Ada A.	D	W	F	May 1888	12	S				MS	AL	GA	
	William F.	S	W	M	Dec 1889	10	S				MS	AL	GA	
	Jennie L.	D	W	F	Dec 1891	8	S				MS	AL	GA	
	Peoples, James	HH	W	M	Apr 1875	25	S				MS	MS	MS	Day Laborer
	Russo, Thomas H.	HH	W	M	Jun 1885	14	S				MS	MS	MS	Day Laborer
95	Epps, Levy	H	W	M	Mar 1864	36	M	6			AL	AL	AL	Farmer
	Nancy A.	W	W	F	Apr 1876	24	M	6	3	2	MS	AL	GA	

1	2	3	4	5	6	7	8	9	10	11	12	13	14	15
	William E.	S	W	M	Nov 1896	3	S				MS	AL	MS	
	Ludiann	D	W	F	Aug 1898	1	S				MS	AL	MS	
96	Smith, Jackson J.	H	W	M	Mar 1855	45	M	21			AL	SC	SC	Farmer
	Margaret	W	W	F	Jan 1850	50	M	21	7	5	GA	SC	SC	
	Martha V.	D	W	F	Jun 1879	20	S				AL	AL	GA	
	Mary E.	D	W	F	Oct 1884	15	S				AL	AL	GA	
	Emma	D	W	F	Feb 1888	12	S				AL	AL	GA	
	Sallie	D	W	F	Jul 1890	9	S				AL	AL	GA	
	John	S	W	M	Aug 1893	6	S				AL	AL	GA	
97	Hester, Joseph P.	H	W	M	Apr 1857	42	M	19			AL	AL	AL	Farmer
	Kizzie A.	W	W	F	Jul 1858	41	M	19	11	9	AL	AL	AL	
	Otheler R.	S	W	M	Jun 1881	19	S				AL	AL	AL	Farm Laborer
	Lee C.	S	W	M	Sep 1882	17	S				AL	AL	AL	Farm Laborer
	Benjamin A.	S	W	M	Jan 1884	16	S				AL	AL	AL	Farm Laborer
	Veto C.	S	W	M	Dec 1885	14	S				AL	AL	AL	
	Zollie W.	S	W	M	Sep 1887	12	S				AL	AL	AL	
	Calvin H.	S	W	M	Jul 1889	10	S				AL	AL	AL	
	Willie P.	S	W	M	Aug 1891	8	S				AL	AL	AL	
	Gerome E.	S	W	M	Apr 1895	5	S				MS	AL	AL	
	Joseph R.	S	W	M	Jan 1898	2	S				MS	AL	AL	
98	Moris, Isaac	H	W	M	Jan 1825	75	S				AL	NC	SC	Farm Manager
	Vaught, Mary J.	Hk	W	F	May 1833	67	Wd		2	1	NC	NC	NC	
	Morison, James	HH	B	M	Jan 1882	18	S				MS	MS	MS	Farm Laborer
99	Deaton, George P.	H	W	M	Oct 1855	45	M	4			MS	NC	NC	Farmer
	Lucy A.	W	W	F	Jul 1869	30	M	4	3	3	MS	AL	AL	
	William W.	S	W	M	Nov 1896	3	S				MS	MS	MS	
	Gradie O.	S	W	M	Mar 1898	2	S				MS	MS	MS	
	Ora R.	D	W	F	Jan 1900	4/mo	S				MS	MS	MS	
	Ruth	M	W	F	Aug 1814	85	Wd				NC	NC	NC	
100	Fuller, Samuel J.	H	W	M	May 1879	21	M	0			AL	AL	AL	Farmer
	Cora B.	W	W	F	Jul 1880	19	M	0	0	0	MS	AL	AL	
101	Clingan, Andrew J.	H	W	M	Sep 1855	44	M	23			MS	TN	AL	Farmer
	Mary E.	W	W	F	Jul 1835	64	M	23	8	3	TN	TN	TN	
	George A.	S	W	M	Feb 1878	22	S				MS	MS	TN	Farm Laborer
102	Deaton, Henry P.	H	W	M	Nov 1853	46	M	23			MS	NC	NC	Farmer
	Louvenia A.	W	W	F	Dec 1858	41	M	23	12	9	MS	AL	AL	
	Luther H.	S	W	M	Jan 1878	22	S				MS	MS	MS	Farmer
	William H.	S	W	M	May 1879	21	S				MS	MS	MS	Day Laborer
	Ziphinah W.	S	W	M	Mar 1881	19	S				MS	MS	MS	Farm Laborer
	Minnie O.	D	W	F	Dec 1882	17	S				MS	MS	MS	
	Tarpley B.	S	W	M	Nov 1884	15	S				MS	MS	MS	Farm Laborer
	Henry A.	S	W	M	Jan 1892	8	S				MS	MS	MS	
	Carrie W.	D	W	F	Apr 1895	5	S				MS	MS	MS	
	Clarence D.	S	W	M	Jul 1897	2	S				MS	MS	MS	
	Mary E.	D	W	F	Feb 1899	1	S				MS	MS	MS	
	Campbell, William M.	FiL	W	M	Jan 1820	80	M	60			AL	PA	TN	
	Rebecca A.	MiL	W	F	Aug 1821	79	M	60	11	5	AL	NC	NC	
103	Dean, James C.	H	W	M	Oct 1850	49	M	23			MS	GA	GA	
	Evie L.	W	W	F	Sep 1855	44	M	23	2	2	AL	AL	AL	
	Sidney B.	S	W	M	Oct 1877	22	S				MS	MS	AL	Farmer
	Terrell H.	S	W	M	Dec 1883	16	S				MS	MS	AL	Farm Laborer
104	Deaton, William	H	W	M	May 1843	57	M	27			NC	NC	NC	Farmer
	Mably E.	W	W	F	Sep 1845	54	M	27	8	5	TN	NC	NC	
	Rutha B.	D	W	F	Jun 1884	15	S				MS	NC	TN	

1	2	3	4	5	6	7	8	9	10	11	12	13	14	15
	Mattie S.	D	W	F	Jul 1887	12	S				MS	NC	TN	
105	Mauldin, David C.	H	W	M	May 1863	37	M	5			MS	MS	MS	Farmer
	Mary C.	W	W	F	Jan 1879	21	M	5	1	1	MS	MS	AL	
	Arnal J.	S	W	M	Mar 1888	12	S				MS	MS	MS	Farm Laborer
	Bettie	D	W	F	Oct 1890	9	S				MS	MS	MS	
	Bula L.	D	W	F	Jun 1892	6	S				MS	MS	MS	
	Lyddy E.	D	W	F	Aug 1899	10/mo	S				MS	MS	MS	
	John	F	W	M	Sep 1837	62	M				AL	AL	AL	Farmer
106	Clingan, James M.	H	W	M	Jul 1864	35	M	13			MS	AL	AL	Farmer
	Martha S.	W	W	F	Jan 1858	42	M	13	4	4	MS	AL	AL	
	Jennie L.	D	W	F	Dec 1887	13	S				MS	MS	MS	
	David T.	S	W	M	Dec 1888	11	S				MS	MS	MS	Farm Laborer
	Andrew W.	S	W	F	Mar 1891	9	S				MS	MS	MS	
	Tabitha E.	D	W	F	Jan 1893	7	S				MS	MS	MS	
	Harrison, Isaya S.	FiL	W	M	Jan 1822	70	Wd				AL	TN	TN	
107	Seaton, Harvey L.	H	W	M	Jul 1875	24	M	4			MS	NC	TN	Farmer
	Georna A.	W	W	F	Aug 1877	22	M	4	2	2	MS	AL	MS	
	Harris D.	S	W	M	Dec 1896	3	S				MS	MS	MS	
	William A.	S	W	M	Dec 1898	1	S				MS	MS	MS	
108	Neal, Annie O.	H	W	F	Mar 1870	30	Wd		4	3	TN	TN	TN	Farmer
	Mary M.	D	W	F	Jun 1892	7	S				MS	MS	TN	
	Evie P.	D	W	F	Jul 1896	3	S				MS	MS	TN	
	Willis G.	S	W	M	Jun 1898	1	S				MS	MS	TN	
109	Burlison, Al.	H	W	M	Oct 1876	23	M	0			AL	AL	MS	Farmer
	Mollie M.	W	W	F	Jan 1881	19	M	0	0	0	MS	MS	AL	
110	Clingan, William D.	H	W	M	Jun 1870	29	M	10			MS	MS	MS	Farmer
	Clara A.	W	W	F	Jul 1876	23	M	10	3	3	AL	AL	AL	
	Oscar	S	W	M	Oct 1892	7	S				MS	MS	AL	
	William H.	S	W	M	Mar 1895	5	S				MS	MS	AL	
	James A.	S	W	M	Jun 1898	1	S				MS	MS	AL	
111	Hicks, Benjamin L.	H	W	M	Apr 1868	32	M	12			AL	TN	NC	Farmer
	Alice S.	W	W	F	Mar 1867	33	12	7	6		MS	KY	MS	
	Calvin L.	S	W	M	May 1888	12	S				MS	AL	MS	Farm Laborer
	Laura B.	D	W	F	Oct 1889	10	S				MS	AL	MS	
	William R.	S	W	M	Aug 1891	8	S				MS	AL	MS	
	Della I.	D	W	F	Dec 1894	5	S				MS	AL	MS	
	Evie C.	D	W	F	Dec 1896	3	S				MS	AL	MS	
	John H.	S	W	M	Sep 1898	1	S				MS	AL	MS	
	Nancy	M	W	M	Jan 1830	70	Wd		7	4	SC	SC	SC	
112	Davis, Willis M.	H	W	M	Oct 1821	78	M	39			AL	TN	GA	Farmer
	Harriett	W	W	F	Oct 1837	60	M	39	12	11	AL	TN	AL	
	George E.	S	W	M	Mar 1875	25	S				MS	AL	AL	Farm Laborer
	Sarah C.	D	W	F	Dec 1876	23	S				MS	AL	AL	
	Garlie V.	D	W	F	Nov 1881	18	S				MS	AL	AL	
	Nancy M.	D	W	F	Feb 1885	15	S				MS	AL	AL	
113	Carr, Joseph B.	H	W	M	May 1848	52	M	30			MS	GA	GA	Farmer
	Ellner S.	W	W	F	Nov 1852	47	M	30	6	4	AL	SC	SC	
	Hettie L.	D	W	F	Jul 1885	14	S				MS	MS	AL	
114	Selvy, Thomas J.	H	W	M	Oct 1836	63	M	28			AL	MD	NC	
	Martha E.	W	W	F	Dec 1847	52	M	28	9	7	NC	NC	NC	
	Thomas L.	S	W	M	Sep 1878	21	S				MS	AL	NC	Farm Laborer
	Cassie C.	D	W	F	Aug 1879	20	S				MS	AL	NC	
	Flora P.	D	W	F	May 1883	17	S				MS	AL	NC	

1	2	3	4	5	6	7	8	9	10	11	12	13	14	15
	Texas J.	S	W	M	Jun 1886	13	S				MS	AL	NC	
	Effie B.	D	W	F	Apr 1890	10	S				MS	AL	NC	
115	Looney, John F.	H	W	M	Apr 1854	46	M	23			MS	TN	TN	Farmer
	Nancy J.	W	W	F	Apr 1858	42	M	23	10	9	MS	AL	AL	
	William L.	S	W	M	Jun 1877	22	S				MS	MS	MS	At School
	Lula A.	D	W	F	Jun 1881	18	S				MS	MS	MS	
	Lola V.	D	W	F	Feb 1884	16	S				MS	MS	MS	
	Joseph A.	S	W	M	Aug 1886	13	S				MS	MS	MS	Farm Laborer
	Henry O.	S	W	M	Sep 1888	11	S				MS	MS	MS	Farm Laborer
	Myrtie B.	D	W	F	Aug 1891	8	S				MS	MS	MS	
	Pearly A.	D	W	F	Dec 1893	6	S				MS	MS	MS	
	Ollie G.	D	W	F	Aug 1896	3	S				MS	MS	MS	
	Autie M.	D	W	F	Oct 1898	1	S				MS	MS	MS	
116	Moore, Henry C.	H	W	M	Nov 1854	45	M	23			AL	TN	AL	Farmer
	Lucy A.	W	W	F	Sep 1856	43	M	23	9	7	AL	GA	GA	
	Dack M.	S	W	M	May 1880	20	S				AL	AL	GA	Farm Laborer
	James W.	S	W	M	Jan 1884	16	S				AL	AL	GA	
	Susie	D	W	F	Dec 1889	10	S				AL	AL	GA	
	Sirlin A.	S	W	M	Jan 1892	8	S				MS	AL	GA	
	John W.	S	W	M	Nov 1893	6	S				MS	AL	GA	
	Ida M.	D	W	F	May 1896	4	S				MS	AL	GA	
117	Jackson, George S.	H	W	M	Aug 1857	42	M	22			MS	GA	AL	Farmer
	Amanda D.	W	W	F	Sep 1855	44	M	22	8	4	MS	AL	AL	
	Jesse C.	S	W	M	Aug 1881	19	S				MS	MS	MS	
	Fannie I.	D	W	F	Sep 1882	17	S				MS	MS	MS	
	William A.	S	W	M	Apr 1882	12	S				MS	MS	MS	Farm Laborer
	Lutha A.	S	W	M	Mar 1890	10	S				MS	MS	MS	
118	Clark, William T.	H	W	M	Dec 1848	51	M	21			AL	AL	AL	Farmer
	Mary L.	W	W	F	Aug 1861	38	M	21	9	9	MS	NC	AL	
	Ella I.	D	W	F	Dec 1879	20	S				MS	AL	MS	
	James R.	S	W	M	Mar 1882	18	S				MS	AL	MS	Farm Laborer
	George H.	S	W	M	Jan 1885	15	S				MS	AL	MS	Farm Laborer
	Martha E.	D	W	F	Feb 1887	13	S				MS	AL	MS	
	William L.	S	W	M	Jul 1889	11	S				MS	AL	MS	Farm Laborer
	John P.	S	W	M	Jul 1891	8	S				MS	AL	MS	
	Thomas G.	S	W	M	Aug 1895	4	S				MS	AL	MS	
	Sam J.	S	W	M	Feb 1898	2	S				MS	AL	MS	
	Mary A.	D	W	F	Mar 1900	2/mo	S				MS	AL	MS	
119	Clark, William A.	H	W	M	Mar 1856	44	M	22			AL	AL	AL	Farmer
	Julia A.	W	W	F	May 1861	39	M	22	2	1	MS	MS	AR	
	Thomas A.	S	W	M	Nov 1882	18	S				MS	AL	MS	Farm Laborer
120	Cornelius, Bettie	H	W	F	Feb 1830	70	Wd		0	0	TN	SC	AL	
121	Hallmark, Jesse C.	H	W	M	Apr 1854	46	M	18			MS	UN	MS	Farmer
	Elizabeth L.	W	W	F	Dec 1859	40	M	18	7	6	MS	SC	AL	
	George C.	S	W	M	Nov 1882	17	S				MS	MS	MS	Farm Laborer
	Drucilla M.	D	W	F	Apr 1885	15	S				MS	MS	MS	
	Thomas E.	S	W	M	Apr 1887	13	S				MS	MS	MS	Farm Laborer
	James W.	S	W	M	Mar 1889	11	S				MS	MS	MS	Farm Laborer
	John L.	S	W	M	May 1894	6	S				MS	MS	MS	
	Birtie A.	D	W	F	Apr 1898	2	S				MS	MS	MS	
122	Shook, Middleton	H	W	M	Jun 1878	22	S				MS	MS	MS	Farmer
	William H.	Bro	W	M	Apr 1875	25	S				MS	MS	MS	Farm Laborer
	Nancy E.	M	W	F	May 1835	65	Wd				AL	AL	AL	
123	Cummins, Britton R.	H	W	M	Sep 1877	22	S				AL	AL	AL	Farmer

1	2	3	4	5	6	7	8	9	10	11	12	13	14	15
	Silas M.	Bro	W	M	Jan 1883	17	S				AL	AL	AL	Farm Laborer
	Norman D.	Bro	W	M	Feb 1885	15	S				AL	AL	AL	Farm Laborer
	Elizabeth	Sis	W	F	Mar 1890	10	S				AL	AL	AL	
	McBee, Ervin	Bro	W	M	Jan 1893	7	S				AL	AL	AL	
	McBee, Macie A.	M	W	F	Sep 1857	42	Wd		9	6	AL	SC	SC	
124	Huffman, Albert M.	H	W	M	Aug 1878	21	S				AL	AL	AL	Farmer
	Darthula S.	Sis	W	F	Sep 1874	25	S				AL	AL	AL	
	Mattie B.	M	W	F	Jan 1860	40	Wd		2	2	MS	AL	AL	
	Feebie	GM	W	F	Mar 1835	65	Wd		6	5	AL	AL	AL	
125	Montgomery, James	H	W	M	Jan 1840	60	M	25			AL	KY	AL	Farmer
	Martha A.	W	W	F	Dec 1834	65	M	25	2	1	AL	TN	IL	
	Gable, Lucinda P.	SiL	W	F	Feb 1829	71	D				AL	TN	IL	
126	Stanphill, Thomas M.	H	W	M	Jan 1853	47	M	12			AL	UN	UN	Farmer
	Mary C.	W	F	M	May 1858	42	M	12	3	3	MS	MS	MS	
	Thomas C.	S	W	M	Jun 1891	8	S				MS	AL	MS	
	Charles K.	S	W	M	Aug 1894	5	S				MS	AL	MS	
	Julia V.	D	W	F	Jul 1897	2	S				MS	AL	MS	
127	Upton, Richard G.	H	W	M	Mar 1878	22	M	3			MS	MS	MS	Farmer
	Cassie A.	W	W	F	Jun 1881	19	M	3	2	1	MS	MS	MS	
	Dosia M.	D	W	F	Aug 1897	2	S				MS	MS	MS	
128	Upton, Thomas	H	W	M	Feb 1874	26	M	4			AL	GA	AL	Farmer
	Emla M.	W	W	F	Jan 1861	39	M	4	3	3	MS	AL	AL	
	Minnie J.	D	W	F	Jun 1896	3	S				MS	AL	MS	
	James M.	S	W	M	Sep 1897	2	S				MS	AL	MS	
	Edward R.	S	W	M	May 1899	1	S				MS	AL	MS	
	Jurnisa J.	Sis	W	F	May 1857	43	S				MS	AL	MS	
129	Byram, James F.	H	W	M	Sep 1853	44	M	27			MS	AL	AL	Farmer
	Eliza M.	W	W	F	Jan 1879	46	M	27	9	8	MS	SC	SC	
	Martha A.	D	W	F	Dec 1880	19	S				MS	MS	MS	Farm Laborer
	Edward A.	S	W	M	Mar 1883	17	S				MS	MS	MS	Farm Laborer
	Mittie A.	D	W	F	Mar 1886	14	S				MS	MS	MS	
	James P.	S	W	M	Feb 1891	9	S				MS	MS	MS	
130	Johnson, Gordon	H	W	M	Sep 1863	36	M	19			AL	GA	AL	Farmer
	Nancy J.	W	W	F	Aug 1864	35	M	19	8	5	AL	MS	AL	
	James W.	S	W	M	Jun 1882	17	S				TX	AL	AL	Farm Laborer
	Joseph A.	S	W	M	Jul 1886	13	S				AL	AL	AL	Farm Laborer
	Mary M.	D	W	F	Jun 1888	11	S				TX	AL	AL	
	Albert S.	S	W	M	Nov 1892	7	S				AL	AL	AL	
	Marcie M.	S	W	M	Oct 1894	3	S				TX	AL	AL	
	Sargent, Ruben C.	BiL	W	M	Mar 1875	25	S				AL	MS	AL	Day Laborer
131	Angland, Thomas	H	W	M	Jun 1823	76	Wd				MS	UN	UN	Too old
132	Angland, Robert	H	W	M	Sep 1855	44	M	19			AL	MS	UN	Farmer
	Martha C.	W	W	F	Feb 1865	35	M	19	11	9	AL	SC	GA	
	Ida B.	D	W	F	Oct 1884	15	S				MS	AL	AL	
	Alice V.	D	W	F	Jan 1886	14	S				MS	AL	AL	
	William P.	S	W	M	Mar 1887	13	S				MS	AL	AL	Farm Laborer
	Thomas L.	S	W	M	Aug 1888	11	S				MS	AL	AL	Farm Laborer
	Robert H.	S	W	M	Jan 1890	10	S				MS	AL	AL	Farm Laborer
	McDaniel	S	W	M	Nov 1891	8	S				MS	AL	AL	
	Mary V.	D	W	F	Sep 1893	6	S				MS	AL	AL	
	Louisa J.	D	W	F	Sep 1896	3	S				MS	AL	AL	
	Washington C.	S	W	M	Oct 1899	7/mo	S				MS	AL	AL	
133	Campbell, William D.	H	W	M	Nov 1856	43	M	22			MS	MS	AL	Farmer

1	2	3	4	5	6	7	8	9	10	11	12	13	14	15
	Sarah J.	W	W	F	Jan 1861	29	M	29	9	7	MS	AL	AL	
	Lila	D	W	F	Jul 1883	16	S	16	S		MS	MS	MS	
	Gerome C.	S	W	M	Nov 1885	14	S				MS	MS	MS	Farm Laborer
	Cordiann R.	D	W	F	Feb 1888	11	S				MS	MS	MS	
	James E.	S	W	M	Apr 1890	10	S				MS	MS	MS	Farm Laborer
	Grover C.	S	W	M	Jan 1893	7	S				MS	MS	MS	
	Edna L.	D	W	F	May 1898	2	S				MS	MS	MS	
134	White, Mahalia	H	W	F	Jan 1827	73	Wd				AL	NC	SC	Farmer
	Mary J.	Nce	W	F	Jun 1855	44	S				MS	SC	SC	
135	Crane, Dennis	H	W	M	Sep 1853	46	M	28			AL	SC	AL	Farmer
	Ophelia G.	W	W	F	Jun 1849	50	M	28	10	9	MS	SC	AL	
	Dovie M.	D	W	F	Dec 1882	17	S				AL	AL	MS	
	Frank, B.	S	W	M	May 1885	15	S				MS	AL	MS	
	Dennis, L.	S	W	M	Feb 1887	13	S				MS	AL	MS	Farm Laborer
	Lucinda O.	D	W	F	Sep 1889	10	S				MS	AL	MS	
	Carus	GS	W	F	Sep 1899	8/mo	S				MS	AL	AL	
136	Guller, Ismus	H	W	M	Apr 1850	50	M	26			AL	SC	SC	Farmer
	Bessie A.	W	W	F	Jul 1851	49	M	26	7	5	AL	NC	AL	
	Laura J.	D	W	F	Jun 1886	13	S				AL	AL	AL	
137	Crane, John W.	H	W	M	Dec 1872	27	M	2			AL	AL	AL	Farmer
	Willie L.	W	W	F	Jan 1881	19	M	2	1	1	AL	AL	AL	
	James L.	S	W	M	Jul 1899	10/mo	S				MS	AL	AL	
138	Fuller, Adolphus P.	H	W	M	Oct 1874	25	M	5			AL	AL	AL	Farmer
	Bessie F.	W	W	F	Apr 1880	20	M	5	3	3	AL	AL	AL	
	Clarence L.	S	W	F	Feb 1896	4	S				AL	AL	AL	
	Canis L.	D	W	F	Sep 1897	2	S				AL	AL	AL	
	Lillie G.	D	W	F	Oct 1899	8/mo	S				AL	AL	AL	
139	Cranford, James F.	H	W	M	Mar 1833	67	M	14			AL	GA	AL	Farmer
	Georgia P.	W	W	F	Feb 1868	32	M	14	2	1	AL	AL	AL	
	Nancy E.	D	W	F	Dec 1892	7	S				MS	AL	AL	
140	Shook, James W.	H	W	M	Jan 1877	23	M	0			MS	AL	AL	Farmer
	Ednar E.	W	W	F	Oct 1879	20	M	0			MS	AL	MS	
141	Shook, Michael	H	W	M	Aug 1834	65	M	45			MS	AL	MS	
	Martha M.	W	W	F	Jul 1839	60	M	45	10	7	MS	AL	MS	
	Emilie A.	D	W	F	Jul 1825	24	S				MS	AL	MS	
	Short, Alma L.	D	W	F	Apr 1870	30	M	7	1	1	MS	AL	MS	
	Olive I.	GD	W	F	Jun 1893	6	S				MS	AL	MS	
	Hallmark, Alford	UN	W	M	Nov 1851	48	S				MS	AL	AL	Farmer
142	McRae, Alexander E.	H	W	M	Jun 1853	46	M	22			MS	NC	SC	Farmer
	Clern S.	W	W	F	Dec 1856	43	M	22	9	8	MS	NC	AL	
	Mary L.	D	W	F	Sep 1878	21	S				MS	MS	MS	
	John A.	S	W	M	May 1880	20	S				MS	MS	MS	Farm Laborer
	Robert B.	S	W	M	Jun 1884	15	S				MS	MS	MS	Farm Laborer
	Carity B.	D	W	F	Jan 1886	14	S				MS	MS	MS	
	Margaret M.	D	W	F	Feb 1889	11	S				MS	MS	MS	
	Addie R.	D	W	F	Sep 1891	8	S				MS	MS	MS	
	William W.	S	W	M	Aug 1894	5	S				MS	MS	MS	
	Kenneth S.	S	W	M	May 1897	3	S				MS	MS	MS	
143	Maulden, William P.	H	W	M	Jan 1859	41	M	19			MS	MS	MS	Farmer
	Sarah I.	W	W	F	Jul 1853	46	M	19	6	4	MS	AL	AL	
	Lodonia C.	SD	W	F	May 1874	26	S				MS	MS	MS	
	Charles	SD	W	M	Aug 1884	15	S				MS	MS	MS	
	Louvenia	GD	W	F	May 1888	12	S				MS	MS	MS	

1	2	3	4	5	6	7	8	9	10	11	12	13	14	15
	Myrtle	D	W	F	Oct 1898	6	S				MS	MS	MS	
	Lester	SD	W	M	Jan 1900	6/mo	S				MS	MS	MS	
	Duncan, Wesley	Bdr	W	M	Oct 1838	61	S				MS	MS	MS	
144	Shook, Carter	H	W	M	Apr 1867	33	M	12			MS	GA	MS	Farmer
	Orlena	W	W	F	Dec 1858	41	M	12	6	5	MS	AL	AL	
	William B.	S	W	M	Aug 1888	11	S				MS	MS	MS	
	Martha E.	D	W	F	Apr 1890	10	S				MS	MS	MS	
	Maye B.	D	W	F	Jun 1892	7	S				MS	MS	MS	
	Thomas O.	S	W	M	Nov 1894	5	S				MS	MS	MS	
	Alva M.	S	W	M	Feb 1897	3	S				MS	MS	MS	
145	Hallmark, John C.	H	W	M	Dec 1853	46	M	22			MS	AL	AL	Farmer
	Elizabeth A.	W	W	F	Dec 1851	48	M	22	6	6	MS	AL	AL	
	Fannie V.	D	W	F	Oct 1880	19	S				MS	MS	MS	
	Laura E.	D	W	F	Mar 1882	18	S				MS	MS	MS	
	Melvertie R.	D	W	F	Jul 1884	15	S				MS	MS	MS	
	John A.	S	W	M	Dec 1890	9	S				MS	MS	MS	
	Luther A.	S	W	M	Dec 1888	12	S				MS	MS	MS	Farm Laborer
146	Wood, John M.	H	W	M	Sep 1864	35	M	9			MS	NC	SC	Farmer
	Addie L.	W	W	F	Jan 1874	26	M	9	5	5	TX	MS	VA	
	Effie E.	D	W	F	Oct 1891	8	S				MS	MS	TX	
	Ethel B.	D	W	F	Jan 1893	7	S				MS	MS	TX	
	Mary E.	D	W	F	Jan 1895	4	S				MS	MS	TX	
	Robert E.L.	D	W	M	Feb 1897	3	S				MS	MS	TX	
	Oliver, H.	S	W	M	Jan 1899	1	S				MS	MS	TX	
147	Willis, Charley	HH	W	M	Feb 1878	21	M	1			AL	IL	AL	Hired Hand
	Fannie	W	W	F	Jan 1881	19	M	1	0	0	MS	GA	GA	
148	Orrick, James S.	H	W	M	Mar 1862	38	M				AL	IL	AL	Farmer
	Erana A.	W	W	F	May 1874	26	M	11	2	2	MS	MS	MS	
	William O.	S	W	M	Jul 1889	10	S				MS	AL	MS	Farm Laborer
	Ida O.	D	W	F	Mar 1893	7	S				MS	AL	MS	
149	Hamilton, Walter G.	H	W	M	Jan 1870	30	M	9			MS	LA	TN	Farmer
	Mary E.	W	W	F	Sep 1869	30	M	9	5	4	MS	MS	MS	
	Malinda A.	D	W	F	Jul 1890	9	S				MS	MS	MS	
	Joseph M.	S	W	M	Jul 1892	7	S				MS	MS	MS	
	Robert L.	S	W	M	Feb 1897	3	S				MS	MS	MS	
	Walter C.	S	W	M	Apr 1899	1	S				MS	MS	MS	
150	Willis, John H.	H	W	M	Nov 1852	47	M	23			IL	IN	IN	Day Laborer
	Martha M.	W	W	F	May 1863	37	M	23	9	9	AL	AL	AL	
	Mary B.	D	W	F	Mar 1891	19	S				MS	IL	AL	
	Annie B.	D	W	F	Sep 1884	15	S				MS	IL	AL	
	John W.	S	W	M	Nov 1886	14	S				MS	IL	AL	
	Mitie E.	D	W	F	Mar 1888	12	S				MS	IL	AL	
	Carrie S.	D	W	F	Oct 1890	9	S				MS	IL	AL	
	James P.	S	W	M	Mar 1892	8	S				AL	IL	AL	
	Robert A.	S	W	M	Sep 1895	4	S				MS	IL	AL	
	Myrtle M.	D	W	F	Oct 1897	2	S				MS	IL	AL	
151	Clark, John H.	H	W	M	Aug 1854	45	Wd				AL	AL	AL	
	Julius N.	S	W	M	Nov 1880	19	S				MS	AL	MS	Farm Laborer
	Martha N.	D	W	F	Mar 1883	17	S				MS	AL	MS	
	Charity R.	D	W	F	Oct 1884	15	S				MS	AL	MS	
	Sallie L.	D	W	F	May 1886	14	S				MS	AL	MS	
	Walter P.	S	W	M	Nov 1887	12	S				MS	AL	MS	Farm Laborer
	John W.	S	W	M	Feb 1890	10	S				MS	AL	MS	Farm Laborer
	James T.	S	W	M	Apr 1892	8	S				MS	AL	MS	
	Henry V.	S	W	M	Aug 1896	3	S				MS	AL	MS	

1	2	3	4	5	6	7	8	9	10	11	12	13	14	15
152	Perry, William M.	H	W	M	Sep 1859	40	M	21			FL	SC	SC	Farmer
	Sallie E.	W	W	F	Aug 1862	37	M	21	7	5	MS	KY	NC	
	Mary A.	D	W	F	Feb 1891	19	S				MS	FL	MS	
	John M.	S	W	F	Jan 1884	16	S				MS	FL	MS	Farm Laborer
	Carrie E.	D	W	F	Aug 1862	13	S				MS	FL	MS	
	Effie C.	D	W	F	May 1889	11	S				MS	FL	MS	
	Elmer D.	S	W	M	Feb 1892	8	S				MS	FL	MS	
153	Vinson, James	H	W	M	Jun 1844	55	M	31			Ga	GA	SC	Farmer
	Lucinda	W	W	F	Feb 1845	55	M	31	11	5	MS	NC	SC	
	James W.	S	W	M	Apr 1876	24	S				MS	GA	MS	Farmer
	Ambrose L.	S	W	M	Jun 1880	19	S				MS	GA	MS	Farm Laborer
	Carra P.	D	W	F	Aug 1888	11	S				MS	GA	MS	
154	Hamilton, Isaac M.	H	W	M	Jul 1874	25	M	2			TN	SC	TN	Farmer
	Louella	W	W	F	Jul 1881	18	M	2	2	2	MS	AL	GA	
	Verna M.	D	W	F	Sep 1895	4	S				MS	TN	MS	
	Hosie I.	S	W	M	Mar 1900	3/mo	S				MS	TN	MS	
155	Cranford, William M.	H	W	M	May 1861	39	M	9			MS	AL	AL	Farmer
	Nora	W	W	F	Sep 1864	35	M	9	6	6	AL	GA	GA	
	Earnest C.	S	W	M	Aug 1885	14	S				AL	AL	AL	Farm Laborer
	Nannie E.	D	W	F	Sep 1891	8	S				MS	MS	AL	
	Ollie D.	D	W	F	Nov 1892	7	S				MS	MS	AL	
	Walter L.	S	W	M	Aug 1894	5	S				MS	MS	AL	
	Autra L.	D	W	F	May 1896	4	S				MS	MS	AL	
	Braxton S.	S	W	M	Dec 1899	5/mo	S				MS	MS	AL	
156	Stacy, Thomas F.	H	W	M	Dec 1836	63	M				AL	NC	SC	Farmer
	Martha E.	W	W	F	Apr 1836	64	M	27	7	6	TN	NC	NC	
	George A.	S	W	M	Oct 1870	29	S				MS	AL	TN	Farm Laborer
	Margaret A.	D	W	F	Jun 1872	28	S				MS	AL	TN	
	Leland W.	S	W	M	Mar 1874	26	S				MS	AL	TN	
157	Stacy, George	H	W	M	Mar 1848	52	M	33			AL	NC	SC	Farmer
	Mary A.	W	W	F	Mar 1850	50	M	33	9	7	AL	GA	GA	
	Mary D.	D	W	F	Aug 1872	27	S				MS	AL	AL	
	Misie J.	D	W	F	Feb 1881	19	S				MS	AL	AL	
	Alphia O.	D	W	F	Dec 1883	16	S				MS	AL	AL	
	Thomas F.	S	W	M	Mar 1886	14	S				MS	AL	AL	Farm Laborer
158	Stacy, George	H	W	M	Dec 1874	25	M	2			MS	AL	AL	Farmer
	Fannie B.	W	W	F	Feb 1882	18	M	2	1	1	MS	AL	AL	
159	Wood, William C.	H	W	M	Mar 1859	41	M	19			MS	AL	AL	Farmer
	Georgia A.	W	W	F	Oct 1864	35	M	19	7	6	MS	SC	MS	
	Leona C.	D	W	F	Oct 1882	17	S				MS	MS	MS	
	Absolom J.	S	W	M	Feb 1887	13	S				MS	MS	MS	Farm Laborer
	George A.	S	W	M	Sep 1889	10	S				MS	MS	MS	Farm Laborer
	Martha R.	D	W	F	May 1893	7	S				MS	MS	MS	
	Lela G.	D	W	F	Sep 1895	4	S				MS	MS	MS	
	Savilla B.	D	W	F	May 1899	1	S				MS	MS	MS	
160	Manuel, Robert	H	W	M	Mar 1859	41	M	8			GA	NC	GA	Farmer
	Bertha	W	W	F	Jan 1865	35	M	8	6	6	AL	AL	AL	
	Alonza	S	W	M	Apr 1884	16	S				AL	AL	AL	Farm Laborer
	Carrie	D	W	F	Apr 1893	7	S				AL	AL	AL	
	Calvin F.	S	W	M	Dec 1894	5	S				MS	AL	AL	
	Myrtle	D	W	F	May 1900	0/12	S				MS	AL	AL	
161	Wood, Sidney J.	H	W	M	May 1867	33	M	5			MS	KY	AL	Farmer
	Margaret	W	W	F	Jan 1874	26	M	5	4	3	AL	AL	AL	

1	2	3	4	5	6	7	8	9	10	11	12	13	14	15
	Pearly A.	D	W	F	Sep 1895	4	S				MS	MS	AL	
	Henry E.	S	W	M	Jun 1897	2	S				MS	MS	AL	
	Vernie	D	W	F	Feb 1899	1	S				MS	MS	AL	
	Charity	M	W	F	Jun 1828	72	Wd		11	7	AL	SC	SC	
162	Ham, Mattie B.	H	W	F	July 1864	35	Wd		7	6	MS	AL	AL	Farmer
	Philix	S	W	M	Feb 1885	15	S				MS	AL	AL	Farm Laborer
	Finus J.	S	W	M	Jul 1887	12	S				MS	AL	AL	Farm Laborer
	Roy D.	S	W	M	Feb 1890	10	S				MS	AL	AL	Farm Laborer
	Willie C.	S	W	M	Jan 1894	6	S				MS	AL	AL	
	Walter F.	S	W	M	Jan 1896	4	S				MS	AL	AL	
	Tressie F.	D	W	F	Dec 1899	5/mo	S				MS	AL	AL	
163	Patterson, John N.	H	W	M	Mar 1863	37	M	14			MS	TN	GA	Farmer
	Sallie E.	W	W	F	Nov 1867	32	M	14	5	5	AL	AL	AL	
	Bary N.	S	W	M	Apr 1887	13	S				MS	MS	AL	Farm Laborer
	Hattie N.	D	W	F	Dec 1889	10	S				MS	MS	AL	
	John C.	S	W	M	May 1897	7	S				MS	MS	AL	
	Finus L.	S	W	M	Apr 1896	4	S				MS	MS	AL	
	Dewey D.	S	W	M	Oct 1898	1	S				MS	MS	AL	
164	Shook, William	H	W	M	Dec 1866	33	M	5			MS	MS	AL	Farmer & Teacher
	Mary E.	W	W	F	Sep 1867	32	M	5	1	1	MS	AL	AL	
	William O.	S	W	M	Nov 1898	1	S				MS	MS	MS	
	Jones, Fannie	Bdr	W	F	Sep 1890	9	S				MS	MS	MS	Bound Girl
165	Steele, Andrew J.	H	W	M	Feb 1876	24	M	5			AL	GA	MS	Farmer
	Nanie	W	W	F	UN 1879	21	M	5	2	2	AL	GA	GA	
	Lee B.	S	W	M	Jun 1898	2	S				AL	AL	AL	
	Jeffie D.	S	W	M	Nov 1899	8/mo	S				AL	AL	AL	
166	White, Andrew J.	H	W	M	Jul 1843	56	M	37			AL	SC	SC	Farmer
	Celie	W	W	F	Aug 1843	56	M	37	3	2	AL	SC	SC	
	Seth T.	S	W	M	Sep 1879	20	S				AL	AL	AL	Farm Laborer
167	Skinner, William P.	H	W	M	Apr 1836	64	M	35			AL	KY	TN	Farmer
	Erline M.	W	W	F	May 1848	52	M	35	8	8	KY	KY	KY	
	Opha	D	W	F	Jan 1885	15	S				MS	KY	KY	
	Sidney C.	S	W	M	Sep 1878	21	S				MS	KY	KY	Day Laborer
168	Garrett, James W.	H	W	M	Mar 1874	26	M	6			AL	AL	AL	Farmer
	Sarah F.	W	W	F	Dec 1875	24	M	6	3	3	AL	AL	AL	
	William O.	S	W	M	Feb 1895	8	S				MS	AL	AL	
	Luke A.	S	W	M	Feb 1897	3	S				MS	AL	AL	
	Benjamin A.	S	W	M	Sep 1899	8/mo	S				MS	AL	AL	
	Rusoe, Bochia J.	SiL	W	M	Apr 1883	17	S				AL	AL	AL	
169	Ewing, Tomes	H	W	M	Jan 1851	49	M	24			GA	GA	GA	Farmer
	Nancy	W	W	F	Apr 1851	49	M	24	10	8	AL	GA	GA	
	William L.	S	W	M	Oct 1879	20	S				AL	GA	AL	Farm Laborer
	Dora	D	W	F	Dec 1882	17	S				AL	GA	AL	
	Allen	S	W	M	Dec 1884	15	S				AL	GA	AL	Farm Laborer
	Lela L.	D	W	F	Apr 1886	14	S				AL	GA	AL	
	Walter H.	S	W	M	Feb 1888	12	S				AL	GA	AL	Farm Laborer
	Robert	S	W	M	May 1890	10	S				AL	GA	AL	Farm Laborer
	Georgia B.	D	W	F	Feb 1894	6	S				AL	GA	AL	
	Albert L.	S	W	M	Apr 1899	1	S				AL	GA	AL	
170	Williams, Sarah F.	H	W	F	Feb 1852	48	Wd		6	5	MS	GA	GA	Farmer
	Armenta C.	D	W	F	May 1879	21	S				AL	MS	GA	
	Susan S.	D	W	F	Aug 1882	17	S				AL	MS	GA	
	Robert L.	S	W	M	Oct 1883	16	S				AL	MS	GA	Farm Laborer

1	2	3	4	5	6	7	8	9	10	11	12	13	14	15
171	Patterson, William H.	H	W	M	Aug 1865	34	M	12			MS	TN	SC	Farmer
	Mary L.	W	W	F	Feb 1867	33	M	12	4	4	MS	UN	NC	
	William H.	S	W	M	Jan 1888	12	S				MS	MS	MS	Farm Laborer
	Thomas O.	S	W	M	Dec 1889	10	S				MS	MS	MS	Farm Laborer
	Benjamin E.	S	W	M	Feb 1894	6	S				MS	MS	MS	
	Martha O.	D	W	F	Jun 1898	1	S				MS	MS	MS	
172	Martin, William A.	H	W	M	Oct 1833	66	M	45			AL	TN	KY	Farmer
	Martha	W	W	F	Oct 1834	65	M	45	3	3	NC	NC	NC	
	Epps, Ward	Crop	W	M	Jan 1876	24	S				MS	AL	MS	Cropper-Farmer
173	Stamphill, Vinson B.	H	W	M	Nov 1847	52	M	32			AL	AL	AL	Physician
	Sarah E.	W	W	F	Nov 1846	53	M	32	8	8	AL	AL	GA	
	Loutehia	D	W	F	Dec 1875	24	S				MS	AL	AL	
	Hosie B.	S	W	M	Jul 1879	20	S				MS	AL	AL	Farmer
	Minnie D.	D	W	F	Sep 1881	18	S				MS	AL	AL	
	Sallie A.	D	W	F	Mar 1885	15	S				MS	AL	AL	
174	Gurley, Marcus	H	W	M	Dec 1879	20	M	0			MS	UN	UN	Farmer
	Ema	W	W	F	Jul 1883	16	M	0	0	0	MS	AL	AL	
175	Stamphill, Thomas A.	H	W	M	Jan 1878	22	M	0			MS	AL	AL	Farmer
	Ida	W	W	F	Jan 1876	24	M	0	0	0	MS	TN	SC	
176	Balard, Charley	H	W	M	Dec 1866	33	M	18			AL	AL	AL	Farmer
	Mahala C.	W	W	F	Apr 1867	33	M	18	6	6	AL	AL	AL	
	Benjamin A.	S	W	M	Jan 1887	17	S				MS	AL	AL	Farm Laborer
	Oscar C.	S	W	M	Mar 1885	15	S				AL	AL	AL	
	Charles A.	S	W	M	Feb 1888	12	S				AL	AL	AL	
	Viola A.	D	W	F	Jan 1889	11	S				AL	AL	AL	
	Thomas M.	S	W	M	Dec 1891	8	S				AL	AL	AL	
	Hosey	S	W	M	Apr 1899	1	S				MS	AL	AL	
177	Nix, James	H	W	M	Oct 1870	29	M	9			GA	GA	GA	Farmer
	Silonia	W	W	F	Nov 1867	32	M	9	7	4	MS	MS	AL	
	John E.	S	W	M	Oct 1892	7	S				MS	GA	MS	
	Oscar C.	S	W	M	Jan 1894	6	S				MS	GA	MS	
	Herbert L.	S	W	M	Aug 1896	3	S				MS	GA	MS	
	Lola May	D	W	F	Jul 1899	10/mo	S				MS	GA	MS	
	Criddle, George	HH	W	M	Dec 1875	24	S				AL	GA	TN	Day Laborer
178	Waddle, Thomas	H	W	M	Jan 1891	19	Wd				MS	MS	AL	Farmer
179	Epps, James I.	H	W	M	Jun 1850	49	M	28			AL	NC	AL	Farmer
	Mary I.	W	W	F	Mar 1855	45	M	28	10	10	MS	TN	AL	
	Mary J.	D	W	F	Sep 1876	23	S				AL	AL	MS	
	Ira S.	D	W	F	Mar 1879	21	S				MS	AL	MS	
	John E.	S	W	M	Feb 1882	18	S				MS	AL	MS	Farm Laborer
	Cora O.	D	W	F	Jul 1884	15	S				MS	AL	MS	
	James O.	S	W	M	Aug 1888	11	S				MS	AL	MS	Farm Laborer
	Ola A.	D	W	F	Mar 1891	9	S				MS	AL	MS	
	Lela M.	D	W	F	Dec 1894	5	S				MS	AL	MS	
	Amie C.	D	W	F	May 1896	4	S				MS	AL	MS	
	Sarah	M	W	F	Jan 1818	82	Wd		1	1	AL	NC	NC	
	Martin, William M.	Bdr	W	M	Mar 1877	23	S				AL	AL	AL	Farmer
180	Mann, William A.	H	W	M	Oct 1857	42	M	27			AL	GA	GA	Farmer
	Dithula	W	W	F	Jan 1853	47	M	27	8	7	IL	AL	VA	
	Idella E.	D	W	F	Nov 1873	26	S				AL	AL	IL	
	Louella C.	D	W	F	Apr 1875	24	S				AL	AL	IL	
	Cinthia	D	W	F	Feb 1883	17	S				AL	AL	IL	
	John W.	S	W	M	Dec 1885	14	S				AL	AL	IL	Farm Laborer
	Ilina J.	D	W	F	Apr 1887	13	S				AL	AL	IL	

1	2	3	4	5	6	7	8	9	10	11	12	13	14	15
	Charles M.	S	W	M	Apr 1889	11	S				AL	AL	IL	Farm Laborer
	Silas M.	S	W	M	Aug 1891	8	S				AL	AL	IL	
181	Byram, Marion	H	W	M	Feb 1863	37	Wd				MS	AL	AL	Farmer
	Nancy K.	D	W	F	Jun 1886	13	S				MS	MS	MS	
	James A.	S	W	M	Dec 1888	11	S				MS	MS	MS	
	Mary K.	D	W	F	Jul 1893	6	S				MS	MS	MS	
	Charles H.	S	W	M	Feb 1896	4	S				MS	MS	MS	
	Sullinger O.	S	W	M	Feb 1898	2	S				MS	MS	MS	
182	Martin, William D.	H	W	M	Feb 1850	50	M	20			GA	SC	SC	Farmer
	Fatima A.	W	W	F	Mar 1860	40	M	20	6	6	MS	TN	AL	
	Percy A.	S	W	M	Jun 1881	18	S				MA	GA	MS	Farm Laborer
	Almer M.	D	W	F	May 1885	15	S				MS	GA	MS	
	Frederick G.	S	W	M	Aug 1887	12	S				MS	GA	MS	
	Carrie B.	D	W	F	Jan 1891	9	S				MS	GA	MS	
	Arkadelphia	D	W	F	May 1893	7	S				MS	GA	MS	
	Willie A.	D	W	F	May 1896	4	S				MS	GA	MS	
183	Harris, Ben	H	W	M	Apr 1830	70	M	47			TN	GA	TN	Farmer
	Polly A.	W	W	F	Aug 1833	67	M	47			TN	GA	MS	
	Stamphill. Finis B.	GS	W	M	Dec 1879	20	S				MS	AL	MS	Farmer
184	Davis, Middleton M.	H	W	M	Jul 1832	67	M	36			AL	NC	AL	Merchant-Farmer
	Mary J.	W	W	F	Dec 1842	57	M	36	5	4	AL	SC	SC	
	Nancy	D	W	F	May 1853	47	S				AL	AL	NC	
	Viannia	D	W	F	Mar 1866	34	S				MS	AL	AL	
185	Davis, Major M.	H	W	M	May 1874	26	M	5			MS	AL	AL	Farmer
	Mollie	W	W	F	Apr 1877	23	M	5	1	1	MS	AL	MS	
	Katie A.	D	W	F	Jun 1896	3	S				MS	MS	MS	
186	Upton, Thomas M.	H	W	M	May 1841	59	M	16			AL	GA	TN	Farmer
	Nancy A.	W	W	F	May 1854	48	M	16	8	4	AL	AL	AL	
	Louisa P.	D	W	F	Apr 1885	15	S				AL	AL	AL	
	Joseph L.	S	W	M	Mar 1888	12	S				AL	AL	AL	Farm Laborer
	Dollie P.	D	W	F	Jun 1892	8	S				AL	AL	AL	
	Martha E.	D	W	F	Feb 1894	6	S				AL	AL	AL	
187	Harris, Marion L.	H	W	M	Aug 1864	35	M	12			MS	AL	TN	Farmer
	Nancy P.	W	W	F	Apr 1869	31	M	12	3	2	MS	AL	AL	
	Charles M.	S	W	M	Oct 1889	10	S				MS	MS	MS	Farm Laborer
	Curtis L.	D	W	F	Jun 1897	2	S				MS	MS	MS	
188	Stacy, John W.	H	W	M	Feb 1845	55	M	30			AL	AL	AL	Farmer
	Martha E.	W	W	F	Mar 1847	53	M	30	11	9	MS	SC	SC	
	Aplha O.	D	W	F	Nov 1880	19	S				MS	AL	MS	
	John V.	S	W	M	Sep 1883	16	S				MS	AL	MS	Farm Laborer
	Lou V.	D	W	F	Nov 1886	14	S				MS	AL	MS	
	Cassie V.	D	W	F	Apr 1889	11	S				MS	AL	MS	
189	Criddle, Enoch	H	W	M	May 1874	26	M	3			MS	AL	AL	Farmer
	Dillie B.	W	W	F	Jan 1877	23	M	3	1	1	MS	AL	MS	
	Lovelma	D	W	F	Nov 1898	1	S				MS	AL	MS	
190	Martin, Sarah E.	H	W	F	Mar 1843	57	Wd		3	3	AL	GA	AL	Farmer
	Charles E.	S	W	M	Feb 1879	21	M	1			TN	AR	AL	Farm Laborer
	Benjamin	S	W	M	Mar 1881	19	S				TN	AL	AL	Farmer
	Virgie L.	DiL	W	F	Mar 1880	20	M	1	0	0	MS	MS	AL	
191	McRae, John	H	W	M	Nov 1818	81	M	49			NC	NC	NC	Miller-Farmer
	Amanda	W	W	F	Feb 1830	70	M	49	8	6	NC	NC	NC	

1	2	3	4	5	6	7	8	9	10	11	12	13	14	15
192	Madison, John M.	H	W	M	Jan 1840	60	M	32			AL	UN	UN	Farmer
	Emily E.	W	W	F	Dec 1845	54	M	32	1	1	AL	AL	AL	
193	Moore, Robert E.	H	W	M	Sep 1868	31	M	11			MS	SC	NC	Farmer
	Mary A.	W	W	F	Feb 1870	30	M	11	3	3	MS	AL	AL	
	William R.	S	W	M	Oct 1890	9	S				MS	MS	MS	
	Annie B.	D	W	F	Jan 1893	7	S				MS	MS	MS	
	Nannie M.	D	W	F	Feb 1899	1	S				MS	MS	MS	
	Hutchenson, Marcard	Nce	W	F	Aug 1875	24	S				MS	MS	AL	
194	Milstead, James B.	H	W	M	May 1857	43	M	18			AL	AL	AL	Farmer
	Amanda B.	W	W	F	Jun 1849	44	M	18	5	3	MS	NC	NC	
	Jessie M.	D	W	F	Nov 1887	12	S				MS	AL	MS	
	Casper B.	S	W	M	Jun 1885	14	S				MS	AL	MS	Farm Laborer
	Maggie E.	D	W	F	May 1889	11	S				MS	AL	MS	
195	Moore, Calan A.	H	W	M	Dec 1826	73	M	18			AL	NC	NC	Farmer
	Martha	W	W	F	Jan 1855	45	M	18	7	7	AL	AL	AL	
	Thomas G.	S	W	M	Aug 1882	17	S				MS	AL	AL	Farm Laborer
	Sopha	D	W	F	Jun 1884	15	S				MS	AL	AL	
	Maud	D	W	F	Feb 1886	14	S				MS	AL	AL	
	Grover	S	W	M	Apr 1888	12	S				MS	AL	AL	Farm Laborer
	Vernetta	D	W	F	Dec 1892	7	S				MS	AL	MS	
196	Tynes, Henry L.	H	W	M	Feb 1850	50	M	27			AL	VA	GA	Physician
	Mattie N.	W	W	F	Jan 1854	46	M	27	11	11	MS	SC	AL	
	Carrie L.	D	W	F	Nov 1873	26	S				MS	AL	MS	
	Hubert A.	S	W	M	Feb 1879	21	S				MS	AL	MS	Farm Laborer
	Robert R.	S	W	M	Oct 1880	19	S				MS	AL	MS	Farm Laborer
	Lucius L.	S	W	M	Oct 1882	17	S				MS	AL	MS	Farm Laborer
	Clara M.	D	W	F	Sep 1884	15	S				MS	AL	MS	
	Henry W.	S	W	M	Dec 1886	13	S				MS	AL	MS	Farm Laborer
	James S.	S	W	M	Aug 1889	10	S				MS	AL	MS	Farm Laborer
	Carl V.	S	W	M	Mar 1891	8	S				MS	AL	MS	
	William P.	S	W	M	Dec 1893	6	S				MS	AL	MS	
197	Dubois, Andrew T.	H	W	M	Jan 1875	25	M	3			AL	AL	AL	Day Laborer
	Nancy I.	W	W	F	Sep 1871	28	M	3	1	1	TN	TN	MS	
	Andrew A.	S	W	M	Jan 1899	1	S				TN	TN	MS	
198	Harris, Charles C.	H	W	M	Aug 1849	50	M	33			NC	NC	NC	Farmer
	Margaret A.	W	W	F	Apr 1851	49	M	33	13	13	MS	MS	AL	
	Mary G.	D	W	F	Apr 1874	26	S				MS	NC	MS	
	Charles W.	S	W	M	Jan 1880	20	S				MS	NC	MS	Farm Laborer
	Martha E.	D	W	F	Feb 1882	18	S				MS	NC	MS	
	Jourdan A.	S	W	M	Nov 1883	16	S				MS	NC	MS	Farm Laborer
	Mack A.	S	W	M	Feb 1886	14	S				MS	NC	MS	Farm Laborer
	Vira I.	D	W	F	Dec 1888	11	S				MS	NC	MS	
	Lee M.	S	W	F	Jul 1890	10	S				MS	NC	MS	
	William L.	S	W	M	Mar 1894	6	S				MS	NC	MS	
	Tipton, James W.	BiL	W	M	Nov 1853	46	S				MS	MS	AL	Farmer
199	Streetman, William J.	H	W	M	Jan 1856	44	M	21			AL	AL	GA	Farmer
	Margaret I.	W	W	F	Oct 1855	44	M	21	8	6	MS	MS	MS	
	John D.	S	W	M	Nov 1881	18	S				AL	MS	MS	Farm Laborer
	George W.	S	W	M	Sep 1885	14	S				AL	MS	MS	Farm Laborer
	James E.	S	W	M	Dec 1888	11	S				AL	MS	MS	Farm Laborer
	David S.	S	W	M	Apr 1891	9	S				AL	MS	MS	
	Walter J.	S	W	M	Dec 1892	7	S				AL	MS	MS	
	Jessie F.	S	W	M	Oct 1895	4	S				AL	MS	MS	
200	Moore, Benjamin F.	H	W	M	Jan 1873	27	M	2			MS	GA	MS	Farmer
	Nancy J.	W	W	F	Mar 1878	22	M	2	1	1	MS	AL	MS	

1	2	3	4	5	6	7	8	9	10	11	12	13	14	15
	Myrtie I.	D	W	F	Jul 1898	1	S				MS	MS	MS	
	Thomas C.	BiL	W	M	Nov 1880	19	S				MS	AL	MS	Day Laborer
201	Hood, John	H	W	M	Nov 1850	49	Wd				MS	NC	SC	Farmer
	Lucinda	Sis	W	F	Jan 1847	53	S				MS	NC	SC	
	Jacola	Sis	W	F	Aug 1852	47	S				MS	NC	SC	
	Waddle, Sarah K.	Nce	W	F	May 1874	26	S				MS	SC	MS	
	Clinton	Nep	W	M	Sep 1894	5	S				MS	MS	MS	
202	Wright, Frank P.	H	W	M	Jul 1852	47	M	23			GA	GA	GA	Farmer
	Sarah F.	W	W	F	Oct 1859	40	M	23	9	8	AL	AL	AL	
	Henry J.	S	W	M	Apr 188?	19	S				AL	GA	AL	Farm Laborer
	John W.	S	W	M	Jul 1884	15	S				AL	GA	AL	Farm Laborer
	Arary F.	S	W	M	Dec 1885	14	S				AL	GA	AL	Farm Laborer
	James A.	S	W	M	Mar 1888	12	S				AL	GA	AL	Farm Laborer
	Laura E.	D	W	F	Oct 1890	9	S				AL	GA	AL	
	Freda B.	D	W	F	Apr 1894	6	S				AL	GA	AL	
203	Clifford, Dave A.	H	W	M	Sep 1850	49	M	23			NC	NC	NC	Farmer
	Mary J.	W	W	F	Dec 1860	39	M	23	5	3	MS	TN	MS	
	Daniel M.	S	W	M	Jan 1879	21	M	0			AL	NC	MS	Farm Laborer
	Thomas A.	S	W	M	Jan 1889	11	S				AL	NC	MS	Farm Laborer
	David O.	S	W	M	Jan 1892	7	S				AL	NC	MS	Farm Laborer
	Malinda J.	DiL	W	F	Sep 1885	14	M	0	0		MS	AL	MS	
204	Ferguson, Will	H	W	M	Oct 1841	58	M	9			MS	MS	UN	
	Belle D.	W	W	F	Apr 1849	51	M	9	2	2	MS	NC	TN	
	Florist A.	D	W	F	Oct 1891	8	S				MS	MS	MS	
	Effie E.	D	W	F	Nov 1893	6	S				MS	MS	MS	
	Gaines, Eliza	MiL	W	F	Nov 1893	83	Wd				TN	KY	TN	
	Allen Lunsford P.	SS	W	M	Dec 1880	19	S				MS	MS	MS	Farm Laborer
	Franks, Pomp	HH	W	M	Jan 1845	55	S				MS	AL	MS	Farmer
205	Bassell, Nathan	H	W	M	Oct 1872	27	M	5			AL	GA	AL	Farmer
	Arminta	W	W	F	Nov 1875	24	M	5	1	1	MS	MS	GA	
	Myrtie A.	D	W	F	May 1896	4	S				MS	AL	MS	
206	Caveners, James	H	W	M	Sep 1875	24	M	0			MS	MS	MS	Merchant-Farmer
	Irene M.	W	W	F	Feb 1877	23	M.	0	0	0	AL	AL	AL	
207	Castleberry, Jack	H	W	M	Dec 1871	28	M	13			MS	SC	SC	Farmer
	Sallie	W	W	F	Jan 1865	25	M	13	6	5	MS	SC	SC	
	Virdie	D	W	F	Feb 1886	14	S				MS	MS	MS	
	Virdine	D	W	F	Jan 1887	13	S				MS	MS	MS	
	Dell	S	W	M	Feb 1892	8	S				MS	MS	MS	
	Mary	D	W	F	Dec 1894	5	S				MS	MS	MS	
	Madison	S	W	M	Jul 1896	3	S				MS	MS	MS	
208	Aldridge, William G.	H	W	M	Nov 1876	23	M	3			MS	MS	MS	Farmer
	Rosie	W	W	F	Jun 1881	19	M	3	2	2	MS	MS	MS	
	John T.	S	W	M	Apr 1898	2	S				MS	MS	MS	
	James W.	S	W	M	Apr 1899	1	S				MS	MS	MS	
	Garrison, Nancy A.	MiL	W	F	Jan 1855	45	S				MS	MS	MS	
209	Moore, Ira M.	H	W	M	Sep 1872	27	M	0			MS	AL	MS	Farm Laborer
	Mary K.	W	W	F	Dec 1872	21	M	0	0	0	MS	MS	MS	
	Green, Daniel E.	Bdr	W	M	May 1880	20	S				AL	AL	AL	Getting out staves
	Joe C.	Bdr	W	M	Mar 1877	23	S				AL	AL	AL	Getting out staves
210	Castleberry, William H.	H	W	M	Jan 1862	38	M	4			MS	MS	SC	Farmer
	Anna G.	W	W	F	Feb 1864	36	M	4	0	0	MS	SC	SC	
211	Jourdan, Enoch	H	W	M	Nov 1834	65	M	33			NC	NC	NC	Farmer

1	2	3	4	5	6	7	8	9	10	11	12	13	14	15
	Nancy C.	W	W	F	Sep 1852	47	M	33	5	2	AL	TN	AL	
	Ezell V.	D	W	F	Oct 1891	8	S				MS	NC	AL	
	Henly, John W.	SS	W	M	Jan 1880	20	S				TN	AL	AL	Farm Laborer
212	Waddle, Melmoth	H	W	M	Oct 1850	49	M	23			GA	SC	SC	Farmer
	Mary J.	W	W	F	Jul 1858	41	M	23	5	5	MS	AL	MS	
	Bordell	S	W	M	Mar 1878	22	S				MS	GA	MS	Farm Laborer
	Bell	D	W	F	Aug 1879	20	S				MS	GA	MS	
	Willie L.	D	W	F	Feb 1881	19	S				MS	GA	MS	
	Jesse	S	W	M	Feb 1883	17	S				MS	GA	MS	Farm Laborer
	Melmoth A.	S	W	M	Feb 1889	11	S				MS	GA	MS	Farm Laborer
213	Weatherford, S.M.	H	W	M	Jul 1855	45	M	20			AL	AL	AL	Merchant-Farmer
	Tennessee A.	W	W	F	May 1860	40	M	20	10	6	MS	AL	TN	
	Amand J.	D	W	F	Feb 1883	17	S				MS	AL	MS	
	Hattie L.	D	W	F	Jan 1888	12	S				MS	AL	MS	
	Yittie M.	D	W	F	May 1890	10	S				MS	AL	MS	
	James C.	S	W	M	Oct 1892	7	S				MS	AL	MS	
	Eddie	D	W	F	Jan 1895	4	S				MS	AL	MS	
	Cleo	D	W	F	Feb 1898	2	S				MS	AL	MS	
	James H.	HH	W	M	Aug 1878	21	S				AL	AL	AL	Farm Laborer
214	Cole, Jesse S.	H	W	M	Mar 1824	76	Wd				SC	SC	SC	Farmer
	Nancy J.	D	W	F	Jul 1846	53	S				MS	SC	TN	
	Sallie E.	D	W	F	Apr 1850	50	S				MS	SC	TN	
215	Wigginton, Silas	H	W	M	Jan 1868	32	M	12			AL	AL	AL	Farmer
	Elizabeth	W	W	F	Jan 1873	27	M	12	4	4	MS	AL	MS	
	Thomas M.	S	W	M	Apr 1890	10	S				MS	AL	MS	Farm Laborer
	Mary E.	D	W	F	Sep 1893	6	S				MS	AL	MS	
	Charnel S.	S	W	M	Mar 1895	5	S				MS	AL	MS	
	Dennis F.	S	W	M	Jan 1898	2	S				MS	AL	MS	
216	Waddle, Malina	H	W	M	Aug 1867	32	M	11			MS	SC	GA	
	Serena M.	W	W	F	Aug 1868	31	M	11	6	6	MS	MS	AL	
	Cora S.	D	W	F	Oct 1889	10	S				MS	MS	MS	
	Sarah A.	D	W	F	Mar 1892	8	S				MS	MS	MS	
	Norah C.	D	W	F	Feb 1893	7	S				MS	MS	MS	
	Ora E.	D	W	F	Oct 1894	5	S				MS	MS	MS	
	Mary A.	D	W	F	Dec 1896	3	S				MS	MS	MS	
	William Jesse	S	W	M	Dec 1898	1	S				MS	MS	MS	
217	Roebuck, Sarah E.	H	W	F	Mar 1840	60	Wd		0	0	SC	SC	SC	
218	Montgomery, James G.	H	W	M	Dec 1874	25	M	3			MS	MS	SC	Farmer
	Lola L.	W	W	F	Jan 1878	22	M	3	2	1	MS	MS	MS	
	Eliza A.	D	W	F	Feb 1899	1	S				MS	MS	MS	
219	Moore, William C.	H	W	M	Jan 1860	40	M	11			MS	AL	NC	Farmer
	Ella T.	W	W	F	Dec 1866	33	M	11	7	7	MS	MS	SC	
	James	S	W	M	Feb 1890	10	S				MS	MS	SC	Farm Laborer
	Elra	D	W	F	Aug 1891	8	S				MS	MS	SC	
	Bardie	S	W	M	Feb 1893	7	S				MS	MS	SC	
	Hardie	S	W	M	Feb 1893	7	S				MS	MS	SC	
	Tinse P.	D	W	F	Aug 1895	4	S				MS	MS	SC	
	Robert	S	W	M	Jan 1897	3	S				MS	MS	SC	
	Belvy	D	W	F	Feb 1899	1	S				MS	MS	SC	
220	Parker, Marcus	H	W	M	Sep 1869	30	M	10			MS	TN	AL	Farmer
	Sarah I.	W	W	F	Jan 1873	27	M	10	3	2	MS	SC	GA	
	Sarah G.	D	W	F	Jul 1894	5	S				MS	MS	MS	
	Willie B.	D	W	F	Oct 1899	8/mo	S				MS	MS	MS	

1	2	3	4	5	6	7	8	9	10	11	12	13	14	15
221	Hammett, Robert J.	H	W	M	Jul 1838	61	M	42			SC	SC	SC	Farmer
	Sarah C.	W	W	F	Mar 1841	59	M	42	3	1	GA	SC	GA	
222	Allen, William	H	W	M	Sep 1870	29	S				MS	MS	MS	Farmer
	Margaret	Sis	W	F	Aug 1873	26	S				MS	MS	MS	
	Dora	Sis	W	F	Mar 1876	24	S				MS	MS	MS	
223	Pharr, Margaret	H	W	F	Aug 1848	51	Wd		2	2	AL	GA	AL	Farmer
	William F.	S	W	M	Jun 1885	14	S				MS	MS	AL	Farm Laborer
	Bolivar S.	S	W	M	Jul 1887	12	S				MS	MS	AL	Farm Laborer
224	Pharr, James N.	H	W	M	Jan 1871	29	M	10			MS	MS	MS	Farmer
	Malinda A.	W	W	F	Sep 1870	29	M	10	7	5	AL	MS	AL	
	David J.	S	W	M	Dec 1891	8	S				MS	MS	AL	
	Willie B.	D	W	F	Dec 1894	5	S				MS	MS	AL	
	Mary S.	D	W	F	Feb 1896	4	S				MS	MS	AL	
	Emilie E.	D	W	F	Sep 1897	2	S				MS	MS	AL	
	Minie P.	D	W	F	Jul 1899	10/mo	S				MS	MS	AL	
225	Ivy, John	H	W	M	Jun 1850	49	M	24			AL	AL	TN	Farmer
	Sarah	W	W	F	Jan 1861	39	M	24	13	11	AL	AL	KY	
	William D.	S	W	M	Feb 1879	21	S				AL	AL	AL	Farm Laborer
	James H.	S	W	M	Jun 1881	18	S				MS	AL	AL	Farm Laborer
	George W.	S	W	M	Mar 1884	16	S				MS	AL	AL	Farm Laborer
	Sinnie	S	W	M	Jun 1886	13	S				MS	AL	AL	Farm Laborer
	Cleveland	S	W	M	Apr 1888	12	S				MS	AL	AL	Farm Laborer
	Samantha B.	D	W	F	Jul 1889	10	S				MS	AL	AL	
	Marion	S	W	M	Dec 1891	8	S				MS	AL	AL	
	Jesse	S	W	M	Mar 1893	7	S				MS	AL	AL	
	Lillie	D	W	F	Aug 1894	5	S				MS	AL	AL	
	Bosie	D	W	F	Jul 1896	3	S				MS	AL	AL	
	Daisie E.	D	W	F	Sep 1899	8/mo	S				MS	AL	AL	
226	Wigginton, William	H	W	M	July 1855	46	M	25			AL	AL	AL	Farmer
	Arrena E.	W	W	F	Mar 1874	26	M	10	2	1	MS	GA	MS	
	Cornelius	S	W	M	Oct 1879	20	S				AL	AL	AL	Farm Laborer
	James E.	S	W	M	Jul 1882	17	S				AL	AL	AL	Farm Laborer
	Modenie C.	D	W	F	Dec 1888	11	S				MS	AL	AL	
	Talitha C.	D	W	F	Sep 1893	6	S				MS	AL	AL	
	Wiggington, Martin	F	W	M	May 1831	69	Wd				AL	SC	SC	Farmer
227	Butler, Joseph T.	H	W	M	Oct 1871	28	S				AL	MS	AL	Farmer
	Emily M.	M	W	F	Oct 1838	61	Wd		4	4	MS	SC	AL	
	Martha E.	Sis	W	F	May 1865	35	S				AL	AL	MS	
	Mary B.	Sis	W	F	Jan 1878	22	S				AL	AL	MS	
	Sidney J.	Bro	W	M	Mar 1882	18	S				AL	AL	MS	
228	Grammar, Francis M.	H	W	M	Feb 1862	38	M	15			MS	AL	SC	Farmer
	Tyrena O.	W	W	F	Mar 1854	46	M	15	2	1	MS	AL	AL	
	William F.	S	W	M	Aug 1885	14	S				MS	MS	MS	Farm Laborer
229	Butler, Angeline	H	W	F	Oct 1862	37	S		6	5	AL	SC	MS	Farmer
	Maud B.	D	W	F	May 1884	16	S				MS	MS	MS	
	Thomas Y.	S	W	M	Aug 1886	13	S				MS	MS	MS	Farm Laborer
	Geneva F.	D	W	F	Sep 1888	11	S				MS	MS	MS	
	Lurnin C.	S	W	M	Aug 1890	9	S				MS	MS	MS	
	Hattie P.	D	W	F	Oct 1894	5	S				MS	MS	MS	
	Tolie U.	S	W	M	Jun 1898	1	S				MS	MS	MS	
230	Hammett, Thomas C.	H	W	M	Jul 1840	59	M	32			SC	SC	SC	Farmer
	Mary E.	W	W	F	Sep 1849	50	M	32	13	7	MS	SC	SC	
	Columbus C.	S	W	M	Jun 1875	24	S				MS	SC	MS	Farm Laborer
	Ollie B.	D	W	F	Oct 1880	19	S				MS	SC	MS	

1	2	3	4	5	6	7	8	9	10	11	12	13	14	15
	Fannie E.	D	W	F	Jun 1888	10	S				MS	SC	MS	
	Myrtie A.	D	W	F	Oct 1892	7	S				MS	SC	MS	
231	Hammett, Price J.	H	W	F	Mar 1872	28	M	7			MS	SC	MS	Farmer
	Amanda M.	W	W	F	Oct 1877	22	M	7	4	4	MS	AL	AL	
	Arnd C.	S	W	M	Dec 1893	6	S				MS	MS	MS	
	Robert L.	S	W	M	Feb 1895	5	S				MS	MS	MS	
	Annie M.	D	W	F	Mar 1897	3	S				MS	MS	MS	
	Willie Thomas	S	W	M	Jan 1900	5/mo					MS	MS	MS	
232	Whitehead, Joseph S.	H	W	M	Oct 1873	26	M	8			MS	AL	AL	Farmer
	Sarah C.	W	W	F	Dec 1870	39	M	8	3	3	MS	SC	MS	
	Grover A.	S	W	M	Sep 1894	5	S				MS	MS	MS	
	Joseph E.	S	W	M	Jul 1897	2	S				MS	MS	MS	
	Dewey F.	S	W	M	Apr 1900	3/mo	S				MS	MS	MS	
233	Whitehead, Joe	H	W	M	Feb 1844	56	M	31			AL	NC	NC	Farmer
	Mahalia A.	W	W	F	Apr 1858	41	M	31	10	10	AL	NC	AL	
	Ludie	D	W	F	Jun 1887	13	S				MS	NC	AL	
	Hinderman	S	W	M	Jun 1890	9	S				MS	NC	AL	
	Hugh	S	W	M	Jun 1895	4	S				MS	NC	AL	
234	Wigginton, Paul	H	W	M	Aug 1870	29	M	7			MS	AL	AL	Farmer
	Margaret A.	W	W	F	Jun 1880	19	M	7	2	1	MS	AL	AL	
	Willie J.	S	W	M	Jan 1898	2	S				MS	MS	MS	
235	Gilbert, William C.	H	W	M	Jul 1866	33	M	9			MS	GA	KY	Farmer
	Annie O.	W	W	F	May 1871	29	M	9	7	7	MS	GA	MS	
	Viola O.	D	W	F	Oct 1891	8	S				MS	MS	MS	
	Syms E.	S	W	M	Nov 1892	7	S				MS	MS	MS	
	Belvy S.	D	W	F	May 1894	6	S				MS	MS	MS	
	Velma C.	D	W	F	Dec 1895	4	S				MS	MS	MS	
	Martha J.	D	W	F	Feb 1897	3	S				MS	MS	MS	
	William T.	S	W	M	Apr 1898	2	S				MS	MS	MS	
	Leno O.	D	W	F	Mar 1900	2/mo	S				MS	MS	MS	
236	Samples, William B.	H	W	M	Jan 1844	56	M	36			MS	AL	AL	Farmer
	Ellen J.	W	W	F	Dec 1842	57	M	36	9	8	AL	TN	TN	
	Daily Y.	S	W	M	Feb 1883	17	S				MS	MS	AL	Farm Laborer
	Florence C.	D	W	F	Feb 1887	13	S				MS	MS	AL	
237	Samples, William R.	H	W	M	Mar 1875	25	M	5			MS	MS	AL	Farmer
	Margaret	W	W	F	Jan 1878	22	M	5	3	3	MS	AL	AL	
	Porter	S	W	M	Feb 1896	4	S				MS	MS	MS	
	Arra	S	W	M	Jan 1898	2	S				MS	MS	MS	
	Dovie	D	W	F	Mar 1900	3/mo	S				MS	MS	MS	
238	Keggle, Loyd	H	W	M	Feb 1865	35	M	13			AL	AL	SC	Farmer
	Martha E.	W	W	F	Sep 1869	30	M	13	4	4	MS	MS	AL	
	Ella V.	D	W	F	Oct 1888	11	S				MS	AL	MS	
	Mary A.	D	W	F	Jul 1892	7	S				MS	AL	MS	
	Loyd M.	S	W	M	Jun 1894	5	S				MS	AL	MS	
	Lola B.	D	W	F	Jan 1897	3	S				MS	AL	MS	
239	Johnson, Thomas J.	H	W	M	Apr 1860	40	M	17			MS	NC	NC	Farmer
	Mary J.	W	W	F	Oct 1867	32	M	17	5	5	MS	MS	AL	
	Lillie B.	D	W	F	Oct 1884	15	S				MS	MS	MS	
	Anna L.	D	W	F	Oct 1888	11	S				MS	MS	MS	
	William E.	S	W	M	Feb 1890	10	S				MS	MS	MS	
	Newton	S	W	M	May 1893	7	S				MS	MS	MS	
240	Whitehead, James H.	H	W	M	Jan 1870	30	M	10			MS	MS	MS	Farmer
	Lucinda E.	W	W	F	Aug 1867	32	M	10	4	3	MS	AL	AL	

1	2	3	4	5	6	7	8	9	10	11	12	13	14	15
	Joseph E.	S	W	M	Apr 1893	7	S				MS	MS	MS	
	Florence A.	D	W	F	Oct 1895	4	S				MS	MS	MS	
	James E.	S	W	M	Jan 1898	2	S				MS	MS	MS	
241	Pharr, George J.	H	W	M	Jul 1875	24	M	2			MS	MS	MS	
	Nancy B.	W	W	F	Sep 1880	19	M	2	2	1	MS	MS	MS	
	Pearl V.	D	W	F	Jan 1900	3/mo	S				MS	MS	MS	
242	White, Lenard C.	H	W	M	Dec 1852	47	M	19			AL	SC	SC	Farmer
	Milda U.	W	W	F	Mar 1863	37	M	19	0	0	MS	MS	MS	
243	Holley, Isac J.	H	W	M	Sep 1850	49	M	9			MS	AL	AL	Farmer
	Nancy A.	W	W	F	Nov 1867	32	M	9	2	2	AL	AL	SC	
	Elijah Thomas	S	W	M	Sep 1862	27	S				MS	MS	AL	Farm Laborer
	Julia M.	D	W	F	Jan 1898	2	S				MS	MS	AL	
	Isac T.	S	W	M	Dec 1899	5/mo	S				MS	MS	AL	
244	Pharr, Jack A.	H	W	M	Aug 1845	54	M	32			MS	SC	TN	Farmer
	Gladis	W	W	F	Sep 1846	53	M	32	11	10	MS	AL	TN	
	Joseph D.	S	W	M	Jul 1880	19	S				MS	MS	MS	Farm Laborer
	Stanley L.	S	W	M	Dec 1882	17	S				MS	MS	MS	Farm Laborer
	Lydia M.	D	W	F	Jul 1885	14	S				MS	MS	MS	
	Thomas C.	S	W	M	Sep 1888	11	S				MS	MS	MS	Farm Laborer
245	Wigginton, Leander	H	W	M	Dec 1858	41	M	21			AL	AL	AL	Farmer
	Mary O.	W	W	F	Nov 1861	38	M	21	8	8	GA	GA	GA	
	Hettie J.	D	W	F	Aug 1880	19	S				AL	AL	GA	
	Leander R.	S	W	M	Jan 1883	17	S				MS	AL	GA	Farm Laborer
	Daniel S.	S	W	M	Aug 1885	14	S				MS	AL	GA	Farm Laborer
	William D.	S	W	M	Apr 1888	11	S				MS	AL	GA	Farm Laborer
	Newton C.	S	W	M	Mar 1891	9	S				MS	AL	GA	
	James E.	S	W	M	Jan 1894	6	S				MS	AL	GA	
	Doctor S.	S	W	M	Jan 1894	6	S				MS	AL	GA	
	Tabitha A.	D	W	F	Oct 1898	1	S				MS	AL	GA	
246	Wigginton, Samuel A.	H	W	M	Sep 1873	27	M	9			AL	AL	AL	Farmer
	Minda J.	W	W	F	Nov 1874	25	M	9	4	4	MS	MS	AL	
	Mary S.	D	W	F	Jul 1892	7	S				MS	AL	MS	
	Leander S.	S	W	M	Mar 1894	6	S				MS	AL	MS	
	James R.	S	W	M	Mar 1896	3	S				MS	AL	MS	
	Nathan S.	S	W	M	Mar 1899	1	S				MS	AL	MS	
247	Haley, Enoch	H	B	M	Apr 1858	42	M	21			AL	AL	AL	Farmer
	Dora A.	W	B	F	Oct 1868	31	M	21	12	6	MS	AL	AL	
	Clifton	S	B	M	May 1882	18	S				TN	MS	AL	Farm Laborer
	Ellie C.	S	B	M	May 1887	13	S				TN	AL	MS	Farm Laborer
	Elonzo C.	S	B	M	Apr 1890	10	S				MS	AL	MS	Farm Laborer
	Harris J.	S	B	M	Jan 1894	6	S				MS	AL	MS	
	Casey A.	S	B	M	Apr 1896	4	S				MS	AL	MS	
	James G.	S	B	M	Jun 1898	1	S				MS	AL	MS	
	Enoch	Nep	B	M	Feb 1887	13	S				MS	AL	AL	Farm Laborer
248	Campbell, John	H	W	M	Aug 1849	50	M	32			MS	AL	AL	Farmer
	Rachel M.	W	W	F	Jun 1848	51	M	32	16	14	AL	NC	SC	
	Enoch A.	S	W	M	Apr 1870	30	S				MS	MS	AL	Farm Laborer
	Finis L.	S	W	M	Feb 1876	24	S				MS	MS	AL	Farm Laborer
	Sarah S.	D	W	F	Apr 1884	16	S				MS	MS	AL	
	Charlie I.	S	W	M	Oct 1885	14	S				MS	MS	AL	Farm Laborer
	Mattie S.	D	W	F	Oct 1887	12	S				MS	MS	AL	
	Carrie A.	D	W	F	Jul 1891	8	S				MS	MS	AL	
249	Campbell, George	H	W	M	Apr 1872	28	M	3			MS	MS	AL	Farmer
	Annie R.	W	W	F	Jun 1873	26	M	3	4	3	AL	GA	AL	

1	2	3	4	5	6	7	8	9	10	11	12	13	14	15
	Hughie W.	SS	W	M	May 1893	7	S				AL	AL	AL	
	Cordelia N.	D	W	F	Jun 1898	2	S				MS	MS	AL	
	Texana	D	W	F	Aug 1899	10/mo	S				MS	MS	AL	
250	Campbell, William F.	H	W	M	May 1869	31	M	10			MS	MS	AL	Farmer
	Lydia L.	W	W	F	Mar 1869	31	M	10	5	3	MS	MS	MS	
	Gladis M.	D	W	F	Oct 1890	9	S				MS	MS	MS	
	Eliza E.	D	W	F	Jan 1892	8	S				MS	MS	MS	
	Willie L.	S	W	M	Feb 1897	3	S				MS	MS	MS	
251	Campbell, Con J.	H	W	M	Sep 1877	22	M	1			MS	MS	AL	Farmer
	Lillie	W	W	F	Sep !883	16	M	1	1	1	MS	MS	MS	
	James R.	S	W	M	Dec 1899	5/mo	S				MS	MS	MS	
252	Thomas, Willie	H	B	M	Jan 1854	46	M	27			MS	MS	MS	Farmer
	Jane	W	B	F	Oct 1853	46	M	27	6	1	AL	SC	AL	
	Nora S.	D	B	F	Oct 1882	18	S				MS	MS	AL	
	Lanstrom, Walter	Nep	B	M	Jun 1885	14	S				MS	MS	AL	Farm Laborer
	Modenia	Nce	B	F	May 1892	8	S				MS	MS	AL	
253	Hopkins, John C.	H	W	M	Jul 1837	62	M	41			KY	SC	KY	Merchant-Farmer
	Elliner A.	W	W	F	May 1840	60	M	41	9	8	NC	NC	NC	
	James B.	S	W	M	Sep 1876	23	S				MS	KY	NC	Farmer
	Charles G.	S	W	M	Jun 1878	21	S				MS	KY	NC	Farm Laborer
	Alphus	S	W	M	May 1886	14	S				MS	KY	SC	Farm Laborer
	Ola C.	D	W	F	Dec 1882	17	S				MS	KY	SC	
254	Wilson, Hepsie A.	H	W	F	Jan 1852	48	Wd				AL	AL	AL	Farmer
255	Sphears, George H.	H	B	M	Oct 1843	57	M	22			KY	MS	NC	Farmer
	Frances	W	B	F	Oct 1849	50	M	22	8	7	TN	MS	TN	
	Oscar L.	S	B	M	Jul 1877	22	S				MS	KY	TN	Farm Laborer
	Hugh R.	S	B	M	Feb 1879	21	S				MS	KY	TN	Farm Laborer
	Eudora	D	B	F	Sep 1880	19	S				MS	KY	TN	
	Anna L.	D	B	F	Aug 1882	17	S				MS	KY	TN	
	Jesse	S	B	M	Jul 1883	16	S				MS	KY	TN	Farm Laborer
	George	S	B	M	Mar 1887	13	S				MS	KY	TN	Farm Laborer
	Florence	D	B	F	Oct 1894	5	S				MS	KY	TN	
256	Criddle, John C.	H	W	M	Jul 1839	60	M	34			AL	GA	TN	Farmer
	Manda M.	W	W	F	Sep 1847	52	M	34	11	10	TN	GA	TN	
	Sarah E.	D	W	F	Jul 1868	31	S				MS	AL	TN	
	Hyram, V.	S	W	M	May 1879	21	S				MS	AL	TN	Farm Laborer
	Mack J.	S	W	M	Aug 1881	18	S				MS	AL	TN	Farm Laborer
	Andrew D.	S	W	M	Jul 1884	15	S				MS	AL	TN	Farm Laborer
	Thomas P.	S	W	M	Dec 1889	11	S				MS	AL	TN	Farm Laborer
257	Criddle, William B.	H	W	M	Jan 1877	23	M	1			MS	AL	TN	Farmer
	Orra B.	W	W	F	Apr 1882	18	M	1	1	1	MS	AL	MS	
	Atra A.	D	W	F	Sep 1899	8/mo	S				MS	MS	MS	
258	Stacy, William M.	H	W	M	Jul 1868	31	M	2			MS	AL	MS	
	Neoma C.	W	W	F	Oct 1869	30	M	2	1	1	AL	AL	TN	
	George A.	D	W	F	Oct 1898	1	S				MS	MS	AL	
259	Cranford, Martin D.	H	W	M	Jun 1842	57	M	40			GA	GA	GA	Farmer
	Nancy J.	W	W	F	Jul 1841	58	M	40	8	7	AL	SC	GA	
	Carlis H.	S	W	M	Sep 1877	22	S				MS	GA	AL	Farm Laborer
	Yarber, Preston	SiL	W	M	Jan 1879	21	M	1			MS	AL	MS	Farm Laborer
	Hation J.	D	W	F	Apr 1881	19	M	1	1	1	MS	GA	AL	
	James L.	GS	W	M	Sep 1899	8/mo	S				MS	MS	MS	
260	Cranford, John R.	H	W	M	Mar 1867	33	M	10			MS	GA	AL	Farmer

1	2	3	4	5	6	7	8	9	10	11	12	13	14	15
	Mary A.	W	W	F	Oct 1869	30	M	10	4	2	AL	MS	MS	
	Many L.	D	W	F	Nov 1890	9	S				MS	MS	MS	
	Webster, S.	S	W	M	Mar 1900	2/mo	S				MS	MS	MS	
261	Beachum, Fannie	H	B	F	Feb 1870	30	S		2	2	MS	MS	AL	Farmer
	Walter L.	S	B	M	Feb 1882	18	S				MS	MS	MS	Farm Laborer
	Clifford R.	D	B	F	May 1883	17	S				MS	MS	MS	
	Tipton, Esther	Nce	B	F	Jul 1891	8	S				MS	MS	MS	
262	Gilbert, William	H	W	M	Apr 1836	64	M	35			KY	NC	KY	Farmer
	Mary J.	W	W	F	Feb 1839	61	M	35	4	4	KY	NC	KY	
	Ella L.	D	W	F	Nov 1870	29	S				MS	TN	KY	
263	Pate, William L.	H	W	M	Apr 1869	31	M	11			MS	NC	MS	Farmer
	Ha Tinie	W	W	F	Dec 1865	34	M	11	6	4	MS	MS	NC	
	John L.	S	W	M	Sep 1889	10	S				MS	MS	MS	
	Amand B.	D	W	F	Aug 1892	7	S				MS	MS	MS	
	Pansy P.	S	W	M	Jan 1897	3	S				MS	MS	MS	
	Daniel D.	S	W	M	Feb 1900	3/mo	S				MS	MS	MS	
264	Gilbert, Carroll B.	H	W	M	Jul 1874	25	M	7			MS	TN	KY	
	Adie M.	W	W	F	Aug 1872	27	M	7	5	4	MS	NC	TN	
	Ermie O.	D	W	F	Jul 1894	5	S				MS	MS	MS	
	Gerome A.	S	W	M	Dec 1895	4	S				MS	MS	MS	
	William A.	S	W	M	May 1898	2	S				MS	MS	MS	
	Greta B.	S	W	M	Sep 1899	8/mo	S				MS	MS	MS	
265	Nix, Luke	H	W	M	Oct 1836	62	M	42			AL	AL	AL	Farmer
	Mary S.	W	W	F	Nov 1837	62	M	42	9	8	MS	SC	AL	
	George O.	S	W	M	Feb 1873	27	Wd				AL	AL	TN	Farm Laborer
	Whitehead, Mary	Ser	W	F	Feb 1850	50	S				AL	MS	AL	Servant
266	Whitehead, Clara	H	W	F	Mar 1840	40	S				AL	MS	AL	Farm Laborer
	William P.	S	W	M	Oct 1887	12	S				MS	MS	AL	Farm Laborer
267	Credille, Willis B.	H	W	M	Feb 1867	33	M	7			AL	AL	TN	Farmer
	Mittie J.	W	W	F	May 1868	32	M	7	2	2	MS	AL	AL	
	John H.	S	W	M	Oct 1893	6	S				MS	AL	MS	
	Marrie L.	D	W	F	Nov 1895	4	S				MS	AL	MS	
268	Brown, Carroll T.	H	W	M	Dec 1873	26	M	6			MS	Eng	AL	Farmer
	Narcis C.	W	W	F	Apr 1875	25	M	6	3	3	MS	AL	AL	
	James W.	S	W	M	Sep 1894	5	S				MS	MS	MS	
	Charles P.	S	W	M	Feb 1897	3	S				MS	MS	MS	
	Virdie B.	D	W	F	Aug 1899	10/mo	S				MS	MS	MS	
269	Mann, Whitfield, C.	H	W	M	Jan 1836	63	M	46			SC	SC	VA	Farmer
	Marinda A.	W	W	F	Feb 1833	67	M	46	1	1	NC	TN	SC	
	Musi C.	GD	W	F	Apr 1893	7	S				MS	AL	AL	
270	Mann, Marion C.	H	W	M	Apr 1872	28	M	8			AL	SC	AL	Farmer
	Georgia A.	W	W	F	Oct 1870	29	M	8	2	2	AL	GA	AL	
	Gerthia	S	W	M	Oct 1872	6	S				AL	AL	GA	
	Pearley M.	D	W	F	May 1895	5	S				AL	AL	GA	
271	Hale, Nepthie D.	H	W	M	Aug 1837	62	M	40			TN	TN	VA	Farmer
	Margaret	W	W	F	Oct 1838	61	M	40	4	3	NC	NC	NC	
272	Jackson, Mion A.	H	W	M	Apr 1866	34	M	14			AL	GA	GA	Farmer
	Mary C.	W	W	F	Oct 1866	33	M	14	6	5	AL	AL	AL	
	Dosia O.	D	W	F	Oct 1886	12	S				AL	AL	AL	
	Walter W.	S	W	M	Oct 1889	10	S				AL	AL	AL	Farm Laborer
	Louisa J.	D	W	F	Sep 1891	8	S				AL	AL	AL	

1	2	3	4	5	6	7	8	9	10	11	12	13	14	15
	Eliza E.	D	W	F	May 1895	5	S				AL	AL	AL	
	George T.	S	W	M	Jun 1898	1	S				AL	AL	AL	
	Joseph	F	W	M	Jul 1823	76	S				GA	GA	GA	
273	Hodges, William E.	H	W	M	Nov 1856	43	M	17			MS	AL	AL	Farmer
	Julia	W	W	F	Oct 1865	34	M	17	10	8	IL	MS	MS	
	Austin	S	W	M	Aug 1883	16	S				MS	MS	IL	Farm Laborer
	Bella	D	W	F	Oct 1884	15	S				MS	MS	IL	
	Pearley	D	W	F	Nov 1887	12	S				MS	MS	IL	
	Nettie	D	W	F	Oct 1891	8	S				MS	MS	IL	
	Essie	D	W	F	Nov 1893	6	S				MS	MS	IL	
	Fred E.	S	W	M	Dec 1895	4	S				MS	MS	IL	
	Odie	D	W	F	Oct 1897	3	S				MS	MS	IL	
	Edith	D	W	F	Oct 1899	7/mo	S				MS	MS	IL	
274	Hale, Mavel J.	H	W	M	Oct 1866	33	M	11			MS	TN	NC	Farmer
	Martha C.	W	W	F	Oct 1868	31	M	11	1	1	MS	KY	NC	
	John M.	S	W	M	Nov 1891	8	S				MS	MS	MS	
275	Henley, George O.	H	W	M	Jul 1853	46	M	8			AL	AL	GA	Farmer
	Emeline	W	W	F	Jul 1860	40	M	8	0	0	MS	SC	NC	
	Albert	Nep	W	M	May 1884	16	S				AL	AL	AL	Farm Laborer
276	Ozbirn, John M.	H	W	M	Sep 1857	42	M	12			AL	GA	GA	
	Almer E.	W	W	F	Dec 1867	32	M	12	4	3	AL	TN	TN	
	Eda E.	D	W	F	Jan 1889	11	S				MS	AL	AL	
	John T.	S	W	M	Jun 1890	9	S				MS	AL	AL	
	Cordelia	D	W	F	May 1892	8	S				MS	AL	AL	
277	Epps, William F.	H	W	M	Dec 1874	25	M	1			AL	AL	MS	Farmer
	Dollie	W	W	F	May 1880	20	M	1	1	1	AL	GA	GA	
	John R.	S	W	M	Jul 1899	11/mo	S				MS	AL	AL	
278	Long, John C.	H	W	M	Apr 1847	53	M	34			GA	NC	NC	Farmer
	Germima D.	W	W	F	Jun 1850	49	M	34	14	12	AL	NC	NC	
	Elizabeth M.	D	W	F	Dec 1871	28	S				AL	GA	AL	
	Andrew J.	S	W	M	Jan 1878	22	S				AL	GA	AL	Farm Laborer
	John W.	S	W	M	Jan 1880	20	S				AL	GA	AL	Farm Laborer
	Emma	D	W	F	Aug 1882	18	S				AL	GA	AL	
	Francis M.	S	W	M	Sep 1883	16	S				AL	GA	AL	Farm Laborer
	George W.	S	W	M	Jun 1885	14	S				AL	GA	AL	Farm Laborer
	Arthur D.	S	W	M	Dec 1891	8	S				AL	GA	AL	
	Cora B.	D	W	F	Jan 1894	6	S				MS	GA	AL	
279	Long, Loyd M.	H	W	M	Mar 1876	24	M	0			AL	GA	AL	Farmer
	Florence M.	W	W	F	Jan 1878	22	M	0	0	0	MS	AL	AL	
280	Patterson, Benjamin F.	H	W	M	Jan 1873	27	M	5			MS	SC	AL	Farmer
	Missouri S	W	W	F	Nov 1877	22	M	5	3	3	AL	AL	GA	
	Benjamin L.	S	W	M	Sep 1895	4	S				MS	MS	AL	
	Henry H.	S	W	M	Jun 1897	2	S				MS	MS	AL	
	Vela E.	D	W	F	Jan 1900	5/mo	S				MS	MS	AL	
	Surrena A.	M	W	F	Feb 1840	60	Wd		2	2	AL	SC	NC	
	Ellen V.	Sis	W	F	Mar 1855	15	S				MS	TN	AL	
281	Sullivan, William H.	H	W	M	Oct 1855	44	M	22			AL	Ire	GA	Farmer
	Louisa	W	W	F	Nov 1854	45	M	22	8	6	GA	NC	NC	
	Mattie P.	D	W	F	Apr 1880	20	S				MS	AL	GA	
	Mary S.	D	W	F	Oct 1883	16	S				MS	AL	GA	
	Samantha C.	D	W	F	May 1886	14	S				MS	AL	GA	
	Thomas J.	S	W	M	Apr 1889	11	S				MS	AL	GA	Farm Laborer
	James T.	S	W	M	Jan 1891	9	S				MS	AL	GA	
	Alpherd L.	S	W	M	Jan 1895	5	S				MS	AL	GA	

1	2	3	4	5	6	7	8	9	10	11	12	13	14	15
282	Tatum, Julia A.	H	W	F	Jul 1839	60	Wd		3	3	MS	SC	AL	Farmer
	Mary D.	D	W	F	Jul 1875	24	S				MS	TN	MS	
	John W.	S	W	M	Jul 1877	22	S				MS	TN	MS	Farm Laborer
	Billon, Ames J.	GS	W	M	Dec 1894	5	S				MS	AL	MS	
283	Mink, Newton B.	H	W	M	Oct 1868	31	M	8			MS	AL	AL	Farmer
	Annie L.	W	W	F	Dec 1862	36	M	8	5	4	MS	AL	MS	
	Horace J.	S	W	M	Jul 1892	7	S				MS	MS	MS	
	Esther O.	D	W	F	Sep 1895	4	S				MS	MS	MS	
	Marcus L.	S	W	M	Jan 1898	2	S				MS	MS	MS	
	Ora O.	D	W	F	May 1900	0/mo	S				MS	MS	MS	
284	Mink, Marvin Ed	H	W	M	Oct 1878	21	S				MS	MS	MS	Farmer
	Mammie E.	M	W	F	Oct 1838	61	Wd		1	1	AL	AL	AL	
285	Fancher, Hayden	H	W	M	Jul 1861	38	M	13			AL	TN	AL	Farmer
	Delpha	W	W	F	Oct 1865	34	M	13	4	2	AL	AL	AL	
	Ellis A.	S	W	M	Aug 1887	12	S				MS	AL	AL	Farm Laborer
	Ednar O.	D	W	F	Jun 1889	10	S				MS	AL	AL	
	Elger F.	S	W	M	May 1898	2	S				MS	AL	AL	
286	Ozbirn, Thomas W.	H	W	M	Nov 1862	37	M	8			AL	AL	AL	Farmer
	Martha J.	S	W	M	Sep 1892	35	M	8	3	3	MS	AL	SC	
	Marony J.	S	W	M	Sep 1892	7	S				MS	AL	MS	
	Effie G.	D	W	F	Aug 1896	3	S				MS	AL	MS	
	Peardelia J.	D	W	F	Sep 1899	7/mo	S				MS	AL	MS	
287	Hale, William J.	H	W	M	Apr 1857	43	M	21			MS	TN	AL	Farmer
	Lillie N.	W	W	F	Jan 1863	37	M	21	7	6	MS	TN	AL	
	Serena C.	D	W	F	Oct 1881	18	S				MS	MS	MS	
	Emily M.	D	W	F	Jan 1884	16	S				MS	MS	MS	
	Lydie E.	D	W	F	Jan 1886	14	S				MS	MS	MS	
	Ellen E.	D	W	F	Dec 1887	12	S				MS	MS	MS	
	Phoelie A.	D	W	F	Nov 1889	10	S				MS	MS	MS	
	Mary I.	D	W	F	Mar 1896	4	S				MS	MS	MS	
288	Dickinson, John	H	W	M	Jun 1873	26	M	2			AL	AL	AL	Farmer
	Roxie N.	W	W	F	Nov 1876	23	M	2	1	1	MS	AL	MS	
	Buta B.	D	W	F	Dec 1898	1	S				MS	AL	MS	
289	Jackson, Ezekial W.	H	W	M	Jun 1855	44	M	23			GA	GA	GA	
	Luann	W	W	F	Oct 1850	49	M	23	6	6	AL	AL	AL	
	Jefferson A.	S	W	M	May 1880	20	S				AL	GA	AL	Farm Laborer
	Martha E.	D	W	F	Jun 1882	17	S				AL	GA	AL	
	Mary S.	D	W	F	Jun 1882	17	S				AL	GA	AL	
	John W.	S	W	M	Jun 1885	14	S				AL	GA	AL	Farm Laborer
	Henry W.	S	W	M	Feb 1890	10	S				AL	GA	AL	Farm Laborer
290	Dickinson, William B.	H	W	M	May 1847	53	M	28			AL	GA	GA	Farmer
	Drucilla C.	W	W	F	Dec 1853	46	M	28	10	8	AL	TN	AL	
	Oscar L.	S	W	M	Mar 1882	18	S				AL	AL	AL	Farm Laborer
	Rosie B.	D	W	F	Apr 1884	16	S				AL	AL	AL	
	Nancy A.	D	W	F	Aug 1886	13	S				AL	AL	AL	
	William C.	S	W	M	Nov 1888	11	S				MS	AL	AL	Farm Laborer
	Virgie C.	D	W	F	Jun 1891	8	S				MS	AL	AL	
	Erta	D	W	F	Oct 1893	6	S				MS	AL	AL	
291	Bostic, Green L.	H	W	M	Sep 1864	35	M	9			AL	GA	GA	Farmer
	Fannie P.	W	W	F	Oct 1873	26	M	9	5	4	MS	KY	NC	
	Lewis L.	S	W	M	Jan 1892	8	S				MS	AL	MS	
	Erie	D	W	F	Nov 1895	4	S				MS	AL	MS	
	John A.	S	W	M	Jul 1897	2	S				MS	AL	MS	
	Clide	S	W	M	May 1900	4/mo	S				MS	AL	MS	

1	2	3	4	5	6	7	8	9	10	11	12	13	14	15
292	Tharp, John H.	H	W	M	Jan 1857	43	M	22			AL	AL	AL	Farmer
	Mary M.	W	W	F	Dec 1858	41	M	22	10	10	AL	AL	AL	
	Savannah A.	D	W	F	Nov 1878	21	S				MS	AL	AL	
	Myrtle M.	D	W	F	Aug 1880	19	S				MS	AL	AL	
	James E.	S	W	M	Jun 1883	16	S				MS	AL	AL	
	Almeada R.	D	W	F	Aug 1884	14	S				MS	AL	AL	
	Martha A.	D	W	F	Jun 1887	13	S				MS	AL	AL	
	Perlina F.	D	W	F	Jul 1888	11	S				MS	AL	AL	
	Garvin D.	S	W	M	Jan 1891	9	S				MS	AL	AL	
	Cass A.	S	W	M	Nov 1893	6	S				MS	AL	AL	
	William C.	S	W	M	Jul 1896	3	S				MS	AL	AL	
	Lafford B.	S	W	M	Dec 1899	1	S				MS	AL	AL	
	Fernando F.	Nep	W	M	Oct 1880	19	S				MS	AL	AL	Farm Laborer
293	Messer, John F.	H	W	M	Oct 1854	45	M	16			GA	GA	GA	Farmer
	Mary L.	W	W	F	Sep 1866	33	M	16	4	4	MS	KY	NC	
	Purley V.	D	W	F	Feb 1885	15	S				MS	GA	MS	
	Cora E.	D	W	F	May 1888	12	S				MS	GA	MS	
	Norma E.	D	W	F	Dec 1889	10	S				MS	GA	MS	
	Flavous L.	S	W	M	Nov 1893	6	S				MS	GA	MS	
294	Butler, James W.	H	W	M	Nov 1867	32	M	12			MS	AL	MS	Farmer
	Cordelia J.	W	W	F	Feb 1868	31	M	12	6	3	MS	ENG	AL	
	Oscar L.	S	W	M	May 1891	9	S				MS	AL	MS	
	Aurorer V.	D	W	F	Jan 1894	6	S				MS	AL	MS	
	Mary J.	D	W	F	Jan 1899	1	S				MS	AL	MS	
295	Hall, James S.	H	W	M	Aug 1846	53	M	20			TN	TN	TN	Farmer
	Nancy C.	W	W	F	Aug 1843	56	M	20	0	0	MS	NC	MS	
	Moore, James	Nep	W	M	Jan 1869	31	S				MS	NC	MS	Idiot
296	Stacy, William J.	H	W	M	Feb 1871	29	M	5			MS	AL	AL	Farmer
	Flora A.	W	W	F	Apr 1878	22	M	5	4	3	MS	MS	NC	
	Carrie D.	D	W	F	May 1896	4	S				MS	MS	MS	
	Fannie A.	D	W	F	Aug 1897	2	S				MS	MS	MS	
	McCoy, ————	MiL	W	F	Jul 1840	59	S				NC	NC	NC	
297	Jackson, Joseph F.	H	W	M	Feb 1878	22	M	5			AL	AL	AL	Farmer
	Mary C.	W	W	F	Mar 1875	25	M	5	3	3	AL	AL	AL	
	Eliza R.	D	W	F	Sep 1894	5	S				AL	AL	AL	
	Nathaniel	S	W	M	Jan 1897	3	S				AL	AL	AL	
	William S.	S	W	M	Feb 1899	1	S				AL	AL	AL	
298	Belue, James R.	H	W	M	Feb 1845	55	M	16			TN	SC	TN	Farmer
	Margaret	W	W	F	Oct 1845	54	M	16	2	1	AL	UN	TN	
	Frederic F.	S	W	M	Mar 1882	18	S				MS	TN	AL	Farm Laborer
	Dellie F.	D	W	F	Feb 1885	15	S				MS	TN	AL	
	Jones, Marrery J.	SiL	W	F	Dec 1861	38	S				AL	UN	TN	
	Butler, Charles W.	Nep	W	M	Mar 1878	22	S				MS	AL	TN	Farm Laborer
299	Jones, William	H	W	M	Dec 1866	33	M	8			AL	TN	AL	Farmer
	Martha A.	W	W	F	Jul 1877	22	M	8	4	4	AL	AL	AL	
	Mary I.	D	W	F	Oct 1892	7	S				MS	AL	AL	
	Sarah M.	D	W	F	May 1895	5	S				MS	AL	AL	
	Effie L.	D	W	F	Jul 1897	2	S				MS	AL	AL	
	William C.	S	W	M	Jan 1898	1	S				MS	AL	AL	
300	Hunt, William H.	H	W	M	Nov 1859	40	M	16			MS	SC	MS	Farmer
	Mourney L.	W	W	F	Nov 1869	30	M	16	4	4	IL	GA	MS	
	Walter R.	S	W	M	Aug 1889	10	S				MS	MS	IL	Farm Laborer
	Oscar L.	S	W	M	Feb 1892	8	S				MS	MS	IL	
	Carl	S	W	M	Jul 1894	5	S				MS	MS	IL	

1	2	3	4	5	6	7	8	9	10	11	12	13	14	15
	Mary L.	D	W	F	Oct 1896	3	S				MS	MS	IL	
301	Crumby, Carroll	H	W	M	Apr 1840	60	M	25			MS	SC	TN	Farmer
	Eucinda F.	W	W	F	Oct 1852	47	M	25	8	7	TN	TN	TN	
	John E.	S	W	M	Sep 1874	25	S				TN	MS	TN	Farm Laborer
	James W.	S	W	M	Nov 1876	23	S				TN	MS	TN	Farm Laborer
	Josephine M.	D	W	F	Nov 1879	20	S				TN	MS	TN	
	Genetta M.	D	W	F	Dec 1882	17	S				TN	MS	TN	
	Sarah F.	D	W	F	Oct 1885	14	S				TN	MS	TN	
	Thomas H.	S	W	M	May 1892	8	S				TN	MS	TN	
	George W.	S	W	M	May 1897	3	S				TN	MS	TN	
302	Ward, Isaac N.	H	W	M	May 1860	40	M	22			AL	GA	GA	Farmer
	Mary L.	W	W	F	Jun 1862	37	M	22	6	6	AL	AL	AL	
	Joseph H.	S	W	M	Jun 1882	17	S				MS	AL	AL	Farm Laborer
	Jesse C.	S	W	M	Jul 1888	11	S				MS	AL	AL	Farm Laborer
	Isaac T.	S	W	M	Jul 1893	5	S				MS	AL	AL	
	Andrew F.	S	W	M	Mar 1897	3	S				MS	AL	AL	
	Evie D.	D	W	F	Nov 1899	7/mo	S				MS	AL	AL	
303	Ward, William H.	H	W	M	Dec 1879	20	M	0			AL	AL	AL	Farmer
	Willie B.	W	W	F	Mar 1878	22	M	0	0	0	MS	MS	MS	
304	Butler, George G.	H	W	M	Feb 1870	30	M	8			MS	MS	MS	Farmer
	Amanda L.	W	W	F	May 1874	26	M	8	3	3	MS	MS	TN	
	William R.	S	W	M	Jan 1893	7	S				MS	MS	MS	
	George C.	D	W	F	Nov 1895	4	S				MS	MS	MS	
	Leora	D	W	F	Dec 1898	1	S				MS	MS	MS	
305	Adams, William A.	H	W	M	Feb 1845	55	M	35			MS	NC	SC	Farmer
	Cinthia C.	W	W	F	Aug 1842	57	M	35	8	7	TN	SC	TN	
	William N.	S	W	M	May 1876	24	S				MS	MS	TN	Farm Laborer
	Cora L.	D	W	F	Oct 1882	17	S				MS	MS	TN	
306	Eaton, John R.	H	W	M	Apr 1867	33	M	11			MS	AL	TN	Farmer
	Fannie S.	W	W	F	Dec 1869	31	M	11	6	5	MS	UN	NC	
	Henry O.	S	W	M	Jan 1890	10	S				MS	MS	MS	Farm Laborer
	Mattie B.	D	W	F	Sep 1891	8	S				MS	MS	MS	
	Emma C.	D	W	F	Dec 1894	5	S				MS	MS	MS	
	John C.	S	W	M	Jan 1898	2	S				MS	MS	MS	
	Carra S.	D	W	F	Oct 1899	7/mo	S				MS	MS	MS	
307	Eaton, James E.	H	W	M	May 1864	37	M	7			MS	AL	TN	Farmer
	Samantha D.	W	W	F	Aug 1871	28	M	7	4	4	MS	AL	AL	
	James W.	S	W	M	Nov 1893	6	S				MS	MS	MS	
	George W.	S	W	M	Oct 1895	4	S				MS	MS	MS	
	Ivie E.	D	W	F	Dec 1896	3	S				MS	MS	MS	
	Fannie L.	D	W	F	Aug 1899	8/mo					MS	MS	MS	
308	Cole, Edmond A.	H	W	M	May 1857	43	M	20			MS	SC	AL	Farmer
	Mary M.	W	W	F	Sep 1871	38	M	20	10	8	AL	AL	AL	
	Bertha S.	D	W	F	Jun 1881	19	M				AL	MS	AL	
	Sebron J.	S	W	M	Dec 1883	16	S				AL	MS	AL	Farm Laborer
	James M.	S	W	M	Mar 1886	14	S				AL	MS	AL	Farm Laborer
	Martha E.	D	W	F	May 1888	12	S				AL	MS	AL	
	Sarah J.	D	W	F	Feb 1891	9	S				AL	MS	AL	
	Mollie B.	D	W	F	Sep 1893	6	S				MS	MS	AL	
	Pherrie P.	D	W	F	Jun 1896	3	S				MS	MS	AL	
	Eddie	D	W	F	Oct 1898	1	S				MS	MS	AL	
309	Harris, Jasper N.	H	W	M	Nov 1858	41	M	15			MS	TN	MS	Farmer
	Emma	W	W	F	Jan 1865	35	M	15	6	6	MS	MS	MS	
	Docia L.	D	W	F	Jan 1886	13	S				MS	MS	MS	

1	2	3	4	5	6	7	8	9	10	11	12	13	14	15
	Charles C.	S	W	M	Oct 1889	10	S				MS	MS	MS	Farm Laborer
	Ira O.	S	W	M	Jan 1891	9	S				MS	MS	MS	
	Melmuth M.	S	W	M	Jul 1893	6	S				MS	MS	MS	
	Mary T.	D	W	F	Feb 1895	5	S				MS	MS	MS	
	Russ D.	S	W	M	Sep 1897	2	S				MS	MS	MS	
310	Castleberry, Thomas	H	W	M	Jul 1879	20	M	0			MS	NC	NC	Farmer
	Lonie L.	W	W	F	Jun 1880	19	M	0			AL	AL	AL	
	Jerry	Bro	W	M	May 1884	16	M	0			MS	NC	NC	Farm Laborer
	Florida R.	DiL	W	F	Sep 1884	15	M	0	0	0	AL	AL	AL	
311	Moore, William R.	H	W	M	Apr 1859	41	M	14			MS	AL	MS	Farmer
	Emily A.	W	W	F	Aug 1862	37	M	14	7	5	MS	MS	AL	
	Eunice E.	D	W	F	Dec 1887	12	S				MS	MS	MS	
	William I.	S	W	M	Apr 1891	9	S				MS	MS	MS	
	John M.	S	W	M	Mar 1893	7	S				MS	MS	MS	
	Berthal R.	S	W	M	Mar 1895	5	S				MS	MS	MS	
	Jeneral P.	S	W	M	Oct 1897	2	S				MS	MS	MS	
312	Angland, Charlie M.	H	W	M	Apr 1866	34	M	14			MS	MS	AL	Farm Laborer
	Sarah E.	W	W	F	Sep 1867	32	M	14	7	5	MS	MS	MS	
	James T.	S	W	M	Oct 1887	13	S				MS	MS	AL	Farm Laborer
	Lydie L.	D	W	F	Jul 1890	9	S				MS	MS	AL	
	Ada V.	D	W	F	Apr 1893	7	S				MS	MS	AL	
	Gerome S.	S	W	M	Feb 1897	3	S				MS	MS	AL	
	Lee C.	S	W	M	Aug 1899	10/mo	S				MS	MS	AL	
313	Selby, David	H	W	M	Oct 1872	27	M	4			MS	AL	MS	Farmer
	Mary F.	W	W	F	Dec 1873	26	M	4	2	2	MS	MS	AL	
	James F.	S	W	M	Dec 1895	4	S				MS	MS	MS	
	Effie B.	D	W	F	Jan 1898	2	S				MS	MS	MS	
314	Clingan, John A.	H	W	M	Aug 1849	50	M	17			MS	TN	AL	Farmer
	Amanda A.	W	W	F	Jul 1855	44	M	17	4	2	MS	AL	MS	
	Wiley E.	S	W	M	Mar 1887	13	S				MS	MS	MS	Farm Laborer
	Joseph A.	S	W	M	Mar 1893	7	S				MS	MS	MS	
	Harrison, Usie B.	Nce	W	F	May 1895	5	S				MS	MS	MS	
315	Smith, Levy	H	W	M	Mar 1870	30	M	10			TN	TN	TN	Teamster
	Manervy	W	W	F	Nov 1864	35	M	10	3	3	AL	AL	AL	
	Thomas J.	S	W	M	Apr 1891	9	S				MS	TN	AL	
	Ruffuis L	S	W	M	May 1893	7	S				MS	TN	AL	
	Buddie	S	W	M	Sep 1895	4	S				MS	TN	AL	
	McBee, Levy M.	Bdr	W	M	Mar 1868	32	Wd				AL	AL	AL	Day Laborer
316	Walker, John W.	H	W	M	Oct 1876	23	M	5			AL	AL	MS	Farmer
	Lonie B.	W	W	F	Nov 1877	22	M	5	3	2	MS	AL	TN	
	Gadston H.	S	W	M	Jan 1898	2	S				MS	AL	MS	
	Lonie B.	D	W	F	Oct 1899	7/mo	S				MS	AL	MS	
	Tackett, Jane	MiL	W	F	Dec 1848	51	Wd		1	1	TN	SC	SC	
317	Tackett, Rebecca	H	W	F	May 1845	55	S				TN	SC	SC	Day Laborer
	Elmira C.	Sis	W	F	Nov 1855	45	S				MS	SC	SC	Day Laborer
318	Carden, John M.	H	W	M	Mar 1847	53	M	12			GA	GA	GA	Farmer
	Callie	W	W	F	Sep 1862	35	M	12	3	2	AL	AL	AL	
	John F.	S	W	M	Jan 1882	18	S				AL	GA	AL	Farm Laborer
	Lemuel C.	S	W	M	Oct 1888	11	S				AL	GA	AL	Farm Laborer
	Millard J.	S	W	M	Feb 1894	6	S				AL	GA	AL	
319	Gook, Berthia	H	W	F	Dec 1851	48	D		2	2	MS	AL	TN	Farmer
	James W.	S	W	M	Jul 1885	14	S				MS	MS	MS	Farm Laborer
	John H.	S	W	M	Feb 1889	11	S				MS	MS	MS	Farm Laborer

1	2	3	4	5	6	7	8	9	10	11	12	13	14	15
320	Mann, James R.	H	W	M	Jul 1861	38	M	17			AL	SC	AL	Farmer
	Mary M.	W	W	F	Jun 1867	32	M	17	7	7	AL	GA	GA	
	Belzie S.	D	W	F	Oct 1883	16	S				AL	AL	AL	
	James M.	S	W	M	Nov 1885	14	S				AL	AL	AL	Farm Laborer
	Dorra E.	D	W	F	Oct 1887	12	S				AL	AL	AL	
	Lou E.	D	W	F	May 1889	11	S				MS	AL	AL	
	Effie L.	D	W	F	Feb 1891	9	S				MS	AL	AL	
	Lou A.	S	W	M	Aug 1897	2	S				MS	AL	AL	
	Lothic M.	D	W	F	Jun 1899	11/mo	S				MS	AL	AL	
321	Long, William W.	H	W	M	Oct 1867	32	M	4			AL	GA	AL	Farmer
	Susan E.	W	W	F	May 1875	25	M	4	2	2	GA	GA	GA	
	Charles E.	S	W	M	May 1896	4	S				MS	AL	GA	
	Harvey M.	S	W	M	Aug 1898	1	S				MS	AL	GA	
322	Long, Charles W.	H	W	M	Apr 1874	26	Wd				AL	GA	AL	
323	Shook, Fletcher	H	W	M	Mar 1876	24	M	1			MS	MS	MS	
	Sarah A.E.	W	W	F	Jan 1884	16	M	1	1	1	AL	AL	MS	Farmer
324	Caine, Elias L.	H	W	M	Jul 1851	48	M	23			AL	AL	AL	Farmer
	Sarah E.	W	W	F	Apr 1855	45	M	23	5	5	MS	OH	AL	
	Neama A.	D	W	F	Aug 1877	22	M	4			MS	AL	MS	
	James M.	S	W	M	Dec 1878	21	S				MS	AL	MS	Farm Laborer
	Larence F.	S	W	M	Dec 1882	18	S				MS	AL	MS	Farm Laborer
	Sarah A.	D	W	F	Jan 1884	16	M				AL	AL	MS	
	Largus C.	S	W	M	Jan 1886	14	S				MS	AL	MS	Farm Laborer
325	Shewball, Elizabeth R.	H	W	F	Dec 1834	65	Wd				AL	SC	TN	
326	McClung, William	H	W	M	Apr 1853	47	M	23			AL	AL	AL	Farmer
	Maggie M.	W	W	F	Sep 1849	50	M	23	6	0	AL	SC	GA	
	Lora L.	GD	W	F	Dec 1895	4	S				MS	MS	AL	
327	Upton, John W.	H	W	M	Nov 1871	28	M	9			AL	AL	AL	Farmer
	Sarah E.	W	W	F	Jan 1875	25	M	9	0	0	AL	AL	AL	
328	Armstrong, Charles M.	H	W	M	Dec 1860	39	M	15			AL	AL	AL	Farmer
	Nancy L.	W	W	F	Aug 1862	37	M	15	5	4	GA	GA	SC	
	Magie O.	D	W	F	May 1888	12	S				AL	AL	GA	
	Florence	D	W	F	Jul 1891	8	S				AL	AL	GA	
	Flossy	D	W	F	Jul 1891	8	S				AL	AL	GA	
	Charlie W.	S	W	M	Jan 1896	4	S				MS	AL	GA	
329	Bridges, George C.	H	W	M	Apr 1854	45	M	15			NC	NC	GA	Farmer
	Julia A.	W	W	F	Aug 1863	37	M	15	7	5	GA	SC	SC	
	John M.	S	W	M	Sep 1886	14	S				MS	NC	GA	Farm Laborer
	Larra F.	D	W	F	Apr 1888	12	S				MS	NC	GA	
	Ratha M.	D	W	F	Oct 1889	10	S				MS	NC	GA	
	Georgia A.	D	W	F	Jul 1895	4	S				MS	NC	GA	
	Sidney S.	S	W	M	Feb 1898	2	S				MS	NC	GA	
330	Breckfield, James	H	W	M	Apr 1878	22	M	0			AL	SC	GA	Farmer
	Allie V.	W	W	F	Nov 1870	29	M	0	0	0	AL	MS	AL	
331	Breckfield. John	H	W	M	Oct 1850	49	M	27			SC	SC	SC	Farmer
	Mary C.	W	W	F	Dec 1852	47	M	27	8	5	GA	SC	SC	
	John	S	W	M	Apr 1884	16	S				AL	SC	GA	Farm Laborer
	David E.	S	W	M	Sep 1891	9	S				MO	SC	GA	
	Marion A.	S	W	M	May 1893	7	S				MO	SC	GA	
	Sarah C.	D	W	F	Apr 1876	24	Wd				AL	SC	GA	
332	Haris, Henry T.	H	W	M	Jan 1853	47	M	7			GA	SC	GA	Farmer-Carpenter

1	2	3	4	5	6	7	8	9	10	11	12	13	14	15
	Sarah A.	W	W	F	Apr 1876	24	M	7	3	3	AL	SC	GA	
	Elsie L.	D	W	F	Sep 1891	5	S				MO	GA	AL	
	Mary E.	D	W	F	Aug 1896	3	F				MO	GA	AL	
	Myrtle	D	W	F	Jul 1899	10/mo	S				GA	GA	AL	
333	Harrison, William C.	H	W	M	Oct 1849	50	M	12			MS	UN	UN	Farmer
	Angeline	W	W	F	Mar 1840	60	M	12	7	4	TN	TN	TN	
	Lillie V.	D	W	F	Mar 1882	18	S				MS	MS	MS	
	Alice	D	W	F	Feb 1884	16	S				MS	MS	MS	
	Minnie V.	D	W	F	Aug 1886	13	S				MS	MS	MS	
	Hamilton, Martha E.	D	W	F	Jul 1873	26	S				TN	TN	TN	
334	McDonald, Francis	H	W	M	Jun 1849	50	Wd				GA	GA	GA	Farmer
335	McDonald, John W.	H	W	M	Apr 1875	25	M	6			MS	MS	MS	Farmer
	Lunara	W	W	F	Nov 1876	23	M	6	4	2	AL	AL	MS	
	Jessie B.	D	W	F	May 1896	4	S				AL	AL	MS	
	Perlie	D	W	F	Feb 1900	3/mo	S				MS	AL	AL	
336	Stamphill, Vince	H	W	M	Sep 1877	22	M	0			MS	AL	AL	Farmer
	Minnie	W	W	F	Jun 1883	16	M	0	0	0	AL	AL	AL	
337	Walker, James W.	H	B	M	Sep 1866	33	M	13			MS	UN	AL	Farmer
	Dorthula	W	B	F	Sep 1872	27	M	13	5	3	MS	MS	AL	
	Georgia C.	D	B	F	Aug 1884	15	S				MS	MS	MS	
	Walter	S	B	M	Aug 1891	8	S				AL	MS	MS	
	Zollie	S	B	M	Mar 1896	4	S				MS	MS	MS	
	Ordie A.	D	B	F	Jan 1899	1	S				MS	MS	MS	
338	Moore, David C.	H	W	M	Mar 1877	23	M	3			AL	AL	AL	Farmer
	Lillie A.	W	W	F	Apr 1882	18	M	3	1	1	MS	AL	AL	
	Homer L.	S	W	M	Jun 1899	1	S				MS	AL	MS	
339	Wedgeworth, John	H	W	M	Jul 1850	49	M	17			AL	SC	AL	Farmer
	Martha E.	W	W	F	UN UN	UN	M	17			GA	GA	GA	
	Bates, Sarah E.	UN	W	F	Jan 1848	52	Wd		3	3	AL	AL	AL	
	Espy B.	D	W	F	Jan 1883	17	S				AL	AL	AL	
	Thomas J.	S	W	M	Mar 1886	14	S				AL	AL	AL	Farm Laborer
	Mary F.	D	W	F	Mar 1890	10	S				AL	AL	AL	
340	Mann, Louisa	H	W	F	Aug 1861	38	Wd		7	7	AL	AL	AL	Farmer
	James H.	S	W	M	Oct 1882	17	S				AL	AL	AL	Farm Laborer
	John E.	S	W	M	Mar 1885	15	S				AL	AL	AL	Farm Laborer
	George M.	S	W	M	Jan 1887	13	S				AL	AL	AL	Farm Laborer
	Rinda E.	D	W	F	Jan 1889	11	S				MS	AL	AL	
	William W.	S	W	M	Feb 1891	9	S				MS	AL	AL	
	Sarah M.	D	W	F	May 1893	7	S				MS	AL	AL	
	Josha D.	S	W	M	Nov 1897	2	S				MS	AL	AL	
341	Mann, Charlie C.	H	W	M	Jun 1867	32	M	14			AL	SC	AL	Farmer
	Dealy	W	W	F	Jun 1868	31	M	14	8	3	AL	AL	AL	
	Delitha A.	D	W	F	Jan 1887	13	S				AL	AL	AL	
	Alice O.	D	W	F	Dec 1888	11	S				MS	AL	AL	
	Rosie E.	D	W	F	Sep 1890	9	S				MS	AL	AL	
342	Ewing, William M.	H	W	M	Mar 1861	39	M	8			AL	AL	SC	Farmer
	Sis	W	W	F	May 1870	30	M	8	3	2	AL	GA	GA	
	Erbie	S	W	M	Feb 1894	6	S				AL	AL	AL	
	Eddie	S	W	M	Feb 1896	4	S				AL	AL	AL	
343	Ewing, James E.	H	W	M	Apr 1859	41	M	19			AL	SC	SC	Farmer
	Asa A.	W	W	F	Nov 1861	39	M	19	8	7	AL	SC	SC	
	Rubin C.	S	W	M	Feb 1883	17	S				AL	AL	AL	Farm Laborer

1	2	3	4	5	6	7	8	9	10	11	12	13	14	15
	Henry W.	S	W	M	Jun 1885	14	S				AL	AL	AL	Farm Laborer
	Perlie S.	D	W	F	Feb 1888	12	S				AL	AL	AL	
	Joseph C.	S	W	M	Apr 1890	10	S				AL	AL	AL	Farm Laborer
	James O.	S	W	M	Aug 1892	7	S				AL	AL	AL	
	Marvin O.	S	W	M	Mar 1894	6	S				AL	AL	AL	
	Babe	S	W	M	Mar 1900	5/mo	S				MS	AL	AL	
344	Gentile, Robert J.	H	W	M	Feb 1845	55	Wd				NC	NC	NC	Farmer
	John W.	S	W	M	Jul 1876	23	S				AL	NC	AL	Farm Laborer
	Debose, D.	D	W	F	Nov 1880	19	S				AL	GA	GA	
345	Hand, John B.	H	W	M	Sep 1862	37	M	4			AL	GA	GA	Farmer
	Georgia M.	W	W	F	Apr 1875	25	M	4	3	3	AL	SC	AL	
	William M.	S	W	M	Nov 1882	17	S				GA	AL	GA	Farm Laborer
	Jessie M.	S	W	M	Dec 1884	15	S				GA	AL	GA	Farm Laborer
	Lee O.	S	W	M	May 1887	13	S				GA	AL	GA	Farm Laborer
	Ader M.	D	W	F	Nov 1899	11	S				GA	AL	GA	
	William Z.	S	W	M	May 1892	8	S				GA	AL	GA	
	Vindex	S	W	M	Jun 1894	5	S				GA	AL	GA	
	John D.	S	W	M	Apr 1897	3	S				AL	AL	AL	
	Ida B.	D	W	F	May 1898	2	S				AL	AL	AL	
	Elbert	S	W	M	Feb 1900	3/mo	S				AL	AL	AL	
346	Harris, Jessie G.	H	W	M	Feb 1860	40	M	13			MS	AL	MS	Farmer
	Eller	W	W	F	Apr 1870	30	M	13	5	5	TN	TN	TN	
	Mary L.	D	W	F	Sep 1888	11	S				MS	MS	TN	
	Robirt L.	S	W	M	Feb 1891	9	S				MS	MS	TN	
	James C.	S	W	M	Mar 1893	7	S				MS	MS	TN	
	Alen	S	W	M	Sep 1896	3	S				MS	MS	TN	
	Rubin	S	W	M	Apr 1899	1	S				MS	MS	TN	
347	Smith, Christopher	H	W	M	Feb 1880	20	M	0			AL	AL	GA	Farmer
	Elemarie	W	W	F	Jan 1878	22	M	0	0	0	MS	MS	AL	
348	Loveless, James A.	H	W	M	Oct 1873	26	M	9			GA	GA	GA	Farmer
	Mary E.	W	W	F	Nov 1872	27	M	9	4	4	GA	GA	GA	
	Frank M.	S	W	M	Oct 1891	8	S				AL	GA	GA	
	Louisa M.	D	W	F	Dec 1892	7	S				TX	GA	GA	
	Joseph L.	S	W	M	Apr 1894	6	S				TX	GA	GA	
	Vinnie M.	D	W	F	Jan 1896	4	S				AL	GA	GA	
349	Timbes, William	H	W	M	Apr 1858	42	M	17			AL	TN	TN	Farmer
	Lucinda E.	W	W	F	Nov 1867	32	M	17	8	6	AL	TN	GA	
	Almeda	D	W	F	Mar 1886	14	S				MS	AL	MS	
	Isaac B.	S	W	M	Nov 1888	11	S				MS	AL	MS	Farm Laborer
	Robert H.	S	W	M	Apr 1890	10	S				MS	AL	MS	Farm Laborer
	Mid M.	S	W	M	Jul 1892	7	S				MS	AL	MS	
	Hosie V.	S	W	M	Oct 1895	4	S				MS	AL	MS	
	Sibrena A.	D	W	F	Jul 1889	1	S				MS	AL	MS	
350	Taylor, Leumel M.	H	W	M	Oct 1843	56	M	38			AL	SC	SC	Farmer
	Messa	W	W	F	Sep 1842	47	M	38	8	6	GA	NC	GA	
	Lilla A.	D	W	F	Oct 1881	18	S				GA	AL	GA	
	Lula E.	D	W	F	Jul 1884	15	S				GA	AL	GA	
351	Breakfield, William L.	H	W	M	Feb 1853	47	M	15			SC	SC	SC	Farmer
	Georgeann	W	W	F	Jul 1865	34	M	15	6	4	TN	AL	AL	
	Martelia A.	D	W	M	Aug 1890	9	S				AL	SC	TN	
	Mathe L.	D	W	F	May 1894	6	S				MS	SC	TN	
	John H.	S	W	M	May 1897	3	S				MS	SC	TN	
	Cordelia	D	W	F	Dec 1899	6/mo					MS	SC	TN	
352	Gentle, Felix	H	W	M	May 1872	28	M	3			AL	NC	AL	Farmer

1	2	3	4	5	6	7	8	9	10	11	12	13	14	15
	Mollie C.	W	W	F	Dec 1877	22	M	3	2	1	AL	SC	AL	
	Rosie D.	D	W	F	Mar 1899	1	S				MS	AL	AL	
353	Ferrell, William M.	H	W	M	May 1852	48	M	21			GA	GA	GA	Farmer
	Martha S.	W	W	F	Sep 1860	39	M	21	13	7	GA	GA	GA	
	Lunnie	S	W	M	Sep 1881	18	S				AL	GA	GA	
	Luther	S	W	M	Sep 1881	18	S				AL	GA	GA	Farm Laborer
	Harrett G.	D	W	F	May 1887	13	S				GA	GA	GA	
	Green	S	W	M	Dec 1889	10	S				GA	GA	GA	
	Odus O.	S	W	M	Jun 1892	7	S				AL	GA	GA	
	Wallis	S	W	M	Jul 1895	4	S				MS	GA	GA	
	Eurel L.	S	W	M	Apr 1899	1	S				MS	GA	GA	
354	Byram, Siqoul S.	H	W	M	Jul 1876	23	M	3			MS	MS	AL	Farmer
	Roxie A.	W	W	F	Mar 1880	20	M	3	2	2	MS	AL	AL	
	Ludie D.	D	W	M	Dec 1897	2	S				MS	MS	MS	
	Odus	S	W	M	May 1900	1/mo	S				MS	MS	MS	
355	Mann, John D.	H	W	M	May 1859	41	M	21			AL	SC	AL	Farmer
	Julia H.	W	W	F	Jun 1860	39	M	21	9	5	AL	SC	AL	
	Arthur V.	S	W	M	Sep 1883	16	S				MS	AL	AL	Farm Laborer
	Almeda E.	D	W	F	Jan 1886	14	S				MS	AL	AL	
	Ider L.	D	W	F	Oct 1898	11	S				MS	AL	AL	
	Jessie A.	S	W	M	Sep 1891	8	S				MS	AL	AL	
	William F.	S	W	M	Mar 1894	6	S				MS	AL	AL	
356	Riggs, Benjamin H.	H	W	M	Aug 1857	42	M	10			MS	TN	MS	Farmer
	Arminda C.	W	W	F	Jun 1865	34	M	10	5	5	AL	TN	AL	
	Esterlee V.	D	W	F	Jun 1880	19	S				AL	GA	MS	
	Ammes O.	D	W	F	Mar 1885	15	S				MS	GA	MS	
	Moorman V.	S	W	M	Aug 1889	10	S				AL	AL	MS	
	Luther J.	S	W	M	Jul 1891	8	S				AL	AL	MS	
	Dyrena C.	D	W	F	Sep 1893	6	S				AL	AL	MS	
	Benjamin F.	S	W	M	Nov 1895	4	S				AL	AL	MS	
	Hillery E.	S	W	M	Mar 1898	2	S				AL	AL	MS	
357	Skinner, William	H	W	M	Oct 1874	25	M	5			AL	AL	GA	Farmer
	Mary V.	W	W	F	Sep 1876	23	M	5	2	2	AL	MS	GA	
	Mattie S.	D	W	F	Feb 1896	4	S				MS	AL	AL	
	Robert H.	S	W	M	May 1899	1	S				MS	AL	AL	
358	Pate, Huner B.	H	W	M	Jan 1828	72	M	14			AL	GA	GA	Farmer
	Mary C.	W	W	F	Apr 1850	50	M	14	0	0	MS	GA	MS	
359	Pruitt, Sidney M.	H	W	M	Mar 1849	51	M	30			AL	GA	SC	Farmer
	Larah F.	W	W	F	Dec 1853	46	M	30	10	8	AL	AL	AL	
	Louis F.	S	W	M	Dec 1878	21	S				AL	AL	AL	
	Martha R.	D	W	F	Jun 1882	17	S				AL	AL	AL	
	William M.	S	W	M	Dec 1885	14	S				AL	AL	AL	
	Johathan	S	W	M	Dec 1888	11	S				AL	AL	AL	
360	Pate, Chrissom B.	H	W	M	Sep 1884	52	M	32			MS	AL	SC	Farmer
	Penelope S.	W	W	F	Apr 1852	48	M	32			MS	MS	MS	
	Dewitt	S	W	M	Apr 1891	9	S				MS	MS	MS	
361	Pate, Hosie L.	H	W	M	Sep 1878	21	M	5			MS	MS	MS	Farmer
	Nancy J.	W	W	F	Oct 1876	22	M	5	3	3	MS	AL	SC	
	Sidney I.	S	W	M	Nov 1896	3	S				MS	MS	MS	
	Thomas E.	S	W	M	Dec 1898	1	S				MS	MS	MS	
	Iler M.	D	W	F	May 1900	1/mo	S				MS	MS	MS	
362	Cornelius, Joe	H	W	M	Aug 1842	57	M	4			AL	AL	AL	Farmer
	Martha U.	W	W	F	Nov 1859	41	M	4			AL	AL	GA	

1	2	3	4	5	6	7	8	9	10	11	12	13	14	15
	Mize, James	SS	W	M	Jan 1892	8	S				MS	AL	AL	
363	Stamphill, John	H	W	M	Jan 1870	30	M	4			MS	AL	MS	Farmer
	Bettie S.	W	W	F	Apr 1877	23	M	4			AL	AL	MS	
	Perlie E.	D	W	F	Oct 1891	8	S				MS	MS	AL	
	Atice O.	S	W	M	Jul 1895	4	S				MS	MS	AL	
	Edner H.	D	W	F	Nov 1897	2	S				MS	MS	AL	
364	Keeton, John A.	H	W	M	Jul 1853	46	M	26			AL	AL	AL	Farmer
	Lougenia A.	W	W	F	Jan 1859	42	M	26	9	8	AL	AL	NC	
	Columbus H.	S	W	M	Nov 1877	22	S				AL	AL	AL	Farm Laborer
	Nancy J.	D	W	F	Jul 1880	19	S				AL	AL	AL	
	John B.	S	W	M	Mar 1883	17	S				AL	AL	AL	Farm Laborer
	Emily L.	D	W	F	Oct 1885	14	S				AL	AL	AL	
	Phillip I.	S	W	M	Jun 1887	12	S				AL	AL	AL	Farm Laborer
	Mary C.	D	W	F	Apr 1889	10	S				AL	AL	AL	
	Jessie S.	S	W	M	Apr 1893	7	S				AL	AL	AL	
	Ada F.	D	W	F	Aug 1896	3	S				AL	AL	AL	
	Ophillia	S	W	M	May 1900	1/mo	S				MS	AL	AL	
365	Messer, Isham Y.	W	W	F	Mar 1875	34	M	6			AL	GA	GA	Farmer
	Dollie I.	W	W	F	Mar 1875	25	M	6	3	3	AL	AL	AL	
	Jessie	D	W	F	Jun 1895	4	S				MS	AL	AL	
	Clrice	D	W	F	Jul 1898	1	S				MS	AL	AL	
	Flavis S.	S	W	F	May 1900	1/mo	S				MS	AL	AL	
366	Picketts, Charles H.	H	W	M	Aug 1866	33	M	0			GA	GA	GA	Farmer
	Zamie	W	W	F	Mar 1870	30	M	0			AL	GA	GA	
367	White, William C.	H	W	M	Aug 1856	43	M	0			AL	GA	GA	Farmer
	Mary A.	W	W	F	Mar 1861	39	M	0			MS	AL	MS	
	Dee	S	W	M	Jun 1882	17	S				MS	AL	AL	Farm Laborer
	William L.	S	W	M	Oct 1886	13	S				MS	AL	AL	Farm Laborer
	Sumpter	S	W	M	Mar 1889	10	S				MS	AL	AL	Farm Laborer
	Noonen	S	W	M	Dec 1893	6	S				MS	AL	AL	
368	Anglin, Thomas J.	H	W	M	Mar 1872	28	M	0			MS	MS	MS	Farmer-Teacher
	Maud E.	W	W	F	Feb 1879	21	M	0	0	0	AL	AL	AL	
369	Ozbirn, Robert	H	W	M	Aug 1852	48	M	20			AL	GA	GA	Farmer
	Sarah A.	S	W	F	Nov 1853	46	M	20	9	7	AL	NC	GA	
	James W.	S	W	M	Aug 1877	22	S				MS	AL	AL	Farm Laborer
	Mary M.	D	W	F	Dec 1879	20	S				MS	AL	AL	
	Florence E.	D	W	F	Nov 1881	18	S				MS	AL	AL	
	Meldy A.	D	W	F	May 1884	16	S				MS	AL	AL	
	Winnie N.	D	W	F	Jul 1889	10	S				MS	AL	AL	
	Richard O.	S	W	M	Dec 1892	7	S				MS	AL	AL	
	David C.	S	W	M	Aug 1896	3	S				MS	AL	AL	
370	Lasley, Jery	H	B	M	Mar 1863	37	M	6			AL	UN	AL	Farmer
	Mattie L.	W	B	F	Sep 1874	25	M	6	3	3	AL	UN	UN	
	Minnie	D	B	F	Jul 1886	13	S				MS	AL	AL	
	Mattie B	D	B	F	Dec 1888	11	S				MS	AL	AL	
	John T.	S	B	M	Feb 1890	10	S				MS	AL	AL	Farm Laborer
	Ogden J.	S	B	M	Mar 1895	5	S				MS	AL	AL	
	Gabriel	S	B	M	Jul 1896	3	S				MS	AL	AL	
	Melvina	D	B	F	Nov 1897	2	S				MS	AL	AL	
371	McCoy, John A.	H	W	M	Jan 1872	28	M	7			MS	MS	MS	Farmer
	Julie E.	W	W	F	May 1873	27	M	7	3	2	AL	GA	AL	
	Nannie D.	D	W	F	Jun 1894	6	S				AL	MS	AL	
	Leander F.	S	W	M	Jun 1898	1	S				AL	MS	AL	

1	2	3	4	5	6	7	8	9	10	11	12	13	14	15
372	Frazier, Columbus	H	W	M	Apr 1829	71	Wd				SC	NC	SC	Mail Carrier
373	Fincher, Nancy	H	W	F	Sep 1856	44	Wd				AL	GA	GA	Farmer
	Cordelia	D	W	F	Sep 1876	23	S				MS	TN	AL	Farm Laborer
	Constine	S	W	M	Mar 1878	22	S				MS	TN	AL	Farm Laborer
	Walter A.	S	W	M	Feb 1879	21	S				MS	TN	AL	Farm Laborer
	Arthur	S	W	M	Apr 1882	18	S				MS	TN	AL	Farm Laborer
374	Ozbirn, Winnie C.	H	W	F	Dec 1831	68	S		1	1	AL	GA	GA	Farmer
	John F.	S	W	M	Sep 1883	16	S				MS	UN	AL	Farm Laborer
	Mary Howard	UN	W	F	UN UN	60	Wd				AL	AL	AL	Mother of 10

End of Enumeration of District #5

Elijah 187
Ellington 12
Elliott 153
Ellis 51, 80, 107, 109
Emerson 100
Emmons 104
Emry 94
Enloe 58
Enlow 107
Epperson 102
Epps 105, 171, 180, 190
Ervin 53
Erwin 16, 25
Estes 107
Evans 14
Ewing 179, 196
Ezell 99

– F –

Fairless 7, 107
Fancher 191
Faris 111
Farris 13, 110
Faust 101, 102
Felker 124, 127
Feltman 74
Ferguson 183
Ferrell 198
Field 66
Fields 122
Finch 112, 161
Fincher 16, 200
Findley 153
Fite 73
Flanagan 37
Flanigan 145
Flemmings 130
Floyd 112, 117, 119, 120
Flurry 131, 133, 168
Flynt 21, 77, 80
Foote 13, 32
Ford 4, 52, 83
Formby 102
Fowler 163
Fraiser 49
Franks 183
Frazier 200
Frederick 132, 162, 166
Fry 4
Fuller 171, 172, 176

– G –

Gable 148, 157, 163, 175
Gaines 59, 86, 183
Galyean 100
Gann 72
Ganong 43
Gant 24
Gardner 128, 144, 154
Garlon 29
Garnett 37
Garrett 13, 179
Garrison 183
Gassaway 20
Gattis 11, 107
Gentile 197
Gentle 197
George 85, 87
Gibson 137
Gilbert 83, 186, 189
Gilchrist 12

Gillian 85
Gillimon 146
Gist 58
Givens 5
Glascow 96
Glasgow 119, 140, 141
Glenn 10, 58, 96, 121
Glover 39, 95
Gober 151, 152
Goddard 141, 142
Godwin 67, 68
Golston 47
Goode 25, 61
Goodloe 52
Goodlow 29
Goodman 30
Gook 194
Gortney 119, 124, 162
Goyer 59
Graham 31
Grammar 185
Gravett 61
Gray 69, 70, 71, 72, 100, 114, 120, 150, 152
Green 22, 23, 31, 48, 134, 135, 142, 161, 162, 170, 183
Greene 136
Gregson 105
Griffin 91, 95, 96
Grimes 107, 118
Grinder 103
Grisham 33, 64, 73
Grizzard 61
Gross 85, 87, 88, 96, 103
Grymes 91
Guller 176
Gunn 130
Gurley 86, 132, 141, 144, 154, 166, 167, 169, 180
Gurney 48
Guthrey 76

– H –

Hadnett 48
Hale 13, 94, 96, 97, 119, 150, 158, 169, 189, 190, 191
Haley 187
Hall 48, 106, 131, 192
Hallmark 174, 176, 177
Halman 137
Ham 179
Hamiel 150
Hamilton 57, 92, 140, 177, 178, 196
Hammerly 58
Hammett 185, 186
Hammon 157
Hampton 132
Hand 197
Haney 19, 51, 56, 57, 58, 105
Hannah 76
Hannon 17
Harden 153
Hardwick 89
Haris 195
Harp 134, 136, 141, 143
Harris 4, 6, 8, 23, 48, 49, 51, 52, 60, 62, 86, 87, 163, 164, 165, 181, 182, 193, 197
Harrison 43, 114, 115, 166, 167, 173, 194, 196

Hart 137
Hartman 108
Harvey 99, 160
Harvill 91
Harwell 22
Hatcher 78, 91, 160
Haygood 161
Hayne 42
Haynes 20, 70
Hearn 50
Hellums 135, 150
Helton 30, 34, 36, 122
Hendrick 37
Hendrix 27, 82
Henley 190
Henly 184
Herd 14
Herrig 51
Hester 172
Hicks 173
Higdon 27
Higginbottom 85, 88
Higgins 38, 85
Hill 19, 23, 27, 32, 48, 50, 117, 128, 129, 130, 133, 152, 165
Hines 103
Hobbs 8
Hodge 157
Hodges 45, 50, 59, 89, 190
Hogeland 166
Hogue 61
Holcom 46
Holcomb 67
Holder 39, 78, 90, 94, 100, 121, 123, 146
Holland 66
Holley 141, 187
Holloway 83
Holmes 48
Holt 107
Honeycutt 74, 75
Hood 183
Hopkins 167, 188
House 40
Houston 48
Howard 50, 123
Howell 141
Hubbard 7, 9, 10, 38, 39, 50, 56, 109, 113, 121
Hudson 30, 33, 34
Huffman 175
Hughes 59, 93, 159, 168
Humble 90
Humphres 118
Hundley 152
Hunt 58, 146, 159, 192
Hutchenson 182
Hutton 101
Hyatt 58
Hyatte 8

– I –

Igo 71
Inlow 155
Ivy 185

– J –

Jackson 6, 30, 38, 45, 47, 66, 174, 189, 191, 192
James 22, 50, 71
Jameson 30

Jamison 15
Jaynes 48
Jenkins 48
Jernigan 70, 116
Johnson 28, 30, 34, 38, 40, 41, 45, 52, 56, 62, 65, 67, 68, 72, 74, 75, 81, 141, 147, 160, 175, 186
Jones 5, 8, 23, 43, 55, 67, 101, 120, 128, 167, 179, 192
Jordan 21, 53
Joshlin 26, 81, 85
Joslin 26, 65, 66, 103
Jourdan 51, 54, 82, 108, 118, 121, 148, 183
Julian 27
Julliam 15

– K –

Kay 146, 148
Keeton 199
Keggle 186
Keith 103
Kelly 48
Kemp 56, 78
Kenell 46
Kennedy 10, 11, 37, 95, 118, 123, 125, 129, 130, 141, 142, 143, 171
Kenneum 10
Kenum 15
Key 137
Kilgore 15
Kimbell 10
Kimberly 16, 25
King 68, 101, 134, 154
Kirk 11, 24, 26
Knot 100
Knowles 59
Kringes 22
Krouce 50

– L –

Laffoon 109
Lamb 69, 70, 74
Lambert 9, 72, 74, 77, 82, 84, 85, 86, 92, 102, 117, 147, 160
Lancaster 130, 145
Langster 26
Lanstrom 188
Lasley 199
Lawry 137, 157
Leatherwood 8, 52, 158
Lee 138, 146
Lenard 27
Lennard 49
Lentz 93
Lewis 24, 98
Lindley 17
Lindsey 79, 101, 169, 170
Linton 12
Little 51
Lock 76, 77
Locket 15, 16
Long 4, 27, 29, 49, 53, 107, 108, 109, 117, 154, 190, 195
Looney 174
Louis 81
Love 71
Lovelace 80, 119
Lovelell 157
Loveless 197
Luker 57

Printed in the USA
CPSIA information can be obtained
at www.ICGtesting.com
JSHW060044150824
68134JS00031B/2632